SECRET MEANINGS IN SHAKESPEARE APPLIED TO STAGE PERFORMANCE:

The Practice of Esoteric Arcana exploring the Plays' Mysteries

WENDY JEAN MACPHEE

AN M-Y BOOKS PAPERBACK

© Copyright 2018
Wendy Jean Macphee

The right of **Wendy Jean Macphee** to be identified as the author of
This work has been asserted by him in accordance with the
Copyright, Designs and Patents Act 1988

All Rights Reserved
No reproduction, copy or transmission of this publication
may be made without written permission.
No paragraph of this publication may be reproduced,
copied or transmitted save with the written permission or in
accordance with the provisions of the
Copyright Act 1956 (as amended).

Any person who does any unauthorised act in relation to
this publication may be liable to criminal
prosecution and civil claims for damage.

A CIP catalogue record for this title is
available from the British Library

ISBN–978-1-911124-91-7

ACKNOWLEDGEMENTS

I am grateful to Gareth Knight for his instruction on all aspects of the esoteric and for his permission to use his terms applied to the Cabala Tree of Life and to Will Parfitt for his guidance in the use of the Tree of Life and for his permission to use quotations from his book *The Qabalah* and the diagrams at Figs. 25 and 26. I am indebted to R. J. Stewart for his insights into the Celtic UnderWorld Journey and Celtic mysticism and to Caitlin and John Matthews for their information on theurgy.

I am grateful for permission to use images from their collections by The Trustees of the British Library: Figs. 4, 5, 7, 8, 11, 13, 14, 16, 24, 27, 31, 45; Trustees of the British Museum Fig. 12; The Warburg Institute: Fig. 6; The Bodleian Libraries, The University of Oxford: Fig. 10. I would like to thank Graham Sergeant and Wendy and Michael Gains for permission to use their photographs of Theatre Set-Up productions.

And finally I thank Susan Brock for her extensive editing of all the contents of this book.

Front cover photo: Leontes: 'O she's warm | If this be magic, let it be an art | Lawful as eating (V. iii. 109). The Philosophers' Stone achieved with Hermione as a living statue; Leontes (Tony Portacio) and Hermione (Morag Brownlie), *The Winter's Tale*, 2006.

Back cover photo: Theurgy. *A Midsummer Night's Dream,* 1983. Bottom (Frank Jarvis) wakes from a dream of his participation in the fairy world.

CONTENTS

PREFACE 1

INTRODUCTION 9

**CHAPTER ONE: ESOTERIC ARCANA I:
GENERAL ASPECTS, ALCHEMY, RENAISSANCE
PLATONISM** 16

Roots of the tradition of encoding esoteric arcana in art 16

The development of encoding esoteric arcana in plays: Shakespeare's forerunners 19

General aspects of the arcana 22

The different arcana in Shakespeare's plays. The identification of sources of their understanding available to Shakespeare 23

ALCHEMY 26

Sources available to Shakespeare 26

History of alchemy 26

George Ripley's twelve gates (stages) of alchemy 27

Alchemy in Shakespeare's plays 29

The Emerald Tablet and Hermeticism 31

The alchemists in the plays 32

The sun and moon 33

The hermaphrodite 33

Puffers 34

RENAISSANCE PLATONISM 34

Sources available to Shakespeare 34

Divine Love 34

The Divided Soul 37

Phaedrus 38

The metaphor of The Charioteer 39

CHAPTER TWO: ESOTERIC ARCANA II: RENAISSANCE MAGIC, THE CABALA, THEURGY AND RITES OF INITIATION 40

Sources available to Shakespeare 40

RENAISSANCE MAGIC 40

THE CABALA 41

The Tree of Life 42

The Pillars of the Tree 44

The sephiroth (spheres) of the Tree 44

THEURGY 48

RITES OF INITIATION 49

CHAPTER THREE: ESOTERIC ARCANA III 51

CELTIC MOTIFS AND MYTHOLOGIES 51

Sources available to Shakespeare of Celtic motifs and mythologies ... 51

The Tudor impulse 51

Aspects of British Celtic culture and mythology applied to Shakespeare's plays 52

THE CELTIC OLD RELIGION 58

THE CELTIC UNDERWORLD INITIATION 58

THE BIBLE 59

Christian Forgiveness 60

ALCHEMY

CHAPTER FOUR: *THE WINTER'S TALE* 68

CHAPTER FIVE: *MUCH ADO ABOUT NOTHING* 87

CELTIC

CHAPTER SIX: *CYMBELINE* 102

CHAPTER SEVEN: *THE MERRY WIVES OF WINDSOR* 125

CHAPTER EIGHT: *ALL'S WELL THAT ENDS WELL* 143

CELTIC, MAGIC, THEURGY

CHAPTER NINE: *THE TEMPEST* 161

CHAPTER TEN: *A MIDSUMMER NIGHT'S DREAM* 188

RITES OF INITIATION

CHAPTER ELEVEN: *THE TWO GENTLEMEN OF VERONA* 219

CHAPTER TWELVE: *LOVE'S LABOUR'S LOST* 236

CHAPTER THIRTEEN: *THE TAMING OF THE SHREW* 256

CHAPTER FOURTEEN: *TWELFTH NIGHT* 266

CHAPTER FIFTEEN: *AS YOU LIKE IT* 281

CHAPTER SIXTEEN: *THE COMEDY OF ERRORS* 311

RENAISSANCE PLATONISM

CHAPTER SEVENTEEN: *ROMEO AND JULIET* 346

CHAPTER EIGHTEEN: *ANTONY AND CLEOPATRA* 364

THE CABALA

CHAPTER NINETEEN: *THE MERCHANT OF VENICE* 380

MERCY AND REVENGE IN THE NEW AND OLD TESTAMENTS

CHAPTER TWENTY: *MEASURE FOR MEASURE* 406

CHAPTER TWENTY ONE: *HAMLET* 432

CHAPTER TWENTY TWO: CONCLUSIONS 456

END NOTES 467

APPENDIX I 491

APPENDIX II 494

BIBLIOGRAPHY 497

INDEX 506

LIST OF ILLUSTRATIONS

All production photos are of Theatre Set-Up. Colour photos by Wendy and Michael Gains, black and white photos by Graham Sergeant.

Cover photo: Leontes: 'O she's warm/ If this be magic, let it be an art | Lawful as eating' (V. iii. 109). The Philosophers' Stone achieved with Hermione as a living statue. Leontes (Tony Portacio) and Hermione (Morag Brownlie), *The Winter's Tale* 2006.

Fig. 1. *Hamlet* 1976, the first performance of Theatre Set-Up. **Above:** Old Hamlet's ghost (Raymond Farrell) appearing at Forty Hall, Enfield, through the gates of the arch thought to be designed by the eighteenth-century architect Inigo Jones. **Below:** Voltimand (Mike Mousley) and Hamlet (Ciaran Hinds) inside the Forty Hall Banqueting Suite.

Fig. 2. *A Midsummer Night's Dream* 1983. **Above**: The four elements as the reconciled lovers. Demetrius as earth (Sean Aita), Helena as Fire (Amanda Strevett), Hermia as air (Gwyneth Hammond) and Lysander as water (David Goudge). The colour changed on the circular plinth to gold signifying the last alchemical stage of the Philosophers' Stone. Our Hieroglyphic Monad attached to the plinth. **Below:** Hermia embodying air and Lysander. The plinth is white, signifying the second stage of four- staged alchemy.

Fig. 3. Diagram of the Cabala Tree of Life. Terms by Gareth Knight, Will Parfitt and Wendy Macphee.

Fig. 4. Christ and the Philosophers' Stone . From: *Rosarium Philosophorum* in *De alchimia opuscula complura veterum philosophorum* (Frankfurt, in officina Cyriaci Iacobi, 1550). Copyright The British Library Board. All rights reserved. 1032.c.1, sig. aiv recto.

Fig. 5. The 'Tail Eater, the Oroubos' as the 'base matter' of alchemy with the red-and-white-rose, 'flos sapientum' (the 'wise' flux of the process). From: Hieronymus Reusner, *Pandora (*Basel, 1588), p. 257. Copyright The British Library Board. All rights reserved. 1032.b.10, p. 257.

Fig. 6. George Ripley's Diagrammatic Wheel of correspondences between the elements, the four directions, the planets, the signs of the zodiac, alchemy and Christianity. From: *Compound of Alchymy* (London: Thomas Orwin, 1591). Photo: Warburg Institute. Innes Collection FGH4920.

Fig. 7. Multiplicatio represented by lion cubs which symbolise the reproductive power of the Philosophers' Stone, here presented as a lion upon which a queen sits holding an additional image of the Stone as a pelican, pecking its own breast to feed its young. From: J. D. Mylius, *Philosophia Reformata,* (Frankfurt: apud Lucam Iennis 1622). Copyright The British Library Board. All rights reserved. 1033.i.7, sig. Q3verso.

Fig. 8. Coniunctio. The chemical wedding of 'The Red King and The White Queen'. From: *Splendor Solis*, attributed to Salomon Trismosin (1582). Copyright The British Library Board. All rights reserved. Ms Harley 3469, fo. 10r.

Fig. 9. The king eats the son. A metaphor for a by-product of the 'base-matter' being consumed within the process in the stage of coniunctio. From: *The Book of Lambspring* (1678) expanded from the original edition 1625. Translated by A.E. Waite, *The Hermetic Museum Restored and Enlarged*, 2. vols (London: Elliott, 1893), I, 301.

Fig. 10. The wolf eats the king. The wolf here represents the chemical antimony. The goal of alchemy is anticipated with a 'resurrected king' emerging in the distance from a purging fire. From: Michael Maier, *Atalanta Fugiens; Hoc est, Emblemata Nova de Secreti Naturae Chymia*, 2nd ed (Oppenheim: Johann Theodor De Bry, 1618). Copyright The Bodleian Libraries, The University of Oxford. VET.D2.e.18, p. 105.

Fig. 11. The raven as symbol of putrefaction. The 'nigredo' eclipse of 'Mercurius Senex' (symbol of Saturn as 'base matter'). From: Herbrandt Jamsthaler, *Viatorium Spagyricum* (Frankfurt am Main, 1625). Copyright The British Library Board. All rights reserved. 1034.k.2, p. 118.

Fig. 12. Melencholia. Copper plate engraving by Albrecht Dürer (1514). Seven-stage alchemy is represented by the seven-runged ladder rising from the stone which represents the Philosophers' Stone. Copyright Trustees of the British Museum.

Fig. 13. The old king drowning and the birth of the new king. A metaphor for the resurrecting aspect of the alchemical process with the precept 'Die to live'. From: *Splendor Solis*, attributed to Salomon Trismosin (1582). Copyright The British Library Board. All rights reserved. Ms Harley 3469, fo. 16v.

Fig. 14. Stages in the alchemical process. 'Base matter' is represented by a dragon at the base of the image and the Philosophers' Stone by a

LIST OF ILLUSTRATIONS

phoenix at the top. For a comprehensive description of all the items in the image see C.G. Jung, *Psychology and Alchemy*, pp. 284-7. From: Andrea Libavius, *Alchymia* (Frankfurt: J. Saurius, 1606). Copyright The British Library Board. All rights reserved. 535.k.5, p. 55.

Fig. 15. Paulina (Wendy Macphee) as alchemist with Leontes (Tony Portacio) as the 'Red King' in *The Winter's Tale*, 2006.

Fig. 16. *Aenigma Regis*. 'The Rebus'(Hermaphrodite) holding serpents and rising from 'base matter' imaged as a three-headed dragon. Seven-stage alchemy is pictured as a flowering tree and the Philosophers' Stone as a lion and pelican feeding its young from its plucked breast. From: *Rosarium Philosophorum* in *De alchimia opuscula complura veterum philosophorum* (Frankfurt, in officina Cyriaci Iacobi, 1550) Copyright The British Library Board. All rights reserved. 1032.c.1, sig. Xiii verso.

Fig. 17. Viola (Emma Reynolds) as symbolic hermaphrodite with Olivia (Susannah Coleman) in *Twelfth Night*, 1997.

Fig. 18. Divine Love, Christianity and initiation: Friar Lawrence (Michael Palmer) marries Romeo (Neil Warhurst) and Juliet (Victoria Stilwell) In *Romeo and Juliet*, 1996.

Fig. 19. Divine Love and Plato's *Phaedrus* metaphor of the charioteer. The dying Antony (Tony Portacio) and Cleopatra (Rosalind Cressy) in *Antony and Cleopatra*, 1998.

Fig. 20. Divine Love. Bassanio (Richard Sanderson) and Portia (Suzie Edwards) in *The Merchant of Venice,* 2010.

Fig. 21. Divine Love. Florizel (Jack Hughes) and Perdita (Karen Boniface) in *The Winter's Tale*, 2006.

Fig. 22. Plato's metaphor of the *Divided Soul*. Antipholus of Ephesus (Daniel O'Brien) and Antipholus of Syracuse (Tony Portacio), in *The Comedy of Errors*, 1986.

Fig. 23. Initiation. The four lovers in *Two Gentlemen of Verona*, 1987. **Above:** Proteus (Tony Portacio). **Below**: Valentine (Anderson Knight), Sylvia (Claire Fisher), Julia (Emma Gibbins), Proteus (Tony Portacio).

Fig. 24. A diagram of the Cabala Tree of Life, contained in a *Vesica Piscis*. Christ is identified with the Tree, with spheres corresponding to parts of his body. At the top right of the Tree in Chockmah is the Horn of Plenty indicating that the right side of the Tree has active, masculine characteristics, and at the top left in Binah is the All-seeing Eye of the Great Mother, designating female passive characteristics. The pelican beside the image of St John symbolises the self-sacrifice of Christ. For a full description see Gareth Knight, *A Practical Guide to Qabalistic Symbolism.* From: *Liber sacrosancti euangelii de Iesus Christo domino & deo nostro ... lingua Syra, ... a Ioh. Evangelista Hebraica dicta* (Vienna: Michael Cymbermannus 1556). Copyright The British Library Board. All rights reserved. 218.h.21, fo. 101 verso.

Fig. 25. The Cabala: The Lightning Flash. The order (Kether, Chockmah, Binah, Chesed, Geburah, Tiphareth, Netzach, Hod, Yesod, Malkuth) in which Spirit (which is believed to exist within every person) becomes incarnated in the flesh of humanity. From: Will Parfitt, *The Elements of the Qabala*, p. 25, with the author's permission.

Fig. 26. The Cabala: The Three Triangles. The top Supernal triangle, which includes Kether, Binah and Chockmah, represents 'The Realm of the Spirit' connecting the individual to others. The middle triangle of Tiphareth, Geburah and Chesed represent 'The Realm of the Soul' referring to the soul of the individual. The lower triangle of Malkuth, Yesod, Hod and Netzach, 'The realm of the personality' refer to the thoughts, feelings and sensations of the individual. From: Will Parfitt, *The Elements of the Qabala*, p. 4, with the author's permission.

Fig. 27. John Dee's Hieroglyphic Monad. The symbol as it appears in his book, *Monas Hieroglyphica*, 1564. Copyright The British Library Board. All rights reserved. 90.i.20, title page.

Fig. 28. The spiritual world represented by Ariel (Morag Brownlie) interacts with Prospero (James Clarkson), in *The Tempest*, 2001.

Fig. 29. Celtic nature spirits: Titania (Libby Machin) and Oberon (Tony Portacio) in *A Midsummer Night's Dream*, 1995.

Fig. 30. Subjects of the alchemic processes and UnderWorld initiation: Posthumus (Tony Portacio) and Imogen (Emily Outred), in *Cymbeline*, 2009.

Fig. 31. The symbolic cave of the alchemists and the Celts: Mountain of the Adepts. Seven-stage alchemy culminating in the Philosophers' Stone represented as a phoenix, within an alchemist's cave-laboratory-temple

LIST OF ILLUSTRATIONS

hidden in a mountain upon whose flanks are gods symbolising the planets and surrounded by the signs of the zodiac and the four elements of fire, air, water and earth. In the foreground is a man investigating knowledge by following his natural instincts, contrasted with one whose ignorance is indicated by his blindfold. From: Stephan Michelspacher, *Cabala: Spiegel der Kunst und Natur (*Augspurg, 1616). Copyright The British Library Board. All rights reserved. 1032.c.3, Plate 3.

Fig. 32. Falstaff (Richard Ashley) as the subject of alchemy in *The Merry Wives of Windsor* 2004 being 'processed' as he is hidden in a laundry basket before being thrown into the Thames by Mistress Page (Morag Brownlie) and Mistress Ford (Angela Laverick).

Fig. 33. Falstaff (Richard Ashley) relates his Dissolution in the waters of the Thames to Ford (David Reakes).

Fig. 34. Falstaff (Richard Ashley) as Herne the Hunter, his antlers suggesting Cernunnos, King of the Celtic pantheon. Taken from *The Merry Wives of Windsor* 2004 programme.

Fig. 35. Triumphant Helena (Elizabeth Arends) as The Philosophers' Stone in *All's Well That Ends Well*, 2008.

Fig 36. *All's Well*, 2008: Parolles attacked by his fellow soldiers. Bertram (Richard Plumley), Dumaine (Peter Lundie Wager), Parolles (Terry Ashe), Florentine soldier (Toby Eddington), Duke of Florence (Tony Portacio).

Fig 37. 1982 Theatre Set-up production of *The Tempest* at Stonehenge (**above**) and Forty Hall **(below).** The spirits as the Celtic Epona (Henrietta Branwell) and Cernunnos (Michael Branwell).

Fig. 38. Nature spirits. Oberon (Charles Abomali) and Puck (Wendy Macphee) in *A Midsummer Night's Dream,* 2000.

Fig. 39. The four lovers as the four elements in *A Midsummer Night's Dream,* 2000: Demetrius (George Richmond Scott) as earth, Helena (Amalia Lawrence) as fire, Hermia (Susannah Coleman) as air, and Lysander (Peter McCrohan) as water.

Fig. 40. Theurgy. *A Midsummer Night's Dream*, 1983. Bottom (Frank Jarvis) wakes from his dream of his participation in the fairy world.

Fig. 41. Programme for *Love's Labour's Lost,* 2005   Photograph of the actress playing Rosaline (Alice James) superimposed on the portrait of Emilia Lanier, possibly Shakespeare's 'Dark Lady'.

xiii

Fig. 42. From the 1994 Commedia Dell'Arte interpretation of *The Taming of the Shrew*. (Libby Machin who also played Katherine) as Biondello. **(left)**

Fig. 43. From the 1994 Commedia Dell'Arte interpretation of *The Taming of the Shrew*. Grumio as Harlequin (Frank Jarvis). **(right)**

Fig. 44. Orlando (Andrew Crabb) and Rosalind (Morag Brownlie) in *As You Like It*, 2002.

Fig. 45. Coniunctio. A metaphor from alchemy signifying the maxim 'From death comes life' being applied in *Romeo and Juliet* as 'The lovers in the tomb'. Woodcut From: *Rosarium Philosophorum* in *De alchimia opuscula complura veterum philosophorum* (Frankfurt, in officina Cyriaci Iacobi, 1550). Copyright The British Library Board. All rights reserved. 1032.c.1, sig. Giv recto.

Fig. 46. Paris (Tony Portacio) mourning at the tomb of Juliet (Victoria Stilwell), is killed by Romeo (Neil Warhurst) in *Romeo and Juliet*, 1996.

Fig. 47. The Cabala: Geburah. Shylock (Tony Portacio) exalts in his forthcoming vengeance in *The Merchant of Venice*, 1992.

Fig. 48. Mercy: Angelo (Tony Portacio) threatens Isabella (Lucy Curtin) who will forgive him, in *Measure for Measure* 1991. Photo: The Press Agency (Yorkshire) Ltd.

Fig. 49. Revenge. Hamlet (Tony Portacio) kills Polonius (Frank Jarvis) mistaking him for Claudius in *Hamlet*, 1993. A bad consequence of the revenge demanded of young Hamlet by Old Hamlet for his murder by Claudius.

PREFACE

The theatre company to which the secret spiritual meanings were applied in performance was Theatre Set-Up Ltd (www.ts-u.co.uk), an international professional theatre company performing Shakespeare's plays in the light of their esoteric arcana in heritage sites in the UK and mainland Europe. Founded in 1976, the company performed mostly out of doors over the 35 years of their summer seasons in a total of 163 beautiful and iconic heritage sites, including Stonehenge, Verulamium, cathedrals, manor houses, abbeys, theatres, museums, gardens and castles throughout the UK, the Channel Islands, the Isle of Man, Norway, Sweden, Denmark, Germany, Belgium, Switzerland, Luxembourg and the Netherlands. They were selected to represent the UK at the MESS festival in Sarajevo in 1997. These venues are listed in Appendix 2.

Theatre Set-Up began as a part-professional, part-amateur company performing Shakespeare's *Hamlet* in various locations in the banqueting suite and grounds of Forty Hall, Enfield in the summer of 1976. Ciaran Hinds's performance of Hamlet at the beginning of his professional acting career was so spectacular, and his influence on the rest of the cast so inspirational, that the reputation of the company made by that production guaranteed its continuance into the future.[1] (See fig.1)

Three other productions, *The Taming of the Shrew* (1976), *A Midsummer Night's Dream* (1977) and *Romeo and Juliet* (1978) followed, with professional actors performing and supporting the amateur members of the company.[2] These professionals included Sean Chapman and Stewart Permutt, who were to become established in the UK theatre scene, and Jennifer Lilleystone, a renowned opera singer and actress who had performed in the Royal Opera House in Covent Garden and had toured internationally.

In 1978, while I was studying with Dorothy Heathcote at Newcastle University for a diploma in Drama-in-Education and then a Master's degree in Education, I was asked by the National Trust to put on performances of a Shakespeare play for them at Wallington Hall in Northumberland and at Beningborough Hall in Yorkshire. To become a touring company employing professional actors, it was necessary to register with British

Actors Equity in order to issue contracts for multiple venues. *Twelfth Night* was the play we performed in 1979 on our first mini-tour of the two National Trust venues after opening performances at Forty Hall. Caroline Funnell and Susannah Best, who took the roles of Olivia and Viola, were to stay with the company for several years, keeping the standards high and helping with production and administration.[3]

The *Twelfth Night* performances established the company's aims and objectives, which were to present the plays of Shakespeare in heritage sites, mostly in outdoor locations, with high quality period costumes appropriate to the style of the historic venues, accompanied by live music matching the selected period of the costumes and played on period instruments.[4] The texts of the plays were to be interpreted in a clear and accessible style, suitable for the many people in the audience who were not regular theatregoers. To break down any barriers, members of the company would interact with audiences before the performances began and during the interval. Performances would continue regardless of the weather (with the notable exception of electric storms!).

It was suggested by actors in the production of *Twelfth Night* that the season be expanded in future years for the length of the summer in venues throughout the UK. During a holiday in the Scilly Isles, I established venues for the summer of 1980 in Tresco Abbey Gardens and the Chaplaincy Gardens in St Mary's, as well as connecting venues in Cornwall and Devon and throughout the UK, which, along with the existing venues in Northumberland and Yorkshire, comprised our national tour.

In order to get the production to the island of Tresco, all of the props, costumes, lighting, sound equipment and changing tents had to be taken down very steep stone steps from the quay at St Mary's onto a launch below. This would then take the equipment and the cast over to Tresco, where they would be loaded onto the back of a lorry and driven to the performance site. This limited the gear we could have in the production for the whole tour. Our objective then became to take professional performances of Shakespeare's plays presented in a very minimalist production style to remote locations not accessible to more cumbersome productions. In subsequent years, these locations included venues in mainland Europe, the Channel Islands, the Isle of Man and the Isle of Wight. We also made

Theatre Set-Up attractive to venues who did not want their lawns scarred by heavy scenery. We always brought along a photo-board with photos of the actors in costume, which was propped up by the 'box office' table at the entrance to venues. In 1996, in spite of our careful efforts, the *Romeo and Juliet* board slid off the steps into the sea at the St Mary's quay, a salutary reminder of the fragility of our enterprise!

As You Like It was our first national production, and we were joined by many professional actors including David Goudge and Julie Le Grand.[5] We performed in venues in England and Wales. Frank Jarvis (1941 - 2010), a well-known film and TV actor, joined us for our 1981 *Much Ado About Nothing* season, and he was with the company for many years, a great favourite with the audience and always helping the young actors who joined us. One of these was Guy Henry, now a familiar face on TV and film with a long and successful stage career, including many years with the RSC.

The 1980 season of performances was pioneering work in the field of theatre, and it established touring Shakespeare out of doors in heritage sites as a genre, since then one of the most prolific forms of theatre in the UK. The simplicity and economy of its production style and the attraction of the venues to non-regular theatre goers gives this genre an economic edge over many established theatres, which are often expensive to maintain.

Theatre Set-Up received a small grant in 1978 for the Forty Hall production of *Romeo and Juliet*, but apart from that was unsubsidised by any Arts Council or government funds and was economically independent, paying the actors' fees, accommodation and allowances, production costs and publicity expenses from guarantees from promoting venues, box office receipts from self-promoting venues, and donations from sponsors and a Friends of Theatre Set-Up scheme.

During the 1980's and 1990's, economic necessity caused us to reduce cast numbers from twelve to seven so that each actor performed several roles. We found that this improved the social health of the company. Not only was the smaller company more friendly, but each actor had more to do on stage and was therefore happier. What actors like best is to act, not sit disconsolately in the dressing area waiting for long periods of time for their cue to go on while others hog the limelight! The touring companies of Shakespeare's day had nine actors.

From 1983 onwards, my doctoral research on arcana in Shakespeare's plays at the Shakespeare Institute of The University of Birmingham and information on the esoteric given to us by members of our audiences was integrated with the aims of Theatre Set-Up, and became a feature of its performances, informing the interpretation of the plays given to the actors and to the audiences through the plays' programme notes.

A boost to our enterprise came in 1993 in the form of performances in mainland Europe. We performed in Norway, Germany, the Netherlands, Belgium, Switzerland, Sweden, Luxembourg and Bosnia-Herzegovina, and the tag 'international' was added to the company's title. Theatre Set-Up was recommended to the venues in these countries by members of the company's audiences and by actors who had been employed in its productions, and we received an endorsement from the British Council. Performances continued in Norway, the Netherlands and Belgium until the company transferred its operations to the Festival Players in 2012, who still continue to perform in our established venues in those countries.

For many years, Frank Jarvis would come out to the audience for at least ten minutes before the start of the show in order to greet people and talk to them. However, the task of talking to the audiences while they found their chairs or cushions in the audience area, long before the play began, usually fell to me as the on-site artistic and executive director (as well as occasional actor) and musician. It gave me the opportunity to discuss what they wanted, liked and disliked, so that their opinions guided me in the choice and style of plays which we performed. Often they asked for lesser-known plays, such as *The Winter's Tale* or *Cymbeline*. A regular loyal audience was established who always turned up early to the performances so that they could establish their places in the front of the audience area. It was through these talks with members of the audience, especially those with expertise in aspects of the esoteric, that I developed my learning about the secret meanings of Shakespeare's plays. From 1983 onwards, this information was integrated with the aims of Theatre Set-Up, and became a feature of its performances, informing the interpretation of the plays given to the actors and to the audiences through the plays' programme notes. Audience members who were interested in learning the secret meanings of the play about to be performed would settle into the audience from about 6 pm in order to read their programmes. The impetus to write this book came from them, along with their impatience that I should get on with it!

Another enlightening aspect of our contact with the audience was our relationship with children who were there with their parents. Sometimes I would be able to take them backstage to the tents to see the workings of the production, and actors often played directly to them during the play. I always made a point of bringing children to the very front of the audience area so that they could be immersed in the play, and many parents brought their children and in later years their grandchildren to our performances, claiming that we had given them a happy foundation in the understanding and enjoyment of classic theatre.

Their picnics were a large feature before and often during the performance, at some venues taking a disproportionate amount of space in the audience area by featuring tables, chairs, tablecloths, candelabra and silver platters, but the advantage of this was that the resultant jovial atmosphere predisposed the audience to enjoy the play. Often some members of the audiences not usually keen to attend theatre events would attend as picnickers and would become drawn into the story of the play and then come to see us every year. The picnic makers were very generous - Frank Jarvis was often to be seen eating a donated chicken leg as he moved through the audience before the play began!

Our professional actors displayed admirable qualities of rigour, creativity, dedication to their craft and physical endurance. These qualities were necessary when performing in all weathers and setting up and striking the production, with its changing tents, lighting and sound fit-ups, and costume and props setting and maintenance (for an example of doubling and trebling of parts taken by actors, see *The Merchant of Venice* story sections pp. 380-404). The tours often featured travelling between many venues, where often only one performance was staged. These qualities also earned them successful careers after their seasons with Theatre Set-Up were finished. It has not been possible to keep track of all of them, but I list a number of the Theatre Set-Up actors in Appendix 1, indicating a conservative account of their many accomplishments. Sadly, this list includes actors who have since died, but they survive in their film and TV appearances. During the early years of the company, John and Joan Field, who have also since died, were charitable administrators and costume and props makers. When they retired due to ill health, Lyndsey Brandolese and Lindsay Royan stepped in, the latter raising the company's standards of movement by taking charge of choreography. Lyndsey Brandolese's artistic knowledge benefitted all visual aspects of the productions, and she also became the Secretary of Friends of Theatre Set-Up. Evelyn Cousins was a much-appreciated costumier in all the company's seasons from 1976 onwards. Professional costumiers Kim Jones and Andrew Fisher assisted us from 1994. Michael and Wendy Gains and Graham Sergeant voluntarily photographed the plays.

I always donated my services as director and actor charitably to the company, and in order to save the expense which would have been incurred in the employment of an additional actor, I often took acting roles in the performances, usually playing mature women. In later years, I realised that I could also take old men's parts, especially when my mobility became limited. Regular members of the audience enjoyed the sight of me making a fool of myself in a beard![6] Thus I became what was mistakenly thought to be an extinct species – an actor-manager.

We were not able to have long rehearsal periods, as our contracts which fulfilled the Equity terms and conditions required that our seasons began with the first day of rehearsal and full wages had to be paid to our actors from that time. It was therefore challenging to give the actors their creative artistic freedom during our two week rehearsal time, as well as keeping the company's own ideas and customs. However, we eventually managed it. As suggested by one of the actors in 1991, a month before the season began we had a day 'dislocated' from the season in which we introduced the ideas for the production, especially the secret meanings, and after lunch our volunteer photographers were able to take the publicity photographs of the actors in costume for which our venues were clamouring.[7]

Actors turned up on the first day of rehearsal with their lines learnt and primed with well-formed ideas of characterisation for their own roles, how they fitted into the arcane significance of the whole play and a good sense of my vision for the production. I was the artistic director of the plays and had the veto on interpretation of text, but due to my increasing lack of mobility could not direct the movement of the play. In the early years, Frank Jarvis assisted with this, and after he had left the company Tony Portacio, and occasionally Terry Ashe, fulfilled that role. Experienced actors such as Allan Collins and Dan Caulfield always assisted with direction and helping younger actors.

We devised a system of holding a number of simultaneous rehearsals in different parts of the grounds of Forty Hall or other locations where we were rehearsing, in order to complete a performable production of the play in the little time that we had. When a scene had been discussed and rehearsed with me as artistic director and Frank, Terry or Tony as co-director, the actors involved would go off, either by themselves or with an experienced actor helping, and 'work' the scene, firming it up. Often actors would be able to present us with a scene almost ready for public performance which they had rehearsed privately in this way. This method also ensured that the actors could enjoy the freedom of having their own input into their scenes within the artistic frame of the production.

In order for the actors to become acclimatised to the outdoor venues, we tried to rehearse outside as much as possible. If we were in a public area such as the grounds of Forty Hall there was considerable interface with members of the public. This was usually pleasant and some people would come each year to watch the production grow before they enjoyed it in performance. It also advertised the play to the public. We had to run the gauntlet of dogs on walks with their owners, who often had to restrain their pets from joining in our stage action! Sometimes we had problems with gangs of youths. This could, however, be beneficial. When they mocked any of our actors by repeating their lines in a loud voice, we knew that those lines sounded artificial, as if they were not being motivated internally, and consequently needed to be re-worked. I found that the best approach to the gangs was to ask for their help, even asking them to prompt us from the director's script. They were usually impressed by the skill of the actors and I often invited them to be our guests at performance. Regulars in our audience entered into the spirit of this, offering them a seat on their rug.

This informality of our audiences and their willingness to contribute to our seasons in any way they could gave our performances a special atmosphere, and audiences were devastated in 2011 when I told them that Theatre Set-Up would have to cease. My lack of mobility was such that I could no longer continue running and financing the company, and neither of the company's other charitable directors had the resources to take it over.

We were exceptionally lucky, and our regular audiences were extremely pleased, when the Festival Players (www.thefestivalplayers.org.uk) bought our costumes, van and gear, and were able to perform in many of our venues during their seasons in following years. The Festival Players, similar to us in their style of performing Shakespeare's plays with a minimum of cast and accoutrements in mostly open-air heritage sites, were able to continue most of the work of our company as well as continuing with their own venues and schedules. In order to facilitate the transfer, two senior actors who had been members of our company for many years, Terry Ashe (a main actor, sometime assistant director and our stage manager), and Tony Portacio, (our lead actor and co-director), joined the Festival Players in 2012 for their performances of *Twelfth Night*. As the application of esoteric arcana to the productions was considered to be integral to the Theatre Set-Up brand and therefore not initially appropriate to The Festival Players company, the secret meanings have not currently been applied to the interpretation of Shakespeare's plays in their productions. That has made it possible for me to write this book, as it would have been tactless to have done so had the Festival Players included the esoteric arcana in their annual performances.

INTRODUCTION

This book records the research that I undertook to clarify the texts of Shakespeare's plays performed annually in heritage sites from 1976 to 2011 by the international professional company, Theatre Set-Up Ltd. The aim of this book is to provide today's actors, directors and audiences with readings of the esoteric arcana in Shakespeare's plays which might have been part of his intent for his audiences then, but have been lost to us in the 21st century. Many Shakespearean audience members would have been well acquainted with the hidden meanings, and thus enjoyed the thrill of experiencing them encoded in the stage action. Knowledge of these meanings can bring us closer to the understanding of Shakespeare's own actors and audiences. Since I studied the esoteric arcana, my enjoyment of many of Shakespeare's plays as a member of the audience has been heightened, as I recognise the esoteric in the subtext. To an extent, I feel that I am experiencing the plays as if I were in an audience of Shakespeare's own time.

During the early years of Theatre Set-Up, the actors were constantly puzzled by what seemed to be anomalies in the text, which seemed to have no explanation in terms of psychological reality, and on the tour the actors were up late at night discussing these problems and disturbing my sleep in an adjacent room! The theatre practitioner Constantin Stanislavsky said that in order for actors to act truthfully they must fully understand the logic of what they are acting, so this enquiring behaviour of the mystified actors was justifiable.[1]

Our lead actress, Susannah Best, suggested that I undertake research in order to investigate these problems. It was possible that mysterious action and aspects of characterisation might be paradigms, allegories or at least metaphors of spiritual or esoteric significance.[2] My resulting PhD thesis defended the notion of allegorical esoteric meanings in the plays, which are set out here in Chapters One, Two and Three.[3]

The research proved to be a Pandora's box, as the uncovering of one secret meaning revealed others. Many possible layers of meaning unveiled themselves. This obviously included the well-explored social and political relevance of much of the stage action and characterisation to times and countries other than those of Shakespeare, which has led to many productions transcribing the settings of the plays to other countries and epochs.[4]

This 'polysemous' nature of Shakespeare's plays (the term implying different levels of meaning in a text) gives them added depth and is part of their lasting appeal. Ludovico Ariosto's *Orlando Furioso*, translated into English by Sir John Harrington in 1591, provides us with a contemporary reference for Shakespeare in a polysemous text which interprets its story on different levels (p. 286).[5]

During the years I carried out this research into the subtexts of Shakespeare's plays, I found in the arcana not only answers to the problems actors were having with those features of the plays which seemed to lack psychological reality, but also found ways in which I could interpret the plays as the director. Chapters Four to Twenty One describe the problems of interpretation we experienced as actors and director, the results of my research into the plays we presented each year, and the influence the arcana had on my interpretations when directing them. I was occasionally reprimanded by audience members for applying the Cabala only to *The Merchant of Venice* and *The Tempest* rather than to all the Theatre Set-Up productions, so in deference to these people, I have also tried to apply the Cabala to all the plays we performed in my analysis of their secret meanings at the end of each chapter as **Cabala: Post Production**.

In planning our 1982 production of *Tempest*, we had already detected some Celtic meanings which gave us the ideas for our production style, but my analysis of these in the play's programme notes was so inadequate that it was challenged in the press. The actors also required an explanation, which I could not give them, of the references to the Italian aspects of the play and the significance of Milan in the story. Shakespeare features Milan in several plays, and the research posited a reading of the name that implied esoteric meaning.[6] The benefit to us of this Celtic-style production, however, was that it attracted the attention of several scholars of the occult. Many came to know of us mainly through the two performances of the play that we gave at Stonehenge in 1982 and the consequent national press and media interest in performances in such an iconic location.

INTRODUCTION

After a performance at Scotney Castle, Kent, in 1983, the esoteric scholar and writer, Gareth Knight, kindly supplied me with much information on the subject of the occult in Britain, giving me his books on the subject and in subsequent years telling me about publications that were just coming into circulation.[7] Will Parfitt, a writer specialising in the Cabala who had seen our productions at Glastonbury Abbey, gave me additional instruction on his subject. This interface with members of the audience who were experts in the research and its application to the production recorded in the play's programme notes became an important part of the process. I wondered if Shakespeare had enjoyed a similar experience, and if fellow associates of Queen Elizabeth's court, such as Dr John Dee and Sir Francis Bacon, had given him esoteric information after seeing performances of his plays.

Of equal importance was the input of the actors to the research and their reaction to the information I gave them. Michael Branwell, an actor in our 1982 production of *Tempest,* was also a scholar of Celtic arcana, and it was with him that I developed ideas for the Celtic content of that play. When we were performing in Bath, the Celtic scholar, Marko Michel, gave us such exciting information on his subject that I was eager to undertake further research into the possibility of finding Celtic meanings in Shakespeare's plays. However, when I undertook the research at the Shakespeare Institute of The University of Birmingham, my supervisor, Dr Tom Matheson, advised me that I should not limit the research to exploring Celtic arcana but to look into all possibilities.

A friend of Theatre Set-Up advised me to consider the alchemic arcana in the plays. "Shakespeare was an alchemist!" she declared. The 1983 production of *Dream* was the first to which I could apply results of my research on alchemy and the Celtic Old World religion. I was nervous about introducing my ideas of these arcana in the play to the cast, but they gave me the support I needed. The actresses taking the parts of Hermia and Helena were particularly encouraging and enjoyed the extra dimension to their characterisation that their significance as the elements of air and fire gave to their parts. All of the actors in that production participated with enthusiasm in our attempt to convey the alchemical and Celtic significance of the play in our stage action, costumes, set and stage props (see fig. 2).

Support from the casts continued in following years when research uncovered further arcana:

- **Renaissance Platonism** adapted from **Plato's *Symposium* and *Phaedrus*,** including the philosophies of **'Pan and Proteus'** (see below p. 221), **'The Divided Soul'** (see below p. 37), **'The metaphor of the Charioteer'** (see below p. 39) **and 'Divine Love'** (see below pp. 34-36)
- **Rites of initiation** (see below pp. 49-50)
- **Theurgy** (see below p. 48)
- **Renaissance Magic** (see below pp. 40)
- **Celtic Mysticism** (see below pp. 51-58)
- **The Cabala** (see below pp. 41-47)
- **Opposing views within the Old and New Testaments of the Bible: Mercy - 'For if ye doe forgive men their trespasses, your heavenly Father will also forgive you' (Matthew 6. 14) versus Revenge - 'Eye for eye, tooth for tooth, hand for hand, foote for foote' (Exodus 21. 24)** (see below p. 60)

As the research progressed, I felt able to solve the mysterious anomalies of *The Winter's Tale* and *Cymbeline* in order to present these plays, which had been requested by some audience members. Most of the cast of *Winter's Tale* in 1988, especially Dan Caulfield, were particularly pleased and encouraging when I was able to interpret the play in terms of exoteric alchemy, which made sense of the strange events of the play, such as the eating of Antigonus by a bear in III. iii. 57, (see below p. 76). It was the first time that the programme notes were set out as a chart, a custom I continued into most future productions.

Of considerable importance to the understanding of *Cymbeline* was its significance in terms of its Celtic mysticism and alchemy. These secret meanings explained the extraordinary events of the play, such as Imogen's embrace of the headless Cloten, mistaking the body for that of her husband Posthumus in IV. ii. 305-332 (see below p. 117). Tony Portacio, who was playing Posthumus, embraced the esoteric significance of the plot and the through line of thought and action that it gave to his performance.

In 1991, the actress who was playing Isabella in the production of *Measure For Measure* made the point, after I gave the actors the secret meanings I had discovered in the play at the end of a week into rehearsal, that she would have appreciated that information some time before rehearsals started.[8] I took due notice of her advice and in following years gave the actors my interpretation of the secret meanings a month before rehearsals began.

This was particularly necessary in 1992 when I interpreted *Merchant* in terms of the Hebrew Cabala Tree of Life in addition to realising its alchemical significance. The cast took this on board and were supportive, each cast member representing a different aspect of Venice and the significance that aspect had within the esoteric arcana of the play.

In 1995, I learnt from studying the books of John Vyvyan the true significance of Renaissance Platonism and Plato's concept of Divine Love in Shakespeare's portrayal of the lovers in his plays, and I incorporated its ideas into our production of *Dream*. This had a very strong impact on the actors, who loved the beauty of the concepts, especially in contrast to the harshness of alchemy, and they willingly incorporated these ideas into the preparation of their parts.

In the following years, the interpretation of Shakespeare's plays in the light of their secret meanings became an integral part of the brand of Theatre Set-Up, and most of the actors accepted and appreciated the depth that the arcana gave to the portrayal of their roles and the production of the plays. This was partly due to the fact that in 1996 I gained my PhD in the subject, which gave authority to the process! I had promised members of our audience that I would research the Cabala for the production of the 2001 *Tempest* and incorporate it into the preparation of the play and the programme notes, along with other arcana and meanings that I would detect. The actors were fascinated by Renaissance Cabala, especially the efforts that its practitioners would make to change themselves and progress up the Cabala's Tree of Life by making use of things associated with the different spheres on the branches of the Tree (see below p. 44).

I often found when researching the plays for performance that a study of their source material was important. Often the alteration indicates a shift in the story to encode an esoteric level of meaning. In fact, sometimes the difference between the original story and Shakespeare's version of it reveals the esoteric arcana. The original story, for example, of *King Lear and his Three Daughters* ends happily with the survival of Lear and all his daughters in spite of the evil enchantment which had threatened them. In *The Chemical Theatre*, Charles Nicholl demonstrates how this change created an allegory of alchemy in the play.[9]

Sometimes, I discovered that an understanding of the arcana of a play threw light on arguments regarding its nature and ethics. A play which poses problems to directors, actors and audiences alike today is *The Merchant of Venice*. Is it a racist play? Does Shakespeare side with the Venetians in their condemnation of Shylock? Much worse, does he join with them in racist abuse against Jews in the punishment given to Shylock in that he must become a Christian (IV. i. 382)?[10] These questions are so emotive that the play is often considered too unethical to be performed. We had discovered through research into the arcana of the play some possible resolution to these issues (see Chapter Nineteen), but when we proposed to perform *Merchant* in our usual circuit of venues, one of them declined to host us that year as it might have offended some of its patrons. Other plays, such as the early comedies, *The Two Gentlemen of Verona* and *The Comedy of Errors*, are considered to be too light, the first just a romantic comedy, the latter no more than a farce (see Chapters Eleven and Sixteen). When we examined *The Taming of the Shrew* in the light of its arcana, we discovered that Petruchio need not necessarily be considered to be a bully, as he was developing Katherina's potential happiness by reforming her and integrating her into society (see Chapter Thirteen).

The chapters on the plays represent the basis of the analyses of the plays given to the actors and, in the plays' programme notes, to the audiences. In order for actors and audiences to understand the arcana (and other meanings such as 'The Body Politic: Political and Historic Meanings' in the analysis of *Winter's Tale*) appropriate to the action of the plays, I divided the stories into numbered sections, each relevant to the different arcana. I list the plays under the headings of the arcana most significant to an understanding of their subtexts. When reading the application of arcana to the different sections of the stories of the plays, please refer to their detailed descriptions in Chapters One, Two and Three. As was done in the plays' programme notes, a brief description of the meanings is often included at the beginning of the chapters on the plays in order to emphasise Shakespeare's varied application of the arcana in the different plays. For example: in *A Midsummer Night's Dream* and *The Two Gentlemen of Verona*, he emphasises the function of the changing of the four elements of earth, air, water and fire in alchemic transmutation by representing them as lovers who switch allegiances to each other through the plays. In *Romeo and Juliet*, he presents a model of the Divine Love of Renaissance Platonism, and in *The Tempest* a full account of initiation in Prospero's treatment as hierophant/guide of the initiate/neophyte, Ferdinand. Often material is repeated in these chapters for the benefit of those readers who prefer selective reading of particular plays.

My analyses of the plays in terms of the Cabalistic Tree of Life, called **Cabala: Post Production**, require reading of my description of the Tree's features in Chapter Two and reference to fig. 3.

Editions referred to throughout this book will be to the 3rd edition of The Arden Shakespeare unless mentioned otherwise. For all references to plays not performed by Theatre Set-Up I use *The Oxford Shakespeare: The Complete Works*.[11] All references to act, scene and line numbers will be shown as: acts in capital Roman numerals, scenes in lower case Roman numerals and lines in Arabic numerals. Single quotation marks will enclose literary quotations and terms used by the arcana and other meanings. For clarity, I highlight in bold the names of the twelve stages of alchemy and the sephiroth (spheres) of the Cabalistic Tree of Life.

The definition of comedy I consider to be most appropriate to Shakespeare's comedies is that probably derived from Dante's *Divine Comedy*; that is, plays or stories of varied natures with a happy ending.[12]

CHAPTER ONE: ESOTERIC ARCANA I: GENERAL ASPECTS, ALCHEMY, RENAISSANCE PLATONISM

Roots of the tradition of encoding Esoteric Arcana in art

Shakespeare's contemporary, Sir Philip Sidney, in his *An Apology for Poetry*, affirms that secret meanings can be hidden in poetry in order to protect them:

> Believe, with me, that there are many mysteries contained in Poetry, which of purpose were written darkly, lest by profane wits it should be abused. [1]

This statement demonstrates the need in Shakespeare's day for writers to hide esoteric arcana in such a way that they would not be derided by 'profane wits' or bring trouble to the author. In all of Shakespeare's plays, the stories and characters are so strong and attractive that, were he challenged with the illegal representation of alchemy in them (as Charles Nichol reports, this was considered an act of felony from 1404 – 1689), he could have justifiably claimed an innocent intention merely to entertain an audience with a piece of theatre presenting people in interesting stories.[2]

However, in his day it was the custom to entertain the public in all forms of art by encoding allegorical and disguised references to systems, people and ideas, thereby adding another dimension of pleasure in deciphering the puzzle contained therein. Archaeologists tell us that Anglo-Saxon artefacts demonstrate that their creators had a love of placing riddles and puzzles in their work. Perhaps this characteristic continued through to later generations of culture! Certainly esoteric practitioners hid their secrets in jokes and games, for example in children's nursery songs and games. Some English pub signs are an example of this practice, such as *The Red Lion* and *The Green Lion* (alchemic references), and *The White Hart* (a Celtic reference to the King of the ancient pantheon of Celtic gods, but also referencing Richard II, the murdered English king whose emblem was the white hart).

An example of more high-minded allegory can be the commonly acknowledged allegorical content of medieval plays such as *Everyman.* This moral characteristic is continued faithfully in Shakespeare's plays which have moral endings, often in a Christian form. For example, the final scene of *Hamlet*, which gives the audience a stage littered with murdered bodies, is resolved by the entrance of Fortinbras, whose swift assessment of the scene and firm commands reassure the watchers that a moral order will be restored.

Shakespeare's debt to a much earlier work of literature, Ovid's *Metamorphoses,* has long been recognised.[3] This poem can be said to be an allegory of transformation, its fifteen books moving chronologically from the legendary transformation of chaos into the order of the universe, to the politically flattering supposed deification of Julius Caesar in Ovid's own time. This work gives an example, probably learnt by Shakespeare at school where Ovid was a common text, of the use of spiritual allegory in writing, which could have inspired him.[4]

In a later period of literature in Italy, Dante in his *The Divine Comedy* might have provided for Shakespeare a pattern of allegory which can also be identified as polysemous, with different levels of meaning implied in the text.[5] Another model of polysemous allegorical literature accessible to Shakespeare is given by his contemporary poet Edmund Spenser in his epic poem, *The Faerie Queene*. Spenser declared in its preface that it was 'continued allegory, or darke conceit'. He made clear that in this poem the 'general intention and meaning' of the allegory was to 'fashion a gentleman or noble person in vertuous and gentle discipline'. To distance his moral allegory from potentially politically risky contemporary references he set it in the 'historye of King Arthur'.[6] I suggest that this indicates the level of fear of political persecution that writers felt in this period of history following any overt criticism of powerful people or institutions in the land or inclusion in their work of suspect ideas which diverged from the accepted norm, which fuelled a need to hide them in allegory.

The allegory itself became suspect when in 1601 Sir Gelly Merrick commissioned a performance from Shakespeare's company, The Chamberlain's Men, of his *Richard II* in anticipation of a successful rebellion of Robert, Earl of Essex against Queen Elizabeth I. She recognised the parallel between the fate of the deposed King Richard II and the fate that Essex wished upon her. 'I am Richard II. Know ye not that,' she proclaimed. Prosecutions and the beheading of Merrick for treason followed. The actors themselves were ultimately excused from punishment, as it was recognised that their inevitable need for money would occasion them to take any offered commission.[7] However, some Freemasons nowadays claim that Shakespeare and his fellows were excused because of their Masonic connections! This was told to me by the custodian of Forty Hall in 1984 when I spoke to him about researching Freemasonry as a possible source of allegory in Shakespeare. "Shakespeare was a freemason himself, as were all his troupe," he said. "That's how they got off being taken to the gallows in the Richard II affair! Merrick was the scapegoat." The custodian was a freemason himself, and the story about Shakespeare was one that was circulated with pride among his associates as an example of the benefits of membership.

Risking prosecution should any proscribed material be detected, artists nevertheless continued to boldly weave a web of meanings in their work. There lurked in Shakespeare's England non-orthodox spiritual systems of transformation, such as alchemy, which came into prominence in his day due to the alternation of the state religion between Protestantism and Catholicism in the sixteenth and early seventeenth centuries depending on the monarch of the day, with violent religious persecution of dissidents. These non-orthodox systems, dangerously encoded into works of art, would have presented a thrilling challenge for artists.

Visual references in graphic art to arcana, such as the alchemical references to alchemy in Durer's *Melancholia* (see fig.12), and an allegory of 'Platonic Divine Love' in Botticelli's *Primavera* had antecedents in the pictures in the Emblem Books, such as Geoffrey Whitney's *Choice of Emblems* (1551).[8] Shakespeare would have had access to these and Henry Green, writing in *Shakespeare and The Emblem Writers*, identifies specific emblems used by the playwright in *The Comedy of Errors:* II. i. 97 – *Eagle renewing its feathers*; II. ii. 167 – *Elm and vine*; III. ii. 27 – *Sirens and Ulysses,* etc.[9] These emblems presented pictures of such varied items as: faith, folly, astrology, love, The Prince, life, death, hostility, revenge, science, marriage, ignorance, and trees.[10] Whitney's own definition of an emblem explains their attraction:

> Something obscure to be perceived at the first, whereby, when with further consideration it is understood, it maie the greater delighte the behoulder, (Green, p. 6) [11]

Such a definition, I suggest, applies to the appeal of the allegories Shakespeare encodes in his plays, the delight he must have had in inventing them, and our pleasure in deciphering them.

The development of encoding Esoteric Arcana in plays: Shakespeare's forerunners

Shakespeare was not alone in this puzzle-making. He was following a developing tradition of his time in England. The playwright John Lyly, a forerunner of Shakespeare, presented his masque-like plays mainly for boy actors. In plays such as *Endimion*, I find many elements in common with *A Midsummer Night's Dream*: the lunar motifs, with the moon personified (Titania in *A Midsummer Night's Dream*, Cynthia in *Endimion*), obliquely referring to Elizabeth I. Hints of alchemic references are made in the specific use of words such as 'earth', 'lead', 'gold' and 'stone', suggesting that the hero Endimion is undergoing alchemic transformation. Other layers of meaning can be detected, such as Celtic motifs suggested by the fountain oracle in Lyly's story, Renaissance Platonism in the interchange between the heroine Cynthia and Pythagoras, and in the transforming effect of love on Corsites, Endimion, Cynthia, Semele, Dipsas and Tellus.

Another writer, Robert Greene, presents us with a very close contact with Shakespeare early on in his career. In his *Groatsworth of Wit* he writes a bitter condemnation of Shakespeare whom he calls:

> an upstart Crow, beautified with our feathers, that with his Tygers hart wrapt in a Players hyde supposes he is well able to bombast out a blanke verse as the best of you: and beeing an absolute Iohannes fac totum, is in his owne conceit the onely Shakes- scene in a country.[12]

D. Allen Caroll and Andrew S. Cairncross have suggested an allusion in the *Iohannes fac totum* to the revolutionary Jack Cade (sometimes called John Mend-All), and argue that Greene's attack refers to a speech that occurs in the scene of Shakespeare's *2 Henry V*, (III. i. 75-78) which introduces this Jack Cade and describes Gloucester:

> Seems he a dove? His feathers are but borrow'd
> For he's disposed as the hateful raven:
> Is he a lamb? His skin is surely lent him,
> For he's inclined as is the ravenous wolves. [13]

If this is the case, then I suggest the possibility that Greene could also have been referring to Shakespeare's coding of esoteric arcana in plays, and complaining that this was a custom copied from Greene and his fellow playwrights. The words 'dove', 'raven' and 'wolf' are key symbols in alchemy (see below p. 26). Shakespeare based the story of his *Winter's Tale*, (which I consider exemplifies chemical, exoteric Alchemy, see below pp. 26, 68-86), upon Greene's story *Pandosto*. Could this perhaps be revenge, or at least mockery?

In his traducing of Shakespeare, in using the term 'our feathers' Greene is referring to his colleague playwrights. One of these was George Peele, whose play *The Old Wives Tale* incorporates elements of certainly Celtic and possibly alchemic mysticism. An example of Celtic subtext lies in the scene containing a *Well of Life* within which are enchanted heads, the first of which offers gifts of corn and the second gold, which as it rises calls:

> Gently dip, but not too deep,
> For fear thou make the golden beard to weep.
> Fair maid, white and red,
> Comb me smooth and stroke my head,
> [...] And every hair a sheaf shall be,
> And every sheaf a golden tree. [14]

CHAPTER ONE

Ann Ross, in *Pagan Celtic Britain*, explains Peele's debt to Celtic tradition in this scene:

> All the elements present in the Celtic tradition are here – the heads in the well of life, their powers of speech and their fertility associations… and prosperity, both mercenary and agrarian, as shown by the bestowal of gold and corn…The combing and the smoothing of the head may be compared with the treatment of a severed head in the early Irish story Cath Almaine. [15]

In *Celtic Elements in Cymbeline*, Shirley Ann Reid notes Shakespeare's debt to this play in its Celtic emphasis, and to others such as *Clyomon and Clomydes*, where the importance of nature and the relationship between characters and Celtic nature spirits is evident.[16] I find this connection important in providing a precedent for the Celtic arcana in *Dream, Merry Wives, Tempest, All's Well that Ends Well* and *Cymbeline*.

There is also a possible alchemical reading of the above passage of Peele's verse in the use of the colours red, white and gold, which symbolise the last three of four general stages in alchemy, and the double emphasis on the gold which is its goal (see p. 26).

The fantastical element with its allegorical style in the work of Lyly, Greene and Peele may owe its nature to masques, the court entertainments. As described by E. K. Chambers in *The Elizabethan Stage*, these were extended metaphors of political and ethical allegory, elaborately costumed and performed essentially by amateurs, particularly members of the court themselves (pp. 56, 57).[17] This tradition would have been known to Shakespeare, a court performer.

Obviously, there have been many writers in later centuries who have enjoyed the pleasure in discovering esoteric arcana in Shakespeare's plays. Among these writers are: G. Wilson Knight in *Myth and Miracle: An essay on the Mystic Symbolism of Shakespeare*, (1929), *The Shakespearean Tempest* (1932), *Shakespeare and Religion* (1967), *The Wheel of Fire* (1978), *Shakespearean Dimensions*, (1984); Nevill Coghill in *The Basis of Shakespearean Comedy* (1950); John Vyvyan in *The Shakespearean Ethic* (1959), *Shakespeare and Platonic Beauty* (1961), *Shakespeare and the Rose of Love* (1960); Frances Yates in *Occult Philosophy in the Elizabethan Age* (1979); David Banes in *Shakespeare, Shylock and Kabbalah* (1978); Paul T. Olsen in *The Kabbala of Shakespeare*; Charles Nicholl in *The Chemical Theatre* (1980); Lyndal Abraham in *The Lovers and the Tomb* (1991), *Alchemical References in Anthony and Cleopatra* (1982); Luminitsa Niculescu in *Shakespeare and Alchemy* (1984); George Trevelyan in *The Merchant of Venice: An interpretation in the Light of the Holistic World-view* (1981); D.S. Savage in *An Alchemical Metaphor in Hamlet* (1952); Robert F. Fleissner, W.A Murray in *Why was Duncan's blood Golden?* (1996); and Peter Dawkins in *Vita Concordia* (1994) and an ongoing body of works. Please refer to the Bibliography for publication details of these works.

An internet search for *esoteric arcana in Shakespeare* brings up many interesting and informed articles and references. The difference between most of those items and this book is manifest in the experience Theatre Set-Up's actors and directors have of applying the esoteric arcana in their understanding of the scripts and implementing them in performance. In that sense there is a similarity between the experience of Theatre Set-Up and that of G. Wilson Knight, whose research was also performance-based.

General aspects of the Arcana
The esoteric arcana I identified in the plays were:

- **Alchemy**
- **Renaissance Platonism**
- **Renaissance magic**
- **The Cabala**
- **Theurgy**
- **Rites of Initiation**
- **Celtic motifs and mythologies, the Celtic Old World religion and Celtic mysticism**
- **The Bible**

All the arcana had features in common:

- Getting in touch with the Divine, often considered to be within all people.
- Improving, even transforming the psyche of the person carrying out the arcane process through surmounting ordeals which they faced.
- Most importantly, taking the experience of the divine and the benefits of a transformed psyche to other people.

Contemporaries of Shakespeare, Dr John Dee and Sir Francis Bacon, observed correspondences between different mystic systems, religions and initiations. In doing so, they followed a Renaissance tradition. Frances A. Yates tells us in *Giordano Bruno and the Hermetic Tradition* that Pico Della Mirandola in his *Apologia* asserts that 'Magia' (our magic') and 'Cabala' (see below p. 41) increased knowledge of the Christian mysteries (p. 106). [18]

An important goal of alchemy, theurgy and the Cabala was 'self-knowledge'. This links with Christianity, as Jesus himself taught "Know thyself". Furthering this syncretic view of alchemy with Christianity, the goal of alchemy, represented metaphorically as the 'Philosophers' Stone', was often pictured as Christ rising from a tomb, reflecting the resurrecting nature of the process (see fig. 4). As I hope to show in following chapters, Shakespeare's plays demonstrate this redemptive quality, especially the comedies, whose plots consist not only of interesting stories, but of processes which change and improve the protagonists.

All the arcana maintain that all matter - humans, animals, plants, the earth and its minerals, the planets of the solar system and the wider universe - are connected, even one and the same. The maxim of the practitioners of the arcana was 'as above, so below'. Recent science, demonstrating that all things are made of 'stardust', has proved those beliefs to be accurate!

The processes of the arcana may be considered to be circular rather than linear, the alchemic symbol of an 'Ouroboros', a snake eating its own tail (fig. 5) and alchemy imagined as a wheel (fig. 6), the symbols of this. Most of the arcana follow this circular pattern of entry of the protagonists into the processes of the arcana and a return, changed and improved, back into everyday life, a pattern followed in Shakespeare's plays. The person (the neophyte) seeking the Divine will take a route through a metaphorical labyrinth fraught with challenges which he/she must overcome, and whose centre contains the Divine, which can only be reached if deserved.[19] In this surmounting of challenges in order to deserve contact with the Divine, the neophyte is assisted by a guide, called a hierophant.

The Cabala, however, presents an additional process in the form of a 'Tree of Life', upon which the neophyte travels in paths connected to the tree-trunk and to its branches (see *The Merchant of Venice*, Chapter Nineteen and fig. 3). Both tree-trunk and branches contain spheres, called 'sephiroth', which Parfitt in *The Elements of the Qabalah* defines as the names 'given to each of the eleven emanations of cosmic manifestations' (p. 132). In *Meetings With Amazing People*, Parfitt defines the Tree of Life as 'a map designed to help us understand ourselves and our place in the cosmos' (p.105).[20] Discussing the Renaissance practice of the Cabala, Yates calls the sephiroth 'names or powers of God'.[21] The path of the Celtic UnderWorld Journey is also tree-shaped, but the neophyte travels downward not upward (see Chapter Six).

The divinity at the heart of the labyrinth will vary according to the culture. In the ancient Greek initiatory rites of Eleusis this was the goddess Demeter; in Renaissance Platonism it was 'Divine Love', in alchemy the 'Philosophers' Stone', but in most initiations the Divine is known as the 'light', or sometimes as the 'word', which Christians identify as Christ (see the Bible, St John 1. 1-5). In Christian practice, the rite of baptism is believed to steep the baptised person in the spirit of Christ, and the plunging into water and subsequent re-emergence symbolises the process of improving transformation that the baptised person should demonstrate thereafter. The Cabala seeks to find the divinity within the Cabalist. I believe that Shakespeare wove these different arcana throughout his plays to give all their benefits to his characters and through them to the audiences of his plays.

The roles of the hierophants obviously also vary. Mostly these are older people who have themselves passed initiation. The neophyte must rarely be alone, which is often considered to be dangerous. Even in alchemy, the alchemist entering the transforming process must always have an assistant (of opposite gender to his own, see Chapter Four). Perhaps the most unusual hierophant is a visualised white cow in the Celtic UnderWorld journey (see Stewart, *The UnderWorld Initiation*, p. 246).[22] The Cabalist can practice alone or with company.

The challenges that the neophyte must face will vary in type and intensity according to the aim of the initiation. These may involve physical torture as in some cultures, fitting the neophyte for survival in a harsh world. These may be such that the neophyte does not survive (see Chapter Seventeen). Patience and toleration of lowly tasks is usually involved (see Ferdinand in Chapter Nine). The alchemist must endure the time lapses of the chemical processes and tolerate the arduous labour of the different stages, while the subject of the alchemy must endure the trials of the process (see Leontes in Chapter Four). The lovers in Renaissance Platonism must remain true to each other in spite of the challenges they face. This can be seen in the relationship between the lovers in the last acts of *Two Gentlemen, Comedy, Love's Labour's, Romeo and Juliet, Dream, Merchant, Merry Wives, As You Like It, Much Ado, Twelfth Night, All's Well, Measure, Antony and Cleopatra, Cymbeline, Winter's Tale* and *Tempest*.

The Cabalist must be grounded in the real world and face challenges in following a path through life which honours the reason for his incarnation: 'The key is to find our own purpose or true will and then to do it', thus achieving the alignment of themselves, 'as souls with the universal spirit, and can actualize the identity between the microcosm and the macrocosm' (see Parfitt, *The Qabalah* pp. 69-70). Cabalist practitioners, in order to attain this result, will work to improve different aspects of themselves and the corresponding names and powers of God as represented by the spheres on the branches of the *Tree Of Life* (see fig. 3). Christians must even face martyrdom (exampled by Christ and his disciples) if faced with challenges to their loyalty to their religion and be sacrificed for the greater good (see *Romeo* and *Juliet*, Story Section 12).

The following sections describe the kinds of esoteric arcana found in Shakespeare's plays, and I identify sources available to Shakespeare.

ALCHEMY

Sources available to Shakespeare
The Compound of Alchymie, written by George Ripley in 1471 but reprinted in London in 1591; *Mirror of Alchemy* by Roger Bacon (London, 1597). Literary allegorical sources are *Metamorphoses* by Ovid, available to Shakespeare both in the original Latin and in Golding's translation (1567) and *The Golden Ass* by Apuleius, translated into English by William Adlington in 1566.[23]

History of Alchemy
The word alchemy is derived from the Arabic term *al kimia*. The exact origins of the practice are not known, but it was established circa 300-200 B.C. both in the Far East, particularly in China, where there were many attempts to produce an *Elixir of Longevity,* and in the West, centred in Greece and Alexandria, where alchemists specialised in working with metals and minerals (see *Alchemy, The Great Work*, by Cherry Gilchrist, p.10).[24] The western schools of alchemy moved to the Arabic world from the fifth to the sixth centuries A.D., until the twelfth century, when Europeans again took an interest in its practice. In the following centuries, the art was practised with enthusiasm throughout Europe, and experiments with chemicals and the distillation of liquid essences fostered scientific techniques later employed in chemistry, physics and medicine.

In *The Chemical Theatre*, Charles Nicholl reports that although alchemy was legally considered a felony from 1404 to 1689, many prominent members of Elizabethan society from Sir Philip Sidney to Sir Walter Raleigh and even Queen Elizabeth I herself followed its practice in its acceptable philosophic form (pp. 13-22).[25] This philosophic practice of alchemy led to the term 'sophic' being added to items in the process such as 'sophic sulphur' and 'sophic mercury', and is classified as 'esoteric alchemy' as opposed to the chemical form of alchemy, 'exoteric alchemy'.

George Ripley's Twelve 'Gates' (stages) of Alchemy

The process assumes 'the oneness of all matter' and the reflection of 'the cosmos' in 'the microcosmos (mankind)'. As a chemical process, 'exoteric alchemy' is designed to refine and transform 'base matter' (also called 'prima materia') into gold through a set pattern of processes which Ripley, the author of *The Compound of Alchymie*, calls 'Twelve Gates' (as if they were the gates of a castle), namely:

1. **Calcination**, wherein 'sophic sulphur' also called the 'Red King', (often imaged as a lion, hence the occasional significance in Shakespeare's plays of names including 'leo', the Latin for 'lion', such as Leontes, Leonato and Leonatus Posthumus (see *Winter's Tale*, *Much Ado* and *Cymbeline*). However, sometimes the lion is used as a symbol for chemicals in the process (see Leonine and Cleon in *Pericles*) and even for the sun. A lioness or a lion represented with cubs signifies the multiplying of the Philosophers' Stone (see fig. 7). 'Sophic sulphur' is combined with 'sophic mercury', also known as the 'White Queen', hence the significance of names in the Greek form of the god Mercury, 'Hermes', such as Hermione and Hermia (see *Winter's Tale* and *Dream*), although this may also signify air. The union of these materials produces 'a new generation of substances' (see fig. 8).
2. **Dissolution**, in which the breaking down of the 'substance' is begun.
3. **Seperation**, (Ripley's spelling) in which the elements are separated.
4. **Coniunctio**, a Chemical Wedding. Here, a by-product of the substance may be consumed by the substance itself, known as 'the King eats his son' (see fig. 9). Other images generated by alchemy at this stage are of a wolf (the chemical antimony) eating the King (see fig. 10). In this image, the goal of alchemy is anticipated with a 'resurrected king' emerging in the distance from a purging fire.
5. **Putrefaction** is a violent, black stage, often represented by a tempest or a raven (see fig. 11) in which all the elements are broken down, and the 'body', the 'Red King' of the substance is 'tried', being continually washed and heated, while it is separated from

the 'spirit', the 'White Queen' of the process, which ascends in the alchemic vessel as vapour into a 'celestial sphere'.

6. **Congelation**, a white stage (often symbolised by a dove), takes a long period of time, wherein the 'flying spirits' are congealed while the 'body' is purged.
7. **Cibation** is a 'feeding' stage to improve the constituents of the process.
8. **Sublimation** is another violent stage, involving further separating and purifying using much water. Sometimes this is imaged as a storm (see *Winter's Tale*).
9. **Firmentation** (Ripley's spelling) a 'red stage', fixes and resolves the solution. There are three 'Ferments', two of which 'be of bodies in nature cleer', and the third is the 'Red Lion', which must be combined with essences 'begat of itself'.
10. **Exaltation**. The 'spirit' or vapour 'descends' into the 'body of the substance' and the goal of alchemy, the Philosophers' Stone (a reddish powder), is achieved.

It is important to note that the image of the 'Stone' has its source in the ancient Greek legend in which the god Saturn, informed by augury that one of his sons would supplant him as king, devours each of his children at birth. However his wife, Rhea, deceives him by replacing his new-born son Zeus with a stone, which he consequently spits out. It is this stone which alchemists selected as a metaphor for the goal of their operation (see fig. 12). It is not, as is sometimes believed, some kind of precious gem! The selection of this stone from the Greek legend relating to the god Saturn, combined with his function as the god of time (the precise timing of each stage of the alchemical process being critical), motivated alchemists to designate him the supervising god or patron of the process. In *Winter's Tale*, Saturn/Time appears as a character, which I think emphasises the play's alchemic significance.

In order to avoid religious persecution and to emphasise their common ground, many of the esoteric arcana were Christianised, hence the 'Philosophers' Stone' was often symbolically presented as the resurrected Christ rising from a tomb (see above p. 23 and fig. 4). Often, this resurrected aspect of the 'Philosophers' Stone' is figured when it is referred to as a 'phoenix', the legendary bird said to have been able to rise alive from its own ashes. Reflecting the self-sacrificing aspect of Christ as the Stone, it is often symbolised as a pelican feeding its young from its own plucked flesh, a misunderstanding due to the unseen feeding pouch beneath the pelican's chest (see figs 7, 16). Sometimes just the chemical goal is remembered in the Stone's identity as 'gold'.

Where the aim of alchemy was to transform a person's psyche, or the self (which was also imaged as a 'king'), a metaphor of an old king drowning and being replaced by a new king was created. The old king being succeeded by the new is very much the theme of the final scenes of *Macbeth, Lear* and *Hamlet* (see fig. 13).[26]

11. **Multiplication**. The transformative red powder, the 'Philosophers' Stone' is cast where change is required (chemically upon lead to turn it into gold). This stage is imaged as a lioness in the process of feeding her cubs (see fig. 7).
12. **Projection**. The benefits of the process are projected widely wherever needed.

Ripley also cites the different combinations throughout the above twelve stages of alchemy of the elements of earth, air, water and fire, imaging this as the 'Wheel of Alchemy'. Until recent, more scientifically-informed times, it was maintained that all matter consisted of these elements, formed in different quantities and combinations (see figs 2, 6 and 39).

Alchemy in Shakespeare's plays
It was believed that alchemy could manifest 'psychological transformation' in the person practising it and even 'improve the nature of the world'. I believe that this latter aim might have influenced Shakespeare in his encoding of it in his plays. Whether it is known and understood or not, any performer of Shakespeare's plays is practising alchemy (and all the esoteric arcana) in their allegorical form, and who is to say that this does not improve the nature of the world? Certainly at any point in time, someone, somewhere worldwide will be putting on a performance of a

Shakespeare play and enjoying its benefits in whatever form they may be found, the esoteric benefits, I believe, being an unwitting consequence of performance.

I thus believe that in his plays Shakespeare practised alchemy in metaphorical form with this intent, the 'base matter' or 'body' of the process being represented in them by a place or institution, or by a character or group of characters who would undergo trials in the course of the stage action. The 'spirit' or 'soul' of the process, which would be forced apart from the 'body' into an 'astral or celestial sphere', would be someone of the opposite sex who would later symbolically descend back into the process so that the 'Philosophers' Stone' could be achieved. Obvious examples of body/spirit separations in the plays occur between Romeo and Juliet in *Romeo and Juliet,* Leontes and Hermione in *Winter's Tale*, Claudio and Hero in *Much Ado About Nothing*, Posthumus and Imogen in *Cymbeline*, Egeon and Emilia in *Comedy*, Proteus and Julia, Valentine and Silvia in *Two Gentlemen*, King Ferdinand, Berowne, Longaville, Dumaine and the Princess of France, Rosaline, Maria, Katharine in *Love's Labour's*, Demetrius and Helena, Lysander and Hermia in *Dream*, Pericles and Thaisa in *Pericles*, Bassanio and Portia, Gratiano and Nerissa in *Merchant*, Orlando and Rosalind in *As you Like It,* Bertram and Helena in *All's Well that Ends Well*, Angelo and Mariana in *Measure for Measure*, Antony and Cleopatra in *Antony and Cleopatra*, Hamlet and Ophelia in *Hamlet*, Macbeth and Lady Macbeth in *Macbeth*, Othello and Desdemona in *Othello* and King Lear and Cordelia in *King Lear*.

Alchemy itself used many metaphorical terms. The 'base matter' (sometimes called 'Prima Materia' or the 'substance'), the 'body' of the process (lead in its chemical practice), was also called 'dragon', 'snake', 'serpent', 'whale', 'earth', 'toad' and 'King' (see above p. 26 and fig. 14). These words are often spoken by characters in the plays at points in the action when the part of the metaphorical process to which they refer is taking place.

Shakespeare implies that Romeo is the 'base matter' of the alchemy of the play when he refers to himself as 'lead': (I. iv. 15) and 'earth': 'Turn back, dull earth, and find thy centre out' (II. i. 2). Juliet refers to him as both a 'serpent' and a 'dragon' in the paradox of his seeming deception of her when she learns of his killing Tybalt: 'O serpent heart, hid with a flowering face | Did ever dragon keep so fair a cave?' (III. ii. 73, 74). She goes on to use other images of alchemy, 'raven', 'dove', 'wolvish' and 'substance': 'Dove-feather'd raven, wolvish-ravening lamb! | Despised substance of divinest show!'(III. ii. 76, 77).

In *Dream*, the character Demetrius can be identified as 'earth', the 'base matter' of an alchemical reading of the play, by his name, which suggests Demeter, an ancient Greek earth goddess. In the same way the 'base matter' of an alchemic reading of *Merry Wives* can be interpreted as Sir John Falstaff as he is referred to as 'lead' by the servant John: 'I had as lief bear so much lead' (IV. ii. 108). He is also referred to as a whale by Mistress Ford: 'What tempest, I trow, threw this whale, with many tuns of oil in his belly, ashore at Windsor?' (II. i. 56). Similarly, Cleopatra whose sobriquet is 'serpent of the Nile', may be the 'base matter' of an alchemical reading of *Antony and Cleopatra*. The king himself is the 'base matter' in *King Lear*.[27] King Leontes performs this function in *Winter's Tale*, as do also the kings in the history plays, and in *Love's Labour's, Cymbeline, Macbeth* and *Hamlet*.

The agent and initiator of the process, sometimes manipulated by the alchemist, was often referred to as 'Mercury'. Examples of Shakespeare's use of this convention in alchemical readings of his plays are Puck in *Dream*, in *Love's Labour's* the messenger Marcade, in *Merry Wives of Windsor* Mistress Quickly, in *Romeo and Juliet* Mercutio and then Friar Lawrence, in *Tempest* Ariel, in *Cymbeline* Iachimo, and in *Winter's Tale* Dion, and later Autolycus. However, alchemical texts and images often refer to the Greek messenger god Mercury as the tortured subject of the alchemy.

Sometimes, Shakespeare provides an alchemical reading of his plays, not in Ripley's twelve stages but summarised in a colour-coded four: black, white, red, gold (see *Dream*, Chapter Ten).

The Emerald Tablet and Hermeticism
A legendary personage with the name Hermes, the Greek form of the name Mercury and also tagged Trismegistus (who, in fact over a sequence of years, was probably a number of different people), was credited as the

author of the *Emerald Tablet*, a treatise which laid down the main precepts of alchemy, giving it the alternative name, especially in its philosophic form, of 'Hermeticism'.[28]

The alchemists in the plays
In what I consider to be Shakespeare's encoding of alchemy in his plays, he himself is usually the alchemist, the twists and turns of the plot carrying out the processes of transformation. However, sometimes characters in the plays perform this function. The most obvious of these is Paulina in *Winter's Tale*. Throughout the play (within the alchemic reading), she controls the action in the Sicilian court from the moment when the death of Mamillius is announced (III. ii. 145), creating an outcome which results in the 'Philosophers' Stone'. In *Much Ado* it is the friar who becomes the alchemist, taking control of the action after Claudio accuses Hero of dishonour. He even cites the alchemic credo 'die to live' (IV. i. 253). The Queen in *Cymbeline* functions as an alchemist. In Theatre Set-Up performances, I sometimes performed these roles with the intention in the forefront of my mind of practising alchemy within the stage action, and found that this gave strength and truthfulness to these characters (see fig. 15). All actors must perform their lines with a clearly-defined intention, and this was mine. Duke Vincentio in *Measure for Measure* can also be regarded as the alchemist directing the action of the transforming process.

I was not the only actor performing roles in Shakespeare's plays with 'alchemic intent'. Mark Rylance, the actor and the Artistic Director of Shakespeare's Globe for many years, who shared my opinion of the arcane content of Shakespeare's plays, told me that he performed the roles he took in the plays 'hermetically'. An example of this was his performance of Richard II in 2003, which showed the depths of character benefiting from this practice. In a spectacular production in 2002 of a dramatized version of *The Golden Ass*, the ancient text of Apuleius whose story is an obvious metaphor of alchemy, Mark performed the role of the Ass, who is the 'base matter' of the alchemy. As his dramatic intent was informed by knowledge of its true meaning, that gave us a truly powerful performance in a magnificent production!

The Sun and Moon
Some characters in Shakespeare's plays can be interpreted as taking on the features of alchemy's 'parents' of the Philosophers' Stone, the sun and the moon, which are conceptualised in the doctrine of Hermes Trismegistus in the mythological *Emerald Tablet*. In *Dream*, Oberon fulfils the role as sun, in *Merchant*, the Doge of Venice, in *Measure* Duke Vincentio, in *Romeo and Juliet* Prince Escalus. In *Comedy*, the role is named less subtly as Solinus, taking the name from the Latin for 'sun'. The feminine moon is less represented: Titania could symbolise the moon in *Dream* and perhaps the Countess of Rousillon in *All's Well*. In images of the very mystifying iconography of alchemy, the sun and moon are often represented as presiding over the operation (see fig. 8).

The Hermaphrodite
Featuring in some alchemic/hermetic iconography is a hermaphrodite figure called a 'rebus' or 'rebis' (see fig. 16). Sometimes this is portrayed as one half man and the other half woman, while often it is a man with female aspects or a woman with male aspects. A hermaphrodite has always been important in the esoteric world, symbolising as it does divinity beyond the limitations of gender. Pharaohs of ancient Egypt were sometimes represented like this, indicating their divinity. There was a belief that the Merovingian Dynasty of France (476-750 AD) inherited the 'seed of Christ' through the legend that Mary Magdalene, pregnant with Christ's child, travelled to the south of France, where she and her descendants lived, becoming kings of the Merovingian dynasty (see Chapter Eight and Chapter Twelve). Sometimes, these monarchs and their descendants were represented as being androgynous; for example, King Francis I was deliberately portrayed as being pregnant (see fig. 80 in Wind, *Pagan Mysteries in the Renaissance*). In Botticelli's *Primavera*, the figure of Flora has a female body but a male face, hinting at divinity in nature (see Wind, fig. 25). Shakespeare has heroines who disguise themselves as men, following this androgynous tradition, including Julia in *Two Gentlemen*, Viola in *Twelfth Night*, Portia in *Merchant*, Rosalind in *As You Like It* and Imogen in *Cymbeline*. All these women are remarkable, and although Shakespeare's purpose may predominantly be expedient in terms of stage

craft as his female characters were played by boys and men, he could also be hinting at their hermetic significance (see fig. 17).

Puffers
The derogatory term 'puffer' was applied to anyone practising alchemy to attempt to gain easy wealth.

RENAISSANCE PLATONISM
Sources available to Shakespeare
Plato's *Symposium*, translated into Latin and mediated by Marsilio Ficino in his *Commentary on Plato's Symposium* of 1484 and accessible to readers of Shakespeare's time through its publication in Latin in Basel in 1561 and in Lugdunum, the modern Lyon, in 1590.[29] T. W. Baldwin in *William Shakspeare's Small Latin and lesse Greek* (1944), asserts that Shakespeare's education at the grammar school in Stratford-upon-Avon would have given him adequate facility in reading Latin. This is corroborated by other writers including F. P. Wilson and Jonathan Bate.[30]

In *Marsilio Ficino's Commentary on Plato's Symposium*, Sears Jayne has made Ficino's translation not only available in English but also established the contemporary English connection to the Italian Ficino revealed in the extant letters dated around 1595 between Ficino and John Colet, Dean of St Paul's, in *John Colet and Marsilio Ficino*.[31] This correspondence demonstrated the interest (and the need in order to avoid the persecution of Christian religious institutions such as the Inquisition) in reconciling concepts in the pagan texts of Plato with Christianity. Ficino's mediation of the Plato text in this way followed a trend established by Neoplatonic writers in medieval times leading up to the Italian Renaissance and exemplified in works by Dante and Petrarch.[32]

Divine Love
I learnt about the Renaissance Platonism concerned with Divine Love in Shakespeare's plays through reading *Shakespeare and Platonic Beauty* by John Vyvyan.[33] In this book and in *Shakespeare and the Rose of Love*, Vyvyan identifies the connection between the Ficino-Plato concepts and Shakespeare's treatment of the lovers in his plays.[34] Following Vyvyan's

lead, I studied an English translation of Plato's *Symposium*, tracing any possible influences of this text upon the Shakespeare play I was directing for Theatre Set-Up each year.[35] In *Shakespeare and the Rose of Love*, Vyvyan demonstrates the development and application in Shakespeare's plays of his dramatic version of Divine Love through Renaissance sources, such as *The Book of the Courtier* by Baldesar Castiglione and Edmund Spenser's *Hymne in Honor of Beautie*.[36] For this reason, in the explanatory notes given to the cast and audiences of Theatre Set-Up's plays, I have retained the title of this philosophy as 'Renaissance Platonism' although sometimes I use the term 'Divine Love'.

The key idea of this philosophy, subsequently developed by Renaissance poets such as Edmund Spenser and given theatrical form by Shakespeare, is that a 'Divine Love' should exist between lovers, their souls' mutual devotion elevating them towards God as they experience a love akin to His for humanity. This should follow a pattern:

1. **Recognising each other from what may have been a previous spiritual existence** (often love at first sight as between Romeo and Juliet). The lovers are considered to be predestined companion souls. Of great importance in the nature of 'Divine Love' is the understanding which the lovers must possess of true beauty, which is the beauty of the inner nature of the beloved, their soul, whose source and nature is Godhead, not their outer appearance. The experience is likened to an illumination of great light, and the trembling which sometimes occurs when people fall in love is identified as a spiritual tremor from the 'Divine Mind'.
2. **The love engendered is via the 'mind-soul' in a quasi-holy context.** Physical consummation may only take place later. If the love is merely physical, without the communing of souls, the love is called 'base love'.
3. **The lovers must remain constant to each other through the trials that assail the course of their love.** It is this constancy and survival of trials which beset the course of their 'Divine Love' (that echoes the love of God for humanity) which creates an 'ascent to God'.

4. **This system of belief holds the notion that individuals, before they became humans, existed as part of Godhead**. Thus in this 'ascent to God', the 'Divine Love' between lovers can redress their previous fall from God down to earth when they are incarnated as humans. In *Merchant*, Shakespeare indicates this belief in 'this muddy vesture of decay', an image for incarnated flesh, which Lorenzo observes to Jessica prevents humans from hearing the musical harmony which he claims the stars they are looking at are creating among themselves, in a 'Harmony of the Spheres' (V. i. 58-65). This pattern of love can be identified in Shakespeare's lovers, the play *Romeo and Juliet* being beyond doubt his work which most exemplifies 'Divine Love' between the lovers (see below Chapter Seventeen and fig. 18) but also can be applied to many other lover-protagonists in his plays who ultimately, as seemingly predestined companion souls, are matched up: see Proteus and Julia, Valentine and Sylvia, in *Two Gentlemen*; Antipholus of Syracuse and Luciana in *Comedy*; Petruchio and Katherina, Lucentio and Bianca in *Shrew*; Ferdinand King of Navarre and the Princess, Berowne and Rosaline, Dumaine and Katharine, Longaville and Maria in *Love's Labour's*; Theseus and Hippolyta, Lysander and Hermia, Demetrius and Helena in *Dream*; Bassanio and Portia (see fig. 20), Lorenzo and Jessica, Gratiano and Nerissa in *Merchant*; Benedick and Beatrice, Claudio and Hero in *Much Ado*; Orlando and Rosalind, Oliver and Celia in *As You Like it* (as Hymen observes, Touchstone and Audrey are mismatched); Orsino and Viola, Sebastian and Olivia, Sir Toby Belch and Maria in *Twelfth Night*; Fenton and Anne Page in *Merry Wives;* Antony and Cleopatra in *Antony and Cleopatra* (see fig. 19); Bertram and Helena in *All's Well*; Duke Vincentio and Isabella, Angelo and Mariana, Claudio and Juliet in *Measure*; King of France and Cordelia in *Lear;* Florizel and Perdita in *Winter's Tale* (see fig. 21); and Ferdinand and Miranda in *Tempest*. The coupling of Angelo and Mariana in *Measure*, and Bertram and Helena in *All's Well* (achieved by the deception of a 'bed-trick' in which the 'companion soul' is joined through love-making to the protagonist by being substituted in bed in a darkened

room for the woman that the protagonist lusts after) is so strange that these have been tagged 'problem plays' (see below Chapters Twenty and Eight).

Plato's *Symposium* consists of a series of speeches on love given by participants over the dessert course of a banquet. The essence of 'Divine Love' summarised above is given in the speech given by Benci in Jayne's translation, as recounted to the philosopher Socrates by the wise woman Diotima. Jayne translates the name of this version of love as 'How the soul is Raised from Bodily Beauty to the Beauty of God' (p. 212).

The Divided Soul
Many different views of the guests at the banquet are expressed in this work of Plato, and many elements find their ways into Shakespeare's plays (see Chapter Sixteen, fig. 22). Of particular significance are the views expressed in the fourth speech given by the guest Aristophanes, entitled *The Myth of Plato on the Ancient Nature of Man is explained*, which we know as 'The Divided Soul'. This story tells of the origins of mankind consisting of three sexes, male born of the sun, female born of the earth, and a third, bisexual, which was a combination of them both, born of the moon. This third sex was a rounded creature with four legs, four hands and two identical faces on either side of the head (see Jayne, p. 154). Their proud moon-born spirits caused them to attempt an attack on the gods and to climb to heaven, in punishment for which Jupiter cut them in half, threatening to split them again if they repeated the offence. Subsequently, each of the two halves of the divided nature of man desired and sought its other half, which it embraced when encountered. To prevent 'privation and inactivity', Jupiter provided each half with a means of intercourse (Jayne p. 154). Thus love is innate in all men, striving to make the divided whole, and to heal mankind (see Jayne, pp. 154-55).

Further interpretation of this story is given in the Platonic text by one of the guest-characters whom Plato calls 'Landino', who claims that the divided body is an allegory designed to conceal sacred secrets from the profane and that the original humans were whole, having two perceptions of 'lights', one a 'natural light' by which they could behold 'inferior and co-equal things', and one a 'supernatural light' which gave them perception of 'superior things' (Jayne p.155). When they threatened Jupiter, he demoted them to being able to perceive only the 'natural light' through their descent into human form. When humans become adolescents, they seek out the 'supernatural light', the other half of themselves. Through the practice of prudence, courage, justice and temperance, they can succeed in knowledge of God by regaining the 'supernatural light' or 'Divine light'. This is represented by a banquet, where those who love God feast on eternal bliss. I believe that Shakespeare adapts features of this story in *Comedy*.

Phaedrus

Other concepts featured in the *Symposium* that find their way into Shakespeare's plays are the beliefs that the guests in the story express concerning the nature of creation as perceived in ancient Greece. In the first story by Phaedrus, love is regarded as a god creating order out of the chaos of a formless world. In *Backgrounds of Shakespeare's Thought*, John Erskine Hankins observes Shakespeare's debt to Plato in *Othello* when Othello claims that to lose the love of Desdemona would return him to a state of chaos (III. iii. 90-92).[37] This has a double meaning, of course, as the state of lunacy (the 'divided soul' born of the moon, 'luna' in its Latin form) in Shakespeare's day was regarded as a descent into chaos and Othello's mind at that point in the play is losing any sense of reason in believing Iago's false accusations of Desdemona, culminating in his insanity in murdering her.[38] The guest Agli continues within the speeches during the banquet to discuss another creation concept, that of the generative power of seeding nature ('nature's germens') which Shakespeare expounds in *Macbeth*. Macbeth demands augury of the witches regardless of the consequences, 'though the treasure/ Of nature's germens tumble all together' (IV. i. 58, 59).

The guest Cavalcanti discusses the relationship of love to beauty. This asserts the Platonic concept that true physical beauty stems from God-given beauty of the soul. In *Measure* Shakespeare demonstrates knowledge of this idea. The disguised Duke praises Isabella's beauty as stemming from her goodness so that it will not diminish as she ages but only increase with time (III. i. 184-188).

I consider that these uses of concepts within his scripts provide evidence of Shakespeare's knowledge of Plato's *Symposium* and its concept of 'Divine Love'.

The Metaphor of the Charioteer in *Phaedrus*

Plato's *Phaedrus* is also significant as a source of another idea in Shakespeare's plays (see Chapter Eleven and Chapter Eighteen). This particular philosophy was developed from the idea that there are two daemons of love, one of which inspires love of the divine in the beloved and the other which inspires procreation, causing abuse of its gifts. Plato develops this idea with the dominant metaphor in *Phaedrus* that souls consist of three elements: reason, spirit and appetite. Reason is presented in the metaphor as a charioteer with wings which can lift the soul to 'ultimate truth' in a chariot harnessed to a white horse, which represents the spirit, and a black horse, which represents the appetite.[39] The steady course of the chariot is conditioned by the charioteer's ability to control the restlessness of the black horse and to balance its urges with the power of the white horse, which will allow the charioteer visions of reality beyond the vault of the sky. Those whose control of their black horse is so poor that they lose their wings fall from the chariot down into matter and into a mortal body.[40]

Plutarch, whose account of the history of Antony and Cleopatra was used by Shakespeare as the source of his play, *Antony and Cleopatra*, observed that the life of Antony exemplified Plato's story of the charioteer. Shakespeare seems to have followed that observation in his play, the black horse being Egypt and Cleopatra, while the white horse becomes Rome with Octavius and his sister Octavia (see below p. 366 and fig. 19). Proteus in *Two Gentlemen* also exemplifies this metaphor (see fig. 23).

CHAPTER TWO:
ESOTERIC ARCANA II: RENAISSANCE MAGIC, THE CABALA, THEURGY AND RITES OF INITIATION

Sources available to Shakespeare

Apuleius, *The Golden Ass*; *Corpus Hermeticum*, translated and mediated by Marsilio Ficino in Italy 1463; *Picatrix*, originally an Arabic text but circulated in Latin translation throughout the 15th and 16th centuries; Marsilio Ficino, *De Triplici Vita,* Italy: 1489; the *Zohar*; Johann Reuchlin, *De Arte Cabalistica,* (Haguenau: 1517); Henry Cornelius Agrippa, *De Occulta Philosphia,* (Antwerp 1533); Johannes Trithemius, *Stenanographia*, (written in 1499 and privately circulated until published in Frankfurt in 1606); John Dee, *Monas Hieroglyphica,* (first published in Latin in Antwerp 1564).[1]

All these arcana are closely linked, and in many of their aspects inter-changeable, a fact which Shakespeare makes use of in *Tempest* (see Chapter Nine). His magus, Prospero, exercises natural magic, while the Cabala and theurgy are integrated into the plot, with Ferdinand the main initiate. *Dream* and *Cymbeline* also have magical content, but I think that its source in those plays is Celtic (see Chapters Nine and Three).

RENAISSANCE MAGIC

The study and practice of magic during the Renaissance was an integral part of academic philosophy in Shakespeare's time. It depended upon the idea that all creation, from Heaven and the stars through humanity to birds, animals, insects, plants, stones and minerals, was inter-linked in a series of 'correspondences', and that by gaining access to the 'spirit' within one of these you could control its associates. In this 'sympathetic magic', every object in the world was believed to hold within itself 'occult sympathies' which flowed into it from the star on which it depended, and the skilled magician could gain control of these by manipulating its correspondences, entering the whole linked system and gaining access to other objects, stars and correspondences. A magician could thus draw power from natural and divine order in 'natural magic', dealing primarily with forces of nature and the elements, what Prospero calls his 'rough magic'. 'Higher' forms of magic, such as 'celestial magic' and 'ceremonial magic', were considered by magic practitioners to be superior to 'rough magic', as their practice depended upon a higher degree of intellectual and moral effort than rough magic, which exploited spirits in nature that they had captured. In order to succeed in achieving this elevation, the magician had to have superior mental strengths and powers, particularly in the application of mathematics.[2]

THE CABALA

Spain was the cradle of the European understanding of the Hebrew mystic system, the Cabala, as written in the *Zohar*.[3] Philosophers such as Raymond Lull used it as early as the 13th century, but after the expulsion of the Jews from Spain in the 15th century it became widely known in Europe, Henry Cornelius Agrippa incorporating it as a magic system in his *De Occulta Philosophia*. There were several important ways in which it became seminal:

- The Hebrew letters themselves were believed to have divine meanings so that by using them, divine powers could be invoked.
- The system of correspondences between all aspects of creation, the human body, the human condition and Divinity, which was called the 'Tree of Life', was used as a system of self-improvement. It was Marsilio Ficino who considered that 'soul' (his term for the psyche) was an inner dimension of all the arcana, and work on them must involve psychological transformation.[4] In *The Occult Philosophy in the Elizabethan Age,* Frances Yates describes how Ficino's pupil, Giovanni Pico della Mirandola, in his 'seventy two Cabalist *Conclusions*' introduced the Cabala into Renaissance thought (see above p. 23). She describes how he advocated a syncretic view of all the arcana, and considered that Christianity could be understood through a study of the ancient Hebrew texts, pioneering the schools of Christian Cabala which followed him.[5]

It is in this Christianised form that the Cabala could have become available to Shakespeare. Yates posits that it was the work (with extended Christian significance) of the Franciscan friar, Francesco Giorgi (1466-1540), who lived in Venice where many Jews lived and worked, that was Shakespeare's introduction to the Cabala. Giorgi's *De harmonia mundi* of 1525 and his other works were in John Dee's library, with free access to all.[6] John Dee, himself a Christian Cabalist, moved in the same court circles as Shakespeare, and it is unlikely that Shakespeare would not have availed himself of Dee's generous provision of his library and thus read Giorgi's Christian version of the Cabala.

The Tree of Life (see fig. 3)
The Syriac New Testament, printed in Vienna in 1555, was also surely included in Dee's library. It was claimed that Syriac, a form of Aramaic, was the language spoken by Jesus Christ and his apostles, and that the New Testament in that language, free of the distortions of subsequent translations, provided a pure version of the text. Included in this New Testament, at the beginning of the Gospel of St John, is a diagram of a Christianised version of the Cabala Tree of Life (see fig. 24). This would provide us with a correspondence of the Tree of Life with the works of Shakespeare and evidence of an opportunity for the playwright to integrate the kind of psychological progression advocated by Ficino (the influence of whose translation of Plato's *Symposium* is demonstrated in his treatment of the lovers in his plays) with his psychological version of alchemy applied in his plays through his characters and stage action. It is logical to presume that Pico's work advocating a syncretic use of these arcana would also have been available in Dee's library, and that it would have guided Shakespeare in this practice, giving his plays additional depth.

It is interesting to make a comparison of this diagram of the Christianised Tree of Life from 1555 with an earlier Hebrew version of 1516. Grillot de Givry, in *Witchcraft and Alchemy,* explains that there is little available Cabalistic iconography, but he displays an engraving of an Israelite Rabbi holding the Sephirotic Tree of Life (the spheres engraved with their original Jewish titles) which he has taken from a rare book, *Porta Lucis haec est porta tetragrammaton, justi intrabunt per eam* by Paulus

Ricius (Augsburg, 1516) in his private collection.[7] The shape of the Tree in this 16th century illustration is similar to the later version of 1555, and the meanings of the spheres, indicated by their Hebrew titles in the 1516 version, are identical. Later versions of the Tree, like those from the books by Will Parfitt and Gareth Knight which inform my understanding of the function of the Cabalistic Tree of Life, have Hebrew names of the spheres which are the same as those used in the 1516 version, but are variously translated into Roman script and the English language.

The core meaning of the Tree of Life is that there has been a descent of Divinity from the sphere called Kether, down through the conditioning spheres, each adding a different quality associated with the names of God that the spheres represent, manifesting the creation of the material world into the sphere at the base, Malkuth, which represents the earth and its living inhabitants, experienced through the senses. This is described as a 'Lightning Flash' (see fig. 25). The task of people living on earth is then to rise up through the paths and spheres of the Tree to experience the Divinity from which they have sprung.

The diagrammatic tree of Shakespeare's day (which I assume to be similar to the 1555 Syriac version) had 10 'divine emanations' or 'spheres' (in Hebrew the 'sephiroth'). These are like fruits at the end of 32 branch-like pathways, radiating from three main stems or pillars (like the trunk of a tree), and representing in the top part the spirit which is common to us all (the spheres presented in the form of a 'supernal' triangle), in the middle the spirit which is our own particular soul (the spheres presented in an inverted triangle) and at the bottom our physical body and the material world (presented also as an inverted triangle), below which is Malkuth (see fig. 26).

Observed nowadays is an eleventh sphere between the spirit and soul triangles called Daath, but as it is not featured in either the 1516 or 1555 versions of the Tree I do not include it in my analysis of Shakespeare's plays, either in *The Merchant of Venice* or *The Tempest* (which embraced an understanding of the Tree in production) or in the **Cabala: Post Production** interpretations of other plays which Theatre Set-Up did not include in its productions, but which members of the audiences of those plays have requested that I include in this book. I place the interpretations of the

Cabalistic Tree of Life at the end of the different chapters of these plays as they might be of use to directors, actors and audiences in understanding the place of this arcana among the others which I dealt with, and apologise to those who lamented the lack of their inclusion in our productions. These interpretations represent my personal understanding of the Tree.

The 'Pillars' of the Tree (see fig. 3)
The Tree and its spheres are divided into three pillars. On the right is the 'Pillar of Mercy', which in the Hebrew version of the Tree is influenced by a male ancestor and is positive and active. On the left is the 'Pillar of Severity', the Hebrew roots of which acknowledge influences from a female ancestor, and which is negative and passive. Between them on the 'trunk' of the Tree, indicating a balanced perspective, is the 'Middle Pillar' of equilibrium or consciousness. I believe that an understanding of the male/female characteristics of the 'Pillar of Mercy' and 'Pillar of Severity' is key to understanding Shakespeare's intentions in *The Merchant of Venice* and to its Cabalistic interpretation (see Chapter Nineteen), and that the pillars are significant in the Cabalistic interpretation of Antony and Cleopatra (see Chapter Eighteen).

The 'Sephiroth' (Spheres) of the Tree (see fig. 3)
There are many levels of meanings, interpretations and applications of the Tree, but a comparison of the 1516, 1555 and modern versions demonstrates a consistency not only in the basic names, but in the basic meanings of the spheres. The first meanings beyond the names given to the spheres are different manifestations of Divinity. Beyond that are lists of corresponding angelic orders and planets. There are correspondences with parts of the human body, as shown in the 1555 Tree of Life, and correspondences in the Christian Cabala with the body of Christ (see fig. 24). Of relevance to the personality development prescribed by Marsilio Ficino as 'soul' yet still very important to contemporary Cabalistic practice and, I believe, to Shakespeare's use of the Tree in his plays, are the characteristics found in the human psyche of each sphere. The target in the Cabalistic use of the Tree in this last way is two-fold: to attain a balanced personality and to access spiritual awareness of Divinity. This numinous sensibility may

include the ecstasy of sex. As Giovani Pico della Mirandola proclaimed in essence, these targets and the means to attain them reflect those of alchemy, theurgy (including initiation) and Renaissance Platonism.

Below is a list of the spheres, tabled in the order of the 'Lighting Flash', with first their given names, then their 'God names', and finally their characteristics within the psyche.[8]

Kether   Crown
                I am or I am become
                The Divine Self (Divinity within oneself)

Chockmah   Wisdom
                The Lord
                Spiritual Purpose

Binah   Understanding
                The Lord God
                Spiritual love

Chesed   Mercy
                God, The Mighty One
                The archetype of Love and Awareness

Geburah   Severity
                God of Battles, God Almighty
                The archetype of Will and Power (judgement)

Tiphareth   Beauty
                God made Manifest in the Sphere of Mind
                The centred self, 'The Silent Witness' (heart)

Netzach   Victory
                Lord of Hosts
                Feelings

Hod Glory
God of Hosts
Thoughts

Yesod The Foundation
The Almighty Living God
Subconscious (which includes traumas)

Malkuth The Kingdom
The Lord and King
Body and Senses (the material world)

In the use of the Tree to attain the targets of personal development, for example, a person who is over-emotional and lacking reason in their way of life would take steps to progress along the path from Netzach to Hod. Conversely, if their life was too cerebral, the path from Hod to Netzach would be attempted. Progress up the Tree is impossible without the clearing of traumas or any other negative psychic factors in the subconscious in Yesod. If the spheres and the paths between them are consciously worked upon, progress can be made. In Shakespeare's plays, the development of his characters can be read in this way, sometimes as individuals (as in Katherina in *The Taming of the Shrew*) and sometimes as part of a greater whole (as is Viola on behalf of Illyria in *Twelfth Night*).

Each sphere has associated with its name attributes and functions, particular colours, minerals, symbols, images, plants, animals, stars, energy centres, feelings and thoughts, so by having contact with them, or concentrating on them, you can strengthen yourself, if that is the need, with that sphere. To be equally balanced on the Tree of Life is to have a rounded, integrated personality and life. This target can be reached by working on the spheres in which you are deficient and the pathways between them (see fig.3).

Since we are all incarnated in this material world, work must always start and end with work on the sphere of the material world, **Malkuth** at the bottom of the Tree, thus becoming grounded. To correct deficiencies in your personality you would work from there sideways and upwards in the Tree, and, to make contact with the immortal aspects of your soul, the Divinity within you, you would work upwards towards the sphere **Kether** at the top of the Tree. Through the associations of the Tree with different parts of the body, you can work on your health. The system is widely used today to improve psychic health and to bring the benefits of spiritual awareness through to everyday life.[9]

I find it interesting that the spheres at the bottom of the Tree, concerned with our physical body and the material world, all relate to aspects of training and performance for actors. These spheres are: **Malkuth** (foundation, the real world appreciated through the senses), **Yesod** (where traumas and other negative features of the personality in the subconscious are cleared away), **Hod** (thoughts), **Netzach** (feelings) and the central part of the trunk of the Tree, bridging to the representation of our particular souls, **Tiphareth** (heart, beauty, calm centre). All relate to aspects of training and performance for actors. As in **Malkuth**, sensory perceptions and their imaginary recreation in the mind must be developed in order to recreate the world of the character being performed; as in **Yesod**, bad physical and mental habits of the actor must be eliminated so that they do not impose upon the character the actor is representing, so that only the movement and thoughts of the acted character are performed; as in **Hod**, the thinking through of character and script must be clear and logical; and as in **Netzach**, the actor must be able to recreate and experience the emotions of the character he is playing. If an actor is to work within a theatre ensemble and also survive performing any psychologically tortured characters, he/she must do so from a 'calm centre' as typified by **Tiphareth**, with the ability to return to it at the end of the performance.[10]

The presence of the Cabala in Shakespeare's plays is well documented. Some examples of this are in *Occult Philosophy in the Elizabethan Age* of Frances Yates; *Shakespeare, Shylock and Kabbalah* by Daniel Banes;[11] *The Kabbala of Shakespeare* by Paul T. Olsen;[12] *Shakespeare, Kabbalah and the Occult* by Daniel Y. Harris;[13] Philip Beitchman in *Alchemy of the Word: Cabala of the Renaissance*".[14]

THEURGY

This is the practice of benevolent magic, carried out for universal benefit. A magician, like a priest, functions as a link between the spiritual and the mundane everyday world, carrying benefits from the former to the latter. The process is similar to that practised in 'Rites of Initiation', the difference being that the practitioner is not an initiate. It is the arcane process at the centre of most mystic systems. In *A History of White Magic* Gareth Knight defines it as:

> The raising of consciousness to the appreciation of the powers and forces behind the external material world in a pious intention of developing spiritual awareness and subsequently helping to bring to birth the divine plan of a restored Earth.[15]

Adults attempting this task have always been aware, as in all the other arcana, of the correspondences between every aspect of creation. Furthermore, those practising in the Renaissance believed in a hierarchy within creation which linked a king (the primate of human society) to stability in nature.[16] Shakespeare demonstrates this belief in the sympathy of nature with the fate of human primates in the storm in the madness of King Lear in *Lear* (III. iv.), the unnatural acts within nature and the storm after the killing of King Duncan in *Macbeth* (II. iv. 6-9), and horrendous events and a storm before the assassination of Julius Caesar in *Julius Caesar* (II. ii. 16-24).

Shakespeare's contemporary, John Dee, was a practising magician who in many ways was an inspiration to the aspiring spirit of Elizabethan England. He expressed his core belief in the correspondences between all aspects of nature relevant to benevolent magic in his creation of the *Hieroglyphic Monad*, a diagram which visually linked them together (see fig. 27). Theatre Set-Up had a representation of this carved in wood as a part of our basic staging, and we attached it to our central rostrum as a declaration of our intent to incorporate Shakespeare's esoteric arcana in our productions until it disintegrated! (see fig. 2).

Part of the Elizabethan belief in this idea of the uniting of all creation within mankind was the concept of the human body incorporating within itself a symbol of the whole cosmos, imaged in the diagrammatic figure of *Adam Cadman*. I think Shakespeare satirised this idea in Dromio's description of Nell in *Comedy* (III. ii. 120-147). Practitioners of theurgy applaud this kind of satire, as the performance of magical practice without maintaining a sense of humour can lead to a lack of balance in its application. As with the Cabala, the person practising theurgy must be grounded in reality, demonstrating a stable personality.

RITES OF INITIATION

The rites of initiation feature a labyrinth into which the initiate (the neophyte) enters with the guide (the hierophant). The neophyte is presented with challenges which he/she must confront and overcome, including a near-death experience. If their bravery and moral strength is sufficient to cope with these challenges presented throughout the course of the labyrinth, he/she qualifies to be granted contact with a Divine presence at the heart of the labyrinth. Then the neophyte, strengthened by endurance and inspired by Divinity, goes out as an ordained graduate by a different route from the labyrinth, taking the benefits of the experience to other people.

This labyrinth may be a real structure, created with foliage or earthworks as borders to the neophyte's path; it may be a dark cave (like the caves of the Dordogne in France, the wall paintings there presenting symbols of the life challenges the neophyte must face); it may be a wood or forest (see *Dream*, *As You Like it*, and *Two Gentlemen* fig. 23); it may be represented as the wanderings of someone who is lost or goes to another domain (see *Tempest*, *Twelfth Night*, *Comedy*, *Shrew*, *Romeo and Juliet* and *Cymbeline*); it may be specifically located, (like the rites at Eleusis); downwards through the trunk of a tree (real or imagined), as in the Celtic UnderWorld journey (see *Cymbeline*) or a series of confined spaces as the prison in *Measure*; or all of these may exist only in the mind as visualisations. The paradigms for the initiatory labyrinth and the trials within it in the post-Christian era represent the wanderings and resisted temptations in the desert of Jesus Christ.

Often rites of initiation consist of two stages. In the first, the 'Lesser Mysteries', the candidate for initiation travels through a labyrinth of often illusory difficulties which represent a kind of Purgatory in which he/she encounters the 'death-experience' until his mind and soul are purged so that he 'knows himself' sufficiently to be ready for the second stage of the 'Greater Mysteries'. Then the candidate undergoes real trials through which he is 'reborn' into a 'Paradise' where he has contact with deities and is united with 'wisdom' or 'truth', a 'celestial bride'. In *Shakespeare's Mystery Play: A Study of The Tempest*, Colin Still demonstrates the application of these two stages in Shakespeare's *Tempest*.[17] Rites of Initiation were considered to be secrets, and it was forbidden to describe them to the uninitiated. However, in *The Golden Ass*, Apuleius gives a limited description of the initiation of his protagonist into the Mysteries of Isis. He describes a 'journey to the margins of death', a 'return to the world of life' and a view of an 'other-world being,' including one which he describes as 'the sun appearing at midnight'. This is a paradigm for the Divinity, the 'Sun-Logos' always appearing to initiates at the heart of the labyrinth, described variously by different cultures as Apollo, Demeter, Mithras or Christ. [18]

Most famous amongst Rites of Initiation were those associated with Demeter at Eleusis in ancient Greece. These rituals, designed to strengthen the initiates' faith in continuing life and rewards and punishments after death, followed the pattern of others described above. They lasted for nine days and incorporated at the climax of the initiation a drama representing a story of the three goddesses from the worlds above and below. Shakespeare refers specifically to this section of the rites in *Tempest*, when Prospero summons spirits to create a mask at the climax of the successful initiation of Ferdinand, who has been subjected to improving trials by Prospero, acting as his hierophant. I give further details of these rites below in Chapter Nine as described by Colin Still in his book on the play.

It is interesting that indigenous peoples throughout the world practice the initiations of their young people (essential for them in their required transition from a childhood attachment to their mothers to adult independence and responsibility within the tribe), in the same way as those described above, but often incorporating physical pain as part of their trials.[19] This universality features in Shakespeare's plays.

CHAPTER THREE: ESOTERIC ARCANA III

CELTIC MOTIFS AND MYTHOLOGIES
A. The Old Religion
B. The UnderWorld Initiation

Sources available to Shakespeare of Celtic motifs and mythologies [1]
The closeness of his birthplace to Wales (the language of which he demonstrates a knowledge of in I *Henry IV,*); his close association with Michael Drayton, whose *Poly-Olbion* has much Celtic content;[2] the Celtic origin of many of Shakespeare's songs; the Welsh epic *The Mabinogion* in its form available in a Welsh translation in Shakespeare's day, *The White Book of Rhydderch* ; Geoffrey of Monmouth, *The History of the Kings of Britain*, in particular the chapter, *The Prophecies of Merlin.*[3] In Shakespeare's day, this was included in a Welsh translation with the text of *The Mabinogion*, to which it is also directly related in its subject matter through its chapter on *The Prophecies of Merlin*, which R.J. Stewart has interpreted as an allegory of Celtic mysticism, thus providing a blue-print for our understanding of this tradition, called 'The Celtic UnderWorld Initiation'.[4] I found this to be a key system in the interpretation of Theatre Set-Up's 1989 production of *Cymbeline* (see *Cymbeline*); songs with Celtic significance such as *The Leaves of Light, Young Tam Lin, Thomas The Rhymer, Lord Bateman, The Daemon Lover, The Wife of Usher's Well, The Cruel Mother, The False Knight on the Road, Down in Yon Forest* indicate an awareness of Celtic meanings in British culture.[5]

The 'Tudor Impulse'
When Henry Tudor came to the throne, having defeated Richard III and thus banished the Plantagenet royal dynasty, he organised research into the Celtic origins of his Welsh ancestry and its connections to the Celtic history of Britain in order to further legitimise his access to the throne of England. Thus Celtdom and Welshness were in vogue in Shakespeare's time under the Tudors. This continued unabated under the subsequent Stuart monarchs, with an added emphasis on Scotland. Shakespeare's

Scottish play *Macbeth* had particular resonance for the monarch, James I, patron of Shakespeare's company, the King's Men, who was remotely descended from the Banquo of the play's story through marriage of a distant ancestor. The story runs that Margaret Bruce, heir to the throne of Scotland, married the chief executive of Scotland, descended distantly from Banquo and called a 'steward'. When she was pregnant with their child, she fell from her horse on the corner of a road in Paisley and was killed. With great presence of mind, an attendant delivered her baby with a dirk, and the first 'Stuart' king was born.

It was therefore reasonable for Celtic elements to feature in some of Shakespeare's plays, and for them to be included to flatter the current monarch. This 'Tudor impulse' seems justified in light of recent archaeology, which has uncovered thousands of years of the Celtic occupation of Britain, leaving a cultural heritage ingrained in its indigenous people, in spite of foreign invasions, conquests and immigrations.

Aspects of British Celtic culture and mythology applied to Shakespeare's plays:

- The Celtic year was divided into two main halves, commencing with the dark calends of winter, starting at 'Samain' on November 1st. As darkness was associated with the supernatural, this festival (now celebrated as Halloween) marked a flow of the supernatural to earth, including the souls of the dead. The light 'calend' of summer began on May 1st, and was named 'Beltane'. Further subdivisions were 'Imbolc' in February and 'Lugnasad' in August.[6] Summer and winter kings were associated with the main two seasonal divisions.
- The four directions, North, East, South and West, had magical significance according to their correspondences:
  North was the direction where magic and the otherworld was located. Its correspondences were the element earth, the colour green and death.
  East was associated with the element air, the colour white and birth.

South represented maturity, the element fire and the colour red. *West* was associated with the element water and colour blue, and was where the dead were thought to reside.[7]
- Boundaries, the 'liminal' in all its aspects, were the portals of the supernatural. This included the margins between night and day, seasons, dates in the calendar and people's properties (especially those marked by stiles where fairies could sit). Political territories (particularly those edged by rivers or lakes) are said by Alwyn and Brinley Rees to have additional supernatural resonances for good (associated with order) or for evil (associated with chaos), and to be particular abodes of the otherworld.[8]
- Natural locations of water (wells, springs, rivers, fords and lakes) were entrances to the otherworld. Caves also performed this function (see Chapter Six and Chapter Nine). Fogs, riverbanks and bogs were considered to be doubly magically potent, as they not only contained water but were liminal. In *Macbeth* the witches make use of this in their invocation, 'Hover through the fog and filthy air' (I. i.). Archaeologists have uncovered many Celtic votive artefacts in riverbanks and supposedly grimly sacrificed 'bog bodies' in bogs from prehistory in countries where Celts were known to live.
- Dew is supposed to have magical properties, with double magic for dew gathered at night. In *Cymbeline*, Belarius observes that the flowers left on the graves of Cloten and Imogen should be left to acquire the additional power of midnight dew (IV. ii. 283-287).
- 'Bel' or 'Belanos' was the name for the Celtic God of Light (perhaps Shakespeare's inspiration for the character Belarius*)*. The god 'Lugh' was associated with Bel and with the sun. Also important in the Celtic pantheon of gods is 'Cernunnos', with the head and body of a man, but with a stag's antlers. He is the 'god of the hunt', his antlers the quarry he will hunt, embodying the principle 'the hunter and hunted are one'. Resonances of this occur in *Merry Wives* in Falstaff disguised as "Herne the Hunter", hunting for money in the wooing of Mistresses Ford and Page but becoming the quarry himself, tormented by the Windsor townsfolk dressed as fairies (V. 5.).

- A female Goddess featuring zoomorphic or shape-changing ways is the 'Morrigan', the 'Triple Goddess', associated with the earth and manifest as a maiden (called 'Etain', and often found by a well), a matron or a crone. In the epic *Tain Bo Cuailnge*, she challenges the hero 'Cuchulainn' at a ford, shape-shifting from a young girl into an eel, a she-wolf, a heifer and then an old woman. She can be represented as a mare called 'Epona' and is a potent energy, with triple control over birth, life and death. In *Merry Wives* she appears as Anne Page, Mistress Page and Mistress Ford; in *Cymbeline* she is represented by Imogen, the ghost of Posthumus's mother and the Queen; in *Tempest* her presence is real in Miranda, but shadowed in Miranda's dead mother and the dead Sycorax, mother of Caliban. Celtic kings were ritualistically married to this goddess who could be represented by a surrogate maiden.
- Zoomorphic religious elements, as well as the horse and stag, continue in the traditional significance of the pig (or wild boar), dog (or wolf), serpent (or dragon), bear, salmon, bull and birds (particularly the owl, wren and raven). A predisposition to shape-changing into animals characterises Celtic legendary heroes and supernatural beings like the 'Morrigan'. Shakespeare reflects this in the transformations of Puck and Bottom in *Dream* and in Falstaff's assuming the costume of a stag's head in *Merry Wives*.
- The important legendary folk hero/god whose Welsh form is 'Bran' is a Herculean giant-like man with a club. He has a magic cauldron from which those who are worthy will go away satisfied and may become immortal, but if unworthy will be poisoned and die (see *Tempest*). The symbol of Bran was a raven and his legend tells that when an injury had made him no longer fit to be king he commanded his followers to cut off his head (following the Celtic tradition of severed heads, see *Cymbeline*) and bury it on a hill in Lud's town (London) to keep Britain free from enemy conquest. Hence we have the tradition of keeping ravens, Bran's symbol, in the Tower of London, on the hill where his head is supposed to be buried. Further traditions maintained in Britain

from its Celtic inheritance are in the figures of Bran and Epona, which appear in the form of giant carvings into the chalk terrain as the Cerne Abbas Giant in Wiltshire and the Uffington White Horse in Oxfordshire.

- A concept of the duality and polarity of nature: summer and winter, night and day, dark and light, hot and cold, dry and wet, life and death permeates the Celtic perception of the human condition, reflected in artefacts of two-faced heads (see Starkey, plate 18). In our Theatre Set-Up productions, we often had a sense of that in the doubling up of characters which could be played by one actor. Some examples of these are: in *Cymbeline* Posthumus/Cloten, Cornelius/Belarius, Cymbeline/Philario, Iachimo/Guiderius; in *Dream* Theseus/Oberon, Hippolyta/Titania; in *Tempest* Gonzalo/Trinculo, Alonso/Stephano, Ferdinand/Sebastian, Antonio/Caliban; in *Winter's Tale* Leontes/Shepherd, Polixenes/clown, Antigonus/Camillo; in *Hamlet,* the Ghost/Claudius; in *Merchant* Shylock/Lorenzo; in *Much Ado*, Don John/a sexton; in *As You Like It*, Duke Senior/Duke Frederick, Oliver/Le Beau; in *Romeo and Juliet* Tybalt/Peter, and in *Measure for Measure* Duke Vincentio/Froth, Angelo/Barnardine, Isabella/Juliet, Pompey/Friar Peter, Lucio/Provost, Francesca/Mariana, Claudio/Abhorson/Elbow, and Escalus/Mistress Overdone. This doubling in the reduced-cast touring form of the plays was also possibly a strategic measure implemented by Shakespeare, himself a theatre practitioner, as the nature of villainous characters was mediated by the double role. Any actors who were inclined to steep themselves too much in the villainous nature of those roles outside the performance were controlled by the moderating nature of the double, a fact that we found socially very convenient when touring the plays! When we first toured Theatre Set-Up, we had limited doubling of characters, as finances were not tight, and thus we suffered from the temperaments of the actors playing villains! The need to tighten the company's economic belt in later years by doubling the villainous characters with more pleasant roles also improved the social health of the company. We also noticed that sometimes the doubles had many characteristics in common; for example, in *Tempest* Antonio and Caliban. One had usurped Prospero's crown, and the other wanted to do the same and kill him. Sometimes the Celts had triple-headed figures. In *Romeo and Juliet*, our triple casting gave us characters from the same family, Prince Escalus/ Mercutio/Paris. In *Merchant,* we used double and triple casting to reflect the different Venetian elements of the play (see Chapter Nineteen).

- In order to ensure social equality, Celtic high-born children were often put up for adoption. The children of the foster family were then adopted by the high status family. This occurs in *Cymbeline* when Posthumus is adopted by Cymbeline, whose two sons are brought up by Belarius.

- Sports and games were held as forms of *augury* (hence perhaps the reason why the historic Sir Francis Drake continued to play bowls at the beginning of the Spanish conflict on Plymouth Hoe). Shakespeare mirrors this with Cloten's game of bowls in *Cymbeline*.

- The Celtic lore of all periods was intrinsically bound up with a respect for nature. Nature spirits were thought to be capable of interacting with humans (see Prospero and Ariel in *Tempest,* fig. 28). This regard for nature was integral to the Celtic Old Religion (see fig. 29 Titania and Oberon as nature spirits).

- A ritual death by several means, 'The Threefold Death', is manifest in 'The Hanged Man' of the Tarot cards, who dies by falling, hanging and drowning. In *The Merlin Tarot*, R.J. Stewart presents a magical view of this personage. Stewart claims, 'The Fool of the Tarot cards has become the Hanged Man'. In this version of the Tarot symbols the Fool represents 'unrealised, unaware potential of humanity but the Hanged Man transcends humanity through profound understanding and merges with divinity'.[9] Archaeologists have discovered that some Celtic 'bog bodies' have been executed by several means, which in northern Europe they term 'ritual overkill' or in the case of kings in Ireland as the 'Triple Killing of Kings', demonstrating this principle. Thus the

CHAPTER THREE

Tarot, the origins of which can be traced back to ancient Egypt, has added Celtic significance.

Although there is no established source of Shakespeare's experience of any version of the Tarot or of this custom, it is worth noting that in *Richard III* Clarence, brother of Richard, is murdered by several means, first by being tricked and stabbed and then drowned in a butt of malmsey (I. iv.). There is a resonance (perhaps ironic) of the multiple death of the Hanged Man there. Certainly the scene is long with Clarence, a fool for his good opinion of his brother Richard, reasoning for his release on the ill effects of their imminent guilt for the hired murders. This follows the account which he had previously given to his keeper of a strange dream about his own guilty conscience. Further references to the Tarot exist in the location of the scene in the Tower of London. The 'Blasted Tower' is another Tarot card which signifies the involvement of an evil usurper and false king. Stewart claims, 'The Tower is the setting in which corruption and delusion are shattered forcibly and instantly' (p.114), applicable in this scene which makes clear, in the commissioned murder of his brother, Richard's villainy and ambition to become the false usurping king. I realised this significance when watching the 1992 RSC performance of the play, and it deepened my perception of the role of Clarence and this scene within the context of the play, which might include overt Celtic aspects of the Tudor impulse, obvious in the general mood of the script which supports the moral claims of Henry Tudor to the English throne over Richard. It is interesting to note that it was Shakespeare who named the symbols of the opposing sides in the Plantagenet/Tudor wars dramatized in his plays as white and red roses, leading to the subsequent naming of those wars as 'The Wars of the Roses'. Perhaps this was intended as a compliment to Elizabeth I. As C.J. Jung points out in *Psychology and Alchemy* (see his List of Illustrations 13, 30, 193), the combined red and white rose symbolised the Philosophers' Stone; this was perhaps a flattering alchemic reference to the English Tudor monarchs, as Henry VII had deliberately combined the Tudor and Plantagenet dynasties (and consequently their symbolic red and white roses, as the Tudor rose) in his marriage to Elizabeth of York.

A. THE CELTIC OLD WORLD RELIGION

Caitlin and John Matthews describe the Celtic Old Religion as a way of life rather than a formal religion, characterised by every aspect of life attracting a special blessing or charm.[10] This native tradition, which shares many of the customs listed above, is still followed today, not only in the oral tradition of blessing people and in the 'Bless this house' images seen in modern homes, but practised as a native spiritual tradition. After our Theatre Set-Up performances of *Dream* in 1983, in which we incorporated customs of the Celtic Old Religion (see Chapter Ten), we received correspondence from a ship's captain who claimed to be a follower of the tradition.

B. THE CELTIC UNDERWORLD INITIATION

I consider that Shakespeare's plays which incorporate Celtic spiritual arcana and folk motifs are *Dream, Merry Wives, All's Well, Tempest, Macbeth* and *Cymbeline*, the last being the only one to exemplify the Celtic UnderWorld Initiation. I believe that just as Geoffrey of Monmouth and the ballad writers had guaranteed the continuance of this secret native mystic tradition in their writings, Shakespeare did so this play. An understanding of this tradition and also of alchemy makes sense of many of its strange features. Only when I had grasped the application of these arcana to the play was I able to direct it so that the actors and audiences could accept its peculiarities.[11]

The initiate who attempts this magical spiritual journey will encounter these features:

- A Goddess of the UnderWorld.
- A Guardian at the entrance who will admit only those strong enough to endure its trials.
- Guides to lead.
- A surge of 'Inner Fire' which will propel the initiate to act correctly.
- An act of love and self-sacrifice by the initiate.
- A change in the initiate's bloodstream (which can even cure ill health).
- Confinement in a prison or cave.
- Contact with ancestors.

- A 'magic dream'.
- A vision of the 'Universal Tree'.

These occur to the protagonists acting out the esoteric arcana of this Celtic initiation in *Cymbeline*. For the account of these features of our 1989 and 2009 productions of the play, please see Chapter Six.

THE BIBLE

Sources available to Shakespeare

The Geneva Bible, translated into English in 1560, and *The Bishop's Bible*, in folio form mainly used in churches from 1572; a quarto edition of the *Geneva-Tomson Bible,* including the *Geneva Old Testament*, the *Apocrypha*[12] and the *Tomson New Testament*, the latter revised in 1576 by Laurence Tomson, with marginal commentaries on the text; the *Psalter*, the hymnal/prayer book used at the time for Morning and Evening prayer services and often included in the *Geneva Bible*.

In *Biblical References in Shakespeare's Comedies*, Naseeb Shaheen identified the Biblical sources within the comedies and the specific Bibles Shakespeare must have used.[13] Information which Shakespeare would have taken from the Tomson commentaries of the *New Testament* made it possible for Shaheen to identify that he mainly used The *Geneva-Tomson* Bible, which seems logical as it is in portable quarto form so that presumably Shakespeare could have had his own copy. Shaheen also considers that Shakespeare's numerous references to the Old Testament Book of Psalms derive from the *Psalter*. I include Shaheen's detailed identification of Biblical references in *Comedy* in order to show the intensive legacy of the Bible to Shakespeare's work, but not in the other comedies dealt with below, as the Biblical influence only falls within the scope of this book in its moral and ethical implications and in its relation to its other arcane meanings. Shaheen's work provides complete identification of Biblical sources in all the comedies for those interested in a comprehensive account.

It was William Tyndale's English translation of the Bible that served as the ancestor of all subsequent English Bibles, a fact that made his martyrdom in Antwerp as a heretic by European Catholic authorities doubly heroic. The Tomson commentaries in the New Testament sometimes glossed the texts in terms of their arcane content, a fact I found enlightening when analysing *Dream* (see *Dream*, Story Section 10), but which drew disapproval from the newly enthroned King James I, always suspicious of anything which might echo of witchcraft. James therefore banned the *Geneva-Tomson* edition, decreeing the version which gained recognition as the *King James Bible*.

All Biblical references below are taken from a 1609 edition of the *Geneva-Tomson* Bible. There are different ways in which Shakespeare uses the Bible:

1. He may take a Biblical character or an event and apply them in a particular context in order to infer an association of meaning, as in *Hamlet*, II. ii. 410, when Hamlet taunts Polonius for his manipulation of his daughter Ophelia, by referring to him as Jeptha, the Hebrew judge who sacrificed his own daughter (see Judges II. 30-39).
2. He may simply distort a biblical quotation as in *Comedy* II. ii. 64-65, when Syracuse Antipholus admonishes his servant for the inappropriate timing of his jesting: 'Learn to jest in good time; there's a time for all things'. This paraphrases Ecclesiastes 1. 1, 4:

To all things there is an appointed time, and a time to every purpose under the heaven...
A time to weepe, and a time to laugh: a time to mourne, and a time to daunce.

3. Shakespeare's plays demonstrate the influence of the Bible on many issues, particularly the Christian New Testament edict on forgiveness, 'For if ye doe forgive men their trespasses, your heavenly Father will also forgive you' (Matthew 6. 14), which characterises the comedies. In *Two Gentlemen*, Julia and Valentine forgive Proteus and the Duke forgives Valentine; in *Comedy*

Solinus forgives Egeon; in *Shrew* Katharine forgives Petruchio; in *Dream* Hippolyta has forgiven Theseus, Theseus forgives Hermia, Hermia forgives Lysander and Helena forgives Demetrius; in *Romeo and Juliet* the Capulets and Montagues forgive each other; in *Merry Wives* Falstaff forgives the citizens of Windsor for his physical torment in the forest as they forgive him for pursuing their wives, and Page and his wife forgive Fenton and Anne. In *Merchant* the Duke grants Shylock his life but also severely punishes him for his attempt on the life of Antonio, and Portia and Nerissa forgive Bassanio and Gratiano; in *Much Ado* Hero forgives Claudio and Benedick forgives his friends but Don John's punishments are predicted; in *As You Like It* Orlando forgives Oliver and a religious hermit persuades Duke Frederick not to pursue his brother, Duke Senior, who forgives him for usurping his dukedom; in *Twelfth Night* Orsino forgives (and embraces) Viola and Olivia forgives Feste, Sir Toby Belch and Maria, but Malvolio threatens revenge for the wrongs done him, a pledge which Orsino hopes to mollify. In *All's Well* everyone forgives Bertram and Parolles; in *Measure* Isabella begs Angelo to show mercy to Claudio and spare his life and forgives Angelo for his crimes, as does the Duke, announcing a general amnesty for all except for Lucio. In *Cymbeline* Posthumus forgives Iachimo, Imogen forgives Posthumus and Cymbeline forgives everyone; in *Winter's Tale* everyone forgives Leontes; and in *Tempest* Prospero forgives everyone.

4. However, the lack of forgiveness and charity in the tragedies follows the Old Testament maxim of 'Eye for eye, tooth for tooth, hand for hand, foote for foote' (Exodus 21. 24). Thus the tragedies (with the exception of *Romeo and Juliet*, in which ultimate forgiveness for all prevails) present a picture of murder and vengeance. The Old Testament maxim of exacting revenge prevails in the tragedies: Hamlet's father's ghost demands that Hamlet should exact revenge for his murder, which ultimately brings about the deaths of Polonius, Rosencrantz, Guildenstern, Ophelia, Laertes, Gertrude, Claudius and finally Hamlet himself.

Macbeth is responsible for the murders of his subjects, Othello for that of his innocent wife, while the vicious Regan and Goneril kill and torture anyone who obstructs them, including their own sister and by default King Lear, their father. This pattern of action also occurs in *Troilus and Cressida* and the Roman and English history plays which reflect the grim realities of human history. An unrepentant villain such as Iago in *Othello* suggests a form of diabolical evil, manifest in the witches in *Macbeth*. Does this ethical difference between the comedies and tragedies indicate a cynicism on Shakespeare's part towards the Biblical precept of Christian forgiveness applied to real life? [14] Does this only occur when reality is distorted as it is in the comedies but prevails as the truth of the human condition in the tragedies and histories, or is it a reflection of the occasional harshness of the Old Testament? However, Shakespeare always contrives a moral outcome by the end of the plays' last acts, with wrongdoers punished and often a new, more righteous order established.

Aspects of the Old Testament books of Genesis 1, 2 and 3 feature in the plays, reflecting the beliefs and social mores of Shakespeare's own time. Firstly, the account of the creation of the world laid down in Genesis is reflected in Western culture and subsequently in Shakespeare's plays.

- In Genesis 1, the separation of darkness from light and water from land created the tradition that a sense of order and cleanliness was virtuous, while disorder, filth and chaos were evil (especially when any of these elements were mixed). Darkness was evil, light was virtuous and storms were portents of evil. In *Julius Caesar* the assassination of Caesar is anticipated with storms and in *King Lear* the storms reflect his madness. In *Macbeth* the witches are heralded by storms.[15] The witches hint to Macbeth that the first three apparitions which they cause to appear to him are from Hell (and should therefore be treated with suspicion) by prefixing their entrances with the thunder which is their hallmark, a fact that is lost on him (IV. i. 69, 76, 86). The chaotic filthy aspect of the nature

of Hell is identified by Lady Macbeth, whose life has become like Hell and tormented by guilt; 'Hell is murky' (V. i. 38).
- In Genesis 1. 26-28, the world created on the sixth day in the image of God himself is given to mankind to use and dominate. The implications of this have been far-reaching in cultures whose faith is based on the Bible, encouraging as it does exploitation of the planet's resources and animals. The influence on an orthodox Christian mind of this aspect of Genesis was brought home to me when I was visiting an uncle of mine in South Uist, in the Outer Hebrides of Scotland. He presented me with the gift of the untreated fur skin of an otter that he had killed by the loch. I must have looked shocked, and he justified the killing by saying, 'All these animals are given to us by God to kill and to eat'. In *As You Like It* both the courtier Jaques and the exiled Duke express regret at wounding and killing the deer in the forest which is their native habitat (II. i. 60-63 and II. i. 21-25). The Princess in *Love's Labour's* also expresses sympathy for the deer that social convention requires her to hunt and kill. This implies a sensitivity in Shakespeare beyond the diktats of Genesis.
- Genesis 2 presents a different view of creation from that of Genesis 1. In this chapter, the first man, Adam, is created from dust of the earth and the first woman, Eve, from one of his ribs. This idea of male supremacy in all creatures on earth including mankind occurs in *Comedy* when Luciana reprimands her sister Adriana for her rebellious attitude towards her husband. She follows the Genesis concept of the hierarchy of men, which are 'more divine' than other creatures (all ruled by the males of their species) that are 'imbued with intellectual sense and souls' and 'masters to their females and their lords'.
- This Biblical idea of the inferiority of women is compounded by the content of Genesis 3, in which Satan appears as a serpent to tempt Eve to eat the forbidden fruit of the Tree of Knowledge of Good and Evil in their paradise of the Garden of Eden. She succumbs to the temptation, gives the fruit to Adam to eat also and they are both punished by being cast out of the Garden of Eden.

> Eve is further punished by God by being condemned, along with all future women, to suffer pain in childbearing and childbirth, and her desire was to be subjugated to that of her husband, who would rule over her. Adam and all future men are also punished by the hard labour needed to win a living from the earth, but Eve and all womankind must bear the additional punishment of guilt for the 'original sin' of yielding to Satan's blandishments. Egeon in *Comedy* reflects this male orthodox view in commenting that his wife Emilia was pleased to suffer the difficulties involved in pregnancy with twins (I. i. 45-46). Luciana upholds the idea of man's supremacy over woman, but is reluctant to undergo the experience of being the submissive object of a man's passion in bed (II. i. 27).

I believe that the Genesis dogma which subjugates women was a distortion of the ancient Sumerian legend which I describe below, subverted in order to facilitate the nomadic lifestyle of the early patristic Hebrews and their subsequent settlement outside the territory of Sumeria from which they emigrated. I actually possess on an artefact purchased at The British Museum, the imprint of an ancient Sumerian seal which relates a much different scenario and which Joseph Campbell identifies in *Masks of God: Occidental Mythology* as the mythic ancestry of the temptation of Eve by the serpent in the Garden of Eden, considerably predating the Biblical Genesis.[16] It is a truism also that the gods of a conquered people often become the devils of the conquerors. The Hebraic Genesis version of the Sumerian legend had supplanted the beliefs of the country not which they had conquered, but from which they had come. Campbell explains that the serpent was an ancient god existing in the Levant for seven thousand years before Genesis was written. The ability of the serpent to slough its skin and thus renew itself made it a symbol of rebirth. Its manner of moving through damp undergrowth, its emergence from the earth like a spring and its movement in water like waves gave it the additional symbolism of water (pp. 9-10). The serpent was linked in all this symbolism with the moon, of which it is sometimes presented as a consort (p. 9). It is often associated in ancient mythologies and graphic representations with a 'World Tree', which it guards from the profane but allows the worthy to partake of as a boon (pp.10-14). In the Genesis story, the serpent displays a likeness to the Greek mythical Prometheus, who gave humans knowledge and in return was punished by the gods. It is also important to note the significance to Greek culture of the healing serpent (which had also become a symbol of Hermes), wound around the caduceus as a symbol of medicine. This Hermetic connection to the serpent explains the role of the snake as paradigm for 'base matter' in alchemy. The divinities associated with the garden of this World Tree are not exclusively male, as in the patristic Hebrew Genesis, but contain female personages (p. 13). This Sumerian version of the story presents an Eve figure in her aspect as mother of all humanity as described in the Bible by Adam, receiving fruit of the World Tree from a female goddess (p 13.). There is no sense of guilt in the pre-Genesis version of the Garden of Eden scenario, but the boon of the knowledge of life is made available to any mortal, male or female who 'reaches for it with the proper will and readiness to receive' (p. 14). In later plays such as *Twelfth Night, As You Like It, Merchant, Much Ado, Winter's Tale, Antony and Cleopatra* and *Cymbeline* the roles of women such as Viola, Rosalind, Portia, Beatrice, Paulina, Cleopatra and Imogen are so strong as to challenge any idea of Shakespeare's belief in the Genesis conception of male supremacy. To return to the ways in which Shakespeare represents Genesis in his plays:

- The view of God as a being outside of creation, the human component of which became tainted by Eve's 'original sin', implies a harsh view of the afterlife as depicted in *Hamlet* by the revelations of Hamlet's father's ghost. He had been poisoned by his brother as he slept in his orchard and had thus not received the Christian religious ritual of the 'Last Rites' which might send him forth into the next world cleansed from his participation in a material existence, his 'days of nature' (I. v. 12). He gives an account of the horrors of the tortures of the Purgatory into which his uncleansed soul has been thrust, so awful that he is forbidden to tell Hamlet the details which would 'harrow up thy soul' (I. v. 16). When Theatre Set-Up performed this play in Salisbury Cathedral, the Bishop's wife commented to me about this harsh Shakespearean view of an 'uncleansed' soul's torture in the afterlife, which is no longer a belief in the Protestant Church. The dogma of the Christian Church maintains that Jesus Christ was sacrificed on the Cross in order to redress 'original sin'. Mankind is to be redeemed from the inherent sin committed in the Garden of Eden by Christ's sacrifice. The experience of Purgatory which Shakespeare presents in the account by Hamlet's father's ghost evidently requires orthodox Catholic intervention in the form of the 'Last Rites' in order for this to be achieved.

We performed the play in the Baroniet of Rosendal in Norway, with the ghost appearing in an upper part of the castle, and members of the audience claimed to have been mentally chilled by it. Audiences of our performances in Carisbrooke Castle on the Isle of Wight reported the same effect when our ghost appeared on the battlements of the castle walls, as they did at Pendennis Castle, Cornwall. Perhaps Shakespeare had this effect in mind when he wrote the scene, terrifying his audiences into a fear of the contemporary Catholic idea of Purgatory, or just taking the opportunity to present scary theatre which emotionally involves the audience. The ghost scene is certainly excellent theatre, commanding engagement from the audience wherever it is performed.

- The paradise of the Garden of Eden from which their sin excluded Adam and Eve has cultural resonances in Shakespeare. In *Measure* a symbol of it exists in the moated grange where Mariana laments her rejection by Angelo (IV. i.). Further reference is made to a paradigm of the Garden of Eden, where Angelo has arranged his assignation with Isabella but where the Duke has conspired to substitute Mariana so that her love for Angelo will be consummated with him there (IV. i. 28). The Forest of Arden in *As You Like It* is regarded by the exiled Duke and his followers as paradise in contrast to the court from which they have been exiled. Their primitive, simple lifestyle there has gained repute in the world outside their haven, and is compared to that of a past paradisiacal age, known as 'the golden world' (I. i.116). In *Love's Labour's*

- the King's grounds are suggested as a paradigm for the Garden of Eden in the consenting sexual sin of Costard and Jaquenetta.
- It is also interesting to note that although the Hebrew religion of the Old Testament claims to be monotheistic, Genesis 3. 22 refers to a collection of gods which the Lord God claims to be part of by his exclamation, 'Behold, the man is become as one of us'. Further inconsistencies perpetuate themselves in Genesis 4. In Genesis 3 Eve was given her name as token of the fact that she was mother of all men. Yet numerous other people, not the children of Eve, are referred to in Genesis 4. 14-26. If Shakespeare had his own quarto copy of the Geneva-Tomson Bible it is likely that he would have detected these inconsistencies and developed sufficient scepticism of the Bible in order to accommodate the acceptance of other esoteric arcana.

Shakespeare adopted in his comedies the Christian New Testament principles of forgiveness and redemption by transformation through Christ (the sun-logos), so like the ideas inherent in Renaissance Platonism, theurgy, alchemy, Celtic Mysticism and the Cabala. Sometimes the ideas in the comedies diverged from the tenets of Genesis in the non-exploitive sympathy shown towards animals in *As You Like It* **and in the strength of so many of his female characters, belying any Genesis-informed inferiority they might have to their male counterparts.** These examples lead me to believe in the likelihood of his acceptance of the alternative spiritual arcana which I believe he encoded in his plays and of which I give a detailed analysis in the following chapters.

In my analysis of *The Comedy of Errors* I include a detailed account of Biblical references to be found in the play, guided by the information in *Biblical references in Shakespeare's Comedies* by Naseeb Shaheen. However, in the Biblical analysis of other plays I only include the moral and ethical implications of the Bible on the plays' actions, referring readers who wish for a more detailed Biblical analysis to the latter publication.

The following chapters on an analysis of the plays performed by Theatre Set-Up are placed in categories which feature their main, but not only, esoteric meaning. The first category is alchemy.

All production photos are of Theatre Set-Up.
Colour photos are by Wendy and Michael Gains.
Black and white photos by Graham Sergeant.

Cover photo:

Leontes: 'O she's warm/ If this be magic, let it be an art | Lawful as eating' (V. iii. 109). The Philosophers' Stone achieved with Hermione as a living statue. Leontes (Tony Portacio) and Hermione (Morag Brownlie), *The Winter's Tale* 2006.

Fig. 1.

Hamlet 1976, the first performance of Theatre Set-Up.
Above: Old Hamlet's ghost (Raymond Farrell) appearing at Forty Hall, Enfield, through the gates of the arch thought to be designed by the eighteenth-century architect Inigo Jones.
Below: Voltimand (Mike Mousley) and Hamlet (Ciaran Hinds) inside the Forty Hall Banqueting Suite.

Fig. 2.

A Midsummer Night's Dream 1983.
Above: The four elements as the reconciled lovers. Demetrius as earth (Sean Aita), Helena as Fire (Amanda Strevett), Hermia as air (Gwyneth Hammond) and Lysander as water (David Goudge). The colour changed on the circular plinth to gold signifying the last alchemical stage of the Philosophers' Stone. Our Hieroglyphic Monad attached to the plinth.
Below: Hermia embodying air and Lysander. The plinth is white, signifying the second stage of four-staged alchemy.

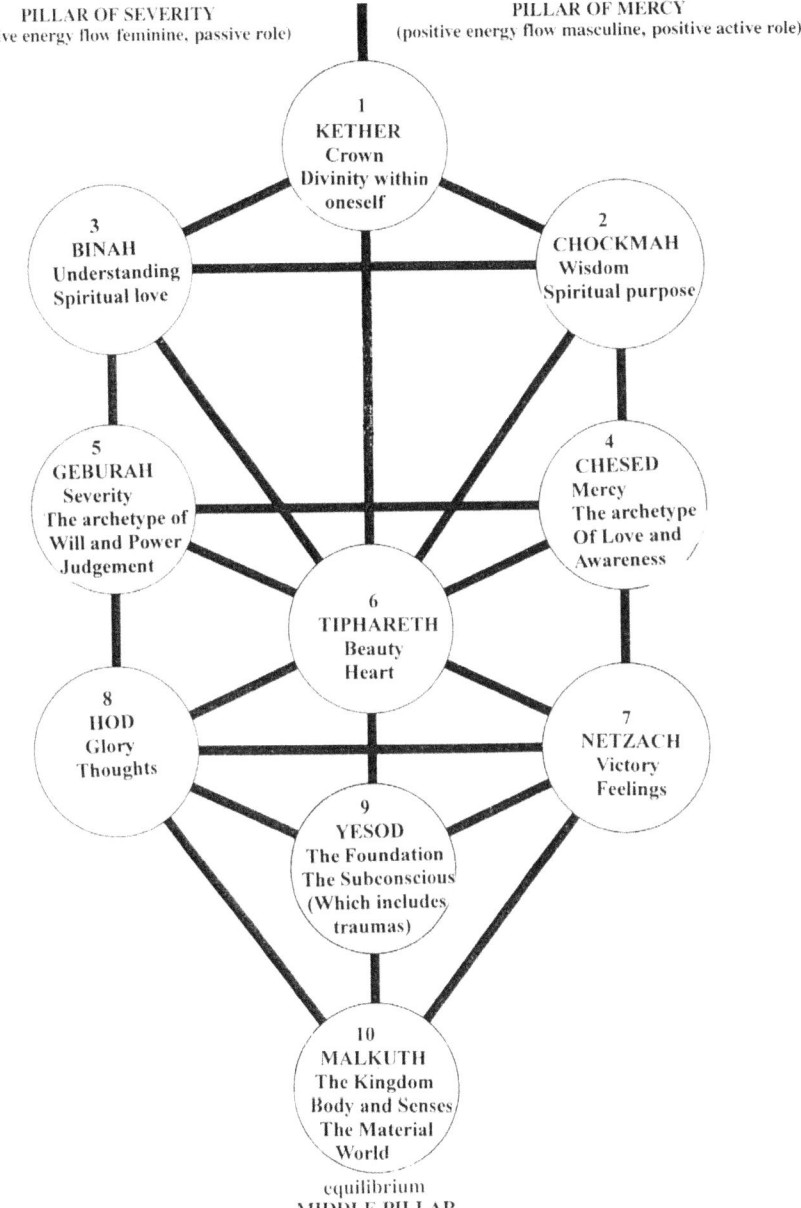

Fig. 3.

Diagram of the Cabala Tree of Life. Terms by Gareth Knight, Will Parfitt and Wendy Macphee.

Fig. 4.

Christ and the Philosophers' Stone . From: *Rosarium Philosophorum* in *De alchimia opuscula complura veterum philosophorum* (Frankfurt, in officina Cyriaci Iacobi, 1550). Copyright The British Library Board. All rights reserved. 1032.c.1, sig. aiv recto.

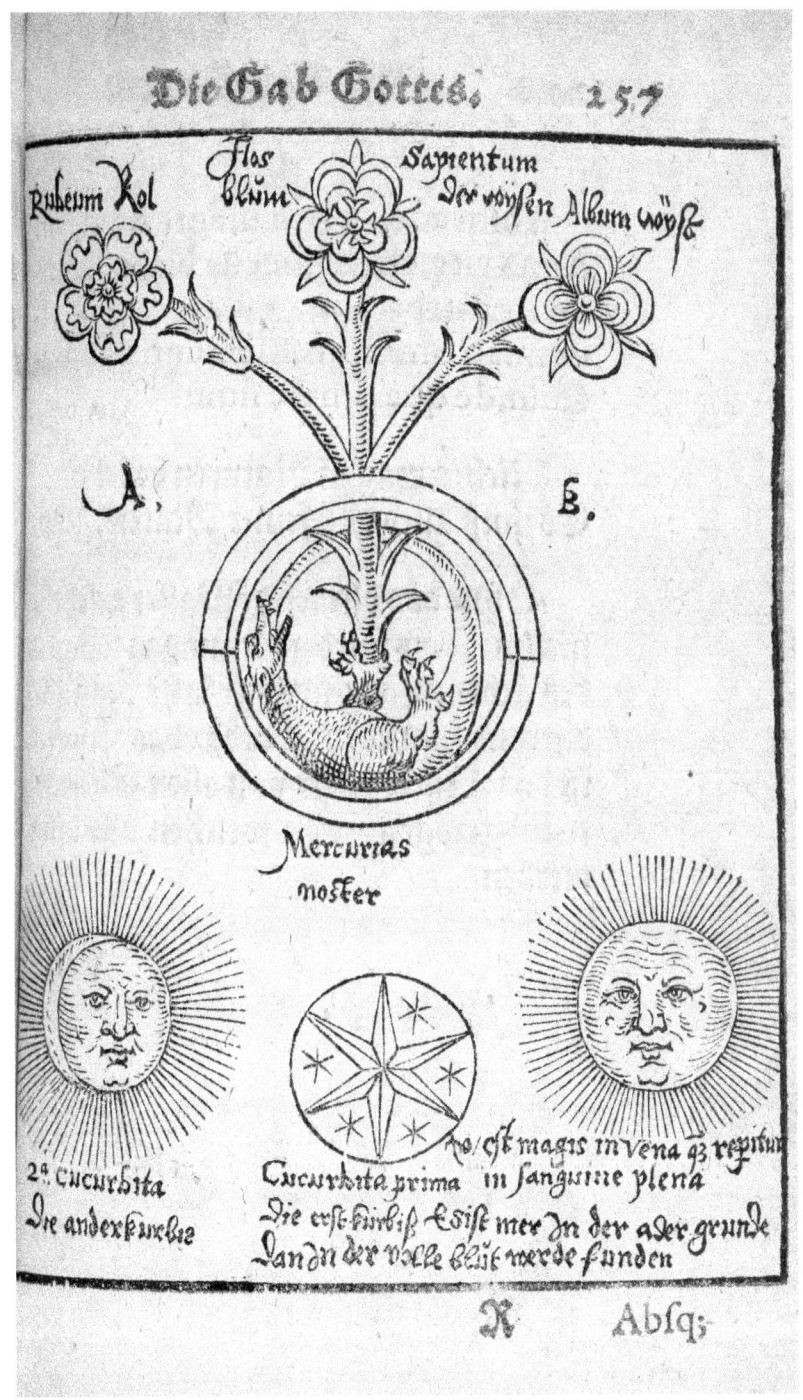

Fig. 5.

The 'Tail Eater, the Oroubos' as the 'base matter' of alchemy with the red-and-white-rose, 'flos sapientum' (the 'wise' flux of the process). From: Hieronymus Reusner, *Pandora* (Basel, 1588), p. 257. Copyright The British Library Board. All rights reserved. 1032.b.10, p. 257.

Fig. 6.

George Ripley's Diagrammatic Wheel of correspondences between the elements, the four directions, the planets, the signs of the zodiac, alchemy and Christianity. From: *Compound of Alchymy* (London: Thomas Orwin, 1591). Photo: Warburg Institute. Innes Collection FGH4920.

Fig. 7.

Multiplicatio represented by lion cubs which symbolise the reproductive power of the Philosophers' Stone, here presented as a lion upon which a queen sits holding an additional image of the Stone as a pelican, pecking its own breast to feed its young. From: J. D. Mylius, *Philosophia Reformata*, (Frankfurt: apud Lucam Iennis 1622). Copyright The British Library Board. All rights reserved. 1033.i.7, sig. Q3verso.

Fig. 8.

Coniunctio. The chemical wedding of 'The Red King and The White Queen'. From: *Splendor Solis*, attributed to Salomon Trismosin (1582). Copyright The British Library Board. All rights reserved. Ms Harley 3469, fo. 10r.

Fig. 9.

The king eats the son. A metaphor for a by-product of the 'base-matter' being consumed within the process in the stage of coniunctio. From: *The Book of Lambspring* (1678) expanded from the original edition 1625. Translated by A.E. Waite, *The Hermetic Museum Restored and Enlarged*, 2. vols (London: Elliott, 1893), I, 301.

Fig. 10.

The wolf eats the king. The wolf here represents the chemical antimony. The goal of alchemy is anticipated with a 'resurrected king' emerging in the distance from a purging fire. From: Michael Maier, *Atalanta Fugiens; Hoc est, Emblemata Nova de Secreti Naturae Chymia*, 2nd ed (Oppenheim: Johann Theodor De Bry, 1618). Copyright The Bodleian Libraries, The University of Oxford. VET.D2.e.18, p. 105.

Fig. 11.

The raven as symbol of putrefaction. The 'nigredo' eclipse of 'Mercurius Senex' (symbol of Saturn as 'base matter'). From: Herbrandt Jamsthaler, *Viatorium Spagyricum* (Frankfurt am Main, 1625). Copyright The British Library Board. All rights reserved. 1034.k.2, p. 118.

Fig. 12.

Melencholia. Copper plate engraving by Albrecht Dürer (1514). Seven-stage alchemy is represented by the seven-runged ladder rising from the stone which represents the Philosophers' Stone. Copyright Trustees of the British Museum.

Fig. 13.

The old king drowning and the birth of the new king. A metaphor for the resurrecting aspect of the alchemical process with the precept 'Die to live'. From: *Splendor Solis*, attributed to Salomon Trismosin (1582). Copyright The British Library Board. All rights reserved. Ms Harley 3469, fo. 16v.

Fig. 14.

Stages in the alchemical process. 'Base matter' is represented by a dragon at the base of the image and the Philosophers' Stone by a phoenix at the top. For a comprehensive description of all the items in the image see C.G. Jung, *Psychology and Alchemy*, pp. 284-7. From: Andrea Libavius, *Alchymia* (Frankfurt: J. Saurius, 1606). Copyright The British Library Board. All rights reserved. 535.k.5, p. 55.

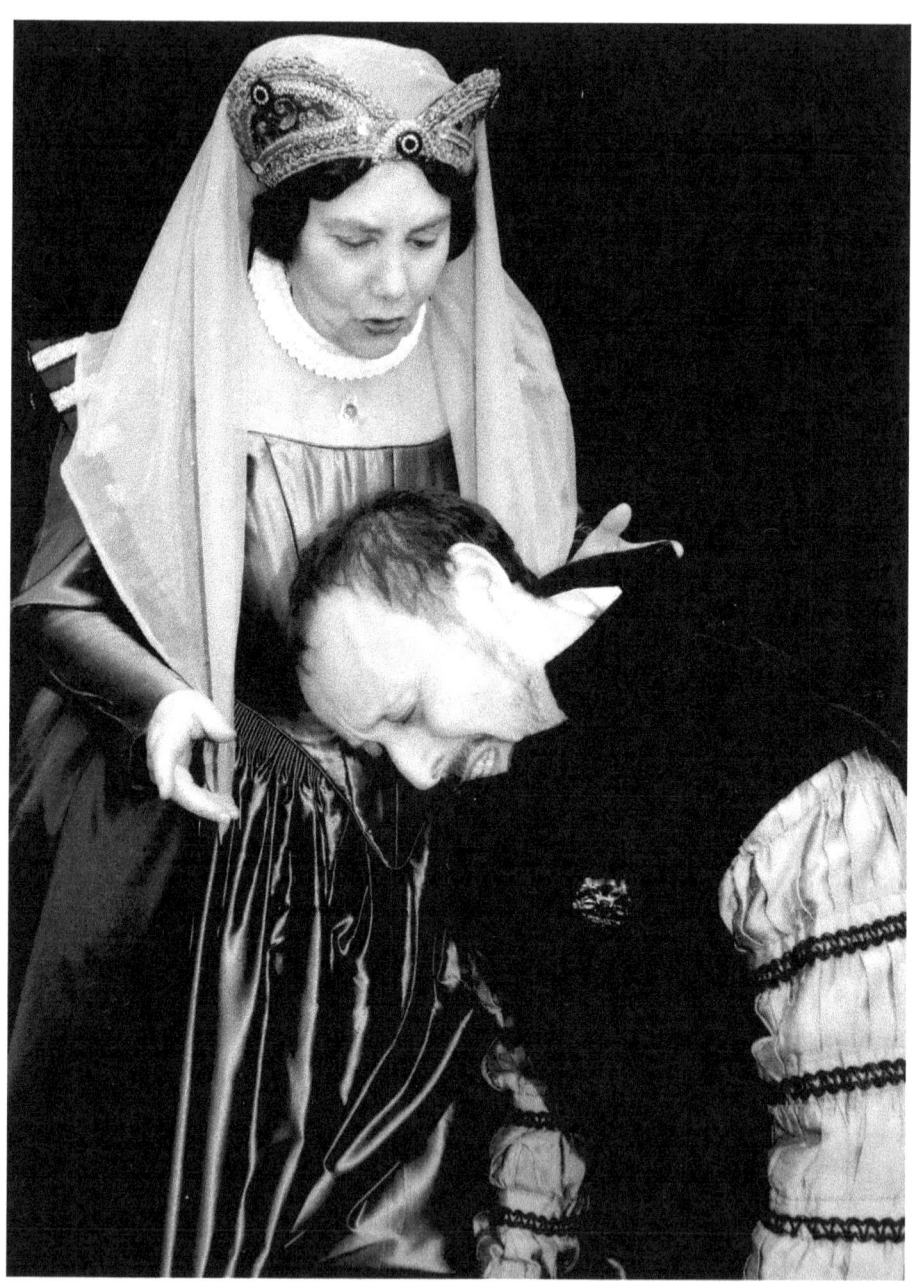

Fig. 15.

Paulina (Wendy Macphee) as alchemist with Leontes (Tony Portacio) as the 'Red King' in *The Winter's Tale*, 2006.

Fig. 16.

Aenigma Regis. 'The Rebus'(Hermaphrodite) holding serpents and rising from 'base matter' imaged as a three-headed dragon. Seven-stage alchemy is pictured as a flowering tree and the Philosophers' Stone as a lion and pelican feeding its young from its plucked breast.
From: *Rosarium Philosophorum* in *De alchimia opuscula complura veterum philosophorum* (Frankfurt, in officina Cyriaci Iacobi, 1550) Copyright The British Library Board. All rights reserved. 1032.c.1, sig. Xiii verso.

Fig. 17.

Viola (Emma Reynolds) as symbolic hermaphrodite with Olivia (Susannah Coleman) in *Twelfth Night* , 1997.

Fig. 18.

Divine Love, Christianity and initiation: Friar Lawrence (Michael Palmer) marries Romeo (Neil Warhurst) and Juliet (Victoria Stilwell) In *Romeo and Juliet*, 1996.

Fig. 19.

Divine Love and Plato's *Phaedrus* metaphor of the charioteer. The dying Antony (Tony Portacio) and Cleopatra (Rosalind Cressy) in *Antony and Cleopatra*, 1998.

Fig. 20.

Divine Love. Bassanio (Richard Sanderson) and Portia (Suzie Edwards) in *The Merchant of Venice*, 2010.

Fig. 21.

Divine Love. Florizel (Jack Hughes) and Perdita (Karen Boniface) in *The Winter's Tale*, 2006.

Fig. 22.

Plato's metaphor of the *Divided Soul*. Antipholus of Ephesus (Daniel O'Brien) and Antipholus of Syracuse (Tony Portacio), in *The Comedy of Errors*, 1986.

Fig. 23.

Initiation. The four lovers in *Two Gentlemen of Verona*, 1987.
Above: Proteus (Tony Portacio). **Below**: Valentine (Anderson Knight), Sylvia (Claire Fisher), Julia (Emma Gibbins), Proteus (Tony Portacio).

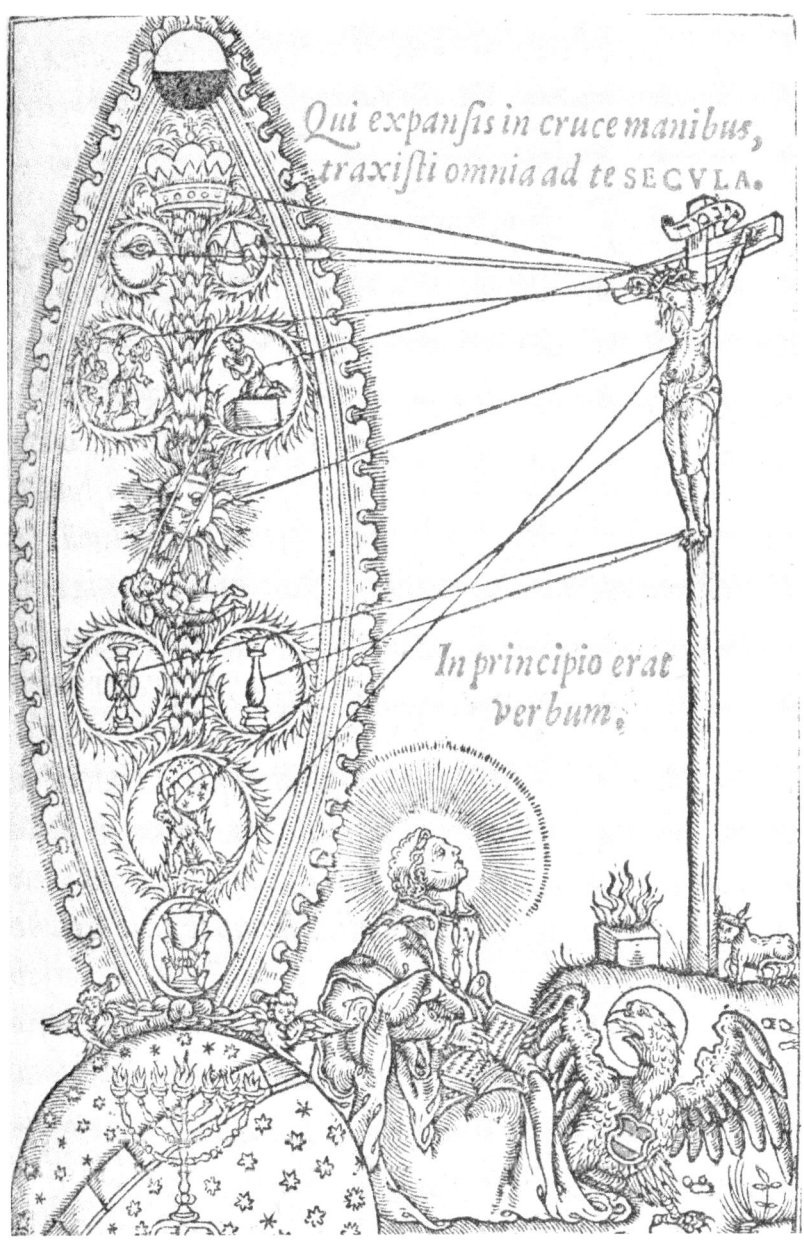

Fig. 24.

A diagram of the Cabala Tree of Life, contained in a *Vesica Piscis*. Christ is identified with the Tree, with spheres corresponding to parts of his body. At the top right of the Tree in Chockmah is the Horn of Plenty indicating that the right side of the Tree has active, masculine characteristics, and at the top left in Binah is the All-seeing Eye of the Great Mother, designating female passive characteristics. The pelican beside the image of St John symbolises the self-sacrifice of Christ. For a full description see Gareth Knight, *A Practical Guide to Qabalistic Symbolism*. From: *Liber sacrosancti euangelii de Iesus Christo domino & deo nostro ... lingua Syra, ... a Ioh. Evangelista Hebraica dicta* (Vienna: Michael Cymbermannus 1556). Copyright The British Library Board. All rights reserved. 218.h.21, fo. 101 verso.

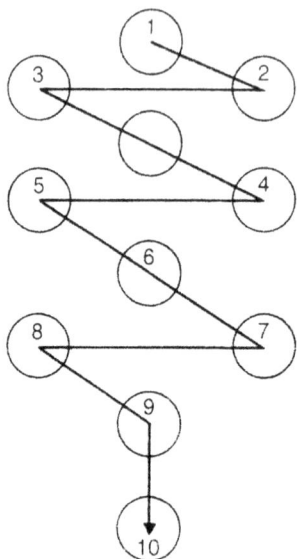

Fig. 25.

The Cabala: The Lightning Flash. The order (Kether, Chockmah, Binah, Chesed, Geburah, Tiphareth, Netzach, Hod, Yesod, Malkuth) in which Spirit (which is believed to exist within every person) becomes incarnated in the flesh of humanity. From: Will Parfitt, *The Elements of the Qabala*, p. 25, with the author's permission.

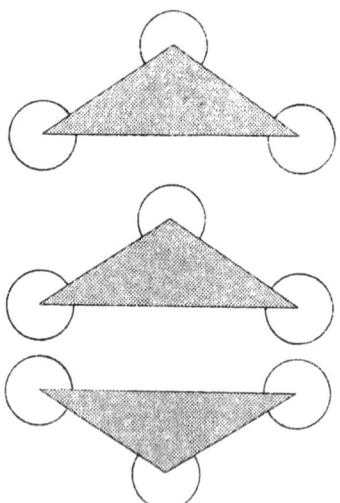

Fig. 26.

The Cabala: The Three Triangles. The top Supernal triangle, which includes Kether, Binah and Chockmah, represents 'The Realm of the Spirit' connecting the individual to others. The middle triangle of Tiphareth, Geburah and Chesed represent 'The Realm of the Soul' referring to the soul of the individual. The lower triangle of Malkuth, Yesod, Hod and Netzach, 'The realm of the personality' refer to the thoughts, feelings and sensations of the individual. From: Will Parfitt, *The Elements of the Qabala*, p. 4, with the author's permission.

Fig. 27.

John Dee's Hieroglyphic Monad. The symbol as it appears in his book, *Monas Hieroglyphica*, 1564. Copyright The British Library Board. All rights reserved. 90.i.20, title page.

Fig. 28.

The spiritual world represented by Ariel (Morag Brownlie) interacts with Prospero (James Clarkson), in *The Tempest*, 2001.

Fig. 29.

Celtic nature spirits: Titania (Libby Machin) and Oberon (Tony Portacio) in *A Midsummer Night's Dream*, 1995.

Fig. 30.

Subjects of the alchemic processes and UnderWorld initiation: Posthumus (Tony Portacio) and Imogen (Emily Outred), in *Cymbeline*, 2009.

Fig. 31.

The symbolic cave of the alchemists and the Celts: Mountain of the Adepts. Seven-stage alchemy culminating in the Philosophers' Stone represented as a phoenix, within an alchemist's cave-laboratory-temple hidden in a mountain upon whose flanks are gods symbolising the planets and surrounded by the signs of the zodiac and the four elements of fire, air, water and earth. In the foreground is a man investigating knowledge by following his natural instincts, contrasted with one whose ignorance is indicated by his blindfold. From: Stephan Michelspacher, *Cabala: Spiegel der Kunst und Natur (*Augspurg, 1616). Copyright The British Library Board. All rights reserved. 1032.c.3, Plate 3.

Fig. 32.

Falstaff (Richard Ashley) as the subject of alchemy in *The Merry Wives of Windsor* 2004 being 'processed' as he is hidden in a laundry basket before being thrown into the Thames by Mistress Page (Morag Brownlie) and Mistress Ford (Angela Laverick).

Fig. 33.

Falstaff (Richard Ashley) relates his Dissolution in the waters of the Thames to Ford (David Reakes).

Fig. 34.

Falstaff (Richard Ashley) as Herne the Hunter, his antlers suggesting Cernunnos, King of the Celtic pantheon. Taken from *The Merry Wives of Windsor* 2004 programme.

Fig. 35.

Triumphant Helena (Elizabeth Arends) as The Philosophers' Stone in *All's Well That Ends Well*, 2008.

Fig 36.

All's Well, 2008: Parolles attacked by his fellow soldiers. Bertram (Richard Plumley), Dumaine (Peter Lundie Wager), Parolles (Terry Ashe), Florentine soldier (Toby Eddington), Duke of Florence (Tony Portacio).

Fig 37.
1982 Theatre Set-up production of *The Tempest* at Stonehenge (**above**) and
Forty Hall (**below**). The spirits as the Celtic Epona (Henrietta Branwell) and Cernunnos
(Michael Branwell).

Fig. 38.

Nature spirits. Oberon (Charles Abomali) and Puck (Wendy Macphee) in *A Midsummer Night's Dream,* 2000.

Fig. 39.

The four lovers as the four elements in *A Midsummer Night's Dream,* 2000: Demetrius (George Richmond Scott) as earth, Helena (Amalia Lawrence) as fire, Hermia (Susannah Coleman) as air, and Lysander (Peter McCrohan) as water.

Fig. 40.

Theurgy. *A Midsummer Night's Dream*, 1983. Bottom (Frank Jarvis) wakes from his dream of his participation in the fairy world.

Fig. 41.

Programme for *Love's Labour's Lost,* 2005 Photograph of the actress playing Rosaline (Alice James) superimposed on the portrait of Emilia Lanier, possibly Shakespeare's 'Dark Lady'.

Fig. 42.

From the 1994 Commedia Dell'Arte interpretation of *The Taming of the Shrew*. (Libby Machin who also played Katherine) as Biondello. **(left)**

Fig. 43.

From the 1994 Commedia Dell'Arte interpretation of *The Taming of the Shrew*. Grumio as Harlequin (Frank Jarvis). **(right)**

Fig. 44.
Orlando (Andrew Crabb) and Rosalind (Morag Brownlie) in *As You Like It,* 2002.

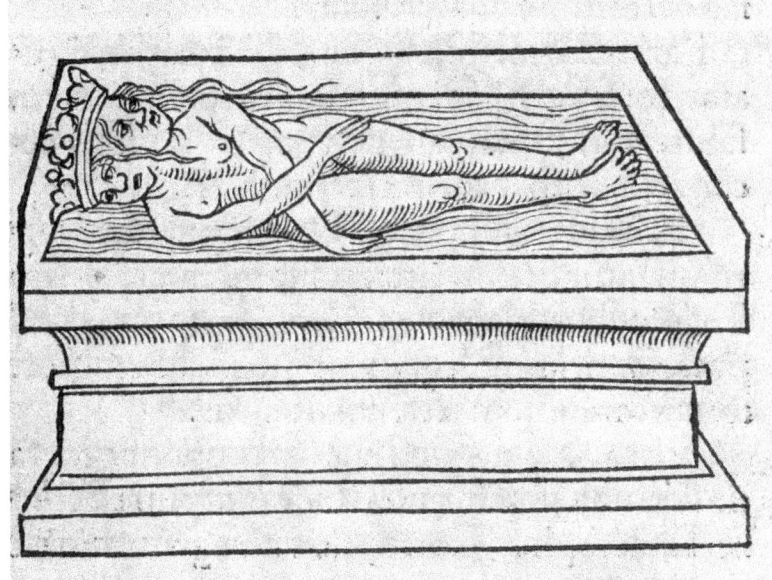

Fig. 45.

Coniunctio. A metaphor from alchemy signifying the maxim 'From death comes life' being applied in *Romeo and Juliet* as 'The lovers in the tomb'. Woodcut From: *Rosarium Philosophorum* in *De alchimia opuscula complura veterum philosophorum* (Frankfurt, in officina Cyriaci Iacobi, 1550). Copyright The British Library Board. All rights reserved. 1032.c.1, sig. Giv recto.

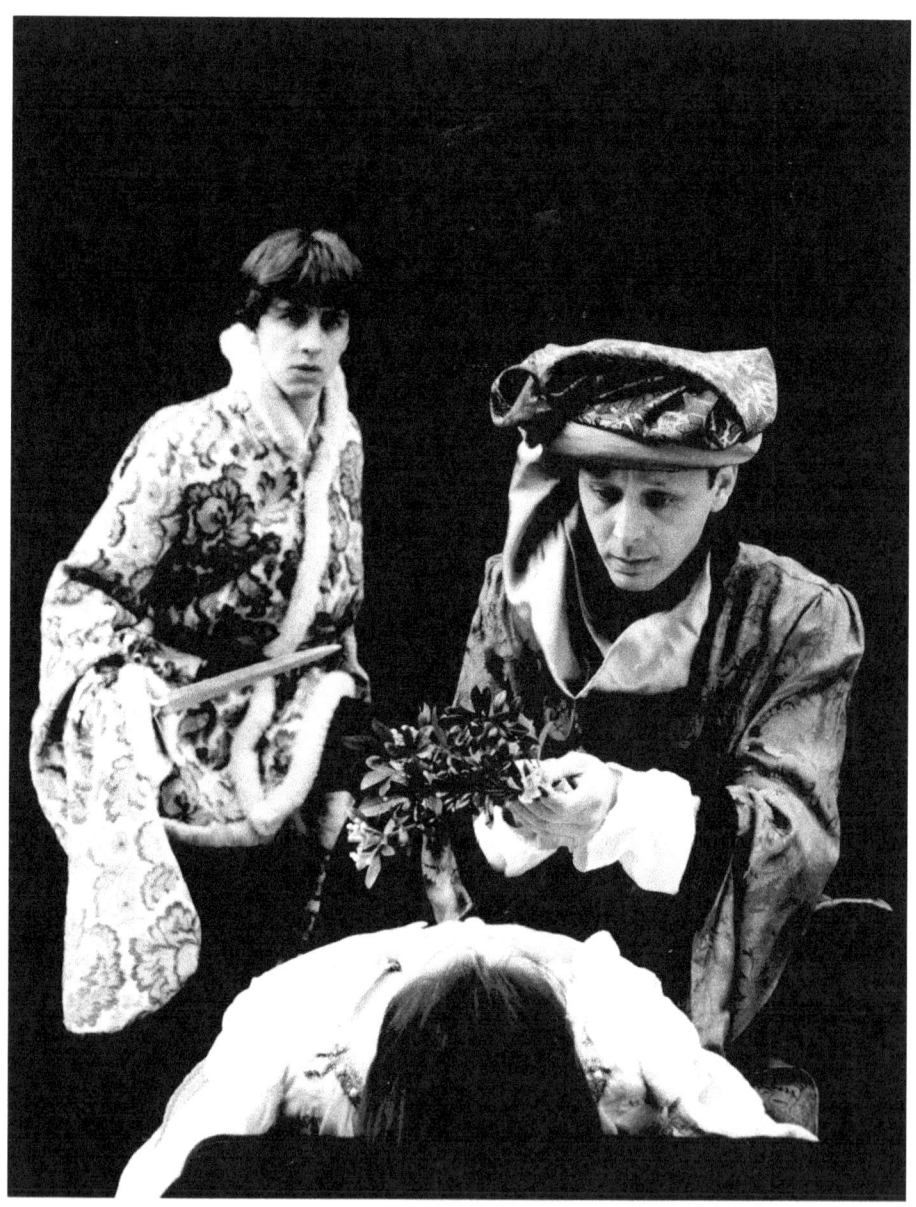

Fig. 46.

Paris (Tony Portacio) mourning at the tomb of Juliet (Victoria Stilwell), is killed by Romeo (Neil Warhurst) in *Romeo and Juliet,* 1996.

Fig. 47.

The Cabala: Geburah. Shylock (Tony Portacio) exalts in his forthcoming vengeance in *The Merchant of Venice*, 1992.

Fig. 48.

Mercy: Angelo (Tony Portacio) threatens Isabella (Lucy Curtin) who will forgive him, in *Measure for Measure* 1991. Photo: The Press Agency (Yorkshire) Ltd.

Fig. 49.

Revenge. Hamlet (Tony Portacio) kills Polonius (Frank Jarvis) mistaking him for Claudius in *Hamlet*, 1993. A bad consequence of the revenge demanded of young Hamlet by Old Hamlet for his murder by Claudius.

ALCHEMY

CHAPTER FOUR: *THE WINTER'S TALE*

It was while preparing this play for production in 1988 that I identified its correlation with George Ripley's *Compound of Alchymie* (see above, pp. 27-29). The identification of the relevance of the work of Ripley's *Compound of Alchymie* to *The Winter's Tale* also solved for me the question of the source of Shakespeare's use of alchemy in the subtext of his other plays and guided me to the alchemical significance of much of their content. So close is this play's action to alchemy as a process of chemistry that I consider the play to be his most exoteric application of this arcana.

The correspondence of the play's action to Ripley's classification of the twelve stages of alchemy into twelve gates of a castle motivated me to present my analysis of the play for the cast and the audience in the programme notes in chart form, which members of the audience found so accessible that they insisted that I do that every year, complaining if I did not do so.

As I identified the role of Paulina in the play as a theatrical projection of an alchemist, I took that role myself, as my knowledge of the mind-set of an alchemist was by then well-developed and I thus understood her intentions at all points in the stage action within that function (see fig. 15).

The understanding of the play's allegory of alchemy solved a number of mysteries for me which can baffle interpreters of the play:

- The existence of a seacoast on land-locked Bohemia.
- The suddenness of Leontes's jealousy of Polixenes and his wife Hermione with the words 'Too hot, too hot!' (I. ii.109).
- The seemingly gratuitous death of young Mamillius.
- The unusual social phenomenon of a woman courtier exerting such power over a king
- The extraordinary eating of Antigonus by a bear, preceded by the quasi-comic stage instruction 'Exit, pursued by a bear' (III. iii. 8).
- Hermione presented to Leontes and Perdita as a statue which comes to life.

CHAPTER FOUR

- The title of the play *The Winter's Tale* when after the first wintry part of the play, spring follows, and the happy conclusion takes place during summer. In the programme notes which I wrote for the 2006 production, the significance of the naming of the season of winter in the play's title was suggested, reinforcing the play's allegory of alchemy:

At the end of *Love's Labour's Lost* Shakespeare presents two songs, one sung by a character named 'Vers' (spring), which is later entitled 'a song of Apollo', while the other song is performed by 'Hiems' (winter) and called the harsh 'words of Mercury'. Mercury was poetically represented as the agent of the harsh practice of alchemy. Thus the title, *A Winter's Tale*, may indicate that Shakespeare is giving us a clue towards the alchemical significance of the play. *The Winter's Tale* is my favourite Shakespeare play, and I find the most poignant moment in all of his plays to be Leontes' realisation that the statue of Hermione is alive as he touches her proffered hand with the words, 'O, she's warm!' (V. iii. 9 and see cover photo). So beautiful is the reunion of Leontes with the wife he had thought to be dead that I believe their total reconciliation must not be doubted. The joy of this occasion is enhanced by the first meeting of Hermione with her daughter Perdita, and the family reunion sees the Philosophers' Stone achieved radiantly with the union of the alchemical 'body' (Leontes) with the 'spirit' (Hermione) and the 'soul' (Perdita).

Theatre Set-Up performed the play twice, in 1988 and 2006, both times costuming it in dress contemporary with Shakespeare's time. In order to realise for the audience the alchemical significance of the play in both productions, Theatre Set-Up built the outline of an alembic vessel placed in front of a structure located at upstage centre (which also served as the curtained surround for Hermione as a statue in V. iii.). Leontes as the 'red king' and Hermione as the 'white queen' made their appearances through this symbolic alembic vessel at the beginning of the play on cue in this specially written prologue: 'We are magicians, practising an ancient art. Alchemists believed that in this vessel they could make magic using chemicals they called the 'red king' and the 'white queen'.'

This was elaborated for those members of the audience who had access to the play's programme by a statement on the front of the programme describing the nature of Theatre Set-Up's presentation of the play:

> As the play's plot is a theatrical projection of alchemy, we present it as if we were a band of magicians performing an experiment linking the alchemic process with people who become, as the story suggests, 'alchemically processed'. The main events of the process are seen to take place in a frame of the alchemists' alembic vessel in the alchemist's tabernacle at the back of the stage area. The magicians aim to create with people the real magic engendered in the alchemic vessel.

It was a popular production with audiences, and we celebrated our 30th anniversary with its performances in 2006.

I found the play to be so profound and multi–faceted that I incorporated six levels of meaning of the story in the programmes notes for the play. These were:

- **Alchemy** (see above pp. 26-32)
- **The spiritual/psychic aspect of alchemy** (see above p. 28)
- **Nature, theurgy and Christianity** (see above p. 48, pp. 59-67)
- **Integration of the personality** (many characters in the play can represent different aspects of the same person)
- **The body politic** (political and historical meanings)
- **Renaissance Platonism** (in particular Divine Love, see above pp. 34-36)

The deeper levels of meanings are all interrelated in the way of Shakespeare's time, when it was thought that there was a certain link (like a chain) between the microcosmic man and cosmic God, and any action taking place at any point along the chain affected all. Thus, an alchemist working with chemicals in his laboratory was thought to be able to effect psychic and spiritual changes in himself and the cosmos as he strove to achieve the Philosophers' Stone. This had to be done within the sights and rules of great Nature. Associated with this was (and still is):

1. The quest for the Divine in all matter, known as 'theurgy' or 'white magic'.
2. The Christian doctrine, which was the spiritual basis of all Renaissance thought.
3. The love of God, which was thought to be reflected in the mutual love of 'companion souls' in the philosophy of Renaissance Platonism (see. p. 34-36)
4. Connected with all this was the 'body politic' and the hope that a time might come when rulers and thus their domains could become enlightened.

The seasonal nature of the play, moving as it does from winter through spring into summer, and indicated in the play's title, links great Nature with man's fate.

Story Section 1 (I. i., ii.)

Leontes, King of Sicilia, becomes unjustifiably suspicious of his pregnant wife Hermione's relationship with his close friend Polixenes, King of Bohemia. He asks his counsellor, Camillo, to poison Polixenes, but instead Camillo warns Polixenes and they both escape from Sicilia overnight.

Alchemy

In the process of **Calcination** the 'red lion' or 'red king' (King Leontes, as the Latin 'leo' in his name implies) or 'sophic sulphur' (the chemical substance) has been combined with the 'white queen' or 'sophic mercury' (Queen Hermione as the feminised form of the name of the Greek God, Hermes, whose Roman form was Mercury) (see fig. 8). Their union has produced a new generation of substances, their son Mamillius and unborn daughter.

The sudden jealous passion of the King, his 'tremor cordis' (I. ii. 110), represents the sudden application of heat in the alchemic process. The beginning of the acceleration of this process is signalled by involvement with Polixenes, King of Bohemia, the home of alchemy in Shakespeare's day. In the context of this play, Bohemia is a metaphorical, not geographical, location, its sea coast part of the allegory, and necessary for the advent of the storms which symbolise later stages in the alchemical process.

Camillo's Italian name, derived from a Latin source, contains the meaning of an acolyte, or an attendant on a priest. In this sense, he functions as the assistant of a woman practising the alchemy. A male alchemist has a female attendant and vice versa.

The Spiritual/Psychic Aspect of Alchemy

The 'lion', Leontes, is the 'body' of the psyche, Hermione the 'spirit' and his unborn daughter the 'soul'. In order to achieve psychic transformation into a better state, these must be separated to undergo individual processes. This separation is initiated.

Nature, Theurgy and Christianity

The Kings Leontes and Polixenes represent the seekers of the truth/godhead that lies in the depths of nature and in themselves. As respective monarchs of Sicilia, in Greek legend the birthplace of the goddess Ceres, and of Bohemia, home of the masculine practice of alchemy, they incorporate the necessary conjunction of feminine and masculine principles in the process. This creates geographic distortion, seeming to give the real Bohemia a sea coast. As the moon was said to be feminine and the sun masculine, the play is set two thirds in Sicilia and one third in Bohemia to achieve Ripley's formula 'one of the sun, two of the moone'.

Integration of the Personality

Leontes is the head of the different elements of the personality (as the lion is a primate of the animal kingdom). Polixenes is his alter-ego, and as the name (which means 'many strangers') suggests, represents the unknown and thus unsuspected aspects of his psyche.

The Body Politic

The dangerous nature of sole rulership is established, the fate of two countries being jeopardised by the foolish whim of King Leontes. Had Camillo complied with the suggested corrupt action requested of him by Leontes and poisoned Polixenes, Sicilia and Bohemia could have been at war.

Two faces of kingship are presented – one tyrannical, the other valued as God-given and protected as such by Camillo.

Renaissance Platonism

Leontes and Hermione are companion souls, but he has lost all sense of this and, becoming inconstant to her, begins an ungodly descent into madness and dishonour.

CHAPTER FOUR

Story Section 2 (II. i.)
Infuriated by the escape of Polixenes and Camillo, Leontes declares them and his wife to be conspirators and traitors. While Mamillius is telling his mother a winter's tale, Leontes parts them, forbidding Hermione to have further contact with the boy. He imprisons Hermione, accusing her of adultery with Polixenes.

Alchemy
Dissolution is the breaking down of the 'substance', the 'base matter' of the alchemical process.
The Spiritual/Psychic Aspect of Alchemy
The 'body' imprisons the 'spirit', which contains the 'soul'.
Nature, Theurgy and Christianity
In order to ultimately gain 'gnosis' or knowledge of the ultimate reality of God, Leontes denies the imprisoned truth, as the disciple Peter did Christ. Mamillius is identified with winter in his telling of 'a winter's tale'.
Integration of the Personality
The psyche sublimates its essential elements.
The Body Politic
The face of unjust tyranny is seen.
Renaissance Platonism
Leontes descends further by the unjust and inhumane imprisonment of Hermione just as she is to give birth to their child.

Story section 3 (II. ii., iii.)
While Hermione is imprisoned, her daughter Perdita is born. Paulina, a court counsellor and physician, presents the child to Leontes, reprimanding him for his unjust behaviour and his courtiers for their sycophancy which allows him to become a tyrant.

Leontes rejects her counsel and commands her husband Antigonus to expose the child to die on some remote shore.

Courtiers, including Dion, are sent to consult the sun-god Apollo at the Oracle of Delphi.
Alchemy
Seperation (Ripley's spelling) occurs. The separating of the elements of

the 'base matter', Leontes (the body) Hermione (the spirit) and Perdita (the soul) commences. Paulina is identified as the female alchemist, taking control of the process, assisted by Camillo and Antigonus. Dion (performed by a cast member who later doubles as Autolycus) is the agent, Mercury, of the alchemical process.

The Spiritual/Psychic Aspect of Alchemy
Outside influences begin to take a hand, but Leontes still rejects his immortal soul (symbolised by Perdita).

Nature, Theurgy and Christianity
Leontes does not recognise his own divine essence and casts out Godhead (Hermione).

Integration of the Personality
The separating of the different parts of the personality is part of the breaking down process that the personality must undergo before being reconstructed and becoming stable.

The Body Politic
In the attempted killing of his own child, the worst face of the tyrant is seen. Paulina criticises the sycophants that feed tyranny and make it possible.

Renaissance Platonism
Leontes' descent is shown in his inability to sleep and in the lunacy of which Paulina accuses him. There was a Renaissance belief that a mad person descended down away from God and then humanity.[1] His ordering the death of his daughter marks the beginning of the nadir of his descent.

Story Section 4 (III., i., ii.1- 141)
During the trial to which Leontes subjects Hermione, the messengers return from the Oracle of Delphi which declares that Hermione, Polixenes and Camillo are innocent and Perdita legitimate. It predicts that Leontes will die without an heir if that which was lost (Perdita) be not found. Leontes rejects the Oracle.

Alchemy
Coniunctio occurs. The conjunction of the 'red king' (sophic sulphur) and the 'white queen' (sophic mercury) is challenged as they come together in the trial.

The sun-god Apollo's Oracle presents the dominant influence of the sun in this critical stage of the alchemical process.

The Spiritual/Psychic Aspect of Alchemy

The truth is exposed and the psychological crisis reached under the influence of the sun, the god, Apollo.

Nature, Theurgy and Christianity

The Oracle pronounces that Leontes will not gain eternal life until he finds his lost soul. Godhead is revealed as truth through the agency of the sun (Apollo).

Integration of the Personality

The psyche takes a futile stand separate from the rest of society, does not accept natural authority and consequently falls.

The Body Politic: Political and Historic meanings

Reference is made to a higher authority and power higher than that of earthly kings.

Renaissance Platonism

The message from the Oracle of Delphi endorses truth, cautions Leontes and halts his descent. The pinnacle of Plato's 'Divine Ascent' was believed to correspond to meeting the eyes of Apollo.[2] In the Christianised version of this, Apollo is identified with a Christian God.[3]

Story Section 5 (III. ii. 142 – 243)

News is brought of the sudden death from grief and shock of young Mamillius, son to Leontes and Hermione. The Queen faints, is carried out, and Paulina announces that she has died, blaming Leontes. He at last regrets his wicked tyranny and vows to do daily penance on the grave of his son and wife.

Alchemy

The violent stage of **Putrefaction** is achieved, in which all elements are severely broken down. The death of Mamillius represents the consumption of a by-product of the substance in the vessel by the substance itself. This was known in alchemic iconography as 'the King eats his son' (see fig. 9). The 'body' (Leontes) of the substance must undergo **Putrefaction** by being continually heated and washed (trial by fire and water). Paulina, the alchemist, symbolically begins doing this to Leontes. The 'spirit', sophic mercury (represented by Hermione), was said to ascend in the vessel as vapour and, later in the process, would descend to be 'reconciled' with the solution. Thus Hermione is seen to ascend away from the world of Leontes.

The Spiritual/Psychic Aspect of Alchemy
The 'body' of the psyche is now separated from 'spirit' and 'soul'. The 'body' begins to be purged and rid of the elements damaging to the psyche.

Nature, Theurgy and Christianity
Leontes denies nature in the form of his own family and is punished by their loss. He begins the expiation of his sins.

The death of Mamillius, which shocks Leontes into the realisation of his sins, begins the healing process. As the name Mamillius (linked to the Latin 'mamilla', meaning a nurturing breast) suggests, the death of plants in winter feeds the new growth of spring.

The Body Politic: Political and Historical Meanings
Tyrants who abuse their subservient wives are remembered in the trials.

Renaissance Platonism
The death of his son and the reported death of his wife makes Leontes realise his fall. Paulina shows him the extent of his descent:

> A thousand knees
> Ten thousand years together, naked, fasting,
> Upon a barren mountain, and still winter
> In storm perpetual, could not move the gods
> To look that way thou wert. (III. ii. 210-214)

Story Section 6 (III. iii.)

Meanwhile, during a storm, the ship carrying Antigonus and Perdita has landed in Bohemia. Antigonus has dreamt that Hermione commanded the child to be left there. He leaves the child with gold and tokens giving evidence of her birth. On his return to the ship he is attacked and consumed by a bear. The ship is wrecked by the storm.

An old shepherd finds the baby Perdita and decides to look after her. His son, a clown, reports that while the old man was finding the living child, he witnessed the death of Antigonus and the ship-wrecked mariners. The shepherd and his son consider the gold left with Perdita to be fairy gold.

Alchemy
The 'nigredo' stage of **Putrefaction** is attained. This 'blackness' occurred in the alembic vessel which was often contained in a bear-shaped still. Thus a bear came to represent this alchemical stage. The eating of Antigonus by a bear symbolises the consumption of an element in this stage. Another symbol for this stage was of a ship being wrecked in a storm.

The distilled vapour, the 'soul' of the substance, could be symbolised in alchemic iconography by a foundling child, a reference to Perdita. That this child should be incorporated in achieving the goal of alchemy is indicated by the 'faery gold' left with her.

This stage of the alchemic process was so severe that Shakespeare uses every catastrophic symbol he can find to represent its violence.

The Spiritual/Psychic Aspect of Alchemy
The soul is discovered and nurtured by benevolent nature (represented by the old shepherd).

Nature, Theurgy and Christianity
The cataclysmic confusion of this section of the story is symbolised by the storm, which the clown claims is a confusion of sea and land as they existed before God separated them and began creation, as reported in the Biblical book of Genesis. The cruel aspect of nature's storms is thus identified with the downward spiral of theurgy, and kindly nature with its upward spiral, as the old shepherd takes in Perdita to be brought up as his daughter in the countryside. She is identified as a nature spirit by the 'faery gold'.

Integration of the Personality
The psyche experiences shocking pain, as felt by Antigonus and the mariners, and begins to be healed when Perdita is nurtured by the old shepherd.

The Body Politic - Political and Historical Meanings
The effects of tyranny on others are shown; Antigonus is cruelly killed, the mariners drowned and the innocent baby exposed to death. However, Antigonus is punished for submitting to a tyrant's law. This is contrasted with the natural goodness of such people as the old shepherd.

Renaissance Platonism
Another story of Divine Love is begun. Reference to Christ (often referred to in the Bible as 'The Good Shepherd') is made in the saving of Perdita by a benevolent shepherd.

Story Section 7 (IV. i.
The fact that sixteen years have passed is reported by the character of Time, a chorus. While Leontes is doing penance for his crimes against his family in Sicilia, Perdita has grown up believing herself to be the old shepherd's daughter in Bohemia. She is loved by the son of Polixenes, Florizel, who has met her while falcon-hunting and is in disguise as a country swain in order to court her.

Alchemy
Congelation, the 'white stage' in which the 'flying spirits' are congealed while the 'body' of the 'base matter' is being 'purged', is symbolised here. Ripley says, 'First purge, and then fixe the elements of our stone| Till together congeale and flowe anon.' This stage would take a long time to attain, hence the passage of sixteen years.

The character of Time, who delivers the bridging narration, refers to the Greek god, Saturn, the presiding influence over the substance of alchemy (see above p. 28 for the ancient Greek legend connecting Saturn with the Philosophers' Stone).

The Spiritual/Psychic Aspect of Alchemy
Time is taken for spiritual purging and healing.

Nature, Theurgy and Christianity
Perdita, the 'divine essence' and 'embodiment of nature' (suggested by the name of the goddess Flora, in whose festive dress Florizel has decked her) is nurtured in the womb of nature while Leontes is purged until he be fit to receive her again.

Integration of the Personality
Time is needed for the damaged psyche to recover and nurture its healing elements.

The Body Politic: Political and Historical Meanings
Time may bring young heirs to inherit power and their reign may bring enlightenment and benevolent rule.

CHAPTER FOUR

Renaissance Platonism
In spite of seeming social differences, Divine Love has brought together Perdita and Florizel.

Story Section 8 (IV. ii., iii., iv. 1 – 418)
Suspicious of his son's disappearances, Polixenes disguises himself and Camillo to seek Florizel out at the old shepherd's sheep-shearing feast. Of great interest to all there is Autolycus, a rogue, pedlar and pick-pocket. Perdita, costumed as the Greek spirit of nature, Flora, is hostess of the feast and much admired by all, including the disguised Polixenes and Camillo.

Alchemy
Cibation is represented by the shearers' feast. Ripley states, '**Cibation** is called a feeding of our matter drie, | With milke and meate.' If this is done moderately he claims, 'Then shall it grow, and waxe ful of courage, | And doe to thee both pleasure and advantage.' Florizel and Perdita can be identified as the subjects of this process.

Autolycus identifies himself as the son of Mercury and refers, in his stealing of sheets put out to dry, to an alchemical practice of collecting morning dew on sheets laid outside overnight to use in the process. His rainbow ribbons represent the stages of alchemy.[4]

The Spiritual/Psychic Aspect of Alchemy
Moderate nourishment brings strength to the awakening soul.

Nature, Theurgy and Christianity
As Perdita is the feminine aspect of nature, Florizel (as the name, a masculine version of Flora, suggests) is the masculine aspect.[5] They begin the spring of the play. He is the ideal seeker of truth whose character is such that he has recognised his 'divine essence' in Perdita instantly, and will never be parted from it.

Nature must always be part of the practice of alchemy, thus Shakespeare makes Florizel, whose name suggests vegetation, a child to Polixenes, the King of Bohemia, home of alchemy.

Integration of the Personality
The psyche has developed new positive elements which begin to assert themselves.

The Body Politic: Political and Historical Meanings
Reference is made in Florizel and Perdita to the hope England was experiencing at the time (the play was written c.1611) in the heir to the throne, the young Prince Henry, made Prince of Wales in 1610, and his sister the Princess Elizabeth, children of James I.[6]

Renaissance Platonism
The extent of the love between this young couple is seen. Florizel vows to be constant to Perdita, even in the face of possible opposition of his father to the match: 'To this I am most constant | Though destiny say no.' (IV. iv. 45, 46)

Perdita indicates the divine nature of their love and her dislike of artifice. Referring to her refusal to plant unnaturally-grafted plants, she claims, 'No more than, were I painted, I would wish | This youth should say 'twere well, and only therefore | Desire to breed by me.' (IV. iv. 101 – 103)

<u>Story Section 9</u> (IV. iv. 418 – 843)
When Florizel declares his intention to marry Perdita, the King reveals his identity, forbids the marriage, and threatens to disinherit Florizel from succession to the throne of Bohemia, and to punish with death or torture the old shepherd, his son the clown, and Perdita.

Florizel declares his intention to abdicate his rights to the throne and to marry Perdita in spite of Polixenes, and he agrees to Camillo's suggestion that they all escape to the court of the now-penitent King Leontes.

They make Autolycus exchange garments with Florizel in order to create a disguise for their escape. Autolycus overhears the old shepherd and his son planning to show Perdita's swaddling clothes and gold to Polixenes to show that she is not their kin, and he dissuades them from doing so, convincing them to board a ship to Sicilia with Perdita and Florizel.

Alchemy
Sublimation is reached here. This is a violent stage involving further separation and purification using much water, represented here by the sea voyage to Sicilia. The hypocrisy and snobbery of Polixenes must be purged, and this is represented by his separation from the young couple.

This stage took 40 days, a period of time mentioned by Autolycus in his fantastic ballad told to the shepherds. (IV. iv. 277)
The Spiritual/Psychic Aspect of Alchemy
Another psychic transformation, that of Polixenes, must be initiated.
Nature, Theurgy and Christianity
Florizel proves constant to his vision of Perdita as his 'divine essence' in spite of trials of fire (the King's anger) and of water (the sea voyage).
Integration of the Personality
The old unregenerative, conservative aspect of the personality threatens to destroy the better nature that has developed.
The Body Politic: Political and Historical Meanings
The relationship between James I and Henry his son is referred to in Polixenes and Florizel. England's hope for a brighter future lay with the enlightened heir.
Renaissance Platonism
Florizel carries out his vow to be constant to Perdita.

Story Section 10 (V. i. ii.)
Polixenes angrily follows Florizel and Perdita to Sicilia, where King Leontes discovers, through the old shepherd, that Perdita is his lost daughter. Polixenes is reconciled to Leontes and gives permission for Florizel to marry Perdita (see fig. 21).

    The kings acknowledge the old shepherd and his son as their kin through adoption, grateful for their nurturing of Perdita.

Alchemy
Firmentation (Ripley's spelling), fixes and resolves the solution. Ripley states that there are three 'firments': 'Two be of bodies in nature cleer' (Perdita and Florizel), and the third is the lion, which must be combined with essences 'begat of itself' (Leontes, who has been 'purged' by Paulina until restored to his lost daughter, Perdita).
The Spiritual/Psychic Aspect of Alchemy
The 'soul' is returned to the 'body'. **Firmentation** 'Is of the soule with the bodie incorporate.' (Ripley)
Nature, Theurgy and Christianity
The revelation of the truth of Perdita's origin restores harmony. Leontes

has found his immortal soul and now can 'inherit eternal life', as the Oracle of Apollo has promised.

Integration of the Personality
The psyche begins to be made whole and to be integrated.

The Body Politic: Political and Historical Meanings
Shakespeare's wishful thinking gives Europe's dissenting monarchs amity through their enlightened children.[7]

Renaissance Platonism
Florizel's constancy to Perdita is rewarded by a happy outcome for the couple.

Story Section 11 (V. iii. 1 - 130)
All are taken to see a statue of the supposed-dead Hermione, which Paulina claims she has had made to an astonishing likeness. It is in fact Hermione herself, who has not died but remained in seclusion, hidden by Paulina until her daughter be found. She returns to life and to Leontes, whose expiation of his crimes is now complete, and to her new-found daughter.

Alchemy
In this stage of **Exaltation**, the spirit or vapour descends into the body of the base matter and the Philosophers' Stone is achieved. Paulina refers to this stage: 'your exultation | Partake to everyone.'(V. iii. 131)

The Spiritual/Psychic Aspect of Alchemy
The 'spirit', Hermione, returns to the 'body', Leontes, made possible by his redemption. As Paulina says, 'for from him | Dear life redeems you.' (V. iii. 102-103)

Nature, Theurgy and Christianity
Ripley refers to Jesus Christ in this stage, which sees the accomplishment of the Philosophers' Stone (with which Jesus was identified): 'Christ saying thus, if I exalted be, | Then shall I draw all things unto me.'

To the ancient Greeks practising the rites of initiation, this stage brought a 'meeting of the eyes of Apollo', to Buddhists the achievement of Nirvana, and to theurgists it attains contact with the essence of Divinity which they consider to be in all living things.

CHAPTER FOUR

Integration of the Personality
The psyche is completely integrated, and the person made whole (well-adjusted in our understanding of psychology).
The Body Politic: Political and Historical Meanings
Political enlightenment is miraculously restored.
Renaissance Platonism
Leontes, having undergone 16 years' penance, during which he has begun the Platonic ascent again, is reunited with his companion soul, Hermione, who 'embraces him' and 'hangs about his neck' (V. iii. 112, 113) in their reconciliation. Shakespeare shows the holiness of the occasion by setting the scene in a chapel.

Story Section 12 (V. iii. 130 – 155)
Paulina tells them to spread their exultation to all. She herself is given in marriage by Leontes to Camillo.

Alchemy
In these stages of **Multiplication** and **Projection**, the Philosophers' Stone (which was in its chemical form a reddish powder) is multiplied and projected on to other base substances (like lead) in order to raise their nature (for instance, turning them into gold). Paulina commands this allegorically in her instruction to those present, whom she calls 'You precious winners all' (V. iii. 131) to spread the happiness of their 'exultation' (V. iii. 131), to others, 'Partake to every one' (V. iii. 132). As the female alchemist she is united with Camillo, a male assistant.
The Spiritual/Psychic Aspect of Alchemy
As the spiritual Philosophers' Stone has been achieved, hopefully some cosmic enlightenment can take place.
Nature, Theurgy and Christianity
No theurgist must make this journey for himself – he/she must go into the 'magic centre' in order to bring out what is there for others' benefit, to 'Partake to everyone' (V. iii. 132). This also applies to Christianity.
Integration of the Personality
The self-adjusted, integrated personality can have the confidence to give benefit to others.

The Body Politic: Political and Historical Meanings

If a political leader is enlightened (that is, willing to be progressive, positive and benevolent in their personal behaviour), as it was hoped that Prince Henry and Princess Elizabeth of England would be in Shakespeare's day, this might become universal through their government. Through Shakespeare's representation of Florizel and Perdita, another reference is made to the hope that the 'Seed of Christ', perpetrated through the children of James I, inheritor of branch of the Merovingian dynasty, would unite Europe.[8] Sadly, Prince Henry, reflected in Florizel, died young, and Princess Elizabeth, married to the Elector of Bohemia and reflected in Perdita, ended up as a refugee in Holland with her husband due to losing an ill-advised war, incidents which occurred after Shakespeare's writing of his last plays, which still glow with optimism for a progressive, non-aggressive Europe and England.

Renaissance Platonism

That the couples have through their mutual love achieved a Divine Ascent which must be shared by others is indicated by Paulina:

> You precious winners all; your exultation
> Partake to every one. (V. iii.131 – 133)

Cabala: Post Production (see above pp. 41-47 and fig. 3)

The different characters, representing different parts of the psyche, take different routes through the Tree. In the early scenes of the play, King Leontes becomes so violent with evil intent that he hardly deserves to be located on the Tree. However, so intense is his negative emotion that he can be placed on **Netzach (feelings)**, his actions against his family and friends showing such a lack of reason that his behaviour indicates a need for him to acquire the characteristics of **Hod (thoughts)** and to be more soundly grounded in **Malkuth (Kingdom, the world as experienced through the senses)** as his behaviour is deluded and not grounded in reality. It is the announcement of the death of his son and his wife that shocks him into an understanding of the truth of **Malkuth**.

Paulina reinforces this with her castigation of Leontes, and he demonstrates a progress towards **Hod** when he accepts her reproof and subsequent declaration to repent. His crimes have been so extreme that it will take sixteen years to eradicate their effect and secure his position on **Hod**. However, his guilt will imprison him in **Yesod (the unconscious, holding traumas)** and only when his daughter and wife are returned to him can he ascend the Tree to **Tiphareth (heart, centre)** and from the calm of a restored family ascend with them to **Kether.**

Polixenes, having escaped the evil intent of Leontes, has been living contentedly in his kingdom in a state equal to **Tiphareth**, but he descends to **Netzach** in his rage against Florizel, Perdita, the old shepherd and his son. His behaviour indicates the presence in **Yesod** of a trauma caused by social snobbery, which is only obliterated when he hears of Perdita's royal birth and subsequently learns to regard the old shepherd and his son as social equals. This enables him to ascend the Tree.

Paulina, Antigonus and Camillo behave in a reasonable and sympathetic manner, showing a balance of **Hod** and **Netzach** and grounded in **Malkuth**. It is these three characters who provide the stable elements in the psyche and demonstrate a balance on the Tree. As Antigonus is killed in his attempt to save Perdita and follow the inspiration of a dream to take her to Bohemia, it can be assumed that he benefits from resurrection in an afterlife which might take him directly to **Kether**. The ascent of Camillo and Paulina up the Tree is dependent on their treatment by the kings they serve. It is these kings who, grateful for the service demonstrating the characteristics of **Geburah (strength, judgement)** and **Chesed (mercy)** that the pair have given their monarchs, provide for their marriage and a possible ascent to **Kether**.

Also functioning as an element serving the main protagonists is Autolycus, firmly grounded in **Malkuth** and never leaving it, the events of the play causing him to at least declare an intention to reform his criminal behaviour. This integrates him into the psyche and places him on **Tiphareth**.

Perdita, the old shepherd and his son are firmly grounded on **Malkuth** and demonstrate a balance between **Netzach** and **Hod**, but Forizel, in courting Perdita in disguise as one of her social class as a shepherd's daughter, shows characteristics only of **Netzach**, lacking the **reasoning**

of Hod that this deception will cause them all grief when revealed. His actions in defying the wrath of his father show a progress towards **Hod,** the subsequent events of the play bringing him to a sense of the reality of **Malkuth**. It is his fortune that Perdita is revealed as the daughter of King Leontes and that his marriage to her is allowed. This takes him to **Tiphareth** and a marriage which will integrate him within the psyche and raise him in time to **Kether.**

CHAPTER FIVE: *MUCH ADO ABOUT NOTHING*

Much Ado About Nothing presents directors and actors with a minimum of implausible action or characterisation to explain and assimilate in performance, but the character of Claudio, lying at the heart of the plot, presents problems.[1] His inability to do his own courting of Hero, requiring Don Pedro to do this for him by proxy, and his gullibility in believing the lies about Hero from Don John with the resulting disgracing and rejection of Hero at the altar of their supposed marriage, makes him an anti-hero. Only the news that upon the reported death of Hero, Don John has fled, and the confession of Borachio bring him to his senses. His remorse for his behaviour is then so extreme that he is prepared to commit himself to marry a girl he does not know and will not see until the marriage has been performed, in recompense to the family he has dishonoured in his denunciation of Hero. Fortunately, this spineless and morally dubious behaviour at the core of the play can be explained by the arcana. Combined with the character of Hero, the victim of his behaviour, Claudio mirrors the basis of the alchemy in the play as well as providing an example of inconstancy in his love for her, his soul companion as defined by Renaissance Platonism. As a flawed character, he is also ripe for progression through the Cabalistic Tree of Life, of which I was sadly unaware in our Theatre Set-Up productions in 1999 and 2011 but which I describe in the post-production section of this chapter. As a young man, Claudio seems eligible for being a candidate of initiation, but lacks an adequate guide or hierophant. Don Pedro does not qualify for this function as he supports Claudio in his unfounded denunciation of Hero.

Ironically, the exuberant and independent characters of Beatrice and Benedict are themselves manipulated, but in a way which makes them realise the intrinsic love they bear for one another, and their resulting alliance provides a moral strength which guides the stage action. The verve of these two characters made the play popular with our actors and audiences, so we chose it as our swansong in 2011.

The different levels of meaning through which I explained the play to the actors and to the audience in the play's programme notes were **Alchemy**,

Renaissance Platonism and Christianity, **Independent thought** (There is a strong theme in *Much Ado About Nothing* of not questioning what seems to be the evidence of the senses and the dictates of society. Beatrice and Benedick (with the exception of believing what they have overheard about their love for one another) think and act for themselves and make judgements based on logic, in contrast to Hero and Claudio who are blown about at the whim of society's customs and their false sensory perceptions. It is almost as if Shakespeare anticipated in this play later philosophies such as those of Descartes on empirical scepticism) and **Watching, Being Watched and Eavesdropping** (In this play, Shakespeare sets forth many aspects of voyeurism. In it most people are eavesdropping, watching or being watched, with good and bad results).

Story Section 1 (I. i., ii.)

Leonato, his wife Innogen (a non-speaking role, often as in our production, omitted from the text and the stage), their daughter Hero, and niece, Beatrice, welcome as house guests a party of soldiers triumphantly returning from battle. These comprise Don Pedro of Aragon and his companions Claudio and Benedick; Don John, his bastard brother; and their attendants.

Beatrice and Benedick engage in a battle of wits, but Claudio falls in love with Hero and seeks to marry her, requesting Don Pedro to speak to her on his behalf. Their conversation is overheard and misinterpreted by Antonio, Leonato's brother, who reports that Don Pedro wishes Hero for himself.

Alchemy

In the first alchemic stage of **Calcination**, Leonato, the 'red lion' (implied in the Latin 'leo') or 'sophic sulphur' has been combined with Innogen, who has functioned as the 'white queen' or 'sophic mercury' (possibly Shakespeare's purpose for including this silent, seemingly-actionless character in his original script) to produce a new generation, their daughter, Hero, whose lover Claudio will become the 'base matter' of the alchemy. Their niece, Beatrice, and her lover, Benedick, will participate in the process.

Renaissance Platonism and Christianity
Hero and Claudio recognise each other as 'companion souls', but Beatrice and Benedick do not, although their witty repartee sets them apart from others and indicates their equality with each other.

Independent Thought
Beatrice and Benedick continually reassess each other by challenging their opponent's position. Hero and Claudio, by contrast, do not even speak directly to each other and Claudio woos her through the agency of Don Pedro, his social superior.

Watching, Being Watched and Eavesdropping
Claudio falls in love with Hero by just watching her. Antonio misunderstands overheard conversation, and demonstrates its dangers, giving his brother inaccurate information.

<u>Story Section 2</u> (I. iii., II. i, ii.)
Don John and his attendants, Conrade and Borachio, plot to create any trouble that they can and to destroy Claudio's marriage plans. Borachio devises a plan to deceive Claudio and Don Pedro into thinking that Hero is a loose woman.

In honour of his guests, Leonato holds a feast and masquerade, during which Hero is wooed on behalf of Claudio by Don Pedro. Beatrice further insults Benedick and their friends plan to match them off in marriage to each other.

Alchemy
As Saturn was the presiding god of alchemy, the Saturnine evil of Don John and his followers, Conrade, 'born under Saturn' (I. iii. 11), and Borachio become the alchemic agent of the process. They challenge the smug self-satisfaction of the returning heroes and ultimately turn them into villains, who are deceived into cruelly wronging a virtuous lady and her father, their kindly host. This is the dissolving process of the second alchemic stage, **Dissolution**. This action, like a quickstone, will also test the jesting Benedick, who proves to be morally superior to his companions in judgement and loyalty.

Renaissance Platonism and Christianity
Don John sets up a test for Claudio's constancy to Hero, which is likely to falter as he has not even had the courage to be direct in his courtship, done for him by proxy. His love for Hero seems based on the false values of superficial appearance and worldly possessions. The plan to match off Beatrice and Benedick will test their identity as companion souls.

Independent Thought
Don John is presented as a caution against too much antisocial independence. He refuses to compromise himself in any way to be accommodating:

> I cannot hide what I am: I must be sad when I have cause, and smile at no man's jests; eat when I have stomach, and wait for no man's leisure; sleep when I am drowsy, and tend on no man's business; laugh when I am merry, and claw no man in his humour. (I. iii. 12-17)

However this is also the credo of a self-confessed villain, 'I am a plain-dealing villain' (I. iii. 30).

Hero does not enjoy such independence and is commanded to marry to please her father, a stricture criticised by Beatrice, who recommends that she should marry to please herself.

Hero is ultimately wooed for Claudio by proxy through her father and Don Pedro, her senses deceived by Don Pedro's mask into thinking that he is Claudio.

Watching, Being Watched and Eavesdropping
Evil results from Borachio's hearing of the intended marriage between Claudio and Hero, as he is eavesdropping while hiding behind an arras. The masks that everyone wears at the masquerade facilitate unobserved watching and deception.

<u>Story Section 3</u> (II. iii., III. i.)
Don Pedro, Leonato and Claudio arrange for Benedick to overhear their discussing Beatrice and himself. They pretend that Beatrice is hopelessly in love with him and they pour scorn on his cruel treatment of her. When they have gone, he resolves to return her love. She is thus mystified by his

changed attitude to her when she calls him to dinner. This mystery seems to be solved when she overhears Hero and her servants discussing her and Benedick. They pretend that he is hopelessly in love with her and scorn her disdain of him. When they are gone she resolves to return his love.

Alchemy
Benedick, in being joined to Beatrice by his friends, is ironically prepared to be separated from them in the third alchemic stage of **Seperation** (Ripley's spelling). His constancy to Beatrice will prevent him from falsely denouncing Hero, an immoral act which will be committed by Claudio, who at this time is being prepared by Don John to be separated, as 'body' of the alchemic process, from Hero, its 'soul'.

Renaissance Platonism and Christianity
The plan to match Beatrice and Benedick succeeds and it takes little for them to recognise their intrinsic love for each other. The motives that they express in deciding to return the other's supposed love are unselfish, founded not on personal desire, as in 'base love', but in a wish to gratify the one who loves them. They recognise in each other their companion souls.

Independent Thought
Beatrice and Benedick appear to be deceived by what they overhear into believing that each is in love with the other. However, it is Shakespeare's trick to make this devised deception the actual truth.

Watching, Being Watched and Eavesdropping
Eavesdropping is used to bring Beatrice and Benedick together.

Story Section 4 (III. ii., iii.)

Don John effects his plan to prevent the marriage of Hero to Claudio by taking him and Don Pedro to overhear a servant, pretending to be Hero, willingly being courted by Borachio below her chamber window. The device is believed to be the truth by the eavesdroppers.

Dogberry, the local constable, and Verges, the local headborough (a parish officer) enjoin the members of the Prince's watch to be careful in the execution of their duties. The members of the watch overhear Borachio bragging to Conrade of the money he has been given by Don John for his part in the plot against Hero and Claudio, and they arrest the villains.

Alchemy
The **Seperation** of Claudio, as 'body' of the alchemic process from Hero, its 'soul', is effected by Don John. At the same time, the means for discovering his deception, rejoining the couple and repairing the process is introduced through the members of the watch.

Renaissance Platonism and Christianity
Claudio falters in his constancy to Hero, is easily taken in by a crude device to discredit her and makes a base resolve to ruin her reputation at a wedding which will be a mockery of love.

Independent Thought
Claudio and Don Pedro are easily deceived by their senses into believing that a servant-woman is Hero, and upon this slim evidence they resolve to condemn her.

Watching, Being Watched and Eavesdropping
Don John and his companions plot to deceive Claudio and Don Pedro by luring them to eavesdrop on a servant-woman masquerading as Hero at her chamber window. However the watch, whose job in the play is to observe others, uncover this plot by overhearing Borachio and Conrade.

<u>Story Section 5</u> (III. iv., v., IV. i. 1-143)
Preparations take place for the wedding at which Claudio now plans to disgrace Hero. Dogberry and Verges try to warn Leonato of the conspiracy against Hero but such is his haste and their manner so inarticulate that he ignores their words and dismisses them.

    The process of the wedding is begun, but Claudio denounces Hero as an 'approved wanton'. Hero faints and Don Pedro, Don John and Claudio leave in disgust. Leonato does not know who to believe and condemns Hero, saying that 'she is fallen | Into a pit of ink.' (IV. i. 139 – 140)

Alchemy
An 'alchemical wedding' called, in the fourth alchemical stage, **Coniunctio**, is halted and turned into the violent fifth stage of **Putrefaction,** wherein all elements of the process are severely broken down and the 'body' and 'soul'

torn apart. This was called the 'black stage', as suggested by Leonato's reference to Hero having fallen into a 'pit of ink'.

Renaissance Platonism and Christianity
Claudio fails his test of constancy and in his false condemnation of Hero begins a moral descent away from God.

Independent Thought
Leonato, in dismissing Dogberry and Verges, underestimates the value of information which can be given by people he finds to be 'tedious'.

Showing little judgement of character, Claudio and Don Pedro attempt to ruin the life and reputation of a lady whom they hardly know. Leonato similarly misjudges in believing the aristocratic men against his virtuous daughter.

Watching, Being Watched and Eavesdropping
Leonato, ignoring Dogberry's garbled account of the report from the watch, loses the benefits of their findings. The worst consequences of voyeurism in the play are realised in Claudio's false condemnation of Hero.

Story Section 6 (IV. i. 143-254)
Hero falls in a faint, but after her accusers have left the stage she recovers. Friar Francis re-assures Leonato that in the 'angel whiteness' of her face he reads Hero's innocence and advises that the story be given out that she has died. This might mollify Claudio's anger, make him sorry for what he has said and done and give time for the correct story to be revealed. If the truth does not emerge and Hero's good reputation not be restored, she should ultimately take refuge in a convent. This advice is taken and Hero led away into hiding.

Alchemy
The sixth stage, **Congelation**, in which the soul ascends into an astral or heavenly sphere is dramatised here as Hero, the 'soul' of the process, pretends to be dead, on the advice of Friar Francis, who functions as the alchemist controlling the action. It was known as the 'white' stage, as her 'angel whiteness' testifies. During this process, the 'body' must undergo purification, as the friar suggests might happen to Claudio should he experience remorse for his treatment of Hero.

Renaissance Platonism and Christianity
It is God's agent, personified as Friar Francis, who suggests a way forward for Hero, who he has accurately perceived to be wronged.
Independent Thought
Only Friar Francis, Beatrice and Benedick demonstrate the good sense of measured judgement in their support of Hero.
Watching, Being Watched and Eavesdropping
Friar Francis, in closely observing Hero's symptoms of distress, correctly diagnoses her innocence.

Story Section 7 (IV. i. 255-334)
Left in misery by the awful condemnation of Hero by Claudio, and shocked by the hideous reality of the situation into a realisation of their own feelings, Beatrice and Benedick pledge their love for each other. In response to Benedick's challenge to Beatrice to test his own constancy in love, she asks him to 'Kill Claudio!' (IV. i. 288). At first he shrinks from such an action, but she convinces him that it is justified.

Alchemy
The alchemic process is supported or 'fed' by Beatrice and Benedick in the seventh stage, **Cibation**, as the declaration of their mutual love strengthens them and they join in the support of Hero. The challenging and testing of Claudio is begun when Beatrice asks Benedick to kill him. It is implied that Benedick should challenge him to a sword fight, and in alchemy swords are symbols for purifying fire.
Renaissance Platonism and Christianity
Their love for each other confirmed in the face of such nastiness, Beatrice and Benedick begin a 'Divine Ascent' in support of the truth and each other. She presents him with a test of his constancy to her, and challenges him to kill Claudio, and in accepting this he strengthens his moral position in defending good against evil in the play.
Independent Thought
Beatrice and Benedick reason sensibly that Hero must be innocent, their compassion drawing them closer together in love.

CHAPTER FIVE

Watching, Being Watched and Eavesdropping
Benedick, in closely observing Beatrice's reactions to the scene, reaches the conclusion that Hero, her cousin, is innocent.[2]

Story Section 8 (IV. ii., V. i. 1-252)
Conrade and Borachio are brought to justice by the local sexton and the crime perpetrated upon Hero is brought to light.

Leonato and Antonio challenge Claudio and Don Pedro to a duel, which they laughingly disdain, but they are more concerned when challenged by Benedick, who tells them that Don John has fled. Claudio's remorse is complete when he learns the truth of the whole situation from the repentant Borachio as he is led to prison.

Alchemy
The eighth, violent stage of **Sublimation**, in which the 'body' undergoes intensive purification, begins. The culprits are tried, Claudio is challenged to fight, and then he is humiliated and plunged into total remorse and self-condemnation as he hears the truth about the lies against Hero and his part in her supposed death. The repentant Borachio also shares in this self-purifying process.

Renaissance Platonism and Christianity
Claudio's recognition of the wrong he has done and his total remorse arrests his descent from God.

Independent Thought
Leonato learns not to value people according to their rank in society, but nevertheless foolishly and illogically (given his old age, contrasted with the youth of his warrior opponent) challenges Claudio to a sword fight.

Borachio points out that the watch and constables, 'these shallow fools', have succeeded in uncovering his treachery, while the more sophisticated nobles have been deceived by it.

Claudio learns how his senses have not only deceived him but have made him act in a way so outside the dictates of society as to render him despicable.

Watching, Being Watched and Eavesdropping
Claudio learns the error of his eavesdropping and Borachio regrets using

it as a means to deceive, as the benefits of the legitimate observations of the men designated as the 'watch' take effect.

Story Section 9 (V. i. 253- 286)
Leonato condemns the now repentant Claudio for his action against Hero (still believed to be dead) but offers absolution from his revenge if he will tell the people of Messina the truth of Hero's innocence, mourn her death that evening at her tomb, on the next day be married to his brother's daughter and give her the marriage rights which had been due to Hero.

Alchemy
Leonato ensures that Claudio (the 'body') undergoes the purifying that his repentance requires, and sets him the punishing trial of demanding that he marry a person he does not know or has not seen. His actions prepare for the ninth stage, **Firmentation**, which fixes and resolves the solution.

Renaissance Platonism and Christianity
It is demanded of Claudio that not only must he carry out restitution of Hero's good name and appropriate Christian rites of mourning, but he must blindly take a wife in a manner opposed to his previous values of assessing a woman according only to her appearance. When he first saw Hero, he proclaimed that she was 'the sweetest lady that ever I looked on' (I. i. 174-175).

Independent Thought
Claudio's remorse causes him to accept an arranged marriage with as much haste and as little regard for his future wife as he has shown for Hero.

Watching, Being Watched and Eavesdropping
Claudio is made to pay for his folly in being deceived into betraying Hero by eavesdropping at her window.

Story Section 10 (V. i. 286-326, V. ii., iii., iv. 1-33)
Amazed at and grateful for Leonato's mercy, Claudio agrees to all his demanded points of action. That night he mourns at Hero's tomb.

Beatrice and Benedick meet, displaying their mutual love. The next day the arranged marriage is prepared, with the real Hero disguised as her cousin whom Claudio expects to marry.

Benedick asks Friar Francis to officiate at his own marriage to Beatrice.

Alchemy
The alchemic stage of **Firmentation** is composed of three 'firments', of which the 'Red Lion' Leonato, must be one and the other two must be 'of bodies in nature cleer' (the virginal Claudio and Hero).[3]

The marriage upon which Leonato insists will not only rejoin the young couple, but will reconcile him with Claudio. Another **Firmentation** or 'fixing' of the process will take place with the marriage of Beatrice and Benedick.

Renaissance Platonism and Christianity
Leonato demonstrates Christian mercy in his attitude to Claudio, who responds with Christian contrition. This Christian dimension is emphasised in the presence of Friar Francis, before whom Claudio must pledge to marry the unknown veiled woman and to whom Benedick applies to marry him to Beatrice.

Independent Thought
Again Claudio's senses deceive him, the veil which Hero wears preventing him from recognition of her.[4]

Watching, Being Watched and Eavesdropping
The benefits of the true observations of Friar Francis, Benedick and the watch take place.

<u>**Story Section 11**</u> (V. iv. 34-71)
When Claudio takes the hand of the veiled woman whom he pledges to marry, she lifts her veil and to his joy reveals herself as the very much alive Hero.

Alchemy
The tenth stage, **Exaltation**, takes place as the 'soul' 'descends' to re-join the purified 'body', and the 'gold' of alchemy is achieved. This occurs when Hero lifts her veil and identifies herself as a living person to Claudio.

Renaissance Platonism and Christianity
When Hero lifts her veil, the illusions of the play disappear, and Claudio

literally recognises his 'companion soul'. Hero demonstrates Christian forgiveness in taking back Claudio as a lover and husband.

Independent Thought
Only when Claudio pledges to act against the gratification of his senses by blindly accepting the wife that society demands he must take in reparation for his crime is Hero's veil lifted so that his perception is corrected.

Watching, Being Watched and Eavesdropping
Claudio receives the benefit of repentance for his previous incorrect observation.

Story Section 12 (V. iv. 72-126)
Beatrice and Benedick almost lose each other in denying their mutual love in provocative banter, but their love is confirmed by sonnets that they have written about each other, discovered by their friends. Benedick commands that they all celebrate their happiness in a dance before the double wedding.

A messenger reports that Don John has been captured in flight from Messina, but this unpleasantness is brushed aside in the general rejoicing.

Alchemy
The 'golden' moment of the reconciliation of Hero and Claudio must be multiplied in the eleventh alchemical stage of **Multiplication**, and shared with other people. This occurs here with the confirmation of the mutual love of Beatrice and Benedick.

The benefits must not be kept in by those achieving this 'gold', but in the twelfth stage, **Projection**, these benefactors must embrace everybody, as Benedick does when he includes them in a joyful dance.

Renaissance Platonism and Christianity
Both couples indicate their joy of the Divine Ascent through love by sharing their joy through dance with all present.

Independent Thought
Beatrice and Benedick almost lose their happiness by asserting their separateness, over-indulging in repartee. The sensory evidence of the sonnets as 'their own hands against their hearts' ironically saves them.

Watching, Being Watched and Eavesdropping
The friends of Beatrice and Benedick have no respect for their written privacy as they steal and read their sonnets about each other with, however, beneficial results.

Cabala: Post Production
Progress up the Tree of Life can be found in the couples Beatrice and Benedick and Claudio and Hero. At the beginning of the play, both Beatrice and Benedick are locked in **Yesod (Foundation, the unconscious – holding trauma)**, Beatrice resenting Benedick's having flirted with her, engaged her heart, and then left her for the war. She confesses as much to Don Pedro, who teases her for the harshness of her invective against Benedick:

> DON PEDRO: Come, Lady, come, you have lost the heart of Signior Benedick.
> BEATRICE: Indeed, my lord, he lent it me awhile, and I gave him use for it, a double heart for his single one. Marry, once before he won it of me with false dice, therefore your Grace may well say I have lost it. (II. i. 261-264)

Benedick resents the sharpness of her criticism of him and the bitterness of her retorts:
'O God, sir, here's a dish I love not! I cannot endure my Lady Tongue' (II. i. 257-258).

The unhappy confessions that both Beatrice and Benedick make about each other to Don Pedro do not correspond with the 'merry war' (I. i. 56), or the 'skirmish of wit' (I. i. 57) that Leonato claims they practise. Both of them are suffering trauma, suppressing feelings of love for each other which Don Pedro detects in his plan to bring them together, although he does claim that this will represent 'one of Hercules' labours' (II. i. 342).

This plan succeeds, both Beatrice and Benedick being released from the restrictions of the inhibiting characteristics of **Yesod**, so that when the grim reality of Claudio and Don Pedro's denunciation of Hero occurs, the emotions engendered by the scene make the declaration of their mutual love possible. This is tested in her challenge to him to 'Kill Claudio' (IV. i. 288), which he accepts, moving up the Tree to **Geburah (strength)** and taking Beatrice with him in his defence of the wronged Hero. Both Beatrice and Benedick forgive Claudio in the character of **Chesed (mercy)**, reconciled in what will become the family relationship within the two marriages of the cousins Hero and Beatrice to Claudio and Benedick. This reconciliation shows features of **Binah (spiritual love)** and **Chokmah (spiritual purpose)** leading to **Kether (the crown of existence, the Divine self)** of married sexual consummation.

Claudio's progress must be a longer journey. His unenlightened attitude to Hero, both in worshipping her from afar, proposing marriage to her by proxy through Don Pedro, believing false evidence against her, and cruelly denouncing her and rejecting her at what was supposed to be their wedding, places him in a wavering position on **Netzach (feelings)**. He cannot even be identified as being grounded in **Malkuth (the real world perceived through the senses)**, although he uses his favour with Don Pedro to get him to doing his wooing for him and expresses interest in Hero as the heir of Leonato. He allows his senses to deceive him into thinking that a servant woman at a window is Hero, not bothering to move closer to the window to investigate the truth. Even when he is told that Hero has died, he does not perceive that his accusation must have been false to cause her death. His jocund response to Benedick's accusation of his guilt is callous. Only Borachio's confession brings about self-confessed guilt, 'I have drunk poison whiles he utter'd it' (V. i. 240). This progress towards **Hod (thoughts)** will also place him in **Yesod**, where his guilt must lie heavy on his heart. The sincerity of his mourning prepares him for ascent up the Tree, and when the forgiving Hero identifies herself as his bride he enters **Tiphareth (beauty, heart, the centred self)** and hopefully in his marriage moves towards **Kether** in the bride bed.

Hero herself lacks the logic of **Hod** in agreeing to marry a man who does not even have the courage to do his own wooing. She is dazzled by him, an impression which is dispelled when he rejects her at the altar with false accusations. This changes her, and under the guidance of Friar Francis she moves to **Hod**, given time to contemplate her situation while in hiding, possibly in a quiet state resembling **Tiphareth**. Her father,

Leonato, is advised by Friar Francis to believe in her innocence, and in his and Antonio's defiance of Don Pedro and Claudio, he holds the position on the Tree of **Geburah (strength, justice)** on her behalf.

Leonato, Antonio and Hero move up the Tree to **Chesed (mercy)** in forgiving Claudio sufficiently to agree to a marriage with him. As a couple benefitting from life-changing events, hopefully in the future life of the characters beyond the script and in the minds of the audience, Hero and Claudio could move up the Tree to **Kether** in their marriage.

CELTIC

Alchemy is also crucial to an interpretation of the following plays, which have Celtic themes.

CHAPTER SIX: *CYMBELINE*

The mysteries of *Cymbeline* are such that I found it impossible to direct a logical production of the play until 1989 when I understood its arcana. In that year, the first clue that I found to the play's mysteries was in Charles Nicholl's *The Chemical Theatre,* which provided an alchemical reading of the strange scene IV. iii. 296-333 in which Imogen, mistaking the headless body of Cloten for her husband Posthumus (as he is dressed in her husband's clothes), embraces the corpse, bathing herself in the blood of his dismembered neck.[1] I developed an understanding of many of the play's other strange features after reading *The UnderWorld Initiation* by R.J. Stewart.[2] There appeared to me to be a direct correspondence between the stages of Celtic mysticism Stewart describes and some of the mysterious events of *Cymbeline*. I list these below for easy reference to my analysis of the play. The initiate who attempts this magical initiation will encounter the following features. The numbers correspond to my identification of them in the play in the section on **The Celtic UnderWorld Initiation** arcana, corresponding to the different sections of the story.

1. A Goddess of the UnderWorld (see Story Sections 1, 4, 10, 17, 21, 28).
2. A Guardian at the entrance who will admit only those strong enough to endure its Trials (see Story Section 12).
3. Guides to lead (see Story Sections 13, 17, 22).
4. A surge of 'Inner Fire' which will propel the initiate to act correctly (see Story Section 23).
5. An act of love and self-sacrifice by the initiate (see Story Section 23).
6. A change in the initiate's bloodstream which can even cure ill

health (see Story Section 23).
7. Confinement in a prison or cave (see Story Sections 12 and 26).
8. Contact with ancestors (see Story Section 27).
9. A 'magic dream' (see Story Section 27).
10. A vision of the 'Universal Tree' (see Story Section 31).

It seemed to me that Shakespeare had encoded this Celtic mysticism in *Cymbeline* to ensure its continuation into the future just as arcana are often preserved in British children's games, riddles, jokes and pub signs. Similarly, in his chapter *The Prophecies of Merlin,* which R. J. Stewart has decoded as a manual of the Celtic mystical tradition, Geoffrey of Monmouth has left a blueprint of this mysticism as a legacy for future readers in his *The History of the British Kings*.[3] In *The UnderWorld Initiation*, Stewart claims that the whole of this book is itself a 'storehouse of magical symbolism, a compendium of traditional initiatory instruction' (p. 54). Shakespeare used historical (often semi-legendary) characters and stories featured in Geoffrey of Monmouth, taken directly or via Holinshed's Chronicles. From this source he takes real ancient British royalty, Cymbeline, Guiderius and Arviragus, as some of his protagonists. I consider that Shakespeare's reference to historical British kings from Geoffrey of Monmouth's *The History of the British Kings*, where there are also Celtic arcana coded in a chapter titled *The Prophesies of Merlin*, suggests a correspondence which justifies my reading of such Celtic arcana in *Cymbeline*.

A further justification for my reading of the play was the obvious Celtic content of the play featuring ancient Celtic society and mythology:[4]

- **The adopting out of high-born children** and their exchange for children of non-royal families in order to equalise society. Posthumus is adopted by King Cymbeline and his two sons by the soldier Belarius.
- **Caves**, such as the one in which Belarius, Guiderius and Arviragus live, represent entrances to the Celtic UnderWorld.
- **The cult of the severed head** (Cloten's), important in the legend of the Celtic God Bran (whose symbol is the raven). His living

severed head, supposedly buried beneath the hill on which the Tower of London now stands, is said to bring well-being to Britain.
- **The Janus-Head** theme of two characters (one the real, the other the false personality which must be purged away in an initiation ritual) being one person. This is represented by Posthumus/Cloten, the main initiate.
- **The male-female polarity of spiritual power**, which sets up an energy of conflict which can generate the events of the ritual. This is represented by the Queen against Cornelius and Belarius (like the legendary Morgan le Fay and Merlin), and Imogen against Cymbeline.
- **Sports games held as augury** such as Cloten's game of bowls.

The Celtic and alchemic arcane content of the play becomes overt in the remarkable scene II. ii. when Iachimo, hidden in a trunk, moved for safe-keeping into Imogen's bedroom, emerges when she is asleep, steals a bracelet from her arm and records details of her bedroom and marks upon her person which will convince Posthumus that he has slept with her, thus winning a wager that he has been able to assail her proclaimed virtue. The Latin meaning of 'arcanum' (usually in the plural form of 'arcana'), is 'a mystery; profound secret'. It is derived from the Latin 'arceo' meaning 'shut up' from 'arca', 'chest'. In this literal sense, Iachimo, hidden in the trunk (another word for 'chest') becomes a metaphor for the mystery he embodies as the initiator of Imogen's entrance into the Celtic UnderWorld Initiation and the processes of psychic alchemy. As he re-enters the trunk, he evokes magical powers which he names as 'dragons of the night' (the symbols of the 'base matter' of alchemy (see fig. 14) 'that dawning| May bare the raven's eye!' (II. ii. 48-49). The raven is the symbol of **Putrefaction**, the violent stage of alchemy during which, in a subsequent part of the story, Posthumus will try to have Imogen killed (see fig. 11). The raven is also associated with the Celtic goddess characterising the UnderWorld, the Morrigan, in her crone or matron aspect of the Triple Goddess, symbolised in this play by the Queen. Iachimo then names the hellish UnderWorld into which he has thrust Imogen, 'Though this a heavenly angel, hell is here' (II. ii. 50). He follows this by echoing the striking clock, 'One, two, three: time, time!' (II. ii. 51), counting her into her future trials and marking his exit as the initiating agent with the number three, significant to Celts as well as to Christians, who observe the Trinity of Father, Son and Holy Ghost. This scene is spellbinding in performance.

Another scene where an apparent anomaly can be resolved by reference to both alchemic and Celtic arcana is V. iv. 29-122, in which Posthumus has a dream featuring his mother, father, two brothers and the Roman god, Jupiter. This may seem to the audience a fiction in the mind of the sleeping Posthumus, but a book containing a mysterious prophecy is found beside the waking Posthumus, implying the real presence of Jupiter and possibly the ghosts of Posthumus's family.

If the mysticism and emotional content of the play is not respected and is not performed by the actors of the scene with sincere emotion, the resolution of the plot in V. v. can seem ridiculous. In this scenario, the members of Cymbeline's family, including Imogen and Posthumus, are brought together and Iachimo confesses his treachery against Imogen. A lack of respect for this scene can make nonsense of the play. As a result of the way the lines are delivered, this moving scene can become comic melodrama, eliciting from the audience constant laughter as each revelation of the coincidences of the story are revealed. Aware of this problem in production, we contrived the performance of this scene in the Theatre Set-Up productions of the play in 1989 and 2009 to be emotionally sincere, with the reunion of the members of the King's family heartfelt so that audiences did not react in this way. Nor did they laugh at the events of V. v. in the RSC production directed by Bill Alexander with Harriet Walter as Imogen, which I saw in The Pit in 1988. The 2016 RSC production of *Cymbeline*, directed by Melly Still, was radical in its interpretation, changing the gender of some of the play's protagonists (for example making King Cymbeline a queen mourning her lost sons), and giving the events of the plot current relevance by transferring the period of the action to a future in which Cymbeline's decision to pay tribute to Rome in V.v. became a 'Brexit'-like political issue challenging payments to the European Union. This distortion of the plot and characterisation, exciting as it may be, demonstrates the extent to which directors feel they must reinterpret a Shakespearean play when the arcane subtext is not understood.

It is important that the resolution of events in the last scene be taken seriously, as it provides evidence of the new wisdom of King Cymbeline in his surprise decision to pay tribute to Rome, although he has won the right not to do so. Here, Shakespeare portrays an ideal political decision, taken not out of the national pride and self-interest that the Queen advocates, but in a spirit of creating peace and harmony. This action also mirrors the target of all spiritual systems, that is, to raise the individual above the level of petty self-interest to union with Divinity through devotion to others. The unity of Rome with Britain in a state of peace also reflects the aim of idealistic and spiritual societies - to achieve a consciousness of oneness above divisions and differences as symbolised by the male/female composite, the hermaphrodite, which Imogen represents as a page boy (see above p. 33).

In the explication of my reading of *Cymbeline* given to the Theatre Set-Up's cast and audiences, I follow the tabular layout insisted upon by the company's regular audiences. I considered there to be thirty-three sections in the story. This number, thought to be of high magical significance (as in the age of Christ when he was crucified) is sometimes used as the number of stages of initiatory rituals. An example of this can be found in the Ancient and Accepted Rite of Freemasonry, which has thirty three degrees of attainment.[5]

> Each numbered section in the story has a specific meaning for **The Celtic UnderWorld Initiation** and **Alchemy.**

Both of these processes are undertaken by individuals to effect changes in themselves which will raise their own spiritual consciousness to the benefit of the world at large. In *The Flaming Door,* Eleanor C. Merry describes the links between alchemy and the practices of the Druids, exponents of Celtic mysticism: 'The Druids prepared the way for the burning, dissolving and binding in the realm of alchemy'.[6]

Story Section 1 (I. i.)
The King of Britain, Cymbeline, banishes a young man, Leonatus Posthumus (the orphaned son of the war-hero, Sicilius Leonatus, and

whom Cymbeline himself has fostered), as punishment for marrying his own daughter, Imogen. She is now heir to the throne since Cymbeline's two sons, Guiderius and his younger brother, Arviragus, were abducted twenty years previously as babies. Although Posthumus is worthy, it has been Cymbeline's wish that Imogen should marry Cloten, the imbecilic and secretly dangerous son of his second wife, the scheming Queen, now stepmother to Imogen and manipulator of all events at court.

The Celtic UnderWorld Initiation
Cymbeline, representing Britain, demonstrates a lack of wisdom in following the advice of the Queen, wishing to force her son Cloten upon Imogen as a husband and banishing Posthumus, who Imogen has married. This unwiseness must be purged for Britain to survive, but Cymbeline is too weak to become an initiate. His adopted son, Leonatus Posthumus, becomes the first initiate who will undergo the transformative Celtic UnderWorld journey on his behalf. Imogen, stronger in mind than he, will soon follow. Cymbeline, freed from the influence of the Queen, will become the third. The Queen demonstrates aspects of the sinister Celtic Goddess, the Morrigan, Goddess of national sovereignty, battle, heroes and the dead. This deity is associated with ravens, crows, cows, wolves and eels, into which she can shape-change. She sometimes uses magical potions as a means to effect her actions. As in this story, in which she has married the warrior-King Cymbeline, she is a sexual figure who marries the heroes she promotes and encourages national sovereignty which will lead to war.[7] The Celtic Goddess at the heart of the Celtic mysteries is Ceridwen.[8] However, the evil, calculating nature of the Queen in *Cymbeline* corresponds more to that of the Morrigan.

The Queen makes it possible for Posthumus to begin his initiate journey by severing his attachments at court. Her son, Cloten, is the 'dark self' of Posthumus, his unregenerate 'double'.

Alchemy [9]
Shakespeare's changing the name of the character in what is probably the source of this plot, Boccaccio's *Frederyke of Jennen,* from Ambrosius of Jennen to Leonatus Posthumus creates an allegorical alchemic reading of the play.[10] Leonatus Posthumus becomes the lion (from the Latin 'leo')

or 'sophic sulphur', and Imogen 'air' or 'sophic mercury', the 'opposing halves', the main ingredients of the 'base matter', also termed a 'dragon', which will transform Britain (see fig. 30). Leonatus Posthumus is the 'body' of the 'base matter' and Imogen the 'spirit'. In their marriage, the first alchemical stage of **Calcination** takes place. They must be separated and 'broken down' for redemptive rebuilding of the 'base matter' to take place.

Base matter is also represented by Cymbeline, the alchemic 'king' (symbolising the self in psychic alchemy). He has lost his son (symbolising his soul in the allegory of alchemy). Thus there are two allegories of alchemic processes symbolised in the play, one for Cymbeline and one for Imogen and Posthumus.

Story Section 2 (I. ii., iii., iv.,)
Posthumus leaves Britain to take up exile in Rome. Imogen gives him her mother's diamond ring in exchange for his bracelet, which he places on her arm. The Queen's son, Cloten, has tried to attack Posthumus, but has been prevented from doing so by courtiers, who try to pacify him while privately mocking his stupidity.

The Celtic UnderWorld Initiation
Posthumus prepares for initiation. His alter ego, Cloten, is revealed to be a violent fool.
Alchemy
Seperation, the separating process, begins, but Imogen and Posthumus are still held together by the interchanged jewellery whose circular shape symbolises the completeness of their relationship.

Story Section 3 (I. v.)
In Rome, at the house of his host, Philario, Posthumus is challenged by a cunning Italian, Iachimo, who wages gold against Posthumus's diamond ring that he can assail and conquer Imogen's chastity. Against Philario's advice, Posthumus accepts the challenge, and Iachimo sails for Britain.

The Celtic UnderWorld Initiation
In a dishonourable wager on the chastity of his wife for gold, Posthumus

demonstrates his own weakness of character which must be purged. It thus becomes necessary for a stronger initiate to aid Britain. This will be Imogen.

Alchemy
The gold which Iachimo wagers is the ultimate goal of alchemy, but for Posthumus, it is an action which does him no credit. He aspires to attain it via a shortcut, without having worked for it or deserved it, and upon a crude wager which dishonours his wife, Imogen, his alchemical 'spirit'.

Story Section 4 (I. vi.)
The Queen is seen making medical potions. Cornelius, a doctor, intercepts her and tells the audience that he has substituted harmless sleep-inducing drugs for the poison she thinks she is using. Pisanio, servant to Posthumus and Imogen, is given a box of this medicine by the Queen as an attempted bribe for him to switch his loyalty from Posthumus and Imogen to herself.

The Celtic UnderWorld Initiation
By giving Pisanio a sleep-inducing drug which he will give to Imogen, the Queen prepares the ground for Imogen to become an initiate on behalf of Britain.

Alchemy
Cornelius is revealed as the real alchemist, the Queen operating under his supervision. Between them they concoct a potion which will transform Imogen and redeem Posthumus.

Story Section 5 (I. vii.)
Arriving in Britain, Iachimo tries to trick Imogen into having an affair with him, but she rebuffs him. In order to gain access to her bedroom, he plans to hide in a trunk of treasure which he has asked her to take into her room for safe-keeping.

The Celtic UnderWorld Initiation
Iachimo, whose nature suggests the trickster of mythology, begins to effect change for the good by ill means.[11] Shakespeare changes the name of John of Florence, the corresponding character in the supposed source

of this plot in Boccaccio's *Frederyke of Jennen,* to an Italianised form of 'Jack', the knave/trickster in a pack of cards.

Alchemy

When Iachimo sees Imogen, he recognises her worth and calls her 'the Arabian bird' (I. vii. 17), the phoenix, one of the terms for the goal of alchemy (as well as gold and the Philosophers' Stone). He finds that he cannot attain her through a short cut to the goal of alchemy without performing all the requisite processes of alchemy needed to achieve the Philosophers' Stone, but must instead deceive with a trick.

Story Section 6 (II. i.)

Cloten loses a wager for a hundred pounds at a game of bowls. Several courtiers report that when reproved by a spectator for swearing, Cloten has broken his skull and cut his ears off. One of the courtiers expresses the country's hope that the 'divine' Imogen (II. i. 56) will be able to withstand the ass Cloten and 'keep unshak'd| That temple, thy fair mind, that thou mayst stand | T'enjoy thy banish'd lord and this great land!' (II. i. 62-65).

At the beginning of this scene in rehearsal, Tony Portacio, who was playing both Posthumus and Cloten, sought to find a modern version of this character in terms recognisable to our audiences. We decided that Cloten's type would have been a violent 'lager lout' in today's society. Such was Tony's skill as an actor that he was able to effect the external change into Cloten from Posthumus with no more than the wearing of an unruly wig and a change of cloak. His internalised 'lager lout' transformed his face, voice, movement and posture to such an extent that it seemed to be another actor performing the part. The character also appeared to be as ridiculous as commented upon by the courtiers in the play.

The Celtic UnderWorld Initiation

Cloten, the 'dark self' of Posthumus, also makes and loses a wager. His dangerous, uncontrolled violence is demonstrated, making evident that he must be removed from society. The hope expressed by a representative of Britain's people on behalf of Imogen confirms the need for her to enter initiation on their behalf.

Alchemy
Imogen's value as the 'spirit' of the alchemical process is confirmed as 'divine'.

Story Section 7 (II. ii.)
That night while Imogen is sleeping, Iachimo emerges from the trunk she has allowed to be put into her bedroom, notes specific details of the room and a distinguishing mark on her body, 'On her left breast | A mole cinque-spotted: like the crimson drops | I' th' bottom of a cowslip' (II. ii. 38 -39). Taking the bracelet Posthumus had given her from her arm, he climbs back into the trunk.

The Celtic UnderWorld Initiation
Imogen's initiation is begun by Iachimo. He signals her entry into the Celtic UnderWorld: 'Hell is here. | One, two, three' (II. ii. 50 -51). Counting to three demonstrates the magical power of triplicity, as significant to the Celtic mysteries as to other spiritual cultures (see Merry p. 90). In Boccaccio's *Frederyke of Jennen*, the telling mark on Imogen's body that John of Florence (the character corresponding to Iachimo) notes is a black wart on her left arm. Shakespeare changes this to a mole on her left breast because this is more intimate, suggesting that Iachimo has enjoyed a physical relationship with Imogen. In the reference to the five spots on the mole, like those in the bottom of a cowslip, and in using the common name for the flower, he gives the mole Celtic significance. The cow is a symbol of the Celtic divinity, Bridget (sometimes called 'Bride').[12] This reinforces the courtier's opinion that Imogen is 'divine'. There is a double significance in this reference to the cow into which the Morrigan could shape-change as well as into the raven of 'the raven's eye' (II. ii. 49), hinting at Imogen's descent into the Hell of the Morrigan's domain. Contrary to my reading of the arcane significance of the 'cowslip', Nosworthy's footnote (p. 51) to this part of the text in the Arden edition of the play comments upon the wisdom of Shakespeare in his decision, following the Boccaccio version of the story, to use a mole on the left breast as in Boccaccio's character Zinevra rather than the black wart on her arm as in *Frederyke of Jennen*. However, he sees no significance in the identifying flower as a cowslip: 'In the French versions of the wager-

story the mole is likened to a rose and to a violet, but Shakespeare's flower analogy is almost certainly coincidental.'
Alchemy
Iachimo, in taking the 'binding' jewellery from the couple, separates them and begins the achievement of the breaking-down stage, **Putrefaction**, the symbol of which is the raven. He declares, 'Swift, swift, you dragons of the night, that dawning | may bare the raven's eye!'
(II. ii. 48-49). The 'dragons' refers to the 'base matter' which is being separated into the 'body' of the alchemical process (Posthumus) and 'spirit', (Imogen).

Story Section 8 (II. iii.)
The next morning Cloten, encouraged by the King and Queen, courts Imogen by serenading her. When she responds by claiming that Posthumus's clothes mean more to her than Cloten's person, he vows revenge for the insult.

The Celtic UnderWorld Initiation
Cloten is identified as the 'dark self' of Posthumus by Imogen associating him with the clothes of her husband.
Alchemy
This device of causing Cloten to wear Posthumus' stolen clothes is contrived in the stage action so that Imogen may later mistake Cloten for Posthumus in order that an unusual alchemic effect can be achieved.

Story Section 9 (II. iv.)
In Rome, Iachimo presents Posthumus with the seeming proofs of Imogen's infidelity – the bracelet taken from her arm and the observed detail of the mole on her left breast. Posthumus believes Iachimo, gives him the diamond ring, and vows vengeance on Imogen.

The Celtic UnderWorld Initiation
Posthumus is shown to be the victim of illusion, made possible by the lack of faith in his own wife, upon whom he has laid a dishonourable wager, and also a belief in the highly suspect Iachimo. He will be punished and purged of this folly.

CHAPTER SIX

Alchemy
Further **Putrefaction** takes place; the 'nigredo' (black) stage of alchemy begins to take effect.

Story Section 10 (III. i.)
An ambassador from the Roman Emperor, Augustus Caesar, demands from Cymbeline the tribute for Rome agreed by previous treaty but not sent. The Queen and Cloten defy Rome and encourage Cymbeline to arm against Rome and raise British national consciousness.

The Celtic UnderWorld Initiation
Cymbeline yields to persuasion to separate the national identities of Britain and Rome. The national pride which the Queen and Cloten advocate is in fact an illusion which will weaken Britain's position in the world and its spiritual identity.

Alchemy
The fire is ignited that must purge Posthumus.

Story Section 11 (III. ii.)
Pisanio receives letters from Posthumus; one letter instructs him to kill Imogen, who he believes has betrayed him, and the other he is to give to Imogen in order to deceive her into going to Milford Haven to meet Posthumus. Once in the woods near the harbour, Pisanio must obey his master and kill her, an action he is reluctant to perform. Imogen adopts a humble disguise in order to escape detection as the princess on her journey to Milford Haven, and leaves with Pisanio.

The Celtic UnderWorld Initiation
Imogen begins her journey of initiation.

Alchemy
Imogen as alchemic 'spirit' is led by Pisanio into the realm where she will be further 'purified'.

Story Section 12 (III. iii.)
In the woods near Milford Haven, Belarius (who has assumed the name 'Morgan'), a former courtier of Cymbeline, and the two young men

whom he has brought up from childhood in a cave there, join the story. Unbeknownst to them, the young men are the King's lost sons, Guiderius and Arviragus, whom Belarius and their nurse Euriphile (who he married and who has since died), abducted 20 years previously from Cymbeline in revenge for his tyrannous treatment of them. The boys have grown up thinking him to be their father and Euriphile their mother, but are now chafing at their rustic confinement, and they long to join society.

The Celtic UnderWorld Initiation
Belarius at the mouth of the cave represents the guardian at the entrance of the UnderWorld who admits those he considers capable of withstanding its trials. This function is also associated by Christians with Christ, who they believe stands at the door of Heaven. Bel was the Celtic God of Light, and the name Belarius suggests this association with Christ, the Son of Light, who was also the mediator at the heart of the initiate's journey.

Alchemy
The King Cymbeline's 'lost sons' are located in a cave, which was the alchemists' symbol of nature's womb, the alchemic alembic vessel, and regarded as an amphitheatre where the drama of alchemic transmutation took place (See fig. 31).[13]

Story Section 13 (III. iv.)
Pisanio cannot bring himself to kill Imogen, showing her his letter of instruction from Posthumus, and recommending that she adopt a boy's disguise and seek employment as a page with the Roman army, now at Milford Haven. He gives her the medicine he had from the Queen, believing it to be a beneficent potion, sends false proof of killing Imogen in the form of her scarf soaked in animal's blood to Posthumus, and returns to court.

The Celtic UnderWorld Initiation
With the showing of Posthumus' letter to Imogen and the suffering it brings, Pisanio as guide begins Imogen's trials on her journey of initiation. Seeing her read the letter from Posthumus which accuses her of infidelity, he comments, 'What shall I need to draw my sword? The paper | Hath cut her throat already' (III. iv. 33-34). Such is her misery that she asks Pisanio

to kill her, but he refuses, advising her that there must have been some treachery enacted against her and Posthumus in Rome.
Alchemy
Pisanio acts as a 'psychopomp', a spiritual guide, leading Imogen into the labyrinth of the alchemic journey. He gives her the potion from the Queen which will transform her, and the page's clothing, which will present her as a symbolic hermaphrodite.

Story Section 14 (III. v.)
War is declared between Rome and Britain. Imogen's absence is noted, and Cloten privately forces Pisanio to reveal her whereabouts to him and give him the clothes of Posthumus that she claimed to prefer to his own person. His aim in doing this is violent and perverted. He intends to dress in the clothes of Posthumus, find Imogen and Posthumus, rape her in his clothes and then kill Posthumus, all for revenge.

The Celtic UnderWorld Initiation
Pisanio guides Cloten, the 'dark self' of Posthumus, into the labyrinth of the UnderWorld.
Alchemy
Cloten, dressed as Posthumus, temporarily assumes his alchemic identity and becomes the 'body' of the process.

Story Section 15 (III. vi., vii.)
Imogen, dressed as a boy, is lost and hungry in the woods. She finds the cave of Belarius and enters to seek food. Belarius, Guiderius and Arviragus return from hunting, find her and offer her refuge. The boys wonder at the strange affinity they feel for this person whom they call their brother, but who is, in fact, their sister.

The Celtic UnderWorld Initiation
Imogen, lost in the labyrinth of the UnderWorld, is protected by its guardian and guides.
Alchemy
Imogen finds Cymbeline's lost son Guiderius, the king's symbolic

Philosophers' Stone and lost soul, in the heart of nature in this alchemic cave. Her eating of the food in the cave represents the feeding stage of **Cibation**.

(Theatre Set-Up omitted III. viii. in performance as we were unable to provide the costumes for it, used only in this scene. It concerns military arrangements in Rome concerning the war against Britain.)

Story Section 16 (IV. i., ii. 1-47)
Cloten arrives before the cave of Belarius. The day after Imogen's arrival in the cave sees her too unwell to join her new friends in their hunting. Left behind to rest in the cave, she decides to try the medicine Pisanio has given her.

The Celtic UnderWorld Initiation
Imogen takes the potion which will cast her into an 'initiatory sleep', from which she will wake to a transformation.
Alchemy
In taking the potion, Imogen assumes a death that represents the complete **Putrefaction** of the 'spirit'.

Story Section 17 (IV. ii. 47-183)
Seeking Posthumus and Imogen, Cloten encounters Belarius, Guiderius and Arviragus. He insults and threatens Guiderius, who fights him and cuts off his head which he throws into a stream, 'And let it to the sea, | And tell the fishes he's the Queen's son, Cloten' (IV. ii. 152-153).

The Celtic UnderWorld Initiation
The UnderWorld guide, Guiderius, rids Posthumus of his 'dark self' in cutting off Cloten's head. The severed head suggests the God-King, Bran, whose symbol, the raven, is shared by the Celtic Goddess, the Morrigan, in her form as the Hag (the symbol of death), who confronts victims in streams as the 'Washer at the Ford'. Thus, the son's head is sent by stream to his mother, the Queen, in her identity as the 'agent of death'.
Alchemy
As the 'dark self', the alter ego of Posthumus, Cloten dies, just as Imogen

seems to die, thus both 'body' and 'spirit' achieve total **Putrefaction**. 'For the matter of alchemy to become transformed, its opposing halves (sophic sulphur and sophic mercury, body and spirit, man and wife) must first be married, then killed, then buried together, and finally revived'.[14]

Story Section 18 (IV. ii. 183-290)
The medicine has cast Imogen into a deep sleep which Belarius, Guiderius and Arviragus believe to be death. They mourn her in song, and in deference to his status as the Queen's son, place Cloten's (now headless) body beside hers for burial.

The Celtic UnderWorld Initiation
Imogen enters the 'initiatory sleep'. This lasted for three days before Christ's resurrection. Theurgists believe that Christ's achievement in the conquering of death that the resurrection symbolises has made this period of time no longer necessary.[15]

Alchemy
The 'opposing halves' (sophic sulphur and sophic mercury, body and spirit, man and wife), are entombed together.

Story Section 19 (IV. ii. 290-332)
After Belarius, Guiderius and Arviragus leave, Imogen wakes and mistakes the headless body beside her for Posthumus, whose clothes he wears. She blames herself for mistrusting him, blames Pisanio for his death and mourns him over the headless body, steeping herself in the blood from his neck.

The Celtic UnderWorld Initiation
This scene presents a further trial for Imogen. She is faced with a grotesque image of death and the belief that it is her husband. This is the nadir of her initiation and the depths of her downward spiral.

Alchemy
Shakespeare dramatically represents the process **Coniunctio**, a 'chemical wedding', a gruesome death-embrace presented here between the two 'opposing halves'. This also imitates an alchemical metaphor cited by Nicholl, in which the process is described as the sister swallowing up

the brother (Cloten is Imogen's step-brother) in an embrace. This is part of the alchemical process which shall redeem Posthumus and Britain.[16]

Story Section 20 (IV. ii. 333-403)
A Roman soothsayer and Caius Lucius, the general of the Roman forces, marching to do battle with Cymbeline, discover Imogen mourning over the body which she says was that of her master. Caius Lucius takes her into his care as his boy-page and they bury Cloten's body.

The Celtic UnderWorld Initiation
Imogen is now led by Caius Lucius, who functions as a guide, leading her out of the labyrinth of the UnderWorld and into the upward spiral of her initiation.
Alchemy
Imogen in her metaphorical role as 'spirit' of the alchemy enters the calmer, 'white' stage of **Calcination** in which the 'flying spirits' are congealed while the 'body' (now only Posthumus), is 'purged'.

Story Section 21 (IV. iii.)
The Queen becomes ill and Cymbeline arms for battle.

The Celtic UnderWorld Initiation
The Queen's metaphorical task, in creating the situations which will send Posthumus and Imogen on their initiatory journeys, must now concentrate on Cymbeline. For this she must simply go away to release him from her influence and bondage. She becomes ill and ultimately dies.
Alchemy
Her contribution to the alchemy having succeeded, the Queen leaves the drama. Cymbeline takes action that will find Guiderius, his 'lost son', the alchemic symbol of his soul.

Story Section 22 (IV. iv.)
The battle sounds surround Guiderius and Arviragus, and Belarius can no longer restrain them from joining in the fray. They all go to defend Britain against the Romans.

CHAPTER SIX

The Celtic UnderWorld Initiation
The UnderWorld guardian and guides now directly assist Britain.
Alchemy
Cymbeline's 'lost son' defends his father's kingdom (also his own).

Story Section 23 (V. i. ii.)
Posthumus, now a member of the Roman army with his Italian friends, regrets Imogen's murder, which the bloodied scarf has led him to believe has been carried out on his instruction by Pisanio. In order to expiate his crimes against Britain by having killed Imogen, whom he believes to have been the heir to the British throne, he casts off Roman uniform and joins the British army, defeating Iachimo in battle. Posthumus hopes to die in the battle, but survives. Cymbeline is defeated, and the remains of the British army flee.

The Celtic UnderWorld Initiation
Posthumus takes positive action in his initiation. His repentance and declared love for Imogen and his willingness to sacrifice himself for her honour begin the change in his blood (represented by the bloodied scarf) necessary for redemption. He begins to make correct decisions and can thus defeat Iachimo, the trickster, and, unbeknownst to him, his enemy. The 'inner fire' of Posthumus is represented by the sword fighting.
Alchemy
Posthumus, the 'body' of the 'base matter', is purged by fire (symbolised by the sword). Cymbeline is defenceless without his 'lost son'.

Story Section 24 (V. iii.)
A British lord describes to Posthumus how Belarius, Guiderius and Arviragus have trapped the escaping British soldiers as they are running away from the battle along a narrow lane, forcing them back into battle with renewed courage as they join them in the defence of Britain.

The Celtic UnderWorld Initiation
The narrow lane represents the difficult, narrow path the initiate should choose rather than the 'primrose path to dalliance' (*Hamlet* I. iii. 50).

Alchemy
Guiderius, the 'lost son', symbol of Cymbeline's soul, begins the defence of his father.

Story Section 25 (V. iii. 1-63)
Belarius, Guiderius and Arviragus, joined by Posthumus, rescue Cymbeline from his capture by the Roman army.

The Celtic UnderWorld Initiation
Posthumus makes the right decision in choosing the narrow path the initiate should follow, seconding in battle the guardian, Belarius, and the guides, Guiderius and Arviragus.

Alchemy
Posthumus, as 'body' of the alchemic process, enters the further violent purging stage called **Sublimation**.

Story Section 26 (V. iii. 64-95, V. iv. 1-29)
The defeated Romans are taken captive, and Posthumus puts on Roman uniform again in the hope that he will be taken and killed. He is put in chains by the British and awaits death.

The Celtic UnderWorld Initiation
Posthumus enters the nadir of his initiation. Druids underwent this process, experiencing the 'shadow of death' in caves and labyrinths underground, or in stone cells which represented 'the prison of the body where the spirit lay captive'.[17] It was a paradigm of dying in the old life before being reborn to the new.

Alchemy
In prison, Posthumus experiences further **Sublimation** of his identity and body.

Story Section 27 (V. iv. 30-151)
While sleeping in prison, Posthumus experiences a dream in which his mother, father and his two brothers who died in battle visit him. They comfort him and accuse the Roman God Jupiter of unjust cruelty in the

fate laid upon him. Descending on an eagle, Jupiter, reassuring them that the trials of Posthumus are over and that he is to be specially blessed, declares, 'Whom best I love I cross; to make my gift,| The more delay'd, delighted' (V. iv. 101-102). Jupiter asserts that Posthumus will ultimately benefit from his trials, 'Happier much by his affliction made" (V. iv. 108). Jupiter then ascends to heaven, leaving for Posthumus a strange book containing an enigmatic prophecy which is later interpreted by a soothsayer. The gaoler of Posthumus is instructed to free him from his manacles and take him to the King.

The Celtic UnderWorld Initiation
Posthumus is rewarded for the endurance of his trials in his cave-like prison, and is blessed with a 'magic sleep' granted to those initiates who attain spiritual fulfilment. In his dream, the ancestors summoned by initiates come to him, and Jupiter blesses him. 'Whoever dares to work magic in the cave is supported and contacted by ancestors who have gone before; it is the cave of initiation, education and ancestral earth power'.[18]

Alchemy
The 'body' of the alchemic process enters the stage of **Firmentation** (Ripley's spelling). There are three 'ferments': 'Two be of bodies in nature cleer' (the mother and father of Posthumus) and the third is the lion itself (as in Leonatus Posthumus).[19]

Story Section 28 (V. v. 1-209)
In Cymbeline's tent, the death of the Queen is reported, along with her confession of all the wrongs she committed against Cymbeline and Imogen. Iachimo confesses his guilty action which gave Posthumus a false report of Imogen.

The Celtic UnderWorld Initiation
The initiates, Posthumus, Imogen and Cymbeline begin to emerge, successful.

Alchemy
Firmentation, which fixes and resolves the alchemic solution containing the 'body' of the 'base matter', continues.

CELTIC

Story Section 29 (V. v. 210-263)
Posthumus and Imogen are reunited. As he clasps her about his neck, he cries, 'Hang there like fruit, my soul, | Till the tree die' (V. v. 263).

The Celtic UnderWorld Initiation
In the reunion of Imogen with Posthumus, now made wiser by his experiences in the labyrinth, Jupiter's prophecy that he will be 'happier by his affliction made' (V. iv. 108) is fulfilled.

Alchemy
As Imogen and Posthumus are reunited, the alchemic stage of **Exaltation**, in which the 'spirit' descends into the 'body' of the 'base matter', takes place. Posthumus also finds his Philosophers' Stone, the 'gold' and goal of the alchemic transformation of his psyche, in his wife, Imogen, imaged by him as the 'fruit' of their alchemic labours.

Story Section 30 (V. v. 264-426)
Cymbeline is reunited with his three children as the true identities of Imogen, Belarius, Guiderius, Arviragus and Posthumus are revealed. Cymbeline pardons everyone, including his Roman prisoners, Caius Lucius and Iachimo.

The Celtic UnderWorld Initiation
Britain is made whole and its well-being assured.

Alchemy
The King Cymbeline finds his lost son (symbolising his immortal soul). As the representative of Britain he makes his country sound in its rulership.

Story Section 31 (V. v. 427-459)
The Roman soothsayer interprets Jupiter's prophetic message to Posthumus: 'When as a lion's whelp shall, to himself unknown, without seeking find, and be embrac'd by a piece of tender air: and when from a stately cedar shall be lopp'd branches, which, being dead many years, shall after revive, be jointed to the old stock, and freshly grown, then shall Posthumus end his miseries, Britain be fortunate, and flourish in peace and plenty' (V. v. 436-443). The soothsayer interprets the lion's whelp as Leonatus, the

air Imogen and the cedar Cymbeline, the branches his once-lost sons. Thus the events of this story are declared by the soothsayer to have been necessary for the well-being of Britain.

The Celtic UnderWorld Initiation
Jupiter's prophecy implies that the initiations of Posthumus, Imogen and Cymbeline were undertaken on behalf of Britain, and indicates the meshing of the Celtic initiation with the alchemic process. The tree imagery suggests the attainment of the Celtic initiation in the Universal Tree. This is usually an ash tree but is here named a cedar, in deference to the cult of the severed head, which was always embalmed in cedar oil.[20]

Alchemy
The prophetic book left by Jupiter for Posthumus suggests the 'Emerald Tablet' which in the alchemic tradition was bestowed upon Hermes Trismegithus by Jupiter and upon which were engraved the principles of alchemy (see above p. 31).[21] Jupiter's prophecy summarises the events experienced by Imogen and Posthumus in alchemical terms.

Story Section 32 (V. v. 459-477)
Cymbeline, aware of Jupiter's blessing upon Britain, pledges to pay the demanded tribute to Rome, even though his defeat of their army has made this redundant. Thus he creates peace and harmony between Britain and Rome.

The Celtic UnderWorld Initiation
Spiritual journeys must always be undertaken for the ultimate benefit of other people, otherwise the point of the initiation, which must not have selfish aims, is defeated. Cymbeline gives the benefit of the successful initiations (of Posthumus, Imogen and himself) to Britain and Rome, and in an ideal political resolution of the conflict between the two countries, creates a peaceful outcome. His act of 'turning the other cheek' to the Romans honours the preacher of that precept, Jesus Christ, the deity at the centre of the labyrinth and goal of all post-Christian initiation.

Alchemy
Cymbeline creates the stage of **Multiplication**, spreading the new-found harmony in his own life to all Britain and Rome.

Story Section 33 (V. v. 478-486)
Processions will take place in Lud's town (London) and the peace with Rome will be ratified in Jupiter's temple and sealed with feasts.

The Celtic UnderWorld Initiation
The British nation's new-found well-being must be celebrated in London to honour the heart of the nation's legendary founding; that is, the site where the head of the god Bran supposedly lies, buried beneath the hill on which the Tower of London now stands. The peace must be given holy sanction and celebrated with feasting, like the celestial banquet that souls were thought to be granted on entry to Heaven. Folk and classic traditions are thus fused together in this proposed celebration, just as Shakespeare fuses the Celtic and alchemic initiations.

Alchemy
In the alchemic stage of **Projection**, Cymbeline bestows upon his subjects the harmony he now enjoys in his family and as ruler of Britain.

The Cabala: Post Production
The Celtic UnderWorld Initiation, for which I find a metaphorical reading in *Cymbeline,* presents an obverse version (manifesting itself underground) to the Tree of Life of the Cabala, which rises from earth above ground towards Heaven. Therefore I do not consider its application appropriate to this particular play.[22]

CHAPTER SEVEN: *THE MERRY WIVES OF WINDSOR*

This is Shakespeare's domestic play. Our Theatre Set-Up actors enjoyed performing in this everyday world where a dinner for guests features hot venison pasty, pippins and cheese and where the host proposes disputes be resolved by drinking his wine. The conflicts are between members of families whose troubles ring true today, such as jealousy within marriage and differing hopes for the marriage of children, and they involve household events and objects such as hunting, greyhound racing, the washing, drying and bleaching of clothes and linen, and a laundry basket. Even an unpopular household aunt, 'the fat woman of Brainford' (IV. ii.70), links the Windsor families to those of today who dread the obligatory visits of certain relatives, while the core resentment of the ordinary citizens of Windsor to being patronised by nobility such as Sir John Falstaff typifies the British sense of democracy. Even some of the exclamations ring of domesticity: 'Good cabbage!' (Falstaff, I. i. 15), 'You Banbury cheese!' (Bardolph, I. i. 121), 'Ay, by these gloves, did he,' (Slender I. i. 142), 'Alas I had rather be set quick i'th'earth, | And bowled to death with turnips.' (Anne, III. iv. 84, 85). However, while relishing the homely context, prose language, fast amusing action and lively characters, it is easy to underestimate the deeper content of the play.

Theatre Set-Up performed the play twice; once in 1985, when my study of the secret meanings was in its infancy, and again in 2004, and the difference in our understanding of the play's depths in the latter production made a great contrast to the earlier production in our respect for the play and its characters, and gave the actors fuller characterisations of their parts.

Some core secret meanings within the play: **alchemy, shape-changing and the Celtic, the hunter becomes the hunted** (as happens to Falstaff), **the Devil and water, the humours, imagination and language**, and **parody** were identified in my research of 1985, but were insufficiently developed to gain respect from the cast, but an understanding of alchemy did assist in understanding the physical torments undergone by Falstaff. If examined closely, these correspond with the stages of alchemy of which he thus becomes the subject on behalf of Windsor, and mitigates the common accusation of Shakespeare's cruelty to what is, in effect, an old man. The actors also embraced the different humours applied to their characters and took that into their performances. We performed the play as a masque in the context of it being a celebration of the installation of George Carey (Lord Hunsdon and the patron of Shakespeare's company) as a Knight of the Garter on April 23rd 1597. Capes and insignia representing the heraldic costumes of the ceremony were worn at the procession beginning the play, but discarded once the play itself began. The ambivalence of the date of the play (with a historical character in Falstaff from the time of English monarchs, Henry IV and Henry V, appearing in a play remembering a ceremony of the time of Queen Elizabeth I) was resolved by a decision to costume the play in the Tudor period of the Knight of the Garter installation in 1597.

In order to avoid repetition, this costumed opening procession did not feature in the 2004 production when the play was staged in general Renaissance costumes, reflecting the ambivalence of the period in which the play is set and celebrating its tone of a festive holiday mood. In both productions, the incidents in IV. iii. and IV. v. concerning the revenge Evans and Caius take upon the Host and the interchange between Simple, Falstaff and the Host were omitted. Significant meanings within the play which guided my interpretation for the actors were summarised in the programme notes for the audience under four main categories with the following explanations of their content particular to this play:

History, Society and the Philosophy of Humours
This is known as Shakespeare's most 'English' comedy, set amongst the people of Windsor. The names and places he chooses are genuine, even now to be found in Windsor records and registers. The character of Falstaff had its origins in the real person of Sir John Oldcastle, a Lollard martyr, executed by Henry V but recorded to have been his boon companion in his youth.[1] This radically-Protestant Lollard background may be the inspiration of the surprising number of Biblical quotations made by Shakespeare's Falstaff, the name-change from Oldcastle needed out of deference to Oldcastle's descendent, Lord Cobham, still important at Elizabeth's court.

The occasion of the first performance of the play to possibly celebrate an Order of the Garter Ceremony has resonances in the play. It is also a 'humours' play. The humours were thought to be substances in the bloodstream which determined a person's prevalent mood and health. Four humours were considered to prevail: 'choleric' (angry), 'phlegmatic' (dull), 'melancholic' (depressed), and 'sanguine' (good tempered). Different characters in this play demonstrate the characteristics of these various humours.

Myths, Legends, Magic and Celtdom

That Falstaff has a mythic status in this and the Henry IV plays is probable. The character has an iconic reputation. He functions like a trickster found in most cultures (turned into Satan in the Hebrew and Christian traditions). In his relationship to Prince Hal of the Henry IV plays, his function may be similar to that of the centaur Chiron to Achilles and other heroes of Greek mythology when the animal roughness and proximity to nature of the half-man, half-horse Chiron acted as a corrective to their fathers and as an education to the real world outside the court. Falstaff functions like this is in some ways in this play, the distraction of his attempted wooing of the women exposing and correcting flaws in the Windsor society. He even appears as an animal in the final scene of the play. In relation to the societies he moves in he is like a Lord of Misrule who in old times in England, on only one day of the year, presided over an inverted social order when chaos was allowed to reign. In this play he is like a scapegoat for Windsor, drawing upon himself the punishment due to the townsfolk for any of their transgressions, such as Ford's jealousy and the Pages' unsuitable choice of husbands for their daughter Anne. In his self-indulgent excesses he is compared to the Roman god Bacchus. All of this is manifest in Windsor Forest where, in his stag's horns, he takes on the appearance of the Celtic God of Nature, Cernunnos.

Alchemy (showing the features of Shakespeare's varied application of the philosophy in this play)

It was believed that the psyche (or character) of a person or group of people, a town, a country, world order or the state of the cosmos could be transformed and improved by being subjected to the processes of alchemy. In a world which drew no distinction between science, art and religion, this could be practised chemically, improving the base metal, lead, into gold. The many stages of alchemy were often represented by the colours of the rainbow. The agent of alchemy was mercury or 'quicksilver'. The goal of alchemy was often called the 'Philosophers' Stone', and to Christians was synonymous with Christ. Those who misunderstood alchemy as not a psychic transformation (as practised by adepts) but as a method of getting rich quickly were known as 'puffers' (see above p. 34 and *Compound of Alchymie* by Sir George Ripley).

Renaissance Platonism (see above pp. 34-39)
Shakespeare's contemporaries thought there to be a 'chain of being', with God and Reason at the top, and animals and 'lunacy' at the bottom.

Story Section 1 (I. i., I. ii.)

Justice Shallow of Gloucestershire, who is visiting his Windsor deer park, complains to his nephew, Slender, and to the local parson-schoolteacher, Sir Hugh Evans, that the courtier, Sir John Falstaff and his retinue have killed deer, beaten his men and 'broke open' his lodge. Evans tries to divert him from his plan of suing Falstaff in court by suggesting that he should focus on making a match between Slender and Anne Page, daughter of wealthy citizens, George and Meg Page. This is proposed, to the satisfaction of Page, who is attracted by Slender's fortune. Falstaff, like Shallow and Slender, Page's dinner guest, is accused of his crimes, openly admits them and laughs at Shallow. Evans and Page make peace between Shallow and Falstaff, and all but Slender go in to dinner. He boasts about a contact with the famous bear, Sackerson. Anne Page, annoyed by the foolish Slender, is sent to fetch him in to join them. Evans sends to Mistress Quickly to solicit her help in Slender's suit of Anne.

History, Society and the Philosophy of Humours

Falstaff exploits his status as courtier in vandalising Shallow's deer park. Shakespeare subjects the Welsh accent of Evans to ridicule. Is this English chauvinism of the time, or just an opportunity to create comic characterisation? The custom of bear-baiting referred to by Slender was often alternated with plays in the theatres of the time but never in buildings used by Shakespeare's company, The Lord Chamberlain's Men (later The

King's Men). The role of the humours is made clear: Slender is of the phlegmatic humour (dull), Page and Falstaff sanguine (good-tempered).

Myths, Legends, Magic and Celtdom

Falstaff is in this section presented as the Lord of Misrule, confessing his riots and laughing at Justice Shallow's threats to sue him. The Celtic stag-headed God, Cernunnos, is already introduced in association with Falstaff in the deer he has killed which has become the 'venison pasty' that Page offers his guests. In his misdoings, Falstaff is being set up to represent another mythic figure, Acteon, of Ovid's classical myth. Acteon, out hunting with his dogs, was caught by the Goddess Diana as he watched her bathe in a river. For his presumption, she transformed him into a deer and he was pursued and killed by his own hounds. The hunter became the hunted. This will be Falstaff's fate.

Alchemy

Falstaff is making trouble in an already troubled Windsor. The local parson, Sir Hugh Evans, and Justice Shallow suggest to the local fool, Slender, that he should woo Anne Page for her money. Anne's father approves of this obviously unsuitable match as Slender also has money. This prospect of trading Anne as if she were property begins to mark out Windsor as needing to be changed and the possible subject of alchemic transformation. Evans, Shallow and Page are all 'puffers'.

Renaissance Platonism

A 'base love' match between Anne Page and Slender is proposed by the parson, Evans, who should know better. It is based on financial considerations, 'Seven hundred pounds, and possibilities, is good gifts' (I. i. 58). Anne's father is also guilty of wishing to force a 'base love' match on his daughter. She later complains of his preference for Slender:

> O what a world of vile ill-favoured faults
> Looks handsome in three hundred pounds a year! (III. iv. 32, 33)

Story Section 2. (I. iii., iv.)

Falstaff, staying at the garter inn with its jovial Host there, discusses with members of his retinue - Pistol, Nym, Bardolph and his page, Robin - his current solution to his eternal need for money. Firstly, he must discharge some of his followers. The Host offers to take on Bardolph as a tapster. Falstaff then proposes to court the wives of rich Page and Ford to access their husband's money, and gives Pistol and Nym the task of delivering love letters to the women. When they object to these demeaning jobs, Falstaff dismisses them and they plot revenge, planning to tell the husbands of Falstaff's ruse. Slender's servant, Simple, gives Evans' letter to Mistress Quickly, housekeeper to the court doctor, the Frenchman Doctor Caius, who himself is a suitor to Anne (favoured by her mother because of his wealth and court connections). Unexpectedly returning home, Caius catches Simple hiding in his closet, learns of Evans' suggestion that Slender should marry Anne and goes off with his servant Rugby to challenge Evans to a duel. The suitor whom Anne prefers, the courtier Fenton, enters, and is told by Mistress Quickly that Anne loves him.

History, Society and the Philosophy of Humours
The celebration of a Knights of the Garter ceremony is hinted at by Shakespeare's naming the inn the 'Garter'. Falstaff was stripped of his Garter knighthood by the crown because of his disreputable behaviour, so has no part in the celebrations. His followers have little respect for him in refusing his requests, and he has little respect for them in sacking them on so trivial an issue. The French doctor to the court is also ridiculed for his accent. He refers to his visit to court, 'la grande affaire', probably a Garter Investiture. The Host is sanguine, and the quick-tempered Caius choleric. Pistol and Mistress Quickly name humours incorrectly.

Myths, Legends, Magic and Celtdom
Falstaff, performing as a Vice figure, overestimates his powers in hoping to trick the wives. As Mistress Page later declares, 'Wives may be merry, and yet be honest too' (IV. ii. 99).

Alchemy
Falstaff now involves himself deeply with the households of Windsor, following their trend of associating love with money. He also becomes a 'puffer'. The local doctor, Doctor Caius, also unreasonably pursues Anne Page, and irrationally challenges the local parson to a duel, the swords to be involved in this representing the purging fire of alchemy. Mistress

Quickly, as her name suggests, represents quicksilver, the alchemical mercury, and, as go-between to all the parties, becomes the agent of the alchemy.

Renaissance Platonism

The ultimate 'base love' is revealed in Falstaff's plan to woo two married women to gain access to their husbands' wealth. The love of Doctor Caius for Anne is also base, as it is not only inappropriate but also unreturned. However, the love between Fenton and Anne is 'Divine Love', and will be tried through ordeals.

Story Section 3. (II. i.)

Mistress Meg Page, indignantly reading her 'love' letter from Falstaff, meets Mistress Alice Ford, who has received an identical letter. They plot to be revenged on the insolent knight by pretending to keep assignations with him, only to punish him. They appoint Mistress Quickly as their go-between to Falstaff. Pistol and Nym tell their husbands of Falstaff's plan. Page trusts his wife not to succumb to Falstaff's attempted seduction, but the irrationally jealous Ford does not and plots to disguise himself as Brooke, and bribes Falstaff to court his wife so that he might seduce her himself. The Host of the Garter Inn has planned to prevent the duel between Doctor Caius and Parson Evans by appointing them different places to meet.

History, Society and the Philosophy of Humours

The high esteem in which honour was regarded in marriage in Elizabethan society is reflected in the wives' indignation over Falstaff's proposals to them. Falstaff is patronising enough to consider that his status as a courtier (in spite of his repulsive physical appearance) will make him attractive to the women and override their marriage vows. However, Falstaff cuts no ice with the respectable wives of Windsor.

Myths, Legends, Magic and Celtdom

In the composition of the women in the play, the Celtic Triple Goddess, the Morrigan, is suggested. She took three alternative forms: of a matron or messenger-raven, hence Mistress Page and possibly Mistress Quickly; of an older potent woman confronting heroes in fords, hence Mistress Ford (who confronts Falstaff); and of a young maiden, hence Anne Page. The number three had spiritual significance in Shakespeare's day, as demonstrated by the Holy Trinity. This is a 'three play'; there are three couples, three punishments for Falstaff, and three suitors for Anne. Pistol refers to the Acteon myth when telling Ford of Falstaff's attempt to cuckold him.

Alchemy
Using Mistress Quickly as agent, the merry wives set up Falstaff to become a kind of scapegoat for the flawed society of Windsor. He will be subjected to processes of alchemy on Windsor's behalf, and through this wrong will be put right. Further flaws in Windsor are seen in the unjustified jealousy of Ford in his marriage. As part of the body of Windsor, Ford will also undergo alchemic transformation. The alchemic stage of **Calcination**, a sudden application of heat to the process, is begun in his jealous passion.

Renaissance Platonism
The baseness of Falstaff's courtship of both wives brings down their revenge on him. They are indignant that he should consider them also so base that they would even consider having an affair with him. The love between Page and his wife stands the test of Falstaff's plan, but Ford is not constant and his love for his wife not yet proved to be 'Divine'. In fact, his jealousy and his plot with Falstaff are very base.

Story Section 4 (II. ii., iii., III. i.)
Mistress Quickly gives Falstaff the letters from Mistress Ford and Page, making an assignation for him with Mistress Ford at her house when her husband is supposed to be absent. Ford enters disguised as Brooke, bribes Falstaff to seduce his wife on his behalf and learns to his horror of this assignation and the plan (as he thinks) to cuckold him. The duel between Caius and Evans is foiled, as planned by the Host, but they are angered at his intervention and plot to be revenged.

History, Society and the Philosophy of Humours
Ford's dread of being cuckolded also reflects the value given to honour in marriage in the Shakespearean period, and also the subject of many comedies and tragedies, for example, *The Winter's Tale* and *Othello*. Ford's humour is melancholic as he takes a negative attitude to his marriage in

his unfounded jealousy of his wife. It was considered to be a dangerous humour, so people who were melancholic could aim to take steps to change or have changed their humour to sanguine. This fortunately happens to Ford during the course of the play. An unhappy fate fell upon those who were by nature sanguine but events made them melancholic (like Hamlet). Worse (usually madness and suicide) befell those (like Ophelia) who suffered extremes of it.[2]

Myths, Legends, Magic and Celtdom
Elizabethans associated God with order and the Devil with chaos. As the book of Genesis in the Bible described God's creation of order on earth in terms of taking the water from the land, the Devil and chaos are associated with water. In taking the name 'Brooke', a different form of water to 'Ford', Ford lurches towards insanity and the Devil.

Alchemy
The heat of Ford's anger increases when he meets Falstaff. This represents the surging heat of the alchemic furnace. Further heat is generated in the process in the falling out between the Host, Caius and Evans. Falstaff identifies Mistress Quickly as a 'She-Mercury'.

Renaissance Platonism
Ford is made to suffer for the base nature of his attitude and actions concerning his wife. Punishments for Falstaff's baseness are prepared by the wives.

Story Section 5 (III. ii., iii.)

Mistresses Ford and Page set up a trick to be played on Falstaff. Mistress Ford arranges with her servants that they should have ready a laundry basket and on her signal should take it up and tip it into a muddy ditch by the Thames where linen-bleaching is taking place. The plan is to pretend that her husband has returned, announced by Mistress Page, and to persuade Falstaff to escape in the basket. However, Ford does really return (ironically forewarned by Falstaff himself), with Doctor Caius as his witness, to catch his wife 'in the act' with the courtier. The two women bundle Falstaff into the basket, which is taken out as instructed, while Ford fruitlessly storms through the house in search of him (see fig. 32). The wives plot another punishment for Falstaff.

History, Society and the Philosophy of Humours
Details of everyday life in Windsor emerge in the households of the Fords which are typical of the rise of middle classes in Elizabeth's reign, including the custom of communally bleaching clothes in the sun (by those called 'whitsters') in Datchet Mead, near Windsor. Falstaff patronises Mistress Ford for her social status, which is lower than his.

Myths, Legends, Magic and Celtdom
Falstaff as the Devil enters his watery domain.

Alchemy
Falstaff undergoes his first alchemic process, **Dissolution**, in which 'substance' is broken down with liquids. The stage of **Seperation** is also reflected here in the separation of Ford in his mind and actions from his wife. Falstaff later defines his experiences to Ford in alchemical terms when he declares the discomfort he suffered in being 'stopped in, like a strong distillation' (III. v. 103, see fig. 33).

Renaissance Platonism
The wives begin their purging of Falstaff's baseness. Mistress Ford also undertakes a testing of her husband.

<u>Story Section 6</u> (III. iv.)
The courtier Fenton and Anne lament that his penury due to the 'riots' (III. iv. 8) of his past behaviour have made her father suspicious that he only wants to marry her for her money. However, he declares that although that was his original motive, he now loves her for herself. Shallow and Mistress Quickly encourage the foolish Slender to court Anne. Mistress Page, when Anne begs her mother to prevent her marriage to Slender, tells her that she intends Anne to marry Doctor Caius. Fenton returns to plead his case with Anne's mother, and she agrees to consider his suit to her daughter. Mistress Quickly pledges to do what she can for all three suitors.

History, Society and the Philosophy of Humours
The vulnerable status of women is shown in Anne's proposed marriage to the fool, Slender, or the French doctor, Caius. There is no reference to Fenton as a fictional or historical companion to the riotous Prince Hal and

Poins in the Henry IV plays, but any association with them would have given a person a bad reputation and squandered their money. Shakespeare creates the story of Anne and Fenton in the form of the Commedia Dell' Arte tradition of lovers who play tricks to deceive their parents in order to marry each other instead of the suitors preferred by the parents.[3]

Myths, Legends, Magic and Celtdom

A threefold ritual of courtship is performed in the three men, Caius, Slender and Fenton, courting Anne.

Alchemy

The next stage, an alchemical 'marriage' of substances called **Coniunctio**, is mocked here in the attempts of three courtiers to marry Anne Page. The true marriage she desires, to Fenton, the one she loves, seems impossible. His confession that once he valued her for her money ranked him as a 'puffer', but now the status of his love has become elevated beyond that as he claims that he finds her of more value:

> Than stamps in gold or sums in sealed bags
> And 'tis the very riches of thyself
> That now I aim at. (III. iv. 15-18)

Renaissance Platonism

Fenton confesses that once his love was base but now it has become true and 'divine'. The trials which Fenton and Anne must overcome are presented in the opposition of her parents and their efforts to force on Anne potential husbands who she despises. Mistress Quickly exemplifies the components which contribute to 'base love' in accepting money as a go-between to all the suitors.

<u>Story Section 7</u> (III. v.)

Mistress Quickly makes the next assignation between Falstaff and Mistress Ford (during which the wives intend to further punish him). Ford, disguised as Brooke, talks with Falstaff and learns how he escaped detection in the laundry basket, and that another assignation is planned that very morning. The furious Ford plans to break in upon this tryst and expose his wife's and Falstaff's treachery to his companions in Windsor.

History, Society and the Philosophy of Humours
Mistress Quickly advises Falstaff to visit Mistress Ford between eight and nine that morning, as their day began at daybreak. She also tells Falstaff that Ford will go 'a-birding' (III. v. 42), a common Elizabethan pastime, wherein small birds were trapped and shot as game.

Myths, Legends, Magic and Celtdom
The cause of Ford's unreasonable jealousy may have its roots in his over-active imagination, which could have led him down the slippery path of associating women with magic and emasculation. Perhaps Falstaff touches a nerve when he calls him a 'jealous rotten bell-wether' (III. v. 100), ironically identifying him with characteristics of a bell-wether sheep, which was considered mad and was usually castrated, and had a bell tied around its neck as it led the flock, just as Ford led his neighbours into his house. The Fords have no children, and Ford seems obsessed with proving to Page the infidelity of their wives. Perhaps his problem may be impotence, which he could believe has been induced by female magic.

Alchemy
The violent alchemical process, **Putrefaction**, is planned as Falstaff exposes himself further to the heat of Ford's wrath.

Renaissance Platonism
Ford and Falstaff become further entangled in the punishment of their baseness.

Story Section 8 (IV. i.)
Mistress Page and Mistress Quickly, bringing the young William Page to school, meet Sir Hugh Evans, the boy's teacher, who tells them that there is a holiday that day. In response to the declaration of Mistress Page that her husband considers that his son is learning nothing at school, Evans promptly tests William on his knowledge of Latin. Mistress Quickly misinterprets the Latin in vulgar terms.

History, Society and the Philosophy of Humours
The holiday to which Evans refers might be that given to celebrate the Garter ceremonies. It has been speculated that Shakespeare, during

the years before 1592 when there is no account of his early life, was a teacher. This scene may indicate this possibility as features familiar to the experience of teachers of any period are shown; for example, parents' complaints about their children's progress, students' logical arguments and the often crude misinterpretation of learning. The Latin Grammar tests in the scene are from the contemporary text book, Lily's *Latin Grammar.*

Myths, Legends, Magic and Celtdom

Reference is made to the core of the current education of Shakespeare's day – a knowledge of classical languages and literature. It is known that Shakespeare would have studied Ovid's *Metamorphoses* in its original language, and this was the source of much of his mythology and is referred to twice in this play.

Alchemy

Reference is made in the Latin lesson to the goal of alchemy, the Philosophers' Stone, in the discussion of lapis, a stone.

Renaissance Platonism

Mistress Quickly's base nature is demonstrated in her vulgar interpretation of innocent Latin words and constructions.

Story Section 9 (IV. ii.)

Falstaff again protests his love for Mistress Ford in their second meeting, but is interrupted by Mistress Page telling them that Ford is on his way, railing against all womankind, marriage and Sir John Falstaff. When Falstaff tries to hide in any corner of the house, Mistress Ford tells him that Ford regularly searches every one of them. As planned, the wives disguise Falstaff in the clothes of a maidservant's aunt, the 'fat woman of Brainford' (IV. ii. 70), a person detested as a witch and forbidden from entering the house by Ford. In order to punish her husband for his jealousy, Mistress Ford teases her husband by having the laundry basket brought out again. Rising to the bait, Ford pulls all the soiled washing from the basket in front of his neighbour while searching for Falstaff. The latter, however, tries to make good his escape, disguised as the fat woman, but Ford beats the 'witch' before casting 'her' out. When it is pointed out that the woman must be a witch as he has a beard, Ford realises the deception and gives chase. The wives now resolve to tell their husbands of their plots against Falstaff and to plan with them a further punishment for him.

History, Society and the Philosophy of Humours
More details are given of life in the Windsor households, such as the custom of firing a gun up a chimney to clear it. Ford exerts a licence to beat the fat woman of Brainford, perhaps a common treatment of suspected witches and an indication of intolerant times in the persecution of elderly women.

Myths, Legends, Magic and Celtdom
Ford's overreaction to the fat woman of Brainford might indicate his fear of her potential witchcraft and the effect it might have had on his married life and sexual potency. The name 'Brainford' suggests that her status as a witch exists only in his brain, as well as referring to modern Brentford, twelve miles from Windsor.

Alchemy
The violent stage of **Putrefaction** is achieved, as Falstaff is beaten by Ford. The servants John and Robert, carriers of the laundry basket, identify Falstaff as a subject of an alchemical process in characterising him as one of its metaphorical names, 'lead':

> Robert: Pray heaven it be not full of knight again.
> John: I hope not. I had as lief bear so much lead. (IV. ii. 6, 7)

Renaissance Platonism
Falstaff is made even baser in women's garments and is further punished. Ford descends down the 'chain of being' away from God and towards apparent lunacy.

Story Section 10 (IV. iv., v. 85-118)
Learning of his wife's true faithfulness and skill in punishing Falstaff, Ford asks her forgiveness and promises never to be jealous again. Evans, Ford, Page and the wives conceive another plot to punish Falstaff. They will invite him to another tryst, this time at midnight at Herne's Oak in Windsor Forest. Mistress Quickly is to persuade him to dress as Herne the Hunter with a stag's horn on his head. The citizens of Windsor plan

to disguise themselves as fairies, which will torment him and then shame him by revealing themselves and all their successful plots against him. Both Page and his wife plan to use this masquerade to dupe each other by arranging elopements for Anne with their respectively preferred husbands for her, Slender and Caius.

History, Society and the Philosophy of Humours
A descendent of the Oak tree still survives in Windsor Great Park, probably because of Shakespeare's preserving the tradition in this play.

Myths, Legends, Magic and Celtdom
Ford seems magically transformed when he learns the truth of his escapades with Falstaff. It is as if his potency is restored when his imagined demons regarding women and Falstaff have been exorcised from his brain. The legend of Herne the Hunter (a forester who, guilty of wrong-doing, was said to have hanged himself from an oak and subsequently haunted it) follows the universal myth of 'The Wild Hunt' wherein a devil-like creature followed by savage hounds mysteriously appears in a terrifying hunt.[4] In this mythic context, the fairies into which the Windsor citizens will costume themselves represent the 'Souls of the Dead'. The Herne the Hunter myth is still associated with Windsor Great Park.

Alchemy
The process is congealed in the stage of **Congelation** as Ford is reconciled with his wife. **Cibation**, wherein the process is 'fed', is also suggested as they feed more ideas into Falstaff's punishment.

Falstaff, complaining to Mistress Quickly of his beating says, 'I was beaten myself into all the colours of the rainbow' (IV. v. 106), naming in the rainbow the symbol of the alchemic processes he has undergone.

Renaissance Platonism
Ford in his return to sanity ascends the 'chain of being' again, but a further descent is planned for Falstaff in his disguise as an animal.

Story Section 11 (IV. vi., V. i., ii., iii., iv., v. 1-206)
Fenton and Anne plan to foil her parents' plans, and arrange to elope together and, with the help of the Host, to marry. They will arrange for two boys to be disguised as Anne, one in green (as Mistress Page instructs) and one

in white (as Master Page orders), and for each to be given the appropriate passwords, and thus 'elope' with Slender and Caius. Falstaff agrees to the forest assignation with Mistress Ford and to the costume he must wear.

All takes place as planned, both Mistresses Ford and Page meeting Falstaff (who declares his ability to make love to both of them), and the Windsor citizens, dressed as fairies, torment him. His reaction when confronted with their tricks upon him is good-humoured as he admits defeat. However, Page and his wife are appalled to find out that their plots to match Anne in marriage to the husbands of their choice have failed, and that both Slender and Caius have mistakenly been 'married' to boys disguised as Anne.

History, Society and the Philosophy of Humours
The masquerade that the Windsor citizens present might have formed part of a masque previously performed by Shakespeare's company for the court. Certainly the speech spoken by Mistress Quickly (V. v. 55-76) seems inappropriate for her, as the figurative style of the language is unlike any of her previous dialogue in the play.

Myths, Legends, Magic and Celtdom
In this play Falstaff takes on, with his antlered head, a mythic form, as the hunter-of-women becomes the hunted (see fig. 34). His forced shape-changing throughout the play (squashed into a basket, dressed as a woman, dressed as a stag) mirrors a Celtic mythic tradition such as that of the Morrigan shape-changing in order to confuse and deceive her victims. It could be considered that Falstaff is gullible in believing the Windsor masqueraders to be haunting fairies. However, given the continuing belief in the Wild Hunt and hauntings in many parts of the world, the superstitious nature of Elizabethans in particular, and the midnight Windsor Forest location, it seems reasonable that his usual scepticism was suspended. As Lord of Misrule, his reign is destined to end when normal social order is restored.

Alchemy
Falstaff undergoes a further violent stage of **Sublimation**. Page, his wife, Caius and Slender are also punished for their puffer-like attitudes to Anne. Falstaff's good humour begins the harmony that will generate the 'Philosophers' Stone', as relationships are corrected, stabilised and 'fixed' in the stage of **Firmentation**.

Renaissance Platonism
Fenton and Anne take the initiative to surmount their trials in constancy to their 'Divine Love'. Falstaff at the nadir of his descent down the 'chain of being' proves worthy in his humility and, corrected, ascends to an acceptable level of humanity.

Story Section 12 (V. v. 207-241)
Fenton and Anne, now married, enter and ask their parents for forgiveness. In their defence, Fenton protests that the unloving alliances that Anne's parents would have forced upon her would have been shameful, dishonest and unholy. Ford reinforces this, claiming that money buys land, not wives. Falstaff rejoices that he is not the only one to have been tricked. Page and his wife accept the marriage of Anne to Fenton in good humour and invite everyone, including Falstaff, to 'laugh this sport o'er by a country fire' (V. v. 234).

Ford comments to Falstaff that his promise to Brooke will be ironically realised, as 'he tonight shall lie with Mistress Ford' (V. v. 241).

History, Society and the Philosophy of Humours
Windsor society, healed, is inclusive and embraces the courtier Falstaff in its rejoicing.

Myths, Legends, Magic and Celtdom
As scapegoat, Falstaff has performed his function in being sacrificed in order to restore the harmony and social health of the Windsor community. As this is a comedy, he does not have to die to achieve this. As Cernunnos he will preside over the festivities, like the figure on the Gundestrop Cauldron.[5] It is possible that relief at not being pursued by supernatural beings tempers Falstaff's reaction to his disgrace.

He is not however the only one present to experience feelings of relief. Ford has been the only person in Windsor to believe it possible that his wife could be seduced by the despicable Falstaff. Now that this demon is totally exorcised and disgraced, it seems that Ford's potency is completely restored, as he ends the play declaring that he 'tonight shall lie with Mistress Ford' (V. v. 241).

Alchemy
In the stage of **Exaltation**, forgiveness, acceptance and good humour

prevail, and, in the laughter and reconciliation around the country fire, the new-minted gold of improved and transformed Windsor will be disseminated to others in **Multiplication** and **Projection**.

Renaissance Platonism

Fenton and Anne affirm the divinity of their love. As Fenton claims, 'The offence is holy that she hath committed' (V. v. 217), and even Ford confirms this, declaring 'In love the heavens themselves do guide the state' (V. v. 224). Page accepts this, saying 'Fenton, heaven give thee joy' (V. v. 228), as does his wife, adding 'Heaven give you many, many merry days' (V. v. 232).

Cabala: Post Production (see fig. 3)

It is Ford whose progress through the play can be detected on the Tree of Life. As a prosperous citizen of Windsor he is grounded in **Malkuth (the material world perceived through the senses)**, but needs to be cleared of his unreasonable jealousy in **Yesod (in which the subconscious is cleared of trauma and guilt)** before he can become a balanced personality. He is all feelings (albeit negative ones) on **Netzach (feelings)**.

His scheming to test his wife can be said to give him placement on **Hod (thoughts)**, which ultimately will direct events so that when his wife tells him of the plotting that she and Mistress Page have carried out to punish the insolence of Falstaff, he at last attains the riddance of his traumatic jealousy in **Yesod** and he can move to **Tiphareth (the centred self, beauty)**, the loving heart of his home and his wife.

Now centred, he moves up the Tree: in his participation in the Windsor Forest plot against Falstaff he attains the strength of **Geburah (strength and severity)**; in the general atmosphere of convivial reconciliation at the end of the play he practises the mercy of **Chesed (mercy, love and awareness)**; in his advice to Page and his wife about the rightful nature of love he demonstrates the wisdom of **Chockmah (wisdom, spiritual purpose)** and the understanding of **Binah (understanding, spiritual love)**, until he ascends to the spiritual sexual ecstasy with his wife, the promise of which crowns the play in **Kether (the Divine self)**.

CHAPTER EIGHT: *ALL'S WELL THAT ENDS WELL*

The 'Problem' Plays

As *All's Well that Ends Well* poses some implausible events and characterisation and, partly, because it contains a social problem, that of social class inequality, it has become known as a 'problem play'. Shakespeare examines issues concerning justice, crime and punishment in *Measure for Measure* (see Chapter Twenty), also considered to be a problem play, and in *All's Well that Ends Well* he considers the issues of social equality, snobbery and respect for nature. It is heavily influenced by Boccaccio's *Giletta of Narbona*, readily available to Shakespeare in William Painter's *The Palace of Pleasure*, vol. I (1566 and 1575) (if not in the original).[1] In turn, the source reflects a traditional folk-story of the girl who wins a noble husband by magic, wit or virtue.

The 'bed-trick'

Both problem plays are linked by the action turning on the results of a 'bed–trick.' In *Measure for Measure* this device is suggested by Duke Vincentio as a means to resolve Isabella's quandary regarding Angelo, who demands that she go to bed with him as a condition for the stay of execution of her brother, Claudio. Mariana, previously engaged to be married to Angelo but currently not married to him, is the one who performs the morally questionable 'bed-trick'. However, in *All's Well that Ends Well* Helena, who devises and performs the trick, does so upon her own husband. The audiences of both plays must question the plausibility of successful and happy marriages resulting from a bed-trick which forces Angelo and Bertram to accept wives whom they have previously rejected. This is mitigated slightly in *All's Well that Ends Well*, as Bertram has begun to feel love for Helena when he hears the rumour that she has died. Also, Helena has only played a trick upon Bertram in response to trick conditions which he has imposed upon her. I think that Shakespeare makes the point that the reasons the men have rejected the women are unethical (Angelo due to Mariana's loss of her dowry and Bertram due to Helena's low social status) but are certainly plausible, in terms of the philosophy of Divine Love in Renaissance Platonism. According to this philosophy, true lovers are 'companion souls'. Sometimes one or even both of the lovers do not recognise their companion soul. In the case of these problem plays, the women recognise the men as their corresponding spiritual partners but the men do not. It takes the bed-trick and consequent action to bring the men to their senses. The stage action involving the two couples, Mariana and Angelo and Helena and Bertram, could be said to demonstrate the problems that can occur when not recognising one's companion soul.

The Legend of the 'Seed of Christ' and its significance to the play

Theatre Set-Up set the 2008 production of *All's Well that Ends Well* in costumes of the period 1603-1604 after the accession of James VI of Scotland to the throne as James I, known through his maternal grandmother to be a descendent of the French Merovingian dynasty, thought to be descended from Mary Magdalene and Christ. This belief was known as the heresy of the 'Seed of Christ'. James I adopted the Burbage-Shakespeare company of players as his own (changing their name to 'The King's Men') and I believe that Shakespeare returned the compliment by references to Celtic themes from Scotland and France (always Scotland's close friend) in this play, which features French locations associated with the legend of the Seed of Christ.

This legend is discussed at length in *Holy Blood and the Holy Grail* by Michael Baigent, Richard Leigh and Henry Lincoln.[2] Although this book is controversial, it supplies several factual links for the belief in Shakespeare's time in the supposed lineal descent from Jesus through the Merovingian dynasty to the Stuarts, including James I of England. It includes a copy of a painting c. 1623, featuring the Crusading hero of the Merovingians, Godfroi de Bouillon (1061-1100) wearing a crown of thorns, thus identifying him with Jesus Christ.[3] This painting was made by Claude Vignon for Claude de Lorraine, presumably at his request, to reinforce and possibly disseminate the belief that Claude de Lorraine had inherited the bloodline of Jesus through a scion of Godfroi de Bouillon. This book also includes a modern chart of genealogies which shows the descent of James I's mother, Mary, Queen of Scots, through her mother, Marie de Guise, from the Dukes of Guise and Lorraine, whose descendent, Claude de Lorraine, had hoped in the painting of 1623 to establish the family's connection to the bloodline of Jesus Christ.[4] Charles de Guise, the brother of Claude de Lorraine, is shown as a cousin of Mary and a contemporary of James I. I suggest that these facts provide evidence that James I must have known of the legend and even have subscribed to it, as did his subjects, such as Shakespeare. In *The Wife of Jesus*, Anthony Le Donne, researching the social customs of the society into which Jesus Christ was born and considering the facts of his ministry as reflected in the accounts given of it in the New Testament and other documents of that time, concludes:

> I think that it is highly unlikely that Jesus was married to Mary Magdalene or to any of his followers during his preaching career. We cannot rule out the possibility that Jesus was previously married (perhaps in his early twenties), but he seems almost 'anti-family' during his teaching and preaching career.[5]

This recent contradiction of the facts behind the legend of the Seed of Christ may echo similar cynicism in Shakespeare's time, but I consider that to be irrelevant as its significance in *All's Well that Ends Well* would have been political, designed to flatter the patron of Shakespeare's company.[6]

One of the locations featured in both the legend and the play is Narbonne, birthplace of Helena and the central location of the 'heresy'. This is Shakespeare's adaptation of the name of the heroine's father, Narbona, as used in Painter's source of the play. The home of the Countess, Bertram and Helena is Roussillon, a core place in the legend's story and an adaptation of Painter's location of Rossiglone. It is significant that Shakespeare changes Helena's sojourn during her journey from Florence to Roussillon from Painter's Montpelier to Marseille, thus further aligning it with the legend which claimed that Mary Magdalene, pregnant with Christ's child, landed in Europe at Marseille.

A further change from the source, which makes a reference to the Magdalene pregnancy in the story of the heresy, is in the condition of Helena, who is pregnant when she confronts Bertram in Roussillon, whereas in the Painter original the heroine is carrying her already-born twin sons. There is a Celtic oral tradition that the legendary 'grail' was in fact twins, a boy and a girl, born to Magdalene and Christ, and these twins had the power to disappear to be reincarnated into Britain at a time when the conditions were appropriate. It is not made clear whether Helena is pregnant with a single child or with twins, although Diana claims, 'She feels her young *one* kick' (V. iii. 294), or if Shakespeare, in choosing to make her pregnant rather than already the mother of twin boys, is referencing this Celtic extension of the Seed of Christ 'heresy'. Had Shakespeare known of this Celtic tradition it is unlikely that he would have clearly acknowledged it, as it would have been considered blasphemous in the context of contemporary Christianity. It can be left for us to speculate upon this possibility.

Another possible interpretation of Shakespeare's reference to Mary Magdalene in the portrayal of Helena is the support that would give to the association of Mary Magdalene with the feminine principle in Christianity. This association, believed by devotees who honoured, even revered, Mary Magdalene, opposed the patristic view of Christianity of the New Testament accounts of the life of Jesus and his disciples.

Shakespeare has shown respect for women in the strength of his female characters

The above indications of the encoding of the Seed of Christ legend in *All's Well* are repeated in the sections of the story in which they occur.

Themes in the play

All's Well that Ends Well also demonstrates a concern that mankind should not lose touch with nature, and it is this issue which makes it so relevant to the present time. Other themes in the play which the production examined and the programme notes declared to be relevant to our own times were:

- The inhumanity of overzealous punishment of wrongdoers. They should be corrected, then cared for (a principle demonstrated by LaFeu's generous treatment of Parolles).
- Loss of contact with and the benefit of natural forces (as demonstrated by Helena's mastery of the 'natural' remedies of her father).
- Over-valuation of man-made hierarchies and institutions rather

than the natural order of things, as Helena is able to cure the King with natural remedies when his official doctors could not.

The different levels of meaning of the story proposed to the actors and to the audiences in the programme notes were **God through Nature versus Man and his Institutions**, **Alchemy** (in the analysis of the play below I followed the four grouped-together stages, coded as 'black', 'white', 'red' and 'gold', with reference to specific stages within them), **Renaissance Platonism**, and **Celtdom and the heresy of the 'Seed of Christ'**.

These legends and traditions are fused in a mythical strain. The influence of the thinking of the ancient philosophers, especially Plato, was transformed by the Renaissance interpreters of their work, such as Marsilio Ficino, and fused with Christianity. This interpretation of the play is explored by John Vyvyan in his *Shakespeare and Platonic Beauty* and I have quoted him freely in the story sections below.[7]

Story Section 1 (I. i.)
Upon his father's death, Bertram has inherited the title of Count Roussillon and is taken by Lord LaFeu from his home to the court of the King of France, who is ill with an incurable ulcer (a fistula). Bertram is accompanied by Parolles, a military captain, and he leaves behind his grieving mother, the dowager countess, and Helena, daughter to a brilliant but poor physician, Gerard du Narbon. Since her father's death, Helena has lived under the protection of the Countess, and, unbeknownst to Bertram, loves him. She resolves to follow Bertram to Paris and to attempt to cure the King's illness by using her father's remedies.

God through Nature versus Man and his Institutions
Helena stands for the spirit of God's natural world. She has inherited medical and magical powers from her father which are enhanced by her own goodness. Her lowly status gives her the common touch, just like that of Christ, born in a stable. She acknowledges that her love for Bertram, like that of a deer for a lion, upsets the social hierarchy, but maintains that although Bertram is like a star out of her sphere, nature intends for people to be matched outside of man-made social hierarchies. She also claims

that God gives people free will to follow their own course in life and that their fate is not laid down by the stars. Those who blame misfortune on their fate lack will and initiative.

Renaissance Platonism

The Platonic idea of love was that it illuminated the mind with an understanding of God's love for mankind and raised the soul to a level from which it could reach God. Material beauty, inspiring love, must lead to contemplation of God. Here, Helena describes that spiritual ascent as she contemplates her love for Bertram and maintains that love and the will of God have freed her from fear of equating her inferior social rank to his noble one in order to pursue the one whom she perceives to be her soul mate. Love for her, besides being physically consummated, is also to be raised to the sphere of the spirit, according to the doctrine of ascent.

Alchemy

In the first stages of the alchemic process, 'nigredo', the 'black' stage (so-called because of the colour of the chemical substances at that point) is effected here upon Bertram who becomes the 'body' of the process of the operation in his separation from his mother, the alchemical 'spirit', and Helena, its 'soul'. Here he is parted from them by Lafeu, whose French name implies the fire of the process in a sombre scene.

Celtdom and the heresy of the 'Seed of Christ'

Helena's circumstances associate her with this 'heresy', wherein it was believed that Christ was married to Mary Magdalene, and their descendants were the members of the French Merovingian dynasty. The location of the opening of the play is Roussillon, where the legend of the Merovingian heresy took root. Its centre was Narbonne, Helena's birthplace.

Central to Celtic mythology was the Triple Goddess as woman, old woman and girl, corresponding to the Widow (who appears later in the play), the Countess and Helena, who govern the play.

Story Section 2 (I. ii.)

In Paris, the King notes a feud in Italy between the Florentines and Senoys. He does not support the case of either side, but gives permission for any young Frenchman eager to see military action to serve in Italy. He welcomes Bertram to the court, remembering in him his honoured father, and he laments his own unfitness to serve his country because of his incurable illness.

God through Nature versus Man and his Institutions
Man's science and medical arts are seen to have failed the King, as the sore which originally troubled him has become ulcerated through medical maltreatment. All attempts to cure him have been abandoned. The King observes that Bertram has inherited the natural form of his noble father.

Renaissance Platonism
'The King of France permits his young nobles if they wish to "stand on either part" – an impartiality which makes it plain that there is no question of a "fearful" Sienna against a "holy" Florence. It is a quarrel in straws!' (Vyvyan, p. 47)

Thus participation in the war is not necessarily in support of some ethical stance and does not merit honour.

Alchemy
The 'body' of the process separated from the 'soul' and 'spirit' must be tried by fire and water, subjected to refinement and purging. A symbol of this kind of fire was a sword. The war is introduced as the arena within which Bertram will be tried by the sword. The 'base matter' of alchemy was also termed the 'king'. The French King and his country are drawn into the alchemic process whose outcome will affect them.

Celtdom and the heresy of the 'Seed of Christ'
It was a Celtic tradition that the king must be a man without physical blemish. A blemished king must be replaced, as his 'scar' would affect his country. This King of France infers this and also uses the bee imagery, symbolising the Christian aspects of the 'heresy'.[8]

Story Section 3 (I. iii.)
A household servant, the clown Lavatch, enters the Countess's room. The Countess is told by a servant that she has overheard Helena tell of her love for Bertram. The Countess forces a confession from Helena and pledges support for Helena's projected curing of the King and pursuit of Bertram, especially when she is made aware of the propitious stars guiding the event.

God through Nature versus Man and his Institutions
The Countess recognises the natural virtue of Helena, thinks it right for her to love Bertram, and gives support to her plan to win the hand of Bertram by curing the King's disease. Helena realises that God through nature intends the project, as the stars are propitious.

Renaissance Platonism
Helena in going to Paris to cure the King does so for love of Bertram:

> 'It was Shakespeare's life-long asseveration that if our values do not "go forth of us" and in effect work miracles, we might as well not have them. The power that makes them go forth is love!' (Vyvyan p.137)

Alchemy
The 'soul' and 'spirit' gather strength for the 'soul' to be joined to the body in an 'alchemical marriage'.

Celtdom and the heresy of the 'Seed of Christ'
The Celtic mother-goddess, represented in a Celtic reading of this play by the Countess, could be manifest as the Christian Saint Bridget, whose symbol was a cow. This is referred to in the French word for a cow, 'la vache', implied in the name Lavatch, given to the clown-servant of the Countess.

Story Section 4 (II. i.)
Bertram is galled by the fact that he is not given permission to join in the military action in Florence. Helena is received by the King, who doubts her ability to cure him when science and conventional medicine have failed. She offers to surrender her life under torture if she fails, and he accepts her pledge with the promise that if she succeeds he will grant her the husband of her choice from among his eligible subjects.

God through Nature versus Man and his Institutions
Helena brings the healing power of God-in-nature to the King and thus through him to all France. In order to achieve this she offers herself as sacrifice, reflecting the Christian view of Christ's salvation of the world through his voluntary sacrifice.

CHAPTER EIGHT

Renaissance Platonism
Helena functions here as a divine agent of God.
Alchemy
Bertram, the 'body' of the alchemic process, longs for trial by fire represented in alchemic iconography by the sword he will use in the war. Helena as the 'soul' is enabled to be 'married' to the 'body', and becomes incorporated in another body, the Kingdom of France.
Celtdom and the heresy of the 'Seed of Christ'
The legends of the Seed of Christ and the flawed king are fused. Helena (the implied Magdalene) cures the King. She does so by the use of the 'triple eye' (as she says herself), the third eye of magical insight (located mid-forehead).

Story Section 5 (II. iii. 1-183)

Helena succeeds in her cure of the King, Lafeu commenting that it was magical and that Helena was in this the agent of Heaven.

The King keeps his promise to her, offering her the husband of her choice. She selects Bertram, but he rejects her as beneath him in social status. He persists in his objection even when the King promises to raise Helena socially. Finally, in response to threats from the King, Bertram agrees to marry Helena, and the wedding takes place immediately.

God through Nature versus Man and his Institutions
Alternative medicine and natural magic succeed where conventional methods have failed. Helena, the agent for God's use of natural medicines and spiritual magic to cure the King, and through him France, is rejected by Bertram, who only recognises man-made hierarchies in which a match between a member of the aristocracy such as himself and a poor physician's daughter such as Helena would be incongruous. He submits to that hierarchy by accepting the King's command to marry Helena in what becomes an unnatural union.
Renaissance Platonism
Helena's curing the King is miraculous, implying Divine intervention. However, Bertram rejects Helena as his companion soul, ignoring the apparent intervention of Heaven in the King's cure and the subsequent matching of Helena to himself in marriage.

Alchemy
The first part of the alchemical marriage takes place.
Celtdom and the heresy of the 'Seed of Christ'
In traditional Celtic society, social rank never presented barriers; King's sons were fostered by lowly families and vice versa. This lack of social discrimination is reflected in the King's honouring of Helena.

Story Section 6 (II. iii. 184-296, II. iv, II. v.)
Lafeu challenges the improper attitude of Parolles towards Bertram and reprimands his general pretentiousness. This is further manifest when Parolles suggests that Bertram escape his unwanted forced marriage by joining the fighting in Florence. Bertram agrees to this and instructs Helena to return home immediately as he must go away on urgent business.

God through Nature versus Man and his Institutions
Lafeu identifies the vainglorious Parolles as the influence which is corrupting the inherited natural nobility of Bertram so that he values only man-made forms such as social hierarchy and military accomplishment.
Renaissance Platonism
In rejecting his soul companion and choosing instead the false military values of Parolles, Bertram moves away from God.
Alchemy
Parolles in this instance is an element of the 'body' that must be purged and worked on by the 'fire', Lord LaFeu. **Putrefaction**, the main separating stage of the 'body' from the 'soul-spirit', is begun when Bertram leaves his wife and his mother.
Celtdom and the heresy of the 'Seed of Christ'
The Celts valued the feminine principle which Helena represents and Bertram rejects.

Story Section 7 (III. ii., III. iii., III. iv.)
Bertram leaves secretly for Florence, sending a letter to his mother informing her of his rejection of Helena as a wife and of his escape from France. He sends another letter to Helena, imposing seemingly impossible conditions upon her:

CHAPTER EIGHT

> When thou can'st get the ring upon my finger, which never shall come off, and show me a child begotten of thy body that I am father to, then call me husband; but in such a 'then' I write a 'never'. Till I have no wife I have nothing in France. (III. ii. 56-59)

The Countess comforts Helena and bitterly criticises Bertram's actions, which she blames on Parolles' corrupting influence. Helena, however, is full of remorse that she has driven Bertram away from his own home and country and into the danger of war. She resolves to secretly leave Rousillon so that Bertram may then feel free to return, and that night she escapes, leaving a letter to tell the Countess that she intends to become a pilgrim of Saint Jacques in order to pray for Bertram's safety in the war.

God through Nature versus Man and his Institutions
Bertram rejects what is in fact a 'natural' match and turns it into an unnatural marriage, only to be normalised ultimately by the conditions, imposed upon Helena in his letter to her; that is, that she should get from him the ring which he always wears on his finger and bear a child of which he is the father. He supposes that these conditions are against nature's natural laws as he has no intention of giving her the ring or impregnating her.

The Countess identifies Parolles as the corrupter of Bertram's nature. She repudiates the 'honour' Bertram is seeking in war in the light of the 'dishonour' of his behaviour towards Helena.

Helena demonstrates her willingness to sacrifice herself for others' benefit and gives up her familiar life and home to be a pilgrim, whose purity of life will strengthen her prayer for the redemption and safety of Bertram.

Renaissance Platonism
'Bertram turns his back on what is, in undermeaning, the road to Paradise. In place of love he chooses war, and later, lust'. (Vyvyan p.145)

Bertram's concept of honour is false as he has repudiated the King and Helena in favour of Parolles. Only Helena's self-sacrificing love can redeem him.

Alchemy
The final separation of **Putrefaction** is achieved when Helena becomes a

pilgrim of Saint Jacques. The 'soul' of the chemical process in ascending to the top of the alembic vessel was said to enter a 'celestial sphere' where it collected beneficent heavenly influences; in human terms, entering a spiritual sphere such as a religious order. This marks the 'white' stage of the process.

Celtdom and the heresy of the 'Seed of Christ'
Celtic stories abound with riddles. Here, Bertram poses one for Helena.

Story Section 8 (III. v., III. vii., IV. ii.)
Bertram distinguishes himself in battle in Florence, capturing the enemy's commander and slaying the treacherous brother of the Duke of Florence. However, he dishonourably courts Diana Capilet, daughter to a Florentine widow in reduced circumstances and now a hostess to pilgrims of Saint Jacques.

While Diana and her mother are watching a street parade of the victorious soldiers, including Bertram, they meet Helena who, as a pilgrim of Saint Jacques, is seeking lodgings. When Helena discovers that Bertram is courting the unwilling Diana, she strikes a bargain with the two women that, in return for sufficient money to provide a good dowry for Diana, they will mislead Bertram into thinking that Diana has agreed to sleep with him and inveigle him into surrendering the ring on his finger to her and promising her marriage on the death of his wife.

In the bed-trick which they all enact, Helena replaces Diana, and she gives Bertram the ring from her finger which the King had given her, receives from Bertram his family's ring, and succeeds in becoming pregnant by him.

God through Nature versus Man and his Institutions
Bertram climbs the ladder in his man-made world. He achieves heroic stature in war and pays court to Diana of the house of Capilet, one of the aristocratic families of Italy. However, the natural nobility of this girl makes her reject Bertram and refer him to his duty to his wife. Heaven makes it possible for her to help this wife and for Helena to achieve the seemingly unnatural terms of Bertram's letter through a chance meeting in the streets of Florence.

Nature assists Helena in granting her a child when the marriage with Bertram is consummated under the illusory circumstances which reflect Bertram's sense of values. So obsessed is he with attaining Diana that he surrenders the ring which is his and his family's natural birth-right. This is substituted for a ring which more accurately reflects his standards, one which comes through Helena from the King of France.

Renaissance Platonism

In allowing himself to unwittingly fulfil the conditions he imposed upon Helena in his letter to her, Bertram demonstrates that 'even in love's phase of blindness – that of shadow-worship – it is nevertheless unconsciously directed towards the true beauty' (Vyvyan p. 153).

Alchemy

Bertram survives his trial by the sword in his Florentine battles. The complete alchemical marriage (**Coniunctio**) takes place, with the conjugation of Helena as 'soul' of the process, with Bertram as 'body'. The rings that are exchanged represent this soul-body bond.

Celtdom and the heresy of the 'Seed of Christ'

Helena proves her worth in solving the task-riddle.

Story Section 9 (IV. iv., IV. iii. 3-4)

In order to allow Bertram to return to France and to give Diana a reason to challenge Bertram with his promise to make her his wife on the death of Helena, Helena has it announced that she has died, and, with Diana to act as circumstantial witness, begins the journey to France in order to seek the help of the King to demonstrate to Bertram that she has fulfilled the terms of his letter to her. It is reported that Bertram expresses regret at hearing the death of Helena, to the extent that he seems to be a changed man.

God through Nature versus Man and his Institutions

The King, whose help Helena seeks, has feet in both camps of the God-through-nature and man-created worlds. As King, he is the natural head of his subjects, and he appreciates the natural virtue of Helena, but as Head of State he represents the top of the ladder which Bertram respects. He is therefore an ideal mediator between Helena and Bertram. The shock of the news of Helena's death gives Bertram pause and begins his reform.

Renaissance Platonism
In feeling sorrow and love for Helena after hearing of her death, Bertram begins to recognise his companion soul. The continuing support of Diana for Helena will ensure the ultimate happy ending. 'They are like Juno's swans […] inseparable' (Vyvyan p. 155).

Alchemy
The benefit of the process will have wider application if the King can be involved, as it incorporates the alchemical metaphor of 'king' as self. In this sense, the integration of the King in the story represents the psychological significance of the process.

Celtdom and the heresy of the 'Seed of Christ'
Helena continues the solution of the task-riddle and has trapped Bertram in one of her own.

Story Section 10 (IV. iii.)
Bertram's companions in arms decide to reveal the true nature of Parolles to him. They ambush Parolles in a trick concerning the recovery of a drum lost in a skirmish, and pretend to be a savage foreign army holding him hostage until he reveals Florentine military secrets (see fig. 36). Parolles betrays these secrets and commits additional treachery against Bertram, who then leaves him, returning to Roussillon.

God through Nature versus Man and his Institutions
Parolles, the main prop of Bertram's unwiseness, is removed, and the path is made clear for Bertram to realign his values. This is symbolised by his departure from Florence to Roussillon.

Renaissance Platonism
The revelation of the true nature of Parolles is necessary before Bertram's own awakening. However, when left alone, Parolles reveals 'that all this disgrace is but an accumulation of dirt, and beneath is an immortal spirit' (Vyvyan p.159).

Alchemy
Parolles, the undesirable element of the 'body' of the process, is tried by the sword (representing fire) and fails (see fig. 36). He is rejected by the now cleansed 'body', represented by Bertram.

CHAPTER EIGHT

Celtdom and the heresy of the 'Seed of Christ'
Parolles is subjected to a trick, similar to that which will trap Bertram in response to that which he imposed upon Helena.

Story Section 11 (V. i.)
Diana and the pregnant Helena arrive in Marseille seeking the King, only to find that he has gone to Roussillon.

God through Nature versus Man and his Institutions
Helena arrives at a place said to have been associated with Jesus Christ in a version of the Christian story called a heresy by the church. She thus identifies herself with the 'feminine principle' (Mary Magdalene) of God.

Renaissance Platonism
In this extended journey, Helena's constancy to Bertram in her love for him is further tested.

Alchemy
Helena, as the 'soul' of the alchemic process, collects beneficent influences from the 'sphere of Jesus Christ'.

Celtdom and the heresy of the 'Seed of Christ'
Perhaps this scene is inserted in the action of the play because in the legend of the Seed of Christ Mary Magdalene, pregnant with Christ's child, was said to have landed at Marseille.

Story Section 12 (V. ii.)
Parolles, tattered and impoverished, returns to Roussillon and begs charity of Lord Lafeu, who takes him in.

God through Nature versus Man and his Institutions
Stripped of his vainglory, Parolles, the previous pillar of the world of hypocrisy and the vanity of man's false endeavour, seeks refuge with Lafeu, a model of true perspectives, integrity and mercy. The opposites are fused and right has won.

Renaissance Platonism
Mercy and forgiveness are exemplified in the charity extended to Parolles by Lafeu.

Alchemy
The 'purged' element of the 'body' is reincorporated into the process by the 'fire'.

Celtdom and the heresy of the 'Seed of Christ'
The Celtic obligation of a nobleman's hospitality is seen at work in Lafeu's attitude towards Parolles.

Story Section 13 (V. iii.)
Believing Helena to be dead, the Countess has agreed that Bertram, repentant of his treatment of Helena and of her subsequent death, should marry Lafeu's daughter, Maudlin, and the King has come to Roussillon to give his royal consent.

Bertram gives as a favour for Maudlin the ring given to him in Florence by Helena. The King instantly recognises it and suspects Bertram of Helena's murder.

Further confusion occurs when Diana enters, claiming Bertram as her promised husband, Helena refutably being dead. As proof of plighted troth she shows the ring given to her by Bertram. Everyone recognises it as the Count's family heirloom and endorses Diana's claim.

However, Helena enters and reveals that she has fulfilled the conditions of Bertram's letter and has won her place as his true wife. He begs her pardon for the wrongs he has done to her in the past and pledges her eternal love.

The King expresses the general joy of the happily-resolved occasion and promises Diana a reward of a generous dowry.

God through Nature versus Man and his Institutions
Bertram is very swiftly stripped of all his pretensions and lies and is made to appear as ridiculous before the King as Parolles was before him. The virtuous Diana as a symbol of unpolluted nature becomes the instrument of this. Only when Bertram stands stripped of falsehood and false values does Helena return to him, and he can appreciate and truly love her as his nature-appointed partner and wedded wife. The joy of this rightful reunion infuses everyone.

Renaissance Platonism
'In the final scene […] it comes very near to being a rite of purification.

(Vyvyan p. 160) It represents 'stripping away of falsity and disguise from the self. (Vyvyan p. 158) […] The hero's union with the heroine also implies his knowledge and recognition of love in himself […]. He finally recognises true beauty 'through the one who is […] (his) predestined companion. And this ultimate clear sight includes self-knowledge'. (Vyvyan p. 154) The reconciliation represents 'the union of the soul with eternal beauty.'(Vyvyan p. 161)

Alchemy
Bertram is subjected to a swift succession of alchemical processes, beginning with **Firmentation**, in which the solution was 'fixed' and 'resolved' by two pure bodies (Diana and Helena) and its own by-product (Bertram's unborn child in Helena, which will 'fix' him to her). Next is **Exaltation**, when the 'spirit' (the Countess) and the 'soul' (Helena) return to the 'body' (Bertram) in the 'red' (Rubedo) stage. The last processes of **Multiplication** and **Projection** are realised when the joy of Helena's reunion with Bertram radiates through the King, and through him, France. Bertram has found his 'phoenix' and the 'gold' of alchemy. The Philosophers' Stone has been achieved (see fig. 35).

Celtdom and the heresy of the 'Seed of Christ'
The number 13 was for the Celts a symbol of magical potency, and thus the quasi-magical outcome is resolved as the story falls into thirteen parts.

Cabala: post-production (see fig. 3)
France, in an analogy of the psyche, is the subject of the Tree of Life in *All's Well that Ends Well*. It is represented by its inhabitants and King. Already having ascended to the higher levels of the Tree are the Countess, Helena and the King. Their positions on the Tree are indicated by their relationship to Bertram, who is the subject, as a young untried man, for progress through the Tree.

Bertram begins the play grounded in **Malkuth, the world experienced through the senses**, and retains its values until he learns the truth about his companion, Parolles. His forced marriage to Helena, his resentment at not being given permission by the King to go into battle and the temptations to betray both his family and his King by running away to fight must have given him traumas in **Yesod, his unconscious**.

The aggression in his nature which caused him to go to war and his base courting of Diana as a mistress demonstrates his prevalence in **Netzach (feelings)**, but his success in battle must demonstrate not only elements of the emotions of bravery which belong to **Netzach** but also strategies which lead to **Hod (thoughts)**. In succumbing to the bed-trick he unconsciously starts to travel towards **Tiphareth (beauty, heart)**, his destiny in Roussillon as husband of Helena, father and responsible Count of Roussillon.

The revelation of the base nature of Parolles, his erstwhile guide and companion, projects him towards **Hod** and ensures his progress towards **Tiphareth**. However, his trauma in **Yesod** regarding his treatment of Helena will not be cleared until he sees her alive. Until that time his shameful behaviour towards Diana before the King and his disgrace before all at Rousillon prevent any ascent of the Tree, and it is the **Geburah (strength, judgement)** of the King and Helena and their kindness to him on **Chesed (mercy)** that redeems him as a person so that he can achieve the understanding of **Binah** and the wisdom of **Chokmah** in his future life, hopefully ascending with Helena to **Kether (the crown of existence)**.

CELTIC, RENAISSANCE MAGIC, THEURGY

CHAPTER NINE: *THE TEMPEST*

During the years preceding 2001, the regular members of our Theatre set-Up audiences had complained that I had not found meanings from the Cabala in Shakespeare's plays (with the exception of *The Merchant of Venice*). I promised that when we presented a production of *The Tempest* in 2001 I would examine the Cabala in relation to the play, incorporate any of its meanings in the production, and display them in the programme notes. We also agreed that as *The Tempest* was the last play that Shakespeare completely wrote himself, it was likely that he would have incorporated in it, through the special medium of Prospero, his master-magician, all the arcana, his magical secret meanings, with which he had encoded his other plays.

In Theatre Set-Up's earlier production of *The Tempest* in 1982 (see fig. 37), we had recognised some of the Celtic content of the play, but many of its features remained a mystery to us, prompting me to undertake the PhD research into arcana in Shakespeare's plays. Equipped with the results of this research, I recognised seven levels of meaning (including the promised Cabala Tree of Life) in the preparation of our 2001 production, much to the delight of those members of the audience with whom I had previously discussed the arcane potential of the play. These levels were: **Social and political (**in which Shakespeare highlights characteristics of a stratified English society which still exists today, issues relating to colonisation of newly-explored lands, and the right to rule applied to political takeovers), **Renaissance philosophies** such as **a) magic** and **b) Platonic Divine Love**, and **Theurgy and rites of initiation**.[1] I also examined levels of meaning in the play based on **The Bible**, **The Cabala**, **Celtic** mythology and **Alchemy**.[2]

The arcana provided answers to mysterious events in the play such as:

- Prospero's declaration that he will break his magic staff, burying it in the earth, and will drown his book.

- His claim that Miranda is 'a third of my own life | Or that for which I live.'
- His possession of Caliban: 'This thing of darkness I | acknowledge mine.'
- His statement, as he prepares to return to Milan, 'That every third thought shall be my grave.'
- The arcana clarified the kind of magic that he was using, his 'rough magic', and his progression within the field of higher magic in his future life.
- It was possible to hazard an informed guess at the books that Gonzalo put in the boat for Prospero.
- The significance of the banquet which Ariel places before King Alonso and his court.
- Colin Still's book, *Shakespeare's Mystery Play: The Tempest,* as well as informing the different levels of initiation which were featured in the play, revealed the significance of the masque of the Goddesses presented to Miranda and Ferdinand.

Important in my reading of the different levels of meaning was Shakespeare's exposition of social and political issues within the story of the play which were prominent in his time. The ethics of the exploration and colonisation of new countries in the world by English adventurers is questioned in Prospero's treatment of Caliban, and the way enemies should be dealt with is explored in Prospero's dealings with his brother and King Alonso and his court. Shakespeare's solutions to these issues are compassionate. The courtier Gonzalo is characterised as a discreet politician who tactfully seeks to make the best of bad situations.

We presented the 2001 Theatre Set-Up production of *The Tempest* as a magic ritual, with the appropriate opening and closing ceremonies. In keeping with the fact that the play was likely Shakespeare's farewell to his full-time theatrical career in 1612, we presented it in costumes which reflected the style of that year. For incidental music and as an accompaniment to the songs, in acknowledgement of the Celtic content of the play and because I considered his music to be magical, I played on a Celtic folk harp the music of the blind composer/harpist, Turlough O'Carolan (1670-1738). The production was a happy one throughout its season of 36 venues in five countries, and the last night saw me dripping tears of regret that it was finishing into my harp at the end of the performance.

Story Section 1 (I. i.)
King Alonso of Naples is returning from the marriage of his daughter, Claribel, to the King of Tunis with his brother, Sebastian, his son, Ferdinand, and his friend Antonio who, twelve years previously, he had helped usurp the Dukedom of Milan from Antonio's brother, Prospero. Also in this court party is Gonzalo, a senior statesman of Milan. A tempest overwhelms the ship, and all its passengers and crew are cast onto the island where Prospero and his daughter, Miranda, have been living since Antonio exiled them from Milan.

Social and Political
During the tempest at the opening of the play, it is made clear that death and disaster do not respect social class, and the royal presence has no restraining effect on the waves. 'What care these roarers for the name of King?' (I. i.16) exclaims the boatswain. In such a crisis, the social order is inverted, as the boatswain orders the court members to keep to their cabins and get out of his way with the abusive 'You do assist the storm' (I. i. 14). He also informs the counsellor Gonzalo that his political power in human affairs holds no sway over nature.

Renaissance Philosophies: a) Magic; b) Platonic Love
a) The storm is an illusion, created by the nature spirit, Ariel, at the command of Prospero, who shows himself, through his control over Ariel, to be an accomplished magus of 'natural magic' (see above p. 40).

Theurgy and Rites of Initiation
King Alonso, his court party and Ferdinand experience the beginning of their initiations, the former entering the Lesser Initiation and the latter the Greater. Prospero is their hierophant. The tempest exposes them to the necessary water-cleansings that take place before initiation.

The Bible
Prospero brings his enemies within his power. Their descent into the seas

which they describe as Hell is a metaphor for their moral descent in their sins against Prospero.

The Cabala

In effecting the magic which has created the tempest, Prospero would have used the Hebrew letters which formed part of casting spells. The crew of the ship are seen to be rooted in the reality of **Malkuth (the real world as experienced through the senses)**, whereas the King and his party are ridiculed by them for their lack of common sense in their behaviour during the storm.

Celtic

The island which Prospero inhabits holds the same magical symbolism in the Celtic Western Way as a labyrinth of initiation.[3] His magic practised through the dominance of nature spirits is Celtic.

Alchemy

King Alonso (and his court) will be the 'base matter' of the alchemy, their transformation into 'improved matter' obviously necessary in their sins against Prospero, who functions as the alchemist with Ariel as his assistant. In the first alchemical stage of **Calcination**, extreme heat is applied in the process, which breaks up the 'base matter' into the different parts which can then be subjected to the different processes. Prospero's tempest does this, Ariel creating the fire of the extreme heat. The different parts of the base matter are King Alonso's party and family, and Alonso's loss is his children.

Ferdinand shares the burden with his father of being the 'body' which must be tried and tested, and Miranda, as his future wife, becomes part of the 'spirit' of the process.

Story Section 2 (I. ii. 1-187)

Miranda accuses her father of creating the storm as she knows his powers as a magician. He acknowledges that he has done so, but reassures her that no-one in the ship has been harmed and that this illusory tempest has been created for her own good. He tells her the story of how they came to be living on the island with only a cave-cell for shelter, and that he is really the Duke of Milan, but, devoting too much time to study, including the learning of magic arts, he neglected his state duties and did not notice the danger of the increasing power of his brother, Antonio.

The time came when Antonio, helped by King Alonso of Naples, usurped Prospero's Dukedom, taking over power completely from Prospero and casting him and Miranda, then three years old, into an old rotting boat. However, the old Lord Gonzalo secretly put food, water, clothing, implements needed for survival and Prospero's most treasured books into the boat, so that when, by chance, the boat landed on the island they now live on, they were able to survive, and Prospero has been able to continue his study so that he is now an accomplished magus, a master-magician.

Social and Political
Prospero gives an account of how his political power was usurped by his brother to whom he had virtually delegated it. He had not respected the duty he owed to his inherited title, but used the resources it brought him to indulge his personal interests.

The role of the counsellor, Gonzalo, is interesting. He retains political power in order to mediate where he can, as when he secretly made sure that Prospero had the means to live and study, although he was obliged to be an agent of Prospero's exile.

Miranda is presented as the innocent victim of Antonio's ambition. He intended that she should die along with her father. This aspect of political conflicts is known now as collateral damage.

Renaissance Philosophies: a) Magic; b) Platonic Love
a) We can guess at the titles of some of Prospero's books which Shakespeare might have known. Any of these would have served Prospero well as manuals of magic: *Picatrix,* written in Arabic in the 12th century and subsequently translated into Latin for Europeans; Marsilio Ficino's *Pimander* and *De Vita Coelitus Comparanda*; *De Occulta Philosophia* by Henry Cornelius Agrippa; Reuchlin's *De Arte Cabalistica*; *Steganographia* of Johannes Trithomius; the *Zohar* and *The Hieroglyphic Monad* by John Dee. In addition to these, there might have been works from the ancient world by Plato and Pythagorus and those attributed to the mysterious ancient authors, Asclepius and Hermes Trismegisthus.[4]

Theurgy and Rites of Initiation
The magician must only practise if no harm comes to anyone and the balance of nature is undisturbed. As the nature of the storm, which Prospero has

created though Ariel, is illusory, and no one is harmed, these conditions are fulfilled in Prospero's tempest, created to bring King Alonso, his court, his son and Antonio within his influence.

The purpose of practising magic is to benefit others, not oneself, as Prospero was doing in his isolated studies in Milan, and thus it is not surprising that ill came from this and he was forced into exile. There, fortunately, he had the opportunity to learn from the books put into the boat by Gonzalo the correct, beneficial magic practice which he is now embarking on as an adept, a magus of the highest potency. In some senses, Gonzalo has been a minor hierophant to Prospero and then to the court.

We understand from Prospero's story that King Alonso and Antonio, Prospero's brother, have committed crimes which necessitate their 'Lesser Initiation' in order for them to be 'redeemed'; that is, corrected and morally improved.

Prospero's cave-cell imitates those in which magicians have always practised, even in locations which are metaphors of a cave. Only those who have passed initiation can enter it, and those not worthy are expelled (as happens in this play).

The Bible

Prospero gives an account of the sins committed against him by his enemies. Prospero's treatment of them will be tested in the light of the New Testament precepts, 'Love your enemy' and 'Turn the other cheek'.

The Cabala

In terms of the Cabala, in his role as Duke of Milan, Prospero was not 'grounded' in the real world of **Malkuth**, but delegated his practical duties to his brother, concentrating his attention exclusively on his own mental life in the sphere of his soul, **Tiphareth**. As his studies were so academic and esoteric, he could be said to have been over-balanced in the sphere of **Hod (thoughts)**, lacking not only a connection to the material world but deficient in **feelings (Netzach)**. This was forced upon him when he was thrust out of Milan and into a boat with his tiny daughter, sustained by his love for her. When they were cast onto a deserted island, **Malkuth** was forced upon him when he had to fend for himself and his daughter.

Celtic

Living in his cave-cell on the deserted island, Prospero is very like Celtic religious hermits, such as St Cuthbert, who lived on Holy Island in Northumberland.[5] Prospero's magic cape represents his 'magic personality'. Naturally, he takes it off when discussing mundane matters with his daughter.

Alchemy

Prospero as alchemist has initiated the alchemical stage of **Dissolution** as the sea-drenched party from Naples emerges from the storm. Prospero describes to Miranda his own **Dissolution**, which took place twelve years previously when he was exiled from Milan and cast onto the sea in a rotten boat. The number twelve is significant as there are twelve stages in Ripley's alchemy.

Story Section 3 (I. ii. 186-377)

Prospero calls up the spirit of the air, Ariel, through whom he is able to practise his magic (see fig. 28). Ariel describes how he has 'performed the tempest', appearing to be a pillar of burning fire on the ship so that all aboard jumped, terrified, into the sea to avoid him. He then made sure that all came safely to land and that the ship itself was safely in harbour. He has, as instructed by Prospero, isolated Ferdinand from the rest of the court party.

When Prospero gives him more tasks, he objects, calling for his promised freedom from toil. Prospero reminds him how he had been imprisoned by the witch Sycorax in a pine tree for twelve years, and only Prospero's art could release him, in return for service. Ariel is promised his freedom in two days' time and commanded to become like a sea-nymph for his next duties.

They discuss the witch Sycorax, banished from Argier for evildoing and brought, pregnant, to this island. Her son, Caliban, 'not honoured with human shape', was born here, and after she died he lived alone on the island until Prospero and Miranda's arrival. He taught them how to survive on the island, and in return they gave him affection, language and education. However, for his attempted rape of Miranda he was imprisoned and enslaved. Caliban is summoned to serve them, and although threatened with further punishments, he curses them for taking power over his island.

Social and Political

Prospero himself is seen as a demanding task-master to those he finds on the island on which he has become exiled. In return for releasing Ariel from torture, he demands service, although for a limited period of time. He had adopted Caliban into his family, but when this part-animal native of the island tried to make use of Miranda sexually, he cast him out and now imprisons him with harsh punishments as a slave. In *The Crown of Life*, G. Wilson Knight is generous to Prospero's attitude to and treatment of Ariel and Caliban, which he equates with the later puritanical colonising impulse of the English, that is 'to raise savage peoples from superstition and blood-sacrifice, taboos and witchcraft and the attendant fears and slaveries, to a more enlightened existence.'[6] I think that in Prospero's treatment of the indigenous beings on the island, Shakespeare demonstrates the testimony of history, that is, that the behaviour of colonialists towards native people was rarely altruistic but always motivated by self-interest in the basic need to survive.

Caliban accuses Prospero of usurping the island from him, its rightful owner through his mother, Sycorax. This loss of birthright territory to a conquering colonialist dominates Caliban's resentment of Prospero. Shakespeare here reflects the plight of many native people punished for appropriation of property in their usurped territory. An example of this is the way Australian Aboriginals hunted and killed the sheep that colonists were grazing on their ancestral hunting grounds.

Prospero's role as a teacher is interesting. He is successful with a capable and pliant pupil like Miranda, but fails with Caliban, a challenging pupil with behavioural difficulties. His use of corporal punishment is excessive and it alienates Caliban further from him.

Renaissance Philosophies: a) Magic; b) Platonic Love

a) We see Prospero manipulating the 'natural order' through the nature spirit Ariel, who also dominates the elements of air, fire and water, as he has demonstrated in his creation of the tempest.

b) Caliban, in his assault upon Miranda, has demonstrated 'base love', which is only carnal and the opposite of 'Divine Love'. In *The Elizabethan World Picture*, Tillyard describes the Renaissance belief, originating in

Plato's *Timaeus* and developed throughout subsequent centuries, in a 'chain of being', stretching from heaven down through humanity to the animals beneath them and further downwards to inanimate objects (pp. 33-44). This belief promoted an unsympathetic view of animals, regarding them as belonging to a much lower order than humans in the cosmos. To act as an animal was to descend away from God. As Caliban is part-animal, 'not honoured with human shape', he is already, according to Renaissance belief, of a lower order of being, and his animal actions seem reasonable to himself although not acceptable to 'full humans'.

Theurgy and Rites of Initiation

Using talismans and spells from his magic textbooks, Prospero is able to practise magic through an agent, Ariel, a spirit of the air who also functions in his mercurial role as a junior guide of initiation to Ferdinand and to King Alonso and his court. Ariel simulates the elements fire and water in his shape-changing.

Identification with the four elements and their associated directions - earth/north, water/west, fire/south and air/east - and an occasional preference to work through one of them is part of a magician's operation. Prospero has preferred air/east. The mother of earthly Caliban, Sycorax, the witch who had practised malevolent magic upon Ariel, imprisoned him in a pine, the tree associated with her earth/north direction (see above p. 52).

The Bible

Caliban appears in the play as a kind of devil who has experienced a fall from grace like the Biblical Satan, who was expelled from Heaven as Caliban was from Prospero's cell. His fall has made him bitter and vengeful.

The Cabala

Shakespeare often presents the characters in his plays as different aspects of the one personality, and in this play Caliban represents the realm of the material world based on **Malkuth**, Prospero the realm of the individual soul, centred on **Tiphareth**, and Miranda the realm of the spirit, rising to **Kether** (see fig. 26). Certainly it was Caliban who instructed Prospero how to survive in the material world of the island and thus become grounded in **Malkuth**, as he should have been in Milan. However, Caliban himself has at this point in the play been thus far unable to raise himself above the lower levels of his 'self'.

Celtic
The witch Sycorax and her son are similar to the Celtic hag Cailloch Beare, whose pursuit of her son or consort (often represented by a bull, as Caliban is called a 'mooncalf') alternates with her son or consort's pursuit of her, representing the changing summer-winter, lightness-darkness seasonal patterns of the year. She is associated with the raven (whose feather Caliban invokes to curse Prospero) and her familiars are creatures of the nights, the 'toads, beetles, bats' of her evil charms.[7] The god associated with her in Celtic mythology, Setebos, is a snake-god (also observed in Shakespeare's day in South America).[8]

When Prospero threatens to imprison Ariel within an oak, he reverses the normal process of Celtic magic. The term for a priest in Celtic magic, 'druid', contains as part of its meanings 'to release the magic from an oak'.[9]

Alchemy
Ariel describes how in the alchemical stage of **Seperation** (Ripley's spelling), he has separated all the members of the ship from each other. Prospero recounts a separation within his own family unit – the casting out of Caliban.

Story Section 4. (I. ii. 378-506)
Ariel, invisible and singing, leads Ferdinand into the presence of Miranda and Prospero. As Prospero had hoped, they fall in love at first sight, but, so that Ferdinand should value Miranda more, Prospero pretends to be suspicious of him, casts a spell upon him and leads him away in captivity.

Social and Political
Prospero, in making Ferdinand's alliance with Miranda difficult, understands that it is human nature not to appreciate anything too easily acquired: 'This swift business I must uneasy make, lest too light winning | Make the prize light' (I. ii. 454-455).

Renaissance Philosophies: a) Magic; b) Platonic Love
a) The staff with which Prospero charms Ferdinand, and which causes him to drop his sword, is a magic staff or rod, a magical implement of ritual magical art.[10]

b) Miranda and Ferdinand, as foreseen by Prospero, are 'companion souls' and recognise each other straight away, instantly experiencing 'Divine Love'. Prospero begins the trials of their love which will test their constancy to each other.

Theurgy and Rites of Initiation

Ferdinand enters the 'Greater Initiation', with Prospero as hierophant. Miranda will be his 'celestial bride'. Such initiates were compelled to fast and eat lowly food, as decreed by Prospero. The young prince is a willing candidate, prepared to undergo any trials in order to be worthy of his celestial bride.

The Bible

Ferdinand must endure trials to test him, as suffered by Biblical personages such as Job.

The Cabala

Within the total personality presented by these characters, another personality aspect is introduced with the character of Ferdinand in the sphere of **Chesed**, the archetype of love and awareness within the realm of the soul. This is strengthened, according to Prospero's plan, by **Geburah**, the archetype within this realm of will and power.

Celtic

When Ferdinand sees Miranda, he thinks that she must be a goddess of the island. In the Celtic sense of the play this is true. The Celts respected an earth-goddess, the Morrigan, who existed in three forms: a hag representing death (Sycorax); a matron representing birth (implied in Miranda's mother); and, representing life, a young girl called Etain, with whom it was the ritual obligation of a hero to mate (Miranda).

Alchemy

Coniunctio, an alchemical wedding, takes place figuratively as Ferdinand and Miranda 'have chang'd eyes' (I. ii. 444).

The song 'Full fathom five thy father lies' (I. ii. 399-406), with which Ariel draws Ferdinand into the presence of Prospero and Miranda, presents an allegory of alchemical transformation that Prospero hopes King Alonso will undergo: the 'coral' of which his bones are made (I. ii. 399-400) was used by alchemists, because of its red colour, to represent the red powder termed the Philosophers' Stone, which could turn lead into gold.

The 'pearls' (I. ii. 401) of his eyes represent the human soul (which will become redeemed by the process), and the 'sea-change' (I. ii. 403) is the transformation itself, now begun by Alonso's purifying 'washing' in the sea-waves of the tempest.

Story Section 5 (II. i.)

King Alonso, grief-stricken over the apparent loss of his son, enters with Gonzalo, Antonio, Sebastian and members of the court. Sebastian, the King's brother, and Antonio mock Gonzalo's attempts to make the best of their situation, and Sebastian criticises King Alonso for bestowing his daughter Claribel in marriage upon the King of Tunis. They are all bemused by the fact that although they have been shipwrecked, their clothes seem fresher than ever before. Gonzalo fantasises on the ideal state that he would create had he the 'plantation of this isle' (II. ii. 139).

Ariel enters, and puts Gonzalo and Alonso to sleep with magic music. Antonio convinces Sebastian to kill King Alonso so that he can take the kingship for himself, but as they raise their daggers to do this, Ariel wakes up Gonzalo and the plot is foiled. Antonio and Sebastian pretend that they have heard a fearful noise of lions, and that they were armed in order to defend their King. All the courtiers resolve to find safer ground.

Social and Political

In his criticism of the arranged match of Claribel with the King of Tunis, Sebastian highlights the unfortunate position of a royal princess, used as a pawn in a marriage of political convenience.

Gonzalo, as counsellor, continues to mediate the situations he finds himself in, striving to cheer up the King, tolerating the verbal abuse of Antonio and Sebastian and protecting the King when they threaten to kill him. In King Alonso's escape from his brother Sebastian's attempt to kill him, the vulnerability of people in high power in Shakespeare's day is demonstrated. No-one, especially close members of the family, could be trusted, and the chances of being killed for acquisition of power were high.

Gonzalo's 'ideal commonwealth' that he described is unrealistic, assuming an unflawed human nature among its inhabitants and an extravagant bounty from nature itself.

Renaissance Philosophies: a) Magic; b) Platonic Love
a) Pythagorus decreed that music imitated the 'harmony of the spheres', and that in its rightful practice, celestial harmony would be reinforced and create a sympathetic harmony in the soul. Music is used with that purpose throughout the play as an instrument of magic.

Theurgy and Rites of Initiation
The courtiers continue their 'Lesser Initiation', noticing that their clothes, in spite of being sea-drenched, seem improved (a sign of their ritual cleansing). King Alonso experiences the imagined death of his son. He and Gonzalo also undergo an initiatory sleep, induced by Prospero to throw into relief the guilt of Sebastian and Antonio. When they are awakened, the guilty pair standing over them with swords (an image from the Rites of Eleusis) make the excuse that they heard a roar of lions or bulls. Gonzalo acknowledges that he heard a strange 'humming' (II. ii. 312). This imitates the 'rhombus', a bull-roarer used in the Eleusis rites.

The Bible
Antonio and Sebastian complete their descent away from Divinity. The King reaps the rewards of his sins in suffering the assumed death of his son.

The Cabala
King Alonso, Sebastian and Antonio represent unbalanced personalities, overburdened in **Yesod** with evil or guilt. The first stage in clearing this away is to expose it, and here Antonio's and Sebastian's evil ambition is exposed. King Alonso's guilt in marrying his daughter against her wishes and everyone's advice, with the catastrophic result of the loss of his son on the voyage back home from the wedding in Tunis, has already been exposed.

Celtic
The music used to effect magic here is common to all Celtic magic practice.[11]

Alchemy
The violent stage of **Putrefaction**, in which all the elements of the process are severely broken down, begins here, as Antonio and Sebastian are further divided from the King by attempting to murder him. The King, devastated by the loss of both his son and his daughter, begins to lose his mind. The 'lions' referred to symbolise the lions (both red as the symbol of 'sophic

sulphur', a basic constituent of the alchemy, and green, the symbol for vitriol, a chemical used to dissolve the 'base matter').

Story Section 6 (II. ii.)

Caliban enters, still cursing Prospero, and falls down in terror, thinking that a spirit has been sent to torment him, when Trinculo, Alonso's jester, enters, looking for shelter from an impending storm. Seeing Caliban and thinking him to be a native of the island, he wonders at his strange shape and speculates that were he able to take him to England, he could make money from displaying him:

> Were I in England now, as once I was, and had but this fish painted, not a holiday fool there but would give a piece of silver: there would this monster make a man; any strange beast there makes a man: when they will not give a doit to relieve a lame beggar, they will lay out ten to see a dead Indian (II. ii. 28-33).[12]

Commenting that this native has probably been struck down by a thunderbolt, he takes refuge beneath Caliban's cape, his 'gaberdine' (II. ii. 39). Stephano, Alonso's butler, enters drunkenly, sees what he imagines to be a monster with two heads and four legs, and speculates that if he were to take him back home he could give him as a gift to the Emperor, presumably for a reward. He gives Caliban a drink from his wine bottle to ease his complaining. When Trinculo recognises Stephano's voice but, believing him to be drowned, cries out, Stephano offers to pour drink into the monster's 'other mouth'. Stephano, alarmed when Trinculo (who he imagines is part of a monster), calls out his name, thinks that the monster must be a devil and goes to leave. Trinculo persuades him that he is indeed his friend, and Stephano confirms this when he pulls him out from Caliban's cape by the legs.

Meanwhile, Caliban considers that the drink he has been given is a 'celestial liquor', and that Stephano must therefore be a god. He kneels to him, swearing to serve him. Trinculo ridicules this, but Stephano, flattered, encourages Caliban, who, rejoicing in his new master and freedom from Prospero's tyranny, leads them to find fresh food on the island.

Social and Political
Members of the lower social orders make their appearance, making more successful attempts to survive than the Court party. The early reaction of both Trinculo and Stephano to Caliban is to speculate on the possibility of taking him to Europe and making money by displaying him as a freak. Shakespeare is ungenerous to them in that their appetites are basic; drink, money, sex, and the advancement of their social position. Caliban, in mistaking Stephano for a god and thus betraying himself into servitude, and in being seduced and destroyed by alcohol, echoes the horrendous history of the indigenous peoples of the Mesa and South Americas, who initially believed that the conquering Spaniards were gods as followers of the mythic Quetzacoatl.

Renaissance Philosophies: a) Magic; b) Platonic Love
b) Just as Caliban has attempted 'base love' (which is deceptive) of Miranda, he finds false gods. Having rejected Prospero's teaching, which might have elevated him above the lowly status into which, as part-human, part-animal, he is born, he begins a descent further away from God. Trinculo and Stephano, in their exploitation and deception of Caliban, also descend.

Theurgy and Rites of Initiation
Trinculo and Stephano, who have undergone the same water-cleansing as the court and Ferdinand, represent a failed initiation.

The Bible
Caliban functions further as a Biblical Satan in creating a false god of Stephano.

The Cabala
Stephano and Trinculo exist entirely in the material world of **Malkuth**. It is natural that they should be joined by Caliban, who is also grounded in **Malkuth**, but whose inner aspirations to ascend the Cabalistic Tree of Life are demonstrated by his need to make a god of Stephano.

Celtic
Celts were fond of imagined creatures that were half-man, half-creature. Caliban is such a being.[13]

Alchemy
Another potential murder, the murder of Prospero, is prepared, as Caliban changes masters, extending **Putrefaction** into another section of the King's party.

Story Section 7 (III. i.)

Ferdinand enters in servitude, carrying logs for Prospero's fire. When Miranda offers to help him he refuses her assistance, saying that he is glad to work in her service. They declare their love for each other, watched by the unseen Prospero, who rejoices at the success of his plan.

Social and Political

Ferdinand is not a snob. He will undertake lowly work if required to. He is also a chivalrous gentleman in his attitude towards Miranda, respecting her and honouring her, although, as far as he knows, she is only one of the indigenous population (usually looked down upon by Europeans) and he believes her to be far beneath him in social status.

Renaissance Philosophies: a) Magic; b) Platonic Love

b) Ferdinand and Miranda pass through their trials of Divine Love and are constant to each other.

Theurgy and Rites of Initiation

Ferdinand willingly undergoes the physical trials of the Greater Initiation.

The Bible

Ferdinand shows Biblical patience in enduring his trials.

The Cabala

The nature of Ferdinand's love in honouring Miranda and his willingness to deserve her by undertaking lowly tasks in her service not only elevates him in **Chesed**, but spirals the nature of their love upwards into the sphere of **Binah, spiritual love**, strengthened by **Chockmah, spiritual purpose**. This ascent is similar to that described in Renaissance Platonism.

Celtic

Miranda functions as the young goddess, Etain, helping the hero.[14]

Alchemy

In willingly carrying out the lowly act of bearing logs (an act beneath his usual dignity as a royal prince), Ferdinand enacts the alchemical stage of **Congelation**, wherein the 'body' of the process is purged. Miranda, as the 'spirit' of the process, is 'congealed' (as in this alchemic stage) in her resolve to be Ferdinand's wife.

Story Section 8 (III. ii.)

Caliban drunkenly leads in Trinculo and Stephano and persuades them that they should kill Prospero, rape Miranda and, under the kingship of Stephano, rule over the island. Ariel, invisible, assumes the voice of Trinculo and plays tricks on them. When they sing, he plays the musical accompaniment to the tune on a tabor and pipe, to the pleasure of Caliban and the amazement of the others. Caliban tells Stephano and Trinculo not to be afraid of the music as it is a joyous feature of the isle, 'Sounds and sweet airs, that give delight and hurt not' (III. ii. 134). He speaks of the benison the music gives him:

> Sometimes a thousand twangling instruments
> Will hum about my ears; and sometime voices
> That, if I then had wak'd after long sleep,
> Will make me sleep again: and then, in dreaming,
> The clouds methought would open, and show riches
> Ready to drop upon me; that, when I wak'd,
> I cried to dream again. (III. ii. 135-141)

Ariel tells Prospero of the plot to kill him.

Social and Political

The corrupting power of drink misleads Caliban, Stephano and Trinculo into false ideas of their own capabilities. Caliban, in his wonderful appreciation of the magical music of the island, shows a finer soul than his behaviour indicates.

Renaissance Philosophies: a) Magic; b) Platonic

a) Caliban's soul is capable of being elevated by the music which Prospero uses on the island as an integral part of his magical practice.

Theurgy and Rites of Initiation

Trinculo and Stephano succumb to every temptation placed before them by Caliban in a debased descent.

The Bible

Caliban becomes truly Satanic in tempting Stephano and Trinculo to commit murder. It is the original, fallen angel in him who appreciates the music of the island.

The Cabala
Caliban, Stephano and Trinculo abuse their participation in the material world, and, abusing their bodies which the Tree represents, will suffer the consequences. Caliban, in his appreciation of music, demonstrates appreciation through the senses of **Malkuth**.

Celtic
In Celtic style, Ariel shape-changes in order to trick people, as does Puck in *Dream*.

Alchemy
The lower social orders of the King's party begin to be satirically 'purged' in this stage as they are punished by Ariel for falling for Caliban's temptations. Caliban shows his 'spirit' potential in his love of the music of the island.

Story Section 9 (III. iii.)
The court characters enter again, exhausted by wandering through the seemingly labyrinthine island in search of Ferdinand. The invisible Prospero dazzles them with a magic display of strange creatures bringing in a banquet for them. However, when King Alonso goes to eat from the banquet, Ariel, in the form of a harpy, dismisses the banquet and accuses Alonso, Antonio and Sebastian of being 'Three men of sin' (III. iii. 53). He reminds them of their cruelty to Prospero and Miranda and declare that 'the powers' (III. iii. 73) have 'pronounced' 'lingering perdition' (II. iii. 77) upon them, including the loss of Ferdinand, until they can demonstrate 'heart's sorrow, | and a clear life ensuing' (III. iii. 81-82). Gonzalo, to whom this apparition did not appear, observes that they seem guiltily deranged as they resolve to join in death the supposedly drowned Ferdinand and to fight the devils of the island.

Social and Political
Occasionally, as here, political malpractitioners get their come-uppance and are made to see the error of their ways.

Renaissance Philosophies: a) Magic; b) Platonic Love
a) Prospero uses magic for benevolent means through the spirits he conjures.

Theurgy and Rites of Initiation
In a wandering search for a lost person typical of the Lesser Initiation

in the purgatory labyrinth of the island, the court members now undergo more experiences typical of the process in the form of the appearance of strange creatures and the presentation and withdrawal of a banquet barred from them by a fury (in this case represented by Ariel as a harpy). Now their guilt is declared, exposed and confronted with the threat of eternal punishment unless they become penitent and transformed. The trauma they suffer from this experience renders them mad.

The Bible
Only when they recognise and confess their guilt can Alonso, Antonio and Sebastian begin an ascent back to grace, which Prospero has put into motion.

The Cabala
Prospero continues the process, through Ariel, of 'cleaning out' repressed guilt and sin from the personalities of the courtiers. Exposing their guilt, he does this by activating the subconscious sphere of **Yesod**, which clears out repressed negative qualities and ultimately reintegrates them into their correct positive spheres.

Celtic
Theatre Set-Up presented the strange shapes which offer the banquet as gods from Celtic mythology (a three-faced god – a tricephalos, the horned Cernunnos, and Epona, the female horse- God see fig. 37).[15] The banquet was presented as Celtic symbols – a representation of the grail cauldron containing the mead of immortality which would poison anyone unworthy (as Alonso is) who drinks it, and a boar's head with silver apples, mythically destined for an elect person and not for anyone who usurps and murders.[16] The possible recognition of the significance of these symbols, added to the actions and words of Ariel as harpy, provoke feelings of guilt from all but the good Gonzalo, who is exempted from Ariel's threat of punishment and tortures.

Alchemy
In the next alchemical stage, **Cibation**, the 'base matter' is 'fed'. This is symbolised by the presentation of the banquet, which the King is willing to eat but prevented from doing so as the next violent stage of **Sublimation** occurs when Ariel as harpy (the raven often used as a symbol for this violent stage) forces King Alonso, Antonio and Sebastian into an awareness of their guilt and, potentially, penitence.

Story Section 10 (IV. i.)

Ferdinand, having passed his trial of Divine Love, is now accepted by Prospero on the condition that his relationship with Miranda remains chaste. Prospero creates for him and Miranda a masque of Greek Goddesses, including Juno, Iris and Ceres, who bless the marriage. He interrupts an additional masque of naiads and reapers when he remembers that he must move quickly to foil Caliban's plot on his life. He muses that life is ephemeral, dream-like, as are the spirits of the masque itself, 'We are such stuff | As dreams are made on; and our little life | Is rounded with a sleep' (IV. i. 156-158).

Ariel has lured Caliban, Stephano and Trinculo through briar and thorn bushes around the island and left them in a cesspit, from which they emerge, only for Stephano and Trinculo to be diverted from their killing mission by a display of 'glistering apparel', which, in spite of Caliban's warnings, they try on. There they are captured by Prospero, who has them tormented and hunted by hounds. Prospero observes, 'At this hour | Lie at my mercy all mine enemies' (IV. i. 252-253).

Social and Political

Ferdinand is rewarded for his chivalry to Miranda in the promise of her as his bride. Prospero's emphasis on his relationship with Miranda remaining chaste until their marriage was not only a social convention of the time but a convention in Shakespeare's plays. The contempt that Caliban shows for Stephano and Trinculo in their greed for the 'glistering apparel' which deflects them from their purpose in killing Prospero resonates with the horror of those civilisations in the Americas at the gold-lust of the conquistadores, and of all indigenous cultures that have been despoiled by European colonialists.

Renaissance Philosophies: a) Magic; b) Platonic Love

b) Ferdinand and Miranda's ascent through their 'Divine Love' is represented by the masque of Goddesses presented to them. The descent of Trinculo, Stephano and Caliban is shown in their fall into the cesspit and their torture by hounds.

Theurgy and Rites of Initiation

Ferdinand, having passed and survived his trials, is granted by Prospero a vision of Paradise in the form of a masque, in which he encounters goddesses who bless his forthcoming union with Miranda, his 'celestial bride'. Trinculo and Stephano are led into the mire, an abyss of Hell, by Caliban, and are pursued by the hell-hounds which a true initiate should defy. They consequently suffer awful physical punishments. Prospero knows that his magnanimity as a true magus is about to be tested, as his enemies lie at his mercy.

The Bible
Stephano and Trinculo are punished for their yielding to Caliban's temptations and Caliban pays the penalty for being the tempter.

The Cabala
That Ferdinand and Miranda have achieved the highest spiritual level in the Tree is indicated by their permitted vision of deities.

Prospero indicates Miranda's function as his 'spirit' in saying that she is 'A third of mine own life | Or that for which I live' (IV. 1. 3), Caliban being the other third. When Prospero warns Ferdinand against sexual intimacy with Miranda until the relationship is sanctified by holy marriage, he is referring to their loss of spiritual attainment that would occur if that happened.

Stephano, Trinculo and Caliban are 'purged', a known pathway, through the correspondences on the Tree, to bringing about a result on the mind.

Celtic
The Goddess Iris (of the rainbow) has a Celtic equivalent, Arionrod, also of the rainbow, and also of a silver wheel. In Celtic legendry, she threw the rainbow across the world to protect it from evil by scaring away violence. She functions in Celtic initiation, her castle being one of death and rebirth. The Celtic equivalent of Ceres (Goddess of agriculture and initiation) is Ceridwen, Goddess of corn and inspiration of the Celtic Mysteries. She possesses a cauldron of rebirth containing an initiatory drink. Her purpose is to inculcate thoughts of responsibility for knowledge and its uses. Here it relates to marriage.[17]

Alchemy
Firmentation (Ripley's spelling) fixes and resolves the solution. The problems of Ferdinand and Miranda are here resolved, and their engagement 'fixed' not only by Prospero, but by images of goddesses in the masque. A

more unpleasant 'fixing' takes place for Stephano, Trinculo and Caliban, as they are led into the cesspool and imprisoned by Prospero.

Story Section 11 (V. i.)
Ariel pleads that Prospero be merciful to his enemies, as they all seem repentant and have been adequately punished. Prospero responds:

> They being penitent,
> The sole drift of my purpose doth extend
> Not a frown further. Go release them Ariel
> My charms I'll break, their senses I'll restore,
> And they shall be themselves.

Ariel sings of his now-imminent promised freedom as he dresses Prospero in his Duke of Milan attire so that the members of the court can recognise him.

Prospero says farewell to all the spirits of nature through whom he has practised his 'rough magic' and pledges to break his staff, burying it in the earth, and to drown his book. He uses music to comfort the courtiers as they enter in a trance, from which he gradually releases them. He is reconciled with them, and his lost Dukedom of Milan is restored to him. Prospero teases King Alonso, claiming that just as the King has lost a son, he has lost a daughter, but to everyone's delight, he reveals Miranda and Ferdinand playing chess. Miranda is astonished to see so many people, 'How beauteous mankind is! O brave new world | That has such people in't' (V. i. 183-184).

Caliban and his fellow conspirators are brought in, pardoned, and dispatched. Prospero invites the court to his poor cell until they can sail to Naples for the wedding of Miranda and Ferdinand and thence to his Dukedom of Milan. Ariel will ensure them a safe voyage.

Social and Political
Problems arise in many situations when the principle of taking revenge is invoked. Here, Prospero avoids that, although he makes clear to all parties concerned that he does not condone evildoing. In the play major

social issues are dealt with in the problem of what to do with your enemies if they fall into your hands, and the treatment of criminals. Prospero's solution is to attempt to reprogramme their minds so that they do not reoffend, and to be charitable to them so that they cease to be enemies. Much to Caliban's surprise, Prospero returns the island to him, although, it must be noted, as the restored Duke of Milan, Prospero does not need it anymore.

Miranda's exclamation on the beauty of mankind in her assessment of the court members, 'O brave new world', expresses Shakespeare's ultimate optimism and belief in humanity.

Renaissance Philosophies: a) Magic; b) Platonic Love

a) Prospero enumerates all the nature spirits through whom he has been able to control natural phenomena and even waken the dead, and he says farewell to them as he resolves to abjure 'this rough magic' (natural magic, operated through control of nature spirits such as Ariel). It is possible that he was aspiring to ascend to a higher grade of magic, taking as a model John Dee, the pre-eminent magician-mathematician of Shakespeare's day, who had applied the mathematics he had acquired for higher magical practice to everyday matters. He thus benefitted the society he served in scientific as well as magical ways.

In order to be an effective magician of a higher order, Prospero must forgive his enemies, as the magus who achieved the top rank of Ceremonial or Religious magic had to be pure and ascetic. Only then, through the intellect, the highest faculty of the soul, can he reach the peak of attainment. By forgiving everyone their sins against him, he proves himself worthy as an adept.

b) Miranda and Ferdinand demonstrate 'Divine Love' in their mental communication through the chess game.

Theurgy and Rites of Initiation

The King and court emerge penitent from their purgatory, and, by restoring the Dukedom to Prospero, are granted the ending of their tormenting illusions when Ferdinand appears with Miranda. Prospero as hierophant has succeeded in conducting both initiations. Gonzalo claims that the members of the Court have attained self-knowledge (which is an essential feature of initiation) in finding themselves, 'When no man was his own'

(V. i. 213). Ferdinand claims that through Prospero he is reborn into a 'second life' (V. i. 196), a result of successful initiation.

The Bible

Prospero forgives his enemies so that they can achieve a return to grace.

The Cabala

The personalities of the court party are integrated as Prospero brings them into his circle. Even Caliban will 'seek for grace' (V. i. 295). Prospero, in forgiving his enemies, displays the essential generous and 'higher' qualities (such as altruism, love, service) of **Tiphareth** (the heart and 'centre' of the individual soul and of the Tree of Life). In his wisdom and compassion in the treatment of his enemies he displays characteristics of **Binah** and **Chockmah**, which will help him to ascend to **Kether** (the Divinity within himself).

He acknowledges the responsibility he has for Caliban as his **Malkuth**, 'This thing of darkness I | Acknowledge mine' (V. i. 275-276). As he goes towards the unknown in Milan he acknowledges the inevitability of his death with, 'Every third thought shall be my grave' (V. i. 311), acknowledging the significance of the Christian Holy Trinity.

Celtic

Prospero associates himself with the Celtic midsummer 'sun-king', dependent upon an auspicious position of the stars for the achievement of his magic and the 'zenith' of his fortunes.[18] However, the ritualistic obligation of this Celtic summer-king (as in many other cultures) was to offer himself to be sacrificed at his retirement. This is symbolised as Prospero casts off his magic powers and gives away his daughter.[19] His staff that he resolves to bury indicates the magic that is personal to him alone. Prospero resolves, 'I'll drown my book' (V. i. 57). He is following in the path of the famous Celtic magician, Merlin, who drowned his book to stop it falling into the hands of an adversary.[20] Prospero must ensure that while he will be involved in matters of state as the Duke of Milan, the book which instructs him in his magic powers should not fall into the wrong hands and be misused for harmful magic.

When Miranda is seen playing chess with Ferdinand she represents the Celtic theme of the young girl, usually the Goddess Etain, who appears as a figure of destiny, the outcome of the chess game deciding fate.

Alchemy
The alchemical process culminates in the stage of **Exaltation**, when the 'body', purified, can be re-united with the 'spirit', and the 'gold' of alchemy is achieved. This takes place when the King is re-united with Ferdinand, now joined to Miranda, who will replace his daughter within his family. All the members of the King's party are brought together for their return to Milan as Prospero regains his lost Dukedom. Gonzalo recommends, marvelling at the wonder of the story, that they, 'Set it down | with gold on lasting pillars' (V. i. 207-208).

<u>Story Section 12</u> - Epilogue
Prospero speaks an epilogue to the audience, begging them to set him free with their 'indulgence' (20).

Social and Political
Theatre consists of social interaction and interdependence between actors and an audience, a fact which Prospero acknowledges in his address to them.

Renaissance Philosophies: a) Magic; b) Platonic Love
a) In addressing the audience, Prospero pleads for them to send him to Milan. Only then, upon returning to a society in which he can benefit, will he be able to begin his ascent to the higher order of magic.

Theurgy and Rites of Initiation
If the audience agree with Prospero that the play has achieved the 'magic of the theatre', he can proceed, vindicated. The actor playing Prospero is simulating, in his direct address to the audience, the magician's role as 'walker-between-the-worlds', in this case the illusory world of the stage and the real world of the audience.[21] The name 'Milan' carries the meaning of 'centre' (see above p. 10), and returning there, Prospero identifies it with the centre of his own labyrinth of theurgy. All magic must have opening and closing sequences, and in asking the audience to help him to return to the Milan from whence he came, Prospero hopes to achieve this.

The Bible
Prospero asks that the charity he has displayed to others be granted to him by the audience.

The Cabala
A Cabalist must not work in isolation but must both give the benefits of his practice to others and work alongside others. In order to do this, Prospero must return to Milan.

Celtic
Prospero asks the audience to assist him in a return to Milan without the trappings of magic, using mental strength alone.

Alchemy
When Prospero addresses the audience he casts the benefits of the 'gold' to them in the alchemic stages of **Multiplication**, and he begs their acceptance of this so that the final stage of **Projection** can be achieved.

Perhaps Shakespeare is also asking for this play to be the culmination of his 'Great Work', the ultimate goal of alchemy.

POSTSCRIPT

When researching and performing Shakespeare's last plays, I was overwhelmed by the beauty and compassion of the grand statements he was making on the human condition. The idea of forgiveness in the realm of crime and punishment explored in *Measure for Measure* was extended into the international political realm in *Cymbeline* when, in order to promote peace, the King decides to pay tribute to Rome, although he has won the right not to do so. In *The Winter's Tale* a tyrant is reformed and forgiven and war avoided between countries, the new-found harmony within his own family reflected in his country's political arena.

In what Shakespeare might have viewed as his last opportunity to promote benevolent ideas on his stage, he extends these concepts in *The Tempest*. Prospero does not exploit his power over his enemies by killing them and thus eliminating them, but he reforms them, forgives them and then joins them in integrating with them into society. The criminality of Caliban, Trinculo and Stephano is detected and punished so that they do not offend again, and then they are forgiven.

The problems arising from the colonisation of foreign lands by Europeans is explored in Prospero's dealings with Caliban. Shakespeare creates him as part-human, part-animal, born of a witch. Often European colonists viewed the humans they conquered and exploited as sub-human, a fact that Shakespeare may have observed in his creation of this Caliban as a reflection of their illusions. Initially in the play's story, there had been harmony in the cultural exchange between Prospero and Caliban, Caliban instructing Prospero on how to survive and in return Prospero teaching Caliban language, music and European knowledge. However, when Caliban's animal nature surfaced in his attempted rape of Miranda, Prospero's treatment of Caliban became intemperate, based on physical torture, behaviour typical of European colonists who went even further in systematically wiping out many of the indigenous population of the countries they conquered.[22] This colonist behaviour was in its infancy in Shakespeare's day, but its increasing prevalence as Europeans dominated new lands in later years marks Shakespeare's observations as prophetic. Although only the colony at Jamestown in Chesapeake Bay had been established by the English in 1606, reports of the Spanish plundering of countries they had conquered years before must have reached Shakespeare's ears. In 1609, a ship sailing for Jamestown was cast by a storm upon the shores of Bermuda, the report of which is supposed to have inspired Shakespeare's writing of *The Tempest*.[23] I think that in the relationship between Prospero and Caliban and its concerns it throws up about colonisation, Shakespeare was informed by more than that event.

Trinculo and Stephano regard Caliban as a freak who could make money for them if they displayed him as such on their return home. Many of the explorers in Shakespeare's day returned not only with plundered booty of the countries they had discovered, but with people and animals to be put on display as curiosities. Shakespeare displays a sensitivity to this in Trinculo's and Stephano's attitude to Caliban. Just as Caliban frequently does, indigenous people that have survived extinction have protested continually against the occupation of their lands and their debasement into second class citizens. Shakespeare's answer to this is to give back the island to Caliban.

CHAPTER TEN: *A MIDSUMMER NIGHT'S DREAM*

The central theme of *A Midsummer Night's Dream* is transformation, physical, spiritual, psychological and theoretical, embodying all the arcana.

Theatre Set-Up presented seasons of the play three times after the research on the secret meanings was begun; in 1983, when only alchemy and the Celtic Old World religion had been investigated (see figs 2 and 40), and in 1995 (see fig. 29) and 2000 (see figs 38 and 39), when the research into arcana (apart from an understanding and application of the Cabala) had been completed. All these productions depended upon the research into the arcana of the play for the thrust of its 'inner line', and found that illogicalities of characterisation and stage action were solved by an understanding of the arcane meanings which were sometimes used as a basis of characterisation. For example:

- The actresses performing the role of Helena could accept the character's plea to Demetrius to use her as his dog (II. i. 202-207) by understanding that the 'soul' of the alchemical process was often symbolised as a dog and, in the alchemical interpretation of the role of Demetrius as the 'body' of the process in the play, she pursues Demetrius into the woods as the 'soul' follows the 'body'.
- The actors performing the roles of Hermia, Helena, Lysander and Demetrius found the changes of love-partnerships within the play acceptable when the metaphorical significance of their roles indicated by analysis of their names gave them the alchemical function of the four elements, changed in their combinations as indicated by Ripley in his *Compound of Alchymie* as a symbolic turning of a wheel in order to create alchemic change (see figs 6 and 39).
- Following my further research, the actors of these same roles in the 1995 production enjoyed the Renaissance Platonic levels of interpretation of their characters reflecting Divine Love and its conditions and trials.

CHAPTER TEN

- Through the Celtic readings of the play, the role of Puck was freed from its usual misinterpretation as a youthful elf and given its Celtic characteristic as a hobgoblin, older and more gnarled than an elf (see fig. 38).

The play is so extraordinary in its characters and plot, so distant from the psychological reality of everyday life, with the participation of supernatural beings, that directors often find it necessary to find an inspiration for the 'inner line' of the production outside the script, with a resultant distortion of characterisation. Theatre Set-Up found that the arcana deepened understanding of the characters in the play for the actors, who thus felt confident in the performance of their roles irrespective of the period in which the production was set, so that contrasting production styles became possible.

Theatre Set-Up productions of *A Midsummer Night's Dream*

In 1983, the production visually realised alchemical aspects of the play, the four lovers dressed in colours representing them as elements, white for Hermia as air, red for Helena as fire, blue for Lysander as water and green for Demetrius as earth. The stages of the alchemical process of the play were marked by the actor in the role of Puck changing covers on a central plinth (from black to white to red to gold –see fig. 2). Oberon and Titania were also costumed as Luna (the moon) and Sol (the sun) as their roles in the play influence the plot in the same way as the sun and moon were thought to condition the outcome of alchemical processes. Reflecting the Celtic elements in the play, the period selected for the style of the costumes, properties and movement of the play was that of the Celtic *Mabinogion*, of around the twelfth century AD. The actresses performing the roles of Helena and Hermia based their characterisations on their alchemical functions as elements (Helena being fiery and Hermia executing very light movements, especially during the lovers' quarrel, when she was swung onto Lysander's shoulder and became virtually airborne for much of the scene (see fig. 2).

The 1995 production was set in 1895, honouring the 100th anniversary of the National Trust, one of our main clients. The actors playing the four lovers benefited considerably in terms of the development of their characters and in the understanding of the play from the Renaissance Platonic interpretation of the different sections, mediated from Ficino's version of *The Symposium* by John Vyvyan. They held in their minds throughout the performances of the play that the two couples, Lysander and Hermia and Demetrius and Helena, were 'companion souls' ultimately destined to be together, the women remaining constant to their lovers through the trials in the woods, which tested their loyalty to them. Oberon, Titania, Puck (still a hobgoblin) and the attendant fairies were presented as nature spirits (see fig. 29).

For the 2000 production we selected the period of ancient Athens, corresponding to the world of Greek legend within which Shakespeare sets the play, in sunrise-coloured costumes to mark the dawn of a new millennium. Also in celebration of the millennium, we included songs from the musical written for the students of Southgate College in 1971 by Terry Hawes, which he called *To the Woods*. This music had nothing to do with the arcana of the play, but enhanced its lyrical and fun qualities. In spite of this, a number of the actors had been in previous Theatre Set-Up productions, so were familiar with the arcana and enjoyed their application to *A Midsummer Night's Dream*. It was a very smooth season, our knowledge of the arcana providing us with leads to characterisation and understanding of the text.

One of the questions the play poses is the undetermined physical relationship between the transformed Bottom and the drugged Titania. Is it Shakespeare's intention that her love for him is consummated? The research suggested an answer to that and a hint of one of Shakespeare's deepest secrets (see Story Section 10).

By this time, audiences demanded that the story and its corresponding levels of meanings be presented in table form in the programme notes which I reproduce here. The story was interpreted in terms of these arcana:

- **Alchemy** (see above pp. 26-32)
- **The Celtic 'Old Religion'** (see above p. 58)
- **Christianity and Theurgy** (see above pp. 48, 59)
- **Renaissance Platonism** (see above p. 34)

In order to clarify the aspects of these arcana particular to *A Midsummer Night's Dream*, I gave descriptions of each of these secret meanings before the analysis of the different sections of the story, repeating material from Chapters One, Two and Three.

Alchemy (showing the features of Shakespeare's varied application of the philosophy in this play)

Alchemy was a practice wherein it was believed that due to a correspondence between all aspects of creation, transformation in a person's psyche and in the moral state of mankind could be effected by working with chemicals to transmute matter. A 'base matter' (sometimes called a toad, dragon, earth, whale, lead, snake, King or a serpent) would be processed by recombining its constituent elements (called 'turning the wheel of the elements') until its 'Divinity', its distilled quintessence (called the 'Philosophers' Stone' and considered to be synonymous with Christ) emerged, and could turn lead into gold (often symbolising humanity redeemed by Christ, or inspired by Divinity to goodness). This was sometimes known as 'finding the jewel in the brow of the toad'. The alchemy would be carried out in a hermetically-sealed vessel (called the 'vase of Hermes') which was placed in a furnace, and the application of different chemicals to the 'base matter' would separate (in the violent 'black' stage) its 'body' (in its dramatic form a man) from its 'soul' or 'spirit' (in its dramatic form a woman). The 'soul' would then 'ascend' to collect 'astral' influences from the 'heavens' (the top of the vessel) in the 'white' stage. The 'body' would be purged by being heated (in a 'trial by fire') and washed (in a 'trial by water') until it was fit to be reunited to its 'spirit' (in the 'red' stage). The resulting 'Philosophers' Stone' (a red-purple powder) was 'multiplied' and 'projected' onto lead to create the 'gold'.

The Celtic 'Old Religion'

Although *A Midsummer Night's Dream* is set in Athens, many of its features and characters are British. The fairies are British, characteristic of the 'Old Religion' which finds spirits in nature and in all aspects of domestic life. It continues to be practised now as a form of Paganism, the remnants of its domestic character still with us in 'Bless this House' pictorial invocations. When this play was written, in the time of Queen Elizabeth I, belief in the supernatural was prevalent and not considered to be incompatible with Christianity.

Christianity, Initiation and Theurgy

Orthodox Christianity informs the moral outcome of the play in spite of the ancient Greek setting, New Testament precepts of mercy causing Theseus to overrule the Athenian law dictating that Hermia should marry Demetrius, the man of her father's choice. However, the location of the woods subverts orthodoxy and presents its own mystic forces.

Theurgy and initiation takes neophytes into its mysteries, deep into the heart of a labyrinth, providing them with hierophants (spiritual guides), which lead them through trials, including an experience of a simulated death, until they are fit to have contact with the Divinity at the centre of the labyrinth. Initiation was practised by young neophytes (in this play the young lovers) and theurgy by older people (Titania and Bottom enacting this rite). In both traditions the participants return to the outer world as successful graduates, giving to others the benefits of their experience. Often theurgy has addressed the issue of the identity and function of Christ outside his role familiar to us in his incarnation as Jesus of Nazareth.[1]

Story Section 1 (I. i. 1-127)

Duke Theseus of Athens has led a war against the Amazonian warrior-women, defeated them, taken captive their Queen Hippolyta, with whom he subsequently has fallen in love, and whom he is to marry in four days' time. To his court comes Egeus, demanding the Duke support him in implementing a law of Athens that condemns a girl to death or to single life if she does not marry the man of her father's choice. Egeus insists that his daughter Hermia should not marry the man she loves, Lysander, but another Athenian, Demetrius, although he was previously betrothed to Hermia's friend, Helena. Lysander accuses Demetrius of a false courtship of Hermia, and calls him a 'spotted and inconstant man' (I. i. 110). Duke Theseus is obliged to uphold the law in supporting Egeus, and allows Hermia the time until his own wedding to decide whether she will marry Demetrius, be executed, or become a nun.

CHAPTER TEN

Alchemy
Theseus and Hippolyta present in their own situation a successfully completed cycle of alchemy. The male-female polarity which alchemists thought necessary to provide the process with energy is symbolised by the violence of the war that has occurred between them, and their marriage represents an evolved harmonious balance of polarities. The poise that Theseus exhibits throughout the play derives from his having survived all the trials that he has suffered.

The alchemy represented in the allegory of this play does not, as in many other of Shakespeare's plays, incorporate the rigid system of Ripley's twelve-stage process but is certainly divided into four stages (as signified by the Theatre Set-Up 1983 stage production). Separate alchemic processes are experienced by Hermia, Demetrius, and Bottom combined with Titania, these all being contained within the frame of an implied cycle of alchemy successfully completed by Theseus and Hippolyta before the play opens.

A new alchemical process is begun with the case brought by Egeus against his daughter Hermia. Greek sources of the names of the lovers indicate their significance as the elements of which the substance, the 'base matter' of alchemy, consists:

- Air in Hermia (the female form of Hermes – the Greek god-equivalent of Mercury, whose element was air);
- Fire in Helen (derived from the Greek 'torch of reeds');
- Water as in Lysander (from the Greek term designating liquid 'chemical loosening', as in 'catalyst');
- Earth in Demetrius (son of Demeter, an earth goddess).[2]

They all have secondary symbolical alchemical functions: Demetrius as earth and the 'spotted and inconstant toad' is the 'base matter' which must be transformed; Helena will also become the furnace fire of the process; Lysander the cleansing water; and Hermia contains the alchemy within her situation (as in the 'vase of Hermes').

The Celtic 'Old Religion'
Theseus refers to the slow waning of the moon. He is waiting impatiently for the time of the new moon and his scheduled wedding. This is later applied

to Titania, whose function in the play suggests the moon (considered to be female by its varying monthly phases, reminiscent of women's monthly fertility cycle). She is disrupting nature by retaining the Indian boy in an allegorical full moon phase which wanes so long that the new moon cannot appear 'like to a silver bow new-bent in Heaven' (I. i. 9-10).

Christianity, Initiation and Theurgy.
Duke Theseus is bound by law to implement a harsh, primitive law which gives little scope for mercy. That he would like to be merciful to Hermia is indicated by his skilful ruse in contriving to leave her alone with her lover while he diverts Egeus and Demetrius (I. i. 123-126). Theseus himself would have undergone a mystery initiation, like all high-born Athenians, in the rites of Eleusis, and he presents us with a model of a graduate, an 'adept'.

Renaissance Platonism.
Hermia's allegiance to her love (in whom she recognises her companion soul) rather than to the law of Athens and filial duty is justified in the light of this philosophy. At the beginning of the play, we see two sets of possible companion souls, Hermia and Lysander and Helena and Demetrius. Demetrius either does not recognise his predestined partner or is just inconstant, and constancy is an important feature of this kind of love.

Story Section 2 (I. i. 128-25, I. ii.)

Left alone, the lovers Lysander and Hermia lament their fate but plot to escape the 'sharp Athenian law' (I. i. 152) that night by eloping through the woods beyond Athens to start a new life in the country with Lysander's rich widowed aunt, who regards him as her only son. They tell their plans to the jilted Helena, who resolves to alert Demetrius so that she may have an excuse to see him again and even gain some gratitude from him.

Meanwhile, a group of workmen, Quince, Snug, Flute, Starveling and Bottom, meet to plan the performance of a play, *Pyramus and Thisbe,* which they intend to offer to Theseus and Hippolyta as entertainment after their wedding feast.

Alchemy
By jilting Helena, Demetrius has initiated the first 'turn of the wheel', in which each element is turned into the other in order to perfect them.

Lysander and Hermia's elopement sets this up, and Helena puts this into motion by her planned pursuit of Demetrius, who pursues Lysander, who in turn seeks to marry Hermia. Thus the sequence occurs of fire-earth-water-air.

Shakespeare sometimes laughs at or even subverts the structures he creates, with the workmen's planned theatrical production of *Pyramus and Thisbe* a parody of his own alchemical theme.

The Celtic 'Old Religion'

In planning to escape to the woods, the lovers put themselves into the power of the nature spirits located there. In the city human laws prevail, but in regions of untamed nature such as the woods, undisturbed spirits hold sway. The workmen will also enter this magical sphere.

Christianity, Initiation and Theurgy

Hermia adopts a Christian sense of martyrdom in facing the trial of her love for Lysander, 'Then let us teach our trial patience | Because it is a customary cross' (I. i. 152-153).

Woods and forests can be paradigms for labyrinths of initiation and theurgy. In these scenes, the lovers are set to enter the labyrinth of the woods as neophytes of initiation. Helena's action in betraying Hermia and Lysander to Demetrius becomes less shameful and illogical in this context, as she, and particularly Demetrius (whose inconstancy in love and selfish pursuit of Hermia demonstrates his need to be transformed), will also become neophytes.

The lovers and the workmen prepare to enter the labyrinth of the woods. It is Shakespeare's skill to prepare to involve them in a metaphor of the deepest secret of theurgy in Bottom's interface with the fairy world.

Renaissance Platonism

In this philosophy it was believed that the mortal body could disguise the soul so that soul companions did not always recognise each other in their earthly forms. 'Love-sight' (now termed 'falling in love'), which Platonism considered to be the recognition of one's companion soul, was presumed to pierce the earthly disguise of the loved one's true identity.

There is a necessary link between self-knowledge and love, and so we may readily understand the Shakespearean-Platonic idea that constancy to the loved one is dependent upon self-knowledge. But this is far from easy, and therefore, as Hermia says to Lysander, 'The course of true love never did run smooth' (I. i. 134). The tests of constancy have begun before the action of the play begins. Helena defines the nature of love as she understands it: that it looks with a 'mind' that does not respond to the real evidence of the senses, thus Demetrius, now loving Hermia, does not perceive, as other people do, that she is as beautiful as Hermia.

Story Section 3 (II. i. 1-145)
In the woods where Hermia and Lysander will meet to elope, another conflict is revealed. The King and Queen of the fairies, Oberon and Titania, are disrupting nature itself by causing unseasonable weather in their quarrel over the possession of an Indian changeling boy. They confront each other in the woods, Titania refusing to give the boy up to Oberon to be his henchman, and they taunt each other with their respective infidelities.

Alchemy
All wishing to find the 'Philosophers' Stone' had to enter a labyrinth, which could be a dark abyss, often either the depths of the sea or a forest. The legend of Duke Theseus relates that in addition to his successful escape from the Minotaur in a labyrinth, he made an initiatory journey to the depths of the ocean, where he was rescued from a rock onto which he had grown. Here the abyss is the woods. All things in alchemy took place in the natural orbits of 'Sol', the sun, and 'Luna', the moon, here represented by Oberon and Titania. The Philosophers' Stone was sometimes referred to as an orphan, often black, hence the demand for the Indian boy, desired by the opposing parties, as the goal of alchemy.

The Celtic 'Old Religion'
The essence of the 'Old Religion' is captured in the persons of Oberon and Titania and their situation. The events of the play take place on May Day Eve, the Celtic 'Beltane', sacred to a female deity in her 'bright aspect' as mistress of wild creatures, and a male deity as 'Lord of the Forest' (these appear in our culture as 'Queen of the May' and 'The Green Man'). They are, as British fairies, heroic, trooping fairies, possibly descended from gods, and are statuesque, amorous and vengeful, with power to manipulate

nature and give fertility to mortals (with whom they have love affairs – see fig. 29).
Christianity, Initiation and Theurgy
In the labyrinth of the woods, the forces of nature that will be the unseen guides of the mortals are revealed. Oberon will take the lead as hierophant-guide and Titania as the female embodiment of nature.
Renaissance Platonism
We see the kind of disturbance in cosmic order that occurs when companion souls of the order of Oberon and Titania are in conflict.

Story Section 4 (II. i. 146-187)
When Titania leaves, Oberon plans revenge and commands his servant, Puck (sometimes called Robin Goodfellow) to fetch a white pansy flower whose purple centre is a wound made by Cupid's arrow and which contains the essence of love. The juice of this flower, applied on anyone's sleeping eyelids, will make them 'madly dote' (I. i. 171) on the 'next live creature' (I. i. 172) that is seen. Oberon challenges Puck to fetch the herb before a whale can travel a league. Puck responds with the promise that he will circle the earth in forty minutes. Oberon plots to humiliate and subjugate Titania by using this flower-juice to cause her to fall in love with something vile, and, while she is in this trance, to obtain the Indian boy.

Alchemy
The love-potion, the white flower stained 'purple with love's wound' (II. i.167) which Oberon is planning to use will have the effect of the transforming chemical 'vitriol' (often symbolised as a green lion). Oberon is using it to sexually separate his wife Titania from himself, thus initiating another alchemical process which will result in his achievement of the 'Philosophers' Stone' as the Indian boy.

The colour-change of the flower from white to purple is alchemically significant, representing alchemy's progress from the white stage to the red-purple. The whale is also an alchemical symbol, representing base matter.
The Celtic 'Old Religion'
Here we see Puck demonstrating some of his mythical powers, in contrast to his more domestic aspect as Robin Goodfellow, revealed earlier in the

same scene. Puck, which means 'fairy' or 'devil', is an old earth deity in Celtic legendry, and as Robin Goodfellow, a 'hobgoblin' fairy, a guardian spirit of the home, (sweeping 'the dust behind the door' (V. i. 375). Lewis Spence relates in *British Fairy Origins: The Genesis and Development of Fairy Legends in British Tradition* how the ancestors of fairies such as Puck were rough and hairy. This gave us in Theatre Set-Up the justification for presenting him as a nuggety earth-creature in our productions (see fig. 38). Thiselton Dyer in *Folklore of Shakespeare* points out that as 'Puki' or 'Puk' the name still survives as a domestic spirit in Iceland, Friesland and Jutland. In England, the mischievous nature of Puck survives in the 'poake' of Worcestershire and in the 'pixie' of Devon, Cornwall and Hampshire. In Wales, a version of the name appears as 'Pwcca' (pp. 5, 6). He is capable of shape-changing himself and others, often into horses, is mischievous, and misleads travellers.

The potent and vengeful nature of Oberon is demonstrated. These are characteristics of supernatural beings featured in Celtic mythology, such as banshees and the spirits of the Tuatha De` Danann, which needed to be propitiated to prevent them causing harm to mortals who might have offended them.[3]

Christianity, Initiation and Theurgy
Oberon unwittingly initiates, in his plan for revenge, Titania's participation in a wider issue reflecting the core belief linking Christ with Western theurgy.

Renaissance Platonism
Constancy tests are also unwittingly set up for the lovers by Oberon through what will become Puck's misuse of Cupid's flower.

Story Section 5 (II. i. 188-268)
Demetrius enters the woods pursued by the infatuated Helena, whom he brusquely rejects. She throws off his insults, telling him that she is prepared to be his 'spaniel' in following him. He escapes from her, leaving her alone. Oberon has seen this event and, sympathetic to Helena, decides to use the love-potion to make Demetrius fall in love with her. When Puck returns with the flower, Oberon, unaware that there is more than one couple in the woods, commands him to put some of the flower's love-juice on the

eyes of an Athenian whom he has seen in the woods and who is loved by a sweet lady whom he disdains.

Alchemy

The 'soul' of the 'base matter' of alchemy was often symbolised as a dog. When Demetrius, as 'body' of the base matter which must be alchemically transformed, enters the wood, his 'soul', Helena, is following him. This she indicates in 'I am your spaniel' (II. i. 203). When Demetrius casts her from him he is separating himself from his 'soul', and thus initiating his alchemical process. By not giving Puck sufficiently precise instructions in the dispensing of the love-potion, Oberon unwittingly sets up another alchemical process which will have an unfortunate effect upon Hermia.

The Celtic 'Old Religion'

The mischief that could be done with misapplied love-potions had a firm place in Celtic legendry, as in the story of Tristan and Isolde when a love-potion, intended for another purpose, was drunk by the protagonists, and thus the tragedy of Tristan and Isolde's illicit love began.

Christianity, Initiation and Theurgy

Oberon takes his place as the guide-hierophant of the lovers who have entered the labyrinth. That there is an even higher power involved who is directing the action is indicated by Oberon's unawareness of the second couple in the woods. This indirectly leads to the wrongful anointing of Lysander's eyes, which in turn leads to the trials that the lovers undergo and their ultimate improvement.

Renaissance Platonism

If Demetrius is indeed her soul companion, Helena is justified in pursuing him into the woods. She reinforces this idea with the statement that to her he is all the world, an echo of the Platonic concept of the microcosm (a person) linked to the macrocosm of Divinity through love. For the situation between them to be redeemed, Demetrius will need to recognise her as his soul's companion. The love-juice from Cupid's flower will be able to effect that.

The inadequate directions given to Puck will cause him to misapply the love-juice, initiating action that will also test the love of Lysander and Hermia.

Story Section 6 (II. ii.)

Titania lies on her bed of flowers wrapped in a snake-skin. Her attendants sing her to sleep with a lullaby, which prohibits snakes, hedgehogs, newts, blind-worms, spiders, beetles, worms and snails from coming near her.[4] The chorus of this song enjoins Philomel as a nightingale to sing with them. She was the mythic character in Ovid's *Metamorphoses* transformed into a bird after being raped and mutilated by Tereus, her sister's husband.[5]

Oberon puts the love-potion on Titania's eyes as she sleeps on her customary flowery bank. Lysander and Hermia, lost in the woods, enter this arena and decide to rest for the night. Hermia insists that modesty dictates that Lysander 'lie farther off' (II. ii. 56) from her. Puck, searching through the forest for the Athenian youth whose eyes he must anoint with the love-potion, sees Lysander with Hermia, seemingly rejected, sleeping at a distance from him. Mistaking him for Demetrius, he anoints his eyes.

Helena enters in pursuit of Demetrius, who casts her off, leaving her alone in the dangerous woods. She discovers the sleeping Lysander and wakes him up. The love-potion takes effect and he declares undying love to her, and she naturally thinks that he is mocking her. He pursues her as she escapes from him, leaving the sleeping Hermia alone. Hermia awakes, terrified by a dream in which a serpent eats her heart out while Lysander watches smiling. She discovers that he has gone and leaves, looking for him.

Alchemy

The Titania-Oberon alchemy is begun with Titania as the 'base matter' suggested by the snake-skin in which she is wrapped, the snakes that are commanded to keep away from her as she sleeps, and the reference to the transmuted Philomel. There is a more sinister reference in the use of the name of Philomel in the lullaby. Oberon is about to enact a species of abuse upon his wife, akin to that of Tereus upon Philomel, but the effect will be beneficial. This imitates the process of alchemy, which incorporates violence to effect ultimate good.

Puck now inadvertently initiates a reverse turn of the wheel of the alchemical elements in causing Lysander to fall in love with Helena. Lysander, referring to her fairness, calls her a 'dove' and the darker Hermia a 'raven'. These terms also symbolised the white and black stages of alchemy. Thus, when he says, 'Who will not change a raven for a dove?' (II. ii. 113) this chemical progression is implied. In the separation of Hermia from Lysander, she enters an alchemical process, the black stage. That she is the base matter, the 'body' of the process, is indicated by her dream of the serpent eating her heart. Lysander will later refer to this when he threatens to shake her from him, 'like a serpent' (III. ii. 261).

The Celtic 'Old Religion'

Oberon is seen to take malicious but not harmful revenge on Titania. He functions as a benevolent nature-spirit in his wish to assist Helena. In the wrong application of the love-potion, the mischievous nature-spirit Puck makes a characteristic mistake which, although unintentional, he later relishes for the amusement it gives him.

Christianity, Initiation and Theurgy

Lysander and Hermia are lost within the labyrinth. Puck as the instrument of Oberon also functions as a guide. He will create the trials and then resolve them. Hermia enters the nadir of her initiation. Before this she had Lysander's support, but now she must face solitude.

Renaissance Platonism

From Lysander's reaction to Helena when he wakes up under the spell of the love-potion on his eyes, we understand its properties. It gives him the instant power to perceive Helena's inner Divinity: 'Transparent Helena, nature shows art | That through thy bosom makes me see thy heart' (II. ii. 103-104). As Vyvyan puts it, 'what has been revealed is a shimmer of divinity like sunlight under water' (p. 86). The drug thus short-cuts the usual hard work the soul has to put in to acquire this ability.

Story Section 7 (III. i.)

The workmen meet in the woods to rehearse their play. Puck discovers them, and, noticing that they are near the sleeping Titania, uses his power to transform the leading actor, Bottom, giving him an ass's head. This terrifies his fellow actors so that they flee, Puck in pursuit.

Titania awakes and falls in love with the transformed Bottom, declares her love to him, and, with her attendant fairies, leads him to her bower.

Alchemy

Puck makes Bottom enter the alchemy of the play. The name 'Bottom' often indicated the bottom rung of a ladder, which represents a scale, grading metals and their associated planets from lead (associated with the Greek god Saturn at whose revels, called Saturnalias, asses' heads were worn), to gold and, by association, to the sun. As 'lead', Bottom is also the base-matter of an alchemical process. Titania, in hoping to 'purge his mortal grossness' (III. i. 153), seems to quote directly from George Ripley's *Compound of Alchymie*.

Puck, leading (and misleading) the mortals through the woods, applying the love-potion and its antidote to their eyes and effecting Bottom's transformations, functions as the agent of alchemy, Mercury. In the psychological aspect of alchemy, he is the 'psychopomp', leading the souls through their Hell, like Virgil in Dante's *Inferno*.

The Celtic 'Old Religion'

Puck exercises his shape-changing power in transforming Bottom and himself, and takes delight in his mischief-making. He characteristically misleads the workmen through the woods. The shape of ass and man combined given to Bottom was not extraordinary within Celtic lore, which enjoyed the idea of mixed creatures and species, reflected in many of their artefacts.[6]

In an understanding of a more mundane aspect of Celtic lore, Bottom instantly recognises Titania's attendant fairies as British herbal medicines. Bottom's greetings to Peaseblossom and Mustardseed refer to the Elizabethan medicinal uses of the pea and mustard plants. He suggests making use of Cobweb as bandaging for a small cut, but he tactfully does not refer to Moth in this context as the medicinal uses of moths required their deaths.[7]

Christianity, Initiation and Theurgy

A parody of trials in the labyrinth is presented by Puck's mischievous pursuit of the workmen. Bottom shows that he is equal to anything, being totally unfazed by his inclusion in the fairy world. He enters his extraordinary role with aplomb.

Renaissance Platonism

Titania's reaction to the love potion is as extreme as Lysander's, and she instantly perceives, through the 'mortal grossness' that she later identifies in Bottom, the 'virtue' that is his divine essence: 'And thy fair virtue's force doth move me | On the first view to say, to swear, I love thee' (III. i. 135-136).

Story Section 8 (III. ii. 1-344)
The triumphant Puck boasts to Oberon of his success in both causing Titania to fall in love 'with a monster' (III. ii. 6) and in anointing the Athenian's eyes. However, his mistaking of Lysander for Demetrius is made obvious by the entry of Hermia, attacking Demetrius for the supposed murder of her lover Lysander, who she cannot believe would otherwise have left her alone in the woods. Puck is unrepentant for his mistake, blaming fate.

Hermia leaves the hated Demetrius, who decides to remain and sleep. Oberon anoints his eyes with the love-potion and commands Puck to find Helena. Puck succeeds in bringing her into the scene, pursued by the adoring Lysander, and Demetrius wakes and falls in love with her. Hermia enters in pursuit of Lysander and a violent quarrel between the four lovers ensues.

Alchemy
The reverse turn of the 'wheel of the elements' is achieved when Lysander enters in pursuit of Demetrius, who is caused to fall in love with Helen, and then Hermia enters in pursuit of Lysander. Thus a contrary circle rotates: air-water-earth-fire (see fig. 39). The process of alchemy was often referred to as 'the squared circle', beginning in a circle of chaos, forming into a triangle, and, after fire has been at its greatest heat, resolving into a perfect square. This can be seen in the pattern of the lovers' changing affections and their subsequent quarrel. As the 'bodies' are tried and tested in this conflict, the white stage is achieved. Words spoken in the scene which are symbols used in alchemy include 'serpent' (III. ii. 261) and 'crow' (III. ii. 142), indicating the alchemical content of the scene.

The Celtic 'Old Religion'
Puck demonstrates his traditional mischievous character in his description of his transformation of Bottom and his pursuit of the mechanicals through the woods. His enjoyment of the results of mistaking Lysander

for Demetrius is also appropriate within this tradition. Oberon persists in his intention to do good to the mortals and bring them within his beneficent power.

Christianity, Initiation and Theurgy

The lovers are in the nadir of their trials in the labyrinth, psychologically isolated from each other by a separate anguish. Oberon acts as benevolent guide, ensuring that they come to no harm. Puck functions more as a hierophant, creating the trials which test them before he leads them out of the labyrinth.

Renaissance Platonism

The lovers' conflict is an example of the kinds of confusion that result from the illusory pursuit of the wrong soul companions. This illusion is given a location and habitation, by the moonlit wood. The association with the planet Venus recalls the importance of her influence in Platonic Love.

Story Section 9 (III. ii. 345 - 463, IV. i. 1-101)

Oberon commands Puck to create an illusion so that Lysander and Demetrius do not kill each other in their fighting, then to cause all the lovers to sleep and to place the juice of Dian's bud, the herb which is the antidote to the love-potion, on Lysander's eyes so that he loves Hermia again. Puck warns Oberon that this must be done in haste as dawn, which signals the time that all spirits must return to their dwelling-places, is imminent. He refers to ghosts returning to their abodes and the damned, who, meriting punishment beyond the grave, are buried in liminal, threshold locations in water and at crossroads. However, Oberon reminds Puck that they, as benevolent spirits, welcome the dawn. After creating a fog to confuse the lovers, Puck leads in the two men to exhausted sleep, brings in the two women, who also fall asleep within sight of their rightful lovers, removes the effects of the love-potion from Lysander's eyes and blesses the two couples.

Titania and her attendant fairies are seen tending Bottom in his transmuted ass's head. The fairy queen is sleeping with him in her arms when Oberon enters. He, now ready to restore Titania to her former state as she has surrendered the Indian boy to him, puts the Dian's bud on Titania's eyes. She wakes and is reconciled with Oberon as they dance together. Puck is ordered to remove the ass's head from Bottom.

Alchemy

Hermia, hitherto the pivot of both men's affections, has been subjected to the reverse experience, yet in spite of the unpleasantness of this, she remains loyal to Lysander, wishing, as she joins the other sleeping lovers gathered in by Puck, 'Heaven shield Lysander if they mean a fray' (III. ii. 447). Thus, allegorically as the 'serpent', the base matter of a process of alchemy relating to her, she emerges from her trials redeemed and successful when Dian's bud restores Lysander to her.

Three symbolic marriages or unions of materials of opposite nature are claimed to take place in alchemy. One of these is the marriage of the four elements (which will take place at the end of the play); the second is of the 'body' with the 'soul' and the 'spirit' (also represented by the lovers' marriages); but the third, between male and female principles (represented by the pairs of lovers, by Theseus and Hippolyta and by Oberon and Titania) must take place in the correct sequence of stages, in the middle of the process. It is out of the question for the mortal lovers to enact any union before their weddings at the end of the play, as Shakespeare upholds the idea of chaste love in his plays and Oberon has divorced himself from Titania's bed, so Shakespeare has arranged an extraordinary 'alchemical marriage', or '**Coniunctio**', between Titania (the spirit of the alchemical processes of the play) and Bottom (signifying its base matter). This is also part of the alchemy that achieves Oberon's goal of the Indian boy as the Philosophers' Stone. The **Coniunctio** that takes place in this play represents a true picture of the union of opposites that alchemy likes to effect in this stage of the process with the contrasting natures of Titania and Bottom. The union marks the turning point of the action, satisfying Oberon so that he obtains the Indian boy, and thus ending the nature-disturbing quarrel between him and Titania, and turning their combined benign attentions towards the pairs of lovers.

The Celtic 'Old Religion'

Oberon persists in his intention to do good to the mortals and bring them within his beneficent power. He and Puck define this benevolence in terms of their ability to remain in the light of day while other tormented ghosts and evil spirits must return to their graves as dawn appears, in the way demonstrated in another of Shakespeare's plays by the unshriven ghost of

Hamlet's father (*Hamlet,* I. v. 89, 90). Puck reveals his ability to control the weather in creating the fog that diffuses the lovers' quarrel. He quotes British country proverbs which describe happy resolutions:

> And the country proverb known,
> That every man should take his own,
> In your waking shall be shown
> Jack shall have Jill,
> Nought shall go ill;
> The man shall have his mare again, and all shall be well. (III. ii. 458-463).

The diminutive aspect of the fairies attendant on Titania is thought to be Shakespeare's own invention, and a contribution that he made with this play to the traditions of British lore. The dances that Titania performs with her fairies and with Oberon when they are reconciled signify social cohesion and unity with nature (IV. i. 84). Puck's observation that damned spirits are buried in locations which Celtic tradition considered to be thresholds between this and the spirit worlds, like waterways and crossroads, brings resonances of Celtic mythology where encounters took place between humans and spirits at such places. For example, the Celtic triple goddess the Morrigan, in her threatening aspect as a hag, challenged Cuchulain at a ford (see above p. 54).

Christianity, Initiation and Theurgy
Oberon as hierophant takes control of the lovers so that they come to no harm. It is dangerous to enter the labyrinth without a benevolent guide. The essential movements of initiation, leading the neophyte into the labyrinth and then out again to take the benefits to the world, are signified in this scene by Oberon's instructions to Puck to resolve the conflicts so that the lovers can return, restored, to Athens. Puck also refers to this, citing the homely country proverb in his casting of his final benevolent spell upon the lovers.

When Titania is released from the spell put upon her, she is able to add her power to Oberon's in giving benediction.

Renaissance Platonism. The antidote to the love-potion destroys the illusions that have separated the lovers and Titania from true perceptions of their soul companions.

CHAPTER TEN

Story Section 10 (IV. i. 101-199, IV. i. 199-217, IV. ii.)
As dawn breaks, Duke Theseus, Hippolyta and Egeus enter on a hunting trip. They see and wake the two sets of sleeping lovers, Lysander with Hermia, and Demetrius with Helena (see fig. 2). The angered Egeus threatens revenge on Lysander, but Demetrius confesses that his love has returned to Helena and the Duke declares a general amnesty, suggesting a triple wedding: 'Three and three | We'll hold a feast in great solemnity' (IV. i. 183-184). He leaves the four lovers to gather their senses, scarcely able to comprehend their changed circumstances, or how they came to be together, so happily paired, in the woods at dawn. Helena rejoices in the return of Demetrius's love for her, 'And I have found Demetrius like a jewel | Mine own, and not mine own' (IV. i. 190-191).

Bottom awakes, remembering his sojourn among the fairies as a dream. His memories of himself with an ass's head are confused:

> Methought I was – there is no man can tell what. Methought I was – and methought I had – but man is but a patched fool if he will offer to say what methought I had (IV. i. 206-209 – see fig. 40).

He decides to suggest to Peter Quince that his dream be performed as a ballad called 'Bottom's Dream', which he could sing as part of the wedding celebrations, but when he re-joins his fellows he is unable to tell them about his 'dream'. They prepare to perform their offering of *Pyramus and Thisbe* after the triple wedding feast.

Alchemy

Harmony is achieved in the alchemical red stage of the rosy dawn as the marriage of the elements, air (Hermia) with water (Lysander), and fire (Helena) with earth (Demetrius) is achieved. Ripley's three alchemical marriages (see above pp. 27-29) are symbolised in the triple wedding which Theseus proposes. Helena refers to the alchemical transformation of Demetrius in referring to him as a 'jewel' like that which is extracted from the transmuted toad (a symbol of 'base matter').[8]

Bottom's memory of his participation in the Oberon-Titania alchemy remains as a dream.

The Celtic 'Old Religion'
Three is the most magical Celtic number. Shakespeare's use of a three-motif always indicates an intended magic. This occurs as the three couples share the reconciliation that comes with the dawn.

Christianity, Initiation and Theurgy
The lovers, as initiates, emerge from the labyrinth in harmony with each other and improved. The events in the woods have managed to subvert the primitive Athenian law so that Theseus can implement mercy. The Christian Trinity is echoed in the proposed triple wedding.

In remembering his experience in the woods, Bottom misquotes a Biblical quotation from I Corinthians 2.9., which is, in the Geneva-Tomson Bible:

> The things which eye hath not seene, neither eare hath heard, neither came into man's Heart, are, which God hath prepared for them that love him.

as:
> The eye of man hath not heard, the ear of man hath not seen, man's hand is not able to taste, his tongue to conceive nor his heart to report (IV. i. 209-212 - see fig. 40).

In its context in Corinthians, this passage discusses the hidden wisdom of God, stating that God prepares things only revealed by His spirit for those that love Him and imperceptible to human eyes, ears and heart. Reference is also made to the preordination of Christ's incarnation in order to redeem mankind. This is glossed as a mysterie, 'Hid Wisdom', described in I Corinthians 2. 7, 8. as:

> 7. But we speake the wisedom of God in a mysterie, even the hid wisedom, which God
>   Had determined before the world, unto our glory.
> 8. Which none of the princes of this world hath knowen: for had they knowen it, they
>   Would not have crucified the Lord of Glory.

In all initiation and theurgy, whether practised by initiates in the ancient Greek rites of Eleusis, by Aborigines in the centre of Australia, or by followers of the mystery traditions of Britain, the Divinity hidden in the centre of the labyrinth is the same: the 'sun-word', identified in Christianity as Jesus. Before the incarnation of Christ as Jesus of Nazareth, initiates always had to undergo a three-day trance-sleep before they were able to have contact with the Divine. Theurgists claim that in the three days between Christ's crucifixion and resurrection he entered the depths of nature and overcame a female force.[9] This action had such an effect that after that time the three-day trance was no longer necessary for initiates.[10] In orthodox Christianity, Christ is said during the three days to have conquered death. Perhaps this event is secretly referred to in the extraordinary interaction between Titania and Bottom, whose ass's head is reminiscent of the ass Christ rode into Jerusalem.

Deborah Baker Wyrick, in 'The Ass Motif in *The Comedy of Errors* and *A Midsummer Night's Dream*', implies that this kind of association of the ass motif with Bottom is valid, as asses in the Bible are 'benign, even exemplary'. She gives an example of the Biblical Balaam's ass in Numbers 22, who was granted a sight of an angel, was made a channel of communication for God, and sustained persecution for righteous action, which precipitated God's reproach and redeemed her master from sin. The ass can thus be regarded as a symbol of wisdom and suffering, characteristics which I consider it would not be blasphemous to attribute to an analogue of Christ. In fact, Wyrick refers to the identification of the ass in the *Folie* of Erasmus with the kind of holy fool that Christ is said to have loved, to the extent that by the end of his book, Erasmus is identifying Christ himself with this holy fool. Wyrick regards Bottom as the epitome of the play's Ovidian metamorphoses, his wish for the transformation within dramatic roles fulfilled in his transformation as part ass, and lover of the Queen of the fairies, more than he could have hoped for. [11]

Renaissance Platonism
Harmony is seen to prevail as, in the dawn of a new day, the lovers wake to find 'their vision restored'.[12] Vyvyan records the Platonic principle: 'When the true beauty is rightly apprehended, concord comes to the world' (Vyvyan pp. 89-90).

CELTIC, MAGIC, THEURGY

Story Section 11 (V. i. 1-355)
Theseus and Hippolyta discuss the strange experiences in the woods which the lovers have recounted. Theseus doubts the truth of the accounts, as he considers that lovers, like madmen and poets, have 'such seething brains' (V. i. 4) that their imaginations create fantasies. He observes that imagination has such power that it can actualise thoughts:

> And as imagination bodies forth
> The forms of things unknown, the poet's pen
> Turns them to shapes and gives to airy nothing
> A local habitation and a name. (V. i. 14-20)

Not only does this passage express the cynicism of those denying the existence of the kinds of spiritual arcana that I claim Shakespeare adumbrates in his plays, but it expounds the principle of the power of drama to activate the imagination of audiences so that they can supply details such as locations of the action, a belief that the actors performing the play are the characters they are representing and a historic truthfulness of the action. Thus the reasoning of Theseus illuminates the real issue to be examined in looking at imagination, dreams and the world of the play, that is, the propensity of the dreamer/audience to be deluded by the dream/play.

The issue of what audiences will accept, and to what extent they will be prepared to exercise their imaginative faculties, is one which constantly teases theatre practitioners in determining exactly how they mount a production. It is one which always tested Theatre Set-Up. As the company had limited financial resources, with a need to perform and travel unencumbered by a surfeit of objects, we were always grateful to Shakespeare for creating scripts and a theatre convention, in which the material world is created by the script, 'bodied forth' by the imagination of the audience and thus allowing for a minimalist style of production. An example of this occurs in the opening lines of III. i. when Peter Quince is selecting a suitable rehearsal location:

> Pat, pat; and here's a marvellous convenient place for our rehearsal. This green plot shall

Be our stage, this hawthorn-brake our tiring house. (III. i. 2-3)

Time of day is indicated by the characters, for example Oberon says: 'Ill met by moonlight, proud Titania. (II. i. 60).
However, the workmen do not understand the extent to which the imaginative faculty of the audience can be exercised by words in the script alone, but are not deluded into thinking that the play is a reality, so that they find it necessary that Snug should identify himself as a person and not the lion he is representing in case he frightens the ladies in his audience:

Then know that I as Snug the joiner am
A lion fell, nor else no lion's dam;
For if I should as lion come in strife
Into this place, 'twere pity on my life. (V. i. 218-221)

They also do not scruple to break character to respond to audience comments. When Theseus comments that the wall, being able to speak, should curse Pyramus, Bottom interjects:

No, in truth sir, he should not. "Deceiving me" is Thisbe's cue: she is to enter now, and I
Am to spy her through the wall. You shall see it will fall pat as I told you: yonder she
Comes. (V. i. 182-185)

In the workmen's attempts at presenting the tragedy of *Pyramus and Thisbe,* Shakespeare presents a paradigm of the very opposite dramatic conventions to those he created in *A Midsummer Night's Dream* (that is, extending the imagination of the audience so that they can accept the reality of supernatural characters). In some senses, he anticipates Bertolt Brecht's alienation effect wherein the illusion of the reality is constantly destroyed in order to focus the attention of the audience on the issues raised by the play. He deconstructs the illusions he has created in previous scenes.
The story of *Pyramus and Thisbe*, in the opposition from their families to their marriage, partly follows that of Hermia and Lysander, but it has the

unhappy ending that Shakespeare avoided in this play and incorporated in *Romeo and Juliet*. In this version of the tale, the love of Pyramus and Thisbe for each other is forbidden by their fathers, whose adjoining properties are divided by a wall, which has a chink through which they whisper and plot to elope. Their plan to meet by moonshine at Ninus' tomb near to a mulberry tree turns to tragedy when a lion scares away Thisbe. In her flight, she drops her mantle, which the lion stains with his bloodied mouth. Pyramus, coming upon the scene, finds this mantle and, assuming that Thisbe has been killed, draws his sword and kills himself. Thisbe, returning to the scene, finds the body of Pyramus and stabs herself with his sword.

Alchemy
The triple weddings signal the achievement of the Philosophers' Stone. The story of *Pyramus and Thisbe* which the workmen perform in their interlude is itself an alchemical allegory from Ovid's *Metamorphoses*. The lion representing the 'green lion' (vitriol), the 'bloody mantle' and the blossom of the mulberry tree (which changes from white to red-purple as in the stages of alchemy), when drenched in the blood of the dying Pyramus, are all significant. Those who wrongfully practice alchemy, known as 'puffers', are represented by Flute, the 'bellows mender' in this parody of alchemy.

The Celtic 'Old Religion'
Bottom and his friends owe little in their style to Athens and much to those loyal artisans, subject to Queen Elizabeth, who made dramatic offerings to her on many royal progressions through her realm. When Theseus agrees to hear the workmen's play, he refers to the kinds of incidents she experienced on these occasions, and to her graciousness in her warm reception of the offerings regardless of their quality. A possible reference to Queen Elizabeth as 'fair vestal enthroned in the west' is made by Oberon earlier in the play (II. i. 158).

Christianity, Initiation and Theurgy
Theseus is charitable in his reception of the workmen's offering. However, this is not sustained and seems hypocritical in the light of his rude and patronising comments during their performance, unsuitable for a graduate initiate. The same applies to the male lovers.

Perhaps this rudeness is caused by ebullience, as all of the mortals are experiencing the benefits of the end of their trials.
Renaissance Platonism
In this play within the play, another pair of star-crossed lovers are seen to be constant to each other. Like the lovers in *Romeo and Juliet* which Shakespeare also wrote at about this time (1595 or 1596), the disguise that the lovers must overcome to perceive their soul companions is the rivalry between their families, symbolised by the wall.

Story Section 12 (V. i. 357-408)

After the mechanicals' play, the three couples retire. Puck, Titania and Oberon enter to bless them and their issue. Puck precedes his master with an invocation to the night:

> Now the hungry lion roars
> And the wolf behowls the moon;
> Whilst the heavy ploughman snores,
> All with weary task fordone. (V. i. 357-360)

He describes their fairy participation in the night:
> And we fairies that do run
> By the triple Hecate's team
> From the presence of the sun,
> Following darkness like a dream,
> Now are frolic; (V i 369-373).

He relates his given role in the blessing:

> I am sent with broom before
> To sweep the dust behind the door (V. i. 375-376)

Oberon instructs his and Titania's attendants to distribute 'glimmering light' through the house as they sing and dance, bestowing blessings on the three couples. He reserves for himself and his wife the privilege of blessing the 'best bride-bed', of Theseus and Hippolyta, whose issue he claims will subsequently be fortunate (V. i. 389, 392). The subsequent children of all three couples, he decrees, will benefit from the fairies' blessing, being free of disabilities and disfiguring birth marks. A final blessing is bestowed on Theseus and his palace.

Alchemy
The stages of the **Multiplication** and **Projection** of the Philosophers' Stone are implied in the blessing of Oberon and Titania upon the three couples and their future children. The alchemy of the play ends here, its twelve stages implied but not followed exactly in the natural divisions of the play's story.

The Celtic 'Old Religion'
Oberon and Titania fulfil their function of blessing couples and bestowing fertility. They have, however, a sense of status. 'To the best bride bed will we' says Oberon, referring to that of Theseus and Hippolyta. Puck is seen in his domestic role, in which he is sent 'To sweep the dust behind the door'.

Christianity, Initiation and Theurgy
The forces of nature enter the realms of the mortals and continue their benediction into the future.

Renaissance Platonism
'Celestial' harmony is seen to be created 'by the constancy of love to its ideal', which has been achieved by all the couples (see Vyvyan, p. 90).

Story Section 13 (V. i. 409-422)
Puck craves the indulgence of the audience to accept the substance of the play as a dream. He pledges, in the name of honesty, and assuming that all escape 'the serpent's tongue', to make amends for any offence given by the players or fairies, and bids the audience goodnight.

Alchemy
The psychoanalyst Carl Jung observed the correlation between dreams of his patients and the images of alchemy which he thoroughly examined, finding the process of alchemy and all its terms to be that of 'psychological individuation' and hence imagination. He discovered that contemporaries

of Shakespeare had observed that functions of the psyche were 'projected' (like the 'shadows', the actors and fairies referred to by Puck) onto alchemical practice in this way.[13] In this play it seems that dreams, illusions of midsummer madness, imagination, poetry, theatre and the psyche are linked through the allegory of alchemy.

Puck implies, in his reference to the serpent's tongue, that the members of the audience have been subjected to the transmutations of alchemy through the catharsis of drama. This has been achieved without any effort on the part of the audience, and the benefits are thus achieved through 'unearned luck'.

The Celtic 'Old Religion'
The number 13 was of special significance to the Celts. It is at this point that Puck addresses the audience.

Christianity, Initiation and Theurgy
The play itself takes the audience into a labyrinth so that the audience undergoes a surrogate initiation. Puck now releases them back into the world outside the theatre.

Renaissance Platonism
Puck refers to the 'visions' of the 'shadows' (the actors and fairies), and implies that the audience must find its own truths beyond these illusions.

Cabala: Post Production (see fig. 3)

I see the Cabala as being applied in this play allegorically on the city of Athens and its environs in the woods as if they were a person, the characters elements of that person's psyche. There are three entrenched problems in the subconscious of this entity as **Yesod (Foundation, the subconscious containing traumas)**. Firstly, there is an unmerciful patristic law which demands that a woman must marry the man of her father's choice, or be executed or become a nun. Secondly, taking advantage of this and insisting on its implementation through Egeus, Hermia's father, who favours him, is Demetrius, a flawed young man who has rejected his erstwhile love, Helena, in favour of her friend Hermia, loving and loved by Lysander. Thirdly, there is conflict between the supernatural beings, the fairies, who influence nature and the well-being of the people of Athens and its environs.

These three flaws lack logic. The patristic, unmerciful law is barbaric and not appropriate to the enlightened Theseus, who is marrying his erstwhile enemy, Hippolyta. As Lysander points out, there is no reason why Egeus should prefer Demetrius to himself, as they are equal in all aspects except that Hermia loves him, Lysander. In addition, Demetrius has courted Helena, won her love and then rejected her, an act for which Theseus himself has intended to reprimand him, and yet pursues to the letter of the law his claim to Hermia's hand in marriage.

The conflict between the fairies, Titania and Oberon, is illogical. Titania refuses to yield a changeling Indian boy to Oberon. She justifies this stance by explaining that his mother who was a fellow votaress died during his birth and she has vowed to rear him in her stead. However, Oberon and Titania are a married couple and share common territory, within which the boy can belong to both of them. Also, it is time for Titania to allow the boy to leave her mothering female realm of influence and enter the more grown-up male sphere of Oberon. As Titania reports, this conflict between them is disrupting nature through unseasonable weather, creating 'rheumatic diseases' (II. i. 105) in humans. In terms of the Tree of Life, Titania should inhabit the supernal sphere of **Binah (Understanding, spiritual love)**, while Oberon should demonstrate **Chokmah (Wisdom, spiritual purpose)** so that they can carry out their benevolent spiritual roles on nature and people. Titania on the other hand is firmly engrossed in the emotions of **Netzach (Victory, feelings)** in her obsession with her mothering of the boy and opposition to Oberon, who is also engrossed by anger that Titania will not do as he wishes, which renders him also characterised by **Netzach**.

Lysander takes a logical step to escape the dire situation that he and Hermia are in by planning and executing an elopement away from Athens and its harsh law to stay in the house of a rich widowed aunt, where they can marry and live. In this act he moves towards **Hod (Glory, thoughts)**. Helena entrenches herself in **Netzach** in warning Demetrius of the elopement and following him into the woods as he pursues Hermia and Lysander. His actions in rejecting Helena after successfully wooing her, in seeking to obtain Hermia through her father and exposing her to the harsh law, and in his rudeness to Helena in the woods, demonstrate such character flaws grounded in the subconscious of **Yesod** that only a miracle will be able to clear them. This miracle will be implemented by Oberon.

Bottom, Peter Quince and their fellow workmen are firmly placed in **Malkuth (Kingdom, the material world experienced through the senses)** and comfortably remain there, but Bottom will make an unexpected journey up the Tree and back during the course of the play.

In losing his way through the woods, Lysander lacks the thoroughness of the logic of **Hod**, and as a result of Hermia's prudery, doubtless instilled into her subconscious in **Yesod** by her upbringing (so that she commands Lysander to lie further from her as they sleep), the couple fall victim to events in the woods, Lysander mistakenly caused by Puck to fall in love with Helena. Oberon also makes Demetrius fall in love with Helena using the miracle of the love-potion, and thus with both men in love with Helena instead of Hermia, there ensues fighting between them all which jettisons them all down to **Malkuth**, from which a journey up the Tree must commence in any case.

Puck functions on the Tree as a traveller on the paths between the spheres of the Tree without showing characteristics of any of them. He is part of the miracle-making of Oberon through use of the love-potion. His greatest achievement in this function is the match he makes between the drugged Titania and Bottom, with his ass's head. This projects Bottom into the supernal realm of the fairies, a transition he accomplishes with poise. Not quite fit to operate in the supernal spheres, however, I think that he descends with Titania to **Netzach**. When he is restored to his normal self and separated from Titania, the memory of his supernatural experience remains as a dream, which resonates with **Tiphareth (Beauty, heart)**.

By restoring Lysander's love for Hermia and Titania to himself, Oberon creates the harmony and balance between the lovers on the one hand and the proper benevolent functions of Titania and himself on the other. He and Titania now demonstrate the characteristics of **Chockmah** and **Binah**, which extends their benevolence to Theseus and Hippolyta. As Demetrius now disclaims the love for Hermia which threatened her, and rejoices in his renewed love of Helena, Theseus feels able to ignore the protests of Egeus that the harsh law against Hermia and Lysander be implemented. Theseus offers a harmonious conclusion to the lovers' stories in a triple wedding to be shared with his own. Cleared of the three impediments in

Yesod which prevented the three pairs of lovers from ascending the tree, they are now able to rise to **Kether** in the consummation of their marriages, blessed by Titania and Oberon, and as harmony is restored in Athens and the woods, the psyche is balanced and restored.

The performance of *Pyramus and Thisbe* by Peter Quince, Bottom and their companions is firmly grounded in **Malkuth**, reminiscent of the fact that magic practice, including that of the Cabala, should begin and end in that sphere, grounded in the reality of the everyday world. The workmen are praised and rewarded for their performances, and, with their Bergomask dance, they are included in the general rejoicing. When the fairies bestow their benedictions on the three couples, all the elements, human and supernatural, of Athens and its environs are integrated, and the psyche is made whole in the balance and ascent of the Tree.

RITES OF INITIATION

These always involve young people (neophytes) who benefit from older guides (hierophants). *The Tempest* and *A Midsummer Night's Dream* also have characters which are subject to 'Rites of Initiation', as well as those mentioned in the plays below.

CHAPTER ELEVEN: *THE TWO GENTLEMEN OF VERONA*

I consider this to be the first comedy that Shakespeare wrote, as the moment in V. iv. 83 when Valentine offers up his lover Sylvia to his friend Proteus is very difficult for the actor performing Valentine. It is almost impossible, given the previous action of the play wherein Valentine has prevented Proteus from raping Silvia, to find the motivation for his action, and this makes his character seem to be that of a very callow youth in regarding his love as no more than a possession to be handed over to Proteus. I can imagine that Shakespeare's fellow actors might have challenged the young playwright for doing that, as few moments like that occur in future plays, in which characterisation is usually consistent and action-motivated. The play is rarely performed, possibly because of this difficult moment. In the 2014 RSC production of the play, the moment is rushed through, covered up by Julia's fainting. Theatre Set-Up performed the play twice, and on both occasions we interpreted the action as Valentine offering his friend not Sylvia, but a share in their happiness. I cannot claim that it was very convincing!

The Christian theme of self-sacrifice is represented in this play by the treatment of his dog, Crab, by Launce, the servant of Proteus. The addition of the rascally dog, on whose behalf Launce bears the constant punishment for Crab's misdeeds in order to save his life, is always a welcome, if unusual addition to the dramatis personae of the play. The arcane theme of sacrifice takes on a poignant significance with the audience's delight in the account by Launce of the scandalous behaviour of Crab and the punishments he has undergone on his dog's behalf.

The problem with the play for actors is that it can seem slight, its plot concerned only with the tangled love affairs of two young men.

This overly romantic style of the play changes suddenly and becomes at odds with the brutish action of Proteus in his attempted rape of Silvia and the implied callousness of Valentine in treating Silvia as a property to be handed over to his callous friend. However, we found that an understanding of the play's deeper significance in terms of the arcana made it possible for the actors to rationalise their characters and gain respect for the plot.

Another problem for literally-minded audiences is Shakespeare's apparent lack of attention to realistic detail in this play in the seeming geographical ignorance evidenced in the sea voyages undertaken by Valentine and Proteus from Verona to Milan, a land journey. I suggest that this journey is a paradigm of the initiatory path which the young men are taking, often represented as a sea-voyage. This geographical distortion also occurs in *Winter's Tale*, which attributes land-locked Bohemia with a seacoast, which I claim is also symbolic (see above p. 71).

The arcana I selected to investigate and apply to the production of *The Two Gentlemen of Verona* play are **Alchemy and the zodiac**, **Renaissance Platonism conventions and philosophies**, **Theurgy and Rites of Initiation**, and **The Bible**.

Story Section 1 (I. i. ii.)
Two gentlemen who live in Verona, Proteus and Valentine, take leave of each other as Valentine departs for the Emperor's court in Milan to begin his social improvement. He scorns Proteus for remaining at home, tied there by his love for Julia. Valentine's servant, Speed, reports to Proteus that he has successfully delivered his master's letter for Julia to her household. Lucetta, Julia's maid, teases her about her suitors, in particular Proteus, whose letter she proffers. Julia coyly rejects it, then tears it up and throws it to the ground, before immediately regretting her action and picking it up.

Alchemy and the zodiac
The cosmic aspects of the play, and perhaps Shakespeare's higher purpose, are revealed by the opposite signs of the zodiac and the corresponding elements (of which all matter was supposed to be made) which the four lovers represent.

- Proteus is of Cancer, changing like the moon, its planet and the generative element, water.
- Julia, whose name means 'descends from Jupiter', is Sagittarius and the 'bringing to maturity element', fire.
- The Aquarian, Valentine, who needs to be valorous to make the planet Mars prevail over the melancholy Saturn (which influences this sign) is the element air, the 'animus mundi' (the spirit of the world), which gives the vital breath to…
- Earth, the element represented by Silvia (Valentine's destined lover), and the embodiment of beautiful nature and Venus, her planet under the sign of Taurus.[1]

Alchemically, the elements are 'turned' three times in a kind of circle or wheel in the first stage of **Calcination**, represented here by these three actions:

1. Valentine parts from Proteus for Milan.
2. In Milan he will find Sylvia.
3. Julia tears up the letter from Proteus.

Renaissance Platonism, conventions and philosophies
The name Proteus (which implies changing from the name of the Greek sea-god of that name who shape-changed) indicates that this gentleman of Verona will change until he finds the 'hidden-god', the Pan within himself, reflecting the Renaissance philosophy, 'Pan and Proteus'.[2]

The name of his friend, Valentine, implies heart, where the hidden god in all people was thought to lie.[3] This hidden god was known as 'Divine Love', or 'eternal good' (often represented as a rose), and its attainment was the goal of changing to achieve self-knowledge or identity, known as the 'essence'. Julia and Proteus are companion souls. If he is constant he will experience Divine Love.[4]

The artificial, remote courtly love exemplified by the Italian poets, Dante and Petrarch, is shown in the exchange of letters between the lovers.

Valentine is yet to find his companion soul.

Theurgy and Rites of Initiation
The name Milan carries the meaning of 'centre', so Valentine's journey there

indicates the beginning of his initiation to the centre of the metaphorical labyrinth through which he must endures trials as an initiate.

The Bible

The play begins with the young people displaying ethical loyalty and love, Valentine and Proteus vowing to pray for each other and Proteus named as a 'votary to fond desire' for Julia.

Story Section 2 (I. iii., II. i., ii., iii.)

Julia replies to Proteus in a letter declaring her love, but the progress of their match is halted when Antonio, the father of Proteus, urged on by a family friend, Panthino, decides to send Proteus to join Valentine in Milan.

Meanwhile, in Milan, Valentine, in spite of his scorn of the lovelorn Proteus, has fallen in love with the Emperor's daughter, Silvia, and she with him.

In Verona, Julia and Proteus part sadly, exchanging rings as proof of their mutual love.

The story of another tearful parting from his family is told by Launce, the servant of Proteus, to his dog, Crab.

Alchemy and the zodiac

The next alchemical stage, **Dissolution**, presents the dissolving of the elements to begin the separation of the constituent parts of the alchemical process from each other. The 'solution' was said to 'bring to light what was hidden'. This is the love now declared between Julia and Proteus ('dissolved' by his departure for Milan) and the love growing between Valentine and Silvia, dissolved by her father's disapproval. The men are the 'bodies' of the process and the women the 'spirits'.

Renaissance Platonism, conventions and philosophies

Valentine finds his companion soul in Silvia and must undergo trials in the form of her father's opposition to achieve her and make the 'Divine Ascent'. The name Panthino also carries, in its source as Pan, the god at the centre of the initiatory labyrinth and the ultimate goal of his journey.

The love-token rings which Proteus and Julia exchange represent their soul-body bonds.

Theurgy and Rites of Initiation
Panthino (the name derived from Pan, who was often invoked in his function as a nature deity and as a spiritual guide) acts as a kind of hierophant in his insistence that Proteus should also go to Milan.[5] The quest for the true identity of the candidate for initiation was often represented by a sea voyage, which is why Proteus and Valentine symbolically sail from Verona to Milan, normally a land voyage.

The Bible
The loyalty of Proteus and Julia towards each other is confirmed in the exchange of the rings and vows. We are introduced to the main carrier of the theme of sacrifice in the play with Launce and his dog, Crab.

Story Section 3 (II. iv., v., vi.)
In Milan, Valentine faces a rival, Thurio (preferred by her father for his possessions) in his wooing of Silvia. When Proteus arrives he tells him that he and Silvia are betrothed to each other and plan to elope, but Proteus has himself fallen in love with Silvia, and, surprised at the transfer of his love from Julia to Silvia, 'as one nail by strength drives another out' (II. iv. 189), plans to pursue her for himself.

Speed, the servant of Valentine, welcomes Launce and his dog to Milan and, laughing at their masters, they make for the alehouse.

Proteus yields to the temptation to betray his friend Valentine and tell the Emperor of their plan to elope.

Alchemy and the zodiac
Proteus, whose name indicates the changes that must take place in the main body of the process, is now separated from his spirit, Julia, in the stage of **Seperation** (Ripley's spelling) in his arrival in Milan and in his infatuation with Silvia.

Renaissance Platonism, conventions and philosophies
Proteus fails to be constant to Julia and descends away from the path of Divine Love. However, he uncovers sinister aspects of his own personality which he must master and thus come closer to self-knowledge, his 'essence'.

Speed and Launce parody their masters' artificiality.

The Emperor himself needs some character adjustment in his wish to marry his daughter to such a person as Thurio for wealth.

Theurgy and Rites of Initiation
Although Valentine has found his 'centre', Silvia, in Milan, he and Proteus are not doing well in their initiatory trials, both of them planning unethical deeds in response to being challenged and tempted. In presenting the trials to the young men, the Emperor is a kind of Hierophant. Silvia's name also suggests the labyrinth-woods of initiation.

The Bible
Both Proteus and Valentine yield to temptation, which we know will be punished.

Story Section 4 (II. vii.)
At home in Verona, unaware of his changed affections, Julia misses Proteus so much that she decides to go to see him in Milan. She tells Lucetta that she will disguise herself as a boy-page. Lucetta doubts the wisdom of this escapade and the loyalty of Proteus.

Alchemy and the zodiac
The next stage, Coniunctio, representing a chemical wedding, is mocked in Julia's plan to join Proteus in Milan. However, in scheming to adopt a disguise as a boy-page she takes on the more significant form of the androgynous hermaphrodite, the symbol which represents the divine universal above the limitations of either sex. Her behaviour in this disguise will be as immaculate as the principle this symbol represents.

Renaissance Platonism, conventions and philosophies
Julia also embarks on a questing journey, hopefully to be reunited with her companion soul, Proteus. However, her maid, Lucetta, has a realistic opinion of men and correctly doubts the loyalty of Proteus. In this play, servants generally represent the way of the real world.

Theurgy and Rites of Initiation.
Julia now sets out on a journey as a candidate of initiation.

The Bible
Julia hazards all in the mistaken belief that the heart of Proteus is 'as far from fraud as heaven from earth' (II. vii.78)

Story Section 5 (III. i. 1-169)
In the hope that he might secure Silvia's love himself, Proteus betrays Valentine and tells the Emperor of the planned elopement. The Emperor claims that he has locked Silvia securely up in a tower so that Valentine cannot gain access to her. Proteus explains that the tower would present no difficulty to the escapees as they have devised a rope ladder up which he can climb to carry her away.

Proteus leaves as he sees Valentine approaching with his rope ladder hidden under his cloak. Pretending that he wishes to court a lady for himself, the Emperor tricks Valentine into revealing the ladder and a letter to Silvia. He not only prevents the elopement but condemns Valentine to exile.

Alchemy and the zodiac
Silvia, remote in the tower into which her father has put her, now becomes, in her remoteness from Valentine, the separated 'spirit' from him as a 'body' of the alchemic process. His trials as the body will be extended with his exile, his need for improvement shown in his lies and deception of the Emperor. This forced parting from his spirit, Silvia, and the further rough distancing of Proteus from both him and his spirit, Julia, become the violent stage of **Putrefaction**.

Renaissance Platonism, conventions and philosophies
Both Proteus and Valentine descend away from their companion souls and from the Divine Ascent. Proteus betrays his friend and Julia. Valentine, facing a trial in the removal of Silvia out of reach in a tower, is uncourtly and uncivilised in attempting to steal away the Emperor's daughter. A ladder, in this philosophy, represented the ascent to Heaven in order to experience Divine Love (see fig. 12). Valentine loses this ladder by his foolish and unethical attempted theft. It is made of rope to indicate that he is still bound to earth through his selfish motive, according to his own words, in wishing to elope, declaring that his happiness is his target.

Theurgy and Rites of Initiation
The Emperor as hierophant sends Valentine into an exile which will mark the true beginning of his successful initiation. Proteus moves further away from the initiatory success in yielding to temptation.

RITES OF INITIATION

The Bible
Valentine is punished for his attempts to steal Silvia from her father, the Emperor.

Story Section 6 (III. i. 170-373)
Desolate at being separated from Silvia, Valentine declares that he is a dead man. Proteus enters to pretend to comfort him as he leaves for exile and encourages him to write to Silvia. His servant Launce guesses at his treachery but is involved with his own love of a milkmaid. He has written down a list of her accomplishments to help him decide whether he should marry her. Speed exclaims at the items on the list, a marked and prosaic contrast to the style of their masters' values in love.

Alchemy and the zodiac
Putrefaction is continued as Valentine faces the reality of his parting from his spirit, Silvia, without whom he feels 'dead'.

Proteus himself descends into a 'death' of his character with his treachery towards his friend, thus purging out of himself by revealing elements of his nature which must be eliminated. However, the next stage, **Congelation**, in which the components of the alchemy should be like wax to 'congeale like pearls' ready to be reunited in the final stages of the process, is indicated in Proteus's description of Silvia's tearful reaction to Valentine's banishment as a 'sea of melting pearl' (III. i. 224).

Renaissance Platonism, conventions and philosophies
When faced with exile and separation from Silvia, Valentine considers himself a dead man, a 'nothing', as she is the core of his being, his essence (III. i. 182). Launce and Speed parody the love letters through which masters court their lovers in the prosaic list of attributes of Launce's milkmaid.

Theurgy and Rites of Initiation
All initiations contain a simulated death experience. Valentine experiences that here.

The Bible
Proteus descends into further sin, a fact recognised by Launce.

Story Section 7 (III. ii., IV. i.)
Proteus proceeds with his plan to win Silvia by deceiving both the Emperor and Thurio into believing that he will further Thurio's courtship of her. He recommends that Thurio should present Silvia with music and love songs performed beneath her chamber window. He also promises the Emperor that he will discredit Valentine as Silvia still mourns his absence.

In exile, Valentine and Speed are captured by a band of outlaws who elect Valentine to be their much-needed leader, their 'king' (IV. i. 67). Encouraged by Speed, Valentine agrees to this as long as they commit no evil deeds.

Alchemy and the zodiac
The stage of **Cibation** marks a moderate feeding of the process. This is mocked by Proteus' feeding lies and deception to the Emperor and Thurio. Valentine, on the other hand, is fed a lifeline in his capture and offer of leadership by the outlaws.

Renaissance Platonism, conventions and philosophies
Proteus further descends away from Divine Love in deceiving Thurio and the Emperor. Valentine enters the symbolic wilderness, the forest in which he will come to terms with his real identity in suffering trials. The outlaws offer him 'kingship or death'. This represents the controls he must gain over himself to save his soul (see Vyvyan, pp. 107-113).

Theurgy and Rites of Initiation
In this wood-labyrinth, symbol of a place of initiation, Valentine is given the opportunity to take control of his nature by being offered the kingship by the outlaws.

The Bible
Valentine begins the road to ethical recovery in accepting leadership of the outlaws only if they commit no evil acts.

Story Section 8 (IV. ii.)
Pretending to Thurio that it is in his name, Proteus performs the love song to Silvia beneath her window. This is overheard by Julia, disguised as a page, who is a guest at an adjacent inn. The Host of the inn comments on her misery. She replies that the musician plays falsely, but is encouraged

when Silvia rejects the overtures of love which Proteus makes to her aloft in her tower and reprimands him for deceiving Julia. Proteus asks Silvia for a picture of her, a 'shadow' of her to which he can make love if he cannot do so in person, and she agrees to send it as it represents his false nature.

The Host tells Julia that Launce has told him that Proteus is indeed courting Silvia for himself, and that Launce must give his dog Crab to Silvia as a present from Proteus, as the dog intended for Silvia has disappeared. Julia asks the Host to take her to Proteus.

Alchemy and the zodiac
The next stage of **Sublimation** sees the meeting of body and spirit as Julia now meets the treacherous Proteus. The violence of this stage is indicated in the unpleasantness of the meeting and the shock that Julia gets from seeing her betrayal.

Renaissance Platonism, conventions and philosophies
The song that Proteus sings to Silvia beneath her window identifies her as 'Love-Beauty-In-Nature'.[6] The picture, the shadow of her which Proteus requests, mirrors his false love of her, reflecting his current false nature (see Vyvyan, p 125). His true companion soul, Julia, is tried, tested and found constant in her loyalty to Proteus in spite of his treachery.

Theurgy and Rites of Initiation
Proteus pursues shadows, not the truth he is expected to follow. Julia successfully undergoes the trials of her initiation.

The Bible
Julia proves stoical in her reaction to the treachery of Proteus. Launce proves his loyalty to his master in the stoical sacrifice-gift of his loved dog Crab as a present to Silvia on behalf of Proteus.

Story Section 9 (IV. iii., iv. 1-61)
Silvia seeks help from a virtuous knight, Sir Eglamour, in her plan to escape from the match with Thurio which her father plans to carry out. She asks that Sir Eglamour meet her at church and then that he should accompany her to Mantua, where she has heard that Valentine is living. He agrees to do this.

Launce brings in Crab, who has disgraced himself as a present to Silvia, stealing from her table and urinating beneath the table on the other dogs and on her farthingale. He reprimands Crab for making him suffer all the punishments he has always undertaken on the dog's behalf, otherwise Crab would have long since been put down. Proteus is also ungrateful for Launce's sacrifice in giving up his dog to Silvia. Launce is commanded to find the elegant dog which disappeared and give that to Silvia.

Alchemy and the zodiac
Firmentation (Ripley's spelling) fixes and resolves the alchemical process. The resolution is begun by Silvia's plan to escape with the help of Sir Eglamour.

Renaissance Platonism, conventions and philosophies
Silvia herself prepares to enter the wilderness to face trials, guided by Sir Eglamour, an example of ideal Platonic Love, still constant to his lover although she is dead. In the relationship between Launce and his dog, Crab, there is another example of constancy in love. In spite of all the problems the dog gives him, Launce even undertakes his punishments to save him out of love. It is another parody of Launce's master, Proteus, who should follow that example. Launce loves his dog more than Proteus loves his betrothed.

Theurgy and Rites of Initiation
Sir Eglamour is a typical hierophant guiding Silvia through the woods-labyrinth of her initiation.

The Bible
We hear of Launce's self-sacrifice on behalf of Crab. In a paradigm of Christ's self-sacrifice on behalf of humanity, Launce has always taken upon himself the guilt of his dog, accepting the punishments himself. Proteus does not appreciate the loyalty of Launce in his gift of his much-loved dog, Crab, to Silvia. Seeing the dog not as a beloved pet but as a disreputable animal, Proteus cannot understand the essence of the Christian story of the 'widow's mite', in which Christ appreciated the small amount of money that a poor widow gave more than a larger gift from richer people as it represented a large proportion of what she owned and genuine self-sacrifice.

Story Section 10 (IV. iv. 40-203, V. i.)
Julia, under the name of Sebastian, has offered herself as a page to Proteus. Not recognising her, he asks her to give the very ring she gave him as love-token for a present to Silvia in return for the promised picture. Silvia rejects the ring, however, knowing it to have been given to Proteus by Julia. Julia, still disguised as Sebastian, thanks Silvia, pretending to have known Julia, erstwhile love of Proteus, in Verona.

She muses on Silvia's picture, which she must give to Proteus, protesting that he prefers that shadow of Silvia to her real self. The real Silvia, meanwhile, has made her escape from Milan, accompanied by Sir Eglamour.

Alchemy and the zodiac
Firmentation is continued by Silvia as she rejects the courtship of Proteus and escapes to Valentine.
Renaissance Platonism, conventions and philosophies
Julia passes another trial when she endures the base action of Proteus in asking her to give the betrothal ring she gave to Proteus to Silvia. The falseness of his perceptions is shown when he does not recognise her dressed as a page-boy as he pursues a false love instead of his companion soul. Julia observes this theme when she reflects on the picture of Silvia that she must give to Proteus.
Theurgy and Rites of Initiation
Julia is tried further, and passes all of her tests. Silvia now prepares to enter the real labyrinth of her initiation with her hierophant, Sir Eglamour.
The Bible
A similar self-sacrifice to that of Launce is repeated by Julia, who, to make Proteus happy, acts as envoy on his behalf to Silvia. She does not even object when he asks her to give to Silvia the very ring she gave to him as pledge of their love.

Story Section 11 (V. ii., iii., iv. 1-72)
Thurio and Proteus (with Julia as Sebastian in attendance) are wrangling over Silvia when the Emperor enters to announce that she has fled to Valentine accompanied by Sir Eglamour. They all go off in pursuit of the fugitives.

However, Sir Eglamour's protection of Silvia is ineffective, and she is captured by members of Valentine's band of outlaws. He is musing on the virtues of solitary life in the woods where he can lament the lost Silvia when she enters with the disguised Julia and Proteus, who has rescued her from the outlaws. Valentine hides to witness a disgraceful scene in which Proteus begs love from Silvia in return for her rescue, and, when she refuses, threatens to rape her. Valentine steps forward to save her and condemns Proteus for his treachery in friendship.

Alchemy and the zodiac
Exaltation is begun as both couples are re-united, the women as 'spirits' returning to the men, the 'bodies' of the process. This occurs after considerable changing of their relationships in this scene, symbolising the 'turning of the wheel of the elements' that they also represent (see fig. 23).
Renaissance Platonism, conventions and philosophies
Thurio, Proteus, Julia and the Emperor all enter the 'wilderness', in which they must undergo trials. Silvia's trials continue in her capture by the outlaws and rescue by Proteus, who promises her a terrifying fate in his threat to rape her. She remains constant in her love of Valentine. Proteus enters the nadir of his Platonic journey in his treatment of Silvia, from which he is jettisoned by Valentine's reprimanding him for treachery and threatened sexual abuse. His progress in the play has been marked by his self-betrayal in the betrayal of others and in his choice of false values until, in the pit of his loss of real identity and integrity, his friend Valentine rescues him by castigating him and forgiving him when he repents. Similarly, his love, Julia, redeems him with her constant loyalty.
Theurgy and Rites of Initiation
All enter the woods, representing the labyrinth. Silvia suffers two physical ordeals, firstly imposed by the outlaws and then by Proteus. Valentine, in rescuing her and castigating Proteus, acts as a graduate initiate himself.
The Bible
Valentine practises an effective reprimanding sermon upon Proteus in the style of a most stern evangelist and achieves a kind of 'road to Damascus' conversion of Proteus.

Story Section 12 (V. iv. 73-171)

Effectively chastened, Proteus genuinely repents and asks for Valentine's forgiveness. Granting this, Valentine offers Silvia to Proteus. At this, Julia faints, and when she revives she discloses her disguise by showing the two rings exchanged between her and Proteus. She reprimands Proteus for reducing her to the humiliation of a male disguise wherein she has changed her shape as he his mind. In reply Proteus declares that were man 'but constant he were perfect' (V. iv. 110), and, resolving to be constant to Julia, reaffirms and re-pledges his love for her.

The outlaws enter with the captive Emperor and Thurio, who claims Silvia. He soon relinquishes his claim when Valentine threatens him with his sword, and the Emperor, disgusted at Thurio's cowardice and recognising Valentine's worth, endorses the match between Silvia and him, agrees to pardon the outlaws and invites all to celebrate. Valentine tells the Emperor that he will tell him the full story behind this happy resolution, teases Proteus about his behaviour and Julia her disguise, and observes that the day of their double marriage shall bring 'one feast, one house, one mutual happiness' (V. iv. 171).

Alchemy and the zodiac.

The turning of the wheel of the elements continues with the repentance of Proteus, his forgiveness by Valentine and his reunion with Julia, until the Philosophers' Stone or the gold of alchemy is achieved in **Multiplication**, as the benefits of the alchemic process are multiplied with the expulsion of Thurio by the Emperor (see fig. 23). These benefits, in **Projection**, are projected in the Emperor's forgiveness of the outlaws and the planned happy return of all to Milan.

Renaissance Platonism, conventions and philosophies

The medieval conflict of love or friendship is here resolved as Proteus recognises Julia as his true love, his companion soul, as is affirmed between Valentine and Silvia. Thurio fails his test and is sent away, and the Emperor then at last gains a true sense of values in bestowing Silvia on Valentine, and all are united in a euphoric conclusion. The promised wedding feast anticipates the feast which Plato declared celebrated and symbolised the attainment of the experience of 'Divine Love'.

CHAPTER ELEVEN

Theurgy and Rites of Initiation
Proteus, in repenting and recognising his centre in Julia; Valentine in forgiving him, challenging Thurio and defying the Emperor in defence of Silvia; Julia in her toleration of the treachery of Proteus and constancy to him; and Silvia in finding Valentine at the end of her physical trials all pass initiation and go forward into adult life. Thurio, in not standing up to Valentine, fails.

The Bible
Christian forgiveness and mercy is shown by Valentine towards Proteus and by the Emperor to Proteus, Valentine, Silvia and the outlaws. Julia is rewarded for her self-sacrificing constancy to Proteus by his love for her.

Cabala: Post Production (see fig. 3)

In this story, a composite group of characters, Valentine, Proteus, their servants Speed and Launce and their loves Julia and Silvia, provide the basis of the Cabala in its form as the Hebraic Tree of Life.

At the beginning of the play, Valentine, Proteus and Julia are seen not to be grounded in **Malkuth (the material world)** in contrast to their realistic servants. The love that Proteus declares for Julia places him on the sphere of feelings in **Netzach**, which Valentine scorns until he experiences love himself (for Silvia) and attains that sphere.

Launce, grounded in the earthly **Malkuth**, demonstrates genuine love, both for his family he is leaving and for his dog, Crab, whereas his master's love for Julia is distanced from the earthly physical senses of **Malkuth** by the romantic letters he sends to her. She, in tearing up his letter demonstrates an unreal love, distanced from the true love of **Netzach** by a feigned rejection of his protestations of love, action which she subsequently regrets, betraying her true feelings for him.

In Milan, Valentine's ascent up the Tree of Life is impeded by his planned deception of Silvia's father in a plot to elope. Proteus, in betraying this plan to Silvia's father and thus betraying his friend, has descended even further than Valentine, but an unpleasant aspect of his nature is revealed on the sphere of **Yesod (the subconscious)**, where he must experience a clearing process of this characteristic of treachery.

Julia, in devising a plan to disguise herself as a boy page and travel to Milan to be with Proteus, shows a balance of the spheres of **Netzach** in her feelings and **Hod** in her thoughts, but as her maid, Lucetta, grounded in **Malkuth**, advises, her ideas and plans lack the reality of the genuine world of **Malkuth**. She will have to learn the truth of this to progress up the Tree.

Valentine learns the reality of the real world of **Malkuth** in the scene of the Emperor's interception of his elopement with Silvia. The Emperor, symbol of life as it is in reality, makes nonsense of Valentine's silly, idealised plan. In being exiled, Valentine will become grounded in **Malkuth**, which will begin his ascent up the Tree. The process of coming to terms with the real world is painful for Valentine, although the sincerity of his love for Silvia projects him towards the spiritual state of love in **Chesed**.

Proteus descends even further in his extended betraying of the non-delivery of Valentine's letter to Silvia, but Valentine is unrealistic in his imperceptive trusting of Proteus. Launce demonstrates a very realistic appraisal of a milkmaid he is considering marrying. In itemising her assets, however, although this is evidence of a sensual and pragmatic **Malkuth**-like awareness of her, there is no sense of the love that would take him to **Netzach**. This occurs in an intensity which projects him in the love of his dog, Crab, to the higher spiritual love of **Chesed**.

An example of the spiritual love symbolised by **Chesed** is given in the knight Sir Eglamour, who is still loyal to his love although she has died. He is not very effective, however, in protecting Silvia from the dangers of the real world of the woods, as she is captured by outlaws. This would jettison her from the romantic fantasy of her escape from the protected environment of her privileged castle home into a world as others experience it, and land her in the reality of **Malkuth**.

Julia, in learning of the treachery of Proteus, has also become grounded in the un-idealised sensual world of **Malkuth**, and through her still loving Proteus in spite of his disloyalty to her, has attained the spiritual level of love in **Chesed**.

When the Emperor, Proteus, Thurio and attendants go into the woods in pursuit of Silvia, movement throughout the Tree becomes inevitable. Proteus descends further in his attempted rape of Silvia, but is saved from iniquity by Valentine, who, on the sphere of **Geburah** as severity and justice, brings him to his senses in a realisation of his guilt, which takes him from **Yesod** to **Malkuth.** Valentine, from the balanced spheres of **Geburah** and **Chesed** offers forgiveness to Proteus and the share of his love in **Chesed**. Julia's revelation of her identity projects Proteus to **Netzach** and then **Chesed**, balanced by **Hod** and **Geburah** (all done a little too quickly for dramatic plausibility but perhaps characteristic of impulsive youth!).

Thurio is thrown away from the Tree, upon which he has never been placed. The Emperor, previously overly grounded in the materialistic aspects of **Malkuth** and stuck on **Hod** and Geburah, acquires the understanding of **Binah** and the feelings of **Neztach**, so that the composite characters can move happily back to Milan towards **Kether** at the top of the Tree.

CHAPTER TWELVE: *LOVE'S LABOUR'S LOST*

Theatre Set-Up performed this play twice, a joy for us to do as the casting required another actress to join us, thus levelling up the gender balance with the company.[1] The 1984 production marked a landmark event for the company, as Tony Portacio joined the cast and continued for many years to play the leading roles in our productions, in the later years also working as co-director of the plays.

The play was fun to do, with good doubling up of parts of both the men and women who were performing the nobles, enjoying the exuberance of performing the variety of the other characters as well. We made good use of masks to make this possible, several women performing men's characters.

The acknowledged problem of the play is the inverse nature of its mood. Usually, Shakespeare's comedies move from unhappiness of at least one of the protagonists to a general state of bliss, including marriage. The reverse occurs in this play, most of which consists in the happy dalliance of nobles and serving citizens until the entrance of Marcade, announcing a death which turns the play sour and severe with the usual marriages deferred and provisional. This results in the alchemy of the play, like the other arcana and the love matches, becoming unresolved and projected into the future. As Berowne complains, 'Our wooing doth not end like an old play' (V. ii. 863).[2]

As the couples go their separate ways, Armado predicts the forthcoming harshness that the young men must undergo before they are fit to marry. The songs which end the play with verses about winter and hard labour follow verses rejoicing about summer and suggested cuckoldry: 'The words of Mercury are harsh after the songs of Apollo' (V. ii. 919-920). Mercury and winter are symbols of alchemy, the strictures of which reflect the future the young men must endure. The course of the play in which the young men spend their time indulging in games, like the 'songs of Apollo', after breaking their oaths to follow an ascetic and academic life, demonstrates their need to be changed, enduring the trials of life by benefitting society.

The neat metrical form of the scenes in the play and the delightful play of language motivated us to investigate plays of one of Shakespeare's

CHAPTER TWELVE

theatre predecessors, John Lyly, whose balanced style is similar, and to try to replicate their charm in our productions.

In preparing our first production in 1984, we also looked at the significance of numerology in the play and its relevance to the theme in the play of Nature versus Art (specifically the significance of the number four, of the four main couples, to Nature). I also decided that the exquisite pattern of some scenes, such as IV. v., were sourced from Lyly and from the masque origins of the play. The research for the first production also included Freemasonry, some of the elements of which I detected in the play, much to the delight of certain members of the audience. However, when I later learned about theurgy, which provided a matrix for Freemasonry, I identified those elements as probably stemming from the older source.

Our later production of the play in 2005 benefitted not only from my research into the arcana that had taken place between then and 1984, but from the notions prevalent at that time about the identity of the 'dark lady' of Shakespeare's sonnets and the relevance of her to this play. Evidently, the version of the play we now have dates from 1598, when he added material to a previous commissioned masque-like entertainment. In his sonnets written near this date Shakespeare calls it a 'Hell of Time'. It is presumed that he was involved in a love-triangle between his mistress, the dark lady of the sonnets (speculated by A.L. Rowse and a number of subsequent scholars to be Emilia Lanier, descended from an Italian and possibly Jewish family of musicians, and ex-mistress of Lord Hunsdon, previously patron of Shakespeare's company), and W.H. (supposedly the 17 year old William Herbert, whom he loved and who was also making love to Emilia). Regardless of her actual identity, we believed that in the character of Rosaline Shakespeare celebrated his dark lady. This gave us a good through line of contact to Shakespeare's depth of feeling in the play and the importance of Rosaline. We celebrated this is in the core artwork for our publicity material and programme cover, superimposing upon a copy of the Hilliard portrait of Emilia Lanier a photograph of the face of our actress, Alice James, playing Rosaline (see fig. 41). The name Rosaline is significant here, as the deity at the centre of the initiatory labyrinth was sometimes referred to as a rose. Rosicrucianism, the symbol of which was the rose, incorporated ideas of alchemy and theurgy, but aimed for personal improvement through changing and helping society (as Rosaline insists Berowne must do).

The arcana I selected to investigate and apply in the production of this play were **Alchemy, Renaissance Platonism, Theurgy and Initiation, Rosicrucianism, the Bible**, and, finally, **Ideas and Circumstances relevant to 1598**, the content of which included discussion of the following:

1. Shakespeare's 'dark lady'.
2. The influence of the poet/playwright/courtier, John Lyly, is strong in this play, in the speech patterns and ideas. The morality theme of his Euphues, 'Wit-Will-Wisdom', takes the form of the men (the wits), by their will, submitting to the wisdom of the women.
3. Many ideas concerning numerology, the significance of numbers, came from the works of Pythagoras, who incorporates in his work elements of the ancient Orphic Mysteries. Numbers, correctly observed and used, were believed to reflect inner harmony with the order of nature.
4. Some of the characters may derive from Commedia Dell' Arte stereotypes.
5. Nature versus Art & Words. The naturalness of the characters in the play is revealed in the way they use or abuse words. Words are power and fun, and are the basis of continuous word games in the play.
6. 'The Mocking Game' as a courtly pursuit.

Story Section 1 (I. i. 1-178)

King Ferdinand of Navarre requires his courtiers, the lords Longeville, Dumaine and Berowne, to pledge an oath that they will remain in his court for three years, and during that time will study, abjure women and abstain from any worldly indulgences. The aim of this is to gain fame throughout the world in their 'little academe' (I. i. 13), that will live after them and so defeat death.

Longeville and Dumaine swear to deny love and worldly comforts, but Berowne challenges the plan, 'O, these are barren tasks, too hard to keep| Not to see ladies, study, fast, not sleep' (I. i. 47- 48). He criticises the barren study of 'continual plodders' (I. i. 86) that excludes nature, and points out to the King that the item which decrees that no man must speak to a woman for three years and no woman should be allowed to come within a mile of the court must be disobeyed, as the Princess of France is imminently due in order to negotiate with the King about the 'surrender up of Aquitaine | To her decrepit, sick and bedrid father'(I. i. 135, 136). The King realises that he must talk with the Princess, and must therefore cancel that part of the pledge.

Out of allegiance to the King, Berowne signs the pledge warning that 'necessity' (I. i. 146) will often make them all forsworn. The King promises them some allowed entertainment in the person of the Spanish braggart Don Adriano De Armado.

Alchemy

As 'King' is a symbol of the self in alchemy, King Ferdinand represents the psychological aspect of the alchemy in this story. He and his courtiers will also represent the 'base matter', the 'Prima Materia', the substance that needs to be transformed into the 'gold of alchemy'. Following Shakespeare's pattern, if the body of the process is a man, the corresponding spirit, soul or vapour, which must be separated from the body so that it can be worked upon, will be a woman. The Princess and her ladies will provide this component of the process.

Alchemy values nature, must take account of nature and takes place within nature, which King Ferdinand is denying in his pledge to abstain from contact with women. His aim is not a noble one either, but a vain ambition for worldly fame that will defeat death. Alchemy accepts the necessity of death, even a simulated one, observing that there must be a cycle of life and death for nature to thrive, expressed as the motto 'Die to Live'.

Renaissance Platonism

Far from considering the love of a woman divine, the King considers it to be a sin and its denial a virtue which will bring fame, which will itself defeat death. He can be said to see through a 'veil of illusion'.[3]

Theurgy and Initiation, Rosicrucianism, the Bible

The King and his courtiers are ripe for initiation and his garden (or field) will represent the labyrinth.

Ideas and Circumstances relevant to 1598

The play may have historical connections, perhaps slightly known to audiences of Shakespeare's time and therefore interesting to them, if not significant. The 'little academe' may mock similar literary/academic groups of the time.[4]

In *The Oxford Companion to Shakespeare*, Michael Dobson and Stanley Wells conjecture that there may have been contemporary historical French references in the names of the men: Henry of Navarre (later Henry IV of France) in the King of Navarre; Charles de Gontant, Duc de Biron in Berowne; Charles Duc de Mayenne in Dumaine; and Henry I d'Orleans, Duc de Longueville, in Longeville. They also consider that there may have been a possible reference to 'a now lost account of a diplomatic visit made to Henry of Navarre in 1578 by Catharine de Medici and her daughter, Marguerite de Valois, Henry's estranged wife, to discuss the future of Aquitaine'.[5] Today's actors can enjoy this lineage of their roles, adding a dimension to the characters and events of the play.

Number was considered to have magical property and the number four (here the number of the King and his courtiers) to be ideal in form – the perfect square, the four elements, the four humours, four seasons and four directions.

Berowne mocks book-learning divorced from nature which the King wishes his court to study, 'Still and contemplative in living art' (I. i. 14). Its folly is immediately realised in betraying decorum in the visit of the Princess.

Story Section 2 (I. i. 179-302, I. ii. 1-178)

King Ferdinand has also imposed a law of chastity on his subjects (the punishment supposed to be a year's imprisonment), and the first culprit to disobey (the clown, Costard) is brought in by the constable, Dull, with an extravagant letter from Armado claiming Costard's transgression with Jaquenetta, a milkmaid whom he is holding for trial himself. Costard's penalty is reduced to fasting for a week on bran and water, and Berowne forecasts that 'these oaths and laws will prove an idle scorn' (I. i. 296).

Armado enters, telling his page, Mote, that he has also signed the King's pledge but that he is in love. He asks Mote to name him great men that have been in love. Mote tells him of Hercules and then of Samson whose love's complexion was 'sea-water green' (I. ii. 80). Armado says that although 'green indeed is the colour of lovers' (I. i. 83), his love is red and white.

When Dull enters with Costard and Jaquenetta Armado declares his love for the latter and arranges an assignation. Armado debates with himself his inner conflict, to love or to be true to his oath, but 'Cupid's butt shaft is too hard for Hercules's club' (I. ii. 9-10).

Alchemy

The King as head of his subjects includes Costard and Jaquenetta in the alchemic process and here Costard is following nature in loving the milkmaid.

The mention of Hercules as a great man who loved links the processes of alchemy and love. Green (as the 'green lion'), represented the vitriol which was used to break down the substance, while the red and white symbolised the 'Sophic Sulphur' (called the 'Red King' or 'Red Lion'), and 'Sophic Mercury', the 'White Queen', the initial constituents of the process. Hercules was associated with alchemy as the labours of Hercules represented the labours involved in achieving the different stages of the alchemic 'Great Work'. Shakespeare's company, the King's Men, used the symbol of Hercules over their Globe Theatre, linking the legend with alchemy and theatre. (Alchemical symbolism aside, the efforts of putting on plays are akin to the labours of Hercules!)

Armado is thus associated with the process of alchemical transformation, which he rejects for the moment, accepting the temptations of Cupid rather than Hercules' club (which, as a soldier, he should wield).

Renaissance Platonism

'Base love' is shown in Jaquenetta, who spreads her favours. Already causing Costard to be punished, she will involve Armado and ultimately suffer herself. Armado acknowledges to himself that she is base and that his pursuit of her (as turns out to be true in his making her pregnant) is base, especially as he will be breaking his vow to the King.

Theurgy and Initiation, Rosicrucianism, the Bible

Specific mention is made of the garden in which Costard and Jaquenetta have sinned. As a costard is an apple, and Jaquenetta a kind of Eve, this hints at the temptation in the Garden of Eden, the apple the forbidden fruit.

Ideas and Circumstances relevant to 1598

Costard and Jaquenetta represent indulgence in nature, which Costard enjoys so much that it makes his punishment worthwhile. Here, nature triumphs over art.

Armado corresponds to the Capitano Spavento of the Commedia Dell'Arte. His use of words is over-embroidered, but he has the sense to know when to be direct, so that his carnal wooing of Jaquenetta makes him the only successful lover in the play.

Mote mocks everyone and displays excellent verbal repartee with them.

Story Section 3 (II. i. 1-248)

The Princess of France enters with her court ladies, Rosaline, Maria and Katherine, and the courtier Boyet and attendants. She rejects what she considers to be Boyet's flattering praise of her beauty, and, aware that King Ferdinand has vowed that no woman should come within his court, sends for him to receive her embassy in the park. When her ladies discuss the King's courtiers, it becomes obvious that they know and are attracted to them. The Princess is told that the King, in order not to break his oath, intends that the Princess and her entourage should be lodged in the field.

When the King enters, he is reprimanded by the Princess for his lack of hospitality, declaring, 'Tis deadly sin to keep that oath, my Lord | And sin to break it' (II. i. 105-106). Her wish to speed up the negotiations is foiled by their need to wait for the arrival of documents which would prove France's claim to Aquitaine.

Rosaline and Berowne talk aside – he declaring love, she mocking him. Dumaine asks Boyet after Katharine and Longeville after Maria. Boyet remarks that the King has obviously fallen in love with the Princess and so the love of the four couples is declared.

Alchemy

The Princess as the spirit of the process, and by association her women as the spirits of the men who are the body of the court, are engaged in the alchemy. It is they who will bring about the changes needed in the men.

This begins when the Princess points out to the King the 'sin' of his vow and the sin to break it.

Rosaline begins the long process of changing Berowne, whose name suggests 'brown' which implies earth, another symbol of the base matter of alchemy.

Mote functions as a touchstone, testing the characters.

Renaissance Platonism.
The four couples experience Divine Love, each only partly recognising the other, as the 'veil of illusion' has not been completely removed from the men's eyes.

Theurgy and Initiation, Rosicrucianism, the Bible.
The Princess enters as a hierophant, already acting as moral guide. Her ladies, however, are also candidates for initiation.

Rosaline as the rose at the heart of the labyrinth will be for Berowne the heart of his quest. To achieve her he must endure trials.[6]

Ideas and Circumstances relevant to 1598
The Princess and her ladies complement the four men, making the eight-pattern of set dances of the time.[7] They represent the nature to which the men must submit. The wisdom of the Princess is made clear in her comments to the King. 'The Word is God', and to break it, as the King suggests he should, is to be perjured.

Rosaline begins her mocking of Berowne. Audacious word-games between man and woman were tantamount to love-making.

Story Section 4 (II. i. 1-202)
Armado sends Mote to quickly fetch Costard to deliver a letter from him to Jaquenetta. Mote declares that he will go 'as swift as lead, sir' (III. i. 55), contradicting the paradox by explaining that the lead is as swift as a bullet fired from a gun.

Returning with Costard (suffering a cut on his leg), Mote quips with Armado, who gives him the lines, 'The fox, the ape and the humble-bee| Were still at odds, being but three', to which Mote adds, 'Until the goose came out of the door | Staying the odds by adding four' (III. i. 87-90).

Armado gives Costard a small tip (which he calls a 'remuneration' (III. i. 128) to take his letter to Jaquenetta.

Berowne enters and also pays Costard to deliver a letter – to Rosaline. In soliloquy, he confesses and laments not only his love but its object:

> A whitely wanton with a velvet brow
> With two pitch balls stuck in her face for eyes;
> Ay, and, by heaven, one that will do the deed,
> Though Argus were her eunuch and her guard! (III. i. 193-196)

Alchemy
Here is featured another symbol of the base matter of alchemy, lead, which the process will transform into 'gold'. Base matter could also be symbolised as a dragon (referred to in the motive of St George, the 'higher self', conquering the dragon, the lower or base self), or a snake, which Mote will later act out strangling in his performance as Hercules.

Renaissance Platonism
Berowne accuses Rosaline of base love, for which there is no evidence in the play. He is punished in the misadventure of his letter. He refers to her not as a lady but in a lowly form as 'Joan' (III. i. 202), a name he again calls her when speaking to the King and which will later be associated with vulgarity in the words of the song of Hiems as 'greasy Joan' (V. ii. 918).

Theurgy and Initiation, Rosicrucianism, the Bible
The bee was also a symbol for Christ, as its disappearance for three months of the year mirrored the three days between Christ's crucifixion and resurrection.

Ideas and Circumstances relevant to 1598
Berowne's tirade against the nature of Rosaline is not appropriate to her character as written in the play and may have been transferred on to her as an expression of Shakespeare's own misery caused by a woman, possibly Emilia Lanier.

A Renaissance interpretation of ancient Orphic Mysteries by way of Pythagoras occurs as paradox here in Mote's 'swift as lead'.[8] Following the traditions of Medieval Bestiaries, there was variable symbolism for the different animals mentioned in the Armado/Mote word game. The 'ape' could signify miserliness or unreliability, or be a symbol of hope; the 'fox' implied cunning or slyness, and 'goose' could have sexual connotations.[9] Nevertheless, in our Theatre Set-Up productions we did not perform these lines according to those meanings but enjoyed them as a kind of surreal word-game which the actors and audiences enjoyed.

Story Section 5 (IV. i. 1-150)
The Princess and her ladies prepare to hunt deer, and although the Princess is loath to do so, she admits it is only to gain praise.

Costard enters, bringing a letter for Rosaline from Berowne. However, he has mixed it up with the one from Armado to Jaquenetta and it is this that is read to the ladies. It is a condescending proposal of marriage emphasising an awareness of the difference in their social class. He compares himself to King Cophetua and the Nemean lion (killed by Hercules) and her to the beggar Zenelophon and a lamb that must submit or be killed.

Rosaline is teased by the ladies about Berowne in hunting terms with sexual innuendo. The women also engage in sexual banter with Boyet. Costard joins in with this, admiring all their vulgarity and also the style of Armado and his page.

Alchemy
Armado's comparison of himself to the Nemean lion which was killed by Hercules is apt, as the flaws in his nature, which even the letter reveals, must be 'killed' in the alchemical process symbolised by the labours of Hercules.

Renaissance Platonism
Armado's letter to Jaquenetta exemplifies base love in its arrogance.
The banter between the ladies, with its sexual innuendos, diminishes the quality of their love for the men and degrades it. Their vulgar teasing of Boyet, admired by Costard, displays the symptoms of base love.

Theurgy and Initiation, Rosicrucianism, the Bible
An elderly candidate in Armado is identified as needing initiation. This can also be seen to be required in the ladies.

The principle laid down in Genesis that all creatures on earth are available for mankind to use and kill is challenged by Shakespeare in the sympathy of the Princess for the deer which she will hunt.

Ideas and Circumstances relevant to 1598
There is a possible reference to the Celtic Old Religion in the guise of the Princess as a hunter of deer, as the King of the Celtic Pantheon at the heart of nature was Cernunnos, the antler-headed God. This allies the Princess with the nature-force of which she is the main representative in the play. Armado's letter to Jaquenetta misuses words and images.

Story Section 6 (IV. ii. 1-163)
Holofernes, a schoolmaster, Nathaniel, a curate, and Constable Dull enter, commenting on the hunting skill of the Princess who has killed a deer (a pricket). Holofernes, much admired by Nathaniel, shows off with his use of Latin and versifying.

Jaquenetta and Costard enter, asking Holofernes to read them the letter she assumes comes to her from Armado. It is, however, the letter to Rosaline from Berowne declaring his love for her in a poem in the courtly style of poets such as Petrarch or Ovid. Holofernes sends Jaquenetta and Costard to the King to deliver the letter, as it gives witness of Berowne flouting the law.

Alchemy
Berowne's self-betraying letter, which will disengage the men from their false path and prepare them for alchemy, is on its way.
Renaissance Platonism
Divine Love should be direct, and communicated through the eyes. Berowne claims this, but declares his love in a false, courtly style.
Theurgy and Initiation, Rosicrucianism, the Bible
The curate Nathaniel, although charitable, is not a good witness for his religion.
Ideas and Circumstances relevant to 1598
The theatre ancestor of the character of Holofernes is the Pedant, the Dottore of the Commedia Dell'Arte, and his friend Nathaniel, the Classical Parasite, the Affirmato.

Holofernes pompously speaks language as it is written and he and his friend Nathaniel eat and drink words and insult one language (English) by adulterating it with another (Latin).

Berowne's letter is courtly and imitative.

CHAPTER TWELVE

Story Section 7 (IV. iii.1-362)

Berowne, bearing another poem to Rosaline, again reprimands himself for his state in loving Rosaline. His wish that he would not mind being forsworn of his oath if the other three were in the same state is granted, as he hides to see the King entering and reading a love poem he has written declaring his love for the Princess. The King in turn hides when he sees Longeville reading a love poem to Maria. All the lovers become involved in the declarations of love when Longeville stands aside to hear Dumaine reading his ode to Katharine. Berowne, in response to Dumaine praising his love's amber hair, calls her a raven. Longeville steps forth to challenge Dumaine but is challenged himself by the King, who is in turn reprimanded by Berowne,

> O me, with what strict patience have I sat,
> To see a King transformed to a gnat!
> To see great Hercules whipping a gig,
> And profound Solomon to tune a jig (IV. iii. 163-166).

However, his own fall from grace is proved when Jaquenetta brings in his letter to Rosaline. The four men agree to yield to their loving, and vie with each other about the relative merits of their ladies. The King teases Berowne that the colour of his 'ebony' (IV. iii. 245) love is, 'the badge of hell, the hue of dungeons and the school of night' (IV. iii. 252-253).

They leave this jesting and the King asks Berowne to justify their 'loving lawful and our faith not torn' (IV. iii. 283). Berowne claims that the vows they made were foolish and treasonous against their youth and that love, 'first learned in a lady's eyes…gives to every power a double power', and gives insights into true knowledge. 'They are the books, the arts, the academes | That show, contain, and nourish all the world' (IV. iii. 303-07, 328-329).

Confidently, the four men resolve to woo their ladies with 'revels, dances, masques and merry hours' (IV. iii. 355).

Alchemy
The self-betrayal of all of the men is complete, and the path that will lead to their transformation begun, referred to by Berowne applying the image of 'Hercules whipping a gig' (IV. iii. 165) to the King confessing his love. That Rosaline will be the cause of Berowne's alchemic transformation is implied in the teasing of him about her dark colouring. Black was the colour associated with the stage of alchemy called **Putrefaction** (when the substance at that stage of the process had been turned black), symbolised by a raven.

Renaissance Platonism
The men acknowledge to each other their love to the women, but plan their courtship in a false way. They display base love in the vulgar repartee over the women. The 'veil of illusion' is not lifted yet.

Theurgy and Initiation, Rosicrucianism, the Bible
In engaging themselves to court the ladies who will act as hierophants, guiding them from their current folly, the men prepare to enter the 'labyrinth' of their initiation.

Ideas and Circumstances relevant to 1598
A John Lyly device in representing stage action four times is used here. The action begins to turn from Art to Nature, although the odes and sonnets in which the men express their love to the women are still far from a state of reality.

Story Section 8 (V. i. 1-150)
Holofernes, Nathaniel and Armado meet, and Mote says of them, 'They have been at a great feast of languages and stolen the scraps' (V. i. 36, 37). Holofernes proves that his learning is all from books (not from experience and life) in his misunderstanding of the pronunciation of silent consonants in words. Costard observes, 'O, they have lived long on the alms-basket of words' (V. i. 48, 49), and then delivers what was the longest English word in existence, 'honorificabilitudinitatibus' (V. i. 41).

Armado, claiming the King as his intimate acquaintance, tells Holofernes and Nathaniel that he has asked him to present entertainments to the Princess and asks for their help. Holofernes decides that they should present the popular masque of *The Nine Worthies* (V. i. 111).

Alchemy
The scraps of the feast of words could ironically refer to the eighth alchemical stage, **Cibation**, in which the base matter of alchemy is fed. However, the main process of alchemy has not really begun yet, as the need for its occurrence is demonstrated in the base nature of the men who will become the body of the alchemy which will transform them.

Renaissance Platonism
The masque of *The Nine Worthies* was originally designed as a moral guide, and Holofernes obviously feels that it is appropriate to put it on before the two courts of the young King and Princess.

Theurgy and Initiation, Rosicrucianism, the Bible
An example of the kind of falseness with the use of words that the men are about to practise is exampled here.

Ideas and Circumstances relevant to 1598
The summation of word-abuse occurs in this 'feast of words'.

Story Section 9 (V. ii. 1-485)
Laughingly the Princess and her ladies show each other the favours their lovers have given them. The King has given the Princess diamonds, Longeville has given Maria pearls, Dumaine's present to Katharine is a pair of gloves and Berowne, it is later revealed, has given Rosaline a pearl. They are warned that the men are coming to woo them disguised as Russians, and the Princess tells her ladies to put on masks and exchange favours and thus identities, so that the men will be courting the wrong women. 'They do it but in mockery merriment, | And mock for mock is only my intent.' (V. ii. 139-140). She also instructs her ladies not to dance if asked, because, to shame them, 'there's no such sport as sport by sport o'erthrown' (V. ii. 153).

Her plans succeed, the men's artifice is humiliated, and they go. When the men return in their own identities, the King invites the Princess and her ladies to enter his court to receive proper hospitality. The Princess disdains to be the cause of breaking his vow.

When Rosaline makes it clear to Berowne, in response to his telling her directly that he loves her, that she knew he was disguised as a Russian, he pledges future honesty and plain speaking, 'henceforth my wooing mind shall be expressed | In russet yeas and honest kersey noes' (V. ii.

42-43). He pleads with all the women to have mercy on their lovers, but they further tease them by revealing that they have courted the wrong disguised men. Berowne is incensed.

Alchemy
The baseness of the base matter is further shown here, as the men sport with love and the women purge their immaturity and falsity.
Renaissance Platonism
The men carry out their silly plans, alienating the women. However, the veil of illusion is lifted slightly when Berowne vows to be more direct in future.
Theurgy and Initiation, Rosicrucianism, the Bible
In this entanglement in the labyrinth of the park, the masks that they all wear will have to be discarded if initiation is to succeed.
Ideas and Circumstances relevant to 1598
The Mocking Game reaches its pinnacle. As a result, Berowne vows in his promise to be plainer and nearer to nature in his expression.

Story Section 10 (V. ii. 486-662)
Costard announces that the masque of the Worthies is ready, and all the courtiers receive this entertainment. However, the men are rude to the well-meaning performers by mocking them, thereby showing off to the ladies, who are not impressed. Neither are Holofernes and Armado who reprimand them, 'This is not generous, not gentle, not humble' (V. ii. 627).

Alchemy
A depth of baseness is reached in the mocking of the well-meaning performers. Mote as Hercules strangling the snake represents a dominant paradigm of alchemy carried out by the labour of the alchemist, conquering the base matter of the process (and in its psychological aspect, alchemically transforming the 'self'). In his attempt to humiliate Holofernes, Berowne sarcastically makes reference to St George (symbol of the higher self or the soul), but the inappropriateness of this is implied in the following comment from Dumaine that in this instance St George is made of lead (which ironically represents base matter).[10]

Renaissance Platonism
Further alienation of the ladies from the men takes place during the masque, when the men's rude behaviour takes them into a descent from Divine Love.
Theurgy and Initiation, Rosicrucianism, the Bible
The young men show themselves to be in considerable need of improvement and maturity, true candidates for initiation.
Ideas and Circumstances relevant to 1598
The masque of *The Nine Worthies*, originally elevating worthy men of history, had become by this time debased by too much inadequate performance, like the interlude of *Pyramus and Thisbe* in *Dream*. Mockery turns on itself as the courtiers forget their courtly duty in cruel mockery of the masquers. Punning and clever word play is misused for mockery, and Berowne abuses language by showing off.

Story Section 11 (V. ii. 663-862)
The masque is interrupted by Berowne telling Costard that Jaquenetta is pregnant by Armado. Costard (still dressed as Pompey) challenges Armado (still performing Hector) to a fight over her.

This farce is in turn interrupted by Monsieur Marcado, a messenger from France, announcing to the Princess that her father has died. The Princess orders arrangements for her departure, but the King tactlessly begs her to stay.

Berowne pleads that it is the fault of the ladies that they have, 'Played foul with our oaths' (V. ii. 751). He claims that their beauty, 'Hath much deformed us' (V. ii. 752). In response, the Princess tells him that they have rated the courtships as, 'pleasant jest, and courtesy' (V. ii. 775).

When the King asks the ladies to, 'Grant us your loves' (V. ii. 784), the Princess replies, 'A time, methinks, too short | To make a world-without-end bargain in' (V. ii. 785-786). She then tells him that as he has broken his oath she cannot trust him, and if he wishes to win her love he must go immediately to, 'some forlorn and naked hermitage, remote from all the pleasures of the world' (V. ii. 790-791), and there for twelve months endure hardship to test his love 'made in the heat of blood' (V. ii. 795). If, at the end of the year, he still loves her, she will be his. Meanwhile, she will shut herself up in a 'mourning house' (V. ii. 803) in remembrance of her father's death.

Katharine imposes similar conditions upon Dumaine, as does Maria upon Longeville, but Rosaline has harsher terms for Berowne. To expiate his cruel indiscriminate mocking, he must for a year visit 'the speechless sick' and talk with 'groaning wretches' (V. ii. 840-841), and use his wit to make them smile.

Alchemy

The entrance of Marcade (whose name implies Mercury, the agent of alchemy) dressed in black, heralds the true beginning of the alchemy. The black he wears not only represents mourning for the King, the father of the Princess, but also the black stage of **Putrefaction**.

The Princess, as the spirit of the alchemical process, enacts this stage of alchemy upon the King, the body or base matter of the alchemy, by insisting that they separate, he to be tried and tested, and she to be isolated in mourning. At the end of that time if he survives the harsh process they will be reunited as the spirit and body reunite in alchemy when the body has been transformed, and then the process may go forward to achieve the gold, the Philosophers' Stone of redeemed matter. The King agrees to the demands of the Princess, and a golden outcome is implied, as indeed it is with all four couples.

Renaissance Platonism

After gross insensitivity to those they claim to love, the men are at last forced to remove the 'veil of illusion' and embark on trials which will, if they are constant, grant them Divine Love and begin their 'ascent to God'.

Theurgy and Initiation, Rosicrucianism, the Bible

The 'death experience' occurs with the announcement of the death of the King of France.

This is obviously felt most by the Princess, but its effect will carry on into the two courts as it will put an end to her visit and the men's courtship.

The beginning of the process of initiation of the men is declared as the women compel them to endure the necessary trials. Rosaline, in giving Berowne tasks to perform within the community, is following the precepts of Rosicrucianism.[11]

Ideas and Circumstances relevant to 1598

The real world interrupts the masque and the courtly games that have predominated over the play so far, with the entrance of Marcade. The women force the men to abandon the artifice of the court and to come to terms with reality. Nature has triumphed over art.

Story Section 12 (V. ii. 863-920)
The women prepare to depart as Berowne protests:

> Our wooing doth not end like an old play;
> Jack hath not Jill. These ladies' courtesy
> Might well have made our sport a comedy. (V. ii. 863-865)

Armado enters to announce that he has vowed to Jaquenetta to 'hold the plough for her sweet love three year' (V. ii. 872), and to present a dialogue composed by Holofernes and Nathaniel, between Vers (spring) in praise of the cuckoo, and Hiems (winter) in praise of the owl. At its conclusion, Armado says, 'The words of Mercury are harsh after the songs of Apollo. You that way; we this way' (V. ii. 919-920).

Alchemy
The final songs of spring, then winter, confirm the alchemic process, as after the merriment in the preceding scenes (as the 'songs of Apollo'), the words of the agent of alchemy, Mercury, initiate the alchemy of the separating couples, the men the body of the process, the women the spirit.
Renaissance Platonism
The trials that the men must face in order to prove their constancy in Divine Love to the women are reflected in the final songs in the 'words of Mercury' of harsh winter after their happy rompings in the 'songs of Apollo'.
Theurgy and Initiation, Rosicrucianism, the Bible
The pattern of the play is mirrored in the songs, and both men and women begin their initiations (heralded by the words of Mercury, considered by the Greeks to be a key spiritual hierophant). Observing the proper decorum, the men go one way, the women the other.
Ideas and Circumstances relevant to 1598
The two songs, in a dialogue between the seasons of nature, are written in plain language with homely images, nature triumphing over art and words.

Cabala: Post Production (see fig. 3)

Like the other arcana relevant to this play, little ascent of the Hebraic Tree of Life is attained throughout most of the action. The King, in his intention to abjure all sensual pleasures in the pursuit of an academic life, commits himself, his courtiers and his subjects to an unbalanced life not grounded in **Malkuth (the material world)** and featuring the sphere **Hod (thoughts)** to the exclusion of all else. That Berowne cautions the King of the folly of this plan singles him out for a possible candidate for progress throughout the Tree. The Spanish braggart, Don Adriano De Armado, whom the King allows for entertainment to the courtiers, proves to be well grounded in **Malkuth**.

Berowne's cautions are realised in the conviction of Costard and Jaquenetta for adultery. Armado falls in love with Jaquenetta and debates the virtues of his love at **Netzach (feelings)** against the restraints of **Hod (thoughts)** as prescribed by the King. He favours **Netzach**.

This will also be the fate of the King and his courtiers, as they fall in love with the Princess and her ladies who have come to the court. However, as they are not grounded in **Malkuth**, the progress of their love on the sphere of **Netzach** will be silly and unconvincing. This is in contrast with the Princess and her ladies, who adopt a balanced view of their relationships with the men, tempering **Netzach** with **Hod**.

The love of Armado for Jaquenetta is patronising and base, fixing it on **Netzach** with no prospect of an ascent to **Chesed (the archetype of love and awareness)**.

Holofernes and Nathaniel display another aspect of **Hod**, academic but not genuine, lacking the balance of **Netzach** and unsuited to ascend to **Geburah (Will and Power)**.

Berowne begins to be grounded in **Malkuth** with future honesty and plain speaking when Rosaline condemns his pretence as a visiting Russian.

The rudeness of the King and his courtiers to the well-meaning performers of the *Masque of Worthies* shows a lack of judgment in their characters, which will have to be addressed if they are to ascend the Tree.

The real world enters as **Malkuth** in the revelation that Armado has made Jaquenetta pregnant and that the father of the Princess has died. The King still demonstrates lack of **Netzach** (as feelings) and **Geburah** (as judgement) when he asks the Princess to remain at his court and not return immediately to the mourning of the death of her father.

The result of this is a demand from the Princess and her ladies of their lovers that they enter the real world of **Malkuth** for a year, giving service to those in need, and at the end of a year they will give an answer to the men regarding their proposals of marriage. The Princess herself will enter the sphere of **Chesed** in mourning for her father.

The play ends with the dialogue between winter (as **Hod, Geburah** and **Binah**) and spring (as **Netzach, Chesed** and **Chokmah (spiritual purpose)**) representing the relationship between the feminine negative energy flow as typified by the women's severe conditions imposed upon the men and the positive masculine energy flow of the tasks the men will undertake to achieve the balance on the Tree of union with the women.

CHAPTER THIRTEEN: *THE TAMING OF THE SHREW*

When performing *The Taming of the Shrew* in 1994, Theatre Set-Up considered this play to be so dominantly a Shakespearean spin-off from the Italian La Commedia Dell'Arte that the play's programme did not follow the pattern of other years. Instead of stating the secret meanings corresponding with each section of the story, the arcana were dealt with in separate paragraphs.

Regular members of our audiences complained about this, so I returned to the charts in future years, but as the historic application of the arcana to the Theatre Set-Up productions of the plays is recorded herein, I follow the practice of that year in the abbreviated form we followed.

Often today the play is discarded for performance because of the bullying treatment that Petruchio metes out to Katherina. In spite of the 'taming' programme, during which her husband succeeds in modifying her behaviour so that she is no longer shrewish, it seems unlikely that the strong and intelligent Katherina should have her spirit broken to such an extent that she should become as submissive and pliable as her speech at V. ii. 137-180 might imply. Besides, such a brutish and insensitive attitude towards women (in spite of the strictures of the Biblical *Genesis*) on the part of Shakespeare is inconsistent with our understanding of his views in his other plays. Taking the arcana into account, we solved this problem to our satisfaction so that a plausible performance from our actress playing Katherina was possible.

Another factor to be considered is that Shakespeare's company performed at the court of the magnificent Queen Elizabeth I, and I think that he would have lacked diplomacy, even strategy, to suggest in one of his plays that women were inferior to men and should be subservient to them!

The emphasis of the 1994 Theatre Set-Up production was on the Commedia style of each of the characters, which were presented in the 18th century form of a Harlequinade, with colourful masks, wigs and costumes, the transformations within the story carried out by the character of Harlequin/Grumio flourishing his slapstick (see fig. 43). The social issues of the play

CHAPTER THIRTEEN

concerning the rights and obligations within child-parent and husband-wife relationships, which are so much the focus of Shakespeare's play, were given prominence within the production. It seemed to us that he showed sensitivity to the problems of women such as Katherina and Bianca in their economic dependence on men, either fathers or husbands, so that they were treated as commodities. In his selection of the Commedia Dell'Arte style of this play he made use of the trickery that young lovers practised on their parents in order to escape from the bondage of imposed marriage settlements, and thus created a comedy from a situation whose outcome was so often tragic for the woman. Our justification for deciding that the play had a Commedia source was Shakespeare's description of Gremio as 'a Pantaloon', an Anglicised form of the Commedia character, Pantalone.[1] Our source of Commedia Dell' Arte information of all kinds including costume, masks, characterisation and movement was the book *La Commedia Dell'Arte* by Cesare Molinari, which we had been given on the subject by the host of one of our venues, Mottisfont Abbey.[2] We performed the play's characters according to the following Commedia Dell' Arte correspondences:

Player in the Interlude, Bianca = young female lover
Biondello = a Zanni (see fig. 42)
Lord in the Interlude, Lucentio (later disguised as Cambio) = young male lover
Curtis = a Zanni
Tailor = a Zanni
Pedant = Il Dottore
Vincentio = father of male lover
Grumio = Harlequin (the main Zanni – see fig. 43)
Baptista – father of the female lovers
Player in the Interlude, Katherina = young female lover
Gremio = Pantalone
Peter = a Zanni
Widow = the Signora
Petruchio = Il Capitano
Tranio = Brighella
Hortensio = young lover, later disguised as Licio = Scapino

We made full use of the character-defining masks and costumes in order to have several people (regardless of gender) perform the same roles, the actors performing Bianca and Katherina doubling as Biondello (see fig. 42) and the actors performing Lucentio and Hortensio doubling as the Pedant. Those same masks and costumes facilitated our usual doubling and trebling of roles and made it more plausible for women to perform comic male roles. Everyone enjoyed the whole process, which was just as well, as we performed in 42 venues in seven countries over a period of five months!

Obviously we studied Petruchio's declared method of taming Katherina in terms of the techniques of falconry in which the austringer uses the regulation of the bird's food and rest to condition its behaviour, this being the justification of his actions which cause her transformation.

The usual benefits of deepening perceptions of character and story were attained through study of the secret meanings, but of greatest help to us in preparing and rehearsing the play was the light they threw on Petruchio's treatment of Katharina and her seemingly submissive speech at the end of the play. Insights into Bianca and her young suitors were also discovered.

We found these meanings and themes most useful:

- **Alchemy**, and, importantly within that, the Renaissance holistic concept of the link between the microcosm (humans) and the macrocosm (the cosmos) in relation to the story.
- **Theurgy / Initiation**
- **Role, disguise and deception** in the play.

The Renaissance Platonism idea of Companion Souls in Divine Love (see above pp. 34-36) can be identified in Katherina/Petruchio and Lucentio/Bianca, but we considered that its role in the play is subjugated by the Commedia Dell' Arte features of the plot, as are any Biblical references.

Alchemy
At the beginning of the play, Tranio recommends that his master, Lucentio, should read Ovid's *Metamorphoses*. This book features metaphors of alchemy, thus hinting at Shakespeare's intentions. It is Katherina who

becomes the 'base matter' of the alchemy of the play. She is obviously unhappy, socially unacceptable, and in need of change. In the alchemical interpretation of the story, Petruchio establishes her as the goal of the alchemy he will practise upon her by declaring as his aim the gold her dowry will give him, 'Hortensio, peace. Thou know'st not gold's effect' (I. ii. 92).

Petruchio's name carries the etymological meaning of 'rock', from the Latin 'petros', meaning 'rock'. This gives us the possible reading of Philosophers' Stone, thus indicating that the goal for Katherina's/gold's alchemic transformation is harmonic union with Petruchio. He certainly undertakes the 'labour of Hercules', Gremio describing Petruchio's intended wooing of her in the terms of the labours of Hercules (Alcides being his alternative name), the paradigm for the process of alchemy:

> Yea, leave that labour to great Hercules,
> And let it be more than Alcides twelve (I. ii. 254-255).

Petruchio certainly undertakes these labours with a sense of destiny and purpose:

> For I am he born to tame you, Kate,
> And bring you from a wild Kate to a Kate
> Conformable as other household Kates (II. i. 269-271).

There are twelve steps to his 'taming', which will beneficially transform her and bring her into line with the potential of her life and psyche, corresponding with the twelve stages of alchemy:

- **Calcination**: he woos her roughly.
- **Dissolution**: he announces his intention to marry her and then departs.
- **Seperation**: he uses 'shock therapy', terrifies her, and begins to separate her from her traditional patterns of behaviour by being late for his wedding and then appearing disrespectfully dressed.
- **Conjunction**: he marries her.

- **Putrefaction**: he totally breaks down her shrewishness through his rough behaviour to his servants, and by starving her and denying her sleep and new clothing.
- **Congelation**: he confirms her renewing self by the tests on the road, culminating with the requested kiss. It is at this point, I believe, that Katherina sees the humour in her situation and turns the tables on Petruchio by exaggerating her requested response to his demands that she should address Vincentio as if he were a young woman:

> Young budding virgin, fair, and fresh, and sweet,
> Whither away, or where is thy abode?
> Happy the parents of so fair a child,
> Happier the man whom favourable stars
> Allots thee for his lovely bedfellow (IV. v. 36-41).

I think that it is at this point that the match between Petruchio and Katherina is made with their shared humour.

- **Cibation**: he rewards her by allowing her to attend Lucentio's feast.
- **Sublimation**: he tests her again in demanding her presence and commanding her to throw her cap underfoot.
- **Firmentation:** he 'firms up' her new nature by asking her to deliver a lecture on wifely duty to the widow. In this speech, the alchemic principle of 'as above, so below', an interdependence between heaven and earth linking the harmony of the cosmos with harmony among humans, is demonstrated. What Petruchio has forcefully taught Katherina is that in order to achieve 'cosmic harmony', she must contribute to harmony within her marriage by playing the role considered appropriate by the society of her time, to be, 'Conformable as other household Kates' (II. i. 271). She is forced to accept this, but in her turn she cleverly uses the speech Petruchio asks her to make to set out what she considers to be his complementary role within the marriage:

> Thy husband is thy lord, thy life, thy keeper,
> Thy head, thy sovereign; one that cares for thee,
> And for thy maintenance; commits his body
> To painful labour both by sea and land,
> To watch the night in storms, the day in cold,
> Whilst thou liest warm at home, secure and safe (V. ii. 147-152).

She also indicates that in return for the forced compromise of her own integrity as an individual in favour of the interests of ultimate harmony (and in accord with the strictures of the Biblical Genesis), she is now prepared to be strategic like her sister Bianca and to manipulate a man by use of feminine wiles in a way that she would not have considered before:

> Why are our bodies soft, and weak and smooth,
> Unapt to toil and trouble in the world
> But that our soft conditions and our hearts
> Should well agree with our external parts? (V. ii. 166-169)

She thus suggests a modification of his ideas of her role. That she is physically flirting with him in pointing out her 'external parts' might be indicated in her classifying them as 'soft and weak and smooth'. This is hardly the impression she has given of her physique in her boisterous behaviour earlier in the play!

- **Exaltation**: he indicates the success of the process with the triumphant words, 'Why there's a wench! Come on, and kiss me, Kate' (V. ii. 181).
- **Multiplication**: he indicates a fecund future for the three couples by saying, 'Come Kate, we'll to bed. We three are married but you two are sped' (V. ii. 185-186). (The two he refers to being the old men, Baptista and Gremio.)
- **Projection**: he leaves Hortensio and Lucentio to follow his methods if they are to attain a like result.

It can also be claimed that in all this process he is acting as the agent of the alchemy, but also being worked on himself. In order to carry through the process on her he must undergo the trials himself. She herself works on him to effect his transformation into a fit partner to achieve the 'gold' of union with her in her homily speech when she subtly suggests that he modify his attitude to become less tyrannical (V. ii. 137-180).

Theurgy and Initiation
Lucentio and Hortensio have, during the course of the play, identified their need to be changed. To woo Bianca, Lucentio adopts the disguise of a scholar and the pseudonym 'Cambio', which means 'change,' but he does not make the kinds of efforts which will transform him and enable him to perceive Bianca's true nature. Hortensio also adopts a physical disguise, which he discards to court the widow as himself, having previously declared of Bianca:

> If once I find thee ranging,
> Hortensio will be quit with thee by changing (III. i. 89-90).

However, that change is external and he does not make sufficient effort to effect a harmonious relationship with his widow.

An indication that Petruchio is himself intended to become a willing initiate lies in his description of his entry into Padua as, 'I have thrust myself into this maze' (I. ii. 54).

The motif of the maze or labyrinth is an ancient one, symbolising the path and journey of an initiate (a neophyte). The psychological journey of trials and ordeals leading to the 'soul centre', where the neophyte is rewarded by an experience of the 'Divine' and then taken outward to give the benefit of the experience to others, is circular, here suggesting the journey of Petruchio and Katherina from Padua to Verona and back.

Katherina is the obvious main neophyte with Petruchio her hierophant, leading her to a knowledge of her true self, but he must also experience the trials she suffers and change to adapt to the new wife he has created for himself, accepting the challenge she gives him in her homily speech of V. ii. so that they can become the compatible couple suggested in V. ii.

177-181. She offers him her hand to be placed submissively beneath his foot, but he takes it to pull her to him for a kiss, 'Why there's a wench! Come on, and kiss me, Kate' (V. ii. 181).

Role, Disguise and Deception
One of the supposed effects of the 'raising of consciousness', as the improved state of being created by a successful initiation was called, was the heightened perception of truth and beauty.

This play deals consistently with false perceptions of truth and beauty, beginning with an induction during which the tinker, Christopher Sly, is persuaded that he is a lord, and a troupe of players enact a play before him which is itself a fiction. Shakespeare demonstrates how subtle deception can be by leading the audience into the play so completely that they forget the reality of Sly's situation as it is absorbed by the overriding interest of the play. In many ways, this comments on the nature of theatre itself, which is untrue but so based on supposed truth that fiction seems reality and fictitious characters take on a life of their own. One of the sources for the material of the plot of *Shrew* is George Gascoigne's *Supposes*, perhaps an inspiration for this aspect of the play.[3] The term 'induction' itself contains the meaning of 'initiation' and, used as it is in this play, could be intended to hint at the use Shakespeare makes of this play as a process of initiation.

Petruchio shows himself to be a potentially successful initiate in immediately identifying the beauty of Katherina's essential self while others condemn her. Her sister Bianca, however, manages to deceive the men around her into feeling false contempt for her. In the final scene of the play, she is revealed as the real 'shrew', and she and Lucentio must both change if they are to attain a harmonious relationship.

Hortensio identifies the need to value inner rather than external beauty:

Kindness in women, not their beauteous looks,
Shall win my love (IV. ii. 50, 51).

However, he still marries for material gold and gets the uneasy marriage he deserves.

Baptista's materialistic false values (shown especially in II. i. 324-391 when he seeks the highest price from her suitors for a marriage with Bianca) are foiled, as he is made the butt of every deception.

The confusion created by the appearance of the real Vincentio in the city where both he and his son are being impersonated is only resolved by his son's decision to be truthful and ask his father's forgiveness. This marks the beginning of Lucentio's successful initiation in the admission of his true self and the discarding of all the disguise and trickery that have attained Bianca as his bride.

'Disguise I see thou art a wickedness' was a theme Shakespeare later treated in greater detail in *Twelfth Night*.

Cabala: Post Production (see fig. 3)

Petruchio is well grounded in **Malkuth (Kingdom, the material world experienced through the senses)**, a man of the world, and a successful soldier, recent heir of his father's estate and money, looking for a rich wife to complete his happiness. His need may be to ascend the Hebraic Tree of Life to become a more sympathetic human being.

Katherina is all chaotic **Netzach (Victory, emotions)**, a mess of feelings leading to unrestrained physical violence, and she needs her confused psyche to be cleared in **Yesod (Foundation, the subconscious)** and to be grounded in **Malkuth**.

Lucentio begins his entry into Padua seeking only to study as the thinking **Hod (Glory, thoughts)**, but is soon captivated by Bianca and acquires the features of **Netzach**. In order to achieve Bianca, he pulls in the features of **Hod** to outwit her father.

The old men, Baptista and Gremio, are cemented into the materialistic aspects of **Malkuth**, Gremio displaying the inappropriate lust of a younger man in a feature of indulgence of the senses in **Malkuth**. Baptista and Gremio lack balance and reason.

Petruchio's psychological technique of taking Katherina's negative statements as positive ones and pretending that everything he does is to her benefit will gradually bring her to **Yesod**, and his physical 'taming', especially when he overcomes her physical violence with his greater physical strength, represents a shock method of shaking her out of her unhealthy emotional condition on **Netzach,** devoid of the balance of **Hod**. His depriving her of food and rest, a known method, which he acknowledges, of controlling birds and animals, will control her emotions and lead to features of **Hod** so that she achieves a balanced personality.

Lucentio's deception of Baptista and his father prevents his ascent through the Tree, but when he confesses his wrongs and apologises to his father, he has enlisted the features of **Yesod** and cleared his guilt so that he can achieve an ascent, his love for Bianca moving through **Tiphareth (Beauty, heart)** to **Chesed (Mercy)** and **Geburah (Strength)**.

The success of Petruchio's actions is realised when Katherina's sense of humour enables her to clear away her psychological problems in **Yesod** and become part of a game she performs with her husband in calling Vincentio a young girl. She has reached **Hod** in accepting the logic of her situation and extending it into **Geburah**. That she genuinely loves Petruchio, so is more happily located on **Netzach**, is indicated in her reluctance to kiss him due to embarrassment in public, but not from lack of love, on the journey back to Padua. She presents an adjusted personality, ready to enjoy humour with an exciting and original husband. I consider that she extends her power through **Geburah, Binah (Understanding, spiritual love)** and **Chesed** in her homily speech, using her sexuality and considerable mental powers to negotiate a more balanced relationship in the marriage. Cabalists regard sexual union as a feature of spiritual ecstasy, and that is promised as Petruchio and Katherina rise to **Kether (Crown, Divinity)** with their kiss and exit to bed at the end of the play.

CHAPTER FOURTEEN: *TWELFTH NIGHT*

This play is a delight to perform, funny, lyrical and romantic, but it suffers from an interpretation of these dramatic qualities as an indication of lightness of content. Its title, which names the day the Christmas and New Year festivities end with rousing celebrations, indicates its function as a festive play. However, the pain and stoicism of its heroine, Viola, saves it from being regarded as the farce into which it could descend with the romping of Sir Toby Belch, Sir Andrew Aguecheek, Feste and their gulling of the pompous Malvolio. The music referenced by Orsino in the opening of the play:

> If music be the food of love, play on,
> Give me excess of it, that, surfeiting,
> The appetite may sicken and so die. (I. i. 1-3)

permeates the play and is key to its enjoyment, both for the performers and audience.

Theatre Set-Up performed the play in 1997 after the secret meanings were researched and the results were available for the play's interpretation. It was a six month long season and included a performance in Sarajevo, Bosnia and Herzegovina, as part of the first presentation of the MESS International Theatre Festival after the War, including the siege of Sarajevo (lasting from 1992-96) that had beset the region.[1] As Shakespeare sets the play in Illyria, the ancient name for that country and several of its neighbours, we costumed it in Balkan dress appropriate to his time. We selected readily available music from nearby Romania for the songs, accompanied on our hammered dulcimer, an instrument prevalent in the Balkans for many centuries.

We presented the play in 48 venues during the six-month season, with several cast changes needed due to their earlier commitments, so it was not an easy passage from late spring, when we started rehearsing, to the end of the season in late autumn. Although the secret meanings were embraced by the cast in the preparation of their parts, their significance became lost amidst the rigours of the tour. However, the audiences appreciated my analysis of the play's arcana in the tabular-form (demanded by our regular audience members) in the play's programme notes, which I produce in modified form below.

The secret meanings were revealed under the headings of **Alchemy**, **Renaissance Platonism** and **British Festivity, Magic, and Rites of Initiation**.

Story Section 1 (I. i.)
We are introduced to the court of the Duke of Illyria, Orsino, whose heart pines for the love of the beautiful countess Olivia, who persistently rejects his courtship and that of all others while she remains in mourning for her recently-dead brother. The courtier, Valentine, tells Orsino that she has vowed to be veiled like a nun for seven years, and, circling around her chamber, to weep in memory of her brother's love.

Alchemy
The 'base matter' of the alchemy, in its psychological application (as researched by Jung, see above p. 26) can be a metaphor for the 'psyche' or 'self' which needs to be transmuted, its different elements improved and integrated so that an adjusted whole personality can be achieved. In this play this self can be interpreted as Illyria, as in *Dream* it was Athens, the different characters in the country treated as if they were different elements of the psyche.

The initial components of alchemy were 'sophic sulphur', often represented as the sun, or as a man who could be the father, brother or husband of the moon or woman, the 'sophic mercury', who could be his daughter, wife or sister. In order for the process to be started, they must be combined and then separated in a kind of death. It was an ancient belief observed by alchemy that only from death can life spring.

Here we learn that Olivia has been separated by death from the brother she had loved. Orsino suffers the delusion that he is allegorically the sophic sulphur to her sophic mercury, but it is her dead brother who performs that function. From his death, new life will be generated into the process. A flaw in the allegorical element of the self of Illyria which

Olivia represents is seen in her obsessive mourning for her brother. As Orsino suggests, her true love should be bestowed on a husband, but she denies that possibility in her nun-like behaviour. Orsino himself mistakes the 'Divinity' (the goal of alchemy, the 'Philosophers' Stone') in his heart for Olivia.

Renaissance Platonism

Orsino is wrong in thinking that Olivia is his companion soul, and although he is constant in his devotion to her, this is misplaced. He indicates this in naming love 'fancy', an artificial form of affection. Flowers were considered to be symbols of sex, so in wishing to lie on beds of flowers, he expresses 'base love':

> Away before me to sweet beds of flowers!
> Love thoughts lie rich when canopied with bowers. (I. i. 41-42)

Olivia's constancy in her mourning is also misplaced, as it denies access to her true companion soul. This obstacle is symbolised by the veil she wears.

British Festivity, Magic and Rites of Initiation

Orsino compares his pursuit of Olivia's heart with hunting a deer or hart. This is significant not only as he identifies himself with the hero of the Greek myth Acteon, who, out hunting with his hounds, caught site of the virgin goddess Artemis while she was bathing, and was subsequently turned into a hart and killed by his own hounds, but also because Cernunnos, the Celtic deer-god, was head of the Celtic pantheon. This might imply a British atmosphere to the play in spite of its Illyrian setting.

The reported mourning ritual of Olivia circling her chamber for seven years has overtones of the magic practice which features the number seven in its rituals. However, neither Olivia nor Orsino show themselves as active enough to undertake initiation or magic on behalf of their country, Illyria.

Story Section 2 (I. ii.)

Viola, saved from drowning by the captain of the storm-wrecked ship in which she had been travelling with her twin brother, Sebastian, is cast on the shores of Illyria. She laments the loss of her brother, but is cheered by the news that he was last seen binding himself to a mast which successfully rode the waves. Needing to find some employment by which to fend for herself, and hearing that the countess Olivia, due to her mourning, is unapproachable, Viola resolves to disguise herself as a man and seek to be a page in the court of the Count Orsino, asking the captain to assist her.

Alchemy

Another sister and brother have been separated, this time by a storm, often the alchemists' symbol of 'Nigredo', the 'black' stage of the process, during which the elements of the alchemic process are brutally torn apart.

However, in her choice of male disguise in order to be accepted as Orsino's page, she is shown to have a larger purpose in the alchemical allegory. As a woman disguised as a man, she represents another symbol for the Philosophers' Stone, the hermaphrodite or 'rebus', a 'one-thing' above the limitations of either sex, and a metaphor for Divinity in all things, often also portrayed as the Greco-Roman god, Mercury (see above p. 33). In this aspect, she thus becomes the goal of the alchemy, and when someone achieves possession of her, the alchemy will be symbolically completed. She demonstrates in her vigorous approach to life the essence of the self which will reanimate the psyche.

Renaissance Platonism

The Elizabethans believed that the sea could be a symbol of chaos from which order could be created.[2] Here Viola, the person who will bring Orsino and Olivia their true companion souls, represents this true order. However, the male disguise she plans for herself will place a veil between her and her companion soul, Orsino, and delude Olivia.[3]

British Festivity, Magic and Rites of Initiation

The sea delivers up Viola, who is fit to be the neophyte for the allegorical representation of rites of initiation for Illyria. She has already endured trial by water. The captain is a guide.

Story Section 3 (I. iii.)

We are introduced to Olivia's household. Her chambermaid, Maria, is hoping for marriage with Olivia's elder cousin, Sir Toby Belch, her house guest, who has introduced as a courtier to Olivia a foolish knight, Sir Andrew Aguecheek, in order to sponge off him.

Alchemy

It is a very important component of the allegory of alchemy in this play that the alchemical process works upon a base matter, the material (a chemical, a mineral such as lead, or the flawed psyche itself) which needs to be improved by being purged and transmuted. Here, Sir Toby Belch and Sir Andrew Aguecheek are seen as some of the base matter. If Maria succeeds in marrying Sir Toby she will perhaps curb his excesses. Sir Toby and Sir Andrew represent uncontrolled elements of the self.

Renaissance Platonism

Sir Toby Belch, inviting Sir Andrew Aguecheek to woo Olivia for her money, incites him to practise a wrongful base love.

British Festivity, Magic and Rites of Initiation

Sir Toby Belch functions as a 'Lord of Misrule', a person appointed to be in charge of festivities and given licence to mock his superiors and invert social order.

Story Section 4 (I. iv. I. v.) Viola, disguised as a page called Cesario, has won favour with Orsino, who sends her as the ambassador of his love to Olivia. She does this reluctantly, as she herself has fallen in love with Orsino. After an unexplained absence, Olivia's fool, Feste, returns to her household and is mocked by her arrogant steward, Malvolio, who also tries to turn from the door the insistent Viola (masquerading as Cesario).

Fascinated by the page's stubborn behaviour, Olivia allows her to enter and present Orsino's courtship, but, in the mistaken belief that Cesario is a man, falls in love with her. Viola realises this and the harm that disguise can bring about, when Olivia sends Malvolio in pursuit of her to give her a ring which, she falsely claims, was an unwanted present given to her by Viola from Orsino.

Alchemy

Viola plays the part of Mercury (as a messenger god) in her role as messenger to Olivia from Orsino. The ultimate success of the alchemical process being achieved through her function as the Philosophers' Stone is hinted at in her love for Orsino, which cannot currently be acknowledged because of her male disguise. The representation by the stage action of many processes of alchemy must take place before this hidden love she feels for him can be acknowledged and returned, symbolising the extraction of the Philosophers' Stone from base matter .

In the graphic representations of alchemy the image of the god Mercury could also represent an agent of alchemy, acting upon the elements of the process, purging and guiding them. Feste demonstrates this essential function as he moves from Orsino's court to Olivia's household, 'catechising' (or purging) his social superiors of their folly. He will also be part of the necessary purging of Malvolio, another element of the base matter of the self. Olivia suffers the delusion that Viola is the Divinity in her heart.

Renaissance Platonism

Companion souls often recognise each other instantly. Viola knows that she has fallen in love with Orsino, but he is confused over his feelings for what he considers to be a boy. As soon as Olivia sees Viola, her soul recognises the outward form of her companion soul, Sebastian, and she falls in love, although it is with a false image. Viola, in commenting on the harm that disguise can do in creating delusions does not realise that she is preparing the way for Olivia's true companion soul, Sebastian. She also reprimands Olivia for 'veiling' her beauty from love.

British Festivity, Magic and Rites of Initiation

Viola continues her trials as a neophyte of initiation in her pain of unrequited love of Orsino. She enters a labyrinth of confusion (which she calls a 'knot') when Olivia falls in love with her.

Feste, Olivia's fool, is the spirit of festival. He moves about taking festivity with him in his music and jesting. The kill-joy, Malvolio, represents the spirit of winter

Story Section 5 (II. i.)

Viola's brother, Sebastian, has been saved from drowning by Antonio who is, however, an enemy of the Count Orsino and therefore in danger of arrest if found near his court. They arrive on the coast of Illyria and Sebastian resolves to go to Orsino's court. Antonio inadvisably decides to follow him.

Alchemy
Sebastian, saved by Antonio, joins forces with Viola as symbolic Mercury. Antonio, as an unruly element of the self, takes steps in his own purging by entering Orsino's territory as a wanted criminal. If he is caught, he will be punished for his crimes.

Renaissance Platonism
Sebastian, Viola's counterpart in bringing order to Illyria, will also bring trust and dispel the illusions created by his sister's disguise. Antonio provides an example of constancy in love, although, on this occasion, Sebastian is not his companion soul.

British Festivity, Magic and Rites of Initiation
Sebastian partakes in his sister's rite of initiation, taken on behalf of Illyria. He has also survived trial by water. Antonio is his guide.

Story Section 6 (II. iii.)
Malvolio puts a stop to a midnight revel which Sir Toby Belch, Sir Andrew Aguecheek and Feste are enjoying and which Maria has not succeeded in curbing. The four plot to humiliate him in revenge and Maria claims that she can write a letter in handwriting like that of her mistress, which should gull Malvolio into believing that Olivia is in love with him.

Alchemy
Some of the composite elements of the base matter of Illyria resist purging by Maria and Malvolio, who is himself prepared for purging.

Renaissance Platonism
Maria, who has recognised her companion soul in Sir Toby Belch, seizes the opportunity to bring about their marriage by devising a trick to gull Malvolio.

British Festivity, Magic and Rites of Initiation

Malvolio, as the spirit of winter, curbs the festivities. Toby, as Lord of Misrule, and his companions justifiably plot his mocking, as it was generally considered unreasonable not to allow festivities that gave warmth and pleasure in winter.

Story Section 7 (II. iv., II. v.)
Viola almost betrays her love for Orsino to him when Feste, upon request, sings a melancholy love song to the court. In an intimate moment with her master, she relieves her unhappy feelings by attributing them to an imaginary sister and is once again sent to Olivia to present Orsino's courtship.

Meanwhile in Olivia's household, Maria's trick upon Malvolio takes hold as he finds the letter forged by Maria which implies that Olivia loves him, requesting him to wear yellow, cross-gartered stockings, smile and generally adopt a style of ridiculous behaviour which Maria knows will annoy Olivia.

Alchemy
Orsino's preparation for the achievement of the Philosophers' Stone manifest as Viola is begun, as is the purging of Malvolio.

Renaissance Platonism
Viola suffers the pain brought about by the deceit of her disguise. Malvolio will also be punished for his base love of Olivia and for the general hypocrisy of his behaviour, which he reveals in this scene.

British Festivity, Magic and Rites of Initiation
Viola demonstrates the right kind of fortitude, like 'patience on a monument' (II. iv. 113), expected of a neophyte in enduring the pain of unrequited love.

Story Section 8 (III. i., III. ii.)
Still deceived by Viola's disguise as the page Cesario, Olivia apologises to her for forcing the ring upon her and confesses her love, which the embarrassed Viola tries unsuccessfully to quench with a sharp response (see fig. 17). Sir Andrew Aguecheek, witness to this scene, protests to Sir Toby and Feste that he will return home, as his suit to Olivia seems pointless in the light of her favouring Cesario. Sir Toby suggests that in order to win some favour from Olivia, Andrew should challenge the page

to a duel over her love. Maria reports that Malvolio has adopted the dress and behaviour as suggested by her letter.

Alchemy
Steps are taken to engage the main violent stages of the alchemic process.
Renaissance Platonism
Viola suffers further punishment for the delusion of her disguise in her embarrassment at being courted by Olivia. Sir Toby merely prolongs the inevitable punishment Sir Andrew will receive for his base love of Olivia in encouraging the duel.
British Festivity, Magic and Rites of Initiation
A ring symbolised the magic circle of wholeness and union. Viola's generosity to Olivia in not embarrassing her before her steward by accepting the ring, in refusing Olivia's further attempted bribery, and in her continuing loyalty to conveying Orsino's courtship, advance her as an initiate.

Story Section 9 (III. iii., III. iv.)

Sebastian agrees that Antonio should continue to accompany him, accepts money from him and arranges to see him later at the inn, the Elephant.

Malvolio appears before Olivia in the terms set out in Maria's letter, is deceived into thinking that Olivia's response to him indicates her love for him, and is mocked by Sir Toby, Feste and Maria. Sir Andrew presents them with his letter of challenge to a duel with Cesario, but Sir Toby considers it too ridiculous to convince the page of its reality and instead confronts Viola himself, presenting the facts of Sir Andrew's challenge and giving a false report of his prowess as a fighter. In turn, he pretends to Sir Andrew that the page is implacable, and the duel between the reluctant pair commences. Antonio, entering upon the scene and mistaking Viola for Sebastian, intervenes, but is arrested as an enemy of Orsino. When Antonio asks Viola to return his purse and she denies all knowledge of him, he accuses her of unkindness. She is amazed at his distress, but pleased when he calls her Sebastian, as she realises that she has been mistaken for her brother. Andrew decides to continue the duel and runs after her as she leaves.

CHAPTER FOURTEEN

Alchemy
As he is part of Illyria's metaphorical base matter, Malvolio's purging is commenced with his being mocked and ultimately imprisoned.

Swords were alchemical symbols for the fire which was used in a furnace to effect the necessary chemical changes in the alchemical process. These also represented the heat of severe pressure applied to the psyche to transform it. The swords of Viola, Sir Andrew, Sir Toby, Antonio and Orsino's officers perform this function.

Renaissance Platonism
The duel between Viola and Sir Andrew is a false test of constancy as neither loves Olivia. Antonio breaks it up and makes way for his friend, Sebastian, to find his companion soul, Olivia.

British Festivity, Magic and Rites of Initiation
The duel between Viola and Sir Andrew becomes a symbolic trial by fire for her. Antonio, in saving her, is at first a guide, then, in his accusations against her, a further trial. Malvolio is mocked by becoming himself like a Lord of Misrule in his inappropriate appearance and behaviour before Olivia.

Story Section 10 (IV. i., IV. ii., IV. iii.)

Feste comes upon Sebastian, whom he mistakes for Cesario, whom Olivia has sent him to find. Sir Andrew upon meeting them makes the same mistake, strikes at him, and receives blows in return. Sir Toby, incensed at this turn of events, challenges Sebastian to a fight. Olivia, fetched by Feste and also mistaking him for Cesario, intervenes, dismisses Sir Toby, apologises to Sebastian, and, to his amazement, invites him to her house, declaring her love for him. To her astonishment, Sebastian, who has fallen in love with her at first sight, accepts her invitation.

Malvolio, imprisoned for his supposed madness in the outrageousness of his behaviour and dress, is tormented by Feste, who feigns to be a curate sent to exorcise him.

Olivia, confused by the supposed Cesario's sudden surrender to her love, proposes immediate marriage to Sebastian, and he accepts.

Alchemy
The fire symbolised by the swords continues with the fighting thrust upon Sebastian. He demonstrates the double alchemic function of Mercury as the Philosophers' Stone (the true goal for Olivia) and as an agent of the process, defeating Sir Andrew and Sir Toby with his sword. Feste shares this latter function with him in the purging of Malvolio.

Renaissance Platonism
Olivia at last meets her true soul companion in Sebastian. He instantly recognises his soul companion in her and agrees to the marriage which will consummate their Divine Love.

British Festivity, Magic and Rites of Initiation
Sebastian undertakes the trial by fire on behalf of his sister, and in his relationship with Olivia he benefits from his sister's ordeal. Malvolio is mocked by Feste as festivity mocks the symbol of winter.

Story Section 11 (V. i. 1-260)
At Orsino's court, Antonio is brought for trial. He accuses Viola/Cesario, standing at Orsino's side, of treachery in denying him when he was in need of support. However, his accusations are dismissed as nonsense, as the facts of the case do not tally with Viola's circumstances.

Olivia enters in search of her husband, Sebastian, and seeing Viola/Cesario, accuses her of breach of faith. When Viola denies any allegiance to her, Olivia refers to the recent marriage, calling the priest who married her to Sebastian as witness. The priest confirms the marriage. The appalled Orsino threatens, then casts off Viola/Cesario for this apparent treachery. Sir Andrew and Sir Toby enter, complaining that Cesario has beaten and wounded them in a skirmish. Sebastian enters to apologise to Olivia for hurting them in self-defence, and the brother and sister at last come face to face, glad to ultimately find each other and happily resolving the confusion caused by Viola's male disguise.

Alchemy
As part of the base matter of Illyria, Sir Toby and Sir Andrew are purged by Sebastian. As the elements of the alchemy come together, the Philosophers' Stone is almost achieved.

Renaissance Platonism
With Olivia married to Sebastian, the way is made open for Orsino to at last be able to recognise his soul companion in Viola.

British Festivity, Magic and Rites of Initiation
Viola suffers the nadir of her trials in being accused by everyone of treachery, a characteristic she loathes. She even patiently endures Orsino's threats of physical violence. However, when she comes face to face with her brother, she emerges from the symbolic labyrinth, her trials over.

Sir Toby is finished as the Lord of Misrule in his marriage to Maria, who may be able to curb him, and in his defeat at the hands of Sebastian.

<u>Story Section 12</u> (V. i. 261-405)
Now reconciled to the idea that Olivia is married to Sebastian, Orsino recognises his affection for his page Cesario as true love for the person he now sees as the woman Viola, especially as she has often made veiled declarations of her love for him. He proposes marriage to her and she accepts his proposal. Olivia offers that the two wedding celebrations should be conducted at her house and at her expense.

She is reminded that Malvolio is still imprisoned there and she instructs that he be brought before her. The indignant Malvolio accuses her of mistreatment, showing her the letter which motivated his behaviour. Olivia recognises Maria's forgery, and the plot to gull Malvolio is revealed, along with the fact that Sir Toby has married Maria as a reward for her part in it. Malvolio departs, threatening revenge on all of them. Olivia agrees that he has been abused, and Orsino requests that he be conciliated.

Alchemy
The Philosophers' Stone is achieved as Orsino at last recognises the Divinity in his heart as Viola and Olivia finds hers as Sebastian. Within the allegory of Illyria as the self, the whole personality is integrated as the different elements represented by the play's characters are linked in harmony. Base matter, purged and improved, is reintegrated with the whole personality (Sir Toby married to Maria and Malvolio entreated to a peace), and the self becomes whole again.

Renaissance Platonism
With the three couples united, the Platonic ascent through Divine Love has been made. Plato symbolised this with a celebratory feast, here offered to all by Olivia.

British Festivity, Magic and Rites of Initiation
Everyone has benefited from Viola's ordeals and Illyria is better for it, its Duke having found true love, achieving the final aim of initiation in bringing the benefits of the neophyte's success to others.

In the marriage of Orsino and Olivia to the brother and sister, Sebastian and Viola, a magic circle of relationships is formed.

Malvolio's threat, 'I'll be revenged on the whole pack of you' (V. i. 375) is not idle, as Twelfth Night is the last day of festivities, and on the next day winter prevails.

Cabala: post production (see fig. 3)
Illyria as a country with its inhabitants is **Malkuth (Kingdom, the material world perceived through the senses)**. The Countess Olivia and the Duke Orsino are self-absorbed in exaggerated emotions, she in mourning the death of her brother, he in a futile courtship of her. They exhibit the characteristics of **Netzach (Victory, emotions)**, and in order to effect balanced personalities with the benefit to their subjects in Illyria, they need to attain aspects of **Hod (Glory, thoughts)**.

Viola is cast upon the coast of Illyria, and demonstrates the characteristics of **Hod** in her swift decisions and actions that she takes in order to survive. When she enters the court of Orsino and falls in love with him, she attracts the elements of **Netzach** but retains balance between **Hod** and **Netzach** in maintaining the disguise she must retain as a single woman in a foreign country. In the grief over the supposed loss of her brother and concealed love for Orsino she suffers trauma as **Yesod (Foundation, the subconscious)** which needs to be cleared before she can ascend the Tree of Life. Her trauma is increased when Olivia falls in love with her, assuming that she is a man.

Firmly positioned in **Malkuth** and overindulging in its worldly pleasures are Sir Toby Belch and Sir Andrew Aguecheek. They are joined by Feste, who joins in their festivities but retains the balance necessary for his job between **Netzach** (displayed in his affection for Olivia) and **Hod** (in his skilful attempts to reason her out of her exaggerated mourning for her brother). Maria, exhibiting all the characteristics of **Hod** in trying to restrain Sir Toby, in seeking to raise her social status by marriage, and in devising and carrying out the means to gull Malvolio, displays a balance with **Netzach** in her love for Sir Toby.

Although in his position as Olivia's steward in the real world of **Malkuth** he displays a professional logic, in his private emotional life Malvolio lacks the logic of **Hod** or the true feelings of **Netzach**. He is imprisoned by his misplaced arrogance and implausible ambition to marry Olivia in traumas such as are found in **Yesod** without the means to clear his subconscious in order to attain a balanced personality and correctly serve Olivia and, through her, Illyria. This will be supplied by his gulling at the hands of Maria, Sir Toby and Feste.

It is the arrival of Sebastian which will make it possible for Orsino, Olivia and Viola to ascend the Tree of Life, and his punishment of the folly of Sir Toby and Sir Andrew will moderate their behaviour and give them a sense of **Hod**, perhaps even steering them in clearing them of their belief that life can be all 'cakes and ale', through **Yesod** into a higher branch of the Tree.

Sebastian's balance between **Hod** and **Netzach** is demonstrated in his swift decision to accept Olivia's unexpected proposal of marriage to him as he has fallen in love with her. This marriage will obliterate Orsino's futile courtship of Olivia and free him to ascend the Tree. When Sebastian comes face to face with Viola, the traumas which have imprisoned her unconscious in **Yesod** are cleared away in swift succession, the grief over her supposedly dead brother wiped away, her predicament over Olivia's courtship of her obliterated, and then her unrequited love for Orsino returned in his proposal of marriage to her. The couples Olivia and Sebastian, Viola and Orsino are projected through their happiness and unity (in Olivia's proposed double celebration of their marriages) to **Tiphareth (Beauty, heart)** at the centre of the Tree. In her firm dealing with Malvolio's protest against her in the belief that the letter written by Maria came from her and motivated his strange behaviour, and her resolve to punish those who wronged him, Olivia demonstrates her ascent to **Geburah (strength, justice)** and **Binah (understanding)**.

In his request that Malvolio should be consoled, in his acceptance that Olivia has married Sebastian and that he can marry Viola, Orsino demonstrates an ascent to **Chesed (mercy)** and **Chocmah (wisdom)**. In their future marriages the consummated love of these two couples will ascend them up the Tree to **Kether (Crown, Divinity)**. Even Sir Toby Belch, in his chastened state and in his marriage to Maria, might have an opportunity to make an ascent up the Tree. In the harmony between these couples the psyche of Illyria is integrated and restored.

CHAPTER FIFTEEN: *AS YOU LIKE IT*

As You Like It is one of Shakespeare's plays which can truly benefit from an explanation of the allegorical significance of otherwise implausible aspects of plot and character. I was in the audience in 1978 in Newcastle-upon-Tyne of an excellent RSC production of the play directed by Trevor Nunn, when a man sitting in the audience near me exclaimed (in very cultured tones) after the play had ended, "What a silly play!" The 'silly' or implausible features of the play include:

- The happy coincidences of lovers' meetings in the Forest of Arden.
- Their coupling made possible by Rosalind's revelation of her true female identity (the recognition of her face not having been achieved by either her lover Orlando or her father).
- The scenario related by Oliver in IV. iii. 104-132 of Orlando rescuing Oliver from a lion and a snake.
- The wedding masque introduced by the supernatural person of Hymen.
- The sudden conversion of the wicked duke by a passing religious hermit.

These unrealistic features of the script were too much for the evidently pragmatic man to accept, spoiling his ultimate enjoyment of the play.

Theatre Set-Up's production of the play

Taking the implausible elements of the play on board, Theatre Set-Up performed *As You Like It* in 2002, in the period when the secret meanings were incorporated into all the company's productions. It was a tough season, presenting the play in 41 venues in three months and often in very rainy weather. Remembering the comment from the audience member in 1978, and hoping that locating the play in a period of distant time when even history became the stuff of irrational myths, we set the production of the play in the medieval period of Richard the Lionheart, as the legends from that time were often as romantic as those Shakespeare refers to in this, his most pastoral play.

Foremost among these legends is that of Blondel, King Richard's minstrel during the time that the king was imprisoned by his enemies in an unknown castle in Europe. Blondel is said to have sought out and found his king by singing a song known only to himself and Richard beneath countless castles windows until an answering refrain to his verse told him where Richard was hidden in the castle in Durnstein. Our production featured costumes and much beautiful music of this period, including (sung by the exiled duke's page) a song reputedly written by Richard himself. In this, the hostage king expresses the loneliness of his captivity and his bitterness that his 'friends' have not ransomed him, a theme of human treachery much dwelt upon by Shakespeare in *As You Like It.*

The different levels of meanings including the arcana were given to the cast a month before rehearsals began as usual and were thus incorporated into the preparation of their characters. As always, audiences appreciated their incorporation in the programme notes. I set them out here followed by the explanations particular to Shakespeare's use of them in this play.

The Pastoral Tradition

Some of the sources from which Shakespeare drew his plot and characters for the play were Thomas Lodge's *Rosalynde*, Robert Greene's *Orlando Furioso* and the Middle English poem *The Tale of Gamelyn*.[1] The first two of these show the characteristics of a literary tradition which followed the conventions of a pastoral style, well-known to us in Sir Philip Sidney's *Arcadia*. In Shakespeare's *Hamlet*, Polonius names several types of pastoral plays in the repertory of the visiting Players, and *As You Like It* seems to be Shakespeare's most identifiable use of the genre. Although Shakespeare makes use of many of the characteristics of the pastoral tradition, it is interesting to note that, even if he accepts their underlying arcane significance, he presents them in a more realistic context, making quite clear the cold, difficult life the exiled Duke Senior and his followers are enduring and their willingness to return to the court. Only the shepherd Corin, accustomed to the country life, praises it.

Characteristics of the pastoral tradition

- Idealisation of the pastoral life, and contrasting of its good simplicity with the corruption of city life.
- It presented dainty shepherds and shepherdesses adorning sylvan glades and pastures in an eternal summer of innocent pleasure.
- This ideal life was often associated with the classical 'Golden Age', and often its participants were exiled from court life.
- They then experienced a 'sojourn', a temporary residence in a wooded or country setting, and in this environment they might experience the delights of love and beneficial transformation.
- Often simple country folk spoke with unexpected wisdom.
- Extraordinary and unlikely events were likely to occur.
- In the pastoral paradise, man was seen to be in harmony with nature.
- This harmony with nature also affected his attitude to time.
- Fortune, good and bad, played its part.
- Lovers were united against the odds.
- Often disguise assisted or confounded the characters.
- Spiritual peace and satisfaction were also valued, so a hermit was sometimes featured.

The whole escapist style of the stories located in unreal settings can be compared to today's genre of science fiction, and like the allegorical style of some of the fantasies that this genre produces, the pastoral tradition really symbolised an imaginary location within the mind and a metaphor for desirable mental processes and ethical values.[2]

Social Realism

Although Shakespeare uses the pastoral tradition as the framework for the play, he is careful to make it plausible to audiences of his time by incorporating the realities of life and some keen social issues of the time.

- He begins the play with a social issue of concern to younger sons. Fathers, in order to leave a prestigious estate intact, willed it to the

oldest son, often with instructions (which could be ignored) for them to provide for the younger sons and daughters. This practice was known as 'primogeniture' and was, at the time, more closely followed in England than in the rest of Europe, to the distress and discomfort of many families' younger sons. The dependence of the younger sons upon their fathers while they lived was simply transferred at their deaths to their older brothers. If the latter were ruthless (as Oliver is), or if insufficient provision was made for them in the father's will, their lives were desperately poor.
- At the same time, it was a period when country peasants like William or household servants like Adam could save their wages and gain independence.
- However, in order to do this, they were still dependent on the good nature of their masters, and Adam is abused in his conditions of service by Oliver, and Corin by his master.
- Dependence upon men was also the condition of women, although Queen Elizabeth was on the throne.
- Adolescent men were also dependent and not encouraged to marry until their mid or late twenties.[3]

Rites of Initiation (see above pp. 49-50)
The young people of this play, especially Orlando and Oliver, undergo the testing and trials associated with initiation.

Alchemy (showing the features of Shakespeare's varied application of the philosophy in this play)
Alchemy was a process by which a red powder, called the 'Philosophers' Stone' (symbolised as a lion or lioness, a phoenix, gold or Jesus Christ of Nazareth), produced by chemical processes from some 'base matter' (symbolised as a snake or serpent, a dragon, a toad, a whale, lead, King or earth) would be cast on to 'base' metals such as lead to turn them into gold. This process could be enacted in the psyche, transforming the mind so that it became 'golden'. If this was successfully achieved, it was thought that the beneficial effects would improve world order.

It was believed that the Philosophers' Stone was actually inherent in all matter as a kind of 'quintessence' which needed to be processed in a set order of stages to distil it from its host. Another paradigm of it was the 'jewel in the eye of the toad' or the 'androgyne', a man-woman (hermaphrodite or rebus, see above p. 33) beyond the limitations of gender. In the dramatic form of alchemy as practised by Shakespeare, if the 'body' of the process which undergoes the firing and cleansing of the process is a man, the 'spirit', which is distilled from it and 'ascends' until the body has been sufficiently purified to re-join it, is a woman. This is the case in this play, but with two brothers as the body. Successful alchemy had to be conducted in harmony with nature, a strong theme of this play.

The Bible

Themes from both New and Old Testaments of the Bible figure in the action of the play.

Platonic Love (see above pp. 34-37)

Story Section 1 (I. i.)

Orlando, youngest son of the deceased Sir Rowland de Boys, complains to Adam, servant of his oldest brother, Oliver, of the latter's neglect of him. Instead of educating him and giving him the upbringing of a gentleman, as his dying father wished and as he has done for the second son, Jaques, he deprives him of education and treats him like a servant. When Oliver enters, he challenges him about his cruel treatment, and the brothers fall to fighting, Orlando forcing Oliver to give him his 1000 crowns inheritance and let him depart. Oliver finds a way to avoid this payment when Charles, a wrestler, warns him that Orlando dangerously intends to accept his challenge to fight before Duke Frederick's court on the next day.

Charles also tells Oliver the 'old' court news (I. i. 98) that Duke Frederick has usurped his throne from his brother, whom he has banished, and who, with his followers, has fled to the Forest of Arden where they live an idyllic existence as 'they did in the Golden world' (I. i. 118-119). He also tells of the banished duke's daughter, Rosalind, still kept at court as beloved companion of the Duke Frederick's own daughter, Celia.

Oliver persuades Charles that Orlando is a treacherous, malicious person who deserves to be put down. He reflects on the illogicality of his hate for his brother, who he hopes will be killed by Charles.

The Pastoral Tradition

The events that will send both Oliver and Orlando into exile into the pastoral world begin. We hear of the exiled Duke, living in the Forest of Arden. The 'Golden World' was a past time associated with the classical legend of Atlantis and the Biblical story of the Garden of Eden. The Duke and his followers have evidently adjusted their sense of time to that of Arden, as they 'fleet the time carelessly', leaving behind the tensions and pace of the city and court.

In contrast to this ethical world of nature, the world of the city and court have produced unnatural behaviour in some of its citizens; Duke Frederick has usurped his brother's throne and sent him into exile, and Oliver, who abuses the rights of the brother he should be caring for, plots to have him killed.

Social Realism

Orlando is a victim of mismanaged primogeniture. Not only has he been left a very small legacy of 1000 crowns in his father's will (insufficient to maintain a life as a gentleman and kept within the purse of his older brother), but his father's instructions to Oliver to educate and care for him have been ignored. This is upon Oliver's personal whim, as he has properly educated and cared for the middle son, Jaques. Often younger sons challenged their ill treatment, as Orlando unsuccessfully does here. A successful challenge is presented in the usurping of Duke Senior by his younger brother, Duke Frederick, and his consequent exile.

Rites of Initiation

Orlando is presented as a young man fit to be a hero and capable of undergoing trials. He endures these at the hands of his older brother, and he chafes at the indignity, shows his courage in challenging his brother and prepares himself for a more noble trial in the wrestling match with Charles. This is made all the more dangerous by Oliver's instructions to Charles. Adam will become Orlando's guide. Oliver is seen as a young man who needs improvement.

Alchemy

The base matter of the process is the dukedom from which the real duke, Duke Senior, is exiled, and the false one, Duke Frederick, is the present ruler. The dukedom is like a person's psyche, the different characters of its subjects its different elements which need to be separated from each other, worked upon and then re-integrated into the transmuted personality. Orlando and Oliver are important components of this base matter and here the first alchemical stage of **Calcination** (in which extreme heat is applied to the matter so that it breaks up and its different parts can be processed), is represented in the angry fight between Orlando and Oliver. Further heat will be applied in the planned contest with Charles. The next stage, **Dissolution**, is begun in the dissolving by Oliver of his ties of blood by planning Orlando's execution at the hands of Charles.

The Bible
The conflict between Cain and Abel is suggested in the conflicts between Duke Frederick and his exiled brother and between Oliver and Orlando. The name Adam is reminiscent of the location of this Bible story, and the Garden of Eden, the lost paradise, also suggested in the comparison of the forest-world of the exiled duke to the legendary Golden World.

Platonic Love
The circumstances of one of the male-female couples are introduced, i.e. Orlando and Rosalind.

Story Section 2 (I. ii.)

At Duke Frederick's court Rosalind and Celia discuss the former's unhappiness at the loss of her father and proper status. Celia assures Rosalind that if she inherits the dukedom she will reinstate Rosalind as its rightful heir. They are musing on the 'sport' (I. ii. 23) of falling in love when Touchstone, the court jester, enters and entertains them. Another courtier, Le Beau, tells them of a 'sport' (I. ii. 92) that they can witness now, a wrestling match between Orlando and the wrestler Charles, who has almost certainly killed the last three contestants, young men now wept over by their old father.

Duke Frederick entreats the two ladies to dissuade Orlando from entering the contest, and they attempt to do this, but Orlando protests that he has nothing to lose should he be killed as none will mourn his death. Orlando wrestles successfully and defeats Charles, but loses his reward from Duke Frederick on acknowledging Sir Rowland de Boys as his father – a man the Duke claims was his enemy. Ashamed of the Duke's behaviour,

Celia and Rosalind congratulate Orlando, and as Rosalind takes a chain from around her neck and places it around Orlando's as a reward for his victory, she falls in love with him, a feeling he returns so strongly that he is unable to speak to her. Le Beau warns him to be gone as the Duke now regards him as an enemy.

The Pastoral Tradition
The love affair between Rosalind and Orlando, which will be developed in Arden, is begun. It is his good fortune to meet Rosalind in this fashion as it will ultimately raise him, through his sojourn in the pastoral world, to a higher status in every way.

Le Beau's statement that the brutal wrestling of Charles, in the fatal breaking the ribs of an old man's three sons and the spectacle of his grief is 'sport for ladies' exemplifies a callousness typical of court behaviour. Its ingratitude and injustice is shown in Duke Frederick's rejection of Orlando's victory because of the identity of his father.

Social Realism
Orlando transfers his physical aggression from Oliver to Charles in a way that makes it clear that had he wished to do so, he could have subdued Oliver. In his victory over Charles, he begins a process involving Rosalind, the true heiress to the dukedom, which will ultimately result in his social elevation to a social position of total supremacy in the state and reigning over Oliver.

The total and whimsical power of rulers is seen in Duke Frederick's rejection of Orlando's claim to reward for his victory.

Rites of Passage
Orlando passes his test of strength against Charles and is rewarded by a glimpse of the 'deity', the 'heavenly Rosalind' whom he will subsequently worship (but not recognise in disguise). The rose (suggested by the name Rosalind) was from ancient times regarded as a sacred symbol, either the reflection of Heaven itself or a symbol of the soul.[4] However, Orlando must pass further trials as a result of his victory over Charles and his inadvertent antagonising of Duke Frederick.

Alchemy
The stage of **Seperation** (Ripley's spelling) occurs as Orlando leaves Oliver and goes to the court. Celia and Rosalind talk of another separation, of

Rosalind from her father, the real Duke.

When Rosalind and Orlando fall in love, and as she places the chain around his neck, they are bound in love in **Coniunctio**, an 'alchemical wedding'.

The Bible
The Duke Frederick's evil is balanced by the goodness of his daughter and niece.

Platonic Love
Rosalind and Orlando, true companion souls, recognise each other in Divine Love, but are instantly tested in their being separated by Duke Frederick's jealous anger of Orlando.

Story Section 3 (I. iii.)

Celia and Rosalind wonder at the suddenness of falling in love when Duke Frederick enters and banishes Rosalind from his court. Celia pledges to run away with Rosalind into exile to the Forest of Arden and they plan to disguise themselves 'in poor and mean attire' (I. iii.107), Rosalind as a boy henceforth to be called Ganymede, and Celia as her sister, to be called Aliena. They resolve to take the jester, Touchstone, with them, along with all of their jewels and wealth.

The Pastoral Tradition
The injustice of the court world continues in the unmerited banishment of Rosalind. It is her cousin Celia who decides to escape into the pastoral world of the exiled Duke, Rosalind's father and her uncle. When they decide to take Touchstone with them, they are removing him from his natural element, one he will be unhappy to leave. Not everyone enjoys the pastoral world. In taking their jewels and wealth with them, they give themselves an unnatural advantage and do not enter the pastoral world on the same basic level as the exiled Duke.

Social Realism
Duke Frederick's dictatorship is also manifest in his dismissal of Rosalind. She indicates the social vulnerability of women in her safe choice of a male disguise when they plan to adventure away from home.

Rites of Initiation

Celia and Rosalind are to go on an initiatory journey as well as Orlando. Celia demonstrates her worth by offering to share its hardships with Rosalind. Touchstone is a parody of a spiritual guide, but he is certainly a practical one.

Alchemy

Orlando and Rosalind must be parted in order for Orlando to undergo the processes as the 'body' of the alchemy and for Rosalind to 'ascend' within the process to become its 'soul' (symbolised within her name as the rose, the symbol of the soul). This is done alchemically in a very long and violent stage called **Putrefaction**, when both are parted by his brother's violence towards him and Duke Frederick's violence towards her. Although Rosalind and Orlando will meet again in Arden, her disguise will separate them. As a woman dressed as a man, she becomes the androgynous symbol of alchemy.

The name Touchstone has alchemical significance, as an implement called a touchstone was used to measure the quality of metals, gold in particular.

The Bible

Celia shows Christian charity to Rosalind in sharing the effects of her father's unreasonable jealousy of her cousin.

Platonic Love

Rosalind shares Orlando's fate in being a victim of Duke Frederick's jealousy and being sent into exile, but it seems that she will never meet Orlando again as she and Celia escape to the Forest of Arden.

<u>**Story Section**</u> 4 (II. i. ii. iii.)

Rosalind's father, the rightful Duke (whom Shakespeare calls Duke Senior), is discovered in the Forest of Arden. He speaks of the superiority of their natural although bleak life in the woods over the treacherous life at court. They laugh over one of their companions, 'melancholy' Jaques and his sorrow over a wounded deer, ignored by a passing herd which Jaques has compared to callous courtiers, citizens and even the hunters themselves. In spite of the mockery of Jaques, the Duke himself questions the ethics of their killing of the native deer for their own survival.

The cruelty referred to by Jaques is seen back at court where Duke Frederick is given to believe that the whereabouts of his missing daughter will be known by Orlando or his brother, Oliver, and they must be hard pressed for information. However, ruthless Oliver has given command that Orlando, returning from his unexpected victory at court, should be killed. Orlando is warned of this by Adam, who offers him the gold of his life's savings as they escape together into exile.

The Pastoral Tradition
We now see the reality of this Duke's pastoral existence in his 'Golden World'. Unlike the pseudo-pastoral inhabitants of the tradition, he experiences the harshness of weather and physical privation, but he ranks it below the cruelty of mankind at court. The accounts of Jaques' sympathy for the wounded deer and his association of its neglect by the rest of the herd with the callousness of the court emphasises the pastoral theme. However, we know that the reality of Jaques' situation and his dependence on food from these animals will ensure that he does not become vegetarian.

Adam and Orlando, exiled by the unnatural behaviour of Oliver, prepare to enter their sojourn in the pastoral world. Oliver, and ultimately Duke Frederick himself, will be jettisoned there by their actions.

Social Realism
Shakespeare emphasises, as he does throughout the play, that the natural world is bleak, not idyllic, with inclement weather and material hardship. This suffering can extend to the animals that inhabit it. The ultimate miscarriage of primogeniture is threatened in Oliver's attempts to have Orlando killed. Adam, abused by Oliver, his master, nevertheless has the independent means to rescue Orlando.

Rites of Initiation
Rosalind's father, the exiled Duke, shows himself to be a person at ease with his harsh lot in life, and confidently survives the trials of his exile, a pattern of successful initiation. We find him in the Forest of Arden, which is a kind of labyrinth. Orlando begins his journey into this labyrinth with Adam as guide.

Alchemy
Within the process of **Putrefaction**, Oliver's violence towards Orlando is realised in the latter's forced exile. Adam's saved gold prefigures the

hoped outcome of the process and represents the 'gold' of his refined nature, tried and tested over many years of humble service.

The Bible

The nature of the Biblical paradise in the Forest of Arden is revealed as an escape from the evil of mankind. Oliver becomes like the Old Testament Cain in his attempt to kill his brother. Adam shows an ideal Christian love in sacrificing the gold which he had saved for his old age to rescue Orlando.

Platonic Love

Orlando's forced exile into the Forest of Arden makes possible the renewal of the love between him and Rosalind.

Story Section 5 (II. iv. v. vi. V. ii.)

Rosalind (as Ganymede), Celia (as Aliena) and Touchstone arrive at the Forest of Arden, and there meet two shepherds, one (Silvius) lovelorn for a shepherdess, Phebe, and the older one (Corin) consoling him. From the latter, they discover that a nearby sheepcote with all its stock is up for sale, and they seek to buy it with the gold they have, employing Corin to work it for them.

In nearby woods, the courtier Amiens sings of the kind ways of the simple country life where only harsh weather is the enemy. 'Melancholy' Jaques is his audience, and in the verse he adds to the song he implies that this country life (which he has willingly entered in loyalty to the exiled duke) does not suit him. They go off to a prepared meal with Duke Senior.

Orlando and Adam (almost dead for lack of food) enter the woods, and Orlando goes in search of food for Adam. Duke Senior and his men hear Jaques describe his happy encounter with Touchstone, who was philosophising about time in the woods. Orlando enters, sword drawn, demanding food, and is surprised by their civil invitation to join them and to bring Adam to their 'table' (II. vii. 105). Jaques compares life and its different stages with the playing of different parts in theatre. As the men eat, Amiens sings to them of the cruelty of man, much sharper than harsh weather. Orlando and Adam are welcomed to stay with Duke Senior and his men in their cave.

CHAPTER FIFTEEN

The Pastoral Tradition

Rosalind and Celia, entering their sojourn in the pastoral world of the Forest of Arden, immediately adjust to it, but Touchstone does not, complaining, 'When I was at home I was in a better place' (II. iv. 13-14). The ladies' gold enables them to buy a means of living in the sheepcote which they purchase. It is their good fortune to meet Corin in this way, a contrivance in the plot. Corin represents the 'noble savage' of the pastoral convention, the wise and dignified shepherd. In Silvius and Phebe we see a typical pastoral scenario, the unrequited love between a shepherd and shepherdess. Amien's song emphasises the pastoral theme of the relative kindness of the natural world, although the weather is harsh compared with the protected indoors environment of the court and city. Jaques does not agree, and his verse lampoons the pastoral world, away from the sophistication of civilisation.

Orlando, threatening Duke Senior with his sword, does so in the manner of the cruel court, and he quickly adjusts to the gentleness of Arden. Jaques' speech on the stages of man shows a court-like cynical approach, and his opinion of old age is belied by the entrance of old Adam, beloved, dignified and the source of Orlando's rescue from his cruel brother. Amien's song, with its sentiment of man's cruelty exceeding the harshness of the winter wind, recalls the cruelty of Oliver and Duke Frederick, and marks Shakespeare's observation that the life in the pastoral tradition is not idyllic but harsh, although less cruel than the treatment of people within so-called civilisation.

Social Realism

The Forest of Arden was in fact not a forest in the sense of an extensive area of trees, but a large tract of land presumably in the English Midlands, consisting of farms with adjacent pastures (usually for sheep) and interspersed with woods like those in which the exiled Duke and his companions take refuge. Rosalind and Celia have arrived in the open pasture lands. There is social reality in the situation of the local shepherds they meet there. Silvius has the ability to buy property, but due to his obsession with Phebe does not do so. His financial status contrasts with the poverty of Corin, who can never rise beyond the lowly status of a dependent hired hand. It is fortunate for them that Celia purchases the property (which we presume she will sell to Silvius when she returns to court) and that Corin finds happy employment with them.

The reality of the inhospitable environment of Arden is focused in the constant hunger of its new arrivals. Orlando's youthful dependence on an older man is realised in his accepting the patronage of the exiled Duke.

Rites of Initiation
Rosalind and Celia survive the first part of their initiatory journey and are rewarded with a comfortable means of survival in the heart of the Forest of Arden. Orlando is prepared to risk his life to protect Adam, but learns in his encounter with Duke Senior and his followers that not all trials are of physical strength and he must learn a new civility. Duke Senior becomes his guide.

Alchemy
Rosalind enters a haven within which she can continue as the 'soul' of the process in the Arden sheepcote. Celia, who goes with her, will also become the soul of the process as the plot unfolds.

Congelation, a purging process, occurs when Orlando is 'purged' of his rough manners by Duke Senior. **Cibation** (a feeding of the process) is then represented by the meal he is given.

The Bible
The 'better days' which Orlando assumes the civil Duke and his friends to have enjoyed are partly typified by Orlando's association of them with a Christian lifestyle, marked by bells knelling them to church (II. vii. 114).

Platonic Love
Orlando and Rosalind both arrive in Arden, but the need for her to maintain her disguise continues to test his constancy to her.

Story Section 6 (III. i. ii.)
The sharp cruelty of man is seen back at court, where Oliver is blamed for the disappearance of Orlando, Celia and Rosalind. Duke Frederick banishes him and seizes his lands and property.

In the milder world of Arden, Touchstone and Corin compare life and values in the country with that of the city and the court. Rosalind and then

Celia read verses in praise of Rosalind which they have found hanging on trees and Celia tells her cousin that they have been written by Orlando, whom she has seen in the woods. He enters, wrangling with Jaques, and Rosalind in character as Ganymede challenges him, riddling about the nature of time and love. Orlando acknowledges that he has written the verses placed on the trees of the woods, and she claims that she can cure him of love, and suggests that they play a game in which she will pretend to be his Rosalind. He agrees to this.

The Pastoral Tradition
Oliver now experiences cruelty himself, as banishment projects him into a sojourn in the Forest of Arden and a change of ethics. The interchange between Touchstone and Corin about the relative merits of life in the city and country gives us a pastoral set-piece, but Corin gives a real, not idealistic, picture of shepherding. The values Corin gives to the simple values of honesty and hard labour echo the pastoral ideal.

Orlando's littering of the woods with his love poems is also a convention of pastorals. He shows that he has absorbed the pastoral values, with its accompanying sense of 'inner time', in contrast to city clock time, which imposes an external artificial restraint on people, when he says, 'There's no clock in the forest' (III. ii. 295-296). The game Rosalind proposes echoes the pastoral tradition of shepherds passing their time in pleasant disputation.

Social Realism
Duke Frederick displays illogical tyranny in blaming Oliver for the loss of his daughter Celia, but he brings about a rough justice in meting out to Oliver the punishment which Oliver himself inflicted upon Orlando.

In the Corin-Touchstone discussion of court versus country, Corin's account of sheep-rearing gives the reality of its nature. Orlando's romanticising of his love for Rosalind in poetry seems so artificial that she feels that she must test the reality of his feelings before she reveals her true identity to him. The shepherds in the play hold their conversations in the heat of the day between noon and two o'clock when the sheep are resting.

Rites of Initiation
Oliver is now sent on his own initiatory journey. Orlando, meeting and

not recognising Rosalind (veiled in her male disguise), enters a different trial, this time of the sincerity of his love.

Alchemy

Sublimation, a further violent stage, takes place in the casting out of Oliver by Duke Frederick. Oliver now becomes part of the body of the alchemical process. Orlando as body meets his soul, Rosalind, but remains parted from her by her disguise so that she remains in the ethereal sphere, and he is further tried and tested.

The Bible

The un-Christian tyranny of Duke Frederick is contrasted with the simple charity of those living in Arden. In Corin, we see the Christian ethic of the contented poor man whose happiness is not dependent on material progress or wealth but on honest devotion to duty.

Platonic Love

Oliver is also banished to Arden, where his companion soul, Celia, is living. However, in his unredeemed state, he does not yet deserve her. Orlando pours out the extent of his love for Rosalind in verses written in her praise. She decides to continue to test the sincerity and constancy of his love.

Story Section 7 (III. iii. iv. v., IV. i.)

Touchstone has found himself a woman, Audrey, who herds goats, and he plans to obtain her through a sham marriage to be conducted in the woods by Sir Oliver Martext. Jaques prevents this and insists on a proper church wedding for them.

    Celia teases Rosalind when Orlando is late for their rendezvous. Corin brings them to see Phebe, whom Silvius adores, but she rejects his courtship, claiming that she cannot love. This is soon disproved, however, when she falls in love with the disguised Rosalind, who reprimands her for her pitiless attitude to Silvius. In musing on how she fell in love with the disguised Rosalind, Phebe speaks the maxim of Platonic Divine Love: 'Who ever lov'd that lov'd not at first sight' (III. v. 82). She deceives Silvius into promising to take a love note to Rosalind, which she claims is a reprimand. Rosalind is teasing Jaques about the nature of his 'melancholy' when Orlando enters. She reprimands him for his late arrival and then they play their 'pretend' game of courtship and a mock marriage takes place.

CHAPTER FIFTEEN

The Pastoral Tradition
Audrey, a shepherdess far from the idyllic pastoral type, enters the picture. In some senses, she parodies the pastoral ideal of honesty and virtue, ethics she claims to uphold but which she may be unlikely to follow, given her association with Touchstone and his city ways. He shows his dishonesty in seeking to obtain her favours in a sham marriage, but he is foiled by Jaques (another city-loving man) who rescues her from this situation, showing that the ways of the city/court people are not all bad.

The behaviour of Phebe towards Silvius follows the pastoral pattern, as does her inevitable falling in love with the unattainable.

Social Realism.
Touchstone's carnal attitude to love is in stark contrast to Orlando's. This is reflected in the object of his desire, a shepherdess of goats, the ancient symbol of sexual potency.

Rosalind understands the realities of love, its fickleness and fallibilities, which she sets against Orlando's romanticism in their 'pretend' game: 'Men have died from time to time and worms have eaten them, but not for love' (IV. i. 101-102).

Rites of Initiation
Other young people, Silvius and Phebe, enter a series of initiatory trials. Orlando continues to be tried by Rosalind.

Alchemy
Touchstone fulfils the function of his name, testing the 'gold' of the alchemic process in his own base courtship of Audrey, which highlights the true-love 'gold' of the love between Orlando and Rosalind.

The Bible
Jaques insists on a proper church wedding to legitimise the relationship between Touchstone and Audrey, emphasising the Christian ethic of sex only within marriage.

Platonic Love
The carnal feeling Touchstone experiences for Audrey is identified here as 'base love' by his desire to obtain her sexually through a sham marriage and then throw her off should he tire of her.

We see another couple, Silvius and Phebe, Silvius proving the constancy of his love at all times. Phebe experiences a false love in loving Rosalind disguised as Ganymede. Often 'companion souls' did not recognise their partners, and this may be Phebe's case, mistakenly identifying her true love in Rosalind rather than Silvius.

Story Section 8 (IV. ii. iii.)

After a successful hunt, a forester sings a song linking the horns of the killed deer with the horns of a cuckolded man. While Rosalind and Celia lament that Orlando is late again for his rendezvous with them, Silvius presents Rosalind with Phebe's love-letter. Rosalind reads this to the suffering Silvius and tells him to charge Phebe to re-direct her love towards him.

They are surprised by the entrance of Orlando's brother, Oliver, who comes from Orlando to apologise for his absence. Giving them a napkin with blood on it, he tells them of the remarkable event that has delayed Orlando. As Oliver was sleeping beneath a tree in the Forest of Arden, a snake had wound itself around his neck and, as Orlando came upon him, was about to bite him but slunk away at Orlando's presence. Then Orlando saw a lioness 'with udders all drawn dry' (IV. iii. 114), waiting to pounce upon Oliver when he woke up. Remembering his brother's cruelty to him twice he turned away, but on the third impulse decided to save Oliver, battled with the lioness and defeated it.

Oliver identifies himself to the ladies as the once-wicked brother of Orlando, but claims that he has been transformed by this event. He tells how he and Orlando have been happily reconciled and given hospitality by Duke Senior, but Orlando, who had been wounded in the fight with the lioness, fainted from the loss of blood and then sent Oliver to apologise for his missed rendezvous. Rosalind faints when shown the bloodied napkin. Celia and Oliver, who have fallen in love with each other, help her home.

The Pastoral Tradition

The pastoral scene and song featuring the forester's triumphant hunt is based on an ancient English pagan rite. However, Shakespeare gives it a realistic punch by turning the song into a mocking of cuckolded men, perhaps a comment on Silvius in the previous and following scenes. (This can be compared with the cuckolding of Falstaff in *Merry Wives*).

The unlikely and spectacular event of Orlando saving Oliver from almost certain death from a snake and lioness follows the pastoral convention of presenting extraordinary and improbable scenes. Shakespeare follows his source in Lodge's *Rosalynde* in the creation of this scenario but, for his own purposes in turning the scene into an allegory of alchemy which will transform Oliver and change his relationship with Orlando, he changes the lion of Lodge's scenario into a lioness which has been suckling her cubs, and he adds the snake. In his claimed self-transformation, Oliver demonstrates the beneficial effects of sojourn in the pastoral world. He is further drawn into this world by falling in love, a sentiment of which he has not demonstrated any experience before. Orlando shows how fully he is imbued with the pastoral virtues of the 'paradise' of Arden in risking his own life to save that of a brother who has mistreated and sought to kill him.

Social Realism

The hunter's victory song 'mocks married men', whose wives cuckold them in reprisal for their married bondage. This is set in social opposition to the concern of Rosalind for Orlando's sincerity in love.

The ill effects of primogeniture between Orlando and Oliver are cancelled when the elder brother is saved from death by the younger.

Rites of Initiation

A report is given of Orlando's passing his most successful trial. He has physically wrestled with and defeated the lioness in defending his brother's life, and has overcome his own reluctance to save him. This double victory of superior character and strength will grant him, at last, a real contact with the goddess at the centre of the forest-labyrinth, Rosalind.

Oliver also reports his own transformation, changed by his suffering to such an extent that his appearance had become that of a 'wretched, ragged man', a state from which he was redeemed by his brother's unselfish act in saving him. He is now fit to have contact with his 'goddess', Celia, which is granted him in their instantaneous love.

Alchemy

The changes Shakespeare makes in this scene from the scenario of his source in Lodge's *Rosalynde*, adding the snake coiled around Oliver's neck and turning the lion into a lioness, create a specific alchemical reading of this section of the story. The snake around Oliver's neck which slinks away at Orlando's entrance represents base matter (see fig 5). The lioness signifies the Philosophers' Stone, usually represented as a lioness with cubs, here implied by the 'udders all drawn dry' to indicate the increasing nature of the Stone (see fig. 7). When Orlando frightens off the snake, he is ridding Oliver of his nature as base matter. When he fights with the lioness, he is wrestling out Oliver's quintessence, the Philosophers' Stone, or higher nature, into his higher consciousness. It is a kind of psychic salvation, equal to saving his physical body. This action sublimates his lower nature to his higher nature in the alchemical stage of **Sublimation**.

In his subduing of the lioness with his bare hands, Orlando is associated with the Greek hero Hercules, the symbol of the difficult tasks of alchemy (see above p. 241).

The Bible

In Orlando's defence of Oliver he exemplifies the Christian ethics of forgiveness and self-sacrifice. He has given his blood for his brother and 'turned the other cheek', thus gaining his love.

Platonic Love

Silvius remains constant to Phebe even when her deception of him is revealed. Oliver and Celia immediately recognise each other as companion souls and instantly fall in love.

Story Section 9 (V. i. ii. iii.)

Touchstone is challenged for the hand of Audrey by a rival, William, a local man, but Touchstone threatens him with violence and he leaves.

Orlando and Oliver comment on the suddenness of falling in love, and Oliver, believing that Celia is indeed Aliena, a local shepherdess, pledges to give up all his inheritance to Orlando and live the humble life of a shepherd. They prepare for the wedding of Oliver and Celia the next day. Orlando laments his bitterness, looking 'into happiness through another man's eyes' (V. ii. 41-43) in the absence of his own love, Rosalind. She, successfully maintaining her masculine disguise, claims that she has knowledge of magic and thus will be able to bestow upon him his own happiness by bringing Rosalind to be married to him at Oliver and Celia's wedding.

CHAPTER FIFTEEN

Silvius enters with Phebe, who accuses Rosalind of betraying the contents of her love-letter to Silvius. They all lament the misery of unrequited love, which Rosalind claims she can resolve if they will all meet at Oliver and Celia's wedding. Audrey and Touchstone, also looking forward to being married alongside Oliver and Celia, are serenaded by Duke Senior's page.

The Pastoral Tradition
Touchstone reveals his callousness in taking Audrey away from William, the man whom she should be marrying, and behaving like a city thug in threatening to kill him.

Oliver shows complete assimilation into the pastoral world by pledging to remain in it. In believing Celia to be the humble shepherdess Aliena and accepting her as his wife, he demonstrates a complete change of values from his previous existence in a way appropriate to the pastoral world. Pastorals often featured magicians, and here Rosalind adopts that role. However, her 'magic' is not real, as Shakespeare's pastoral world never steps out of alignment with the real one until the entry of the god Hymen, who presents Rosalind to Orlando.

Social Realism
Audrey is portrayed as one who might have done better for herself in life had she accepted the hand of William. It is likely that Shakespeare represents him as one of the peasant class of pastoralists who were able to purchase their own property and stock in the epoch of his play. William certainly claims to be 'so, so' rich (V. i. 24).

The love relationship between Oliver and Celia is practical, with no romantic delusions delaying its consummation.

Rites of Initiation
Another young man, William, is given a trial in the threats of Touchstone to kill him if he pursues Audrey. He fails this test and loses Audrey.

Orlando feels his endurance sorely tried as he sees the happiness of Oliver in the soon-to-be-consummated love of his lady, an outcome he contrasts with his own situation. However, the tougher the trial the better the reward, and Orlando's reward will be considerable.

Oliver shows character in being prepared to cast off high social status in order to marry his love. He will be rewarded for passing his test.

Alchemy

In the stage of **Firmentation**, which fixes and resolves the solution, Rosalind promises to resolve all problems and fix all the couples in wedlock.

The Bible

Oliver and Celia follow the Christian principle of marriage before sex. Rewards for ethical behaviour are promised all around by Rosalind.

Platonic Love

It is possible that William and Audrey are portrayed by Shakespeare as companion souls, but William is not constant in his love for Audrey, fails the test by succumbing to Touchstone's threats and thus loses her.

Oliver is constant to his companion soul, Celia, in being prepared to lower his social status to marry her as Aliena.

In the complaints against unrequited love that the four couples make, the misery of separated companion souls is demonstrated.

Story Section 10 (V. iv. 1-149)

Duke Senior wonders at Ganymede's claim that 'he' can bring his daughter, Rosalind, to be Orlando's bride. Rosalind enters with Celia, Silvius and Phebe, extracting from the latter a promise to marry Silvius if something should occur to prevent her from marrying Ganymede, and from the Duke a promise to bestow Rosalind upon Orlando. Rosalind and Celia exit to make good their transformation, Rosalind's 'magic', and Touchstone entertains the party with a set piece of jesting.

Rosalind and Celia, dressed in their true identity as princesses and in wedding attire, enter in a masque in praise of Hymen, the God of marriage, who presents them to the assembled company. Duke Senior receives his daughter and bestows her on Orlando. Phebe recognises that she cannot marry the woman, Rosalind, and she accepts Silvius. It is observed that the marriage between Audrey and Touchstone is a mismatch.

The Pastoral Tradition

The beneficial effects to their sojourn in the pastoral Arden, with lovers married and a family reunited, are realised.

CHAPTER FIFTEEN

Social Realism
Hitherto Rosalind, in her male disguise, has enjoyed independence and a certain degree of control over the people and events round her, but when she abandons her male role she accepts subjection, both to her father, Duke Senior, and to Orlando, her husband.

Orlando, in marrying her through an unlikely series of events, achieves pre-eminent social status. Both he and Oliver have succeeded in marrying well and at an age probably earlier than that allowed to most young men in Shakespeare's day.

Rites of Initiation
Orlando is granted his goddess at the heart of the forest-labyrinth when Rosalind casts off her disguise (see fig. 44). This is implied in the masque of Hymen, in which Rosalind is presented as if she comes from Heaven. Silvius is rewarded for his loyalty to Phebe in spite of her disloyalty to him. Phebe is beneficially changed by her patient endurance of seeing her loved one, Ganymede, turned into a woman, Rosalind, and claims that the faith Silvius has demonstrated towards her has made her love him.

Alchemy
In the alchemical stage of **Exaltation**, the 'souls' of Rosalind and Celia are joined to the 'bodies' of Orlando and Oliver, and 'gold' is achieved.

The Bible
The marriage of the four couples cements their Christian unions.

Platonic Love
In the marriage of the four couples, happiness is predicted for Rosalind and Orlando and Celia and Oliver, who are portrayed as the companion souls which Phebe and Silvius might be if Phebe can prove constant. However, Audrey and Touchstone are definitely not companion souls, Audrey being the victim of Touchstone's 'base love' for her, and their marriage is thus doomed to failure as Jaques predicted.

Story Section 11 (V. iv. 150-197)
A message is brought to Duke Senior that his brother, Duke Frederick, had marshalled a military force and come to the Forest of Arden in order to kill him, but at the edge of the woods he met an 'old religious man'

(V. iv. 159), who diverted him from his purpose and converted him to the virtue of a hermit's life. He has renounced his dukedom, restored his exiled brother to his previous possessions and crown, and remained with the hermit.

Duke Senior welcomes all present to return to the court with him to share his new fortune after they have celebrated the weddings with music and 'rustic revelry' (V. iv. 176). Not attracted by any of this, Jaques resolves to seek out the religious life that Duke Frederick has undertaken, gives his blessing to the couples and departs as the dancing proceeds.

The Pastoral Tradition
The pastoral Arden transforms the wicked Duke Frederick as soon as he enters it, the 'old religious man' corresponding to the traditional pastoral hermit. At last the time that the court people have spent in Arden is established as the temporary stay of the pastoral sojourn, a fact that they had not known until this moment. When they return to the court they will take the benefits of the pastoral Arden with them and hopefully transform its nature and values.

Jaques, the city and court man who has not been transformed by Arden, voluntarily begins a sojourn there, with the hermit as a guide. As Touchstone has not been transformed by Arden but has retained his city ways and values, it is implied that his match with Audrey will be unhappy.

Social realism
Another unlikely event, Duke Frederick's conversion, redresses the wrongs wrought upon Rosalind's father by his younger brother. He, his followers and the newly-weds are not so unrealistic as to prefer the privations of the woods and pastures to the comforts of the court to which they will return.

Rites of Initiation
Duke Senior is rewarded for his successful endurance of his trials by the returning to him of his dukedom and the preservation of his life. His brother, Duke Frederick, has been transformed by a conventional spiritual guide, the 'old religious man'.

Alchemy
The golden joy of **Exaltation** is increased to include the exiled Duke Senior

and his brother Duke Frederick, as the dukedom is at last purified and redeemed in the alchemic stage of **Multiplication.** This is also implied in Jaques' comment on the numbers of couples, 'There is sure another flood toward and these couples are coming to the ark' (V. iv. 35-36).

In the analogy of this process as a disintegration, curing and then integration of the personality or psyche, this stage represents the reformed wholeness of an adjusted psyche that has been experiencing previous difficulties. However, the element that Jaques represents does not wish to be integrated into the harmonious whole, so he leaves.

The Bible
A Christian conversion of Duke Frederick by the 'old religious man' completes the play's progress through the Bible from incidents in the Garden of Eden represented by the Forest of Arden, to a conversion as sudden and as beneficial to others as that recorded in the New Testament of Saint Paul on the road to Damascus (The Acts of the Apostles 9.).

Platonic Love
The unions are celebrated.

Story Section 12

The actor playing Rosalind steps forward to give the play's epilogue.

The Pastoral Tradition (V. iv. 198-220).
Shakespeare points to the double disguise of this play, twice more than usual in the pastoral tradition. Not only has Rosalind stepped out of her disguise as the boy, Ganymede, but the boy actor, who in Shakespeare's day would have been playing her part, steps out of his disguise as a woman. The actor playing the part must also ensure that the audience (unlike Duke Senior, who, even though he is given back his court dukedom, wishes to remain in Arden to complete the wedding festivities) is prepared for its return to the working-day world away from the pastoral fantasy of Arden.

Social Realism
The ultimate reality of the play is presented – the Rosalind of the play is a boy-actor.

Rites of Initiation
The benefits of the successful initiations of the characters in the play are

given directly to the members of the audience, as the actor playing Rosalind comes out of the labyrinth of Arden and out of the play and 'conjures' or blesses them.

Alchemy
The achieved gold, (the Philosophers' Stone) of the process is projected in the final alchemic stage of **Projection** to the audience by the actor playing Rosalind.

The Bible
The actor playing Rosalind asks the audience for a charitable reception.

Platonic Love
The actor of the epilogue pleads for the play's approval by the audience in the name of the love between the men and women which he observes exists between them, but ends the epilogue by declaring that if he were a woman he would practise 'base love' upon the men. In the cynical manner of Jaques, this ironically implies that the audience might expect that kind of love from a lowly actor. (Theatre Set-Up often experienced this kind of derision from members of the public in their tours. The actors called it the 'rogues and vagabonds' syndrome).

Cabbala: post production (see fig. 3)

The psyche which needs to be redeemed by ascent of the Tree of Life is represented by the dramatic action performed by the main actors in the play, who become threads in the tapestry of the whole.

The early scenes represent all of these characters grounded in **Malkuth (the world perceived through the senses)**: Orlando, Oliver and Adam in Oliver's household; Rosalind, Celia, Touchstone and Duke Frederick in the latter's court, wrongfully usurped from his older brother, Duke Senior. Another kind of world is represented in the Forest of Arden, in which Duke Senior and his followers, including the 'melancholy' Jaques and local shepherds and shepherdesses, Corin, Phebe, Silvius and Audrey, dwell.

Orlando, in protesting against his unlawful treatment by Oliver, his brother, demonstrates his position on the Tree in **Netzach (feelings)** and, in taking steps to escape from his humiliating bondage to him, attempts to moves up the Tree to **Hod (thoughts)**, but retains in **Yesod (the subconscious)** resentment against Oliver which must be cleared before he can ascend the Tree. Oliver, his brother, is deeply entrenched in an unethical state within **Netzach**, due to unreasonable feelings of hate towards his brother. These negative feelings are doubtless seated within a trauma in **Yesod** as he does not treat the second brother, Jaques, in that way. He must not only be cleared of this trauma but be purged of evil intent towards Orlando before can move up the Tree.

A similar situation occurs in the relationship between Duke Frederick and his exiled brother, Duke Senior, and the manifestation of his misplaced jealousy of Rosalind. His forcing her out of the court suggests that it might be an evil envy, lodged in his subconscious in **Yesod**, which has been the cause of his cruelty to his brother.

In the Forest of Arden, Duke Senior, in taking refuge within the wildness of nature, in doing so with endurance and even pleasure, and in surviving with his followers in such a way that his state as a 'Golden World' is reported with admiration. He has escaped the trauma of **Yesod**, moved through the logic of **Hod** and demonstrates a poise and calmness worthy of **Tiphareth (heart, the centre self)**. The nature of the Forest of Arden itself, providing a home for refugees from the world of the court and survival for its inhabitants, can be regarded as a metaphor for **Tiphareth** itself, and Duke Senior has become centred there. In exercising control of his situation he can even be regarded as having ascended the Tree to **Geburah (strength)**, but his sorrow at the loss of his daughter, dukedom and possessions holds him back from ascent to **Chesed (mercy, the archetype of love and awareness)** and continuation up the Tree.

Rosalind experiences the heights of **Netzach** in falling in love with Orlando. When she is condemned to a forced exile from the court it is her cousin, Celia, who demonstrates a progression to **Hod** and makes it possible for Rosalind to join her there as they plot their escape together. Celia, being free of the jealousy of Rosalind's popularity, which Duke Frederick names as his justification for exiling her, escapes any danger of being embroiled in traumas in **Yesod**, and passes with Rosalind into the heart of **Tiphareth** in the Forest of Arden.

Orlando also finds himself in the refuge of **Tiphareth** due to the **spiritual love (Binah)** and **spiritual purpose (Chokmah)** of Adam, who has ascended to the spiritual heights of the Tree by the manner of his saving Orlando (whom he loves on **Netzach**) by saving his earnings for a worthy purpose (on **Hod**), having the strength of **Geburah** to defy Oliver and save Orlando (on **Chesed**).

Corin, in his humble life of working for the benefit of others, is similar to Adam. He does not have pretentious ambitions, but finds contentment in successfully caring for his sheep. His job satisfaction places him in **Tiphareth** and his solicitousness for Silvius on **Chesed**. His reward is the chance to gain good employment with Rosalind and Celia at a time when future unemployment and dire poverty threatened. There are no impediments to his ascent of the Tree and he forms part of the whole of the psyche represented by the play in the final reaching of **Kether (the crown of existence)**.

Silvius, totally absorbed in his frustrated love of Phebe, exists only on **Netzach**, ignoring aspects of **Hod** which would improve his material status (which might have increased his potential as a husband in Phebe's eyes) and wantonly wasting his means. His obsession with Phebe impedes not only his conscious but his unconscious in **Yesod**. Only when Phebe accepts him will he become part of the successful ascent of the Tree.

Phebe is also absorbed in the feelings typical of **Netzach**, firstly by persistent rejection of Silvius, then by the pursuit of Rosalind disguised as Ganymede. Her ardour for Rosalind suggests an element of snobbery in her subconscious nature, an aspect of **Yesod** which will only be removed when Rosalind's disguise is removed. Then, she acquires the logic of **Hod** in valuing the constancy of Silvius along with the perception of her love of a false idol in worshipping Rosalind as a man, and she becomes part of the whole ecstatic psyche.

The course of the relationship between Rosalind and Orlando in the Forest of Arden consists of Rosalind testing Orlando's ability to adopt a more rational attitude to love and marriage than he demonstrates in plastering the Forest of Arden with poems in praise of her. She is attempting to move him from **Netzach** to **Hod**, but his basic resentment against his brother's treatment of him in his subconscious keeps him in the bonds of

Yesod. This is signified by his twice turning away from saving his formerly cruel brother from the lioness. Revenge against the cause of his misfortunes is doubtless pre-eminent in his mind on those occasions. However, on the third impulse of his nature he overcomes his reluctance to rescue Oliver by fighting with the lioness, when his self-sacrifice in undertaking such a dangerous task not only clears his trauma against his brother in **Yesod** but that of his brother against him. In his actions, Orlando has practised the strength of **Geburah** and the mercy of **Chesed**. Both men are then able to progress up the Tree, Oliver being granted the love of Celia and Orlando ultimately the hand of Rosalind in marriage.

Touchstone and Audrey are retrograde elements of the psyche, their relationship being illogical, far from **Hod** and not even truly located on **Netzach**. Touchstone's desire for sexual gratification with someone unsuited to him places him in **Yesod**, as does Audrey's desire for social advancement, but their marriage joins them with the other elements of the psyche in progress to **Kether**.

Rosalind's casting off her disguise resolves many impediments that the characters of the play suffer which block the psyche's progress to **Kether**. Orlando finds his 'lost' love, and thus can move to the realms of **Binah** and **Chokmah**. Phebe recognises the virtue of Silvius in the rational aspect of **Hod** and comes to love him for it, centring herself in **Tiphareth**, and showing the strength of **Geburah** to show the mercy of **Chesed** to Silvius, demonstrating the spiritual understanding of **Binah** with the spiritual purpose of **Chokmah**. Silvius wins Phebe and can move to **Hod** and so up the Tree as his happiness frees him from **Yesod**. Oliver, already freed from the evil intent and actions towards Orlando which had locked his subconscious in **Yesod**, and rewarded with the love of Celia, becomes an integral part of the family of Duke Senior, which is moving up the Tree towards **Kether**. His daughter having been returned to him, only Duke Senior's loss of his dukedom and possessions holds him in **Yesod**, and this is changed by the revelation by the brother of Oliver and Orlando that Duke Frederick has been converted from his evil intent to murder Duke Senior, to whom he has returned his dukedom and possessions. It is implied that a return to court signifies ascent to **Kether** with a redeemed psyche ready to benefit the dukedom's subjects. The wholeness of the integrated family, completed by the arrival of Jaques, brother to Orlando and Oliver, signifies the ascent of the psyche up the Tree to **Kether**.

Only melancholy Jaques is exempt. He has stubbornly remained on **Hod** throughout the play, casting his cynicism upon any evidence of love between the couples, but he accepts the chance of being converted to a different kind of love in the religious sphere of the holy hermit. In this sense, he and Duke Frederick may also contribute to the whole of the psyche by reaching **Kether** through a different route.

In the practice of the Cabbala it is necessary to return to **Malkuth** after achieving **Kether**, or in fact any of the spheres. The actor playing Rosalind does this in the epilogue, taking the audience with him as he steps out of his fantasy role in the play and into the real world of the theatre.

CHAPTER SIXTEEN: *THE COMEDY OF ERRORS*

The sources of aspects of Shakespeare's plot are already known: translations by William Warner of *The Menaechmi* and *Amphitruo* of the Roman playwright Plautus; John Gower's *Confessio Amantis*; and George Gascoigne's *The Supposes* (see Geoffrey Bullough's *Narrative and Dramatic Sources*).[1] As with all of Shakespeare's plays, I consider that the differences between the sources and the actual play reveal the arcana. The reason I chose to seek out spiritual arcana in this play as the focus of my PhD research was the challenge it posed because its nature as a bizarre action play rendered any spiritual content unlikely. This was in contrast to *Dream*, the fairyland characters of which made spiritual content more obvious. My thinking was that the polarity of these two plays might provide a touchstone of the spiritual arcana.

The main problem when facing production of this play is a true definition of its nature. It is generally regarded as no more than a rough farce, an opinion which results in a sickening exaggeration of its action and stereotyping of its characters. There have been obvious exceptions to this type of production, significantly the 1976 RSC production directed by Trevor Nunn, with a young Judi Dench as a lively Adriana, her movement enhanced by a hair style full of bouncing curls. Her rendition of the line: 'I see two husbands, or my eyes deceive me' (V. i. 331) was definitive, setting a bench mark for future interpretation. With a stellar cast performing psychologically realistic characters, the line between comedy and farce was skilfully drawn in a memorable production.

Theatre Set-Up performed the play in 1986 and 2005, the second time emphasising the arcana by setting the play within a frame of an ancient Greek banquet/symposium with characters from the Plato story of the Divided Soul (see above p. 37) in a prologue wherein the feasters at the symposium became the protagonists of the play, the character of Socrates becoming Egeon and narrating the opening story of the members of his family's separation from each other. This was mimed by all the actor/feasters taking on the roles in the story as it was spoken, and thus its meaning was clarified and the beginning of the play given action.

The arcana I identified and applied in production were **Alchemy**, **Renaissance Platonism**, **Theurgy and Initiation**, and **The Bible**. The identification of sources in the Bible in this play comes from *Biblical references in Shakespeare's Comedies*, by Naseeb Shaheen.[2]

Story Section 1 (I. i.)
Following a law of exclusion existing between Ephesus and Syracuse whereby, unless a levy of a thousand marks can be raised, citizens of one city are condemned to die for trespass in the other, Solinus, Duke of Ephesus condemns to death Egeon, a man from Syracuse.

Egeon explains that he has come to Ephesus in search of his son, Antipholus, and his servant, Dromio, who left Syracuse in search of their twin brothers from whom, along with Egeon's wife, Emilia, they became separated as children during a storm. Egeon relates the story of how his family became parted from each other. The ship in which he and his wife with their twin sons (both called Antipholus) and their attendant twin servant boys (both called Dromio) had been travelling from Epidamnum to Syracuse had been wrecked in a storm. His wife bound herself, the elder Antipholus and the elder Dromio to a small spare mast, while Egeon likewise bound himself to the other end of the mast with the younger Antipholus and Dromio.

When the ship split up, the family was saved by this device as the mast floated away from the wreck and, as the seas calmed, travelled towards two ships, one from Corinth, one from Epidaurus, which were making their way toward them. However, the mast was broken in two by being cast against an intervening rock, and the family were divided and picked up by different ships, which travel at disparate speeds, making reunion impossible.

The Duke, in sympathy for Egeon's hapless fate, defers sentence of death until evening, in the hope that a ransom can be found.

Alchemy
The alchemical process of the play is begun with the stage of **Calcination**, in which the 'base matter' is purged, first by the joining of 'sophic sulphur', the 'red lion' or 'red king' (represented by Egeon) and 'sophic mercury', the 'white queen' (represented by Emilia), to make, after the course of one year,

the 'Calx', a new generation of substances (represented by the Antipholus twins) and then 'mortified' (as the family was divided during the storm and as Egeon is condemned to death). This signals the beginning of the 'black' stage of the process. Solinus, whose name implies 'sun', oversees the process.

Renaissance Platonism

This story presents a classic blueprint of a Platonic scenario: in which love is described as originating from chaos, represented by the storm and ship-wreck; in which the twin-born love is characterised into two kinds, the heavenly (the Antipholus twins) and the earthly (the Dromio twins); in which the 'Divided Soul', when it reaches early maturity (Antipholus at the age of eighteen) seeks its other half; and in which, through love (implied by the meaning of Antipholus' name), the Soul, seeks to be reunited with the Divinity from which it fell into a human body.[3] Just as the 'divine soul' is imprisoned in the human body, so Egeon is imprisoned for the course of the play.

Egeon seeking Antipholus, and Antipholus seeking his twin, can also be interpreted as an analogue for the creation myth of 'mind' creating order from chaos in turning towards Divinity in the quest for the loved one. In this metaphor, the Dromios reflect the consequent process of the 'body' of the world turning through an impulse of love towards God and the 'World-Soul'.

Theurgy and Initiation

The family of Egeon and Emilia, comprising their twin sons and their attendant servants, form a composite soul-initiate, of which Egeon and Syr. Antipholus are the main neophytes.[4] A frame for this initiation is suggested by their home in Syracuse, which was a Doric city in Sicily, the home in Greek legendry for Ceres/Demeter, Goddess of corn, fertility, marriage, law and order and the prevailing deity of the rites of Eleusis, which imitate the winter descent of her daughter Persephone into the underworld and Persephone's spring re-ascent to the light and to her mother, a scenario represented by Egeon's quest for his son.

The sun that the neophyte experiences, as Apuleius describes for us, is suggested by Solinus, the name of the Duke. However, not until Egeon's identity is completed by his reunion with his family, so that like the successful neophyte, he truly 'knows himself', can this 'sun' illuminate his life by sparing it.

The Bible

Syracuse and Ephesus were both associated with St. Paul. In Acts 19. 1, St. Paul travels to Ephesus where, as a result of his Christian ministry, so many conversions took place that much of the witchcraft practised there was abandoned, and silver statuettes of the Goddess Diana were no longer required (see accounts of St Paul's ministry in Acts 18. 19.23-40. 2 Timothy 4.14 and 1 Corinthians 16.8.). The vast Temple of Diana at Ephesus, one of the Wonders of the Ancient World, made the city a centre of the worship of this deity and was so magnificent as to be considered the source of the architectural imagery in the Epistles St Paul wrote while there: Ephesians 2.19-22, 1 Timothy 3.15, 6.19 and 2 Timothy 2. 19-20.

It is connected with St. John in being the scene in Revelations 1.11 and 2.1 of the most important of the churches of the Apocalypse, as the location of the latter part of his life and in being the site of his tomb. It is possible that his contributions to the Bible were written there.

Syracuse was also associated with St. Paul, as reported in Acts 28.11-12, when he spent three days there while on board a ship named after the legendary twins Castor and Pollux en route from Malta, where he had been shipwrecked, to Rome.

It could have been the thematic biblical associations with these places that determined their inclusion by Shakespeare in the play to give us clues to intended interpretations. The opening versions of St. John are significant to those people, amongst whom Shakespeare might be included, who link Christ with theurgy, and St. Paul makes a similar statement in Ephesians 3.9 on Christ's existence at the heart of creation from the beginnings of time. Speaking of his purpose in preaching the mystery of Christ to Gentiles, he says:

> And to make cleare unto all men what the fellowship of the mysterie is, which from thebeginning of the world hath bene hid in God, who hath created all things by Jesus Christ.

He also expresses the view that Divinity is immanent (i.e., in living nature) in Ephesians 4.6. Maintaining the monotheism of the Christian faith, he declares there to be:

'One God and Father of all, which is above all, and through all, and in you all.'

The Tomson marginal comment glosses the statement that God is 'in you all' as, 'Who onely is joined together with us in Christ'.

St. Paul also preached extensively on morality and marriage, a dominant theme of this play, in Ephesians 5. 22-23 and in Corinthians 7. Other themes are shared between the play and Paul's Epistle to the Ephesians. Resistance to temptations of the flesh, a key issue relating to Eph. Antipholus, is tackled in Ephesians 5. 3-21 and 6.10-17, when St. Paul applies a metaphor of wearing the armour of God to successful resistance to the temptations of evil powers. The atmosphere of the Epistle itself is charged with a sense of bonds and imprisonment, as St. Paul was himself imprisoned in Rome at the time of writing it. He refers to this not with resentment, but with the same sense of benefit that is applied to the restricting of Eph. Antipholus in the play:

For this cause, I Paul am the prisoner of Jesus Christ for you Gentiles, (3.10). Therefore being prisoner in the Lord, pray that yee walke worthy of the vocation whereunto ye are called, (4.1).

However, at the end of the Epistle he asks the Ephesians to pray for his release, a condition secured in the play for Eph. Antipholus.

Story Section 2 (I. ii.)

Egeon's son, Syr. Antipholus and his servant, Syr. Dromio, have also landed in Ephesus and are advised by a merchant to disguise their origin in order to escape the law of exclusion. Syr. Antipholus gives Syr. Dromio gold to the value of one thousand marks to take to the inn, the Centaur, where he must wait until his master's return from sight-seeing in the town.

The merchant leaves Antipholus and he laments his unhappiness in the loss of his brother and mother, in whose quest he feels as a drop of water lost in the ocean:

> I to the world am like a drop of water
> That in the ocean seeks another drop
> Who, falling there to find his fellow forth,
> (Unseen, inquisitive) confounds himself.
> So I, to find a mother and a brother,
> In quest of them, unhappy, lose myself. (I. ii. 35-40)

His servant's twin, Eph. Dromio, the servant to his own twin, Eph. Antipholus from Ephesus, where he has lived under the protection of Duke Solinus for many years, and with whose blessing he has married Adriana, a wealthy woman of Ephesus, enters, and, mistaking Syr. Antipholus for his master, upbraids him for being late for his dinner which awaits him at his house, the Phoenix. Syr Antipholus, mistaking Eph. Dromio for Syr. Dromio, rebukes him for the folly of attributing to him a wife which he denies having, and asks where he has disposed of the gold and why he has returned from the Centaur. Eph. Dromio denies any knowledge of the gold, insisting that Syr. Antipholus should return home for his dinner, and is beaten by Syr. Antipholus, who concludes that Dromio has been bewitched by one of the many sorcerers said to inhabit Ephesus.

Alchemy
Syr. Antipholus represents 'base matter', here in the process of **Dissolution** where it has dissolved. He expresses the experience of this as if he were a droplet of water lost in the ocean. The sister referred to in this stage by Ripley is represented by Syr. Antipholus' sister-in-law, Adriana, who contacts him through the servant Eph. Dromio. Later, she will become Ripley's 'agent' with her husband as the 'patient'.

The name which Shakespeare gives to the home of Adriana and Eph. Antipholus, the Phoenix, adds to the alchemic metaphor of the play. The phoenix, the legendary bird which is supposed to have risen from its own ashes, is a paradigm for the Philosophers' Stone, the goal of alchemy.

Renaissance Platonism
The love-quest of the soul continues. Syr. Antipholus, in comparing himself to a drop of water lost in the ocean, reinforces the idea of the individual soul's incorporation in the whole of Divine creation, exemplified in this

metaphor in which his identity is of the same substance as the chaos from which all creation was thought to have been made. Thus mankind, the microcosm, adumbrates the greater world, the macrocosm.

Although Syr. Antipholus and Syr. Dromio have located the goal of their quest, Shakespeare delays its revelation so that the Antipholus twins can learn to distinguish the 'divine light' from the 'natural light'. For Syr. Antipholus, this will be Luciana, for Eph. Antipholus his wife Adriana whom he neglects, under the influence of his 'natural light', for the charms of the courtesan.

That the two sets of twins are so identical as to be mistaken for each other even by their masters or servants indicates that they represented the cloned Divided Souls of Plato's imagery.

Theurgy and Initiation

A second neophyte, Syr. Antipholus, enters the final arena of his initiation. His initiation specialises not in the confrontation with death, undertaken by his father, but in his quest for his mother and brother and thus for a knowledge of his full identity as exemplified by the motto of the Mysteries of Eleusis, 'Know Thyself'. His initiatory journey began with his seven-year long wanderings between Syracuse and Ephesus to locate his missing family. Now that he has actually reached the place where they live, the further trials he will now undergo in order to achieve the goal of initiation, to truly know oneself, will consist of confusions of that identity and of the false magic in which Ephesus was said to specialise, a fact he knows himself (I. ii. 97-102) and which Pinch exemplifies (IV. iv.).

His rank as a young initiate is suggested by the name of the inn he is staying at, the Centaur. A centaur was a Greek mythical creature which was half horse, half man, and one of these, Cheiron, along with Phoenix had been entrusted with the teaching of the legendary Greek hero, Achilles.[5] This name might also intend a reference to Cheiron as one of the spiritual guides, the 'gods of the . underworld', as Apuleius calls them, that assist the neophyte in initiation.

He enters a metaphorical labyrinth of confused identity when Eph. Dromio mistakes him for Eph. Antipholus.

The Bible

Eph. Dromio, in reprimanding Syr. Antipholus for being late for the dinner at which Eph. Antipholus is expected, speculates that he may already have eaten while his household members are obliged to undergo the kind of feast appropriate to religious devotion or penitence:

> You have no stomach having broke your fast;
> But we that know what 'tis to fast and pray,
> Are penitent for your fault today. (I. ii. 50-52)

There are many Biblical references for this association of fasting and praying: Acts 13.3, 14.23, Luke 3.37, 5. 33, I Corinthians 7. 5, Matthew 17.21, Mark 9.29, Nehemiah 1.4. This anticipates the theme of punishment for wrongful indulgence of the flesh which pursues Eph. Antipholus throughout the play.

The Ephesian sorcerers mentioned at I. ii. 97-102, an addition to the plot of Shakespeare's main source, *Menaechmi* of Plautus, probably derives from their mention in the account in Acts 19 of the effect of St. Paul's teaching on those practising witchcraft (named 'curious arts' in the Bible) in Ephesus. Such was his power of conversion that they publicly burned their very valuable books on the subject:

> Many of them which used curious arts, brought their books, and burned them before all men, and they counted the price of them, and found it fiftie thousand pieces of silver. (Acts 19. 19).

Story Section 3 (II. i.)

Adriana, the over-jealous wife of Eph. Antipholus complains of his tardiness and is reproved by her sister, Luciana, for her impatience and lack of obedience (which she cites as part of a natural world order of hierarchies) to her husband. Adriana, whose riposte to Luciana's reproof has been that only 'Asses will be bridled so', claims that it is Luciana's servile attitude that keeps her unwed. Luciana replies that her reluctance is due to 'troubles of the marriage bed', but she affirms her willingness, should she marry, to obey her husband. Adriana responds that experience like her own would teach Luciana otherwise.

Eph. Dromio enters with the news of the extraordinary behaviour of his supposed master, who had beaten him and denied the existence of any wife. Adriana laments this denial and her continual unhappiness at the hands of her seemingly unfaithful husband. She reminds her sister that her husband promised her a gold chain, which he has not bought her. However, she would not regret the missing jewel if only he would keep faithful to her, as jewellery can be worn away, whereas integrity can never be diminished. She claims that he neglects her because she has lost her beauty which, she protests, he himself has dissipated.

Alchemy

The gate of **Seperation** (Ripley's spelling) is entered as the 'spirit', Adriana, is distanced from the 'body', Eph. Antipholus, by the mistaken report of Eph. Dromio. The nature of Eph. Antipholus, here referred to by his wife and later explicated in his behaviour as an impatient, even unruly person, is most apt to become the subject of alchemy, ripe for improvement.

The gold represents the metaphorical gold of alchemy, which will never be attained by Eph. Antipholus, the main subject of the alchemy of the play, until all the stages of alchemy have been achieved. The chain may well also symbolise this principle, effectively linking Egeon's fate with that of his sons.

Renaissance Platonism

Adriana, as the 'divine light' whose love will lead his soul back to the path to Divinity, feels that she is diminishing in lustre as her husband persists in following his 'natural light'. However, some of this dimming seems self-inflicted (as the 'dark' component of the meaning of her name implies), caused by the excessive jealousy and nagging of her husband, which has blocked their love from developing into the transcendental state which Plato claims true love attains.[6] She expresses an unwillingness to act her role of divine light for her husband.

As Luciana's name (the component 'Luc' for the Latin 'lux', meaning light) and expressed sentiments imply, her potential as divine light is high and the confusion created by the twins' mistaken identities will ultimately bring about its realisation.

Theurgy and Initiation

Another hierophant is suggested by the house name of Phoenix, the home of Eph. Antipholus. The co-teachers of the hero Achilles, the Centaur

Cheiron and Phoenix are referred to in the residences of each twin, hinting at these locations as places of initiation.

The need for Eph. Antipholus to be engaged as co-neophyte with his brother is suggested by his wife's unhappiness in the marriage. Moral instruction as well as mystical illumination is a key feature of all initiatory rites. He is introduced in his absence into the dark labyrinth of confusion by the mistaken report given to his wife by Eph. Dromio.

The Bible

Luciana demonstrates in her attitude to marriage a total belief in the strictures as laid down in Genesis. She takes at face value the Biblical curse laid by God on women as punishment for the sin of Eve in Genesis 3.16, 'thy desire shalbe subject to thine husband and he shall rule over thee'. The latter edict she feels able to cope with (see II. i. 15-25, 29), but the former fills her with dread.

Her homily on submission to Adriana echoes 1. 26-28 and Psalms 8. 6-8, which lay down the superiority of men over all beasts and creation. Adriana's association with submission and beasts is, however, also biblical:

>Luciana: O, know he is the bridle of your will.
>Adriana: There's none but asses will be bridled so. (II. i. 13-14)

This follows Proverbs 26. 3, 'Unto the horse belongeth a whip, to the asses a bridle', and implies that Adriana considers submission to be merely bestial. Luciana has additional Biblical backing to lend authority to her views: St Paul in Ephesians 5. 22 claims wifely submission to be holy, 'Wives, submit yourselves unto your husbands, as unto the Lord'. He also asserts this in I Corinthians 11.3, 'But I will that ye know, that as Christ is the head of every man: and the man is the woman's head: and God is Christes head'; and again in Titus 2. 5, saying that wives should be 'subject unto their husbands that the word of God be not evill spoken of'. The Apostle St. Peter also advocates wifely submission so that this decorous behaviour may win converts to Christianity: 'Likewise let the wives bee subject to their husbands that even they which obey not the word, may without the word bee wonne by the conversation of the wives' (I Peter 3.1).

CHAPTER SIXTEEN

This New Testament reinforcing of Genesis might imply Shakespeare's agreement with the principle of wifely submission, and is consistent with his sympathetic treatment of the character of Luciana throughout the play, validating her characterisation as the divine light of Syr. Antipholus in the Platonic interpretation of the play.

Story Section 4 (II. ii.)

Syr. Antipholus is astonished to find that Syr. Dromio has, as instructed, taken the gold to the Centaur and is looking for him. Syr. Dromio, upon finding his master, is rebuked and beaten for the interchange Syr. Antipholus had in fact with Eph. Dromio. He tries to mollify his master by jesting on time and baldness:

> Syr. Antipholus: Why is Time such a niggard of hair, being (as it is), so plentiful an excrement?
> Syr. Dromio: Because it is a blessing that he bestows on beasts, and what he hath scanted men in hair, he hath given them in wit. (II. ii. 76-80)

Adriana and Luciana enter, and, mistaking him for Eph. Antipholus, Adriana reprimands Syr. Antipholus for the diminishing of his husbandly devotion to her. She delivers a homily to him on the unity of marriage:

> For know, my love, as easy mayst thou fall
> A drop of water in the breaking gulf,
> And take unmingled thence that drop again
> Without addition or diminishing,
> As take from me thyself, and not me too. (II. ii. 125-129)

She holds fast to Antipholus, claiming the bonds of marriage:

> Come I will fasten on this sleeve of thine;
> Thou art an elm, my husband, I a vine,
> Whose weakness married to thy stronger state,
> Makes me with thy strength to communicate. (II. ii. 173-176)

The terrified Syr. Dromio thinks that he is in fairyland:

> This is the fairyland; O spite of spites,
> We talk with goblins, elves and sprites. (II ii 190-191)

Luciana calls him a snail and a slug for not replying to them, and for a moment Syr. Dromio believes himself to be transformed into an ape or the ass which his master then calls him. Syr. Antipholus, wondering if he is in a dream and doubting the truth of reality and Syr. Dromio, convinced that Adriana and Luciana are supernatural and best obeyed, follow them into dinner.

Adriana promises Syr. Antipholus special attention, and commands the door to be locked and Syr. Dromio to guard the gate.

Alchemy
The time jested upon by Syr. Dromio refers alchemically to Saturn, its prevailing deity. This section of the story represents the stage of **Coniunctio**, the alchemical wedding, in which the opposites of body and spirit that were separated in the previous stage are now joined together again. The state of marriage is upheld by Adriana, but she ironically betrays it herself in mistakenly bestowing her favours upon her husband's brother instead of her husband. Thus the body with which she seeks to be joined has a dual identity. Another conjunction is begun in the developing love between Syr. Antipholus and Luciana.

Renaissance Platonism
Adriana ironically reinforces Syr. Antipholus' metaphor of identity merged in a greater whole expressed in terms of a drop of water lost in the ocean. This recalls the Platonic idea and Hermetic principle of the microcosm linked to the macrocosm, and links it to the Platonic concept of the merging of identities in love. Believing Syr. Antipholus to be her husband, she applies the image to the ideal condition of the married state, exemplifying the Platonic concept which she implies once existed between her and her husband. As Ficino expresses it:

> When you love me, you contemplate me, and as I love you, I find myself in your contemplation of me; I recover myself, lost in the first place by my own neglect of myself in you, who preserve me.[7]

CHAPTER SIXTEEN

The Renaissance association of descent from sanity with descent down the ladder of the hierarchy of being from humanity to animals begins to be reflected in the play in the constant references in the play to animals, especially when the mistaken identities create illogical action and speech. This chain-like descent is emphasised in the play by the introduction of a golden chain, commissioned by Eph. Antipholus from Angelo for Adriana and causing, in its deviant passage from its true recipient, such disorder (see above p. 70). The entry of the chain onto the play from the time it is mentioned by Adriana in II. i. 106 seems to signal the confusions of the protagonists, which are represented by animal associations, culminating with the Duke's reference to Circe at V. i. 271.[8]

Theurgy and Initiation

Syr. Antipholus is merged in his function as neophyte with Eph. Antipholus, exchanging identities with him through his wife. His trial of self-knowledge is tested as his own identity is temporarily subsumed in another's, and as he wrongly believes that negative black magic seems to prevail.

The Bible

Syr. Antipholus recommends biblical propriety of behaviour to his servant with the lines: 'Learn to jest in good time – there's a time for all things' (II. ii. 64-65). This imitates Ecclesiastes 3. 1., which recommends, 'To all things there is an appointed time, and a time to every purpose under the heaven'. This both underlines the limitations placed by the demands of time on the characters of the play, and provides a satirical comment on the constant mistimings in the stage action which cause so much misunderstanding and the delay in the two sets of twins recognising each other.

A further biblical echo from Genesis 25. 25-34 links the twins Esau and Jacob with the twins of the play. In jesting on time, hair and wit, reference is made to Esau's hairiness and lack of wit contrasting with Jacob, the 'plaine man'. Esau gave up his birthright to Jacob in exchange for some 'bread and pottage of lentils'. The marginal comment in the Geneva edition, citing a later passage in the New Testament book of Hebrews (Hebrews 12.16), moralises on this event, criticising Esau as one who lives only for the material things of the moment, thereby relinquishing God-given benefits. This reference thus reinforces the prevailing moral tone of the play, which punishes material indulgence.

Although she defies the ruling of Genesis regarding man's supremacy over woman, Adriana invokes the edict of Genesis 2. 24 decreeing that a man should leave his parents and 'cleave' to his wife with whom he 'shalbe one flesh' in admonition of Syr. Antipholus, in the mistaken belief that he is her husband (II. ii. 119-142). She also cites the Biblical authority of Psalms 128. 3 in describing him as an elm around which she entwines as a vine (I. ii. 174), and, contradicting her earlier sentiments to Luciana, flatters him (in II. ii. 175) with a claim to the feminine dependency advocated in I Peter 3. 7: 'Likewise ye husbands…giving honour unto the woman, as unto the weaker vessel'.

Story Section 5 (III. i.)

Meanwhile, Eph. Antipholus reprimands Eph. Dromio for charging him with denying his wife and demanding of him the whereabouts of a thousand marks of gold (an incident that had, in fact occurred with Syr. Dromio).

He negotiates the purchase of the promised gold chain for Adriana with the goldsmith Angelo, whom he invites home to dinner. However, he finds the door of his house locked, with Syr. Dromio maintaining his guard at the door. Even the maid, Luce, whom he summons to let him in, refuses to believe that the person knocking at the door is the master of the house, as it seems to her that the master is already upstairs dining with Adriana who, disturbed by the noise, comes down to the door and sends her husband away in the belief that he is a 'knave' (III. iii. 72).

During this scene, much animal imagery is used, associated with the confusion: 'mad as a buck', 'when fowls have no feathers, and fish have no fin' (III. i. 79); 'If a crow help us in, sirrah, we'll pluck a crow together' (III. i. 83).

Angelo advises Eph. Antipholus to leave quietly until the situation resolves itself and to dine at the inn, the Tiger (III i 85-105). However, Eph. Antipholus decides to dine at the Porpentine (which means a porcupine), where he will give the golden chain to the courtesan, the charming hostess there (III i 107-121).

Alchemy

The violent stage of **Putrefaction** is enacted wherein the 'killing' (the breakdown of the marriage between Adriana, the spirit, and her husband, the body, is graphically represented in the verbal abuse exchanged on both sides and in the attempts of Eph. Antipholus to beat down the door. He and his servant refer to a symbol of this stage, a crow.

Renaissance Platonism

The chain that Eph. Antipholus has commissioned from Angelo is a further symbol of the bonds of the flesh into which his soul has descended. It also symbolises false worldly values and will be the later cause of his actual arrest and imprisonment. The chain, representing false value, will not find its rightful owner but will be cast about as much as the attentions of Eph. Antipholus.

His over-familiarity with the courtesan, the hostess of the Porpentine, indicates the degree to which he is descending down the ladder away from the love of his wife which would assist in his re-ascent back towards Divinity. This is reinforced by his decision to give the chain to the courtesan. In this respect, his actions exemplify the yielding of his will to temptation in the manner of the charioteer being misdirected by the black horse in the Platonic metaphor in *The Phaedrus* (see above p. 38).

The name 'Angelo' can be taken to refer to the coin, an angel, in the currency prevailing in Shakespeare's day. However, it can also represent the daemons, re-named as Angels by Dionysius the Areopagite, which, in the Platonic system, were thought to be 'governors of the lower world' (that is, of earth) and who, as good Angels, protect people, but as bad Angels, tempt them. The circumstances surrounding the character Angelo in the play are consistent with this possible interpretation of his character. He is initially benevolent in terms of his Platonic function: he has made a golden chain for Eph. Antipholus to give to his wife, thus increasing the bonding between them and assisting their Platonic ascent towards Divinity. However, this is a material object and therefore an illusion or shadow, and it ultimately only serves to divide husband and wife when it is pledged to the courtesan and given to Syr. Antipholus. In this respect, Angelo becomes a bad, misleading Angel.

A characterisation of the lesser, natural light is presented in the character of Luce, the servant, contrasting with Luciana, a divine light.

The device of separating the two sets of twins at this point by a wall and door and Adriana's mistaking Syr. Antipholus for her husband points to the illusory deception of the senses which Plato claimed only register, in the material world, the shadows of the true forms of all parts of creation in Heaven. This can lead to moral deception, as Adriana is unaware that the man she is entertaining is not her husband so that her husband's accusations against her are, in fact, true.

Theurgy and Initiation

Eph. Antipholus is engaged as a neophyte, his trials beginning with his exclusion from his own home where he also suffers the loss of his own identity which is supplanted by that of his brother. The bristling anger of his response is reflected in the names of the inns, the Tiger and the Porpentine (a porcupine), his familiarity with the hostess of the latter suggesting his moral looseness.

The Bible

Eph. Antipholus is punished for his worldly values and the implied fleshly over-indulgence regarding the courtesan by being prevented from entering his own house and thus being humiliated before his would-be guest.

Adriana is punished for her hypocrisy in citing Biblical authority for her claims on her husband, when she has rejected Biblical authority for her own behaviour within her marriage by being deceived into unfaithfulness to her husband with his brother.

Story Section 6 (III. ii. 1-163)

Syr. Antipholus has fallen in love with Luciana who, embarrassed by the attentions of one she considers to be her sister's husband, reproves him for infidelity to his wife. That the love is returned is suggested by her advocating subtlety in the declaration of any false love:

> Teach sin the carriage of a holy saint,
> Be secret false; what need she be acquainted? (III. ii. 14-15)

CHAPTER SIXTEEN

Syr. Antipholus denies any relationship with her sister, and protests his true love for her, his 'soul's pure truth' (III. ii. 37), deeming her to be a transforming god, or a mermaid, whose singing should not drown in Adriana's tears but lure him to herself:

> O, train me not, sweet mermaid, with thy note
> To drown me in thy sister's flood of tears;
> Sing, siren, for thyself, and I will dote;
> Spread o'er the silver waves they golden hairs,
> And as a bed I'll take thee, and there lie. (III. ii. 45-48)

He imagines that a death by drowning in such a light as hers to be a gain, although his love is not light and will not drown (III. ii. 50-52). She accuses him of madness, in a fault stemming from his eyes, which he affirms, claiming that it is from gazing on her, the sun. He identifies her as his 'better part':

> Mine eye's clear eye, my dear heart's dearer heart,
> My food, my fortune, and my sweet hope's aim,
> My sole earth's heaven, and my heaven's claim. (III. ii. 61-64)

Abashed, Luciana escapes, but Syr. Dromio enters with news of a courtship made to him by a kitchen wench, so beastly in appearance that her attachment to him makes him feel like a mounted ass. The woman, Nell, is so large and greasy that he imagines making a tallow lamp of her that could last forever: 'If she lives till doomsday she'll burn a week longer than the whole world' (III. ii. 97-98).

He continues her description in terms of these cosmic proportions: even Noah's flood could not wash the grease from her; she is spherical, like a globe; Ireland stands in the bogs of her buttocks; Scotland in the barren palm of her hand; France is a growth in her forehead, warring against her heir; England is in her chin, identified by the salty 'rheum' dividing it from France; Spain in the heat of her breath; while Belgium and the Netherlands were too low in her person to allow notice (III. ii. 104-137). Syr. Dromio relates that this monstrous person lays claim to him, citing marks about his body as evidence of their relationship. He concludes that she must be a witch and would have turned him into a dog had he not been firm in his religious faith (III. ii. 137-145). Syr. Antipholus concurs that they must escape from this seemingly enchanted place as soon as possible, and dispatches Dromio to find a ship to take them thence.

Alchemy

The moderate sixth gate of **Congelation**, the 'white' stage in which the 'spirits' are fixed, is entered. Within this allegory, the spirits are the women, Luciana, who Syr. Antipholus wishes to attach to himself, and the satirically-presented Nell, who wishes to fix herself to Syr. Dromio.

The 'wax' nature of the compound at this stage is represented by the compliant manner (albeit furtive) of Luciana, and the greasiness of Nell, of which Syr. Dromio claims he could make a candle.

Renaissance Platonism

Syr. Antipholus has found in Luciana his 'divine light', and would be set on his ascent through mutual love with her back to his soul's divine source, but this is delayed by the confusion of the mistaken identities. He again speaks in terms of the water-metaphor, representing his identity as a drop of water in the ocean (Plato's image of the divine essence of which the individual is part) in associating her with waves of the ocean, a further identification of his recognition and loving of the divinity in her. In this he presents a classic example of the ideal Platonic Love.

This whole idea is comically parodied (in an example of Shakespearean deconstruction) in the description by Syr. Dromio of Nell. She is posed by master and servant as a literal example of the microcosm represented in the macrocosm, her vastness equating the scale of the material world itself. The image of her as a tallow candle, burning for eternity, at once parodies the idea of her as an eternal divine light and presents her literally as a natural light. In fact, she is the love of Eph. Dromio, and as such presents the Socratic ideal of loving a person in spite of their ugly body.

There is political satire in this description, the hot Spanish breath being the anecdote about Prince Arthur after his wedding night to Catherine of Aragon claiming that he was thirsty after being 'in the heat of Spain all night'. Thus his brother, Henry VIII, who had subsequently married her, felt able to annul his marriage as unlawful (although Catherine, denying the truth of the story, claimed that the marriage to Arthur was never consummated).

Elizabeth I, daughter of Henry VIII, is also referenced in her support of the protestant Henry IV of Navarre to the throne of France when challenged by Catholics. The Catholic attempt to dispossess the heir to the French throne is indicated by Dromio in his identification of France in Nell's forehead, 'armed and reverted, making war against her heir'.

I believe that this double analysis of the imaging of Nell as a globe, incorporating the suggested political satire and the Platonic metaphor, provides an excellent example of the skill of Shakespeare's method. Both meanings could be considered controversial, and could be substituted one for the other if either were challenged as offensive, libellous or blasphemous. By providing alternate levels of meaning for the play, the playwright secures himself from attack.

The identification by Nell of body marks on Syr. Dromio because they are identical to those on Eph. Dromio distinguishes their twinship as the kind of cloning described in the Platonic idea of the Divided Soul. They are a mirror image of each other and as such provide a reference for another Platonic image connected with lovers in which love imprints the reflection of one soul upon the soul of the other. Thus the loved one recognises himself in the soul of the lover and returns that love.

Theurgy and Initiation

Syr. Antipholus makes contact with Luciana, the one who gives him the true illumination of self-knowledge through love. She functions as a component of the 'sun at noon' cited by Apuleius.

Dromio undergoes a contrary experience with Nell.

Syr. Antipholus reinforces in his assertion at III. ii. 51-52 that he is prepared to undergo a metaphorical death (like the death experience faced by neophytes) if his love is not considered genuine.

The Bible

Syr. Dromio draws on Biblical sources in his description of the cosmic proportions of Nell. In his description of her, 'If she lives till doomsday, she'll burn a week longer than the whole world' (III. ii. 99-100), he invokes the account of the world's burning end in 2 Peter 3. 12:

> That day of God, by which the heavens being on fire, shall be dissolved, and the elements shall melt with heat.

Her vastness is also invoked in his reference to Noah's flood of Genesis Chapters 6-8 being insufficient to wash the grease from her. He uses St. Paul's metaphor in Ephesians 6. 13-17 in a similar context (at III. ii. 145) of employing Christian defences against evil powers and witchcraft.

Story Section 7 (III. ii. 164-184, IV. i. 1-85)
Angelo enters and gives the amazed Syr. Antipholus the gold chain ordered by Eph. Antipholus, deferring the offered payment until later that day (III. ii. 164-184). Angelo, however, immediately regrets deferring payment for the chain, as he is instantly accosted by another merchant for payment of a similar owed sum.

Eph. Antipholus enters from the Porpentine, commanding Eph. Dromio to buy a rope to give his wife in revenge for his treatment that day. Angelo requests from him payment for the chain, of which Eph. Antipholus repeatedly denies receipt. As the merchant to whom Angelo owes money will arrest him for debt if he does not secure the money for the chain, he has Eph. Antipholus arrested for avoidance of due payment in his stead.

Alchemy
Eph. Antipholus, finishing his dinner in the Porpentine, signals the seventh gate of **Cibation**, during which the 'substance' is fed. This has not, presumably, been to the degree of moderation advocated by Ripley, so the 'diet' which should be imposed is suggested by the arrest of Eph. Antipholus, here representing the substance of the alchemy, the 'body' of the process.

Renaissance Platonism
The chain now begins to imprison Syr. Antipholus in the bonds of the flesh. It is for this that his brother is arrested and he is mistaken for his brother by Angelo. It will increase confusion for other people in further linking his identity with that of his brother and will distance him from Luciana, the real gold.

Within the Platonic metaphor of the play, the nominal arrest of Eph. Antipholus for the chain of gold imitates his imprisonment in flesh in his continuing descent from Divinity. This is further represented by the rope with which he seeks to thrash his wife and household.

Theurgy and Initiation

In the depths of the confused labyrinth of the stage action, Eph. Antipholus undergoes the trials he needs as a correction for his intemperate behaviour. His arrest and restraining bonds provide a corresponding punishment for the inappropriate humiliation he plans for his wife, to be inflicted by the rope he ordered Dromio to purchase.

The Bible

The reference by Angelo to Pentecost is not so much a textual Biblical reference as the fixing of a date. The imprisonment of St. Paul during his writing of his Epistle to the Ephesians is imitated in the arrest of Eph. Antipholus.

Story Section 8 (IV. i. 86-114, IV. ii. 52-62)

Syr. Dromio, entering with the news for his master that a ship from Epidamnum is waiting to take them away from the port, is ordered by Eph. Antipholus to go to Adriana to get bail for him, which will be provided by a sum of ducats in a purse contained in a chest covered with a Turkish tapestry.

Luciana is telling Adriana of her supposed husband's illicit courtship of her when Syr. Dromio enters in search of the purse. In answer to Adriana's asking of his master, he replies that he has been taken prisoner and is in 'Tartar limbo, worse than Hell, taken by a devil, a wolf, a hound, one that, before the judgement carries poor souls to Hell' (IV. ii. 32-40). He riddles about the chain that binds his master and about Time.

Alchemy

The eighth gate of **Sublimation**, a violent stage, signified by the violence of the stage action that forces the spirit to descend to the body, is entered.

The information that Luciana and Eph. Antipholus give Adriana will force her to descend into the street to interact with her husband. One of the symbols for this stage, a wolf, is named by Syr. Dromio.

Renaissance Platonism
The effects of the imprisonment of the soul in the flesh are increased. The riddling of Syr. Antipholus on Time, the restricting limitations of which are another image of temporality, reflects this Platonic idea patterned throughout the play: Eph. Antipholus should be home for dinner time; when Syr. Dromio experiences pressure from the mixed identities confusions he riddles on time (see also II. ii. 63-107); and all events move towards the inexorable hour of five o'clock, the time fixed for Egeon's execution.

Theurgy and Initiation
Eph. Antipholus is kept in the imprisonment he needs to test him as an initiate by the dispatch of the wrong Dromio for his ransom. Adriana is engaged as part of the process of his initiation. She will drive him further into the correcting labyrinth.

The Bible
The 'Tartar limbo, worse than hell' that Syr. Dromio tells Adriana her husband is in, has several meanings. Limbo itself has the Christian meaning of a place where the good souls of people who were born before Christ or have died without Baptism reside. It is therefore a place of technical non-redemption where souls who have inadvertently missed out on salvation wait until their situation changes. Christian doctrine promises that this will occur for them after the Second Coming of Christ to Earth. A tartar limbo would be worse to Christians than the Christian limbo or hell as it is not even in the Christian sphere.

Story Section 9 (IV. iii.)
Syr. Antipholus enters, commenting that everyone in town seems to know him, giving him money, inviting him, thanking him, offering him things to buy and bespoke clothes to such an extent that he concludes that 'Lapland sorcerers inhabit here' (IV. iii. 1-11).

Syr. Dromio enters, offering him the bail-bond money and expressing amazement that he is no longer restrained by the officer/executioner whom he refers to as 'old Adam…he that goes in the calf's skin that was killed for the prodigal… he that came behind you, sir, like an evil angel and bid you forsake your liberty' (IV. iii. 13-19).

CHAPTER SIXTEEN

The conviction that they are in a place of illusory witchcraft is reinforced by the over-familiar approach of the courtesan, hostess of the Porpentine, who claims that the chain she sees around the neck of Syr. Antipholus was promised to her. He charges her with being the Devil, which Syr. Dromio qualifies by saying that she is worse, being the 'Devil's dam', disguised as a 'light wench' (a pun on the meaning of 'light' as immoral) against whom he cautions, as the Devil can appear to men disguised as angels of light (IV. iii. 49-54).

The courtesan, believing them both to be jesting, invites them to supper. Syr. Antipholus conjures her, as the sorceress he believes her to be, to be gone. She agrees to do this if he will return the diamond ring she claims that she gave him in expected exchange for the chain he now refuses to give her. With cries of 'avaunt thou witch' and 'fly pride says the peacock', both men escape (IV. iii. 76-77).

The courtesan concludes that Antipholus must be mad, else he would not dishonestly disclaim the exchange of the ring, worth forty ducats, for the chain. She plans to go to his home and try to reclaim the ring by telling his wife that in a lunatic fit he ran into her house and stole the ring (IV. iii. 42-93).

Alchemy
The stage of **Sublimation** continues with Syr Antipholus as the compound, suffering a similar torment to that of his brother. However, whereas his brother is threatened by a physical power, Syr. Antipholus imagines black magic to be the enemy attacking him. This provides a reference for the black colour of the water resulting from the purging of the compound. Syr. Dromio mentions a peacock, the symbol, through its rainbow of colour, for the changing states and colour of alchemy.

The number of days required to achieve this stage was forty, the quantity of ducats the courtesan claims as the value of the ring she has exchanged with Eph. Antipholus for the promised gold chain. The number forty also has significance as the number of weeks of human gestation, a fact which indicates the extent to which alchemy was considered to be a living process.
Renaissance Platonism
The exchange of a ring in promise for a chain with the courtesan further

indicates the bonds of the flesh into which Eph. Antipholus is descending. Syr. Antipholus is embroiled in this by his wearing of the chain and he suffers, through acceptance of the chain, the same fate as his brother, taking him further from the divine light of Luciana.

Theurgy and Initiation

In the depths of the metaphorical labyrinth, Syr. Antipholus suffers the loss of all sense of reality, mistaking a very worldly courtesan for an evil sorceress. He is being presented with trials, from which he emerges successful, although confused. He does not succumb to the charms of the courtesan, unlike his brother.

Syr. Antipholus and Syr. Dromio seem suspended, believing either that they or everyone else is transformed, like a neophyte mid-initiation.

The Bible

Syr. Dromio makes use of a series of Biblical references to express his confusion in seeing his master free instead of imprisoned. In the same metaphor he cites Old and New Testament stories and preaching that refer to mankind's temptation by the Devil, thus implying that they are encircled by evil witchcraft. He enquires of the arresting officer with whom he last saw his master as 'the picture of Old Adam new apparelled', paraphrasing and combining Genesis 3. 7, 'They sewed figge tree leaves together and made themselves breeches', Genesis 3.21, 'unto Adam also and to his wife did the Lord God make coates of skinnes, and clothed them', and the reference in Ephesians 4.22-24 to the sinning Adam as 'olde man' which must be shed to be replaced by the redeemed 'newe man' in Christ. This also puns on the double meaning of 'suit' as clothes and lawsuit.[9]

He then merges the image of Adam, symbol of man's original sin, keeper of the Garden of Eden, with the idea of an evil angel dressed in a buff jacket of a skin from a calf like that killed to celebrate the return of the Prodigal Son to his father (Luke 15. 23). This juxtaposition of Biblical stories adds to the sense of confusion in the scene, as Syr. Dromio and his master are themselves the victims of contradictory stage action. Further anomalies are implied in the image of the officer as an evil angel arresting Syr. Antipholus in contrast to the Biblical account of the imprisoned St. Peter being released from prison by an angel of God (Acts 12. 5, 7, 11). Syr. Dromio offers Syr. Antipholus the bail money intended for Eph.

Antipholus with the words, 'Here are the angels that you sent for to deliver you' (IV. iii. 39), in terms of a distorted Biblical quotation from Acts 12. 11: 'The Lord hath sent his Angell, and hath delivered me'. In response, Syr. Antipholus seemingly invokes heavenly protection by quoting directly from Acts 12. 9, 'we wander in illusions' (IV. iii. 41).

The atmosphere associating evil with chaos and confusion is heightened at the entrance of the courtesan. Syr. Antipholus again tries to protect himself against apparent evil incarnated as the courtesan, by citing the Bible directly as 'Satan avoid' (IV. iii. 46), the words used by Christ in his resistance to Satan in the wilderness, 'Avoide Satan' (Matthew 4.10). This biblical scene is later recalled by Syr. Dromio with the prefix to the words applied to the courtesan as Satan, 'it is written' (IV. iii. 53), which cite Christ's response to Satan in Matthew 4. 4, 7, 10 and Luke 4. 4, 8, 10. The imagery associated with angels, sin and evil becomes a reality for the two men as they truly believe the courtesan to be a disguised devil. Syr. Dromio (at IV. iii. 51-56) refers to St. Paul's warning in 2 Corinthians 11. 14 that 'Satan him selfe is transformed into an Angel of Light'. Christ's admonition of Satan is again invoked by the terrified men as protection against the supposed evil of the courtesan in IV. iii. 48 before they escape from the scene.

Story Section 10 (IV. iv.)

Promising the officer that he will be freed by the money he sent for from his home, Eph. Antipholus appears with the officer. However, it is Eph. Dromio who enters with the rope that he had been asked to purchase for the humiliation of Adriana, and it is this rope, instead of the expected gold ducats, that he offers to his master, who beats him with it. The officer advises Eph. Antipholus to be patient, which Eph. Dromio claims is applicable to him, as he is the one in a state of adversity, for which his master calls him an ass. Dromio accepts the validity of this epithet, as his tolerance of the beatings he continually receives from Eph. Antipholus is asinine (IV. iv. 1-37).

Adriana enters with Luciana and Pinch, a schoolmaster and a proclaimed conjurer of spirits, to exorcise Eph. Antipholus of the evil spirits that they believe to be causing the supposed lunacy of his extraordinary behaviour. All of the self-contradictions of the action caused by the mistaken identity of the two sets of twins are exposed by the verbal exchange of the ensuing scene, which is resolved in a diagnosis by Pinch of both Eph. Antipholus and Eph. Dromio, requiring them both to be bound and kept in a dark room. Adriana pays the fine owed by her husband, and has him and his servant taken, bound together, to a dark room in their house.

To the consternation of all, who flee, thinking Eph. Antipholus and Eph. Dromio to be so possessed that they have escaped their bonds and fled from the darkened room, Syr. Antipholus and Syr. Dromio enter, swords drawn against the witchcraft they presume to prevail in the town, which they resolve to escape from as soon as possible.

Alchemy

The ninth gate of **Firmentation** (Ripley's spelling) is established in this action, during which Adriana and Luciana function as the two 'pure firments', while Eph. Antipholus is the 'lion', the compound of the alchemy, which must be given drink 'till his belly burst', action which is replicated in this scene by the exorcising, restraint and ultimately imprisonment to which he is subjected. The binding of Eph. Antipholus and Eph. Dromio together and their imprisonment also signifies the strengthening nature of this stage.

The gold with which the compound must be combined at this stage is symbolised by the bail-bond money Adriana pays to free her husband.

The swords which are wielded by Syr. Antipholus and Syr. Dromio were often used in alchemic imagery to symbolise the alchemic furnace fire, an image which I consider to be here applied in the burst of heat needed for this process, here represented by their fury.

Renaissance Platonism

The flesh-imprisonment of Eph. Antipholus becomes literal when he is bound together with Eph. Dromio and cast into a darkened room. That this will initiate the action that will release him and re-link him to Adriana so that his interrupted ascent can recommence is symbolised by the entry of his alter ego, his brother, Syr. Antipholus.

The illusory nature and false value of material things is symbolised by the rope that is presented to Eph. Antipholus instead of the gold which he expected would procure his release. The implication is that a dependence on material gold may release the body but it increases the imprisonment of the soul.

CHAPTER SIXTEEN

Adriana suffers a double illusion in mistaking Syr. Antipholus for her husband, and in trying to employ witchcraft to cure him. She does not function as the 'divine light' in their relationship. It will take the advice and action of Emilia to correct this.

Theurgy and Initiation

Eph. Antipholus encounters further trials in the confrontation with his wife and the attempted exorcism by Pinch, which is resolved by his and his servant's imprisonment in a dark room. This provides an analogue for the dark labyrinth into which neophytes, in mystery initiations, were committed for trials designed to throw them into a 'state of painful suspense and expectation' before being exposed to almost-blinding light and mystic revelation.

The Bible

Eph. Dromio cites the Biblical doctrine of Job 2.10 prescribing patience in adversity, 'Nay, 'tis for me to be patient, I am in adversity' (IV. iv. 19). The proverbial patience in adversity of Job is not a quality that has been hitherto displayed in his master and mistress and both must learn to practise it before their trials are accomplished.

The attempted exorcism by Pinch of Eph. Antipholus draws Biblical authority from incidents described in the New Testament, wherein Christ cures people by driving out devils (Matthew 9. 32-34, 17. 18, Mark 5. 2-17 and Luke 4. 33-35). Matthew 9.1 reports Christ conferring the power to cast out devils upon his disciples, an action that probably motivated subsequent exorcists. Pinch's reference to Satan being 'hous'd in Eph. Antipholus' (IV. iv. 54) quotes a Biblical incident in Matthew 12. 22, in which Christ is reported curing a man who was 'bothe blinde and dumbe' and 'possessed by the devil' (whom he calls an 'uncleane spirit'), whose soul has become as an inviting 'house' to the devil who will enter it again, this time with seven more of his confederates. The 'state of darkness' to which Pinch exhorts Satan, assumed to be possessing Eph. Antipholus to return to Hell, is that set forth in Genesis associated with chaos and evil and re-appearing in that context throughout the Bible.

Eph. Antipholus also employs a Biblical reference against his wife in response to the attempted exorcism. Believing her to be colluding with

Pinch to cover up her own misdeeds, he distorts in his threat to her, 'But with these nails I'll pluck out these false eyes', the sentiments of Matthew 5. 29, 'Wherefore if they right eie cause thee to offend, plucke it out and caste it from thee'.

Her responding order to bind him (IV. iv. 104) and the observation of Pinch that it is the Devil causing him to speak in that manner, 'the fiend is strong within him' (IV. iv. 104), reflect the futile restraining of the madman cured by Christ in Mark 5. 3-4.

Story Section 11 (V. i. 1-329)

Angelo and the merchant to whom he owes the money for the chain for Eph. Antipholus enter, wondering at his untypically dishonest behaviour in refusing payment for the chain, which he claims not to have received. Syr. Antipholus, wearing the chain, and Syr Dromio enter, and are accosted by Angelo, who reprimands Syr. Antipholus for his shameful behaviour in denying receipt of the chain. Syr. Antipholus draws his sword against this insult, and the merchant draws his sword in reply, but they are prevented from fighting by the entrance of Luciana, the courtesan and Adriana, who protests the lunacy of her husband and demands that the master and servant be bound and taken to her house. However, the two men escape, taking sanctuary in a nearby priory.

Emilia, the Lady Abbess of this priory, emerges to quieten the disturbance. Adriana demands to be allowed entrance to the priory to take her mentally ill husband from thence to a place of recovery. Emilia searches out the reason for his supposed illness and draws from Adriana that her nagging jealousy may have driven her husband insane. The Abbess insists that she will cure him herself with approved means such as herbal medicines and prayers, and, re-entering the priory, refuses to allow Adriana access to him.

Adriana is advised to appeal against Emilia to Duke Solinus, imminently due to implement the execution of Egeon. On the arrival of the Duke she appeals to him, giving an exaggerated account of the day's mishaps but succeeding in persuading the Duke to intervene with Emilia. They are interrupted by a messenger who comes to warn Adriana that her husband and his servant have escaped their bonds, tormented Pinch and his attendants with fire, and that they threaten to do the same to his wife. All present claim this to be impossible as they have just seen the pair enter the priory.

However, Eph. Antipholus and Eph. Dromio enter and appeal to the Duke, whose life, he reminds him, he once saved during a battle. He accuses his wife, Angelo, Pinch and all associated with them for gross mistreatment. On hearing the contradictory accounts of the day's events from the appellants, the Duke concludes that they have all become bewitched, as if drugged by Circe who turned people into animals with a drinking draught, 'I think you all have drunk of Circe's cup' (V. i. 271).

Egeon, seeing one whom he presumes to be his son, appeals to him for the money that will redeem him from death. Eph. Antipholus and Eph. Dromio, to the distress of Egeon, disclaim all knowledge of him, the necessary truth of which is verified by the Duke, who testifies that he has been patron to Eph. Antipholus for the past twenty years.

Alchemy

The stage of **Exaltation** is begun with the action that brings Emilia into the process. In one sense, reinforced by her years in the pure environment of the priory, she is the 'spirit' of the process, which is represented by the composite 'body' of the family. When Syr. Antipholus and Syr. Dromio escape to the sanctuary of her sphere, her integration back into her family is begun. She is the one who holds the key to the family's identity and to the reunion which will symbolise the achievement of the Philosophers' Stone. She demonstrates this in her effective chastisement of Adriana, which removes the barrier of jealousy obstructing her from being reunited with Eph. Antipholus. This realises in stage action, Ripley's description of the compound being 'crucified', echoing the torments undergone by Eph. Antipholus, and 'examinate', as Adriana is by Emila before being re-joined as husband and wife and then 'revived' by the 'spirit of life' (Emilia).

Eph. Antipholus is brought out of his torments by the agency of the Duke Solinus (as the sun in the process).

Egeon again enters the process as part of the corporate 'body', ready to be reunited as Sophic Sulphur, the Red King, with his wife as Sophic Mercury, the White Queen.

Renaissance Platonism

Both Syr. Antipholus and his brother enter the state from which they will emerge with a full sense of their real identities and be united with their true loves as 'divine lights'. In her function in this role, Luciana prevents Syr. Antipholus from fighting with the merchant. In his escape into the priory, an arena of spiritual light itself, he initiates the discovery of his mother, who, as Abbess, will become a guiding light to her sons and, as Emilia, will restore to Egeon the divine light by which he will commence his own ascent to Divinity.

Emilia begins to work on Adriana to rid her of the jealousy which Ficino observes has no place in 'the chorus of the blessed', thus purifying the divine light for one son, while she provides refuge for the other.

Ficino posits that the human soul finds bliss in Divinity along a route led in sequence by four virtues: Prudence, Courage, Justice, and Temperance. This scene presents these guiding virtues characterised as Luciana (Prudence), Egeon (Courage), Solinus (Justice), and Emilia (Temperance). Syr. Antipholus has been prudently rescued by Luciana; the general situation is contained by the exemplary courage in the face of adversity of Egeon; Eph. Antipholus relies on the justice of Solinus to extricate him from the turmoil he finds himself in; and Emilia tempers the pursuit of Syr. Antipholus and the jealous impatience of Adriana.

Solinus expresses the Renaissance view that a descent from sanity dehumanises people into animals by his reference to Circe. To him, the contradictory accounts of events given in this scene are lunatic. The critic Hankins explains that the Renaissance imaged Circe as a metaphor for lust as libido, impressing men's souls with bestial vices (p. 20).[10]

Theurgy and Initiation

Syr. Antipholus is about to escape from the darkness of the labyrinth, a fact that is heralded by the appearance of Luciana, the light of his initiation, preventing him from possible death at the hands of the merchant. This shift into the light is further symbolised by his entry into the sanctuary of the priory, whose abbess is his mother Emilia, functioning in this sense as a kind of Ceres/Demeter.

Egeon as neophyte is brought to the threshold of death in facing his planned execution.

That Pinch is a false guide is proved by the escape of Eph. Antipholus, who breaks free into the light shed by the Duke Solinus, who now guides the action. Egeon faces a further trial in his son's denial of him.

The Bible

The Christian church itself, with all its authority and mastery of Biblical doctrine, asserts control over the confused protagonists through Emilia. With firm assurance, she calmly addresses the problems suddenly put upon her, offering Christian sanctuary to Syr. Antipholus and Syr. Dromio and wise advice to Adriana.

In the patient acceptance of his fate, her husband Egeon exemplifies the Biblical patience in the face of adversity lacking in his son.

Story Section 12 (V. i. 330-426)

Emilia enters with Syr. Antipholus and Syr. Dromio and the two sets of twins face each other for the first time in the play. Egeon is recognised, first by Syr. Antipholus and Syr. Dromio and then by Emilia, who proclaims herself as his lost wife and the mother of his sons, the Antipholus twins. She describes how she had been separated from her son and his servant when Corinthian fishermen stole them from her, leaving her to proceed to Epidamnum and from thence to go to Ephesus and take up her life in the priory.

All the problems of the day's mishaps are resolved, the Duke remits Egeon's death sentence, Eph. Antipholus is reconciled with Adriana, the courtship of Luciana for Syr. Antipholus is allowed, the courtesan's diamond ring is returned to her, and the comedy of errors is deciphered by Syr. Antipholus:

> I see we still did meet each other's man
> And I was ta'en for him, and he for me,
> And thereupon these errors are arose (V. i. 386-388).

Emilia invites all into the Priory to enjoy a feast, during which they can exchange the stories of their separated lives. She rejoices at her reconciliation with her sons:

> Thirty three years have I but gone in travail
> Of you, my sons, and till this present hour
> My heavy burden ne'er delivered (V. i. 400-402).

Her words sum up the happy resolution of the family's tragic history:

> After so long grief, such nativity (V. i. 406).

The Dromio twins are left regarding each other with pleasure and amazement:

> Methinks you are my glass: and not my brother
> I see by you that I am a sweet-faced youth (V. i. 418-419).

They decide that no priority due to the elder of them shall prevail in their brotherhood:

> We came into the world like brother and brother,
> And now let's go hand in hand, not one before another (V. i. 426).

Alchemy

The Philosophers' Stone is achieved with the reunion of the family, as the stage of **Exaltation** is continued and achieved with Emilia's words, 'After so long grief, such nativity'. Their entry into the priory symbolises the Ripley description of the Philosophers' Stone as re-joined man and wife being exalted up to heaven, where it will influence 'other bodies'.

The Philosophers' Stone comprises three couples, Egeon and Emilia, Eph. Antipholus and Adriana, and Syr. Antipholus and Luciana, signalling the play's magic content. The Dromio twins, representing another aspect of the body, will enter the priory later, thus duplicating the action of the others and suggesting the stage of **Multiplication**.

The final stage of **Projection**, in which the Philosophers' Stone transforms base matter into gold, is realised in the behaviour of the Dromio twins, courteous and considerate to each other, exemplifying the ideal principle of equal brotherhood among men.

Renaissance Platonism

A reascent is effected for the family as Emilia removes all the intervening barriers (see fig. 22). The three pairs, Egeon and Emilia, Syr. Antipholus and Luciana and Eph. Antipholus provide individual soul-ascents, but there is also a corporate one for the united family, implying a sense of the benefits of their bliss being relayed to the macrocosm.

Ficino describes the summation of the bliss of souls who succeed in their ascent through love to Divinity as participation in a heavenly feast, for which the feast in the priory to which Emilia invites all can be said to be a paradigm.

The twin Dromios express the image of the mirror in which they see themselves in the other, and affirm the effects of that reflection in the brotherly love with which the play concludes.

The Bible

Christian redemption is reflected in the happy conclusion of the play, symbolised by the entry of all the participants into the Christian embrace of the abbey.

This most Christian of endings supports the tenet of the critic Northrop Frye that New Comedy, especially in its Shakespearean form, tends to be idealised, with analogies to religion. I consider that the theme adumbrates the arcana, that the family is a metaphor for a composite soul and that the family reunions at the ends of the mentioned plays represent an integrated personality and a redeemed soul.[11]

Cabala: Post Production (see fig. 3)

The play begins with a view of opposing spheres on the Hebraic Tree of Life, Duke Solinus represents **Geburah (Strength, as severity)** and Egeon as **Chesed (Mercy**, in its manifestation as a higher form of love) putting himself into danger in the search for his loved son. Both Solinus and Egeon are grounded in **Malkuth (Kingdom, the material world)** through their status and experience.

In their quest to find their lost brothers, Syr. Antipholus and his servant Syr. Dromio display a similar balance between Netzach (Victory, emotions), in their feelings for their brothers, and Hod (Glory, thoughts) in their mental efforts to succeed in their search. They seem grounded in **Malkuth** in their common sense practicality to make their way in Ephesus and to disguise their Syracusian nationality, which could be dangerous. However, this will all become disrupted with the errors caused by their mistaken identities with their brothers, a course initiated by the confusion between Syr. Antipholus and Eph. Dromio.

An unbalanced relationship between Adriana and her husband Eph. Antipholus is shown requiring attention. Both of them seem to be grounded in **Malkuth** (Eph. Antipholus too much so) but firmly fixed on **Netzach** where their unrestrained feelings lack the mediation of **Hod** as thinking. The gold chain becomes a symbol of the over indulgence of Eph. Antipholus in the sensual and materialistic attributes of **Malkuth**. Luciana, by contrast with her sister and brother-in-law, is fixed by her thoughts on the limitations of marriage on **Hod**, and unable to achieve a balance with the emotions of **Netzach**.

Malkuth is challenged in Adriana's mistaking of Syr. Antipholus for her husband and the scene resulting in Eph. Antipholus being locked out of his own home. This precipitates his removal from too much indulgence in **Malkuth** and presents the possibility of his future ascent throughout the Tree.

Syr. Antipholus moves strongly to the sphere of **Netzach** in falling in love with Luciana. She also has at last a taste of the feelings of this sphere in her responding love for him, but that is blocked by **Hod** as she believes the love to be improper as she mistakes him for Eph. Antipholus, her sister's husband.

A relationship homed entirely in **Malkuth** is described in Syr. Dromio's description of Nell who claims him as her lover, Eph. Dromio.

Eph. Antipholus is distanced from the delights of **Malkuth** in his arrest and imprisonment. One of its forbidden pleasures appears in the form of the Courtesan, whose hospitality he has now antagonised with the mistaken action involving Syr. Antipholus, her lowered opinion of the integrity of Eph. Antipholus and her subsequent loss of a diamond ring.

A physical and psychological thrashing out of the fleshly **Malkuth** obsession of Eph. Antipholus is undertaken with the actions of Pinch and his incarceration, bound to his servant, in a darkened room. This may be intended to clear his mind of guilt in **Yesod (Foundation, the subconscious)** but as he escapes and inflicts violence on Pinch, this may not have been achieved.

Syr. Antipholus and Syr. Dromio regard Ephesus as a place entirely lacking in reason on the **pillar of severity** with **Hod**, **Geburah** and **Binah (Understanding, the archetype of will)**.

Emilia, whose life in the priory has granted her the spiritual wisdom and love of **Chokmah (Wisdom spiritual purpose)**, and who as the mother of the twins can be regarded as **Tiphareth (Beauty, heart)**, enters, and in a balance with **Binah** as understanding and **Geburah** as strength and severity, begins to unravel the lives of her unrecognised family. The Duke Solinus, who hitherto has been fixed on **Geburah**, adopts a feature of **Netzach** in forgiving Egeon his death penalty.

The appearance of both sets of twins together and Emilia's recognition of her husband Egeon, and subsequently her sons and their servants, restores balance and harmony. Luciana is allowed to realise her love for Syr. Antipholus, and he to marry her and fulfil his love as **Netzach**, hopefully rising to **Chesed** and balanced with **Binah (understanding)** as the anomalies of Ephesus are removed and his lost family discovered. Hopefully, Eph. Antipholus and Adriana will settle into a more harmonious relationship with a balance of **Netzach** and **Hod** (watched over by his mother no doubt), and Emilia takes all into the spiritual realm of the priory to feast in the achievement of **Kether (Crown, the Divine Self)**.

Shakespeare's application of Plato's theory of the 'Divided Soul' to *The Comedy of Errors* links it to the next category of 'Renaissance Platonism'. The first of the plays in this group, *Romeo and Juliet*, also features, in its young protagonists, the secret meaning in this category of 'Rites of Initiation'.

RENAISSANCE PLATONISM
CHAPTER SEVENTEEN: *ROMEO AND JULIET*

Shakespeare exemplifies all the features of Divine Love in his story of the young lovers, Romeo and Juliet. Theatre Set-Up produced the play in 1996, performing in 46 venues in seven countries. Making her professional debut as Juliet was Victoria Stilwell, later to appear on our TV screens as the animal behaviour expert in *It's Me or the Dog* (see below p. 493). This love of animals became evident during the tour, when I missed a cue as the nurse while we were enthusing about my neighbour's dog and the games that it enjoyed. Her Romeo was Neil Warhurst, and most of the direction was done by Michael Palmer, who had begun his professional theatre career with us in 1987, as I was trying to prepare my PhD manuscript for its deadline submission. The tour was a joy for me as an actor, as I was playing the part most suited to me – Juliet's nurse. While most of the venues in which we performed were in the UK, including five cathedrals and a church in Wales, we presented an extended mainland European month-long tour, exploring new venues in Belgium and Germany.

We set this famous tragedy in the chivalric period of the fifteenth century, when the philosophies that underlie the play were most prevalent. I considered that the theme of sacrifice which the play carries made the play especially appropriate for the season's ecclesiastical venues. The only scenery we had was a circular plinth, placed centre stage. This symbolised the centre of the labyrinth in the paradigm of initiation in the play, gave extra height to players in important moments in the story and represented Juliet's window.

The main problem in this play is the interpretation in performances of the logistics of II. ii., in which Romeo courts Juliet at her window. Often this window is designated to be a balcony, and Romeo is often presented as being able to climb up to Juliet so that they can touch each other. The logic of this seems to me to be flawed as the words in the script (II. ii. 23-5) indicate that they cannot touch or clearly see each other. Besides, it was the practice of fathers in Italy to place their daughters safely in inaccessible bedrooms. I suggest that the secret meaning of Divine Love which Shakespeare establishes that the lovers experience at their first meeting in I.v. (see below in Story Section 3) should be extended by keeping the lovers separate in II. ii. (see below in Story Section 4).

The arcana which I found in *Romeo and Juliet* were so particularly adapted by Shakespeare to the play that I detail them here, as well as referring to their full description in Chapters One, Two and Three.

Alchemy (see also above pp. 26–34)
Alchemists believed that they could improve or redeem 'base matter' (the metal lead or the human psyche) which they termed earth, lead, serpent, whale, dragon or toad, snake or King , by transforming it in chemical processes the goal of which was to raise it to 'gold' by means of a red powder called the 'Philosophers' Stone', often regarded as being synonymous with Jesus Christ. The hermetic vessel where this was done was often called a 'cave'. There are twelve specific stages in alchemy which can be grouped into four main colour-coded stages, which I found to be evident in the scenario and language of *Romeo and Juliet*. The correspondences are explained in detail in the 'Story' sections of the chapter.

- In the first 'black' stage (often called a raven, wolf or crow) the 'body' of the process would be separated by extreme heat (often symbolised by swords) from its 'soul' (the vapour in the chemical process) which would ascend into an 'astral sphere' (just as the vapour ascended in the hermetic vessel).
- In the second 'white' stage (sometimes called a dove), the 'body' would be tried and tested, purified by many processes (in the chemical form of alchemy these were washing and heating), while the 'soul' was refined in the 'astral sphere'.
- In the third 'red' stage, the body and soul were joined together again when the soul would descend into the 'improved' body.
- In the fourth and last 'gold' stage, the red powder called the Philosophers' Stone was achieved, projected onto the base matter and the 'gold' of alchemy realised.

A dominant metaphorical feature of alchemy was the ultimate good resulting from difficulties, expressed as redemption coming through death in the maxim 'die to live', which followed the pattern in nature of new growth springing from old.

Renaissance Platonism and Christianity (see above pp. 34-37, 59)

By Shakespeare's time, the philosophies of Plato had been fused with Christianity. Plato wrote that all creatures had descended into their bodies from Divinity, and always carried a wish, held in their memories of their Divine origin, to reascend to Divinity. Shakespeare's concept of 'Divine Love', based on Plato's views, maintained that this ascent could be achieved through a holy or divine love of a 'companion soul'.

This unselfish love would be so ennobling that the lovers could experience the love of the Divine and their souls would begin the ascent back to Divinity. The ascent would progress as the lovers were tested for constancy and self-sacrifice. 'Base love', however, which was only interested in the gratification of the flesh, would drag the soul further away from Divinity.

Christians saw in this beautiful Platonic scenario a foreshadowing of the ministry of Jesus Christ, who taught 'God is Love' and, according to Christian belief, whose self-sacrifice for the love of mankind was designed to redeem it and bring it closer to God.

Rites of Initiation and Augury (see above pp. 49-50)

From time immemorial, all societies have put their young through rites of initiation (also called rites of passage) during which the young (neophytes) enter a labyrinth in which they must endure pain, fear, suffer a near-death experience and then at the centre of the labyrinth enjoy a mystic sense of divine revelation. The rites of Eleusis, of which Plato himself was a neophyte, were typical of these and provided a blue-print for subsequent mystic systems with which Shakespeare would have been familiar in Britain.

The divine revelation in Western and Middle Eastern mysticism was the 'sun-logos', Jesus Christ as described in the Bible by St John as 'the Word' and 'the light', and indicated as being throughout all time 'at the right hand of God'.

Linked to this mysticism was a sense of destiny patterned in the stars, a prevalent theme in this play.[1]

CHAPTER SEVENTEEN

Story Section 1 (The Prologue, I. i.)
A Chorus introduces the story of Romeo and Juliet, describing the feud between their parents which was dissolved by the 'misadventur'd piteous overthrows' of the star-crossed lovers.

The rival families of Montagues and Capulets are seen feuding in the street of Verona. A young Montague, Benvolio, tries to stop servants of the rival families fighting, but he is challenged by Tybalt, nephew to Lord Capulet. The Lords Montague and Capulet try to enter the skirmish themselves but are restrained by their wives. Many are injured, and the Prince Escalus of Verona intervenes, forbidding any of them to fight again on pain of death.

Lord Montague and his wife discuss the strange behaviour of their only son, Romeo, with his friend, Benvolio. When Romeo enters, Benvolio learns from him that he is in love with Rosaline, who disdains his courtship.

Alchemy
Verona's feuding Capulet and Montague families are the base matter of the alchemy which needs to be transmuted.

Renaissance Platonism and Christianity
Verona is despoiled by the hatred between the Capulets and Montagues, a fact despised by Romeo. However, when complaining to Benvolio that he is frustrated because a lady, Rosaline, that he desires, rejects his advances when she will not 'Ope her lap to saint-seducing gold' (I. i. 212), he demonstrates that this love is 'base love', motivated by physical lust.

Rites of Initiation and Augury
The Chorus indicates before the play begins that the lovers are doomed, being 'star-crossed'. It is as if they have been selected for sacrifice. Romeo is singled out as the main neophyte, but the other young people of Verona, Juliet, Benvolio, Mercutio and Tybalt are also candidates. Benvolio displays a maturity of attitude that almost suggests that he is a graduate of initiation.

Story Section 2 (I. ii., iii.)
Lord Capulet accepts the suit of Paris for the hand of his only child, his daughter Juliet, and plans a feast at which they can become acquainted.

Romeo and his friends, Benvolio and Mercutio, intercept the invitation list to this feast, see the name of Rosaline on it and plan to crash the party disguised in masks. Benvolio suggests that Romeo's ardour would decrease by comparing Rosaline with other ladies at the Capulet feast.

Juliet and her nurse are informed by Lady Capulet of the proposed match with Paris. Juliet is acquiescent to her parents' suggestion of marriage to whoever they choose for her. The nurse prattles of the physical aspects of love.

Alchemy
Romeo will represent the body of the base matter on behalf of the Montagues, and here he is being set up to undertake this task.

Renaissance Platonism and Christianity
Juliet's compliant attitude to the suggestion that she marry Paris demonstrates that so far in her life she has had no knowledge of or expectation of love. The loveless arranged marriages that she and her mother must expect are soul-destroying. Her nurse demonstrates the attitudes of base love.

Rites of Initiation and Augury
Juliet is presented as an initiate. She is the picture of uninitiated innocence.

Story Section 3 (I. iv., v.)
Romeo and Benvolio are joined by Mercutio in going to the Capulets' feast. Romeo claims that he cannot dance as he has 'a soul of lead' (I. iv. 15). When Romeo speaks of a dream he had that night, Mercutio claims that he has been visited in his sleep by Queen Mab, 'the fairies midwife' (I. iv. 54). However, Romeo confesses that his mind 'misgives | Some consequence yet hanging in the stars' (I. iv. 106-107). He feels that his dream is a premonition of 'Some vile forfeit of untimely death' (I. iv. 111), but he will yield to his fate.

This premonition of the forceful hand of fate is realised when he sees Juliet at the Capulets' feast, 'Did my heart love till now? Forswear it, sight. | For I ne'er saw true beauty till this night' (I.v. 51- 52).

Tybalt identifies Romeo by his voice and wishes to challenge the Montague for his impudence in gate-crashing the Capulet feast, but Lord Capulet prevents him from doing so. The angered Tybalt threatens revenge.

Romeo and Juliet fall instantly in love with each other. The words of love that they speak to each other are expressed in terms of religion. Romeo calls his extended hand to her 'This holy shrine' (I. v. 93) and his lips 'two blushing pilgrims' (I. v. 94). Her response echoes the religious metaphors which continue throughout their first meeting:

Juliet:	Good pilgrim, you do wrong your hand too much,
	Which mannerly devotion shows in this;
	For saints have hands that pilgrims' hands do touch,
	And palm to palm is holy palmers' kiss.
Romeo:	Have not saints lips, and holy palmers too?
Juliet:	Ay, pilgrim, lips that they must use in prayer.
Romeo:	O then, dear saint, let lips do what hands do:
	They pray: grant thou, lest faith turn to despair.
Juliet:	Saints do not move, though grant for prayer's sake.
Romeo:	Then move not, while my prayer's effect I take.
	[He kisses her]
	Thus from my lips, by thine, my sin is purg'd.
Juliet:	Then have my lips the sin that they have took.
Romeo:	Sin from my lips? O trespass sweetly urg'd
	Give me my sin again. [He kisses her] (I. v. 96-109)

Both Romeo and Juliet are devastated to learn that each is from a rival family. Romeo exclaims, 'Is she a Capulet? | O dear account. My life is my foe's debt' (I. v. 117). Juliet echoes this complaint:

My only love sprung from my only hate.
Too early seen unknown, and known too late.
Prodigious birth of love it is to me
That I must love a loathed enemy. (I. v. 137-140)

Alchemy

On behalf of the Capulets, Juliet will represent the soul of the base matter, and she is here linked with Romeo, the body of the alchemical process, identified in this function as his reference to his soul being made of lead.

Mercutio, true to his name, will be the agent, Mercury, which instigates the violent stages of the alchemy.

Renaissance Platonism and Christianity

Plato wrote of the instant recognition of companion souls in Divine Love. This is the experience of Romeo and Juliet. That Shakespeare intends that their love should be a model of Divine Love is demonstrated in the religious metaphors they use in their words of love to each other when they meet.

Rites of Initiation and Augury

Romeo and Juliet pass their first test, daring to love their enemy.

Story Section 4 (Prologue, II. i., ii.)

The Prologue narrates the difficulties that the lovers must experience and overcome as members of enemy families, stating, 'But passion lends them power, time means, to meet, | Tempering extremities with extreme sweet.'

Romeo climbs a garden wall and hides in the Capulet garden, hoping to see and talk with Juliet at her window, 'Can I go forward when my heart is here? | Turn back, dull earth, and find thy centre out' (II. i. 1-2). From outside the wall, Mercutio and Benvolio call to Romeo, thinking that he is still enamoured of Rosaline and unaware that he has fallen in love with Juliet. Romeo responds painfully to Mercutio's jesting, 'He jests at scars that never felt a wound' (I. ii. 1). He sees Juliet at her window, confessing her love for him to the night. The space between them is indicated by his wish to be close to her:

> Romeo: See how she leans her cheek upon her hand.
> O that I were a glove upon that hand,
> That I might touch that cheek. (II. ii. 23-25)

These words indicate how important it is that the lovers maintain the distance between the ground where Romeo stands and Juliet at the window above so that the love between them remains Divine. There is no mention in the script of his climbing up to her window (or balcony), a circumstance that her father would have been expected to make impossible in the allocation of her sleeping quarters, safe from intrusion. When Romeo ultimately does enter her bedroom after they are married, it is via a rope ladder that he has been given, indicating that it would be impossible to reach Juliet's bedroom by climbing up to it. In the Theatre Set-Up production of the play, this distance was represented horizontally, Juliet standing on the circular plinth in the centre of the stage and Romeo remaining at a distance.

Romeo takes his cue for revealing himself from her pledging to forsake her name as a Capulet if he should swear his love for her and forsake his name as a Montague. He comes forward and she expresses embarrassment that he has heard her confessing her love for him:

> Juliet: Thou knowest the mask of night is on my face
> Else would a maiden blush bepaint my cheek
> For that which thou has heard me speak tonight. (II. ii. 85-87)

This also demonstrates that they can only see each other dimly, a further feature of the Divinity of their love, the usual senses of touch not possible, and sight limited. She comments on his bravery in daring to enter the private Capulet garden, where, if he were found by any of her male relatives, he would be killed. He protests that love of her is his defence and has given him the power to scale the garden walls. Only lack of her love could kill him. Bereft of being able to touch each other and see each other clearly, they pour forth their mutual love in a torrent of words charged with beautiful images. When she is called in by her nurse and re-enters at her window, Romeo calls her his soul, 'It is my soul that calls upon my name' (II. ii. 164). The lovers resolve to marry the following day.

Romeo seeks out Friar Lawrence to perform this secret marriage and the Friar agrees to do so, in the hope that the union might resolve the conflict between the feuding families.

Alchemy

The lovers affirm their alchemic roles. Romeo actually names himself as 'earth', one of the metaphors for base matter: 'Turn back, dull earth'. He also calls Juliet his 'soul'.

We see Friar Lawrence gathering herbs for his practice of the alchemy taught by Paracelsus, who gave instruction in the use of herbal medicines.

Renaissance Platonism and Christianity

The ascent to Divinity that Romeo and Juliet will make is represented by her presence at a window, high above Romeo. The achievement of their love, although they are physically separated, is further testimony to the fact that their love is divine, not base. The Platonic nature of this love, embracing the soul and mind as well as the body, is revealed in their use of words such as 'friend', 'company', 'home', 'talk' and 'soul'. Shakespeare reinforces their natures as companion souls in the beauty of their language, mutually spoken in imagery which indicates the equality of the intense communication of their minds.

Rites of Initiation and Augury

Romeo expresses his entry into the labyrinth when he resolves to seek out Juliet in a journey like a labyrinth, where he will 'find thy centre out'. In his association of Juliet with the sun, it is implied that for him as a neophyte she represents the Divinity at the centre of the labyrinth. The metaphor is echoed with her later references to him as 'sun' and 'stars', indicating that Romeo is in turn the centre of her labyrinth.

The initiates in the labyrinth always had a spiritual guide, and Friar Lawrence performs that function for Romeo and later for Juliet.

Story Section 5 (II. iv., v., vi.)

On the following morning, Benvolio and Mercutio wait for Romeo, noting that he did not go home the previous night and assuming that he still lusts for Rosalind. When Romeo arrives, Mercutio notes that he no longer shows signs of sexual frustration, 'Without his roe, like a dried herring' (II. iv. 38). When he responds in like kind to Mercutio's jesting, Mercutio praises his changed mood, 'Why, is not this better now than groaning for love?' (II. iv. 88-89)

Juliet's nurse enters with her man Peter, and the young men tease her and flirt with her, mocking her age and gender. She has been chosen by Juliet to act as the go-between for the young lovers, and Romeo arranges with her that Juliet and he should meet at Friar Lawrence's cell that afternoon to be married. That night, Romeo's man will bring the nurse a rope ladder for her to let down to him below Juliet's window so that he can climb up to her bedroom and the marriage can be consummated.

Meanwhile Juliet impatiently waits for the nurse to bring her news of Romeo's response to her sending the nurse as a go-between. The nurse teases her by delaying telling her of Romeo's plans and makes it clear by her praising of Romeo's physical attributes, that again her view of love conforms to the features of base love. Throughout the play, the nurse sets out the conditions of base love, which the young lovers ignore.

As planned, the lovers are married by Friar Lawrence in his cell. When Friar Lawrence cautions Romeo to 'love moderately', he does so in response to Romeo defying death in the daring of this secret marriage between the children of feuding families. Romeo has tempted fate with his words:

> Then love-devouring death do what he dare:
> It is enough that I may call her mine. (II. vi. 7-8)

Alchemy
The lovers are joined so that they can become the redeemers of their debased families. This also represents the alchemical stage of **Coniunctio**, a chemical wedding.

Renaissance Platonism and Christianity
The physical effects of Divine Love are manifest in Romeo after he has met his soul's companion. Although there has been no sexual gratification, this occurrence has so satisfied him that no longer does he show the signs of physical sexual frustration or the moodiness that typified his base love for Rosalind.

The love is blessed by the friar, who wishes it to be holy and to have a beneficial effect on other people, namely the members of the feuding families (see fig. 18).

Rites of Initiation and Augury
The marriage commits the two young neophytes to the trials of their initiation. The danger of their situation also makes them vulnerable to inauspicious astral influences.

Story Section 6 (III. i., III. ii.)

However, Tybalt is still seeking out Romeo to punish his trespass at the Capulet feast. Tybalt tries to engage Romeo in a fight, but Romeo, remembering that Tybalt is now his cousin by marriage, turns away from him. Mercutio, ashamed at what he sees as Romeo's cowardice, and spoiling for a fight with Tybalt, engages swords with him, but Romeo, trying to prevent the fight, blocks Mercutio and Tybalt deals him a death blow. As he realises that he is dying, Mercutio accuses Romeo of making it possible for Tybalt to kill him, and he curses the feuding houses that have cost him his life. Romeo cries out that Juliet's beauty has made him 'effeminate' (III. i. 116) and when Tybalt enters again, challenging Romeo to join Mercutio in death, they fight and Romeo kills Tybalt. As Benvolio hurries Romeo away, Romeo cries, 'O, I am fortune's fool' (III. i. 138).

The citizens of Verona, including the senior Montagues and Capulets and Prince Escalus, enter, horrified at the carnage. Lady Capulet claims that Romeo should be killed as punishment for taking Tybalt's life, but Prince Escalus modifies Romeo's punishment to banishment, exiling him from Verona.

Unaware of the deaths of Mercutio and Tybalt and the banishment from Verona of Romeo, Juliet waits for him in her bedroom. Her nurse brings in the rope ladder given to her by Romeo's man and tells Juliet of the fighting and the deaths. At first Juliet condemns Romeo, but then pledges her support of him as he is her husband, lamenting his forthcoming banishment.

Alchemy

In order for the stages of alchemy to be followed, the body and soul of the process must be separated, and this violent 'black' stage of **Putrefaction** is represented by the killing of Mercutio and Tybalt, which will force the body, Romeo, into exile and separate him from the soul, Juliet.

When Juliet first hears that Romeo has killed her cousin, Tybalt, she uses the alchemic terms 'dragon', 'cave', 'dove', 'raven' and 'wolvish' in her shocked outcry against him.

Renaissance Platonism and Christianity

In yielding to base revenge, Romeo descends back from Juliet and from

Divinity. However, his exile and the subsequent events will test the constancy of his love and his ability for self-sacrifice.
Rites of Initiation and Augury
Mercutio and Tybalt die in the labyrinth of Verona's feud. Romeo suffers the death experience through his friend and goes deep into the labyrinth.

Story Section 7 (III. iii.)
The nurse comforts Juliet and Friar Lawrence consoles Romeo. The young husband climbs a rope ladder to Juliet's room to spend his last night in Verona with Juliet before he begins his exile in Mantua.

Alchemy
In spending their first and last night together, the lovers enact **Coniunctio**, in which opposites are united. Romeo as the body begins, with his exile, the trials which represent the purifying alchemical process.
Renaissance Platonism and Christianity
The rope ladder represents the ascent that Romeo must attempt to make again and that he will achieve through his love of Juliet. A ladder was sometimes used in arcane visual images to symbolise the ascent of the soul towards Divinity, often represented by Jacob's ladder in the Bible story. It also had significance in alchemy.[2] (see fig.12)
Rites of Initiation and Augury
In the consummation of married love, Romeo reaches the sun in the centre of the labyrinth.

Story Section 8 (III. iv., v.)
Lord and Lady Capulet decide that Juliet's wedding to Paris should be brought forward to comfort her in her extreme grieving that she claims to be caused by her cousin Tybalt's death.

After the lovers' night together, Romeo must leave before sunrise to avoid capture before going into exile in Mantua. They appear at her window and both are reluctant to part, but the nurse tells them that Lady Capulet is coming to see Juliet, and Romeo descends. As he reaches the ground, both lovers have premonitions of their doomed fate:

Juliet:	O God, I have an ill-divining soul!
	Methinks I see thee, now thou art so low,
	As one dead in the bottom of a tomb.
	Either my eyesight fails, or thou look'st pale.
Romeo:	And trust me, love, in my eye so do you.
	Dry sorrow drinks our blood. Adieu, adieu. (III. v. 54-59)

When Lady Capulet and then Lord Capulet tell her of her wedding to Paris that they have planned to take place on the following Thursday, they are amazed when she tells them that she does not want to marry Paris, but they compel her to obey their wishes. Juliet asks her nurse for advice, and the nurse recommends that she forget Romeo and marry Paris, who she claims to be a better man than Romeo. Juliet rejects her nurse as a counsellor and confidante, and decides to seek help from Friar Lawrence, resolving to die rather than dishonour her marriage to Romeo.

Alchemy
Juliet is tried and tested as the soul of the alchemic process. In *The Lovers and the Tomb: Alchemical Emblems in Shakespeare, Donne and Marvell*, Lyndy Abraham identifies the alchemical image of lovers embracing in a tomb in the mating, farewells and premonitions of the lovers in this scene.[3] She cites images illustrating this metaphor from woodcuts in the 1550 *Rosarium Philosophorum of* Cyriaci Jacobi (see fig. 45) which predate Shakespeare's writing of the play.[4] Abraham explains the meaning of the image as signifying the alchemic stage of **Coniunctio** merging into the death of the old unregenerated base matter so that the Philosophers' Stone can be achieved.[5] This is certainly the significance of the scenario in the doomed lovers' final embrace before they next meet at the Capulet tomb where their deaths will redeem the base matter of flawed Verona in the Philosophers' Stone of reconciliation of the feuding families. This will be celebrated in the raising of gold statues of the lovers. Abraham cites examples of the themed wedding/tomb in other sections of the play, for example: I. v. 133-4; III. ii. 135-137; III. v. 140; V. iii. 101-120.

Shakespeare's rendering of the alchemical significance of the play gives an example of a secret meaning being achieved by divergence from an original source. Abraham points out that the time between the union of the lovers and their deaths is only two days, a period indicating the alchemically significant symbiosis of the events, whereas in the source of the play, Arthur Brooke's poem *The Tragicall Historye of Romeus and Juliet,* a period of several weeks elapses.[6]

Renaissance Platonism and Christianity
Juliet's constancy in love is tested. She resists the suggestion from the nurse that she should descend to base love in marrying Paris. Both lovers are constant to each other.

Rites of Initiation and Augury
Juliet's trials are intensified as she enters a psychological labyrinth forced on her by her parents in their insistence that she should marry Paris when she is already married to Romeo. Romeo begins a journey to Mantua and enters a metaphorical labyrinth that will see him return back to Verona in trials of his integrity and love for his wife.

Story Section 9 (IV. i.)
Juliet asks help from Friar Lawrence, who suggests, after she has threatened to take her own life with a knife, that she take a potion which he has prepared that will make her seem as if dead for forty two hours, during which time he will be able to send a letter to Romeo in Mantua that he should come to the Capulet vault where she will be laid out on a tomb. They can then escape together from Verona.

Alchemy
Juliet is prepared for her role as the soul ascending to the stars. This is a metaphor for the alchemical white vapour in the alchemic process rising to the top of the alembic vessel. Friar Lawrence carries out his function as a benevolent alchemist, the potion he gives to Juliet a medicine/chemical which will effect the process.

Renaissance Platonism and Christianity
Juliet will face the ultimate test, a simulated death for her love, a fact which Friar Lawrence respects when offering her the potion.

Rites of Initiation and Augury
Friar Lawrence becomes Juliet's spiritual guide, and through the potion he creates for her gives her the simulated death experience necessary in initiation.

Story Section 10 (III. ii., iii., iv.)
Juliet agrees to take the potion, returning home to pretend that she acquiesces to the wedding plans. In solitude, with the task of taking the drug, she expresses a fear that the potion may indeed kill her, an irony that she does not realise in light of the subsequent scenario. After much trepidation, she drinks the potion and falls into a death-like sleep. Her family mourn her death, and, advised by Friar Lawrence, lay her out in the family vault.

Alchemy
In her simulated death-sleep, seeming to ascend to Heaven, as Friar Lawrence preaches to her family, Juliet represents the ascending soul. In the alchemical reading of the play this symbolises the 'white' stage, **Congelation**.

Renaissance Platonism and Christianity
Juliet faces another test in being brave enough to take the drug and suffer its unknown consequences. The love of her family for her, shown wanting in their cruel forcing of her marriage to someone repellent to her, is, however, realised with her apparent death.

Rites of Initiation and Augury
Juliet experiences her brush with death.

Story Section 11 (V. i., V. ii.)
The letter which Friar Lawrence sends to Romeo by way of Friar Peter does not reach him due to a plague in Mantua. Romeo purchases poison from an apothecary, resolving to die over Juliet's body. When Friar Lawrence learns that Friar Peter has not been able to deliver the news to Romeo that Juliet's death is not real, he hastens to the Capulet tomb to alert Juliet and take her to his cell until Romeo arrives.

Alchemy
Romeo as body prepares to be recombined with Juliet, the soul of the

process. The apothecary is a malevolent alchemist, practising the craft for financial gain and called in Shakespeare's time a 'puffer' (after the bellows used to increase the fire used in the process, see above p. 34). His potion, unlike that of Friar Lawrence, is a deadly poison, exchanged for money. In her article on the alchemic significance of *Romeo and Juliet*, Abraham identifies Shakespeare's knowledge of the trappings of 'puffer' alchemists in the items Romeo describes in the apothecary's premises, the hanging tortoise, stuffed alligator and fish, which were 'shop signs' of alchemy. That he has been unsuccessful as a puffer is indicated in Romeo's description of him as miserable, meagre, and bony with tattered clothes and an ostentatious attempt to display empty and worthless items significant to alchemy in his premises. It is his puffer's inability to turn lead into gold, resulting in his abject poverty, which motivates Romeo to approach him for a dangerous poison to be exchanged for the money which Romeo observes that he needs.

Renaissance Platonism and Christianity

Romeo faces a test of his Divine Love for Juliet in his response to the news of her death.

Rites of Initiation and Augury

Romeo's harsh challenges in the labyrinth of his experiences have enabled him to face the prospect of real death.

Story Section 12 (V. iii.)

Paris, who has come to the Capulet vault to mourn Juliet, challenges Romeo when he enters the vault and, in the ensuing fight, is killed by Romeo (see fig. 46). Taking the supposedly-dead Juliet in his arms, Romeo drinks the poison and dies. Friar Lawrence enters the vault and tries to persuade the now-awakened Juliet to leave with him and enter a nunnery. She refuses, and, taking Romeo's dagger, kills herself to join her husband in death.

Alerted by the news of the death of Paris, Prince Escalus, Lord and Lady Capulet and Lord Montague enter the vault, find the bodies of Romeo and Juliet, and mourn the couple's death. Friar Lawrence, who has been apprehended and brought to the scene, tells the assembled company the story of the doomed lovers. Lord Montague and Lord and Lady Capulet are reprimanded by Prince Escalus for the feuding which has killed their children. The bereaved parents resolve their feud in a pledge to raise statues of gold to the ill-fated lovers.

Alchemy

The 'red' stage of alchemy, prefiguring the red powder which, cast upon lead, would turn it into gold, is symbolised in the blood of Paris and Juliet. In their self-sacrificing deaths, which create harmony in Verona between the Capulets and Montagues, Romeo and Juliet achieve the Philosophers' Stone, the goal of alchemy, symbolised by the gold statues of them that will be raised as monuments to them as their families are reconciled.[7] Prince Escalus, in marking the peace between the Capulets and Montagues that the death of their children has created, conveys, in the alchemical stage of **Projection**, the realisation of this benefit to Verona to the audience.

Renaissance Platonism and Christianity

Romeo and Juliet practice the ultimate self-sacrifice in their suicides, which they undergo for their Divine Love for each other, and the benefits to others are immediately made manifest. The implication at the end of the play is that they are united in Divinity. Lord Capulet acknowledges that the lovers have been sacrificed by the families' feud, 'Poor sacrifices of our enmity' (V. iii. 302). Prince Escalus identifies that Romeo and Juliet's love and deaths seem to be ordained by heaven to reconcile the Capulet/Montague enmity, 'See what a scourge is laid upon your hate | That heaven finds means to kill your joys with love' (V. iii. 291-2).

Rites of Initiation and Augury

Sometimes initiates died as a result of their trials in the initiatory labyrinth, an outcome which awaited Romeo and Juliet, as they seem to have been selected by fate to be sacrificial victims who must die to redeem Verona.[8]

Cabala: Post production (see fig. 3)

Verona is the subject of the progress through the Cabala Tree of Life, represented by its young and by its mature citizens. Benvolio and Mercutio are the only youths grounded in **Malkuth**, the reality of the world understood through the senses. Among the adults, only Friar Lawrence and Prince

Escalus are grounded in **Malkuth**, with the difficult task of trying to make peace in Verona.

Tybalt, Romeo, and all other Capulets and Montagues, including the adults of those families, are imprisoned in the traumas of **Yesod**, the subconscious, by their endless tradition of feuding, thus preventing Verona from progressing up the Tree.

However, when Romeo and Juliet meet and fall in love they escape from the traumas of **Yesod** by disregarding the feud which divides their families. This enables them to move up the Tree to **Netzach**, representing feelings, and then to proceed to **Tiphareth (centre, heart, beauty)** by way of **Hod (thoughts)** whose logic causes them to marry with the help of Friar Lawrence. It is their story which will redeem Verona, release it from the traumas in **Yesod** and, with a consequent peace, allow it to progress up the Tree.

The destructive features of **Yesod** are demonstrated in the deaths of Tybalt and Mercutio and the banishment of Romeo. In spite of the efforts of Friar Lawrence to circumvent the effects of **Yesod** on the young lovers by devising a scheme for them to escape from Verona, they are destroyed by the effects of the feud, but in doing so release their parents and Verona from the tradition of their enmity in **Yesod** so that a peaceful Verona can move to the heart of **Tiphareth**. Prince Escalus enacts the justice of **Geburah** and the mercy of **Chesed** on the Capulets and Montagues, whose promise to raise statues in gold to the lovers indicate the presence of Verona on **Tiphareth**. Such have been the disastrous effects of the feuding traumas of **Yesod** on Verona that a further progression up the Tree from **Tiphareth** cannot be envisaged at the end of the play, with Prince Escalus declaring, 'Some shall be pardon'd and some punished' (V. iii. 307).

CHAPTER EIGHTEEN: *ANTONY AND CLEOPATRA*

Antony and Cleopatra doubly illustrates Renaissance Platonism in the Divine Love between Antony and Cleopatra and in the conflict of loyalties this creates between his love for Cleopatra and his duty to Rome, exemplified by Plato's metaphor of the charioteer in *Phaedrus*.

Theatre Set-Up presented their production of *Antony and Cleopatra* in 1998 in 38 venues in six countries with nine actors, including myself as director and actor and Paul Brennan, the company/stage manager, also taking acting roles. We were lucky in having Dan Caulfield before he retired as co-director and Enobarbus, giving a much-admired gravitas to the performances. Rosalind Cressy was a stunning Cleopatra and Tony Portacio her Antony. We benefitted considerably from the contribution to the production of our own choreographer, Lindsay Royan, whose instruction to Rosalind Cressy on ancient Egyptian dance gave her interpretation of Cleopatra the sinuous, beautiful movements which characterised her performance, emphasising her symbolism as the 'serpent base matter' of the alchemic allegory. Our professional costumiers, Kim Jones and Andrew Fisher, delighted in creating new costumes based on ancient Egyptian and Roman dress, while our wardrobe mistress, Evelyn Cousin, adapted costumes we already had into the Roman style. Our music was composed by Terence Hawes for wind and string instruments and pre-recorded by Adrenaline Productions. The resulting production gave a vivid sense of ancient Egypt and its arcane significance. We used six of our small rostra curved into an arc as basis for our staging. This provided a sense of different locations in the play: of a Roman forum, Pompey's ship, rocks near a battlefield, or Cleopatra's court and her monument. Such a minimalist staging marked the change in attitudes to the mounting of productions over the years. When in 1955 I studied the play at school, I was informed that there were so few productions of the play because it was impossible to produce and quickly change the scenery needed to convey the play's various locations. Having left behind the extravagant staging of the Victorians, it is now realised that the locations are in the language and do not need to be represented by scenery. Of all the productions that we mounted over the years, *Antony*

CHAPTER EIGHTEEN

and Cleopatra gave us the most pleasure in its preparation and excitement in performance.

Our printer also accepted the challenge of creating a sense of the ancient Egyptian locations of the play and an addition to its arcane meanings, in the shape of the play's programme, which we discovered could be presented as a pyramid, a 42cm square of glossy paper being divided from its corners and folded from its centre, providing four sides on the outside of the pyramid for basic information on the play and on the inside three corresponding meanings to the story on the fourth side. The information was presented in ascending order up the sides of the pyramid from the bottom as if it were being climbed. I provided this accompanying narrative as an instruction to reading the programme:

> People in the ancient world built pyramids as metaphors of the ascent of man towards God. In climbing them or in performing rituals which ascended them, they put into physical motion this spiritual ascent. As Shakespeare's plays (like the works of his contemporary artists and writers) embody secret meanings which are also metaphors of spiritual ascent, we present the ones in *Antony and Cleopatra* which have formed the basis of our production as a pyramid for you to climb in your reading of it. The way to move around any ancient building to read its stories is to the left. We ask you to do the same with this programme as the secret meanings are all linked to each other.

The mysterious crux of the play occurs in IV. xiv in Antony's words to Eros when, having lost a sea battle to Caesar due to Cleopatra's betrayal, his forces have deserted him and joined with Caesar's. He has not been able to forgive Cleopatra and has driven her away. He asks Eros if he can see him, commenting that a cloud can deceptively take the shape of a living creature, or a material object.

> Antony: My good knave Eros, now thy captain is
> Even such a body. Here I am Antony,
> Yet cannot hold this visible shape, my knave. (IV. xiv. 12-14)

Antony wonders if he has become invisible as he feels that his body has become as indistinct as a shape-changing cloud. This moment has a specific meaning in terms of the alchemy of the play. A 'serpent' is one of the metaphors for the 'body' of 'base matter'. If Cleopatra, as the reference to her as a 'serpent of old Nile' (I. v. 26), suggests, is the body of the alchemical process, her male partner, Antony, must be the spirit of the process. Throughout the play he has been too substantial in worldly terms to qualify for this function, but now, Shakespeare makes clear that he has become, literally as Antony himself experiences it, the alchemical spirit.

I found that the story divided into ten sections with three arcane meanings: **Alchemy**, **Divine Love**, and **Plato's *Phaedrus*** (see above p. 38). I give a brief description of these arcana below to emphasise the particular use Shakespeare makes of them in this play.

The Story[1]
The main source of the historical details of Shakespeare's play *Antony and Cleopatra* is an English translation by Sir Thomas North in 1579 of *Parallel Lives of the Greeks and Romans* volume 2 by Plutarch, written in 75 A.D.[2] In his alteration of the historical facts of the story to fit his play, Shakespeare, as so often, distorts fact to achieve certain effects which can be felt in the arcane dimensions of the drama. Examples of this are:

- The scene IV. xiv.
- The decision to make Antony's wife Octavia childless so that she seems more restrained and identifiable with the 'white horse' of Plato's metaphor of the charioteer, although Plutarch records that Olivia had children by Mark Antony as well as by her first husband.
- The creation of the role of Enobarbus, who comments on the action.

An example of Enobarbus's perception of Antony's dilemma in his incline to the 'white horse' of Rome and his new wife, Octavia, being pulled away by the 'black horse' of Egypt and Cleopatra, is his response to the comment by Maecenas in II. ii. 243 that Antony, being newly married to Octavia, must leave Cleopatra. Enobarbus replies:

> Never! He will not.
> Age cannot wither her, nor custom stale
> Her infinite variety. Other women cloy
> The appetites they feed, but she makes hungry
> Where most she satisfies: for vilest things
> Become themselves in her, that the holy priests
> Bless her when she is riggish. (II. ii. 243-250)

Alchemy (showing the features of Shakespeare's varied application of the philosophy in this play)

Alchemy is a holistic philosophy/science originating in ancient Egypt (see above p. 26), and the Egyptian goddess, Isis, was its goddess. The philosophy holds that general good will come into the world if 'base matter' is elevated, improved and transmuted to a higher substance or state. Shakespeare and other playwrights practised alchemy metaphorically in their plays, as is done in *Antony and Cleopatra*. The alchemical process was thought to be a circular one and was presented as an 'ouroboros', or a snake biting its own tail, an image created in this play when Cleopatra, described by Antony as his 'Serpent of old Nile' (I. v. 26), kills herself with the bites of asps (a species of snake), which she applies to her breast and arm.

Correspondences between Plato's metaphor of the charioteer in *Phaedrus* and the story of the play[3]

In *Phaedrus*, Plato presents a metaphor of the life of a lover as a winged chariot harnessed to two horses, one black, one white. The charioteer will incline his rein to one of these horses, thus altering the course of his love and the passage of his soul according to the nature of the horses. The black horse is passionate and rebellious, and represents fleshly appetites, while the white is obedient and controlled, representing restraint. Plutarch himself commented that the course of Antony's life mirrored Plato's metaphor:

And in the end, the horse of the mind, as Plato termeth it, that is so hard of rein (I mean the unrefined lust of concupiscence) did put out of Antonius head all honest and commendable thoughts: for he sent Fonteius Capito to bring Cleopatra into Syria.
(Plutarch, *Parallel Lives of the Greeks and Romans* trans. by Thomas North, vol.II)

Divine Love from Plato's *Symposium* (showing the features of Shakespeare's varied application of the philosophy in this play)
Another work of Plato that influenced Shakespeare's writing was his *Symposium*. This work concerns the nature of true love and supports the myth that people's souls have had previous existences, during which 'companion souls' are formed. In this life, he suggests that everyone seeks the happiness of being re-united with their companion soul. If companion souls meet, recognise each other and love each other with a 'Divine Love', this will be so ecstatic that they will have a glimpse and understanding of the love of God, an experience which will raise their consciousness, a process called the 'Divine Ascent'.

Story Section 1 (I. i., ii., iii., iv., v., II. i.)
Mark Antony, who shares rule of the Roman world with Lepidus and Octavius Caesar, his fellow triumvirs, is neglecting his Roman duties in his obsessive love affair with Cleopatra, Queen of Egypt. However, news of the death of Fulvia, his wife in Rome, and of a successful revolt against Rome at sea by Sextus Pompeius (Pompey) and Menas, a pirate, persuade him, in spite of Cleopatra's protests, to leave her luxurious court and return to Rome. In his absence Cleopatra longs for him, but Caesar, hitherto sickened by Antony's self-indulgent revelling in Egypt, welcomes the news of his impending return. Pompey is surprised and flattered that his revolt can draw Antony away from Cleopatra.

Alchemy
The play opens with a world divided by a conflict of values polarised into the Roman insistence on military might and self-discipline contrasted

with the Egyptian riotous enjoyment of life and love. This conflict, which must be resolved in order for peace to be established is the base matter of the process. Cleopatra's reference to Antony's calling her 'my serpent of old Nile' (I. v. 26) establishes her identity as the representative of the base matter, the body which must be purged. However, in the theatrical metaphor of alchemy that Shakespeare presents in his plays, if the body is a woman, her male partner is the spirit which must be separated from the body for the alchemy to be achieved. At the start of the play, Cleopatra's partner, Antony, (already combined with her as the principle male/female components of the alchemy in the stage of **Calcination**) is possessor of a third of the Roman world, of a magnificent army, of much treasure and of the most beautiful woman in the world, and is thus hardly qualified to be regarded as the spirit of the process. His separation from the body, as in the alchemical stage of **Seperation** (Ripley's spelling) and from his own worldliness as in **Dissolution**, is begun with his departure for Rome.

Plato's *Phaedrus*

At the outset of the play, Cleopatra and her court are identified as the 'black horse' of the metaphor by the Roman soldier calling her a gypsy, implying her dark-coloured skin. He condemns Antony for abandoning his former restraint and descending into a life of gratification for this 'gipsy's lust' (I. i. 10). Antony is well aware of the Roman disdain of his 'black horse' way of life in Egypt, and as a Roman himself, regrets that he might lose himself 'in dotage' (I. ii. 123). When he returns to Rome, he exemplifies 'white horse' behaviour. In Egypt, Cleopatra identifies herself more completely with the black horse, commenting on her sun-tanned appearance, 'That am with Phoebus' amorous pinches black' (I. v. 29).

Plato's Divine Love

Here, Shakespeare's treatment of this theme is reversed from ascent to descent. There is no conventional Divine Ascent of the protagonists throughout the play as at the commencement of the drama, Antony and Cleopatra are already experiencing such a Divine Love that their expression of it is cosmic, as if through this love they can see Paradise. Whenever they speak of their love for each other, even after they have been bickering, it is always in terms of cosmic imagery and language. In I. i. 17, Antony describes his boundless love as 'heaven' and 'earth' and, in embracing

Cleopatra in I. i. 35-36, 'Here is my space | Kingdoms are clay'. Cleopatra refers to their past love, 'Eternity was in our lips and eyes' (I. i. 36), and names him in his absence as 'the demi-Atlas of this earth' (I. v. 24). In triumph after battle, Antony calls her, 'O thou day o' th' world' (IV. viii. 13). At Antony's death, Cleopatra titles him, 'the crown o' th' earth' (IV. xv. 65), and cries, 'His face was as the heavens, and therein stuck | A sun and moon which kept their course and lighted | The little O, the earth' (V. ii. 77-79).

Story Section 2 (II. ii., iii., iv.,v.)

In Rome, Lepidus, mediating between Antony and Caesar, is relieved by their reconciliation and promotes the suggestion put forward by Agrippa that Antony, widowed while in Egypt, should marry Caesar's sister, Octavia. Enobarbus, Antony's friend, comments that it is unlikely, in spite of Antony's pledges to the contrary, that he will not return to Cleopatra. A soothsayer warns Antony that Caesar's fortune will always subvert Antony's and that he should keep away from him. Antony agrees, observing that his skills are always overpowered by Caesar's luck, and he resolves to return to Egypt and Cleopatra, in spite of his vows of loyalty to Octavia, 'And though I make this marriage for my peace | I'th'East my pleasure lies' (II. iv. 38-39).

The Romans prepare to do battle with Pompey. In Egypt, Cleopatra, although enraged at hearing of Antony's marriage, is confident that he will return to her.

Alchemy

The mis-conceived marriage between Antony and Octavia functions at this stage of the alchemical process as **Coniunctio**, an 'alchemical marriage' which will lead the process into the depths of the stage of **Putrefaction**, where the body will be tried by fire and water. The anguish of Cleopatra first represents this, to be closely followed by the chaos and civil wars that will divide the Roman world.

Plato's *Phaedrus*

Determined to maintain his 'white horse' persona, Antony keeps a strict profile in Rome. Octavia represents this white horse, and in agreeing to marry her, he reinforces his intention. Enobarbus understands how deeply rooted the 'black horse' is in Antony's nature, that his marriage to Octavia is a sham, and that he must return to his way of life in Egypt.

Plato's Divine Love
It is a rule that the Divine lovers should be constant to each other, and Antony, in his alliance with Octavia, is not true to Cleopatra. He will be punished for this. This principle is the opposite of the black horse/white horse ethic, in which he should favour not the black horse of Cleopatra but the white horse of Octavia, and represents the dichotomy in Antony's life which will strip him of everything, including his worldliness, and make him suitable to be the spirit of the alchemy.

Story Section 3 (II. vi., vii.)
Caesar, Antony and Lepidus avert further war with Pompey by negotiating a settlement. In celebration of their reconciliation, Pompey invites them to a banquet on board his ship. Enobarbus tells Menas that, far from uniting Antony and Caesar, Antony's marriage to Octavia will separate them. During the riotous and drunken evening, Menas suggests that if Pompey were to instruct him to kill the triumvirate he could gain control of the world. Pompey declines the offer.

Alchemy
Pompey's refusal to kill the triumvirs prevents the abortion of the alchemic process. Lepidus shows an interest in the alchemy for which Egypt was famed in his statement, 'Your serpent of Egypt is bred now of your mud by the operation of your sun' (II. vii. 26-27). The 'serpent' represents alchemy itself, the 'mud' is base matter, and the 'operation' is the practice of alchemy, which was supposed to take place under the cosmic effect of the sun. Shakespeare's use of this imagery demonstrates his alchemical knowledge and its application in this play.

Plato's *Phaedrus*
At the feast which he is giving, Pompey encourages his Roman guests to indulge in riotous black horse behaviour, and had he not had scruples in refusing the offer of Menas to kill them, they could have lost their lives to the lack of caution in their revelry. Caesar, the ultimate example of restrained white horse behaviour, finds the rioting unpalatable.

Plato's Divine Love
Antony, in cementing his Roman loyalties, further distances himself from his companion soul.

Due to the lack of the additional cast and costumes which performance of the scene would require, Theatre Set-Up omitted III.i.

Story Section 4 (III. ii., iii., iv., v., vi.)
Antony and Octavia are married. In Egypt, Cleopatra demands a false description of her rival. The concord between Caesar and Antony does not last for long and Octavia laments her conflict between loyalty to Antony, her husband, and Caesar, her brother, and she suggests that she should try to mediate between them. Antony, angered with Caesar for joining with Lepidus in murdering Pompey in a treaty-breaking conflict and then dismissing Lepidus from the triumvirate, returns to Cleopatra. Caesar is incensed at the excesses of Antony's defiance of him in Egypt, where he has publicly given Roman territories to Cleopatra and their illegitimate children, and he declares war on him. His anger is compounded when Octavia, unaware of Antony's betrayal of her, comes unheralded to Caesar to plead his reconciliation with her husband.

Alchemy
The alchemic effect of the **Coniunctio** takes place and **Putrefaction** sets in, manifested as Caesar's anger at Antony and making war against him, thus setting up the process which will turn Antony into the spirit of the alchemic process and purge Cleopatra as body. Caesar reports that Cleopatra often appeared in the guise of alchemy's goddess, Isis.[4]

Plato's *Phaedrus*
In returning to Egypt, Antony yields to the 'black horse' which drives him to such unreasonable excesses of behaviour that the 'white horse' of Caesar makes war on him. In Plato's metaphor, when this happens, both horses fall upon their haunches from the violent tugging of the charioteer.[5]

Plato's Divine Love
Antony has betrayed Cleopatra in his marriage with Octavia. He also betrays Octavia in returning to Cleopatra, although his relationship with

Octavia is a false love. Divine Love was often tested, and Cleopatra's love of Antony survives his betrayal of her in his marriage with Octavia.

Story Section 5 (III. vii., viii., ix., x., xi.)
Caesar and Antony prepare to do battle at Actium. Against all advice, Antony, in order to please Cleopatra, engages Caesar not on land, where his army has superior strength, but at sea. Antony is shamefully defeated when he deserts the battle to follow Cleopatra, who has fled. This disgrace causes many of his followers to desert him for Caesar. Antony, ashamed of his behaviour and noble in defeat, does not blame them and gives permission for other soldiers to leave him, giving them rewards for past services. He is reconciled with Cleopatra.

Alchemy
The operation of the elements of air, fire, earth and water were part of the process of alchemy. Cleopatra is here associated with water, an element that Antony should avoid as his previous strength was by land (earth). However, his shift to her element, unsuccessful for him in the worldly sense, promotes the shift of elements in the alchemical process and hastens his transformation into 'spirit', devoid of his worldly status and possessions, corresponding to Cleopatra's function as the 'body' of the alchemical process.

Plato's *Phaedrus*
In fleeing from the battle of Actium, Cleopatra exemplifies the nature of the 'black horse'. Antony is punished, in his loss of the battle, for allowing her to control his behaviour.

Plato's Divine Love
Cleopatra, in fleeing the battle of Actium, is not constant to Antony for the first time in the play. However, in following her rather than remaining to fight the battle, Antony is constant to her. He also proves his love in forgiving her.

Story Section 6 (III. xii., xiii.,)
Antony, conceding defeat and requesting that he be allowed to live in Egypt or Athens and that Cleopatra's heirs retain the crown of Egypt, sends his schoolmaster to Caesar as an ambassador. Caesar will submit

to the request concerning Cleopatra's heirs only if she will exile or kill Antony. He sends Thidias as ambassador to Cleopatra to persuade her to do this. Antony, after his failed attempt to gain mercy from Caesar, foolishly proposes single combat with him. The loyalty of Antony's close friend Enobarbus begins to waiver.

When Antony sees Caesar's ambassador, Thidias, kiss Cleopatra's hand in greeting, he rages and has him whipped. Cleopatra achieves Antony's pardon for flirting with Thidias, but Enobarbus finally decides to leave Antony.

Alchemy
Caesar, a metaphorical agent of the alchemy, in trying to effect the final parting of Cleopatra from Antony, promotes their essential separated alchemical functions. In dividing Antony from his worldly status and possessions, he furthers his identity as the 'spirit' of the process.

Plato's *Phaedrus*
Antony's punishment for allowing the 'black horse' nature of Cleopatra to shamefully draw him from the battle of Actium is increased when he sees her disloyalty to him in her flirtation with Caesar's ambassador.

Plato's Divine Love
Cleopatra's love of Antony is tested by Caesar, who claims that he will grant her heirs succession to Egypt's throne if she will kill or exile Antony. She is true to Antony, but fails him in her seduction of Thidias. Only further vows of her undying devotion to him reconcile them.

Story Section 7 (IV. i., ii., iii., iv., v., vi.,vii., viii., ix.)
Refusing the absurd suggestion that he should fight Antony in single combat, Caesar declares war on Antony again. Antony's followers hear strange music under the earth, signifying that the god Hercules is leaving Antony. Enobarbus also leaves Antony, who, forgiving him, sends his possessions to him in Caesar's camp. Antony fights this battle on land and wins it. Cleopatra and Antony celebrate their victory with a feast, and Antony commands Cleopatra to allow his trusted soldier Scarus to kiss her hand. Enobarbus, tortured by Antony's generosity in the face of his own disloyalty to him, kills himself.

CHAPTER EIGHTEEN

Alchemy

The combined military success of Antony and Cleopatra represents the alchemical stage of **Congelation**, the elemental shift to earth of Antony's land assault being alchemically appropriate at this stage. Their celebratory feast after their victory is the alchemical stage of **Cibation** (in which the base matter is fed). The desertion of both the god Hercules and Enobarbus further strip Antony of substance.

Plato's *Phaedrus*

Antony demonstrates 'white horse' behaviour, fighting on land in the way advised by his 'white horse' Roman soldier companions, and is rewarded for it by success in battle.

Plato's Divine Love

In demonstration of his trust in her constancy, this time, Antony asks Cleopatra to allow her hand to be kissed without jealousy.

Story Section 8 (IV. x., xi., xii., xiii., xiv. 1-105)

Caesar challenges Antony and Cleopatra once more by sea, but again she deserts Antony, whose forces go over to Caesar. This time Antony will not be reconciled with Cleopatra, but he declares that he will kill her. Her attendant, Charmian, suggests that she should send word to Antony that she has killed herself, in order to soften his heart towards her.

Alone with the soldier, Eros, Antony declares that he feels as if he exists only as a vapour. Cleopatra's messenger tells him that she has died. He demands that Eros should kill him to avoid dishonour, but Eros refuses, killing himself instead to avoid this. Now entirely alone, Antony falls upon his sword, mortally wounding himself.

Alchemy

In the violent stage of **Sublimation**, the sea battle achieves the alchemically necessary separation of Cleopatra as body and Antony as spirit, which he himself declares that he has become. Stripped of his part of the Roman world, of his army, his possessions, of his god, Hercules, and of Cleopatra, he now feels so insubstantial that he only wishes to dissolve what is left of his life. Believing Cleopatra to be dead and losing his sole remaining military companion, Eros, he destroys his body and becomes the spirit of the alchemical process.

Plato's *Phaedrus*
Cleopatra, deserting Antony again in battle, is true to her 'black horse' nature. Antony punishes Cleopatra in the way that Plato's charioteer subjugates his horse, reducing her 'to torment'.[6] However, in Shakespeare's treatment of the play and particularly in this section of it, it can be seen that some good can come from Antony's anger and rejection of her, as had he not done so, he would not have been stripped of his worldliness and become the spirit that was needed for the alchemy to be achieved.

Plato's Divine Love
In her desertion of Antony, Cleopatra is once again not constant to him and to their love. This time he cannot forgive her. When she further betrays him with the false news of her death, he takes his own life, demonstrating the extent of his Divine Love for her.

Story Section 9 (IV. xiv. 105-142, xv., V. i., ii. 1-331)

Too late to anticipate Antony's attempt to kill himself, Cleopatra sends word to him that she is alive and that she and her women are safely locked in her monument. Antony asks his soldiers to take him to her, and he is born aloft to her, where he dies in her arms. Cleopatra resolves to take her own life.

Caesar mourns the death of Antony and captures Cleopatra in her monument. Warned by Dolabella that she will be paraded in triumph through the streets of Rome, she and her women escape from this fate by poisoning themselves with bites of asps brought to them in a basket of figs.

Alchemy
The alchemical spirit was said to 'ascend' in the alembic vessel, a process here represented by the elevation of Antony to the monument (see fig. 20). When Antony and Cleopatra, as spirit and body, are together again, they are both transmuted; she is purged by suffering the consequences of her own actions and the trials of fate, he is transformed into a materially humbled person who is generous at every malign twist of fate, and alchemically,

the spirit which will effect the alchemy of the play represented by peace between Egypt and Rome. Thus, purified, together they achieve the stage of **Firmentation**. She indicates her transmuted state by identifying herself with the elevated elements of fire and air, 'My other elements| I give to baser life' (V. ii. 288-289). The other elements from which she has become elevated are earth and water.

This death in love scene represents the cycle of death and rebirth of alchemy as in nature. As body and spirit they are united beyond death when she poisons herself to join him in the 'gold' of the **Exaltation** which she expresses in her final speech, 'As sweet as balm, as soft as air, as gentle - | O Antony!'

In using an asp (the poison of which was mythically supposed to bestow immortality and which was associated with the goddess Isis whom Cleopatra imitated) to kill herself (as 'serpent of old Nile'), she achieves the circular alchemical 'ouroboros', imaged as a snake eating its own tail.

Plato's *Phaedrus*

In Plato's metaphor, the influence of the 'white horse' prevails in the deaths of Antony and Cleopatra as both become ennobled by the Roman custom of self-inflicted death in order to avoid dishonour.

Plato's Divine Love

The lovers are united in death. Previously disdainful of the conventional morality of marriage, Cleopatra now calls Antony 'husband' (V. ii. 286) as she waits to join him in the paradise for which their love has qualified them.

Story Section 10 (V. ii. 332-365)

Caesar mourns the death of Cleopatra, and decrees that she shall be buried beside Antony and that their funeral shall be marked with 'great Solemnity' (V. ii. 365) by the Roman army before their return to Rome.

Alchemy

In the alchemic stages of **Multiplication** and **Projection**, Caesar, in being generous in praising the couple who had been his enemies, 'No grave upon the earth shall clip in it| A pair so famous' (V. ii. 358-359) and granting them honourable burial, declares a generous resolution to the conflict disrupting the Roman world. This projects the benefits of

Antony and Cleopatra's alchemic transformation to the rest of the world, now benefiting from peace.

Plato's *Phaedrus*
The 'white horse' dominance is symbolised by Caesar, whose Roman rule now prevails. He exemplifies this in his generosity to the lovers, hitherto his enemies, in his arrangements for their being buried together and given respect by his army.

Plato's Divine Love
Caesar does not condemn the lovers, and Shakespeare's implication is that their love transcended all worldly considerations. Praising this unmarried love, the morality of the story is unusual for Shakespeare, constrained, however, by the facts of history.

Cabala: Post production (see fig. 3)
If the conflict between Rome and Egypt can be regarded as the subject of the Cabala in the play, with Antony the protagonist of that conflict, Rome and Octavius Caesar have a correspondence with the left hand **Pillar of Severity**, typifying the logical element of the Tree of Life, and Egypt and Cleopatra correspond with the right hand **Pillar of Mercy** typifying the element of emotion. The aim would be to achieve a balance between these polarities on the mid **Pillar of Equilibrium** and thus bring about peace with the resolution of the conflict. However, as Antony is constantly torn between his conflicting loyalties to Rome and subsequently to his wife, Octavia, there, and his love of Cleopatra in Egypt, it is impossible for him to achieve the **Pillar of Equilibrium** on behalf of the conflict.

Thus the behaviour of both Antony and Cleopatra must be changed in order to shift their stance from the emotional **Pillar of Mercy**, and Octavius Caesar must moderate his stance representing Rome on the **Pillar of Severity**. In the final scenes of the play, these transformations are achieved. Both Antony and Cleopatra adopt the severe Roman custom of committing suicide rather than accepting dishonour. Octavius Caesar moderates his severity against them in the merciful decision to allow them to be buried together and be honoured by his army. Thus the conflict is resolved and peace achieved. I think that Shakespeare also grants Antony and Cleopatra a kind of apotheosis in the nobility of their deaths which, like the deaths of Romeo and Juliet, benefit others, and may thus grant them the bliss of **Kether**. In the Introduction to the 1995 Arden Edition of *Antony and Cleopatra*, John Wilders comments that Shakespeare gives Antony and Cleopatra a 'sense of transcendence' not found in Plutarch's text.

THE CABALA

It is possible to find the Cabala in all of the plays featured in this book except *Cymbeline*, but I find that an identification of it in *The Merchant of Venice* is essential in understanding the play's ethics.

CHAPTER NINETEEN: *THE MERCHANT OF VENICE*

Hebrew scholars have indicated meanings which have particular reference to Hebrew culture, the Cabala and the Hebraic linguistic significance of aspects of the *The Merchant of Venice*. Most importantly in 'A Hebrew Source for *The Merchant of Venice*', S. J. Schonfeld agrees with other scholars that there was a Hebrew source for the play in a story which predates and could have influenced the sources we know to have been available to Shakespeare.[1] He points out the correlation between the intrinsic meanings of the play and the Hebraic interpretation of the names of the characters, and gives us a new understanding of Shylock's bond. He tells us that in the original Hebrew story it was likely that Shylock was the Devil himself (as he is often called in the play), and that in this Hebrew text he carries out a devilish trick on the person corresponding to Antonio in writing out the bond in Hebraic script, thus making use of a double meaning in the Hebraic word for 'bond', which gives him the right to take flesh nearest Antonio's heart. In Shakespeare's play, this part of the body to be cut for flesh is included in the wording of Shylock's bond, and Portia acknowledges Shylock's right to take the flesh from there, but points out that Shylock's bond fails him in its lack of foresight in specifying an exact quantity of flesh to be taken (an impossible task to perform) and excludes the spilling of any blood. If the bond were written in Hebrew, Shylock has overlooked the pun on the word 'money', a word which had an alternative ancient meaning of 'blood'. He stipulates that he requires no forfeit of 'money', 'and take no doit/ Of usance for my moneys' (I. iii. 136-137), and thus, according to the possible Hebrew pun, no blood.

CHAPTER NINETEEN

For an actress taking the role of Portia, it is helpful for her to know what information was given to her by Bellario in her consultation with him before she becomes the advocate in the trial scene. It is possible to suggest to the actress that the above information concerning the nature of the bond, especially if it can be considered to have been written in Hebrew with its implications of the puns on the words bond and money, is what Bellario imparted to Portia. This would make sense for the actress of the procedures which Portia initiates in the courtroom, leading Shylock up to the moment when he is preparing to kill Antonio (IV. i. 300) so that the intention of his guilt is demonstrated. However, she knows that he cannot proceed legally according to the terms of his bond. Portia's intervention, 'Tarry a little, there is something else | This bond doth give thee here no jot of blood' (IV. i. 301-302) becomes premeditated, not only in the obvious meaning of the bond but in its Hebrew association, which Bellario has understood. Shylock's reaction would then also be interesting as he would blame himself for missing the pun on the word money. Of course, if the Hebrew context of the bond is ignored, Bellario could have advised Portia how to proceed in allowing Shylock to incriminate himself and then to prevent the killing by pointing out an omission in the bond regarding the shedding of blood. However, an interpretation of the bond being written in Hebrew makes the actions of Portia and the reaction of Shylock to his oversight of the pun on money much more exciting for the actors taking those roles.

This play also benefits considerably in its interpretation by an understanding of its arcana, the main one, given its focus on Jewishness, logically being the Cabala. The key speech in the play is that given in IV. i. 180-201 on the nature of Mercy by Portia, disguised as a man, to Shylock, a man professing the Hebrew religion. A key to aspects of the Hebrew faith is the Cabala Tree of Life, representing the paths, all stemming originally from Godhead, which a devotee might take in a quest to find God through personal improvement. The trunk of the tree holds stabilising core elements and the connecting branches ending in significant fruits or spheres (see above pp. 41-48 and fig. 3).

There are different modern interpretations of gender input into the Tree. Parfitt in The *Elements of The Qabalah* holds the view that the right and left hand pillars have no specific gender reference, while Knight in *A Practical Guide to Qabalistic Symbolism* identifies the left hand pillar as female and the right hand pillar as male. The diagram of the Tree of life from the Syriac New Testament, Vienna, 1555 (see fig. 24) shows the sphere of Binah at the top of the left hand pillar figuring a female symbol of an all-seeing eye, keeping watch of the Great Mother over creation, while the sphere Chokmah at the top of the right hand pillar presents male symbols of the Horn of Plenty and the Horn of the Divine Herald.

I believe that Shakespeare, doubtless familiar with this diagram in the Syriac New Testament, was referring to the form of the Tree in which the right hand side of the Tree is masculine, called the Pillar of Mercy, with a positive flow of masculine energy in a positive active role, and the left hand side is called the Pillar of Severity, with a negative energy flow and feminine, passive role. On the right hand, masculine side, the sphere specifically representing Mercy is Chesed, which a man such as Shylock would observe if he were loyal to his faith, but his unbalanced behaviour and mental stance locates him practising exclusively the characteristics of the opposite feminine sphere of Geburah, which represents Strength and Fear. Portia disguises herself as a man and advocates the maxim of the sphere of Chesed herself, instructing Shylock that a masculine representation of Mercy is appropriate to him as a practising Jew, but he ignores her and is consequently stripped by the Venetian Court of his religion, which he has dishonoured. The Court itself practises mercy in allowing him his life, which, according to the law of Venice, his crimes warrant he should forfeit.

Frances Yates in part two (on John Dee and Shakespeare) of *Occult Philosophy in the Elizabethan Age* agrees with the inferences relating the trial scene to the Hebraic Tree of Life, which she considers exemplifies the sephiroth, specifically as explained by Giorgio.[2] In *The Kabbala of Shakespeare* Paul T. Olson also interprets the trial scene in terms of the Hebraic Tree of Life. He considers that Portia, embodying love (which is Chesed) must herself take the role of severity (Geburah) to teach Shylock that Mercy should modify justice.[3] Olsen conceives yet another interpretation of the trial scene in terms of the relation of the protagonists in the scene to the spheres on the tree in *The Provocative Merchant of Venice*.[4]

However, although he envisions as I do that Shylock is overbalanced on the sphere of Geburah, he posits that Antonio is located on Chesed in its meaning of love and Portia resides on the mediating central pillar as Tiphareth (heart), to which he also gives the attributes of beauty and mercy.

Shylock is a prodigious role that many actors aspire to play, the ranging depths of Shakespeare's character far exceeding the Devil in the Hebraic source play. Harris (see above p. 47) not only agrees to his dominance of the severity sphere of Geburah but exalts in the Jewish grandeur of his portrayal, giving him a proud Jewish title, 'Kadmonik Shylock who resonates with a powerful life-creating force' (p.10).[5] He regards the portrayal of Shylock as not only that of a strong person but the ancestor of others among Shakespeare's great dramatis personae:

> Shylock is a dignified, albeit rapturous human being and the most powerful voice that Shakespeare produced in *The Merchant of Venice* a music-of-the-spheres poetry that would be rivalled only by Hamlet and Sir John Falstaff (pp. 9-10).

The fact that Shakespeare is a playwright creating roles and stories for theatrical effect is often overlooked in the criticism of the ethical judgement of his characters. I believe that Shylock is one of these, on stage an electrifying presence, his behaviour in the trial scene chilling and theatrically potent, a character in the theatre world that actors aspire to perform and who thrills audiences, not the butt of antisemitic acrimony.

Another aspect of the play that is often overlooked in the assessment of its racial stance is the character of Tubal, who as a Jewish business person of Venice might also have attracted the kind of racial abuse suffered by Shylock. This is indicated in III. i. 70-71 by Solanio at Tubal's entry, 'Here comes another of the tribe - a third cannot be match'd, unless the devil himself turn Jew'. However, Tubal has become wealthy enough to lend Shylock three thousand ducats and seems to have been capable of rising above response to racial abuse, although he obviously resents it as he shares Shylock's pleasure at Antonio's misfortune. He mollifies Shylock's distress at the news concerning his daughter's miscreant behaviour with information of Antonio's losses at sea, 'But Antonio is certainly undone'

(III. i. 114), and seems willing to act as agent for Shylock in the subsequent court action. If Shakespeare had a message to give through the character of Tubal, it might be that abuse should be ignored while personal gain is possible. Perhaps Tubal has practised what Shylock claims to have done in response to Antonio's previous racial abuse of him:

> Still I have borne it with a patient shrug,
> (For suff'rance is the badge of all our tribe) (I. iii. 104-105).

Shylock gains no benefit from not behaving according to this principle he cites, but, by responding to abuse with the vitriol of revenge, loses all.

A warning can also be detected to those delivering abuse. Antonio has subjected Shylock to unacceptable racial abuse:

> Shylock: Signior Antonio, many a time and oft
> In the Rialto you have rated me
> About my moneys and my usances:
> Still I have borne it with a patient shrug,
> (For suff'rance is the badge of all our tribe)
> You call me misbeliever, cut-throat dog,
> And spet upon my Jewish gabardine,
> And all for use of that which is mine own. (I. iii. 101-108)

Antonio does not deny this and reaffirms that, although requesting a loan from Shylock, he will do so again:

> Antonio: I am as like to call thee so again
> To spet on thee again, to spurn thee too. (I. iii. 125-126)

Underestimating the latter's bitter resentment and increasing it by insulting the principle of usury, he then unwisely puts himself into danger with Shylock in suggesting that the loan be made in the spirit of enmity:

CHAPTER NINETEEN

> If thou wilt lend this money, lend it not
> As to thy friends, for when did friendship take
> A breed for barren metal of his friend?
> But lend it rather to thine enemy,
> Who if he break, thou may'st with better face
> Exact the penalty. (I. iii. 127-132)

Shakespeare gives Antonio a severe punishment for his racism and his folly in underestimating its effect in the penalty Shylock suggests in his response:

> If you repay me not on such a day
> In such a place, such sum or sums as are
> Express'd in the condition, let the forfeit
> Be nominated for an equal pound
> Of your fair flesh, to be cut off and taken
> In what part of your body pleaseth me. (I. iii. 142-147)

Antonio's false confidence in the safety of his investments and misunderstanding of Shylock's purpose, coupled with his crime of racial abuse, results in the ultimate reality of a grim death at Shylock's hands. As this play is a comedy, Portia, advised by Bellario, rescues Antonio from death, but the torture of its expectation, up to the moment of the knife's near incision in the flesh nearest his heart, is tangible. Bassanio senses the danger in the bond that Shylock suggests:

> You shall not seal to such a bond for me,
> I'll rather dwell in my necessity. (I. iii. 150-151)

However, his greed in wanting to appear rich before Portia and thus qualify as a suitor to her in marriage prevails in allowing Antonio to risk his life. He is punished for this selfishness in the guilt of being responsible for what seems inevitable, as the torture and death of Antonio when the terms of Shylock's bond become due. Bassanio and Gratiano are also punished for their racism and even racist comments in court not only in the anticipated 'death experience' of their friend but also in the revenge (although that is a fairly good-natured jest) which their wives take upon them for their denial of them in court. The play gives us an even stronger message in implying that constant abuse of a person, such as is heaped upon Shylock, may create the vengeful person he becomes.

Portia herself makes a racist comment against the Prince of Morocco. When he fails in the selection of the correct casket that will guarantee her as a wife, she rejoices:

> A gentle riddance, - draw the curtains, go,-
> Let all of his complexion choose me so. (II. vii. 78-79)

For this, she is punished by the delay of her wedding night due to her husband's need to leave immediately after the wedding in order to attend to the imprisoned Antonio. She is also punished in the pain of hearing herself denied by her husband in court:

> Bassanio: Antonio, I am married to a wife
> Which is as dear to me as life itself,
> But life itself, my wife, and all the world,
> Are not with me esteem'd above thy life.
> I would lose all, ay sacrifice them all
> Here to this devil, to deliver you.
> Portia: Your wife would give you little thanks for that
> If she were by to hear you make this offer (IV. i. 278-285).

Shakespeare has, I consider, been falsely accused of personal racism in this play, but I believe that an examination of its internal evidence shows that he demonstrates the evils of and dangers of racism and racial abuse, especially as practised upon a victim as 'red-raw' traumatised as Shylock.

Theatre Set-Up's production of the play

In preparing the play with the actors and giving the gist of that preparation to the play's audiences in its programme notes, I personalised the arcana for each actor who was taking on interconnected multiple roles within the play that they were performing. There were benefits in this system, as the meanings in their roles were specifically focused for each actor. When we first produced the play in 1992, the parts of Portia and Jessica were performed by the same actress, giving us in Jessica an obvious alter ego to Portia, but our 2010 production spared the actress playing Portia that burden, and the role of Jessica was doubled with the part of Solanio and with the minor role of Portia's servant. I record the latter version as it includes the part of Solanio (omitted in 1992) as well as Salerio, both important in the play. The arcana were **Alchemy**, **Renaissance Platonism**, **Theurgy and initiation**, **The Cabala**, and **The Bible**.

These arcana relevant to the different sections of the story were set out according to the functions of the name 'Venice' within the play as performed by each of the seven actors. Venice was interpreted as the subject of the play, allegorically representing the self, a part of Divinity, 'Ain Soph' and 'Ultimate Truth'.

As the chapters on Shakespeare's plays performed by Theatre Set-Up take the form of the plays' programme notes as requested by members of the audience who demanded that this book be written, the nature of *The Merchant of Venice* programme is reproduced here. The research on the play's arcana (and a study of the source material, accessible in the appendices of the Arden edition) uncovered the unique importance to the themes of the play of the city-state of Venice itself, so the parts of each actor were classified according to their significance to Venice and the resolution through the arcana of its problems. During Shakespeare's time, Jews lived and traded freely in Venice, but Shakespeare must have wondered if they suffered the same racial prejudice that he would have observed them experiencing in England. He makes this a central theme in the way he deals with the basic facts of the stories in the source material.

With 'V E N I C E' spread across the top of the chart that comprised the inside fold of the 1992 and 2010 programme notes, and the letters of the city serving as the headings of vertical columns which contained the names of the seven actors, the parts that they were playing, and their functions in the meanings of the play, corresponding with the different parts of the story which went down the chart to the left of the

VENICE columns, this system worked very well. However, to present this in book form is more cumbersome.

For clarity, when discussing the arcana corresponding to the numbered parts of the story, I will need to name the actors in the 2010 season, the different parts they are playing and the functions of those parts in the context of the drama. **Only the actors performing in any scenes of the story are mentioned (their names and their roles underlined). When actors are not named in the categories corresponding to sections of the story, the effects on their functions in the drama of Venice are recorded. The correspondence to the actors' functions as components of Venice with the letters of the name of VENICE are indicated below (as in the chart of the play's programme notes) but subsequently omitted in the numbered sections of the story.**

<u>V</u> <u>Steven Rostance</u>, personified as **the people of Venice:** in the roles of Gratiano, the Doge, Lancelot Gobbo.

<u>E</u> <u>Richard Sanderson</u>, personified as **the young initiate** in the roles of Bassanio, Prince of Morocco, Prince of Arragon.

<u>N</u> <u>Tony Portacio</u>, personified as **the touchstone of chauvinism in Venice** in the roles of Shylock, Lorenzo.

<u>I</u> <u>Suzie Edwards and Jamie Blake</u>, personified as **the 'soul' of the initiates**. Suzie Edwards represents their 'higher selves' and their 'spiritual guide and hierophant' in the role of Portia, and Jamie Blake is personified as the alchemical 'soul' of Shylock and Lorenzo and the alter-ego of Portia in the roles of Jessica, Portia's assistant, and Solanio, a friend of Antonio.

<u>C</u> <u>Terry Ashe</u>, personified as **the provider** in the roles of Antonio, Tubal, Old Gobbo.

<u>E</u> <u>Elizabeth Arends</u>, personified as **the narrative and reflective element** in the roles of Salerio, Nerissa.

In the following account of actual performance details, a sense can be gained of the switching around of scenes to effect costume changes needed for only seven people to perform the play and the skill of the actors in performing contrasting characters, even of opposite genders to their own. Actors not involved in scenes or in their own costume changes are critical in assisting others with theirs.

CHAPTER NINETEEN

Story Section 1 (Act I. i. 1-185)
Bassanio, a young Venetian, needing money to pay court in Belmont to the beautiful and rich heiress Portia, with whom he has fallen in love, requests a loan from his adoring and indulgent relative Antonio, a merchant of Venice. However, as all his funds are entailed in his ships currently at sea, Antonio offers to stand as collateral if Bassanio can arrange a loan from someone. Antonio's friends, Gratiano and Solanio, mock his sober mood while Salerio comments on it.

(Steven as Gratiano) **The People of Venice**
Gratiano's garrulous behaviour and insensitivity to others' pain represents the superficiality and cruelty of Venice which must be purged in order for Venice to be transmuted into a better place.

(Richard as Bassanio) **The young initiate**
Bassanio, undergoes trials on behalf of Venice, in its alchemic process from lead to the attainment of gold. He is the base matter upon which the alchemy of the play is worked. The alter egos of this personification, the Prince of Morocco and the Prince of Arragon are also part of this base matter. The lower self and the body of the alchemic process, Bassanio, attempts to join the soul, of the process, Portia. Bassanio as an initiate prepares for his pilgrimage to attain his soul and the gold of alchemy, but demonstrates his need to be transformed in his false sense of materialistic values which stain his motives in seeking to marry Portia and thereby expose his relative, Antonio, to risk. He also shows a lack of independence and self-reliance, squandering borrowed money and asking for further indulgence.

(Tony as Shylock) **The touchstone of chauvinism in Venice**
The arena is set up within which Shylock will draw forth his own evil and that of Venice. As a touchstone, he reveals the inherent evils of Venice. He is also a shadow initiate, in alchemy transforming figuratively from serpent to phoenix. He boasts of his Jewish heritage, to which he should be true. His alter ego is Lorenzo.

(Suzie as Portia, Jamie as Solanio) **The 'soul' of the initiates**
Portia, representing the 'soul' and 'higher selves' of the initiates, is also their spiritual guide and alchemist.

(Terry as Antonio) **The provider**
Antonio is seen as the patron of Bassanio. His attachment to this relative of his is unhealthy, spoiling his character with over-indulgence. His depression over the news that Bassanio has met his future life's partner indicates the possessive nature of his attachment, although he is prepared to fund Bassanio's courtship.

(Elizabeth as Salerio) **The narrative and reflective element**
Salerio observes Antonio's melancholy and discusses the dangers that his argosies might meet at sea.

Story Section 2 (II. ii. 1-115)
In Belmont, Portia expresses impatience with her situation. She may not choose a husband for herself but must submit to the terms of her father's will, which requires any suitor for her hand in marriage to submit to a lottery consisting of three caskets of gold, silver and lead, in which the selection of the casket with Portia's picture in it grants possession of her as wife. If the suitor fails, he must remain forever unmarried. Portia affirms her resolve to uphold the terms of her father's will, in spite of her dislike of the current suitors. She and Nerissa wish that Bassanio might become one of the suitors.

The people of Venice
Belmont is contrasted with Venice. Portia's wise father has devised a lottery which will select a husband for her who does not have the superficial monetary values of Venice.

The young initiate
The scene of the initiate's first test is set and the terms are laid out. Portia's longing for Bassanio to become a suitor represent the soul's longing to be integrated with the self.

The touchstone of chauvinism in Venice
The opposing force of good which will defeat the evil of Venice and purge it out is introduced in the person of Portia, who will defeat Shylock in court.
(Suzie as Portia, Jamie as Portia's servant) **The 'soul' of the initiates**
In Belmont (meaning 'The Beautiful Mountain'), a sphere of benevolent influences, still governed by the wisdom of Portia's dead father, we meet

in Portia the 'high priestess' of the initiations and the alchemist who is also the 'soul' of Bassanio, longing for union with him. Portia's servant participates in the preparation of the 'trials by casket'.

The provider
The nature of Portia, rival to Antonio for Bassanio's affection and also the possible provider for him in the future, is seen.

(Elizabeth as Nerissa) **The narrative and reflective element**
Nerissa questions Portia on her opinion of all her suitors, narrates the story of the lottery of the caskets and suggests that Portia already loves Bassanio, endorsing him as a suitable husband for her.

Story Section 3 (I. iii. 1-175)
Bassanio secures a loan of 3,000 ducats against Antonio being bound by a contract to the money-lender, the Jew, Shylock. He seems unaware of the strained relations between the Venetian Antonio, who lends money free of interest, and the alien Shylock, who (like modern financiers) sells loans. For a 'merry sport' (I. iii. 141), and against Bassanio's will, Shylock lends the 3,000 ducats without interest but against a collateral of a pound of flesh to be taken from any part of Antonio's body should the money not be repaid within three months.

The people of Venice
The chauvinism of Venice is shown in the treatment of Shylock.

(Richard as Bassanio) **The young initiate**
The baseness of the initiate is further seen in Bassanio's delivering his benefactor into the hands of his enemy for his own gains. He is, however, engaged in a higher battle between good and evil from which he will emerge improved.

(Tony as Shylock) **The touchstone of chauvinism in Venice**
The conflict is engaged with a plot devised by Shylock to take Antonio's life should he not pay the owed money by the due date, by tricking him in the bond. By writing it out in Hebrew, he will be able to use the word 'bond' also in the sense of 'chest', i.e. 'nearest the heart', and so take the pound of flesh where it will kill Antonio. He reinforces this by stating that the flesh is to be taken 'In what part of your body pleaseth me' (I.

iii. 147). He seeks to deflect suspicion by magnanimously stipulating that he requires, beyond the payment of the principal, no 'money', the Hebraic writing of which can be interpreted as 'blood', a fact which, to his later cost, he overlooks. He is abusing his Hebraic culture in misusing it for evil means. As a kind of wily serpent, he begins his own process of alchemic transformation which will purge Venice of evil. He exposes the evil chauvinism and hypocrisy of Venice in his protest against Antonio's habitual mistreatment of him.

The 'soul' of the initiates
The situation is set up which will bring the body (Bassanio) of the process to the soul (Portia) and will provide the arena for the body's further trials. Through Shylock's malevolence, the plot is set up which will completely free Jessica from Shylock, transferring the captive soul from an unworthy body.
(Terry as Antonio) **The provider**
Antonio's love for Bassanio is so binding that he cannot see the danger to himself in engaging in a bond with Shylock. This proves not only dangerous to himself but destructive of others.

The narrative and reflective element
Had other Venetians been present at the contract between Shylock and Antonio on behalf of Bassanio, they would surely have advised against it. Shakespeare omits them to further the plot.

(Theatre Set-Up merged the next scene, II. i. 1-45, with II. vii. 1-79 to facilitate necessary costume changes within their casting of the play).

Story Section 4 (II. ii. 1-197, II. iii., II. iv. 1-39, II. v. 1-39, II. vi. 1-68)
Things are not well at Shylock's house: his servant, Lancelot Gobbo, can no longer stand the grim household and the 'kind of devil' (II. ii. 23), Shylock, and seeks re-employment with Bassanio. His father, Old Gobbo, visits him, bringing him a present for his present employer, Shylock, which Gobbo uses to ingratiate himself with Bassanio. Shylock's oppressed daughter, Jessica, who considers the house to be a 'hell' (II. iii. 2) takes Shylock's money and jewels and elopes with the Christian, Lorenzo, during a masque and a feast, to which the scheming Venetians have invited Shylock.

CHAPTER NINETEEN

(Steven as Lancelot Gobbo) **The people of Venice**
Lancelot Gobbo, in seeking to leave the 'kind of devil', Shylock, for the 'initiate', Bassanio, indicates the willingness of Venice to be transformed and regenerated.

(Richard as Bassanio) **The young initiate**
Bassanio provides the feast, under cover of which Lorenzo is able to elope with Jessica, and thus engages in the conflict with evil, but does so in a manner which is not honourable. In employing Lancelot Gobbo with Shylock's approval he is uniting Venice in his initiatory pilgrimage and thus also representing it.

(Tony as Lorenzo, then as Shylock) **The touchstone of chauvinism in Venice**
The separating stage of Shylock's alchemy (**Nigredo**) is begun when the 'soul' (his daughter, Jessica) of the 'base matter' he represents leaves him and is ultimately taken by his alter ego, Lorenzo, to the 'spiritual sphere' of Belmont. Meanwhile, his alter ego, Lorenzo, behaves badly as a spendthrift, deliberately opposing his miserliness. In the departure of Jessica and Lancelot Gobbo, Shylock is left symbolically separated from Venice and is isolated as a 'soul' initiate.

(Jamie as Jessica) **The 'soul' of the initiates**
In going to Belmont, Jessica, Shylock's 'soul', enters Portia's sphere. In leaving Shylock, Jessica initiates his alchemical transformation.

(Terry as Old Gobbo) **The provider**
Antonio's alter-ego, Old Gobbo, turns up at just the right moment to provide a gift to enhance his son, Lancelot's, chances of changing employers. In this role, he is a humble father-provider.

(Elizabeth as Salerio) **The narrative and reflective element**
Salerio assists in the elopement of Lorenzo and Jessica, reflecting cynically on the contrast between old and new love: 'all things that are, | Are with more spirit chased than enjoy'd' (II. vi. 12,13).

(Theatre Set-Up interposed scenes II. i. 1-46 and II. vii. 1-79 between II. iv. 1-39 and II. v. 1-55 and II. ix. 1-101 between II. viii. 1-53 and III. i. 1-120 to facilitate costume changes)

Story Section 5 (II. i., II. vii., II. ix.)

The Prince of Morocco unsuccessfully attempts the riddle of the caskets, selecting the gold. The Prince of Arragon is also unsuccessful, choosing silver.

The people of Venice

The monetary values so upheld in Venice are rejected in Belmont.
(Richard as the Princes of Morocco and Arragon) **The young initiate**
The alter-ego initiate of Bassanio, personified as the Prince of Morocco, is unsuccessful in terms of the alchemy of the play, as the gold of 'The Great Work' of alchemy cannot be attained before being earned. As Prince of Arragon, he attempts a lesser goal, known as 'The Little Work' in the quest for silver, but that has not been earned yet either.

The touchstone of chauvinism in Venice

Shylock's opponent in the person of Portia is being prepared as the way to the right suitor in Bassanio. Her marriage to him will bring her as advocate into the trial of Antonio versus Shylock.
(Suzie as Portia, Jamie as Portia's servant) **The 'soul' of the initiates**
Portia demonstrates a chauvinistic flaw similar to the Venetians in her racist comment about the Prince of Morocco after his failure to win her as his wife. She will be punished later for this. Portia's servant assists in the casket trials.

The provider

The way is cleared for Antonio's protégé to enter the lists of the casket trial.
(Elizabeth as Nerissa) **The narrative and reflective element**
Nerissa reflects on Portia's wishes in the failure of Morocco and Arragon and assists in the trials.

Story Section 6 (II. viii., III. i. 1-120)

Salerio and Solanio mock Shylock's reaction to his loss of his daughter, Jessica, and the ducats and jewels which she has stolen from him and speculate on the possibility that he will take revenge on Antonio, whose argosies at sea may be lost. Shylock condemns the Venetians for aiding the elopement of his daughter. He pleads for the common humanity of Jews with Christians, but uses this as a reason for exacting revenge, as

CHAPTER NINETEEN

Christians themselves do. The bereft Shylock learns from his kinsman, Tubal, that Jessica and Lorenzo have been squandering Shylock's money and jewels but also that Antonio's ships have been lost at sea so that it is unlikely that he will be able to repay the loan. Bitter at his daughter's betrayal of him and at the duplicity of the Venetians, he vows to take his revenge by exacting the penalty of a pound of Antonio's flesh.

The people of Venice
Venice is about to be punished for its cruelty and chauvinism by Shylock's actions.

The young initiate
Shylock prepares the initiate's greatest trial: the death experience predicted for his benefactor.
(Tony as Shylock) **The touchstone of chauvinism in Venice**
Shylock suffers the pain of the **Nigredo** (the black stage) of alchemy in the loss of his 'true soul', (Jessica), and his 'false soul' (his money and jewels). Instead of submitting to this as a learning and purging process, he responds by feeding an evil impulse to revenge and kill. Tubal eases his pain by telling him of Antonio's losses, but the information he gives him about Jessica's wanton spending spurs on Shylock to plotting revenge. A key to the trauma of Shylock's inner suffering is given in his reference to the loss of his dead wife, Leah, whose gift of a ring to him Jessica has stolen and squandered. Her cruelty to Shylock in this act triggers his subsequent insatiable violent rage His plea for the universal human condition of different races (III. i. 52-66) stands as a plea against racism.
(Jamie as Solanio) **The 'soul' of the initiates**
The conflict which Portia will resolve is engaged. Jessica, Shylock's symbolic 'soul' in the ritual of the play betrays him and he becomes barbaric without her. Solanio mocks Shylock just as Jessica has done.
(Terry as Tubal) **The provider**
The provider to Shylock, Tubal, takes centre stage in informing Shylock of Jessica's betrayal and of Antonio's losses.
(Elizabeth as Salerio) **The narrative and reflective element**
Salerio narrates Shylock's reaction to the elopement of his daughter with

his money and jewels and accurately predicts that Shylock will take his revenge upon Antonio.

Story Section 7 (III. ii., III. iii.)

Unaware of Antonio's misfortunes on his behalf, Bassanio in Belmont attains Portia in marriage by choosing the lead casket. Portia gives him a ring, which will symbolise the value he places on her and their relationship. His friend, Gratiano, and the maid, Nerissa, announce their betrothal, also decided by Bassanio's success, with the gift of a similar ring. However, this double joy is destroyed by the news, brought by Lorenzo, of events in Venice. Portia gives Bassanio three times the amount of the bond-money with which to persuade Shylock to spare Antonio's life. The two couples marry before the men return to Venice, but they decide not to consummate the marriages until they return with Antonio. Shylock confronts Antonio and his gaoler in the street and rejects all his attempts to plead for his life. Antonio accepts his cruel fate at the hands of Shylock.

(Steven as Gratiano) **The people of Venice**
Venice is linked to the initiatory process born by Bassanio by a 'shadow' process begun by Gratiano's pilgrimage to Belmont and confirmed in his marriage with Nerissa, his soul or higher self. The ultimate wholeness of Venice is symbolised by the ring.

(Richard as Bassanio) **The young initiate**
Bassanio increases Antonio's risk by having selfishly delayed in Belmont (which will modify the triumph of his success at the caskets). However, he passes his first great trial, proving in his selection of the lead casket that his materialism is superficial and that he is a worthy candidate. Alchemically, he enters upon the beginning of the process by being identified with the lead casket and with the metal which represents the base matter upon which the process is carried out and which will be transformed into gold. He finds in Portia his soul or higher self, with whom he is linked by the ring, a symbol of wholeness and integration. Because he has not undergone all his necessary trials, he will not yet be granted full union with his higher self.

(Tony as Lorenzo, then Shylock) **The touchstone of chauvinism in Venice**
The opposition to Shylock is strengthened by Portia's marriage to Bassanio. Shylock's implacable desire for revenge, motivated by traumas he has suffered from racist abuse, makes him a formidable opponent.

(Suzie as Portia, Jamie as Jessica) **The 'soul' of the initiates**
An alchemist would need an assistant who (in order to achieve the energy of polarity) had to be of the opposite sex. If Portia is the alchemist, her dead father, represented in the lottery of the three caskets, is her assistant. We feel the wisdom of his presence here as Bassanio, the right suitor for Portia and allegorically (in terms of alchemy) the 'body' counterpart to her as 'soul', wins her as his wife. The ring exchanged between them is the circle-symbol of the unity of body and soul, and the ultimate integration of the personality within itself and the Divinity, which is the aim of all magical rituals. As alchemist, Portia directs the proceedings which will result in the attainment of this goal. She calls Bassanio 'Hercules' (III. ii. 60), symbol of the labours of alchemy (represented – as are the labours involved in presenting theatre performances – by the statue of Hercules outside Shakespeare's Globe theatre). Although they can marry they cannot consummate the marriage, as the 'body' is flawed and must undergo trials until purged. Portia is punished for her earlier racist comment against the Prince of Morocco in the over-dependent attachment Bassanio has for Antonio, which stands between them in their marriage. Jessica, as Lorenzo's 'soul', moves to her new life.

(Terry as Antonio) **The provider**
Antonio makes a fruitless attempt himself to gain mercy from Shylock. His attachment to Bassanio threatens the latter's relationship with his wife, Portia. The request that Bassanio should be present at his death demonstrates his wish to appear as a martyr to his affection.

(Elizabeth as Nerissa) **The narrative and reflective element**
Nerissa and Gratiano shadow Portia and Bassanio's courtship and marriage and undergo a parallel alchemical process.

Story Section 8 (III. iv., IV. i. 1-170)
Portia leaves Lorenzo and Jessica in charge of Belmont, pretending that she will go into a monastery to pray for a safe outcome in Venice for Antonio.

However, she goes to Padua to consult the learned doctor of law, Bellario (also consulted by letter by the Doge of Venice), about Antonio's plight, and, armed with his advice, and recommended by him to the Venetian court presided over by the Doge, she adopts the male disguise of a young doctor of law, Balthazar, with Nerissa disguised as the doctor's clerk. They are received by the Doge in the Venetian court and take control of the court proceedings governing the imminent execution of Antonio by Shylock.

(Steven as the Doge) **The people of Venice**
The Doge is powerless, confronted by the results of an evil which Venice itself has generated.

(Richard as Bassanio) **The young initiate**
Bassanio is undergoing a trial of the death experience in watching his benefactor being prepared for a death brought about by his own self-interest. This is controlled by Portia, his higher self, whom he does not recognise.

(Tony as Shylock then Lorenzo) **The touchstone of chauvinism in Venice**
Shylock's arena of possible transformation is prepared. Portia becomes the instrument of this, the spiritual guide and mentor to Shylock. Lorenzo, his alter-ego, and Jessica, his soul, are in control in Belmont, ethically contrasted with Venice.

(Suzie as Portia, Jamie as Jessica and Solanio) **The 'soul' of the initiates**
Portia becomes a high priestess of the initiation and the alchemist. Another alchemist's assistant is suggested in the learned doctor, Bellario. Solanio, the friend of Antonio, assists in the court-purging of Shylock.

(Terry as Antonio) **The provider**
As one who has committed chauvinistic acts of racial discrimination against Shylock and his fellows, Antonio represents that aspect of Venice in this scene and will suffer the punishment of the 'death-experience' for it.

(Elizabeth as Nerissa) **The narrative and reflective element**
Nerissa as the clerk now reflects the action of the court in writing.

Story Section 9 (IV. i. 170-290)
Portia upholds the Doge's recommendation to Shylock that he should be merciful to Antonio and accept Bassanio's offer of thrice the amount of the original bond, but Shylock is implacable in insisting that the terms

of the bond be implemented. He insists on his rights in law which must be granted if the Venetian state is to be credible. Bassanio states in court that he would willingly sacrifice his wife, dear as she is, if it would save Antonio's life. Gratiano asserts that he would also sacrifice his wife to save Antonio.

(Steven as the Doge) **People of Venice**

Venice, through seeing one of its citizens suffering as it has imposed suffering on others, undergoes a salutary punishment.

(Richard as Bassanio) **The young initiate**

The young initiate, Bassanio, fails in the rejection of his higher self, Portia, for a childlike adherence to old allegiances (Antonio). He is prepared to sacrifice his 'soul' to redeem a situation caused by flaws in his own character.

(Tony as Shylock) **The touchstone of chauvinism in Venice**

As a self-styled practiser of the Hebrew faith, Shylock should follow its maxims and be merciful. When he fails to respond positively to the Doge and Portia, he damns himself and distances himself from his culture and religion, which he is bringing into disrepute. He is referred to as a 'wolf', an alchemical symbol of the breaking-down agent which initiates the stage of Nigredo. Here he is breaking-down and exposing the chauvinism of Venice. He makes the Venetians aware of their chauvinism in their treatment of other races as non-persons, as mere possessions in the form of slaves and as objects of verbal abuse and racial discrimination. In the venom of his desire for revenge upon those who have alienated his culture and subsequently abused him, he demonstrates the ill consequences of this malpractice (see fig. 47).

(Suzie as Portia) **The 'soul' of the initiates**

Portia attains enormous stature in her speeches and manner as court advocate, appropriate to her allegorical roles. She orchestrates the court proceedings as a high ritual to lead Shylock into setting a trap for himself, which will resolve the case and force his transformation into a state of humility and acceptance of his guilt. In terms of the Hebraic Tree of Life, she has had to assume male attire to teach Shylock that the Pillar of Mercy, with its sphere **Chesed**, representing mercy, is male, and that of **Severity**, the sphere of which, **Geburah**, which he assumes, is female. She is herself further punished for her racist comments about the Prince of Morocco in

Bassanio's court rejection of her, his wife, in favour of Antonio. Shylock is also proved unworthy of his 'soul', his daughter Jessica, who, in spite of her cruelty to him in the irreverent disposal of Leah's ring, is justified in leaving him.

(Terry as Antonio) **The provider**
The unwholesome nature of Antonio's attachment to Bassanio is manifest in the latter's rejection of his wife for him in the court.

(Elizabeth as Nerissa) **The narrative and reflective element**
Nerissa reflects Portia's anger at being rejected on behalf of Antonio by her own husband, Gratiano.

Story Section 10 (IV. i. 290-403)

At the moment when Shylock is about to take the flesh from Antonio's breast, Shylock's claim on the bond which Antonio has signed, Portia intercepts him to point out that he must be sure to take only flesh, no blood, which according to Venetian law, if he sheds, would render his lands and goods confiscate to the state of Venice. He must also make sure that he takes exactly a pound of flesh or he will forfeit his life. Shylock, defeated, asks first for a sum of three times the bond, as offered, and then for merely his principal, the original 3,000 ducats. He is refused both the money and permission to leave the court because he has infringed the Venetian law which forbids, on pain of death, aliens, such as Shylock, to seek the life of a Venetian citizen. He begs mercy of the Doge, who grants him his life but takes a fine of his property. Antonio demands that Shylock becomes a Christian.

Steven as the Doge) **The people of Venice**
Venice is redeemed by the higher wisdom of Belmont, demonstrated in mercy towards Shylock.

(Richard as Bassanio) **The young initiate**
The soul of the initiate, Portia, also the hierophant of his initiation, takes Bassanio beyond the death experience.

(Tony as Shylock) **The touchstone of chauvinism in Venice**
At last, Shylock is forced to learn and transform. He is 'hoist with his own petard', as Portia demonstrates his oversights in his drawing up the terms of

the bond. Not only has he omitted a right to spill blood, but in specifying an exact quantity of flesh to be taken has made the task of removing exactly a pound of flesh impossible. If it can be assumed that Shakespeare, as Schonfeld suggests, sourced the story of Shylock from an ancient Hebrew text, and that Shylock's original bond was written in Hebrew, the implications of which Bellario understood, an extra dimension to Shylock's failure to implement his bond becomes evident. Just as he uses the pun on the word 'bond' to mean 'chest', his use of the term 'no money' written in Hebraic can also mean 'no blood'. In his final response, 'I am content', he demonstrates the knowledge that he has brought his own troubles on himself. Allegorically, it means that he accepts his ritualistic transformation as an initiate. He is punished for his abuse of his culture and religion in being stripped of them when Antonio insists that if the payment of a fine be modified, Shylock must become a Christian. This also has alchemic meaning. Christ was symbolised as the 'phoenix', one of the terms for the goal of alchemic transformation (see fig. 4). In forcing Shylock to become a Christian, it is implied that he is being forced to achieve the alchemic transformation from 'serpent' (the Devil in the Hebrew story's source), to 'phoenix'. It is also likely that he has taught the Venetians a lesson and that they might think twice again about treating an alien as a non-person, as they have been punished for this by suffering the death experience.

(Suzie as Portia) **The 'soul' of the initiates**
At a stroke as keen as Shylock's knife, Portia defeats Shylock, and as his alchemist and instructor, in preventing him from committing murder, she pares away all those elements which align him with Hell and the Devil rather than the Divinity dwelling in him, in Hebraic terms the 'Ain Soph', with which he must ultimately become identified. She also rescues Antonio, making it possible for the initiate Bassanio to ultimately free himself of his immature attachment to him. The transfer of Jessica to Lorenzo, Shylock's alter-ego, is completed.

(Terry as Antonio) **The provider**
Antonio is delivered from death by Portia, and it is he who stipulates that Shylock become a Christian, in this becoming the alchemist's assistant, a variation in his role as provider. Shylock must be stripped of the religion he has dishonoured.

(Elizabeth as Nerissa) **The narrative and reflective element**
Nerissa draws up the documents which will resolve the case.

Story Section 11 (IV. i. 404-453, IV. ii.)
Bassanio offers a reward to the disguised Portia as thanks for being instrumental in saving Antonio's life. She will accept nothing but the ring on his finger. At first he refuses but Antonio persuades him to surrender it. Nerissa also succeeds in getting Gratiano's ring.

(Steven as Gratiano) **The people of Venice**
As symbolic representative of the people of Venice, Gratiano fails in the test of the supposed improved state of the city, by not understanding that a new allegiance to a higher state (symbolised by his marriage) should prevail over old loyalties to previous values (symbolised by Antonio).

(Richard as Bassanio) **The young initiate**
In the surrender of the ring at Antonio's insistence, the initiate Bassanio confirms his failure to value Portia (his symbolic "soul") and he loses ground in his initiation.

The touchstone of chauvinism in Venice
The presence of Shylock is still felt, his conflict with the Venetians bringing out into the open flaws in their behaviour which must be purged.

(Suzie as Portia) **The 'soul' of the initiates**
Portia, as hierophant and alchemist, continues to test Bassanio in demanding the ring from him. Jessica, the "higher self" of Shylock, is established at Belmont, the "heart" of the process.

The provider
Portia tackles the problem of Bassanio's immature attachment to Antonio by demanding the ring. A graduated initiate must demonstrate adulthood. Bassanio shows his continuing dependence on the will of Antonio who demonstrates his wish to retain possession of the young man's affection by insisting that he parts with the ring, regardless of the offence to Portia.

(Elizabeth as Nerissa) **The narrative and reflective element**
Nerissa shadows Portia in obtaining Gratiano's ring, proving the immaturity of her own husband.

CHAPTER NINETEEN

Story Section 12 (V. i.)
The couples return to Belmont, the men (bringing Antonio with them) unaware of their wives' participation in the events in Venice. Nerissa first challenges Gratiano with the loss of their betrothal ring and then Portia accuses Bassanio of breaking faith by parting with the ring that she gave him. Antonio apologises that he has caused this division between them, and only when he pledges with his soul that Bassanio will never break faith again does Portia become reconciled with her husband and give him the ring which he recognises as that he gave the advocate. Both she and Nerissa punish their husbands by pretending that they obtained the rings by sleeping with the advocate and his clerk. She resolves their distress by revealing documents which prove their identities as that same advocate and clerk, and which also indicate that Antonio's ships have safely returned, and which give Lorenzo and Jessica a portion of Shylock's estate upon his death. The play concludes with Gratiano's pledge to only fear the 'keeping safe Nerissa's ring' (V. i. 304-305).

(Steven as Launcelot Gobbo, then Gratiano) **The people of Venice**
In the return of Gratiano to Belmont (reinforced by the presence there already of Lancelot Gobbo), Venice prepares for final improvement, undergoes a last trial in the quarrel over the ring and resolves never to break with its higher self again.

(Richard as Bassanio) **The young initiate**
Bassanio is punished for his immature adherence to Antonio in the threatened loss of Portia. Antonio is here like an overprotective parent/guide, who at last lets the initiate act for himself and attain maturity. This releases Bassanio so that he can move forward to union with his higher self, Portia. In the symbolic alchemy of the play, the body of the process, the base matter, Bassanio, has undergone trials which have purified and tested him so that, recombined with Portia, the soul of the process, transformation has taken place and the gold of enlightenment, the Philosophers' Stone, is attained.

(Tony as Lorenzo) **The touchstone of chauvinism in Venice**
Shylock has performed his function as a touchstone of Venice. He has provided the frame within which the evil can be purged, and has, as subject and object of that evil, been the cause of its transformation. We see him in

the form of his alter ego Lorenzo, left in charge of Belmont and reminding us of the link and correspondence between the larger universe (the cosmos) and the individual person (the microcosm), which alchemists believed made it possible for their transformations performed with chemicals to affect personalities and ultimately the world order. Within the allegory of the play it could be claimed that Shylock and Bassanio transformed can improve Venice and the nature of the world. Lorenzo also expounds the Renaissance theory of the Harmony of the Spheres (V. i. 60-65), a belief that the harmonic movement of the spheres created music. This harmonic state of mind of Shylock's alter-ego suggests a successful transformation.

(Suzie as Portia, Jamie as Jessica) **The 'soul' of the initiates**
Portia has much to do on her return, pre-eminent among which is to free Bassanio from his attachment to Antonio. This done, she can unite with him and, within the allegory of the play, the gold of their transmutation will influence Venice and world order (see fig. 20). Her semi-magical presentation to Antonio of the news of his three safely-returned argosies smacks of the Divine, a fact observed by Lorenzo when he is presented with the deed-of-gift forced from Shylock, "Fair ladies, you drop manna in the way | Of starved people" (V. i. 293-294). Portia's alter-ego, Jessica, is deputising for her in Belmont and possibly finding that the Christian ways need adjusting to. As Shylock's "soul" she has shared his treatment with a culture shock and is not entirely at one with his alter ego, Lorenzo. However she becomes part of the Paradise-Belmont, united with Lorenzo.

(Terry as Antonio) **The provider**
Antonio realises that he must give up his patronage of Bassanio, pledging on his soul to Portia that her husband will keep his allegiance to her.

(Elizabeth as Nerissa) **The narrative and reflective element**
Nerissa shadows Portia in punishing Gratiano for unfaithfulness, and the play ends with Gratiano's resolve to be faithful to her, in keeping her ring safe. As Gratiano partially represents the people of Venice, this implies that Nerissa becomes part of its soul, integrating Belmont with Venice. In typical Shakespearean lack of reverence, his statement also implies sexual innuendo, a fitting ending for a romantic comedy.

CHAPTER NINETEEN

In *The Merchant of Venice*, Shakespeare dwells on the theme of the mercy prescribed by the New Testament of The Bible contrasted with the revenge featured within the Old Testament. Mercy dominates the outcome of the Shakespeare's comedies, especially in *The Tempest*, *The Winter's Tale* and *Cymbeline*. The next category features two plays, the plots and outcomes of which are specifically determined by this contrast between mercy and revenge in the New and Old Testaments.

OPPOSING VIEWS WITHIN THE OLD AND NEW TESTAMENTS OF THE BIBLE:
MERCY 'For if ye doe forgive men their trespasses, your heavenly Father will also forgive you' (Matthew 6. 14) **VERSUS REVENGE** 'Eye for eye, tooth for tooth, hand for hand, foote for foote' (Exodus 21. 24).

CHAPTER TWENTY: *MEASURE FOR MEASURE* (MERCY)

This play is so clear in its story, characters and its themes of morality, ethics, crime and punishment that I would have thought that no explanation of any arcana was necessary for the actors' understanding of the script. However, it was after a week's rehearsal in 1991 when I gave the actors my view of the underlying meanings of the play as set out in the play's programme notes that the actress who was performing the characters Isabella and Juliet, complained that she and others in the cast would have benefited from the information I was giving them long before the beginning of the rehearsal period. One of the factors that caused her appreciation of the notes I gave the cast was the inclusion of the ideas on the play expressed by John Vyvyan in *The Shakespearean Ethic*.[1] The Theatre Set-Up actors often found John Vyvyan's ideas and interpretation of Shakespeare's scripts useful for their understanding of the plays and their roles within them. In subsequent years, the actress's response prompted me to present my views of the plays' arcana and themes one month before the beginning of the rehearsal period so that the actors came prepared with a deeper understanding of the script.

Problems with the play

- One of the problems with the play that some people have expressed is the deception of Duke Vincentio in pretending to be a friar in the prison. The underlying meanings of the play make sense of his disguise as Friar Lodowick, indicating his function in role as alchemist and educator of his people.

CHAPTER TWENTY

- *Measure for Measure* and *All's Well that Ends Well* are often included among Shakespeare's 'problem plays'.[2] One aspect of the 'problem' with these plays is that both use the plot device of the 'bed-trick', in which a male protagonist is deceived into making love to a woman he has rejected but who is lawfully his partner, by making him believe that she is another woman whom he desires.
- The two plays are also deemed to be problem plays because of their dark nature, often dealing with social issues. In *Measure for Measure*, Shakespeare deals with social issues involving political corruption, ethics, crime and punishment through his main protagonist, Vincentio, the Duke of Vienna.
- Another problem with the plausibility of the scenario in *Measure for Measure* occurs when the Duke unexpectedly proposes marriage to Isabella at V. i. 489-491, a proposal which she is usually presumed to accept. The way we found to give that a reasonable interpretation was to make Isabella and the Duke fall in love at first sight when they meet in III. i. He continues to love her, guiding her to become fit to be Duchess of Vienna, she suppressing her initial feelings as she believes that he is a friar and she is to become a nun. It is reasonable to suggest this scenario as the Renaissance Platonism which Shakespeare applied to the lovers in his plays decrees that many 'companion souls' recognise each other instantly, thus falling in love. As Phebe in *As You Like it* says, 'Who ever lov'd that lov'd not at first sight?' (III. v. 82). According to this interpretation, Isabella is relieved when Vincentio's identity as the Duke is revealed to know that her feelings for him at their first meeting have not been shameful, and she realises when he proposes to her that it is her destiny to become his wife and not a nun.
- He plays some mystifying games with his subjects and has often been accused of cruelty in allowing them to believe in the death of Isabella's brother.

In fact, Vincentio is following a bold course of social and psychological reform, and setting up a model of mercy instead of vengeful punishment. He strives to cure wrong-doers and replaces execution and fines with social reparation.

The means by which he does this include:

- Facilitating learning by the adoption of an appropriate role, i.e. that of Friar Lodowick.
- Using teaching by exposure of his 'pupils' to simulated experiences.
- Using role models.

These techniques are well-known to contemporary teaching and psychiatry. He replaces vengeance with love and mercy. In our own times, when violent acts are endlessly repeated as political reprisals, this moral philosophy has a poignant relevance.

Theatre Set-Up's Production of the Play

As much of the play shows illusions, characters and situations seeming to be what they are not, and as it seeks to expose and destroy a moral hypocrisy that was very prevalent in the Victorian period, in 1991 Theatre Set-Up set the play in the late nineteenth century as if it were a Victorian touring theatre company. Performing as Shakespeare did on tour (and as did small Victorian theatre companies) with a reduced number of players, we found that each actor played two different kinds of character in the play; one straight-laced, which was reflected in the singing of Victorian parlour songs, and one naughty, conveyed by music-hall numbers.[3] Actors asked the audiences to join in the singing of the choruses of these songs, printed on the back of the play's programme. We included the songs because their themes reflected the meanings of the script, sometimes replacing lines in the script which modern audiences find difficult to digest. For example, instead of the lines III. ii. 6-10, in which Pompey discusses different facets of usury in terms unknown to modern audiences, he sang the Victorian protest song against justice and fortune favouring the rich over the poor:

> It's the same the whole world over,
> It's the poor what gets the blame.
> It's the rich what gets the pleasure
> Ain't it all a blinking shame.

Although the meaning is not exactly the same as that in the original text, it gave the gist of Pompey's feelings of social injustice to the audience and in a way was emphasised by their own joining in singing the chorus. The Victorian parlour songs performed at the beginning of the play and at the end of the interval with 'Love's Old Sweet Song' and 'Drink to me only with thine eye' set a false romantic tone which masked the sinister events of the play and implied a hypocrisy in the society of both Victorian and Jacobethan times. Audiences enjoyed this whole approach.

The arcana in the play

I found the underlying meanings of the play to be so dense that the story fell into 33 sections rather than the usual twelve or thirteen sections of other plays. I analysed the story in terms of only two levels:

- The first was **alchemy** (see above pp. 26-34). I did not analyse the alchemy of the play into its usual twelve stages but grouped them into the four general stages of their colour symbolism of black, white, red and gold. In this play I consider that Vienna is the 'base matter'.
- The second was **morality, ethics, crime and punishment** (and what the Duke is doing as an instrument of Shakespeare's philosophy).[4] The ideas of **Renaissance Platonism** and **the Bible** are included in this level.

Much of the material in this analysis of the story is sourced from *The Shakespearean Ethic* by John Vyvyan.[5] Often, his work recognises Shakespeare's interpretation of the Renaissance philosophies of his time, usually derived from sources in ancient Greek writings. Vyvyan tells us that the play:

> Contrasts three methods of dealing with offence: punishment, indulgence and regeneration [...] to show, in what way creative mercy differs from mere indulgence, the one bringing regeneration while the other brings only chaos to society. [...] (The Duke's) intention is to cure his subjects instead of punishing them. [...] We are watching,

not simply a play, but an experiment in psychiatry. […] The main characters receive a wakening jolt, by being confronted with the prospect of death. To face them with death, and prepare them to meet it, is the Duke's shock-therapy, and is the preliminary to helping them discover their true selves […] to make for them 'heavenly comforts of despair'. (pp. 63-67)

He also considers that the ethics of *Measure for Measure* reflect those of the New Testament, and contrasts the play with *Hamlet*, in which Hamlet's father's ghost instructs his son to take revenge in the way featured in the Old Law of the Old Testament stories. The contrasting outcomes of the action of both plays reveals the effect of these opposing beliefs; *Hamlet* concludes with most of the protagonists killed whereas *Measure for Measure* sees the marriage of four couples and other protagonists praised or forgiven. In fact, Vyvyan claims that throughout his plays Shakespeare 'lays emphasis increasingly on the ethics of the New Testament and repudiates those of the Old' (p. 91).

With hindsight, I see that the Duke acts within the play as hierophant to the young people, Isabella, Juliet and Claudio, in a metaphor of their **initiation** (see above pp. 49-50), so I include that level at the end of the following exposition of the play's different levels of meaning (mostly as set out for the audience and cast in the programme notes), along with an interpretation of the play's **Cabala: Post Production.**

Story Section 1 (I.i.)

Duke Vincentio of Vienna announces his departure from Vienna to his statesman Escalus and makes the strict Lord Angelo his deputy, delegating to him the task of enforcing laws, which, being neglected, have led to moral decay and disease in the city.

Alchemy

The base matter needing to be redeemed is Vienna. This is represented in its different aspects by four couples: its government by the Duke and Isabella and Angelo and Mariana, its people by Claudio and Juliet and Lucio and

Kate Keepdown. These will subjected to processes, as 'body' and 'soul', which will, if successful, regenerate the immoral Vienna. Here, the Duke, who should stand for the body of Vienna, knowing that he has been unfit for the job and with a plan that needs him to function as an alchemist himself, steps down from governing Vienna and puts Angelo in his place.

Morality, Ethics, Crime and Punishment
For the last fourteen years the Duke has been too lenient to his subjects so that the law has fallen into disrepute and there is confusion in society. He hands over control to Angelo, who has a spotless reputation and who will not hesitate to be rigorous in application of the laws.

Story Section 2 (I. ii.)
Angelo implements these laws, closing all brothels and forbidding by law any loose sexual behaviour. The effect of this is seen on Pompey, a pimp, and Mistress Overdone, a madam. They decide to re-name their brothels 'bath houses'.

In order to make an example of him, Angelo arrests and condemns to death the young Claudio, whose illicit partner, Juliet, is pregnant. Claudio and Juliet, paraded through the streets by Angelo, meet their friend Lucio and request him to tell Claudio's plight to his sister Isabella, just that day entering the nunnery of St Clare, and to beg her to intercede on his behalf with Angelo. Lucio agrees.

Alchemy
Angelo is now part of the body of Vienna. As its head, he cleanses and purifies it, attempting to get rid of impurities such as the brothels of Pompey and Mistress Overdone. However, his purges become excessive. The imprisoned Claudio and Juliet become the surrogate for the immoral people of Vienna, Claudio the body and Juliet the soul.

Morality, Ethics, Crime and Punishment
An ancient Viennese law has declared that an adulterer must be put to death. In the current moral looseness of Vienna, that would take out much of the population. So Angelo decides to make an example of Claudio, who protests that he and Juliet, genuine lovers, are affianced and therefore in the eyes of the law, married. 'Claudio is less guilty than most other characters

in the play; but a warning example is to be made of him, so that 'justice' is itself unjust' (Vyvyan, p. 65).

Story Section 3 (I.iii.)
The Duke, meanwhile, has gone to a friar's cell to request a disguise as a friar so that he can return to Vienna and observe Angelo's actions. He suspects that Angelo's moral uprightness might be corruptible when he is given political power.

Alchemy
The Duke now prepares to adopt a different role, as the alchemist or guiding soul of Vienna; like a spirit moving unseen he will be unrecognised in the friar's disguise. This role will enable him to be the actual instrument of moral reform in his city.

Morality, Ethics, Crime and Punishment
The Duke is reported to have gone on a journey. However, in his disguise as a monk he will be able to carry out his deeper intention […] to cure his subjects instead of punishing them. […] He will show that Angelo, the judge is worse than thecondemned (Vyvyan p. 64).

Story Section 4 (I. iv.)
Isabella is about to enter the nunnery of Saint Clare. Shakespeare demonstrates here that her concept of holiness is conditioned by a life-denying self-restraint as she complains that the privileges of the nunnery are too numerous. Lucio is admitted and is successful in persuading Isabella to leave the nunnery to plead for Claudio's life. Her reputation for eloquence is such that she is confident of success.

Alchemy
Isabella, on entering the nunnery, enters the realm of the spirit, but her purity has marked her as the one who must undertake the trials of the body of the government of Vienna. She is the corresponding half of the Duke. At the beginning of the play he was in the body of Vienna and she in its churchly spiritual realm. Now they must change places – he a friar, she treated as a laywoman in the world of the body.

CHAPTER TWENTY

Morality, Ethics, Crime and Punishment
Angelo will be tested by being confronted by Isabella, saintly but severe and cold like him. Both need to understand true virtue and compassion.

Story Section 5 (II. i.)
Lord Escalus is seen as a true diplomat and ideal statesman, attempting to moderate Angelo's severity and dealing appropriately with a case brought by the constable Elbow against Pompey and the foolish Froth, in a situation brought about by the re-naming of the brothels as bath-houses. Elbow's wife has entered one of these places, not knowing what it really was, and has been indecently propositioned.

Alchemy
Escalus is revealed as the constant, true element of the government of Vienna. His integrity is tried and found to be true. Like an alchemist himself, he does some purging.

Morality, Ethics, Crime and Punishment
This scene showing Escalus, a man of tact, justice and mercy, presents us with a foil to the next scene between Angelo and Isabella. Shakespeare also highlights the problems that can occur when euphemistic names are given to places of ill-repute as innocent people like Froth's wife can be deceived and compromised.

Story Section 6 (II. ii.)
The Provost of the prison also questions Angelo's harshness and is pleased to support Isabella in her attempt to mitigate the sentence against her brother. So appealing is her virtue and eloquence that Angelo desires her, not giving her an immediate answer to her request for clemency to Claudio, but asking her to return the following day. He questions the nature of his infatuation that has never been stirred before by a woman until he saw this novice nun. He attributes his feelings to temptations from Hell.

Alchemy
Angelo as part of the body of Vienna faces the first trial in his lust for Isabella. Her trials as body on behalf of Vienna begin with his illicit feelings for her.

Morality, Ethics, Crime and Punishment
In this scene, in which Isabella is striving to intercede on behalf of Claudio her brother, her very purity tempts Angelo to commit the same sin for which he intends to have Claudio executed. Rather than give him the understanding of an emotion which should make him compassionate, he regards his feelings as a temptation from Hell. In this, he is not observing the Platonic rule – that all love ennobles and ultimately teaches understanding of the love of God himself.

Story Section 7 (II. iii.)
The Duke, disguised as a friar, begins ministering in the prison and confesses Juliet, about to give birth to her child.

Alchemy
The Duke as alchemist takes up duty and successfully tries and tests Juliet, the soul of part of the people of Vienna.

Morality, Ethics, Crime and Punishment
We see in this small scene the two techniques the Duke is to use – trying and testing the subject until genuine change and repentance is achieved and using the shock-therapy of the confrontation with death, although he knows that Claudio will not die because he will ultimately prevent it. 'Juliet has seeming sin and real love: (the Duke) builds upon her love to create virtue […] a seed of true human love in the heart will blossom as divine love in the soul' (Vyvyan p. 79).

Story Section 8 (II. iv.)
When Isabella visits Angelo again he propositions her and tells her that if she gives him love he will release Claudio. She refuses and threatens to tell the world of his behaviour, but he points out that his reputation is so spotless that no-one will believe her (see fig. 48).

Alchemy
Angelo fails in his trial by not accepting Isabella's refusal of him and by being grossly corrupt. Isabella succeeds in her trial by refusing to be

corrupted but fails in her lack of charity to the suffering Claudio. This marks the 'black' stage of Vienna's alchemy.

Morality, Ethics, Crime and Punishment

Angelo is seen to sink in sin lower than the man he has condemned to death. If Isabella does not yield to him he will not only proceed with the execution of Claudio but subject him to painful torture. However, Isabella's attitude to her brother's plight is questionable: 'Then Isabella, live chaste, and, brother die| More than our brother is our chastity' (II. iv. 83-184).

With these harsh and seemingly selfish words, Shakespeare removes Isabella from the audience's sympathy and aligns her kind of virtue with that Angelo has hitherto demonstrated in his appearance to the world, characterised by a false and self-regarding pride. 'Angelo and Isabella […] are tempted and fall by what they believe to be their virtues' (Vyvyan p.73).

In this aspect of the plot Shakespeare not only examines human integrity within the justice system but also the issue of trading favours for the conditional release of prisoners or hostages. The plot will prove this to be fruitless. Social inequality affecting justice is also demonstrated in the hopelessness of Isabella's possibility of publicly condemning Angelo, as he himself points out.

Story Section 9 (III. i.)

In the prison, the Duke confesses Claudio and overhears Isabella telling Claudio of Angelo's proposition. She is angry with Claudio when he begs her to yield to it. The Duke pacifies them both and privately suggests a solution to Isabella: that she should consent to Angelo but that Mariana (a lady once betrothed to and cruelly cast off by Angelo when her promised dowry was lost in a shipwreck at sea which also drowned her brother) should take her place in the bedroom where Angelo's violation of Isabella is due to take place.

Alchemy

The Duke as alchemist tests Claudio, who succeeds in his acceptance of death but fails in his attitude to Isabella's refusal to save him. As alchemic 'soul' of the government of Vienna, the Duke meets, and probably falls in love with, Isabella. She possibly returns that feeling, although she immediately suppresses it, assuming, in his identity as a friar and hers as a novice nun, that it is shameful. Alchemically, Isabella is the corresponding body of the process to him as soul, and he begins her preparation for this role in her transmutation and in that of Vienna.

Mariana, the alchemic soul of Angelo, has already suffered the separating **Nigredo** from him in the 'black' stage and now in a moated grange (a symbol of a water-surrounded magic sphere) in the 'white' stage awaits their reconciliation in the 'red' stage of **Rubedo**. This is begun by the planned bed-trick union between them, which will provide the alchemic process with its **Coniunctio**, the alchemical 'marriage'. Mariana will also become an alchemist's assistant to the Duke (as a male alchemist had a female assistant and vice versa).

Morality, Ethics, Crime and Punishment

The Duke practises his psychology on Claudio, who is faced with the prospect of his own death, trying to teaching him stoicism and acceptance of death. However, he obviously does not succeed, as when Isabella tells him that there is a possibility that Angelo might free him if she gives up her virtue, Shakespeare gives Claudio a speech which manifests the horror of the prospect of dying, especially before one's time:

> Ay, but to die, and go we know not where;
> To lie in cold obstruction, and to rot;
> This sensible warm motion to become
> A kneaded clod; and the delighted spirit
> To bath in fiery floods, or to reside
> In thrilling region of thick-ribbed ice;
> To be imprison'd in the viewless winds
> And blown with restless violence round about
> The pendent world: or to be worse than worst
> Of those that lawless and incertain thought
> Imagine howling, - 'tis too horrible.
> The weariest and most loathed worldly life
> That age, ache, penury and imprisonment
> Can lay on nature, is a paradise
> To what we fear of death. (III. i. 117-131)

This passage shows Shakespeare's sensitivity to a fear of the unknown territory of death.

Isabella demonstrates a lack of grace when he appeals to her to save him, 'O you beast [...] Die, perish [...] Mercy to you would prove itself a bawd | 'Tis best you die quickly' (III. i. 135-148). This venom hurled at a brother whom they both believe is to be tortured to death is in stark contrast to her invocation to Angelo to be merciful in II. ii. 57-63.

Story Section 10 (III. ii.)

The disguised Duke sees some other of his subjects in the prison and the effects of his hitherto lax rule of Vienna. He sees the pimp, Pompey, arrested and refused help by Lucio, who castigates and slanders the Duke unknowingly to his face. The madam, Mistress Overdone, accuses Lucio of informing against her although she has maintained his illegitimate child by Kate Keepdown, who had been promised marriage by him. The Duke muses on Angelo's corruption and sin and the evils of Lucio's calumny.

Alchemy
The alchemist Duke faces a tough task in the trial of the people of Vienna with Pompey and Lucio as they do not accept the need for Vienna's reform and their own moral improvement. He faces a trial himself in suffering Lucio's slander of him.

Morality, Ethics, Crime and Punishment
The Duke is faced with a trial of his own sense of mercy in confronting Lucio's calumny against him. Lucio also ultimately betrays his dishonesty in revealing his behaviour towards Kate Keepdown.

Story Section 11 (IV. i.)

In a moated grange, Mariana is solaced by music. The disguised Duke and Isabella put to her the bed-trick plan, to which she agrees.

Alchemy
We see Mariana, the soul of Angelo and, in her unselfish constancy to him, the eternal soul of Vienna.

Morality, Ethics, Crime and Punishment
Isabella is presented with Mariana, her role model, who rescues her from her dilemma. In accepting this convenient solution she shows a moral double standard, for which the Duke will later challenge her. Mariana undertakes the course of action wherein she will redeem Angelo with her lasting love.

Story Section 12 (IV. ii.)
In the prison, Pompey is offered a lenient sentence in return for his services as assistant to the executioner, Abhorson. The disguised Duke enters, expecting Claudio's reprieve as a result of Angelo believing that Isabella has fulfilled her part of their bargain. However, a message affirms Angelo's insistence not only that Claudio should die, but that his head should be sent to him within several hours. Also ordered is the execution of Barnardine, a condemned murderer. The Duke, still in disguise as the friar, tells the Provost (by the authority of his presentation of the Duke's seal which he has about him) to save Claudio and to send Barnardine's head instead of Claudio's.

Alchemy
The alchemist Duke tries to organise the further trials of Angelo, Claudio and now Barnardine, who can be identified as the worst element of criminality in the state. In this function, Barnardine refuses to be purged on the basis of the Duke's previous neglect of the powers of the state, which has allowed criminality to flourish.

Morality, Ethics, Crime and Punishment
Circumstances make it difficult for the Duke to keep up the role of the friar, which sustains the psychotherapy he is practising. He must have faith in order to come out of role now to save Claudio's life. The pointlessness of compromise in trading favours with criminals in order to secure the release of prisoners or hostages is made clear by Shakespeare in Angelo's failure to keep his part of the bargain he made with Isabella.

Pompey is promised a lenient sentence if he will act as assistant to Abhorson, the executioner. The practice, noted here by Shakespeare, of promising either a more lenient sentence or even pardon from being executed to a prisoner if they will act as executioners of their own people or faction is a universal one, even followed in the death camps during World War II. The professionalism of executioners is given voice in Abhorson's objection to Pompey being compelled to be his assistant: 'A bawd sir? Fie upon him, he will discredit our mystery' (IV. ii. 26-27).

Story Section 13 (IV. iii. 1-109)
Barnardine's head is denied as a substitute for Claudio's, as his extensive criminal connections have ensured that he is never executed. He refuses to be executed as he has been supplied with alcohol by his associates from outside the prison and become drunk, and therefore he rightly declares himself unfit to die as his soul will be perjured.

Another head, one more like Claudio's, is supplied by the Provost from the pirate, Ragozine, who has just died of a fever. This head is sent to Angelo, who believes it to be Claudio's.

Alchemy
Fortune, in the form of Ragozine's death, aids the alchemic process.
Morality, Ethics, Crime and Punishment
A real 'power divine' seems to be giving the Duke encouragement in his course of action by supplying him with an already dead head to substitute for Claudio's.

Story Section 14 (IV. iii. 110-177)
Isabella, expecting to hear of Claudio's reprieve, is told by the disguised Duke (who resolves to reserve the news of Claudio's escape for a later time) that Claudio has been executed. She declares revenge on Angelo and that she will 'Pluck out his eyes' (IV. iii. 119). The Duke counsels her that, aided by Mariana and Friar Peter, she could get her revenge upon Angelo by declaring his guilt to the Duke when he returns the next day. Lucio enters to share Isabella's grief and to further provoke the Duke with slander against him.

Alchemy
Isabella as the body demonstrates an imperfection of impatience and desire

for revenge, which the Duke as alchemist must purge out. He will enlist the assistant alchemist, Mariana, to do this.

Morality, Ethics, Crime and Punishment

Isabella, when told of Angelo's perfidy, falls from grace again. The words she utters are far from the sense of mercy she has earlier demanded of Angelo, in her wish to pluck out his eyes. This desire for revenge does not demonstrate the charity of the New Testament precept of 'Love thy enemy' practised by the nunnery Isabella is due to enter, but exemplifies the dated Old Testament law, 'An eye for an eye, a tooth for a tooth'. Isabella also succumbs to the suggestion that she should perjure herself in claiming that it was she whom Angelo has bedded.

Story Section 15 (IV. iv.)

Angelo and Escalus are confused by the letters sent to them by the Duke. These command them to re-deliver their authorities to him outside the city gates and 'proclaim it an hour before his entering, that if any crave redress of injustice, they should exhibit their petitions in the street' (IV. iv. 7-9). Alone, Angelo confesses his fear of Isabella and regret for his supposed deflowering of her and also for the killing of Claudio, which he authorised in fear of his taking revenge on behalf of his violated sister.

Alchemy

The Duke in his temporal role prepares for the purging of Angelo as part of the alchemic body of Vienna. Angelo acknowledges the need for this in his confession of guilt.

Morality, Ethics, Crime and Punishment

Angelo privately confesses his horror of the immoral acts he has committed:

> This deed unshapes me quite […]
> Alack when once our grace we have forgot
> Nothing goes right: we would, and we would not.' (IV. iv. 19-32)

Story Section 16 (IV. v, vi.)
The disguised Duke organises Friar Peter, Isabella and Mariana to carry out the final details of his plot.

Alchemy
The Duke prepares for the purging of Isabella as part of the alchemic body of Vienna. The blessing of Heaven is indicated in the presence of Friar Peter.

Morality, Ethics, Crime and Punishment
In order to sustain the illusion of his role as a friar when he reveals himself as the lay Duke, he enlists the help of a real friar to give weight to the spiritual authority of his plan.

Story Section 17 (V. i. 1-106)
Now out of his disguise, the Duke greets his subjects and praises Angelo for the 'goodness of his justice' in his absence (V. i. 6). Isabella, led by Friar Peter, pleads for justice against Angelo and claims that he has violated her and killed Claudio against his promise.

Alchemy
Using temporal power, the Duke as alchemist sets Isabella up for her purging as the body of Vienna.

Morality, Ethics, Crime and Punishment
Isabella justly accuses Angelo but falls from grace in the lie that he has defiled her.

Story Section 18 (V. i. 107-138)
The Duke pretends not to believe Isabella, accuses her of slander of Angelo and has her arrested. He inquires after the Friar Lodowick (himself in the friar's disguise) to whom she refers, questioning the authority of this man and demanding for him to be called to the scene.

Alchemy
The Duke begins to purge Isabella, as part of the alchemical body of Vienna, of her willingness to lie under observation.

Morality, Ethics, Crime and Punishment
The Duke must punish Isabella for being immoderate in her speech and for allowing herself to be ill-advised. She should have the courage to do only what she knows is right. Friars can easily not be what they seem and their advice could be evil. He himself was masquerading as Friar Lodowick and was in fact not ordained of the Church but a layperson, adopting a disguise for his own purposes. In this respect, he could be accused of deceiving people in the prison such as Juliet and Claudio into a belief that his advice was sanctioned by the Church. However, in his role as Friar Lodowick he is acting as an alchemist and educator for benevolent purposes.[6]

The Duke is also giving Isabella a brief taste of what imprisonment and the threat of death is like so that she can more readily sympathise with Claudio and soon with Angelo.

Story Section 19 (V. i. 139-169)
Friar Peter, in collusion with the Duke in his purposes, accuses Isabella of falsehood in claiming violation by Angelo, and presents the veiled Mariana as witness to this.

Alchemy
Mariana, as assistant alchemist, helps the Duke in his alchemical purging of Isabella, sanctioned by Heaven in Friar Peter.
Morality, Ethics, Crime and Punishment
Friar Peter and Mariana correct Isabella's lie.

Story Section 20 (V. i. 170-232)
Mariana claims Angelo as a husband who has unknowingly made love to her thinking she was Isabella. She unveils and reveals her identity as Angelo's erstwhile betrothed. He acknowledges this fact but disclaims her story.

Alchemy
Mariana faces Angelo as his returning alchemic soul, which he still does not acknowledge.

Morality, Ethics, Crime and Punishment

Angelo has already been saved from violating Isabella by Mariana, his true love; now Mariana proceeds to make their union honourable.

Story Section 21 (V. i. 233-276)

The Duke pretends not to believe Mariana and departs, intending to adopt the disguise of Friar Lodowick again, leaving Angelo and Escalus in charge of the case. They call for Isabella, who has been sent to prison, to be re-examined.

Alchemy

The Duke, in order to achieve the purging of Angelo and Isabella, re-adopts the cleric role in which he could function as an alchemist and pretends to disbelieve Mariana. This marks the 'white' stage of Vienna's alchemy.

Morality, Ethics, Crime and Punishment

The Duke, in order to sustain the process against Angelo, puts Mariana on trial, with Angelo and Escalus as judges, and in order to pursue the accusations against Angelo, re-adopts the friar's role:

> Angelo, on whom the duke is now cunningly at work, is first allowed – or lured, to judge his own case, for to make a rigorous application of one's own precepts to one's own practices is conducive both to knowledge of oneself and mercy towards others – two lessons which the duke is determined to teach. (Vyvyan p. 83).

Story Section 22 (V. i. 277-354)

The Duke, again disguised as the Friar Lodowick, re-enters with Isabella and accuses Angelo of villainy. He is reprimanded by Escalus for this and Lucio denounces him, pushing off his hood, accidentally revealing his true identity.

Alchemy

The cleric and lay roles of the Duke as alchemist are fused. This emphasises the spiritual/psychological aspect of alchemy, which aims to transmute the psyche of the alchemist. The syncretic nature of arcana such as alchemy and Christianity is also indicated.

Morality, Ethics, Crime and Punishment
When Angelo realises that the Duke and Friar Lodowick are one, he realises that his guilt is exposed.

Story Section 23 (V. i. 355-377)
The Duke now resumes authority in his own guise. Angelo, who now knows that all his actions have been observed by the Duke as Friar Lodowick, confesses guilt and begs execution. The Duke orders him to marry Mariana to safeguard her reputation. This is done offstage by Friar Peter.

Alchemy
The Duke completes the purging of Angelo and creates the **Rubedo** stage in Angelo's alchemic transformation when, in his marriage to Mariana, the body and soul of the process are united.

Morality, Ethics, Crime and Punishment
Angelo, when his guilt is revealed, commits himself according to his own code of ethics: 'I crave death more willingly than mercy; | Tis my deserving, and I do entreat it' (V. i. 474-475).

Story Section 24 (V. i. 378-397)
The Duke now turns to Isabella and places himself at her service, as he was as her friar. He sees that she cannot understand why he seemed not to save Claudio. He claims to have been overtaken by the speed of the event.

Alchemy
The Duke initiates the union of himself with Isabella, the body and soul at the core of Vienna's alchemic transformation.

Morality, Ethics, Crime and Punishment
The Duke opens the way for the love between him and Isabella which will complete his own and Vienna's redemption.

Story Section 25 (V. i. 398-414)
When the now-married Angelo enters with Mariana, the Duke claims that Isabella must claim his life in revenge for Claudio's, and he condemns him to death.

Alchemy
The Duke sets the ultimate purging of Isabella. If she has been truly purged as the 'body', she will not agree to the death of Angelo.

Morality, Ethics, Crime and Punishment
The Duke throws Isabella another challenge. By passing the death sentence on Angelo, he is testing her ability to forgive and be merciful. He also puts Angelo through his shock therapy of facing a person who needs improvement with the prospect of their death. With this device, he intends to improve their way of life: 'Be absolute for death; either death or life | Shall thereby be the sweeter' (III. i. 5, 6).

Story Section 26 (V. i. 415-440)
Mariana protests against the death sentence imposed upon her new husband, Angelo. She begs Isabella to plead with her to save Angelo's life.

Alchemy
Mariana, as the alchemist's assistant, creates the situation which will complete Isabella's alchemic transformation in her pleading for Angelo's life.

Morality, Ethics, Crime and Punishment
The role model, Mariana, reacts in the way the Duke knew she would and creates the climax of the play – the request to Isabella to plead for Angelo's life:

> Shakespeare has placed Isabella morally in the dock beside Angelo; and now, although she does not suspect it, she is on trial with him. Angelo is her enemy. If she forgives him and intercedes for him, she will be saved; and the Duke will offer her his love (Vyvyan p.85).

Story Section 27 (V. i. 441-454)
Isabella kneels and pleads for mercy for Angelo, but the Duke pretends to ignore the pleas of both Isabella and Mariana.

Alchemy
Isabella demonstrates that the purged and tried 'body' is ready to be united

with the 'soul', but the impediment of Claudio's supposed death must be removed for that to occur.
Morality, Ethics, Crime and Punishment
Isabella is redeemed by her plea for mercy for Angelo. She is psychologically whole. But in order for her to be rewarded with love, the illusion of Claudio's death which has been sustained to achieve that condition must be destroyed.

Story Section 28 (V. i. 455-487)
In response to a query from the Duke regarding the prisoner Barnardine, he is led in with the muffled Claudio. Barnardine is pardoned on condition that the Duke's mercy makes him a better man. Claudio is revealed to be alive.

Alchemy
Two impediments are removed: Barnardine's reform is undertaken and Claudio, alive, is revealed, transformed and ready for the stage of **Rubedo** in his marriage with Juliet.
Morality, Ethics, Crime and Punishment
Now no illusion lies between Isabella and the destiny chosen for her by the Duke as Duchess of Vienna.

Story Section 29 (V. i. 488-491)
The final barrier between them removed in the revelation of Claudio's escape from death, the Duke proposes marriage to Isabella, who, although she does not speak an acceptance of the proposal, is assumed to agree to their betrothal, as the Duke then acknowledges Claudio as his brother.

Alchemy
The Duke, the alchemic soul of Vienna, and Isabella, the purified body, are joined in a betrothal, the **Rubedo** of their alchemic transformation and that of the government of Vienna. In embracing Claudio as brother, the Duke links government to the people.
Morality, Ethics, Crime and Punishment
The Duke, now more fit to rule Vienna himself having undertaken its and his own moral repair by a very unusual route, gains a consort fit to reign with him.

CHAPTER TWENTY

Story Section 30 (V. i. 492-496)
Angelo, now safe from the charge of Claudio's murder, is released and enjoined to love his new wife, Mariana.

Alchemy
Angelo, freed from the guilt of having Claudio executed and now joined to Mariana, is also part of the alchemically transformed Vienna.
Morality, Ethics, Crime and Punishment

> 'To Angelo he displays the power of creative mercy, which it was the purpose of the play to reveal: "Joy to you, Mariana, love her Angelo." We are let to suppose that Angelo does; and that, because he does, his lifeless virtues become forth-going powers' (Vyvyan p. 86).

Story Section 31 (V. i. 497-522)
For Lucio's slander of him, the Duke first pretends to condemn Lucio to be whipped and hanged. But the Duke forgives him the crimes against himself, causing him, however, to make reparation of his wrongs against Kate Keepdown, and he is ordered to marry her.

Alchemy
The unregenerate Lucio, part of the people of Vienna, is briefly purged. His marriage to Kate Keepdown marks the **Rubedo** of his transformation. Given his resentment at having been compelled to marry the wronged mother of his child, it is doubtful whether his alchemic transformation will ever achieve 'gold'.
Morality, Ethics, Crime and Punishment
The Duke demonstrates his own charity in his forgiving Lucio the calumny against himself, and he shows his sense of social justice in forcing Lucio to make reparation to the wronged Kate Keepdown.

Story Section 32 (V. i. 523-534)
The Duke commands Claudio to marry Juliet, wishes Angelo and Mariana joy, praises Escalus and confirms the coming marriage with Isabella.

Alchemy

The alchemic transformation will be sealed with Claudio's projected marriage to Juliet. This gives us a total of four couples in the story and thus it can be said that 'the circle is squared' (a metaphorical term for alchemic transformation, see above p. 203).

Morality, Ethics, Crime and Punishment

With another social reparation effected in Claudio and Juliet's projected marriage and praise for those like Escalus and the Provost who have demonstrated constant integrity, the Duke is ready for a triumphant entry into Vienna with a programme of social reform exemplified in his treatment of Isabella, Juliet, Claudio, Angelo, Barnardine and Lucio, especially in his prescription of mercy instead of vengeance.

Story Section 33 (V. i. 535-536)

All prepare to re-enter Vienna and the Duke's palace.

Alchemy

The 'gold' of alchemy, the Philosophers' Stone, is achieved for Vienna as the symbolically regenerated couples enter its gates. The magically significant number thirty three into which the incidents in the story fall indicates the play's magical content.

Morality, Ethics, Crime and Punishment

Like all good leaders, employers, teachers and psychiatrists, the Duke caps successful achievement with reward and celebration.

Rites of Initiation and Theurgy: Post Production

I regard the prison in which most of the action takes place as a metaphor for the labyrinth of initiation. In taking on the role of Friar Lodowick, the Duke is enabled to function as a hierophant there, guiding the initiates Isabella, Claudio and Juliet through their trials to emerge improved and ready to give the benefit of their experiences to others. Each is faced with trials which they must overcome in order to progress through and out of the labyrinth, and each suffers contact with simulated death in the threatened executions of Claudio and Angelo. The deity with which they are allowed to have contact, having survived their trials, is the principle of love and mercy. In a Christian interpretation of the play, this would be Jesus Christ as portrayed in the New Testament.

Angelo himself functions in the play as a kind of initiate, guided by the Duke. However, his trials take place mostly outside the prison and are located within the labyrinth of his mind. He is older than the young initiates and his progress to a redeemed person follows the course of theurgy, practised by mature adults. His trials, the temptations to violate Isabella, break promise with her and authorise the execution of her brother, are self-imposed, although he attributes them to Hell. The Duke rescues him from committing these sins, although he pretends to impose the death sentence on him so that its experience will enlighten both him and Isabella. His goddess, a symbol of selfless love, is Mariana, and through her he graduates within a successful path of theurgy to a changed life and a reformed part of Vienna's government.

Cabala: Post production

At the beginning of the play Isabella is about to renounce the material world of **Malkuth** in her entry as a novice into a nunnery. Events take her out from there in an attempt to rescue her brother, but she demonstrates in her lack of charity to Claudio a lack of the feelings of **Netzach** and a prevalence of the thoughts of **Hod** in her fixed life-denying principles. The trauma of her predicament in denying her brother his life at the expense of her loss of virginity to Angelo and her subsequent belief that Angelo has not kept his promise and had Claudio executed must have plunged her into the traumas of **Yesod**. This confusion would only have increased if she 'changed eyes' with the Duke, falling in love with him at III. i. 152, or at III. i. 179 disguised as Friar Lodowick, but this feeling would have begun her progress towards **Netzach**. Presented with Mariana as a model of lasting love, her progress towards **Netzach** is increased. She is able to clear her feelings of revenge towards Angelo, harbouring in **Yesod**, when she joins Mariana in pleading for his life and she demonstrates the qualities of **Chesed (mercy)**, but trauma regarding her brother remains until he appears before her alive and well. Only then is she freed from **Yesod**, knowing that her 'changing eyes' was with the Duke and not with a friar. She realises that her path in life must not be in a nunnery but at the side of the Duke, with whom she can fully ascend the Cabalistic Tree of Life to Divinity in **Kether**.

Angelo begins the play in **Malkuth** with the reputation of dwelling entirely on **Hod**, devoid of the feelings of **Netzach**. However, to his surprise, this changes when he acquires lustful yearnings for Isabella. These feelings he attributes to Hell, and he develops deep feelings of guilt which will fix him in the traumas of his subconscious in **Yesod** until he learns that he has not violated Isabella or killed Claudio at the end of the play. His love-making with Mariana, who becomes his wife and, in spite of his mistreatment of her, begs the Duke to save his life, I interpret as changing his life direction and his future to one that can ascend the Tree, hopefully avoiding the **severity of Geburah**, which has characterised his previous behaviour.

Claudio and Juliet are well-grounded in **Malkuth** in their carnality but not in the restraint they should have exercised in their relationship until their public marriage could be consecrated. Thus they have demonstrated that they are positioned on **Netzach** with a need to acquire the qualities of **Hod**. Their punishment for their indiscretions is extreme in being paraded shamefully through the streets, in Juliet's confinement in prison and Claudio's threatened execution. This will certainly have given them the most severe traumas, which place them on **Yesod** until the end of the play when Claudio is released and they are given permission to marry by the Duke.

The Duke himself undergoes a journey along the Tree during the course of the play. He begins in **Malkuth** as governor of Vienna, but as such confesses that his government has been weak, perhaps showing too many characteristics of **Netzach**. He demonstrates the elements of **Hod** in wisely going into role as Friar Lodowick so that he can secretly observe and guide the actions of his people left in charge, especially those of Angelo. Like any teacher, psychiatrist or leader, he learns much about the subject he is dealing with along the way. The problems he faces with Angelo's misdoings sharpen his wits on **Hod**. He pretends to be fixed on **Geburah** when he is pretending to put Isabella and Angelo through trials when he comes out of role as the Duke, but throughout the play he is the very symbol of **Chesed (mercy)**, which he promotes, with the wisdom of **Chokmah** and the understanding of **Binah**, as the principle quality which must characterise government and justice. Through the action of the play he also meets Isabella, who he recognises as his future wife, and he guides her to fill that role and take them both to **Kether (the crown of existence)**. He also shows that the guiding principle of love, residing in **Tiphareth (heart, beauty)**, must also condition human existence.

CHAPTER TWENTY ONE: *HAMLET* (REVENGE)

Hamlet was the play with which Theatre Set-Up was launched in 1976, with a mixed amateur and professional cast, and with a brilliant young Ciaran Hinds at its helm as Hamlet. In 1993, another production was mounted, benefitting from my PhD research, and with a fully professional cast, including Tony Portacio as Hamlet. It was a long season, from June 10th to September 30th 1993, playing in 41 venues in five countries, including performances in a number of cathedrals.

Hamlet has a sensational plot, verbal brilliance and a philosophical profundity, and is open to many interpretations. However, I found certain features of the play so particular to the period in which it was written (around 1601) that I set it in a style reflecting those times. Some of the key characteristics of the plot, such as the catching of the disease 'adust melancholy', as suffered by Ophelia, and being brought under the influence of the planet Saturn, as experienced by Hamlet, are so particular to Shakespeare's time that a modern interpretation can be difficult for actors to achieve.

It is very much a play that dwells on thresholds, between life and death, between sanity and insanity, and among changing states of social, ethical and political consciousness. Of importance to the plot of the play is the changing of the Old Testament 'old order' insisting on vengeance, reflected by the standards of the Old King Hamlet, to the raised consciousness of the Renaissance philosophies and New Testament principles taught at the University of Wittenberg where Hamlet, Horatio, Rosencrantz and Guildenstern are students.[1]

Requisitioning the stage properties for the play (particularly the funeral and grave items, including several skulls, and appropriate armour and dress for the ghost of Hamlet's father), a director is made very much aware that the play is a myth about death. My own definition of myth is: 'A mesocosm (as a story, event or symbol) which links the microcosm (mankind) to the cosmos (God)'.[2] It explores or defines a mystery of human existence. The myth about death is linked to that of the self-sacrifice which young Hamlet, as the true King of Denmark, understands that he must endure, as he faces up to the task given him by his father's ghost of cleansing Denmark of the corrupt Claudius.

In this sense, Hamlet knows that he is the subject of another myth, that "the true King must die" on behalf of his people.³ This purging of 'something... rotten in the state of Denmark' (I. v. 90) is achieved through an alchemical transformation in which Denmark, Hamlet and those characters in the play who surround him, and, according to Renaissance belief, the world-order, is redeemed.

Hankin discusses Hamlet's state of mind as an example of 'the melancholic man':⁴

> Whatever Hamlet's temperament may have been in former years, he is melancholy throughout the course of the play and, for dramatic purposes, exemplifies the melancholy man. (p. 139)

The Elizabethans of Shakespeare's day believed that any state of mind or mood was conditioned by the presence of humours, blood, phlegm, choler and melancholy, which were ever-changing in the body. Hankin explains that a person is melancholy because of a presence of black bile in the body, and reasons that Hamlet has become melancholy because of events in his life. This has caused the humours in his body to become unbalanced in favour of melancholy.

However, I believe that in *Hamlet* Shakespeare shows a perception of human nature beyond the limitations of theories of his time concerning people's mental health. In *Macbeth* and *Hamlet* at least, I think that Shakespeare presents in his characters symptoms of psychological illness which he may have observed. My opinion in this was conditioned by my experience while teaching drama, including plays by Shakespeare, to an evening class of adults in a local college. During that time, there were two students whose professional day job involved working with mentally ill people. They both expressed astonishment at Shakespeare's accurate portrayal of the symptoms of mental illness in certain scenes of *Macbeth*. One of these students diagnosed Macbeth as suffering from paranoid schizophrenia and Lady Macbeth in V.i. as demonstrating the symptoms of OCD (obsessive-compulsive disorder).

In *Hamlet* for example, Shakespeare demonstrates an understanding of psychological complexities faced by people placed in situations in which self-contradictory actions are expected of them or imposed on them. This dichotomy results in what is nowadays referred to as a mentally paralysing double bind, in which it is impossible to enact one action as it is contradicted by the demands of another. Hamlet, Ophelia, Gertrude, Claudius, Rosencrantz, Guildenstern and Laertes all experience this psychological malady.

One question which can be considered to be an anomaly raised by Shakespeare's intentions in the play concerns Hamlet's sanity. Hamlet assumes a cloak of madness in order to disguise the task given him by his father's ghost of killing Claudius, but does Shakespeare make that mental instability a reality? The answer to that question involves the consideration of what is now termed 'transference', the symptoms of which Shakespeare describes in this play, and which can become an illness. In this condition, the patient transfers characteristics, and particularly transgressions, from one person to another. Hamlet indicates this disturbance of his mind by the sleep-walking reported in II. i. by Ophelia to her father. Clearly Hamlet has transferred the horror of Gertrude's disloyalty to his father upon Ophelia, compounded by her rejection of his courtship at a time when he most needs support from her. It torments his mind so that he enacts it in his sleep-walking, assuming himself the role of his father's ghost. His instability occurs again when he abuses Ophelia in III. i. and, ultimately, at her funeral when he attacks Ophelia's brother in her grave. Hamlet himself acknowledges this temporary madness in the latter scene in his apology to Laertes, 'His madness is poor Hamlet's enemy' (V. ii. 235). I find that the answer to the question of Hamlet's sanity is not answered by any of the arcana, but by Shakespeare's keen observation of human nature. So many pressures are imposed upon the young Hamlet:

- The unexpected death of his father and the incestuous marriage of his mother to his uncle, who has taken the throne which should have been Hamlet's by inheritance.
- The terrifying appearance of his father's ghost and its description of the horrors of the afterlife.
- The revelations that the ghost makes to him of his murder by his brother, which has made it possible for Claudius to become King of Denmark and husband of Queen Gertrude.

- The task the ghost gives him to kill his uncle but not to trouble his mother.
- Ophelia's rejection of his love.
- His knowledge that as the true king he should rid Denmark of Claudius, and his instinct that such an action would instigate his own death, for which, as a young man, he is not ready.
- His mother's request that he should not resume his studies at Wittenberg but remain at Elsinore.
- His accidental killing of Polonius.
- His betrayal by Rosencrantz and Guildenstern.
- His accidental discovery of Ophelia's suicide at her funeral.

It is not surprising that at times Shakespeare portrays Hamlet as losing control of his mind.

Although the terms 'double-bind' and 'transference' were not known to Shakespeare, I think that he had observed the symptoms of these mental conditions and portrayed them in the play. I therefore honour his keen observation by giving them their modern names in discussing their presence in the scenes in which they occur.

The question of Hamlet's procrastinating behaviour, delaying the killing of Claudius until his own death is imminent at the end of the play can, however, be partially explained by one of the arcana, the process of alchemy in the play. Often the real subject of the play, the state of Denmark, can be overlooked, as the compelling character of Hamlet himself takes centre stage. In the alchemic reading of the play, Hamlet must act as the protagonist of the alchemy through all its consecutive stages in order to achieve the goal of alchemy, the Philosophers' Stone, a transmuted and redeemed Denmark.

Honouring this reading of the play by placing a central importance on the country which Hamlet must cleanse of its criminal King Claudius gives another interpretation in which the different characters represent separate facets of the same personality (a metaphor for the country of Denmark), and the plot charts the narrative of their psyches.[5] The integration into a single 'personality' represents Denmark made whole. In addition, aspects of changing social and political trends are emphasised in the play, highlighted by events which affect the characters and plot and ultimately put right a corrupted Denmark.

I found that the play could be divided into 12 story sections, each with six different levels of meaning; **The Psyche**, **Integration of the personality – a metaphor for Denmark**, **Politics and Society**, **Alchemy**, **The Myth 'The True King Must Die'**, and **The Play as a Myth of Death**.

Story Section 1 (I. i.)
The ghost of the dead King of Denmark appears to watchers, including Hamlet's friend Horatio, on the battlements of Elsinore Castle.

The Psyche
The part of the psyche that lives after death appears.

Integration of the personality, a metaphor for Denmark
The ghost is the untimely and wrongly disembodied spirit, perturbed and seeking retribution for his murder and the restitution of the state of Denmark, represented by the characters, Claudius, Gertrude, Polonius, Laertes, Ophelia, Rosencrantz, Guildenstern and Fortinbras, who make up the 'whole person' of the country.

Politics and society
The rightful King of Denmark appears armed from beyond the grave to initiate forces that will cleanse his usurped kingdom. We learn from Horatio, speaking to Marcellus, about the dead king's style of kingship, drawing on old-fashioned codes of conduct in having accepted a personal challenge to fight the King of Norway, whom he then killed in combat, and, as a result, taking land now disputed by Prince Fortinbras of Norway.

Alchemy
Calcination: Old Hamlet, the true 'king' or 'self', declares himself, although a spirit, ready to initiate the alchemic process that will transform Denmark. He represents the 'sophic sulphur', which in this stage has been combined with the 'sophic mercury' (Gertrude) to produce a 'new generation' of substances (young Hamlet) that will effect the process.

CHAPTER TWENTY ONE

The Myth 'The True King Must Die'
The Other-World engages with Denmark through the spirit of its murdered true king.
The play as a Myth of Death
A spirit visits from the world of death.

Story Section 2 (I. ii.)
Claudius, brother to the dead King and now King of Denmark, reveals to the court his plan to avoid war with Norway by strategic negotiation. He announces his marriage to his brother's wife, Queen Gertrude, who joins him in requesting her son, Prince Hamlet, still in deep mourning for his father's death, to throw off his melancholy and not to return to his studies at Wittenberg. Laertes, son of the counsellor Polonius, is granted leave to return to France.

Alone, Hamlet reveals the depth of his unhappiness and his disgust at his mother's incestuous and hasty marriage to her husband's brother, which makes him feel contaminated, wishing for death, 'O that this too sullied flesh would melt'(I. i. 129). He claims that he would kill himself but his religion forbids it. It is a wonder to him that Gertrude should marry Claudius, who to him seems like a satyr compared with his Hyperion-like father, who was exemplary in his love and protection of Gertrude, who in turn, 'would hang on him | As if increase of appetite had grown | By what it fed on' (I. i. 143-145). He comments that ill will come of this marriage.

Hamlet's friend, Horatio, tells him of the appearance of the late King's ghost on the battlements. They plan for Hamlet to try to communicate with the ghost that evening.

The Psyche
Gertrude puts Hamlet's emotions into a double bind of conflicting stresses. On one hand, she has betrayed the love of Hamlet and his father by marrying Claudius; on the other, she asks Hamlet to prove his love for her by not returning to Wittenberg. The depth of melancholy into which his situation at court has plunged him is indicated in his first soliloquy, in which he states that disillusionment has soured his whole life.

Elizabethans believed that if a person became truly melancholic, it could draw them into the influence of the planet Saturn and change their nature. An example of Shakespeare's use of this belief in the influence of Saturn on character is in Titus Andronicus, II. iii 30-31, in which Aaron contrasts Tamora's amorous nature with his own, 'Madam, though Venus govern your desires, | Saturn is dominator over mine'. However, a benefit of this Saturnine influence could be a development of powers of augury which Hamlet later manifests in his premonition that the duel with Laertes will prove fatal to him. He informs Horatio of this, 'Thou wouldst not think how ill all's here about my heart; but it is no matter' (V. ii. 208-209). When Horatio advises him to avoid the duel, Hamlet replies, 'Not a whit. We defy augury' (V. ii. 215).

Integration of the personality, a metaphor for Denmark

Hamlet is one aspect of the young psyche representing Denmark, while Claudius and Gertrude represent the mature aspect. Horatio is the stable element of the young personality, constant and reliable. Polonius represents the element corrupted and made foolish by senility.

Politics and society

In contrast to his brother, who killed the King of Norway in single combat, thereby creating problems between Denmark and Norway, Claudius shows himself to be an astute politician in avoiding war with Norway by strategic negotiation.

In a different sphere of society, Hamlet can be identified as a new age philosopher, following ideas from the Renaissance and the New Testament which he learnt as a student at Wittenberg University, which was at the forefront of breaking from medieval traditions at the time of Shakespeare.[6]

The transition which Shakespeare demonstrates from the Old Testament code of revenge to the New Testament precepts of mercy and forgiveness, as displayed by contrasting the Old Testament ethics of Hamlet's father in *Hamlet* with the New Testament codes in *Measure for Measure*, is commented on by John Vyvyan. In *The Shakespearean Ethic*, he states, 'the ethics of the Old Testament must be repudiated before it is possible to live by those of the New' (p.93). Young Hamlet's reluctance to carry out his father's command to kill Claudius could be explained by his adherence to the New Testament teaching.

Alchemy
Dissolution (a breaking-down stage): The false king (the term 'king' in alchemy being a metaphor for the self) is seen with the usurped Kingdom and its 'soul symbol', Gertrude. In alchemy, the 'base matter' to be worked on (in this play, Denmark) was separated into 'body' (the substance to be refined and transformed) and 'soul' (in the chemical process, a vapour which 'ascended' into the top of the alembic vessel), to be later combined with the base matter at the end of the process. In its metaphorical form in a play, a woman was the soul of a man if he was to be put through the trials of the body. Four agents of the alchemic process that will regenerate Denmark are presented – Hamlet, Laertes, Horatio, and, later, Fortinbras.

The Myth 'The True King Must Die'
Hamlet is identified as the son of the true King and thus the real King of Denmark. It is he who must act to save Denmark from corruption, although he risks death, and would probably prefer to ignore this and return to his student life in Wittenberg.

The play as a Myth of Death
In his first soliloquy, Hamlet wishes to die and become spirit by the natural dissolving of his flesh, or by a Heavenly dispensation that would allow him to commit suicide. Disillusionment with life makes death desirable.

<u>Story Section 3</u> (I. iii.)
Laertes takes leave for France and cautions his sister, Ophelia, that she should not take Hamlet's protested love for her seriously, as he will be obliged to make a more politically advantageous marriage on behalf of Denmark. Her father, Polonius, not only agrees with this but forbids her to accept Hamlet's courtship.

The Psyche
Ophelia is put in a double bind of loyalties between her loyalty to her family and to her lover, Hamlet.

Integration of the personality, a metaphor for Denmark
Laertes, a young man of action, is misguided in his opinion that Hamlet's

love to Ophelia is not sincere. He is a part of the metaphor of the integrated personality of Denmark. Ophelia is wrongfully advised by her family into separating from Hamlet.

Politics and society

Hamlet and Ophelia are seen as political pawns, considered not free to follow their natural love for one another. Laertes refers to the marriage of royalty for political expedience, 'His greatness weigh'd, his will is not his own | For he himself is subject to his birth' (I. iii. 17-18). The assumption made by Polonius and Laertes that Ophelia will not be considered a politically and socially suitable wife for Hamlet is in fact false, which Gertrude makes clear at Ophelia's grave when she says, 'I hop'd thou shouldst have been my Hamlet's wife' (V. i. 236), but it destroys the couple's happiness.

Alchemy

Seperation (Ripley's spelling): As Hamlet is a protagonist of the alchemy on behalf of Denmark and thus the body of an alchemical process, Ophelia represents the corresponding soul to his body. Her family separates her from him, and he enters the trials which he will undergo to effect the alchemical transformation of Denmark.

The Myth 'The True King Must Die'

The would-be consort, Ophelia, of the real King (Young Hamlet) is separated from him, and he is thus weakened without her support in the ordeals to come.

The play as a Myth of Death

Hamlet's links with earthly life are further loosened in the distancing of his love, Ophelia, from him.

Story Section 4 (I. iv. v.)

The ghost appears again on the battlements and tells Hamlet that he was murdered by his brother, Claudius, who poured poison into his ear as he was sleeping in his orchard. Because he did not receive the last rites absolving him of past sins, Old Hamlet is tormented in Purgatory. He charges Hamlet to revenge this act and to cleanse Denmark of the stain of regicide and fratricide by killing Claudius. He criticises Gertrude's incestuous marriage to Claudius, but cautions Hamlet to leave her punishment to Heaven.

CHAPTER TWENTY ONE

Hamlet resolves to feign madness as a cover for any action he will take against King Claudius. He enjoins his companions to secrecy.

The Psyche
Hamlet's father's ghost puts him in several double binds. He commands Hamlet, a person of philosophic frame of mind, to commit the primitive and violent act of killing his King, who is also his uncle, but not to let it taint his mind. He also criticises Gertrude, but instructs Hamlet not to reprimand her. It is not surprising that Hamlet decides to assume madness as a cover. It will, however, allow his psyche expansion in the licence it will give his behaviour.

Integration of the personality, a metaphor for Denmark
The spirit of Denmark, its murdered King, representing legitimate kingship, seeks integration with his past Kingdom through the envisioned action of his son.

Politics and society
Hamlet's father calls on him to honour the old-fashioned code of taking violent revenge on behalf of wronged family. This will contradict the new-age thinking against the taking of reprisals that young Hamlet has been learning in the texts of the New Testament.

Alchemy
More alchemic **Seperation** occurs as Hamlet is isolated from those about him by the horror of the murder told him by his father's ghost and the violent revenge for it that he is commanded to perform (although he subsequently confides this information to Horatio). He is further separated from his mother and from Ophelia by associating his lover with a woman disloyal to him, as his mother was disloyal to his father's memory. The command that he should kill Claudius not only separates him from the court, but divides his conscience.

The base matter, often referred to as a serpent, is in this scene identified by the ghost as Claudius: 'The serpent that did sting thy father's life | Now wears his crown' (I. v. 39-40). It is the ghost's wish that Hamlet should become the protagonist that should work on this base matter. However Hamlet himself, in spite of his seeming enthusiasm to enact the command of the ghost, 'And thy commandment all alone shall live |

Within the book and volume of my brain' (I. v. 102-103), is not yet ready to act, and must undergo transformations himself in order to become the agent of transmutation. All stages of alchemy must be enacted before its aim is achieved. The work of alchemy was often referred to as 'the tasks of Hercules', and Hamlet has commented in his first soliloquy that he is unlike this hero (I. ii. 153).

The Myth 'The True King Must Die'
Hamlet is given his kingly task – he must rid the country of the usurper, at whatever cost to himself. He does not relish the task: 'O cursed spite, | That ever I was born to set it right' (I. iv. 196-197).

The play as a Myth of Death
A grim picture of Purgatory in the world of death is presented by the ghost of Hamlet's father. This hardly gives Hamlet encouragement to risk the same fate by killing Claudius.

Story Section 5 (II. i.)
Ophelia reports to Polonius that she has been frightened by Hamlet's appearance in her room, sleep-walking, partially-dressed, pale, one hand held over his brow, gripping her wrist, shaking her arm, gazing at her, nodding his head up and down three times and then sightlessly leaving her. Polonius attributes this disturbed behaviour to her rejection of his love.

The Psyche
The extent to which Hamlet's psyche is disturbed is shown in this scene, in which he is transferring the situation between his dead father's ghost and his mother onto himself and Ophelia. He enacts the ghost (the hand over his brow mimes the ghost's raised beaver on his helmet), and as Ophelia describes him, he is ghost-like, 'Pale as his shirt, his knees knocking each other, […] | As if he had been loosed out of Hell' (II. i. 81-84).

Integration of the personality, a metaphor for Denmark
Hamlet, traumatised by the horror of his father's ghost's appearance and its revelations, is suffering from dissociation from Ophelia, his soulmate. In this scene, the personality of Denmark becomes disintegrated.

Politics and society
The effects of trauma from politically-motivated violence (as in the murder

of his brother by Claudius), political misinterpretation of circumstances and interference in people's lives (as in the instructions given to Ophelia by Polonius that she must reject Hamlet's love because he would not be allowed to marry her) are seen in Hamlet's disturbed mind.

Alchemy
Coniunctio: In a mock alchemical wedding of soul with body, Hamlet enters Ophelia's closet, but not for the act of love, instead to re-enact the horror of his mother's faithlessness to his father, which he projects onto the situation between himself and Ophelia.

The Myth 'The True King Must Die'
In his disturbed mind, Hamlet's subconscious lives out his concern that his nature is not suited to the task given him of killing Claudius. He has already expressed this reservation in I. v. 196-197.

The play as a Myth of Death
Hamlet's subconscious relives the terror of his meeting with his father's ghost and its revelations of the horrors of the afterlife.

Story Section 6 (II. ii.)
Polonius tells the King and Queen that the cause of Hamlet's strange behaviour is Ophelia's rejection of his love for her. Hamlet mocks Polonius, who confronts him while he is walking and reading in the court. During this confrontation, Hamlet expresses an unwillingness to die.

The King and Queen have summoned to court Hamlet's fellow students, Rosencrantz and Guildenstern, supposedly to cheer him up, but in reality to spy on the cause of his generally strange behaviour. The students have arranged for a band of strolling players to perform at court to divert Hamlet, who asks one of them to perform a scene from the ancient story of the Trojan War. The actor performs this with such empathy that there are tears in his eyes. Hamlet then asks the actors to present a play whose story mirrors the murder of his father. He wishes to test the guilt of the King and the credibility of the ghost. He soliloquises that his lack of resolve in carrying out his father's command to kill Claudius contrasts, to his shame, with the genuine emotion expressed by the actor in his sympathy for a legendary person.

The Psyche
Rosencrantz and Guildenstern are put in a double bind by the King and Queen, who encourage them to spy on their friend. Hamlet confesses to them the depth of his depression.

Integration of the personality, a metaphor for Denmark
Rosencrantz and Guildenstern are other aspects of the personality which is Denmark. They represent the aspect of a person which easily yields to becoming sycophantic.

Politics and society
Political abuse of power is shown in the manipulation of Rosencrantz and Guildenstern by the King and Queen, making them pawns in the power-struggle between Claudius and Hamlet and forcing them to choose between their loyalty to the throne and to their friend.

Alchemy
Rosencrantz (wreath of roses), and Guildenstern (golden star), whose names suggest the 'Rosy Cross' of Rosicrucianism, a philosophy associated with alchemy and the 'gold' goal of alchemy, bring the players, whose interlude will bring about the breaking-down stage of **Putrefaction** in the King, and, by association, in Denmark.[7]

The Myth 'The True King Must Die'
The advent of the Players strengthens Hamlet in his role of ridding Denmark of Claudius, but as he has said to Polonius, he is not yet ready to die.

The play as a Myth of Death
Hamlet seeks to clarify his doubts about the honesty and reality of the ghost by testing the guilt of Claudius in the presentation of a play which reflects the story of his murder of Hamlet's father.

Story Section 7 (III. i.)
Hamlet soliloquises his wish to die by killing himself, but cannot do so for fear of the afterlife.

To test if the cause of Hamlet's mad behaviour is the rejected love of Ophelia, Polonius and Claudius spy on Hamlet as Ophelia returns love tokens to him. He rages abusively at her. Alarmed by the threatening comments Hamlet has made about his own life, Claudius resolves to send him away from Denmark to England.

CHAPTER TWENTY ONE

The Psyche

In debating his possible suicide, Hamlet dwells on his mental conflict: the wish for death but the fear of what may follow; the wish to carry out the task given him by his father's ghost yet an inability to act, fudged by 'the pale cast of thought' (III. i. 85).

It is reasonable that Ophelia should think, in his intemperate raging at her, that he has lost his mind. The intensity of his insults reveals the extent to which he has transferred onto her the failings of his mother. In *The Shakespearean Ethic*, John Vyvyan observes, 'Ophelia is lost in Hamlet's self-destruction' (p.87). Vyvyan also comments that Hamlet's coarse speeches to Ophelia foretell Hamlet's tragic outcome, as 'degradation of Love is one of Shakespeare's regular indications that a soul is moving towards the tragic act' (p.112).

Integration of the personality, a metaphor for Denmark

Ophelia, as the soul-mate and possible consort of Hamlet, the true King of Denmark, is separated from him by his abuse of her. She represents a powerless element of the psyche, unable to act independently and ultimately destroyed by others.

Politics and society

Ophelia is abused by Hamlet, by her father and by the King in the rejection of Hamlet which she is forced into carrying out. As a woman of Shakespeare's time, she does not have the social or political right to act other than as she is instructed by her elders and social superiors. This is something that Hamlet does not seem to understand, and he despises her for not behaving according to her convictions.

The effect of the bad counsel Polonius gives her is worsened by his continuing an action he knows to be based on false premises in order to demonstrate a pet theory (i.e. by forcing Ophelia to return his love tokens when he has already decided that the cause of Hamlet's madness is rejected love).

Hamlet threatens Claudius and Polonius who are spying on him: for Polonius, 'Let the doors be shut upon him, that he may play the fool nowhere but in's own house' (III. i. 133-134); and for Claudius, 'Those that are married already – all but one – shall live' (III. i. 149-10).

Alchemy

In this scene, Hamlet also reveals his dangerous intentions towards his uncle. On behalf of Denmark Hamlet has begun a state of alchemic **Putrefaction** (a stage of violent disintegration).

The Myth 'The True King Must Die'
In his soliloquy, Hamlet demonstrates that he is unready to die should he risk his life by killing Claudius. He is un-kinglike in his discourteous and violent behaviour towards Ophelia.

The play as a Myth of Death
Hamlet again contemplates suicide, but this time with the reservations about the horrors of the afterlife given to him by his father's spirit.

Story Section 8 (III. ii., iii., iv., IV. i., ii.)

The reaction of Claudius to the Players' performance of the play which Hamlet calls 'The Mousetrap' (III. ii. 232), and has been adapted by him to include scenes that imitate the murder of Hamlet's father by Claudius, proves the King's guilt, and also reveals to him that Hamlet knows about his crimes of fratricide and regicide. Hamlet, coming upon Claudius unguarded as he is praying to Heaven to free his guilty soul, goes to kill him, but decides that that would only despatch his soul to Heaven and it would be better to kill him when his behaviour is such that his soul will go to Hell.

Offended at The Mousetrap's criticism of second marriage and the seeming distress caused by this to Claudius, Gertrude summons her son to reprimand him and Polonius hides behind an arras in order to spy upon the scene and support Gertrude in her resolve to take Hamlet to task. Alarmed by Hamlet's aggressive manner to her, she cries out, the concealed Polonius responds, and Hamlet kills him through the curtain in the belief that it is Claudius. Hamlet tells the distressed Gertrude that this killing cannot rank with the fratricide committed against his father by Claudius. He reprimands her for her incestuous marriage, and his father's ghost appears to Hamlet (although not visible to Gertrude) to intercede on her behalf. She repents her behaviour. Hamlet is not punished for the murder of Polonius due to the 'diminished responsibility' of his declared madness and his privileged status as a prince.

The Psyche
The virtuous side of the psyche of Claudius is revealed; he has a conscience.

His sin in killing his brother, usurping his throne and marrying his wife evidently lies heavily upon him and is spoiling his enjoyment of the fruits of his actions. He is also honest in that he freely admits that in order to be freed of his guilt and to merit Heaven's salvation he must give up the benefits he has attained from his sin. However, he cannot bring himself to do this, so is caught himself in a double bind between his need for salvation and his ambition.

It is ironic that Claudius does not believe that his prayers have been effective, yet they have stayed the hand of Hamlet from killing him. Also ironic is Hamlet's assumption that Claudius is, in his prayers, in a state of grace, though Claudius claims that his attempts to pray have failed, as his 'thoughts remain below | Words without thoughts never to heaven go' (III. v. 97-98).

Hamlet's ability to act (and kill) only in the heat of the moment is seen in his killing of Polonius in the belief that it is Claudius concealed behind the arras. Gertrude's consciousness of her own sin is aroused by Hamlet's words to her. She is put into a double bind between her loyalty to her husband, Claudius, and her son, Hamlet, and his father.

Integration of the personality, a metaphor for Denmark

The trial of the mature protagonists of Denmark (Gertrude and Claudius) is begun and the senile aspect (Polonius) is wiped out.

Politics and society

The Players are used as political pawns in the game between Hamlet and Claudius. The ultimate dangers of espionage are revealed when Polonius is killed while he is spying on Gertrude and Hamlet. The potential success in concealing a political murder is demonstrated by Gertrude's ignorance of her husband's murder by Claudius.

Patronage and conspiracy to conceal evidence occurs in the protection of Hamlet from the consequences of his killing of Polonius. Personal motives in wishing to retain the favours of Gertrude drive Claudius to this injustice to Polonius, just as his personal fear of Hamlet instigates his subsequent moves to have him killed.

Alchemy

The total 'Nigredo' stage of **Putrefaction** (in which, during the chemical form of alchemy, black substances were formed) is achieved: for Claudius in the exposure of his guilt; for Hamlet in his accidental killing of Polonius (see fig. 49); for Gertrude in the revelation that Claudius killed her former husband and in the comprehension of her incestuous relationship with her husband's brother that follows from the murder; and for Ophelia in the killing of her father by her lover. The raven, symbol of this stage of alchemy, is represented by Hamlet's prompt to the actor playing Lucianus, 'Begin, murderer. Leave thy damnable faces and begin. Come, the croaking raven doth bellow for revenge' (III. ii. 247-248).

The Myth 'The True King Must Die'
The guilt of Claudius is proved and thus the ghost's command is validated. Fate gives Hamlet the chance to achieve his task while Claudius seems to be praying, but Hamlet misses this opportunity and instead rashly kills Polonius, supposing him to be Claudius. His father's ghost again appears to reinforce his purpose.

The play as a Myth of Death
Hamlet has a taste of inflicting death in his killing of Polonius. In taunting Claudius, Hamlet expounds the grisly fate of bodily flesh after death and its social levelling:

> A man may fish with the worm that hath eat of a king, and eat of the fish that hath fed of that worm [...] a king may go a progress through the guts of a beggar. (IV. iii. 27-31)

Story Section 9 (IV. iii., iv.)
The killing of Polonius gives Claudius a ready excuse to despatch Hamlet to England. There he plots to have him killed, with Rosencrantz and Guildenstern carrying the instructions to that effect in a sealed document, a device which Hamlet guesses at, claiming that he can see a cherub who tells him of Claudius's intentions.

As Hamlet is about to embark for England, he sees the young Prince Fortinbras of Norway leading an army on a justified but minor mission to Poland, and he rebukes himself for his own lack of commitment to his father's command in contrast to the resolve and action of Fortinbras.

The England-bound ship carrying Hamlet is attacked by pirates, and Hamlet, joining in a swordfight against them, boards their vessel, having taken action against Rosencrantz and Guildenstern. He negotiates a deal with the pirates for his return to Denmark.

The Psyche
Hamlet demonstrates his Saturnine power of augury in understanding the evil intent of Claudius in sending him to England. He expresses this as a metaphor of seeing a cherub who warns him of the King's purpose.

He contrasts his lack of action against Claudius with that of Prince Fortinbras, whom he calls 'a delicate and tender prince' (IV. iv. 48) risking death in an enterprise which Hamlet commends as being a 'quarrel in a straw' (IV. iv. 55).

Integration of the personality, a metaphor for Denmark
Fortinbras, in his courage and principled behaviour, represents an admired aspect of the young people of the personality (Hamlet, Laertes, Horatio, Rosencrantz, Guildenstern and Ophelia), and he is destined to become the King of Denmark.

Politics and society
Fortinbras upholds the principle of defending a just cause with no regard to the effect or cost. Hamlet himself engages himself in political intrigue in discovering the treachery of Claudius and substituting the murder of Rosencrantz and Guildenstern for his own.

Alchemy
Often the **Putrefaction** stage of alchemy was symbolised by misadventure at sea. This occurs in the pirate attack on the ship carrying Hamlet, Rosencrantz and Guildenstern, and the action Hamlet takes to rid himself of the latter.

The Myth 'The True King Must Die'
The possibility of killing Claudius is made less likely for Hamlet by his removal to England. He sees in Fortinbras a contrast to his own procrastinating behaviour and he reproves himself in not carrying out his task. However, his subterfuge against Rosencrantz and Guildenstern and his vigorous response to the attack by the pirates shows that he is capable of action.

The play as a Myth of Death
Hamlet accepts his deserved exile to England as punishment for his killing of Polonius, but plans the deaths of Rosencrantz and Guildenstern in foiling the plan of Claudius to have him murdered. Their deaths demonstrate political executions.

Story Section 10 (IV. v., vi., vii., V. i.)

Another young man of action, Laertes, returning to seek revenge for the death of his father and offended by his curtailed funeral rites, unworthy of his station as counsellor, is further grieved to see his sister, Ophelia, her mind distracted with grief over the death of her father, wandering through the court, giving flowers to those she sees and singing bawdy songs.

Claudius, learning that Hamlet has escaped his plot to murder him in England and that he has returned to Denmark, plans with Laertes to kill him during a fencing duel with a poisoned sword and drink.

Gertrude reports that Ophelia has fallen into a brook while gathering flowers, and, still chanting songs, she has drowned. Hamlet, returned to Denmark and meeting with Horatio, sees a grave being prepared and questions the gravedigger about the rotting of bodies in their graves. The gravedigger disputes wittily with him and shows him the skull of Yorick, who had been the court jester in Hamlet's childhood.

The King, Queen, Laertes and courtiers enter the graveyard, following the coffin of a person whose 'maimed' rites show that suicide was believed to be the cause of death. Hamlet learns that the dead person is Ophelia, and, maddened with grief for her, he leaps into her grave, where he attacks the grieving Laertes.

The Psyche

Ophelia demonstrates suffering from what the Elizabethans called 'adust melancholy'.[8] Her grief has caused a black powder that formed itself in her stomach to rise to her brain and drive her to insanity. The inevitable consequence of this illness was thought to be suicide. Ironically, Ophelia's real insanity, like that which Hamlet assumed, gives her a similar licence to criticise Gertrude and Claudius. The flowers she gives them correspond to their natures. To Claudius she gives fennel (which symbolises the flattery which has won him Gertrude and the loyalty of his courtiers) and columbine (thanklessness – as Claudius, in not giving proper funeral status to Polonius, has been thankless about his life's service). She gives Gertrude rue (symbolising the sorrow of Hamlet's killing of Polonius and departure for England) and a daisy (symbolising the 'light o' love' of her marrying Claudius).

She regrets that all the violets (that represent faithfulness) withered when her father, always faithful to the throne of Denmark, was killed and not given an honourable burial. To her brother, Laertes, she gives rosemary (for remembrance) and pansies (thoughts).

At her funeral, Hamlet's mind is again overwhelmed as he leaps into her grave, claiming, 'I lov'd Ophelia. Forty thousand brothers | Could not with all their quantity of love | Make up my sum' (V. i. 264-266).

Integration of the personality, a metaphor for Denmark
Ophelia as the 'soul' of Hamlet and the hope for Denmark as its future queen, is destroyed. The personality becomes flawed in its loss of its young female element, who has died as a victim of action taken by Hamlet, another element of the personality with whom she should have been combined.

Politics and society
Ophelia is an innocent victim crushed between powerful opposites. She loses her mind and then her life. She is denied full funerary rites by the Church and even in her grave her body is the scene of conflict as two men fight over her. It is ironic that the grave-diggers believe her to be privileged because of her high social status.

Alchemy
During this alchemic stage of **Congelation** (in which white substances were formed), the 'flying spirits' are congealed like the pure white of the daisies that Ophelia names. Ophelia's spirit as the soul of the operation ascends in death while Hamlet, the body of the base matter is being purged by fire (represented by the sword fight with the pirates) and water (the return sea-voyage). Hamlet has passed this trial as he returns from the sea-voyage transformed, ready to act and die if necessary.

The Myth 'The True King Must Die'
Hamlet has returned to Denmark as the King who must die on behalf of his country, now practised in action and ready to act his allotted task.

The play as a Myth of Death
In the scene in the grave-yard, the material aspect of death and the grisly remnants of dead flesh and bone are dealt with. Death is the leveller. The ethical question of suicide is treated in the maimed rites of Ophelia.

When Laertes leaps into his sister's grave as the first spadeful of earth is flung in, he exemplifies a behavioural characteristic that sometimes occurs during a funeral when a mourner realises for the first time that the person is actually dead. The actor performing the part of Laertes in our 1976 production of *Hamlet* had experience of this when his father suffered a heart attack at his mother's graveside. I saw it myself in the funeral of a friend's step-father who had committed suicide. At the moment when the priest denied further rites due to the fact that the man had taken his own life, my friend and her mother, who had been calm up to that moment, both clung on to each other and wept loudly. I think that this response to death needs to be understood in the behaviour of both Laertes and Hamlet, as it would seem from his creation of the actions of these two mourners that Shakespeare was familiar with this phenomenon. In addition, Hamlet's reaction to the burial of Ophelia and Laertes' grief is not only shock at her death but a realisation that he loved her.

Story Section 11 (V. ii. 1-365)
Hamlet tells Horatio of his adventures at sea en route to England and his providential return to Denmark. He reveals that he substituted the order from Claudius that England should kill Hamlet, as inscribed in the documents that Rosencrantz and Guildenstern were carrying, for an instruction that they themselves should be killed.

The courtier Osric presents Hamlet with a challenge to a seemingly friendly duel with Laertes. Hamlet accepts, but tells Horatio of a premonition that ill will befall him. He fends off Horatio's advice to refuse the challenge by declaring that he is ready for his death should it occur.

During their duel, such is Hamlet's fencing skill that Laertes finds it difficult to touch him with his poisoned sword, and can only wound him by lunging at him between bouts. Seeing the wound on his body from Laertes' unprotected sword, Hamlet suspects foul play, and during the following fight he exchanges swords with Laertes and stabs him.

The Queen, toasting Hamlet's success, drinks from the poisoned cup that Claudius has prepared for Hamlet and dies. Laertes, now dying himself from his poisoned wound, declares Claudius the guilty cause. Hamlet kills Claudius with the poisoned sword and drink.

The Psyche
Hamlet's power of augury warns him of approaching death. However, his psyche has been strengthened by the ordeals he has suffered, especially of the death-experiences in killing Polonius (and ultimately Rosencrantz and Guildenstern) and enduring in the loss of Ophelia. It is, however, only after a succession of violent events including the death of his mother and Laertes (who blames Claudius for the poisoned sword and drink) and his own imminent death inflicted on him from the poison on Laertes' sword that he can kill the King.

Integration of the personality, a metaphor for Denmark
The marred aspects of the personality are removed: Rosencrantz, Guildenstern, Claudius, Gertrude and Laertes (who has plotted with Claudius to dishonourably kill Hamlet with an unbated sword).

Politics and society
Rosencrantz and Guildenstern lose their lives by becoming political pawns. Hamlet claims that they deserved their fate by enjoying their exploitation of political power: 'they did make love to this employment' (V. ii. 57). Laertes is punished for his criminal collaboration with the King. His whole family have been destroyed by Hamlet's procrastination in ridding Denmark of the corrupt Claudius. When Claudius is killed by Hamlet, he experiences the just fate of the ambitious person who kills even his own kin to achieve and keep power.

Many people have died because of Hamlet's procrastination in carrying out the task given him by his father. Firstly Polonius, then Ophelia, Rosencrantz, Guildenstern, Gertrude, Laertes and finally Hamlet himself, die needlessly. Hamlet's father's ghost told him of a crime which Hamlet concealed from general knowledge for personal reasons inherent in his nature, thereby preventing punishment of the criminal and further crimes. The danger of hesitation can be seen from the outcome of Hamlet's concealing of the criminality of Claudius.

Hamlet's fate exemplifies that of a person's freedom sublimated to their public duty through birth or inheritance. Their high social status is not enviable.

Alchemy
Cibation (a 'feeding' stage of the alchemic process) is ironically symbolised by the wine which poisons Gertrude and ultimately Claudius.

This is also an oblique reference to the Celtic tradition of Bran's cauldron, the contents of which would grant immortality to the virtuous but kill the unworthy.

The very violent stage of **Sublimation** is symbolised by the sword fight, and the killing of Claudius which achieves the stage of **Firmentation** as the base matter of the country is fixed and resolved, Hamlet's task is at last attained, and Denmark freed of its corrupt King.

The Myth 'The True King Must Die'

Hamlet has been strengthened by the events at sea and he has carried out a premeditated killing in the despatch of Rosencrantz and Guildenstern. He indicates to Horatio that at last he is ready to die:

> If it be now,'tis not to come; if it be not to come, it will be now; if it be not now, yet it will come. The readiness is all. (V. ii. 216-218)

He is at last ready to die on behalf of his country by ridding Denmark of Claudius.

The play as a Myth of Death

Death is triumphant in the last scene of the play as all the main players perish. As Fortinbras later observes:

> This quarry cries on havoc. O proud Death,
> What feast is toward in thine eternal cell,
> That thou so many princes at a shot
> So bloodily hast struck? (V. ii. 369-372)

Story Section 12 (V. ii. 365-408)

On the death of Claudius, the dying Hamlet enjoins Horatio to tell the world his true story and he nominates Prince Fortinbras of Norway his successor to the throne of Denmark. Returning from his successful campaign in Poland, Fortinbras enters the court and accepts the Kingship. He praises Hamlet and gives orders for him to receive a soldier's rites: 'For he was likely, had he been put on | To have prov'd most royal' (V. ii. 402-403).

The Psyche
Freed at last in his conscience, the poisoned Hamlet dies.
Integration of the personality, a metaphor for Denmark
Those Hamlet most admires, Horatio and Fortinbras, are the survivors in the cured and integrated metaphorical psyche of Denmark.
Politics and society
The story has an idealistic political resolution and Denmark is fortunate in its new King Fortinbras.
Alchemy
Exaltation, the Philosophers' Stone, a synonym for the gold, the goal of alchemy, is achieved when the philosopher Hamlet, having rid Denmark of Claudius, becomes the King, nominates Fortinbras as his successor and then joins Ophelia, his alchemic soul, in death.

Multiplication (the multiplying of the Philosophers' Stone) will be achieved by the rule of the good Fortinbras over the now cleansed Kingdom. The stage of **Projection** of the Philosophers' Stone will be reached in the honouring of Hamlet's body by Fortinbras and by Horatio telling the world Hamlet's true story.
The Myth 'The True King Must Die'
As Denmark's true King, Hamlet's death on behalf of his country will ensure that Denmark can look forward to a new improved era.
The play as a Myth of Death
Horatio and Fortinbras honour Hamlet in death.

Cabala: Post Production
It is impossible for Denmark, Hamlet, or any of the protagonists of the play to advance up the Cabalistic Tree Of Life until Claudius is killed, as too much trauma relating to his fratricide and regicide is held in the sphere of the unconscious **(Yesod)** which blocks progress. When Hamlet succeeds in killing Claudius, his traumas of fear of death and guilt at not carrying out his father's commands are removed and he swiftly ascends the Tree to the bliss of **Kether (the crown)** anticipated in Horatio's wish for him at his death, 'Good night, sweet prince, | And flights of angels sing thee to thy rest' (V. ii. 364-365).

CHAPTER TWENTY TWO: CONCLUSIONS

As artistic director of the plays performed by Theatre Set-Up, I found the information gained from research into the secret meanings invaluable, especially in contrast to my attempts to interpret the plays during the early seasons when I was floundering to explain anomalies in the script such as the scene described by Oliver in IV. iii. of *As You Like It*, in which Orlando rescues Oliver from a snake and a lioness. This scene and other mysterious actions in the scripts, such as Prospero's intent in *Tempest* to break and bury his staff and drown his book, were explained to me, and his relationship with Caliban clarified, when I understood the arcana that Shakespeare had encoded in the subtext of his plays.[1]

Sometimes, the arcane symbolism of characters in the plays made sense of their actions. For example, the identification of the four lovers as the elements, fire, water, air and earth constantly recombined in the turning of the wheel of alchemy in *Dream* and *Two Gentlemen* made sense to the actors and to me of the shifting loyalties of the male lovers.

An understanding of exoteric alchemy made it possible for me to produce *Winter's Tale* as requested by members of the audience, who also were pleased when my understanding of alchemy and Celtic mysticism realised performances of *Cymbeline*. Ethical issues posed by the plays, such as the cruel physical treatment of Falstaff in *Merry Wives*, the seeming bullying of Katherine by Petruchio in *Shrew* and the forcing of Shylock to become a Christian in *Merchant*, were also resolved. The thorny question of racism in the latter play was also settled to the satisfaction of actors and audiences.

The beautiful concept of Divine Love which inspires Shakespeare's treatment of the lovers in his plays made the interpretation of the love stories in the plays very clear to the actors and to me. We understood that this notion had rules of behaviour which needed to be obeyed to ensure the right outcome. That Romeo and Juliet's adherence to these rules led to their deaths is true, but in the Christian spirit of self-sacrifice for the benefit of others, which also features in the play, their deaths healed an ailing Verona. I found that this New Testament Biblical influence was prevalent in the comedies, especially in the plays in dealing with conflicts between ideas of mercy and revenge. *Measure* sets out, through Duke Vincentio acting in role as Friar Lodowick, Shakespeare's ideas on crime and punishment, with mercy the governing practice. That *Hamlet* had such a tragic outcome due to the governing principle of taking revenge urged by the old King Hamlet was obvious to the actors and to me as director.

Importantly, arcane levels were exposed in comedies such as *Comedy of Errors* and *Two Gentlemen*, usually considered to be light, even farcical, so that they could be appreciated on a deeper level. Plays such as *Twelfth Night* and *Much Ado*, which pose no problems in terms of the real world they inhabit, gained from the addition of the exposition of arcana lying in their depths.

The guiding by characters which function as hierophants to young characters in the plays undergoing the rituals of initiation was interesting. It seemed to me that when older characters, lacking the essential virtuous qualities of hierophants, influenced young characters in the plays, the consequences were dire for the young initiate. Examples of this are Parolles misleading Bertram, and Don Pedro, easily deceived by his brother, Don John, misleading Claudio. However, good hierophants such as Prospero guiding Ferdinand, Petruchio guiding Katherina, Duke Vincentio guiding Isabella, or Oberon guiding the four lovers could effectively bring young initiates through their trials to adulthood.

Sometimes, baffling language became clear, as in the songs at the end of *Love's Labour's Lost*, which present the hard tasks the King and courtiers must undertake under the banner of Mercury's alchemical demands, contrasted with the Apollonian party atmosphere the young people have enjoyed until the entrance of Marcade as Mercury, the agent of the alchemy to which the young men must be subjected. The interpretation of these songs in terms of their alchemical significance solved the riddle of the unusual ending of the play with the usual coupling of the young lovers deferred. The substance of the play has indicated that they are not yet fit to marry, and must undergo the trials of alchemical processes and the Rites of Initiation to give them the adult moral strength required by marriage.

It became obvious to me that often the course of the stage action followed the processes of the arcana. Some examples of this are:

- The different stages of alchemy exemplified in all the plays that Theatre Set-Up produced (but not beginning in *Love's Labours* until the entrance of Marcade).
- The adherence by its main protagonists to the strictures of Divine Love in *Romeo and Juliet.*
- The correct sequence of the initiatory trials experienced by Ferdinand and guided by Prospero as hierophant in *Tempest.*
- The stages of the Celtic UnderWorld journey marked by the stage action in *Cymbeline*.

I discovered that often Shakespeare achieves this outcome by the changes he makes between his play and the source material. I often found that of equal importance to an understanding of the spiritual arcana in the plays were levels of social and political meanings relevant to Shakespeare's time:

- The identification of the reference in the character of Helena and in locations mentioned in *All's Well* to the Merovingian heresy of the 'Seed of Christ', of which King James I, the patron of Shakespeare's company, was said to be an inheritor, gave an added significance to the play.
- Shakespeare's accurate presentation of the pastoral world and the problems experienced in the treatment of younger sons in *As You Like It* created a reality within which the actors were able to perform with conviction.
- In the relationship between Prospero and Caliban in *Tempest*, problems arising from the colonisation by European countries of places outside Europe were exposed and resolved.
- Political tyranny and the danger to subjects of dangerous kings feature in *Hamlet* and *Winter's Tale*.
- Problems arising from an inferior social position of women, dominated by men, often their fathers, are exposed in *Hamlet* (in the treatment of Ophelia), *Shrew*, (in the treatment of Katherina), *Dream* (in the dilemma faced by Hermia over her father's choice of husband for her), *Cymbeline* (in her treatment by her father and

her husband), *Merry Wives* (in the choice of inappropriate husbands for Anne by both her parents), in *Much Ado* (in the treatment of Hero), in *Romeo and Juliet* (in which Juliet's father tries to force her to marry Paris), and in *Two Gentlemen* (in which Sylvia's father wishes to marry her to the unsuitable Thurio). Contrasted with this is the strength of Shakespeare's women characters presented as the alchemical man/woman rebus – Julia, Portia, Viola, Rosalind and Imogen.

Shakespeare's application of the literary traditions of Plato in its modified form of Renaissance Platonism (in addition to the ideal of Divine Love mentioned above) I judged to be important in *Comedy of Errors* (which followed the story of "The Divided Soul" in the *Symposium*), and in *Antony and Cleopatra* (in the identification, also observed by Plutarch, that the course of Antony's life followed that of the Charioteer in *Phaedrus*), and this metaphor also applied to the actions of the character of Proteus in *The Two Gentlemen*.

I regretted not having researched all the plays for our productions of them in terms of the Cabala Tree of Life, which I discovered to be crucial to their interpretation when examining them in **Cabala: Post Production**. I had found how important an understanding of its significance was in *Merchant* and *Tempest*, but had not had the opportunity to apply it to other plays. When I applied the Cabala Tree of Life retrospectively to the plays we had performed, I found that the sphere of **Yesod** (the unconscious, revealing trauma) was most important in terms of the drama, preventing progress up the Tree if trauma was held in there. Thus in the comedies where trauma was less prevalent, ascent up the Tree could take place moderately easily, but in the tragedies where trauma predominates, Hamlet included, ascent could not take place (if at all) until the end of the play when the trauma could be eliminated.

It always seemed to me that stage instructions implied by the text were sometimes significant to ideas in the subtext. For example, in *Hamlet*, the implications of Hamlet associating Ophelia with Gertrude and himself with his father in II. i. are suggested by Ophelia's description of Hamlet's hand held over his brow imitating the raised beaver on his father's helmet. I consider this to be is a key stage action deliberately created by Shakespeare to indicate Hamlet's disturbed state of mind and his consequent attitude to Ophelia.[2]

Just as this detail in the stage action suggests Shakespeare's intentions regarding a relationship within the play between characters and puts down a clue to the interpretation of a protagonist, so I believe that he leaves broad hints about his intended metaphors of arcana in the language he uses.

Some examples of this for readings of **alchemy** include:

- The names of the lovers representing the four elements in *A Midsummer Night's Dream*.
- Falstaff's description of his tumble in the Thames in alchemic terms in III. v.
- Juliet's use of alchemic terms in III. ii.
- The names of King Leontes and Queen Hermione representing sophic sulphur and sophic mercury in *Winter's Tale*.
- The name of Solinus representing the function of the sun in *Comedy of Errors*.

The predominant example of a reading of **Renaissance Platonism as Divine Love** is the religious language in the meeting of Romeo and Juliet in I. v.

The most significant linguistic key to a reading of the **Cabala** is in Portia's speech (IV. i. 180-192) prescribing mercy (the Sphere of Chesed on the Masculine Pillar of the Tree of Life) in *Merchant*.

Celtic arcana are suggested in the name of Puck in *Dream*, Belarius in *Cymbeline* and the nature spirits named in V. i. 33- 40 in *Tempest*.

Rites of Initiation are identified by the names, Juno, Iris and Ceres, of the three goddesses which Prospero conjures up (which occur in the Rites of Eleusis) in a masque for the entertainment of Ferdinand and Miranda.

The **Bible's Old Testament** features in:

- The name Adam, the good old man in *As You Like It*.
- The description of his sufferings in Purgatory by Hamlet's Father's ghost in I. v. 10-21 and his insistence on revenge for his murder.

The New Testament is suggested in Prospero's words forgiving his enemies in V. i. 24-30 in *Tempest* and Isabella's pleading for the life of Angelo in V. i. 442-452.

Prospero's words in V. i. 41-57 create the world of **Renaissance Magic**.

Shakespeare does this also in scenes in which he locates the stage action, as in *All's Well*, implying the 'Seed of Christ' heresy (see above p. 144) and the properties used by characters within the stage action, such as Yorick's skull in (V. i.) in *Hamlet* reinforcing the play's theme of death.

When I had learned the details of the arcana, it seemed to me that Shakespeare integrated obvious clues of their presence in his plays, and I enjoyed unravelling their mysteries for my benefit as interpreter of the scripts of the plays, for the audience in their deeper understanding of them and for the actors in their clear performances.

Opinions of the actors on the usefulness of the information on the secret meanings to their understanding of the plays and to the performance of their roles in them.

I asked some of the actors who had performed in the Theatre Set-Up seasons from 1983 (when the research into the arcana became integral to the productions, especially in the later years when I had detected a number of secret meanings) if they had found the information useful.

Tony Portacio, who was lead actor in most of the plays from 1984 to 1999 and from 2006 to 2011, said, when I first asked him, that the knowledge increased his understanding of the characters he was playing and created a deeper level of performance of the plays. On another occasion, he commented that any information given to actors about their roles gave details that assisted them in presenting precise characterisation.

Terry Ashe, who played a variety of roles in most of the seasons from 1998 to 2011 as well as being the stage manager for the tours, found the information given at the meeting one month before the beginning of the rehearsal period generally useful from an actor's point of view. During the two-week rehearsal period, although I did not discuss the secret meanings then as we had so little time to realise the actual production, he felt that the research had given me a clear interpretation of the texts we performed, which guided the actors in their understanding of their roles and of the scripts. He said that I had the information in my head during those weeks even if I did not talk about it.

Christopher Terry, who was with the company in 2006 and 2007, commented that the information I gave the actors connected the plays with what was going on in Shakespeare's time, increasing the reality of the scripts. He found that the understanding of the secret meanings gave him a key to unlock what the character he was performing was doing.

Suzie Edwards, who performed Portia in the 2010 Theatre Set-Up production of *The Merchant of Venice* and Hero in the 2011 production of *Much Ado About Nothing*, found the information given to her at the meeting a month before the rehearsals began very useful. Firstly, she was taken by surprise at the depth of the interpretation of the play and of her role within it because, as an actor, she had not been given material like that about Shakespeare before. She said that the information on the secret meanings in the play made it possible for her to think about the play and her role at a different level from the usual action of the plot and the characterisation of Portia.

The information I gave Suzie Edwards helped her intentions at critical moments in the play. One of these moments was her preventing Shylock from inserting his knife into Antonio at IV. i. 301. The information I had given her about the possibility that Balthazar had understood the pun on 'blood' and 'money' in Shylock's bond had it been written in Hebrew

CHAPTER TWENTY TWO

(see above p. 380) prepared her to know the outcome of the case should Shylock continue with his intention to kill Antonio. She decided that she and Balthazar had given Shylock the chance to save himself from humiliation and punishment by her advice that he should be merciful. Balthazar had also told her the punishments due to Shylock in Venetian law applicable to miscreant aliens. Thus her actions in the courtroom were premeditated and not spontaneous. Suzie claimed that this 'gave weight to the knife point'. She found my interpretation of the play as a warning by Shakespeare of the dangers of racism convincing, especially when Portia herself makes a racist comment against the Prince of Morocco and is subsequently punished by Bassanio's comments against her in the courtroom

However, much as she was so pleased to be performing Portia, a role to which most actresses aspire, and as she benefitted a great deal from the extra information given her from my notes at our pre-production meeting, the notes helped her even more in her performance of Hero. She explained that the part is difficult in being silent for much of the play, so her character is undetermined. Without my information that Hero is the alchemic 'soul' to the transforming alchemic process in the play of Claudio as 'body', she felt that Hero could be interpreted as a weak girl who should have been crushed by Claudio's treatment of her. Suzie understood that in order to survive the horror of being falsely accused of immorality at the altar of her wedding with Claudio and therefore to be rejected as his bride (IV. i.) required considerable mental stamina, especially as she subsequently forgives him and agrees to marry him. By being part of the alchemical process which transmutes him into a fit person for her to marry, she felt vindicated as a character in agreeing to marry a man who had treated her so badly. She also commented that the scene (III. i.) in which Hero and Margaret (a character I was playing) plot to match Benedict with Beatrice (who can overhear the conversation) was important in clarifying the intention of Hero in the scene, as she became an agent for the part of the alchemy which changes Claudio by making Benedict challenge him on behalf of Beatrice, and ultimately also creates her cousin's happiness.

Susie Coleman, who performed with the company in 1997 and 2000, wrote: 'The information which Wendy gave me from the programme notes on both *Twelfth Night* and *A Midsummer Night's Dream* certainly helped me gain more rounded characters in both these plays as it helped me to re-create these characters with as many layers and as much depth as possible.'

Mark Bodicoat, who was with the company in 2002 and 2003 and who still runs the company's archive website, wrote: 'While directing the Shakespeare productions for Theatre Set-Up, Wendy frequently made reference to the 'secret meanings' behind the story and text. For the audience, it provided an insight to the play's relevance in its day; for the actors involved, it provided an explanation for the through-line of the story and for some of the routes the characters take on their journey. In order for the characters to make sense to the modern audience, however, an actor needs to base their individual choices on previous circumstances, the events that take place and the interactions with other characters. These motivating factors are usually very real and tangible - the characters know nothing of the secret meanings because they are secret. So as an actor, I was often intrigued by the academic investigation of the different levels of meaning, but usually found my characterisation and motives in the text itself. Shakespeare has written such rich and well-rounded characters, that they come to life in a very real way, and their secrets are revealed as things we recognise in our own lives.'

Morag Brownlie performed with Theatre Set-Up and was its tour company manager from 2000 to 2005, and writes as follows: 'An actor's preparation before a rehearsal process begins includes getting under the skin of the play to understand where the playwright is coming from. Wendy's 'Secret Meanings lecture' as she took us through her programme notes proved invaluable in this. Getting a glimpse into the mind of Shakespeare and Elizabethan culture helped inform the company's understanding of the play and gave inspiration for individual character work. I certainly gleaned many ideas to help my characters live for today's audiences. Over the years I worked for TSU, it was often commented on by audience members and reviewers how 'clear' our productions were – I'm guessing that Wendy's passed-on understanding of the plays helped to achieve this.'

Angela Laverick, who performed with the company in 2001 and 2004, writes also on behalf of her husband **David Reakes**, who was with us in 2004: 'I have been thinking about the programme notes and how useful and interesting they were. It was great as an actor to have an extra resource to help to understand the characters I was taking on. Two themes, in particular were very useful; that of Platonic Love (especially when it came to understanding the character of Miranda in *The Tempest*) and the theme of alchemy, which runs through all of Shakespeare's plays. It was a magical experience to perform the plays with this in mind and to be part of what was often a magical evening.

I know that David found the notes very interesting and useful too. We often think back to our time with Theatre Set-Up and remember how much fun it was.'

Elizabeth Arends and **Richard Sanderson**, who are currently working in the USA, wrote:

> 'We found the programme notes really useful. The information gave great depth to the characters instead of just the standard of reading the lines. I also think the audience really enjoyed getting the programme each year to go through and take home. An added bonus for sure.'

My own experiences of the usefulness of the arcana to my portrayal of roles I was acting varied. I applied the method followed by Mark Bodicoat to comic characters like the pantaloon Gremio (whom I based on pictures of Pantalone as a lecherous old man fruitlessly chasing young girls) in *Shrew*, like Verges in *Much Ado* and Snug the joiner in *Dream* (both copying someone I had known). But the core of others benefitted from the arcana. Paulina, in *Winter's Tale*, Friar Francis in *Much Ado* and the Queen in *Cymbeline* carried the function of alchemists in my through-line of thought for the roles. Mistress Quickly, in *Merry Wives*, Puck in *Dream* and the Nurse in *Romeo and Juliet* I experienced as the mercurial messenger-agents of alchemy. These three had added significance in terms of the arcana. Mistress Quickly and the Nurse exemplified 'base love', and the Puck I presented was a gnarled hobgoblin. The part in which I floundered was the Countess in *All's Well*. I sensed that there was a subtext of spiritual significance in addition to the Celtic reference (see above p. 150), but could not identify it. Only when I analysed the play in terms of the Cabala for this book did I realise that she exemplified the higher levels on the Tree of Life of **Chokmah (Wisdom, Spiritual Purpose)** and **Binah (Understanding, Spiritual Love)**. Had I applied that knowledge to my preparation for the part, I might have made my performance more plausible.

END NOTES

Notes to the Preface

1. Ciaran is now a well-known actor from his many TV and film appearances and his work with major theatre companies, including Glasgow Citizens Theatre, the National Theatre and the Royal Shakespeare Company, these latter which I subsequently abbreviate to NT and RSC.

2. Repeated titles of Shakespeare's plays within the text shall be abbreviated. The short titles, indicated within double quotation marks, are as follows for the plays discussed in this book: *The Two Gentlemen of Verona*, "Two Gentlemen"; *Love's Labours Lost*, "Love's Labours"; *The Comedy of Errors*, "Comedy"; *The Taming of the Shrew*, "Shrew"; *The Merchant of Venice*, "Merchant"; *The Merry Wives of Windsor*, "Merry Wives"; *A Midsummer Night's Dream*, "Dream"; *Twelfth Night* and *As You Like It* remain unchanged; *Much Ado About Nothing*, "Much Ado"; *Measure for Measure*, "Measure"; *All's Well that Ends Well*, "All's Well"; *The Winter's Tale*, "Winter's Tale"; *Cymbeline* remains unchanged; *The Tempest*, "Tempest"; *Romeo and Juliet*, *Hamlet* and *Antony and Cleopatra* remain unchanged. Other plays mentioned, *Pericles, Macbeth, Richard III, Julius Caesar, Othello* and *King Lear* remain unchanged.

3. They both continued their careers in the UK and internationally, both in performance and direction. Caroline promoted and cast performances in Germany and the UK, and Susannah led the English Shakespeare Company on a world tour as staff director for Michael Pennington and Michael Bogdanov, before working as part of the staff producer's team in the Royal Opera House Covent Garden and teaching and performing internationally for the British Council with her own company, Shakespeare Link, which still runs theatre events from her home at Penlanole in Wales. She became a trustee of Theatre Set-Up, and with her actor-husband, Philip Bowen, hosted its performances for many years in their Living Willow Theatre in the grounds of Penlanole.

4. The selection, arranging and performance of the music was my responsibility, initially playing a lute and in subsequent seasons a

folk harp, hammered dulcimer, portable organ and dulcimer. For some of the seasons, Andrew Field, a singer/actor, played additional musical instruments, such as a Celtic drum and chanter for *Cymbeline*. Morag Brownlie, also a singer/actor, often assisted in selecting, arranging and performing the music. Our audiences preferred live music to recorded. They declared that they did not mind if there were mistakes made in the playing of the music, as long as they could see the musician(s) performing on period instruments appropriate to the period in which the play was costumed! We had to use recorded brass music for *Antony and Cleopatra* and recorded music for our 2000 orchestrated musical version of *Dream* and audience members were not pleased with me!
5. Julie has since become a renowned actress for national venues including the NT, RSC, and Chichester Festival Theatre and the West End as well as doing much TV and film work, and David Goudge has been an established West End stage and BBC radio actor for many years.
6. In addition to playing the music and performing female roles, I enjoyed performing the friar and Verges in *Much Ado*; Corin in *As You Like it*; Gremio and the cook in *Shrew*; Snug the joiner in *Dream* and the arresting officer in *Comedy*. I also played Puck in our 1995 and 2000 productions of *Dream* as he is a hobgoblin (like my gnarled, ageing self), not the elf as usually portrayed.
7. The actors' services on this day were compensated with an extra day off during the season joined to regular days off when they were able to be at home.

Notes to the Introduction
1. *An Actor Prepares* (London, New York: Routledge, [1936], reprinted 1989) p.15.
2. For 'spiritual meanings' also read arcana, the esoteric, secret meanings, hidden meanings.
3. PhD for the Shakespeare Institute, The University of Birmingham 1996. This thesis is available at etheses.bham.ac.uk/3126/Wendy Jean Macphee, 'Arcana in Shakespeare's Comedies with specific reference to *The Comedy of Errors* and *A Midsummer Night's Dream*'.

4. Noteworthy among these productions were those from a wide range of countries presented by Shakespeare's Globe Theatre for their World Shakespeare season in 2012.
5. Edited with an introduction by Robert McNulty (Oxford: Oxford University Press, 1972).
6. For further details see p. 185.
7. Key to my understanding were publications by these experts in the study and practice of the esoteric and their books: John and Caitlin Matthews, *The Western Way*; R. J. Stewart, *The UnderWorld Initiation* (the capitalisation of the 'W' in UnderWorld is Stewart's means of distinguishing the term from that describing areas other than the realm of Celtic mysticism); Gareth Knight, *A History of White Magic*, *A Practical Guide to Cabalistic Symbolism,* and *The Secret Tradition in Arthurian Legend*; Will Parfitt, *The Qabalah* and *Meetings With Amazing People*. For full details of these books, please refer to the Bibliography.
8. It is worth noting that professional actors prepare for their roles long before the rehearsals start and they must turn up to rehearsals with the lines learnt.
9. (London, Boston and Henley: Routledge and Kegan Paul, 1980, pp. 136-224). For the original source of *King Lear* and other Shakespearean plays please see *Narrative and Dramatic Sources of Shakespeare* by Geoffrey Bullough, 8 vols (London: Routledge and Kegan Paul, 1977-1997).
10. The Arden Shakespeare edition, edited by John Russell Brown, (London: Routledge, 1989).
11. Ed. by John Jowett, William Montgomery, Gary Taylor and Stanley Wells, 2nd edn, (Oxford: Oxford University Press, 2005).
12. See OED definition of comedy: 'In the Middle Ages the term was applied to other than dramatic compositions, the 'happy ending' being the essential part of the notion.' Reference is made to this style of comedy used by Dante in his *Divine Comedy*, called by its author *La Comedia* because 'in the conclusion, it is prosperous, pleasant, and desirable'.

Notes to Chapter One: Esoteric Arcana I

1. Ed.by Geoffrey Shepherd (London: Thomas Nelson & Sons Ltd, 1965), p.142.
2. *The Chemical Theatre* p. 13.
3. See for example: T.W Baldwin, *William Shakespere's Small Latine and Lesse Greek*, 2 vols (Urbana: University of Illinois Press, 1944), Jonathan Bate, *Shakespeare and Ovid*, (Oxford: Clarendon Press, 1993).
4. See my alchemical interpretation in *Dream* of the Pyramus and Thisbe interlude, sourced from Book IV in the Ovid poem. For Ovid in the curriculum of Shakespeare's school see T.W. Baldwin, *William Shakespeare's Small Latine and Lesse Greek* and F.P. Wilson 'Shakespeare's Reading', *Shakespeare Survey* 3 (1950), pp. 14-21).
5. John Vyvyan in *Shakespeare and the Rose of Love* considers that Shakespeare in his inherited allegorical treatment of Divine Love from Dante's *Divina Commedia* has created a more merciful vision than that presented by Dante; 'his hell has no gate' (London: Chatto & Windus, 1960), p.194.
6. See the *Prefactory letter written by Spenser to Sir Walter Raleigh on the Fairie Queen* selected by Charles W. Eliot in The Harvard Classics 1909-14, <http://www.bartleby.com/39/14.html [accessed 3 April 2016] and preface to *The Faerie Queene, Complete Works of Edmund Spenser,* edited by R. Morris (London: Hamilton, 1879), p. 3.
7. E.K. Chambers *William Shakespeare*, 2 vols (Oxford: Clarendon Press, 1963), pp. 325-327.
8. For an image of Botticelli's *Primavera* with enlightening commentary see Edgar Wind, *Pagan Mysteries in the Renaissance*, (Oxford: Oxford University Press, 1980), List of Illustrations 25.
9. (London: Trubner, 1870), pp. 411-425.
10. *Andreae Alciatoi Emblematum Flumen Abundans or Alciat's Emblems in Their Full Stream*, a photolith facsimile of the Lyons edition by Bonhomme, 1551 (London, 1871).

11. 'Shakespeare and the Emblem: Studies in Renaissance Iconography and Iconology', *Papers in English and American Studies*, vol 3, ed. By Tibor Fabiny, revised by Zoltan Iszilassy, Kathleen Woal and Maurice Cassidy (Egyetem, Hungary: Department of English, Attila Jozset University, 1984).
12. E.K. Chambers, *William Shakespeare,* II p.188.
13. 'Johannes Factotem and Jack Cade', *Shakespeare Quarterly* 40 (1968), 461-462.
14. *The Minor Elizabethan Drama* vol 2 (London: Dent, 1951) p. 156.
15. (London: Columbia University Press, 1967), pp. 110-111.
16. Unpublished thesis, The University of Birmingham (1977), p. 13.
17. 4 vols, 2nd edn, (Oxford: Clarendon Press, 1974) IV.
18. (London: Routledge and Kegan Paul, 1964).
19. A labyrinth is sometimes not to be confused with a maze, the intent of which, when a game, is quite different. See Sig Lonegren, *Labyrinths, Ancient Myths &, Modern Use*, (Glastonbury: Gothic Image Publications, 1991).
20. (Shaftesbury, Dorset: Element, 1991) (Glastonbury: PS AVALON, 2017).
21. *Giordano Bruno and the Hermetic Tradition,* p.84.
22. (Wellingborough: The Aquarian Press, 1988).
23. *The Compound of Alchyemie* was dedicated to Edward IV in 1471. (Imprinted, London: Thomas Orwin, 1591) It is now available on <http://www.alchemywebsite.com/tcbcompound.htm [accessed 3 September 2016]. It also appears as a hardback, *Compound of Alchymy*, edited by Stanton J. Linden (Farnham: Ashgate, 2001). *Metamorphoses* by the Roman poet Ovid was completed in 8CE and translated by William Caxton in 1480. The Golding translation was in 1597. Currently available is the translation into English by Mary M. Innes (Harmondsworth: Penguin, 1955, 2007); *The Golden Ass* was translated into English by William Adlington in London in 1566 and reprinted in 1571, 1582 and 1596. Available also is the translation by Robert Graves, (Harmondsworth: Penguin, 1960, 1998 and Oxford: FSG Classics, 2009).
24. (Wellingborough: The Aquarian Press, 1984).
25. (London: Routledge & Kegan Paul, 1980).

26. The psychological implications of alchemy are discussed by C.G. Jung in *Psychology and Alchemy*, second edition, translated by R.F.C. Hull (London: Routledge & Kegan Paul, 1968). I came to understand the processes and significance of alchemy from studying this book.
27. See *The Chemical Theatre*, pp. 136-224.
28. This text, the basis of many ideas on the practice and philosophy of alchemy, was originally reported to be a green tablet found in the grave of Hermes Trismegisthus, its source material attributed to diverse countries and authors, but mostly recognising the Egyptian god of wisdom, Thoth. It was subsequently translated and published in many books and articles. Available to Shakespeare would have been the Latin text from *De Alchemia* by Chrysogonus (Nuremberg: Johannes Petreius, 1541).
29. Translated into English by Sears Reynolds Jayne in 'Marsilio Ficino's Commentary on Plato's *Symposium*, (Columbia: *The University of Missouri Studies*, vol 19, no.1, 1944) pp. 1-247.
30. See F. P. Wilson, 'Shakespeare's Reading', *Shakespeare Survey* vol 3 (1950) pp.14 – 21 and Jonathan Bate, *Shakespeare and Ovid* (Oxford: Clarendon, 1993), pp. 20 – 23.
31. (Oxford: Oxford University Press, 1963).
32. Details of this trend are established by Nesca Robb in *Neoplatonism of the Italian Renaissance* (London: George Allen & Unwin, 1935).
33. (London: Chatto & Windus, 1961).
34. (London: Chatto & Windus, 1960).
35. The text I used was: Plato *The Symposium*, ed.by E.V. Rieu (Harmondsworth: Penguin Classics 1959).
36. Baldesar Castiglione, *The Book of the Courtier,* Venice: (1528) trans. by Thomas Hoby. (London: Wyllam Seres, 1561); Edmund Spenser *Hymne in Honor of Beautie* (London: William Ponsonby, 1596).
37. (Hassocks, Sussex: The Harvester Press, 1978).
38. Hankins p. 81. See Plato's discussion on melancholy, turning what he calls 'black bile' brown and thereby infecting the person with a madness which descends them into the nature of a beast. (Jayne's translation of Plato's *Symposium* p. 230). This must have been the origin of what, in Shakespeare's day was called 'adust melancholy', as recorded in Hankin and Tillyard.

39. See Shen Lin, *The Element of Platonic Love in the Tempest: An Exercise in the Iconological principle*, unpublished Thesis, The Shakespeare Institute, The University of Birmingham (1984).
40. See Shen Lin, pp. 24-25 and Plato, *Phaedrus and Letters VII and VIII* trans. by Walter Hamilton (London: Penguin Books, 1973) pp. 50-66.

Notes to Chapter Two: Esoteric Arcana II

1. The *Picatrix* is a 400-page manual of magic and astrology originally written in Arabic by Ghayat Al Hakim in Spain during the 11th century, where it was subsequently translated into Latin in 1256. Never published as a book, it was nevertheless circulated in other forms and used by many scholars such as Ficino and occultists such as John Dee. The Zohar consists of a collection of books containing core information on the Cabala and commentaries on many aspects of the Hebrew religion. It was published in the 13th century by Moses de Leon who ascribed its original authorship to Rabbi Shimon bar Yochai in the second century A.D. Rabbi Isaac Luria (1534 – 1572), made it available to the general public. John Dee (1527-1608), graduate of Cambridge University, was a Renaissance magus, academic, mathematician, mechanic and alchemist who had travelled and lived throughout Europe from 1547-1587. His home in Mortlake, London, became an intellectual centre for arts and sciences from the late 1560's to the late 1580's. His library, which he made freely available to anyone who wished to consult his collections, contained over 3,000 manuscripts, over 1000 printed books, and maps which England's navigators such as John Hawkins consulted before making their journeys. See the commentary by Diane di Prima to John Dee's *The Hieroglyphic Monad* (New York: Samuel Weiser, 1977).
2. See Yates, *Giordano Bruno and the Hermetic Tradition* (London: Routledge & Kegan Paul 1964), pp. 20-156).
3. For details and explanations of this work see Gershom Schlem, *Major Trends in Jewish Mysticism* (Jerusalem: [n.pub.], 1941).
4. See Thomas Moore, *The Planets Within* (USA: Associate University Press, 1982), Introduction, pp. 29-34, 38-62).

5. See Frances Yates, *The Occult Philosophy in the Elizabethan Age* (London: Routledge & Kegan Paul, 1979 and 1999) p. 20. For a full description of the Renaissance Cabalistic theorists and practisers, please consult this book.
6. See Yates *Occult Philosophy*, pp.112, 148-156.
7. (New York: Dover Publications, 1971), p.207.
8. The God-names are those stated by Gareth Knight in *A practical Guide to Qabalistic Symbolism* (Kent: Kahn & Averill, 1986) p. 249. Characteristics of the psyche are from Will Parfitt *The Qabalah* (Dorset: Element 1991), pp. 31, 33, 34.
9. See Knight in *A practical Guide to Qabalistic Symbolism* and Parfitt *The Qabalah*.
10. Actors in any theatre company nowadays who do not have a 'calm centre' can have difficulties when working within an ensemble.
11. (USA: Malcolm House Publications, 1978).
12. (<http:// www.spunk.org/texts/misc/sp00277.txt [accessed 3 October 2016]).
13. See <http://www.danielyharris.com/pdfs/Shakespeare-**Kabbalah-and-the-Occult.pdf**. [accessed 3 October 2016].
14. (Albany, New York: Suny Press 1998). <http://books.google.co.uk/books? ISBN = 079143737X [accessed 3 October 2016].
15. (London: Mowbrays, 1978) p. 26.
16. See E.M.W. Tillyard, *The Elizabethan World Picture* (Harmondsworth: Penguin Books, 1979), p. 91.
17. (London: Palmer, [1921], facsimile reprint Whitefish, MT: Kessinger Publishing, 2003).
18. As translated by Robert Graves (Harmonsworth: Penguin Classics, 1960), p. 286.
19. See Joseph Campbell, *Masks of God,* 4 vols (New York: Viking Penguin, [1959], revised Harmondsworth: Penguin Arkana, 1991), I, pp. 94-98.

Notes to Chapter Three: Esoteric Arcana III

1. For a full list of sources, please consult my PhD Thesis vol. I pp. 177-183.
2. An accessible edition of this work is edited by J. William Hebel, Michael Drayton, *Poly-Olbion*, 4 vols, IV (Oxford: Basil Blackwell, 1933).
3. This was originally written in Latin in 1136, translated from earlier Welsh texts. In 1587, Jerome Commelin edited and printed the Latin text in Heidelberg.
4. R. J. Stewart, *The UnderWorld Initiation* (Wellingborough: The Aquarian Press, 1985) and *The Prophetic Vision of Merlin* (London: Arkana, 1986).
5. For detailed description of the significance of these and for a complete account of the Celtic UnderWorld Initiation, see R.J. Stewart, *The UnderWorld Initiation*.
6. *Celtic Heritage*: *Ancient Tradition in Ireland and Wales,* (London: Thames and Hudson, [1961], repr. 1978), pp. 89-92. See John Sharkey, *Celtic Mysteries*, (Singapore: Thames and Hudson, 1981) for further details.
7. Ancient graves and cathedrals have an east-west orientation respecting these customs.
8. See items displayed in the section called 'Kingship and Sacrifice' in the National Museum of Archaeology in Dublin and information relating to boundaries in Rees, p. 94.
9. (Wellingborough: The Aquarian Press, 1988), p.133.
10. (The Western Way I), p. 27.
11. See Stewart, *The UnderWorld Initiation*.
12. The *Apocrypha* was a further section of *Old Testament* books which also record parts of the religious history of the Hebrew people, but were judged not to merit inclusion in those parts of the Bible suitable for religious devotion, 'books which were not received by a common consent to be read and expounded publicly in church' (from the introduction to the *Apocrypha*, the *Geneva-Tomson Bible*, 1609).
13. (Newark: University of Delaware Press, 1999).

14. John Vyvyan, in *The Shakespearean Ethic* with specific reference to the contrasting attitudes to revenge and forgiveness displayed in *Hamlet* and *Measure For Measure,* notes the principle of forgiveness as laid down by Christ in the *New Testament* prevailing in the Shakespearean plays which end happily: 'He lays emphasis increasingly on the ethics of the New Testament and repudiates those of the Old', p. 91, (London: Chatto & Windus, 1959).
15. This also links with the alchemic stage of nigredo, where violent separation of the body and soul of the substance takes place.
16. New York: The Viking Press [1964], 2nd edn London: Souvenir Press, 1974, pp. 13, 14.

Notes to Chapter Four: *The Winter's Tale*
1. See Hankins on adust melancholy, p. 81 and Tillyard p.78. Adust melancholy (see n. 38 in End Notes to Chapter I).
2. See the account of the philosophy of love as told to Socrates by the wise woman Diotima in *The Masks of God: Occidental Mythology* by Joseph Campbell, pp. 230-232.
3. See the Jayne translation of 'Marsilio Ficino's Commentary on Plato's Symposium', pp. 212-215.
4. In alchemic iconography a rainbow is used to represent alchemy consisting of seven stages corresponding to the seven colours of the rainbow. When I was first studying Shakespeare's use of alchemy in his plays, I examined this seven-stage alchemic process in relationship to the plays, but ultimately concluded that Shakespeare followed Ripley's twelve-stage alchemic process. Sometimes, as in *Dream*, Shakespeare prioritises the alchemic process in the four main colour-coded stages of black, white, red and gold.
5. In order to create this meaning, Shakespeare has changed the name of this character from Dorastos in his source in Robert Green's novella.
6. See Frances Yates, *Shakespeare's Last Plays: A New Approach* (London: Routledge & Kegan Paul, 1975), pp. 12, 13, 19, 20, 32, 33, 134.
7. An example of this unifying of Europe through their monarch's children is the marriage of Princess Elizabeth to Frederick, the Elector Palatine

(whose castle was in Heidelberg) in 1613. She was briefly the Queen of Bohemia. She was courted by a number of crowned heads of Europe as a dynastic match before she was married. In 1994, during my site visit to Heidelberg Castle, where we subsequently performed for five years, my knowledge of these facts and Shakespeare's connection with the castle through its importance to alchemy which had been fostered by Elizabeth and Frederick delighted the castle's managers. They gave me a privileged visit to the ruins of the section of the castle built for Elizabeth. This had consisted of a seven-storey high tower, on the top storey of which was constructed a theatre modelled on the Globe Theatre where Shakespeare's company, The King's Men, performed in London. The castle's managers told me that they believed from evidence in the castle records that Shakespeare's company had performed in this theatre for Elizabeth and Frederick, but that there was no record of Shakespeare himself being with the company. Sadly, this tower with its theatre was destroyed by Napoleon's troupes and is now considered too dangerous to allow entrance for the general public.
8. Detail concerning the legend about the Merovingian dynasty, called 'The Seed of Christ', is dealt with in the chapter on *All's Well that Ends Well*.

Notes to Chapter Five: *Much Ado About Nothing*

1. This links with another weak character whom Shakespeare names Claudio in *Measure for Measure*, who also acts irresponsibly.
2. Such is Shakespeare's skill in creating the reality of the events of IV. i., that in our productions of the play the actresses performing the roles of Hero and Beatrice were genuinely reduced to tears during its performances throughout the seasons, not just in the early days of the tour when the reactions to the events of the scene were fresh, but consistently from the first night until the last. This also created an emotional response from the actors performing Benedick so that the mutually declared love between Beatrice and Benedick became unforced and compelling. The demand that the actresses playing

Beatrice made through their genuine anger and tears that Benedick should kill Claudio in revenge for his action against Hero, her cousin, was always so strongly motivated that the actors playing Benedick felt no hesitation in accepting the challenge. Audiences were also very moved by this scene.
3. See Ripley's *Compound of Alchymie.*
4. See *Lifting the Veil* by Charles Berner.

Notes to Chapter Six: *Cymbeline*
1. See Nicholl, pp. 227-235 for an alchemical reading of this scene and the events that precede it. For a description of the principles of alchemy see above pp. 26-34.
2: See above p. 58.
3. R.J. Stewart, *The Prophetic Vision of Merlin,* (London, Boston and Henley: Arkana, 1986). Geoffrey of Monmouth *The History of the Kings of Britain,* translated with an introduction by Lewis Thorpe (Harmondsworth: Penguins Books, 1976). In *The UnderWorld Initiation* Stewart claims that the whole of this book is itself a 'storehouse of magical symbolism, a compendium of traditional initiatory instruction', p. 54.
4. See Powell, *The Celts* and Rees, *Celtic Heritage* and above pp. 51-58.
5. M.de Pace *Introducing Freemasonry* (London: Lewis Masonic, 1983) p. 47.
6. (Edinburgh: Floris Books, 1983) p. 186.
7. See:<http://www.corupriesthood.com/the-morrigan/ [accessed 23 January 2017].
8. See Merry, p. 146.
9. For Ripley's twelve 'gates' as the stages of alchemy, see above pp. 27-29.
10. James Nosworthy, the editor of the Arden Edition of *Cymbeline* (London: Methuen, 1974), has reprinted in Appendix A (b), the 1560 version of Boccaccio's *Frederyke of Jennen* which he considers to be the source of Shakespeare's story of Iachimo's wager with Posthumus against Imogen (pp. 191-204).

11. See Joseph Campbell *The Masks of God: Primitive Mythology* (New York: Arkana, 1991) pp. 273-25.
12. See Stewart, p. 110.
13. See Charles Nicholl's explanation of the alchemic symbolism of the cave in *Cymbeline,* including an illustration from Heinrich Khunrath's book *Amphitheatrum Sapientiae Aeternae* printed in the same year, 1609, the probable date of the writing of *Cymbeline* (pp. 227-231).
14. Nicholl, p. 233.
15. See Merry, pp. 143-144.
16. Nicholl, p. 233-236.
17. Merry, p. 186.
18. R. J. Stewart, *The Merlin Tarot* (Wellingborough: The Aquarian Press, 1988), p. 89.
19. See Ripley.
20. See R. J. Stewart *The Under World Initiation* p. 224.
21. See above p. 31 and Nicholl pp. 49, 116, 148.
22. See Stewart pp. 144-149.

Notes to Chapter Seven: *The Merry Wives of Windsor*

1. The Lollards were followers of John Wycliffe (1330-1384), whose puritanical religious views, prescribing that Christians should have direct contact with the Bible and should follow the New Testament precepts of poverty and service to others, anticipated the 16th century Protestant Reformation. They were regarded as heretics by the Catholic Church, persecuted for their beliefs and often executed.
2. See Plato's discussion on melancholy, turning what he calls 'black bile' brown and thereby infecting the person with a madness which descends them into the nature of a beast (Jayne's translation of Plato's *Symposium* p. 230).
3. See the same tradition followed in the story of Bianca and Lucentio in *The Taming of the Shrew*. The deception of Juliet's pretended death in *Romeo and Juliet* demonstrates an unsuccessful use of this kind of ploy, resulting in the deaths of the young lovers.
4. The European myth of the 'Wild Hunt' featured a ghostly horde of

savage hunters in the sky, often riding a storm and accompanied by a pack of wild hounds, pursuing the souls of the living. The appearance of the 'Wild Hunt' was considered to be an ill omen. The leader of the hunters was variously named, culminating in versions of the myth with his being identified as the Devil. The identity of the ghostly hunters was also considered to be varied, but usually contained a reference to them as tortured souls. In <http://cassandraeason.com/folklore_legend/the-wild-hunt.htm [accessed 4 April 2016], the authoress claims that the Saxon version of the myth features Herne the Hunter, in his form as the horned god (whom Celts call Cernunnos) leading the hunt not in the sky, but in the woods of Windsor Great Park in Berkshire. It would seem that this is the version of the myth in *The Merry Wives of Windsor*.
5. See A. Ross, *Pagan Celtic Britain*, pp. 136-167 and fig. 42.

Notes to Chapter Eight: *All's Well that Ends Well*
1. Printed in full in the Appendix of *The Arden Shakespeare* ed. by G.K. Hunter, (London and New York: Methuen [1959]; reprinted 1986), pp. 145 – 152. Used throughout for this discussion of the play.
2. 1st edition, Jonathan Cape [1982]. Reprinted Aylesbury: Hunt Barnard Printing, 1983.
3. Facing p. 385, Plate 35.
4. p. 174.
5. London: Oneworld Publications 2013, p.128.
6. Claude de Lorraine and his brother, Charles, Duke of Guise, were tutored by Robert Fludd, author of many occult works, particularly on Rosicrucianism (see Frances A. Yates, *The Rosicrucian Enlightenment*, (St Albans: Granada Publishing Ltd., 1975, 2nd edition) and who, it is likely, supported the legend and discussed it with his tutees, as he is named in *Holy Blood and the Holy Grail* as a Grand Master of the Priory of Sion, an institution linked with the legend. See p. 133.
7. London: Chatto & Windus, 1961.
8. <http://symbols.ehibou.com/bee [accessed 5 December 2016] tells that the bee in Christian symbolism represents the immortality of the soul and Christ's resurrection. This is because during the three months

of winter bees are not seen, corresponding to the three days during which Christ disappeared after His crucifixion.

Notes to Chapter Nine: *The Tempest*

1. All interpretation of the Greater and Lesser Rites of Initiation in *The Tempest* are taken from *Shakespeare's Mystery Play: The Tempest* by Colin Still, first published in [1921] but reprinted since. See above n. 17 to Chapter Two.
2. The reference books used for identifying many Celtic features of *The Tempest* were: Gareth Knight, *History of White Magic;* Caitlin and John Matthews, *The Western Way* vol I; Eleanor Merry, *The Flaming Door;* Anne Ross, *Pagan Celtic Britain;* Alwyn Rees and Brinley Rees, *Celtic Heritage;* R. J. Stewart, *The Prophetic Vision of Merlin, The UnderWorld Initiation* and *Celtic Gods and Goddesses;* and T. G. E. Powell, *The Celts.* For details of all the above publications please refer to the Bibliography. Much of the material was through personal communication with scholars such as Marko Michell and George Trevelyan.
3. See 'Blessed Isles' in Caitlin and John Matthews, *The Western Way* 2 vols (London, Boston and Henley: Arkana, 1986), I, p. 107-109.
4. For details of all these books please see Frances Yates, *The Occult Philosophy in the Elizabethan Age* (Oxford: Routledge Classics, 2001 first published by Routledge & Kegan Paul 1979).
5. For a Celtic mythological cave see Rees, p. 303.
6. London and New York: Methuen, 1969), p. 255.
7. See Matthews, p. 79 and Ross, p. 219.
8. See note 375 to I. ii. in the Arden edition of the play.
9. See Ross, discussing the authenticity of the oak being part of the name of 'druid'. She notes that the source may be from the Welsh cognate from 'druwids' meaning 'wise man of the oak' or 'the very wise man', p. 33 fn. 3.
10. For a magic staff used in magic practice see Matthews p. 18 and for the staff as 'The White Rod' see Stewart, *The Prophetic Vision of Merlin* p. 93.

11. See Matthews, p. 210, 115.
12. See footnote no. 34 of II. ii. in the Arden edition of the play. This comments on the money-making displays of 'Indians' at exhibitions after 1576, especially during the reign of James I.
13. See Ross, fig. 73a.
14. See Powell, p. 121.
15. For an illustration of a Tricephalos see Ross p. 77; for a horned god fig. 42 – Cernunnos on the Gundestrip cauldron; for Epona p. 199.
16. See for the cauldron Merry, p. 108, 136-152 and Powell, p. 122; for the apples Stewart *The UnderWorld Initiation*, p. 85 and Ross, p. 214. For boar see Ross, pp. 308-321.
17. See Merry 136, 142, 150-152 and Matthews, p. 79.
18. For the importance of star-lore, see Matthews, p. 51.
19. See Stewart, *The Prophesies of Merlin*, p. 40 and oral information from Marko Michell.
20. See Merry, p. 27.
21. See Matthews, p. 29.
22. An example of this is the systematic killing off of Aboriginals in regions of South Australia by poisoning their water holes, a practice which was carried out without compunction by farmers in the Flinders Ranges into very recent times.
23. See: <https://www.khanacademy.org/humanities/ap-us-history/period-2/apush-early-english-settlement/a/intro-to-english-settlement. [Accessed 14 February 2017].

Notes to Chapter Ten: *A Midsummer Night's Dream*
1. For further reading on this see my PhD thesis: *Arcana in Shakespeare's Comedies*, Chapter 9.
2. For the Greek roots of these names see *A Comprehensive Etymological Dictionary of the English Language* by Ernest Klein (Oxford: Elsevier, 1971).
3. See Lewis Spence *British Fairy Origins* (Wellingborough, Northamptonshire: The Aquarian Press [1946], 1st paperback edition 1981), pp. 89, 90.

4. Shakespeare's imagination creates a sense of the fairies by naming small creatures which would seem dangerous to them.
5. *Metamorphoses*, VI 440-668.
6. For an image of a Celtic artefact merging with an animal (in fact a bird) with a human see A. Ross, *Pagan Celtic Britain*, fig. 73a.
7. See Lou Agnes Reynolds and Paul Sawyer in 'Folk Medicine and the Four Fairies of *A Midsummer Night's Dream'. Shakespeare Quarterly* 10, (1959), pp. 513-521.
8. For a graphic representation of the process of alchemy allegorically worked upon a toad as "base matter" please see *Alchemy: The Philosophers' Stone,* Allison Coudert (London: Wildwood House [1980], Australia: Bookwise, 2000), pp. 145-146.
9. This information was given to me orally by George Trevelyan and see Merry pp.143-144.
10. Oral information also given by George Trevelyan from its source in Merry.
11. *Shakespeare Quarterly*, 33 (1982), pp. 432-447.
12. Vyvyan *Shakespeare and Platonic Beauty* p. 89.
13. See C.G. Jung, *Psychology and Alchemy*, 2nd edition, translated by R.F.C. Hull (London: Routledge & Kegan Paul (1968).

Notes to Chapter Eleven: *The Two Gentlemen of Verona*
1. See Richer, Jean, *Prestiges de la Lune et Damnation par les Étoiles dans le Théâtre de Shakespeare* (Paris: *Les Belles Lettres*, 1982).
2. Wind, pp. 191-217.
3. Wind, pp. 218-235.
4. For a detailed analysis of Platonic Divine Love in this play and references enclosed within my analysis, see Vyvyan, *Shakespeare and the Rose of Love*, pp. 99-135.
5. See Wind, pp. 191-217.
6. See Vyvyan, p. 120, 135.

Notes to Chapter Twelve: *Love's Labour's Lost*

1. We usually had two actresses plus myself in the cast with the balance of the cast male actors. An unhappy exception to this was *Hamlet*, which, taking into account the possible doubling of parts, requires only one young actress.
2. The edition used for this play is The New Penguin Shakespeare (1996).
3. See Vyvyan, John, *Shakespeare and the Rose of Love* (London: Chatto & Windus, 1960) p. 67. For a discussion on this eternal concept of the 'Veil of Illusion' see *Lifting the Veil*, by Charles Berner, <http://www.Charlesberner.org/Lifting_the_Veil.pdf [accessed 4 April 2016].
4. See Bradbrook, M.C., *The School of Night* (Cambridge: Cambridge University Press, 1936); Yates, Frances A., *A Study of Love's Labour's Lost* (Cambridge: Cambridge University Press [1936] paperback edition 2013) and *The French Academies of the Sixteenth Century* (London: Routledge & Kegan Paul, 1947).
5. (Oxford: Oxford University Press, 2001), p. 264.
6. See *The Rose of Love*, p. 40.
7. See Barber, C.L. *Shakespeare's Festive Comedy*, (Princeton: Princeton University Press, 1972).
8. See Wind figs 52, 53, 54 'Festina lente'.
9. See *The Continuum Encyclopaedia of Symbols,* Editor Udo Becker (London: Continuum International Publishing Group [2000], reprinted 2005). <http://www.bloomsbury.com/us/continuum-encyclopaedia-of-symbols-9780826412218/ [accessed 4 April 2016]
10. There are many interpretations of the story of St George and the dragon. George Trevelyan, whom I met and talked with in 1987 and who acted as my consultant on spiritual arcana for several years afterwards, gave me the occult interpretation of the legend. This depicts St George as the Higher Self (the moral, spiritual soul of a person), conquering the Lower Self (the sometimes immoral worldly aspect of a person). See his *Magic Casements* (London: Coventure, 1980), *Summons to a High Crusade* (Forres, Scotland: The Findhorn Press, 1986), *A vision of the Aquarian Age* (London: Coventure, 1977), and 'The Merchant of Venice: An Interpretation in the Light of the Holistic World-View' *The Wrekin Trust*, no.114 (1981).

END NOTES

11. See Yates, *The Rosicrucian Enlightenment* (London: Routledge & Kegan Paul, 1972).

Notes to Chapter Thirteen: *The Taming of the Shrew*
1. See stage instruction I. i. 48 (Enter…Gremio, a pantaloon).
2. (Milano: Arnoldo Mondadori, 1985)
3. *Supposes* is reprinted in full in *Narrative and Dramatic Sources of Shakespeare* ed. Bullough l. I pp. 111-158.

Notes to Chapter Fourteen: *Twelfth Night*
1. This annual MESS festival welcomes theatre presentations from countries throughout the world and usually takes the form of a competition. However, it was not a competitive spirit which initiated or governed this festival in 1997 but rather a very brave declaration that hostilities had ceased and that cultural events such as the MESS theatre festival had resumed their place in the fragile society of Sarajevo. Many of the buildings of Sarajevo, and certainly our young hosts, were badly scarred. One of the actors and I still communicate with officials from the Festival who have become our friends. We had unbounded admiration for the young people who organised the event, and British Actors Equity, who had asked us to represent the UK at the MESS Festival, covered our fee (which we needed to pay our actors' wages), when it was learnt that the festival was struggling financially. With enormous resourcefulness MESS had already covered the costs of our plane and bus travel, hotels and food!
2. See Hankin, p. 38.
3. See *Lifting the Veil* by Charles Berner.

Notes to Chapter Fifteen: *As You Like It*
1. See: *The Arden Shakespeare*: *As You Like It,* ed. Agnes Latham, *Introduction*, (London: Methuen [1975], reprinted 2000), pp. xxxi-xlvi.

2. See David Young, *The Heart's Forest: a Study of Shakespeare's Pastoral plays* (New Haven: Yale University press, 1972), pp. xii.-210)
3. See Louis Adrian Montrose 'Of Gentlemen and Shepherds: The Politics of Elizabethan Pastoral Form' *ELH,* 50 (1983), 61-94; 'The Place of a Brother in As You Like It: Social Progress and Comic Form', *Shakespeare Quarterly,* 32 (1981), 28-54.
4. See Gareth Knight, *A History of White Magic* (London: Mowbrays, 1978), p. 39 and *The Secret Tradition in Arthurian Legend* (Wellingborough: The Aquarian Press, 1983), pp. 15, 122, 275.

Notes to Chapter Sixteen: *The Comedy of Errors*
1. Geoffrey Bullough, *Narrative and Dramatic sources of Shakespeare* (London: Routledge & Kegan Paul, 1958).
2. Naseeb Shaheen, *Biblical references in Shakespeare's Comedies* (New Jersey: University of Delaware Press, 1993).
3. In Murray J. Levith's *What's in Shakespeare's Names* (London: Allen & Unwin, 1978), Antipholus' name is glossed as 'one who returns another's love'. The 'Soul' seeks to be reunited with the 'Divinity' from which it fell into a human body.
4. The names of Antipholus and Dromio from Syracuse are prefixed by Syr., and their twins by Eph.
5. Phoenix was a human who later became one of the Myrmidons, the warriors of Achilles in the Trojan War.
6. The name has a Latin source, Hadrianus, or Adria, of the Adriatic, hence the implication of 'dark', as in the hair and skin of people living in that region.
7. Jayne on Ficino, p.145.
8. In ancient Greek legendry, Circe was an enchantress who could change visitors such as Odysseus to her island into animals.
9. The reference to 'breeches' in this edition of the Bible has resulted in its tag as a 'Breeches Bible'.
10. Hankins, p. 81.
11. *A Natural Perspective: The Development of Shakespearean Comedy and Romance* (New York: Columbia University Press, 1965).

Notes to Chapter Seventeen: *Romeo and Juliet*

1. See *Prestiges de la Lune et Damnation par les Étoiles: Dans le Théâtre de Shakespeare*, (Paris: *Les Belles Lettres*, 1982), pp.16-25.
2. See Fig. 12.
3. *Emblematica* 2, 5 (Winter 1991), 301-320.
4. *Rosarium Philosophorum* is part of *De Alchimia Opuscula complura Veterum Philosophorum* (Frankfurt: [n.pub.], 1550).
5. An illustration of other woodcuts on this theme can be seen on <https://www.google.co.uk/#q=woodcut+oflovers+in+the+tomb+in+1550+Rosarium+Philosophorum&* [accessed 17.03.2017].
6. See Appendix II in the Arden edition of the play.
7. That Shakespeare intended this alchemical outcome is indicated in his changing the substance of the statues that the families will raise to their children to gold from the marble of the play's source in *The Tragical Historye of Romeus and Juliet.*
8. See Joseph Campbell, *The Masks of God: Primitive Mythology*, (Harmondsworth: Penguin Books, 1987), p. 98.

Notes to Chapter Eighteen: *Antony and Cleopatra*

1. For its instructive Introduction I recommend the edition I used for the preparation of *Antony and Cleopatra,* The Arden Shakespeare ed. John Wilders, Third Series, General Editors Richard Proudfoot, Ann Thompson and David Scott Kastan (London: Routledge, 1995).
2. Plutarch, *The Life of Marcus Antonius* and *The Life of Julius Caesar* trans. Sir Thomas North, in *Narrative and Dramatic Sources of Shakespeare*, ed. Geoffrey Bullough, vol. 5 (London: Routledge and Kegan Paul, 1977). Also available at <http://oll.libertyfund.org/titles/plutarch-shakespeares-plutarch-vol-2 [accessed 03.04.17].
3. See Plato, *Phaedrus and Letters VII and VIII* trans. by Walter Hamilton (London: Penguin Classics, 1973). Also available at <http://classics.mit.edu/Plato/Phaedrus.html (accessed 03.04.17).
4. On Cleopatra as Isis see Introduction by John Wilders to the Arden edition of the play pp. 67-69.
5. *Phaedrus*, p. 63.
6. See n. 4 above.

Notes to Chapter Nineteen: *The Merchant of Venice*
1. Edited by Yehuda T. Radday, *Shakespeare Survey* Vol. 32.
2. From *Selected Works of Frances Yates,* VII (reprinted Oxford, USA, Canada 2001) pp. 127-131. Francisco Giorgio of Venice was a Franciscan monk and Christian Cabalist who wrote *De Harmonia Mundi,* a work which promoted occult syncretism in 1525.
3. <http://www.spunk.org/texts/misc/sp000277.txt [accessed 3 October 2016]
4. (Chicago 1975), pp. 102-103, 106.
5. Harris uses the term 'Kadmonic' in the adjectival sense of 'Adam Kadmon', a worldly manifestation of Godhead and a kind of primordial human being described in a classification of Godhead by the Jewish Cabalist Luria, (1534-1572).

Notes to Chapter Twenty: *Measure for Measure*
1. (London: Chatto & Windus, 1959).
2. W.W. Lawrence in *Shakespeare's Problem Comedies* (New York: Macmillan, 1931) considers that these two plays present problems because although they are not tragedies they are not comedies in the usual meaning of the genre. As I believe that Shakespeare's form of comedy follows that of Dante, i.e. a story that ends happily, and these two plays are resolved happily, I classify them as comedies, their nature as 'problem plays' lying elsewhere in the scripts.
3. The doublings were: Vincentio, Duke of Vienna/ Froth, a foolish gentleman; Isabella, sister to Claudio/ Juliet, beloved of Claudio; Pompey, servant to Mistress Overdone/ Friar Peter; Francesca, a nun/ Mariana, betrothed to Angelo; Escalus, a lord/ Mistress Overdone, a bawd; Claudio, a young gentleman/ Elbow, a constable/ Abhorson, an executioner; Lucio, a light gentleman/ Provost, in charge of the prison.
4. A short title, **Morality, Ethics, Crime and Punishment** is used in following sections.
5. (London: Chatto & Windus, 1961).
6. Actors upon the stage could be accused of deception in the assumption of characters in roles which only represent reality but that illusion is

usually understood by audiences. In film and Television the illusion is often not comprehended and the actor is identified with the character being represented in the same way as the Viennese identify the Duke with Friar Lodowick.

Notes to Chapter Twenty One: *Hamlet*

1. See <https://learnearnandreturn.wordpress.com/2011/07/30/hamlets-university [accessed 20.05.17] for a commendation of Shakespeare's placing of Hamlet at Wittenberg University, associated with Martin Luther and Dr Faustus.
2. Macphee, Wendy, *Drama as a Mesocosm* Unpublished dissertation, University of Newcastle-Upon-Tyne, (1978). This diploma dissertation describes a link between myth and drama.
3. This is an analogue of Christ's self-sacrifice for mankind. J. G. Frazer in *The Golden Bough* (New York: Macmillan, 1922) sets out in Chapter 24 worldwide historical and anthropological occurrences of the sacrifice of kings.
4. For the debate on Hamlet's change from being a sanguine to melancholic man, see pp.138-143.
5. Oral information given to me by Dr T. P. Matheson.
6. This new code of ethics had been advanced by Martin Luther, professor of moral theology at the University of Wittenberg in 1517 in his *Ninety Five Theses*.
7. For detail of Rosicrucianism, see Gareth Knight, *The Rose Cross and The Goddess*, (Wellingborough: The Aquarian Press, 1985) pp. 78-111 and Frances Yates, *The Rosicrucian Enlightenment* (London, Boston and Henley: Routledge & Kegan Paul, 1972)
8. For detail of adust melancholy applicable to Ophelia, see Hankin. He states 'Under stress of violent emotion any of the humours may be burned by the furnace of the heart, leaving an injurious black substance called "adust" or burnt melancholy… If not purged from the body, it will clog the passages of the veins and arteries, causing madness and finally death' (p. 81). Also see n. 38, Chapter One.

Notes to Chapter Twenty Two: CONCLUSIONS
1. In the 2017 RSC production of *Tempest,* Prospero handed his broken staff to Caliban. According to the Celtic magical tradition which indicated that a magician's staff was personal to him alone and which cited Merlin drowning his book so that no-one could misuse its magical powers (see above p. 184), this might have been a dangerous move (although in the RSC production Caliban decided to discard it).
2. In the stunning Brett Dean opera of *Hamlet*, a wonderful performance of which I saw at Glyndebourne in July 2017, the ghost of Hamlet's father was simply presented with a whitened bare head and torso, presumably in the state in which he was being tortured in Purgatory. As the production was being staged in contemporary times and dress, a helmet with the beaver raised would not have been plausible. However, in order to make the connection between Hamlet's raised hand and the raised beaver as in Shakespeare's version of the story, I wished at the time that he could have been presented in contemporary military dress with some item of headwear suggesting the position of the raised beaver, or placed his hand as if in stress over his brow, as the implications of this for Hamlet's mental state and his attitude to Ophelia are key to an understanding of the plot. I saw this production in the same week as attending the RSC *Tempest*, where the meaning of Prospero's broken staff was not understood and I felt that in these instances knowledge of the contents of this book relevant to those production points might have been useful!

APPENDIX 1

A tribute to the talent and rigour of the Theatre Set-Up actors exemplified in their work following their seasons with the company. This is a conservative account of these actors' accomplishments. Most actors perform in some films and TV in addition to their stage work so that is assumed as part of the C.V.s of the actors in all the lists.

1. **Maintaining theatre work in the UK, often serving the needs of local communities and performing in repertory and regional theatres as well as London mainstream, and in fringe and outdoor locations**
Terry Ashe, Richard Ashley, Mark Bodicoat, James Clarkson, Sean Chapman, Alan Collins, Andrew Crabb, Jonathan Gunning, David Holmes, Peter Landi, Tim Lowe, Peter Lundie Wager, James Morley, Daniel O'Brien, Deborah O'Malley, Emily Outred, Paul Rainbow, Anthony Taylor, Richard Plumley, Simon Startin, Kyra Williams.

2. **In addition to performing in the UK, acting/directing/producing outside the UK** Sean Aita (Europe), Elizabeth Arends (USA), Sue Appleby (world tour), Susannah Best (world tour), Paul Brennan (China), Morag Brownlie (Europe), Kim Evans (Europe), Andrew Field (Europe), Simon Furness (Europe), Jonathan Hartman (Canada and USA), Tim Heath (Europe), Ciaran Hinds (world tour), Jenni Lea-Jones (Europe), Libby Machin (Middle East), Alex Marshall (Europe), Jo Price (USA), Emma Reynolds (Europe), Christopher Terry (world tour).

3. **Establishing their own companies**
Sean Aita, Iain Armstrong, Susannah Best, Henrietta and Michael Branwell, Morag Brownlie, Rosalind Cressy, James Kingdon, Alexa Jago, Angela Laverick, Libby Machin, Chris Pavlo, David Reakes.

4. **Writing – books and scripts for stage and TV**
Sean Aita, Jack Hughes, Deborah O'Malley, Anita Parry, Chris Pavlo, Stewart Permutt, Chris Robbie, Emma Reynolds, Simon Startin, Tim Heath, Neil Warhurst, Anthony Young.

5. Teaching - voice, drama, workshops, in theatres, drama schools, university and schools

Sean Aita (university professor), Susannah Best (international workshops for the British Council), Alison Breminer (voice and text coach RSC), Mark Bodicoat (Schools), Henrietta and Michael Branwell (ballet – to own company in Harlow and Pineapple, Morley College and Central School of Ballet in London), Lucy Curtin (varied venues), Tess Dignan (voice and text coach RSC), David Eadon (Schools), Kim Evans (schools), Gordon Fleming (acting instruction to ballet dancers), Simon Furness (varied venues), Melanie Jessop (voice and drama coach/ tutor/ director in drama schools including RADA and Webber Douglas), Michael Loney (Arts establishments, Australia), David Norell (schools), Michael Palmer (tutor, drama schools), Tony Portacio (schools), George Richmond-Scott (voice and text coach RSC).

6. Performing in the National Theatre

Charles Abomali, Sean Aita, Lynette Edwards, Guy Henry, Ciaran Hinds, Fabian Cartwright, Julie Le Grand, Deborah O'Malley.

7. Performing in the Royal Shakespeare Company

Charles Abomali, Sean Aita, Sean Chapman, Simon Clerk, Derek Crewe, Steven Elder, Guy Henry, Ciaran Hinds, Sarah-Jane Holm, Melanie Jessop, Julie Le Grand, Matthew Rixon, Chris Robbie.

8. Diversified within theatre in addition to stage/TV/film

Julia Ackerman (voice overs), Sean Chapman (voice overs), Susie Coleman (voice overs), Suzie Edwards (role playing), Caroline Funnell (casting director, UK and Europe), David Goudge (radio), Tim Heath (director), Kevin Howarth (horror movies actor), Daniel Hunt (director), Alexa Jago (executive film director), Frank Jarvis (director), Chris Jordan (director/producer/theatre manager), Hugh Kermode (radio/creative director), Michael Loney (marriage celebrant Australia), James Mitchell (magic), Peter O'Dwyer (producer), Geoffrey Owen (performance coach), Anita Parry (artistic director), Chris Pavlo (executive director, radio), Jacqueline Quella (executive producer of major events, film and other media), Emma

Reynolds (voice over, direction), Alex Richardson (film director), Amanda Strevett-Smith (drama therapy), Elliot Tiney (stand-up comedian), David Wylde (role play – in addition to drama school teaching).

After her performances in the West End, Victoria Stilwell (who had played Juliet in our 1996 production of "Romeo and Juliet"), became an animal behaviour expert specialising in dogs, with her own business and TV shows in the UK and the USA. Particularly famous was the TV series, "It's Me or the Dog" (see above p. 346). She took the precaution of warning me of this in case I should suffer shock at unexpectedly seeing her in this capacity on my TV screen. Sean Chapman (who played Benvolio in our 1978 production of "Romeo and Juliet"), was the narrator in some of those episodes.

APPENDIX II

Venues in which Theatre Set-Up performed during their seasons from 1976 to 2011.

1. In the UK, the Channel Islands and the Isle of Man:
Abbotsbury Sub Tropical Garden, Dorset; Albury Park, Surrey; Alnwick Castle, Northumberland; Appleby Castle, Cumberland; Arlington Court, North Devon; Arreton Manor, Isle of Wight; Beningbrough Hall, Yorkshire; Bicton Park, Devon; Binchester Roman Fort, County Durham; Blickling Hall, Norfolk; Bowhill Country Park, Scottish Borders; Broadlands, Hampshire; The Bothey, Avenue House Grounds, London N3; The Bridgwater Amphitheatre, Lakeside Arts Centre, Nottingham; Bristol Cathedral; Broxbourne Civic Hall Gardens, Hoddesdon; Buckden Towers, Cambridgeshire; Carisbrooke Castle, Isle of Wight; Carlisle Cathedral; Castle Rushen High School; The Chaplaincy, St Mary's Isles of Scilly; Chatley Heath Semaphore Tower, Cobham, Surrey; Chatsworth House Gardens, Derbyshire; Corfe Castle, Dorset; Corn Exchange, Bury St Edmunds; Cossington Manor Gardens, Somerset; Cotehele, Cornwall; Cricket St Thomas, Somerset; The Crush Room, Royal Opera House; Dilston Castle, Northumberland; Dunster Castle, Somerset; Durham Cathedral; Dyrham Park, near Bath; Ely Cathedral; Erdding Garden, Wales; The Evesham Festival; Fenton House, Hampstead, London; Forty Hall, Enfield; Ford Park, Cumbria; Fountains Abbey, North Yorkshire; Fountain Garden, Westmere, Birmingham; The Glade in the Forest, Rosliston Forestry Centre, Derbyshire; Grand Square, Royal Naval College, Greenwich; Great Bidlake Manor, Devon; Great Garden, Nash's House & New Place, Stratford-upon-Avon; The Greater London Theatre, County Hall, London SE1; The George Inn, Southwark, London SE1; The Georgian Theatre Royal, Richmond, North Yorkshire; Glastonbury Abbey, Somerset; Guildhall, Bath; Hall's Croft, Stratford-upon-Avon; Hanbury Hall, Worcestershire; Harlow Carr Botanical Gardens, Harrogate; Hatfield House Gardens, Hertfordshire; Heathfield Walled Garden, Croydon; Hereford Cathedral; Holland Park Open Air Theatre, London; Holme Pierrepont Hall, Nottingham; Hutton-in-the-Forest, Penrith; Ingatestone Hall, Essex;

APPENDIX II

Kedlestone Hall, Derbyshire; Kenilworth Castle, Warwickshire; Kentwell Hall, Suffolk; Killerton Gardens, Exeter, Devon; Kirby Hall, Northampton; Kirby Muxloe Castle, Leicestershire; Lacock Abbey, Wiltshire; Lamport Hall, Gardens, Northamptonshire; La Seigneurie, Sark, Channel Islands; Liverpool Cathedral; The Lost Gardens of Heligan, Cornwall; Marble Hill, Richmond, London; The Medieval Hall, The Cathedral Close, Salisbury; Millfield Theatre, Edmonton London N18; Milntown, Isle of Man; Mont Orgueil, Jersey, Channel Islands; Mottisfont Abbey, Romsey; Mount Edgecumbe House and Park, Cornwall; The National Trust, Sutton Hoo, Suffolk; Norwich Cathedral; The Noverre Suite, The Assembly Rooms, Norwich; Oakhill Park Arena, London EN4; The Orangery, The Royal Botanical Gardens Kew; The Orangery, Kenwood, London NW3; Pavilion Theatre, Brighton; Peel Castle, Isle of Man; Pencarrow, Cornwall; Pendennis Castle, Cornwall; Penlanole Living Willow Theatre, Wales; Priors Hall Barn, Essex; Penshurst Place, Kent; Peterborough Cathedral Cloisters; Powderham Castle, Devon; The Pump Room, Bath; Production Village Open Air Theatre, London NW2; Rangers House, Black Heath, London SE10; Ripon Cathedral; Richmond Castle, North Yorkshire; The River Gardens, Pembroke Arms Hotel, Wilton, Wiltshire; The Roman Theatre, Verulamium, St Albans; The Rookery, Streatham Common, London SW4; Rothley Court, Leicester; Royal William Yard, Plymouth; Rushen Abbey, Isle of Man; St. Andrew's Church, Plymouth; St Gabriel's Church, Cwmbran, Wales; Salisbury Cathedral; Saltram House, Devon; Scotney Castle, Kent; Southwark Cathedral; Speeds Farm, Shepton Mallett; Speke Hall, Liverpool; "Starveacres", Radlet; Stonehenge, Wiltshire; Stourhead, Wiltshire; Stokesay Castle, South Shropshire; Sudbury Hall, Derbyshire; Sudeley Castle, Cheltenham; Sun Pavilion, Valley Gardens, Harrogate; Sutton Park, North Yorkshire; Tatton Park Old Hall, Knutsford, Cheshire; Theatre Royal, Bury St Edmunds, Suffolk; Temple Amphitheatre, Chiswick House Gardens, London W4; The Tivoli Theatre, Wimborne Minster; Trelissick Garden, Cornwall; Tresco Abbey, Tresco, Isles of Scilly; Trevarno, Helston, Cornwall; Tewkesbury Abbey; Upstairs at the Gatehouse, Highgate, London N6; Ventnor Botanic Garden, Isle of Wight; Wallington, Northumberland; Wenlock Priory, Much Wenlock, Shropshire; Wesley Memorial Church, Oxford; Weston Park, Shropshire;

Witley Court Grounds, Worcestershire; Winchester Cathedral; Wollaton Hall, Nottingham; Worcester Cathedral.(138)

2. In mainland Europe:
"Arkadenhof", Rheinische Friedrich-Wilhelms-Universität Bonn, Germany; Baroniet Rosendal, Norway; Bierkorf Theaterzaal, Brugge, Belgium; Chateau De Prangins, Geneva, Switzerland; Chateau De Waleffe, Belgium; De Groenzaal, Gent; Das Schloss Theater im Neuen Palais im Park, Sanssouci, Potsdam, Germany; De Nieuwe Kerk, Dam, Amsterdam, The Netherlands; Domein De Renesse, Belgium; Glimmingehus, Sweden; Gravensteen, Gent; "Hof des Alten Schlosses", Württembergisches Landesmuseum, Stuttgart, Germany; Kasteel Ammersoyen, The Netherlands; Kasteel Doorwerth, The Netherlands; Königsaal, Schloss Heidelberg, Germany; Landcommanderij, Alden Biesen, Bilzen, Belgium; Muiderslot, The Netherlands; Rijksmuseum Gevangenpoort, Den Haag, The Netherlands; Salle Paroissiale, Limpertsberg, Luxembourg; Sarajevo The MSS Festival; Slot Loevestein, The Netherlands; Stadsschouburg Koninklijke, Brugge, Belgium; Stadthalle Offenburg, Germany; Theatermuseet I Hofteatret, Copenhagen, Denmark; Ten Weyngaert VZW Brussels, Belgium.

BIBLIOGRAPHY

Abraham, Lyndal, 'The Lovers and the Tomb: Alchemical Emblems in Shakespeare, Donne and Marvel', *Emblematica: An Interdisciplinary Journal for Emblem Studies* 5 no. 2 (New York: 1991), pp. 301-320.

----- 'Alchemical References in Antony and Cleopatra', *Sydney Studies in English*, 8, (1982-3), pp.100-104

Albertus, Frater, *The Alchemist's Handbook* (York Beach, Maine: Samuel Weiser (1960), revised 1974, paper editions 1987, 1989)

Apuleius, *The Golden Ass,* translated into English by William Adlington in London in 1566 and reprinted in 1571, 1582 and 1596. Also translated by Robert Graves, (Harmondsworth: Penguin, 1960, 1998 and Oxford: FSG Classics, 2009).

Ariosto, Ludovico, *Orlando Furioso,* edited by Robert McNulty (Oxford: Oxford University Press, 1972)

Baigent, Michael, Richard Leigh and Henry Lincoln, *The Holy Blood and the Holy Grail* (Aylesbury: Corgi, 1983)

Baldwin, T.W. *William Shakespeare's Small Latine and Lesse Greeke,* 2 vols (Urbana: University of Illinois Press, 1944)

Banes, Daniel, *Shakespeare, Shylock and Kabbalah* (USA: Malcolm House Publications, 1978).

Barber, C.L. *Shakespeare's Festive Comedy*, (Princeton: Princeton University Press, 1972).

Bate, Jonathan, *Shakespeare and Ovid* (Oxford: Clarendon Press, 1993)

Becker, Udo, *The Continuum Encyclopaedia of Symbols* (London: Continuum International Publishing Group, 2000, reprinted 2005)

Beitchman, Philip, *Alchemy of the Word: Cabala of the Renaissance* (Albany, New York: Suny Press 1998).

Bible, The Geneva-Tomson Bible (London: 1609)

Bradbrook, M. C., *The Growth and Structure of Elizabethan Comedy* (London: Chatto and Windus, 1955)

------ *The School of Night* (Cambridge: Cambridge University Press, 1936).

------*The Living Monument* (Cambridge: Cambridge University Press, 1976)

Bullough, Geoffrey, *Narrative and Dramatic Sources of Shakespeare* 8 vols (London: Routledge and Kegan Paul, 1977, New York: Columbia University Press)

Campbell, Joseph, *The Masks of God* 4 vols (New York: Viking Penguin (1959), revised Harmondsworth: Penguin Arkana, 1974, 1991)

Carrol, Allen D., 'Johannes Factotum and Jack Cade', *Shakespeare Quarterley*, 40 (1989) pp. 461-462.

Castiglione, Baldesar, *The Book of the Courtier*, Venice: (1528) trans. by Thomas Hoby (London: Wyllam Seres, 1561), translated by George Bull (Harmondsworth: Penguin, 1967)

Chambers, E. K., *The Elizabethan Stage* 4 vols 2nd edn, (Oxford: Clarendon Press, 1974) IV.

------*The Medieval Stage*, vol. 1 (London, Oxford: Oxford University Press (1903), 8th impression 1978)

------*William Shakespeare*, vols 1 and 2 (London, Oxford: Oxford University Press (1930), reprinted 1963)

Coghill, Nevill, 'The Basis of Shakespearean Comedy', *Essays and Studies*, 3 (London: 1950, pp.1-28)

Cooper, J. C., *Fairy Tales: Allegories of the Inner Life* (Wellingborough: The Aquarian Press, 1985)

Coudert, Allison, *Alchemy: The Philosophers' Stone* (London: Wildwood House, 1980)

Dawkins, Peter, *Vita Concordia*, prospectus of the Bacon Research Trust (Warwick: 1994)

------*The Wisdom of Shakespeare in 'The Tempest'* (Warwickshire: I C Media Productions, 2000)

Dee, Dr John, *The Hieroglyphic Monad*, translated by J.W. Hamilton-Jones (New York: Samuel Weiser, 1977)

De Pace, M., *Introducing Freemasonry* (London: Lewis Masonic, 1983)

Dobson, Michael, Stanley Wells, *Oxford Companion to Shakespeare* (Oxford: Oxford University Press, 2001)

Drayton, Michael, *Poly-Olbion*, 5 vols, 4th volume of his works ed. by J. William Hebel (Oxford: B. Blackwell, 1933)

Eliade, Mercia, *Myths, Dreams and Mysteries,* translated by Philip Mairet (Glasgow: Collins, 1977)

Fabiny, Tibor, 'Shakespeare and the Emblem: Studies in Renaissance Iconography and Iconology', *Papers in English and American Studies*, vol. 3 ed.by Tibor Fabiny, revised by Zoltan Iszilassy, Kathleen Wodal and Maurice Cassidy (Egytem, Hungary: Department of English, Attila Jozset University, 1984)

Fleissner, Robert F., 'Hamlet's Flesh Alchemically Considered', *English Studies* 59 (1978) pp. 508-509

Fowler, Earle B., *Spenser and the System of Courtly Love* (New York: Phaeton Press, 1968)

Frazer, J. G., *The Golden Bough: A Study in Magic and Religion,* abridged edition (London: Macmillan, 1967)

Freher, D. A. *The 'Key' of Jacob Boehme,* translated by William Law (Grand Rapids, MI, USA: Phanes Press, 1991)

Frye, Northrop, *A Natural Perspective: The Development of Shakespearean Comedy and Romance* (New York: Columbia University Press, 1965).

Ghayet Al Hakim, *Picatrix,* written in Arabic and translated into Latin in 11th century.

Geoffrey of Monmouth, *The History of the Kings of Britain,* translated by Lewis Thorpe (Harmondsworth: Penguin, 1966)

Gilchrist, Cherry, Alchemy: *The Great Work* (Wellingborough: The Aquarian Press, 1984)

Givry, Grillot de, *Witchcraft, Magic and Alchemy* (New York: Dover Publications, 1971)

Gollancz, Sir Israel, *Allegory and Mysticism in Shakespeare* (London: Geo. W. Jones, 1931)

Gombrich, E. H., *Symbolic Images: Studies in the Art of the Renaissance* (Edinburgh: Phaidon, 1972)

Green, Henry, *Shakespeare and the Emblem Writers* (London: Trubner, 1870)

Greene, Robert, *Groatsworth of Witte, bought with a million of Repentance* (London: William Wright, 1592)

Hankins, John Erskine, *Backgrounds of Shakespeare's Thought* (Hassocks, Sussex: The Harvester Press, 1978)

Harries, Frederick J., *Shakespeare and the Welsh* (London: T. Fisher Unwin, 1919)

Harris, Daniel Y., *Shakespeare, Kabbalah and the Occult,* <http://www.danielyharris.com/pdfs/Shakespeare-**Kabbalah**-and-the-Occult.pdf. [accessed 3 October 2016]

Jayne, Sears Reynolds, 'Marsilio Ficino's Commentary on Plato's *Symposium' The University of Missouri Studies,* 19 no. 1, (Columbia, 1944) pp. 1-247

------ *John Colet and Marsilio Ficino* (Oxford: Oxford University Press, 1963)

Jacobi, Cyriaci, *De Alchimia Opuscula complura Veterum Philosophorum* (Frankfurt: [n.pub.], 1550).

Jung C. G., *Psychology and Alchemy* 2nd edition, translated by R. F. C. Hull (London: Routledge & Kegan Paul, 1968)

Klein, Dr Ernest, *A Comprehensive Etymological Dictionary of the English Language* (Oxford: Elsevier, 1971)

Knight, Gareth, *A History of White Magic* (Oxford: A. R. Mowbray, 1978)

------*The Rose Cross and the Goddess: The Quest for the Eternal Feminine Principle* (Wellingborough: The Aquarian Press, 1985)

------*The Secret Tradition in Arthurian Legend: The Magical and Mystical Power sources Within the Mysteries of Britain* (Wellingborough: The Aquarian Press, 1983)

------*A Practical Guide to Qabalistic Symbolism* 2 vols, vol.1 (London: Kahn & Averill, 1986)

Knight, Wilson G., *Shakespearean Dimensions* (Sussex:

------*The Shakespearean Tempest* (London: Methuen Harvester, 1984)

------Myth and Miracle: *An Essay on the Mystic Symbolism of Shakespeare* (London: E. J. Burrow, 1929)

------*Shakespeare and Religion* (New York: Barnes and Noble, 1967)

------*The Wheel of Fire* 4th edition (London: Methuen, 1978)

------*The Crown of Life* (New York, London: Methuen, 1982. First published by Oxford University Press, 1947)

Kristeller, Paul, Oskar, *Renaissance Thought: The Classic, Scholastic and Humanistic Strains* (New York: Harper & Row, 1955)

Laroque, Francois, 'Transformations in *A Midsummer Night's Dream*, *The Merry Wives of Windsor* and *As You Like It', Cahiers Elizabethains* 25 (1984) pp. 23-36

Le Donne, Anthony, *The Wife of Jesus* (London: Oneworld, 2015)

Levith, Murray J., *What's in Shakespeare's Names?* (London: Allen & Unwin, 1978)

Lawrence, W. W., *Shakespeare's Problem Comedies* (New York: Macmillan, 1931)

Lonegrin, Sig, Labyrinths: *Ancient Myths and Modern Uses* (Glastonbury: Gothic Image Publications, 1991)

The Maginogion, translated by Geoffrey Gantz (Harmonsworth: Penguin, 1981)

Mac Cana, Proinsias, *Celtic Mythology* (Middlesex: Newnes Books, first published (1968), revised 1983)

Macphee, Wendy Jean, 'Drama as a Mesocosm', unpublished dissertation, University of Newcastle Upon Tyne (1978)

------ 'A Process Account of Making Shakespeare Accessible within the community, "You can Never Bring in a Wall" ', unpublished M.Ed. thesis University of Newcastle upon Tyne (1981)

------ unpublished PhD thesis: 'Arcana in Shakespeare's Comedies', 1996

Maier, Michael, *The Laws of the Fraternity of the Rosie Crosse.* Facsimile reprint of the original English edition of (1656). (California: The Philosophical Research Society, 1976)

Mataraly, F. V. *The Masonic Way* (London: John M. Watkins, 1936)

Matthews, Caitlin, *Mabon and the Mysteries of Britain: An Exploration of the Mabinogion* (London: Arkana, Penguin, 1987)

------ *The Western Way*, 2 vols (London: Arkana, 1985)

Merry, Eleanor, *The Flaming Door* 2nd edition (Edinburgh: Floris Books, 1983)

Molinari, Cesare, *La Commedia Dell'Arte* (Milano: Arnoldo Mondadori, 1985)

Moore, Thomas, *The Planets Within* (Great Barrington, MA, USA: Lindisfarne Books, 1989)

Murray, W. A., 'Why was Duncan's Blood Golden?' *Shakespeare Survey* 19 (1996) pp. 34-44

Nicholl, Charles, *The Chemical Theatre* (London: Routledge & Kegan Paul, 1980)

Niculescu, Luminista, 'Shakespeare and Alchemy: Let us not Admit Impediments', *REAL: The Yearbook of Research in English and American Literature*, 2 (1984) pp.165-198

Olsen, Paul T., *The Kabbalah of Shakespeare* <http://www.spunk.org/texts/misc/sp00277.txt [accessed 3 October 2016]

Ovid, *Metamorphoses*, completed in [8CE], translated by William Caxton in [1480]. Golding translation in 1597, translation into English by Mary M. Innes (Harmondsworth: Penguin, 1955, 2007);

Parfitt, Will, *The Qabalah* (Dorset: Element, 1991)

------*Meetings with Amazing People* (Glastonbury: PS AVALON, 2017)

Plato, *Phaedrus and Letters VII and VIII* trans. by Walter Hamilton (London: Penguin Classics, 1973)

------ *The Symposium*, ed.by E.V. Rieu (Harmondsworth: Penguin Classics 1959).

Powell, T. G. E. *The Celts* (London: Thames and Hudson, 1960)

Purdon, Noel, "The Words of Mercury' Shakespeare and English Mythography of the Renaissance', *Elizabethan and Renaissance Studies*, edited by Dr James Hogg (Salzburg: 1974)

Rabbi Shimon Bar Yochai, *The Zohar*, published by Moses de Leon in the 13th century and by Rabbi Isaac Luria in the 16th century

Read, John, *The Alchemist in Life, Literature and Art* (London: Thomas Nelson and Sons, 1947)

Rees, Alwin and Brinley Rees, *Celtic Heritage: Ancient Tradition in Ireland and Wales* (London: Thames and Hudson, 1978)

Regardie, Israel, *The Philosophers' Stone*, (St Paul, Minnesota: Llewellyn Publications, 1978)

Reid, Shirley Ann, 'Celtic Elements in Cymbeline', part of an unpublished M.A. thesis, The University of Birmingham (1977)

Reynolds, Lou Agnes and Paul Sawyer, 'Folk Medicine and the Four Fairies of *A Midsummer Night's Dream*,' *Shakespeare Quarterly* 10 (1959) pp. 513-521

Richter, Jean, 'Prestiges de la Lune et Damnation par les Etoiles: Dans le Theatre de Shakespeare' (Paris: *Les Belles Lettres*, 1982)

Robb, Nesca A., *Neoplatonism of the Italian Renaissance* (London: George Allen & Unwin, 1935)

Ripley, George, *The Compound of Alchymy*, dedicated to Edward IV in [1471]. (Imprinted, London: Thomas Orwin, 1591), Hardback copy, edited by Stanton J. Linden (Farnham: Ashgate, 2001). <http://www.alchemywebsite.com/tcbcompound.htm [accessed 3 September 2016]

Ross, Anne, *Pagan Celtic Britain: Studies in Iconography and Tradition* (London: Routledge & Kegan Paul, 1968)

Rowse, A. L., *Shakespeare's Self-Portrait* (London: Macmillan, 1985)

Rutherford, Ward, *Celtic Mythology: The Nature and Influence of Celtic Myth from Druidism to Arthurian Legend* (Wellingborough: The Aquarian Press, 1987)

Savage, D. S., 'An Alchemical Metaphor in Hamlet', *Notes and Queries* 197 (1952) pp.157-160

Schlem, Gershom, *Major Trends in Jewish Mysticism* (Jerusalem: [n.pub.], 1941)

Scragg, Leah, 'Shakespeare, Lyly and Ovid: The Influence of Gallathea on *A Midsummer Night's Dream*', *Shakespeare Survey* 30 (1977) pp. 127-134

Shaheen, Naseeb, *Biblical References in Shakespeare's Comedies* (New Jersey: University of Delaware Press, 1993).

Shakespeare, William, *All's Well that Ends Well,* The Arden Shakespeare ed. G.K. Hunter (London: Methuen, 1986)

------ *Antony and Cleopatra,* The Arden Shakespeare ed. John Wilders (London: Routledge, 1995).

------ *As You Like It,* The Arden Shakespeare, ed. Agnes Latham (London: Methuen, 1975, reprinted 2000).

------*The Comedy of Errors*, The Arden Shakespeare, ed. R.A. Foakes (London: Routledge, 1993)

------*Cymbeline,* The Arden Shakespeare, ed. James Nosworthy, (London: Methuen, 1974),

------ *Hamlet*, The Arden Shakespeare, ed. Harold Jenkins (London: Routledge, 1992)

------*Love's Labour's Lost* ed. John Kerrigan (London: Penguin Books, 1996)

------*Measure for Measure*, The Arden Shakespeare, ed. J. W. Lever (London: Routledge, 1988)

------*The Merchant of Venice*, The Arden Shakespeare, ed. John Russell Brown (London: Routledge,1985)

------*The Merry Wives of Windsor*, The Arden Shakespeare, ed. Giorgio Melchiori (Surrey: Thomas Nelson & Sons, 2000)

------*A Midsummer Night's Dream*, The Arden Shakespeare, ed. Harold F. Brooks (London: Methuen, 1979)

------*Much Ado About Nothing*, The Arden Shakespeare, ed. A. R. Humphreys (London: Routledge, 1994)

------*Romeo and Juliet*, The Arden Shakespeare, ed. Brian Gibbons (London: Routledge, 1994)

------*The Taming of the Shrew*, The Arden Shakespeare, ed. Brian Morris (London: Routledge, 1993)

------*The Tempest*, The Arden Shakespeare, ed. Frank Kermode (Surrey: Thomas Nelson & Sons)

------*Twelfth Night*, The Arden Shakespeare, ed. J. M. Lothian and T. W. Craik (Surrey: Thomas Nelson & Sons, 1998)

------*The Two Gentlemen of Verona*, The Arden Shakespeare ed. Clifford Leech (London: Methuen, 1986)

------*The Winter's Tale*, Arden Shakespeare ed. J. H. P. Pafford (London: Methuen, 1986).

Sharkey, John, *Celtic Mysteries: the Ancient Religion* (London, Singapore: 1975, reprinted 1981)

Shen Lin, 'The Element of Platonic Love in the Tempest: an Exercise in the Iconological Principle', unpublished M.A. Thesis, The University of Birmingham, 1984

Shumaker, Wayne, *The Occult Science in the Renaissance* (California: University of California Press, 1972)

Sidney, Sir Philip, *An Apology for Poetry or, the Defence of Poesy,* edited by Geoffrey Shepherd

(London: Thomas Nelson & Sons Ltd, 1965)

Spence, Lewis, *British Fairy Origins* (Wellingborough: The Aquarian Press (1946), 1st paperback edition 1981)

Spenser, Edmund, *The Faerie Queene, Complete Works of Edmund Spenser,* edited by R. Morris (London: Hamilton, 1879).

------*Hymne in Honor of Beautie* (London: William Ponsonby, 1596).

Stanislavsky, Constantin, *An Actor Prepares* (London, New York: Routledge, first published (1936), reprinted 1989)

Stewart, R. J., *Celtic Gods, Celtic Goddesses* (London: Blandford, 1990)

------*The Prophetic Vision of Merlin* (London: Arkana, 1986)

------*The Merlin Tarot* (Wellingborough: The Aquarian Press, 1988)

------*The UnderWorld Initiation* (Wellingborough: The Aquarian Press, 1985)

Still, Colin, *Shakespeare's Mystery Play: A Study of The Tempest* (London: Cecil Palmer (1921)

The Minor Elizabethan Drama 2 vols, vol 2 (London: J. M. Dent, 1958, reprinted 1968)

Thiselton, Rev. T. F. Dyer, *Folklore of Shakespeare* (London: Griffith & Furan, 1883) (Whitefish, Montana: Kessinger Publishing, 2004)

Tillyard, E. M. W. *The Elizabethan World Picture* (Harmondsworth: Penguin Books, 1979)

Tobin, J. J. M., *Shakespeare's Favourite Novel: A study of 'The Golden Asse' as Prime Source* (Lanham Md: University Press of America, 1984)

Trevelyan, George, *Magic Casements* (London: Coventure, 1985)

------*Summons to a High Crusade* (Forres, Scotland: The Findhorn Press, 1986)

------*A Vision of the Aquarian Age* (London: Coventure, 1977)

------'*The Merchant of Venice:* An Interpretation in the Light of the Holistic World-View', *The Wrekin Trust*, no. 114 (1981)

Vyvyan, John, *The Shakespearean Ethic* (London: Chatto & Windus, 1959)

------*Shakespeare and Platonic Beauty* (London: Chatto & Windus, 1961)

------*Shakespeare and the Rose of Love* (London: Chatto & Windus, 1960)

Wind, Edgar, *Pagan Mysteries in the Renaissance* (Oxford: Oxford University Press, 1980) Wilson, F. P. 'Shakespeare's Reading', *Shakespeare Survey*, 3 (1950) pp.14-21

Whitney, Geoffrey, *A Choice of Emblems* (Leyden: Plantin 1586)

Woodman, David, *White Magic and English Renaissance Drama* (Vancouver: Fairleigh Dickinson University Press, 1973)

Wright, Dudley, *Druidism: The Ancient Faith of Britain* (London: Ed. J. Burrow, 1924)

Wyrick, Deborah Baker, 'The Ass Motive in *The Comedy of Errors* and *A Midsummer Night's Dream,*' *Shakespeare Quarterly* 33 (1982) pp. 423-447

Yates, Frances A. *Giordano Bruno and the Hermetic Tradition* (London: Routledge & Kegan Paul, 1964)

------*The Rosicrucian Enlightenment (*St Albans: Granada Publishing Ltd., 1975, 2nd edition)

------*Shakespeare's Last Plays: A New Approach* (London: Routledge & Kegan Paul, 1975)

------*The Occult Philosophy in the Elizabethan Age* (Oxford: Routledge Classics, 2001 first published by Routledge & Kegan Paul 1979)

-------*A Study of Love's Labour's Lost* (Cambridge: Cambridge University Press 1936, paperback edition 2013)

------ *The French Academies of the Sixteenth Century* (London: Routledge & Kegan Paul, 1947).

Young, David, *The Heart's Forest: a Study of Shakespeare's Pastoral plays* (New Haven: Yale University press, 1972)

Zimbardo, R. A. 'Regeneration and Reconciliation in *A Midsummer Night's Dream*' *Shakespeare*

Studies 6 (1970) pp. 35-55

INDEX

adust 432, 450, 472 n. 38, 476 n.1, 489 n. 8
alchemy 26-34
history of alchemy 26 puffers 34, 128, 129, 212
the sun and the moon 33 'base matter' as:
lead 19, 29, 30, 31, 83, 171, 191, 202, 250, 284, 347, 361, 389, 396
earth 19, 30, 189, 191, 193, 243, 284, 347, 353
whale 30, 31, 191, 197, 284, 347
serpent (snake) 30, 31, 65, 191, 201, 203, 205, 215, 284, 347, 364, 366, 369, 371, 392, 401, 441
toad 30, 191, 193, 207, 284, 285, 347, 483 n.8
dragon 30, 104, 108, 112, 191, 244, 284, 347, 356, figs 14, 16
king 27, 30, 31, 69, 71, 149, 191, 239, 241, 252, 284, 312, 347, 439
alchemy in Shakespeare's plays 29
the alchemists in the plays 26, fig. 15
George Ripley's Twelve Gates (stages) 27-29
Calcination 27, 71, 88, 108, 118, 132, 164, 221, 259, 287, 312, 369, 436
Dissolution 27, 73, 89, 134, 167, 222, 259, 287, 316, 369, 439, fig. 33
Seperation 27, 73, 91, 92, 108, 134, 170, 223, 259, 288, 319, 369, 440, 441
Coniunctio 27, 74, 92, 117, 135, 155, 171, 205, 224, 289, 322, 355, 358, 370, 372, 416, 443, figs 8, 9, 45

Putrefaction 27, 75, 77, 92, 104, 112, 113, 116, 117, 136, 138, 152, 153, 173, 175, 225, 226, 248, 252, 260, 290, 291, 325, 356, 370, 372, 444, 446, 447, 449, fig. 11
Congelation 28, 78, 93, 139, 176, 226, 260, 294, 328, 360, 375, 451
Cibation 28, 79, 94, 116, 139, 179, 227, 249, 260, 294, 330, 375, 453
Sublimation 28, 80, 95, 120, 140, 179, 228, 260, 296, 300, 331, 333, 375, 454
Firmentation 28, 81, 96, 97, 121, 140, 159, 181, 229, 230, 260, 302, 336, 377, 454
Exaltation 28, 82, 97, 122, 141, 159, 185, 231, 261, 303, 304, 339, 342, 377, 455
Multiplication 29, 83, 98, 123, 142, 159, 186, 214, 232, 261, 305, 342, 377, 455
Projection 29, 83, 98, 124, 142, 159, 186, 214, 232, 261, 306, 342, 362, 377, 455
four stage alchemy 133, 159, 300, 350
Abraham, Lyndal 22, 358, 359, 361
antimony 27, fig.10
Apuleius 26, 32, 40, 50, 313, 317, 329
Arcana 1, 4, 8-16, 18-25, 28, 29, 40-42, 45, 48, 51, 58, 59, 67, 68, 102-105, 161, 162, 188-191, 210, 220, 236-238, 254, 256, 267, 282, 311, 312, 343, 347, 366, 381, 386-388, 406, 409, 423, 434, 435, 456-458, 460, 461, 468 n n. 2, 3
Ariosto, Ludovico 10
Baigent, Michael, Richard Leigh & Henry Lincoln 144
Baldwin, T.W. 34, 470 n n. 3& 4

INDEX

Banes, Daniel 22, 47
Barber, C.L. 484 n.7
Bate, Jonathan 34, 470 n. 3, 472 n.30
Becker, Udo 484 n. 9
Beitchman, Philip 47
Bible 12, 24, 59, 60, 63, 65, 67, 78, 161, 163, 166, 169, 171, 173, 175-177, 179, 181, 184, 185, 208, 209, 222-224, 226-231, 233, 239, 241, 243-246, 248-253, 285, 287, 289, 290, 292, 294, 296, 297, 300, 302, 303, 305, 306, 312, 314, 317, 318, 320, 323, 326, 329, 331, 332, 334, 335, 337, 341, 343, 405, 406, 486 n. 9
  Old Testament 12, 59, 63, 65, 67, 133, 171, 208, 209, 245, 285, 287, 292, 305, 318, 320, 323, 334, 335, 337, 357, 405, 406, 475 n. 12
  New Testament 12, 24, 59, 60, 78, 166, 209, 229, 233, 244, 285, 305, 314, 318, 320, 323, 334, 335, 337, 348, 405, 406, 461 n.14, 479 n.1
Bradbrook, M. C. 484 n. 4
Bullough, Geoffrey 311, 469 n. 9, 485 n. 3, 486 n. 1, 487 n. 2
Cabala 41-47, figs 3, 24 -26, 47
Cailloch Beare 170
Campbell, Joseph 64, 474 n. 19, 476 n. 2, 479 n. 11, 487 n. 8
Carrol, D. Allen 20
Castiglione, Baldesar 35, 472
Cave 31, 49, 53, 58, 102, 103, 114-116, 121, 166, 347, 356, 479 n. 13, 481 n. 5, fig. 31
Celtic, Celtdom 11, 12, 16, 19-21, 24, 25, 40, 49, 51-59, 67, 102-125, 127, 129-141, 144-152, 154-159, 161-164, 166, 170, 171, 173, 175, 176, 178, 179, 181, 184, 186, 188-191, 193, 195-199, 201-203, 205-208, 212, 214, 215, 246, 268, 454, 456, 458, 460, 468 n. 4, 469 n. 7, 475 n n. 5, 6, 478 n. 4, 480 n n. 4, 5, 481 n n. 2, 5, 483 n. 6, 490 n. 1
Ceres 72, 180, 181, 313, 340, 460
Ceridwen 107, 181
Cernunnos (Herne the Hunter) 53, 127, 129, 138, 139, 141, 179, 246, 268, 480 n. 4, 482 n. 15, figs 34, 37
Chain (of Being) 70, 128, 138, 139, 141, 169, 323
Chambers, E. K. 21, 470 n. 7, 471 n. 12
Christ, Seed of Christ 23-25, 28, 29, 33, 42, 44, 66, 67, 78, 82, 106, 117, 145, 146, 148, 150, 151, 157, 192, 198, 208, 209, 229, 244, 284, 314, 315, 230, 332, 335, 337, 338, 348, 401, 429, 476 n. 14, 480 n. 8, 489 n. 3, figs 4, 35
Coghill, Nevill 21
Commedia Dell' Arte 135, 238, 242, 246, 256-258, figs 42, 43
Coudert, Allison 483 n. 8
crow 19, 107, 203, 324, 325, 347
Dawkins, Peter 22
Dee, Dr John 11, 23, 40, 42, 48, 165, 183, 382, 473 n. 1, fig. 27
Demeter 24, 31, 50, 193, 313, 340
De Pace, M. 478 n. 5

Divine Love 13, 15, 18, 24, 34-39, 78, 79, 131, 141, 143, 161, 168, 171, 176, 180, 183, 188, 221, 223, 225, 227, 232, 243, 246, 251-253, 258, 276, 278, 289, 296, 346-348, 352, 355, 361, 362, 364, 368, 369, 371-378, 414, 456, 458-460, 470 n. 5, 483 n. 4, figs 18-21

Dobson, Michael, Stanley Wells 240 Dove 20, 28, 31, 200, 201, 347, 356

dragon (see alchemy 'base matter')

Drayton, Michael 51, 475 n. 2

elements (as earth, water, fire, air) 11, 15, 29, 41, 168, 169, 188, 189, 203, 205, 207, 220, 221, 231, 232, 240, 373, 456, 460, figs 2, 39

Eliade, Mercia 498

emerald tablet 31-33, 123

Epona, 54, 55, 179, fig. 37

Etain 54, 171, 176, 184

Fabiny, Tibor 471, n. 11

fairy 77, 195, 198, 202, 204, 213, 311, 322, 482 n.3, fig. 29

feast 38, 79, 89, 124, 194, 207, 232, 248, 249, 260, 278, 311, 318, 341, 343, 349, 350, 356, 371, 374, 375, 392, 393, 454

Ficino, Marsilio 34, 40-42, 44, 147, 165, 190, 322, 340, 343, 472 n. 29, 473 n. 1, 476 n. 3, 486 n. 7

Fleissner, Robert F. 22 Frazer, J. G. 489 n.3

Frye, Northrop 343

Ghayet Al Hakim (Picatrix) 40, 165, 473 n. 1

Geoffrey of Monmouth 51, 58, 103, 478 n. 3

Gilchrist, Cherry 11

Givry, Grillot de 42

Green, Henry 18

Greene, Robert 19-21, 282

Hankins, John Erskine 38, 340, 472 n. 38, 476 n. 1, 486 n. 10

Harris, Daniel Y. 47, 383, 474 n. 13, 488 n. 5

hermaphrodite (rebus, rebis) 33, 106, 115, 224, 269, 285, 459, figs 16, 17

Herne the Hunter (see Cernunnos)

initiation 15, 23-25, 45, 48-51, 58, 59, 82, 87, 102-124, 161-166, 169, 171, 173, 175-181, 183-185, 192, 194, 195, 197-199, 201, 202, 204, 206, 208, 209, 212, 214, 215, 219-231, 233, 239, 241, 243-246, 248-254, 258, 262-264, 267-278, 284, 286, 289, 291, 294, 295, 297, 299, 301, 303-305, 312, 313, 317, 319, 320, 323, 326, 329, 331, 332, 334, 337, 340, 345, 346, 348-350, 352, 354, 355, 357, 359-362, 387, 391, 398, 400, 402, 410, 428, 457, 460, 469 n. 7, 475 n n. 4, 5, 11, 478 n. 3, 479 n. 20, 481 n n. 1, 2, 482 n. 16

Iris 180, 181, 460

Jayne, Sears Reynolds 34, 37, 38, 472 n n. 29, 38, 476 n. 3, 479 n. 2, 486 n. 7

Jacobi, Cyriaci 358

Jung C. G. 57, 214, 267, 472 n. 26, 483 n. 13

Juno 156, 180, 445

Klein, Dr Ernest 482 n. 2

Knight, Gareth 11, 21, 22, 43, 48, 168, 469 n. 7, 474 n n. 8, 9, 481 n. 2, 486 n. 4, 489 n. 7

Knight, Wilson G. 21, 22, 168

ladder (also see chain) 154, 155, 202, 225, 323, 325, 353, 354, 356, 357, fig. 12

Lawrence, W. W. 488 n. 2

Le Donne, Anthony 145 Levith, Murray J. 486 n. 3

INDEX

lion, lioness 16, 27-29, 71, 72, 81, 88, 97, 107, 121, 122, 147, 172, 173, 197, 211-213, 241, 245, 281, 284, 298-300, 309, 312, 456, figs 7, 16

Macphee, Wendy Jean 468 n. 3, 489 n. 2, figs 15, 38

Matthews, Caitlin & John 58, 469 n. 7, 481 n n n n. 2, 3, 7, 10, 482 n n n n. 11, 17, 18, 21

mercy 12, 44, 45, 61, 85, 96, 97, 100, 101, 142, 157, 160, 180, 181, 192, 194, 208, 233, 250, 265, 280, 307, 309, 343, 363, 374, 378, 381-383, 397, 399, 400, 405-409, 413, 417, 420, 423-430, 438, 457, 460, fig. 48

Merry, Eleanor 106, 478 n. 8, 479 n n. 15, 17, 481 n. 2, 482 n n n. 16, 17, 20

mesocosm 432

microcosm 25, 27, 70, 199, 258, 317, 322, 328, 404, 432

Michell, Marko 481 n. 2, 482 n. 19

Molinari, Cesare 257 Moore, Thomas 473 n. 4

Morrigan 54, 104, 107, 111, 116, 131, 140, 171, 206, 478 n. 7

Murray, W. A. 22

Nicholl, Charles 14, 22, 26, 102, 117, 478 n. 1, 479 n n n n. 13, 14, 16, 21

Niculescu, Luminista 22

Olsen, Paul T. 22, 47, 382

Ouroboros 23, 367, 377, fig. 5

Ovid 17, 26, 129, 137, 200, 209, 212, 246, 258, 470 n n. 3, 4, 471 n. 23, 472 n. 30

Parfitt, Will 11, 24, 25, 43, 381, 469 n. 7, 474 n n. 8, 9, figs 3, 25, 26

Peele, George 20, 21

Pelican 29, figs 7, 16, 24

Phaedrus 12, 38, 39, 325, 364, 366, 367, 369-378, 459, 473 n. 40, 487 n n. 3, 5, fig. 19

Philosophers' Stone 23, 24, 27-30, 32, 33, 57, 69, 70, 78, 82, 83, 110, 116, 122, 128, 137, 140, 159, 171, 191, 196, 197, 205, 212, 214, 232, 252, 259, 268, 269, 271, 273, 276, 277, 284, 300, 306, 316, 339, 342, 347, 358, 362, 403, 428, 435, 455, 483 n. 8, figs 2, 4, 7, 12, 14, 16, 31, 35

phoenix 29, 110, 159, 284, 316, 317, 319, 320, 389, 401, 486 n. 5

Picatrix (see Ghayet Al Hakim)

Plato 13, 34, 35, 37-39, 42, 75, 165, 169, 232, 278, 311, 317, 319, 326, 345, 348, 352, 364, 366-378, 459, 472 n n n. 29, 35, 38, 476 n. 3, 479 n. 2, figs 19, 22

Plutarch 39, 366-368, 379, 459, 487 n. 2

Powell, T. G. E. 478 n. 4, 481 n. 2, 482 n. 14, 16

puffers (see alchemy)

Rabbi Shimon Bar Yochai 473 n. 1 rainbow 79, 128, 139, 181, 333, 476 n. 4

raven 20, 27, 31, 54, 103, 104, 107, 111, 112, 116, 131, 170, 179, 201, 247, 248, 347, 356, 448, fig. 11

redemption 66, 67, 82, 109, 118, 119, 153, 160, 166, 172, 191, 199, 205, 208, 209, 231, 252, 296, 299, 305, 306, 309, 332, 334, 339, 343, 347, 348, 355, 358, 362, 363, 399, 400, 410, 418, 424, 426, 429, 433, 435

Rees, Alwin and Brinley Rees 53, 475 n. 8, 478 n. 4, 481 n n. 2, 5
Reid, Shirley Ann 21
Renaissance Platonism 13, 15, 19, 22, 24, 25, 34-39, 45, 67, 70-76, 78-84, 87-98, 128-139, 141-143, 147-153, 155-158, 176, 194, 195, 197-202, 204, 206, 209, 213-215, 220-232, 238, 239, 241, 243-246, 248-253, 258, 267-278, 312, 313, 316, 319, 322, 325, 328, 330, 332, 333, 336, 340, 343, 345, 346-364, 366, 368, 370, 372, 374, 376, 378, 387, 407, 409, 459, 460
revenge 12, 18, 20, 61, 96, 112, 114, 115, 126, 130-132, 182, 197, 198, 201, 207, 272, 277, 278, 309, 330, 350, 356, 384, 386, 394-397, 399, 405, 406, 410, 419, 420, 424, 429, 438, 440, 441, 448, 450, 457, 461, 476 n. 14, 478 n. 2, fig. 49
Reynolds, Lou Agnes and Paul Sawyer 483 n. 7
Ripley, George 26-29, 31, 68, 72, 73, 78, 79, 81, 82, 91, 121, 128, 167, 170, 181, 188, 193, 202, 207, 223, 229, 288, 316, 319, 330, 336, 339, 342, 369, 440, 476 n. 4, 478 n n. 3, 9, 478 n. 9, 479 n. 19, fig. 6
Rites of Eleusis 24, 49, 50, 173, 194, 209, 313, 317, 348, 460
Robb, Nesca A. 472 n. 32
Ross, Anne 21, 480 n. 5, 481 n n n. 2, 7, 9, 482 n n n. 13, 15, 16, 483 n. 6
Rowse, A. L. 237 Rylance, Mark 32
Saturn 28, 78, 89, 202, 221, 322, 432, 438, 449, fig. 11

Savage, D. S. 22
Schlem, Gershom 473 n. 3
Serpent, snake (see alchemy, 'base matter'), fig. 16
Setebos 170
Shaheen, Naseeb 59, 67, 312, 486 n. 2
Sharkey, John 475 n. 6
Shen Lin 473 n n. 39, 40
Sidney, Sir Philip 16, 26, 282
sophic (sophic sulphur, sophic mercury) 26, 27, 32, 71, 74, 76, 88, 108, 117, 173, 241, 267, 312, 339, 436, 460, fig. 8
Spence, Lewis 198, 482 n. 3
Spenser, Edmund 17, 35, 470 n. 6, 472 n. 36
Stanislavsky, Constantin 9
Stewart, R. J. 25, 51, 56, 57, 102, 103, 469 n. 7, 475 n n n. 4, 5, 11, 478 n. 3, 479 n n n n. 12, 18, 20, 22, 481 n n. 2, 10, 482 n n. 16, 19, 491 n. 4
Still, Colin 50, 162, 481 n. 1
theurgy 22, 23, 40, 45, 48, 49, 67, 71-79, 81-83, 161, 163, 165, 169, 171, 173, 175-178, 180, 183, 185, 192, 194, 195, 198, 199, 201, 202, 204, 206, 208, 209, 212, 214, 215, 220-231, 233, 237-239, 241, 243-246, 248-253, 258, 262, 312-314, 317, 319, 323, 326, 329, 331, 332, 334, 337, 340, 387, 428, 429, fig. 40
Thiselton, Rev. T. F. Dyer 198
Tillyard, E. M. W. 68, 472 n. 38, 474 n. 16, 476 n. 1
transmute 191, 200, 204, 207, 267, 270, 287, 349, 367, 376, 377, 389, 423, 435, 463
Trevelyan, George 22, 481 n. 2, 483 n n. 9, 10, 484 n. 10

Triple Goddess 54, 104, 131, 148, 206
Vyvyan, John 13, 21, 34, 35, 147, 149, 150, 153, 155, 156, 159, 190, 201, 209, 214, 227, 228, 406, 409, 410, 412, 414, 415, 423, 425, 427, 438, 445, 470 n. 5, 476 n. 14, 483 n n n. 12, 4, 6, 484 n. 3
Wells, Stanley 240
Wind, Edgar 33, 470 n. 8, 483 n n n. 2, 3, 5, 484 n. 8
whale (see alchemy, 'base matter')

Whitney, Geoffrey 18
wolf 20, 27, 54, 213, 331, 347, 399, fig. 10
Wyrick, Deborah Baker 209
Yates, Frances A. 22-24, 41, 42, 47, 382, 473 n. 2, 474 n n. 5, 6, 480 n. 6, 481 n. 4, 484 n. 4, 485 n. 11, 488 n. 2, 489 n. 7
Young, David 486 n. 2
The Zohar 40, 41, 165, 473 n. 1

www.ingramcontent.com/pod-product-compliance
Lightning Source LLC
Chambersburg PA
CBHW071327080526
44587CB00017B/2757